Diverse Voices of Women

Diverse Voices of Women

Susan Frank Ballentine
Diablo Valley College

Jessica Barksdale Inclán
Diablo Valley College

Mayfield Publishing Company
Mountain View, California
London • Toronto

Library of Congress Cataloging-in-Publication Data

Diverse voices of women / [compiled by] Susan Frank Ballentine, Jessica Barksdale Inclán.
p. cm.
Includes index.
ISBN 1-55934-194-7
1. American literature—Women authors. 2. American literature—20th century. 3. Women—Literary collections. 4. Women. I. Ballentine, Susan Frank. II. Inclán, Jessica Barksdale.
PS508.W7D58 1994
810.8′09287—dc20 94-7137
CIP

Manufactured in the United States of America
10 9 8 7 6 5 4 3 2 1

Mayfield Publishing Company
1280 Villa Street
Mountain View, California 94041

Sponsoring editor, James Bull; production editor, Merlyn Holmes; manuscript editor, Margaret Moore; text designer, Jean Mailander; cover designer, Donna Davis; manufacturing manager, Martha Branch. The text was set in 9/11 Palatino by G&S and printed on 50# Butte des Morts by Banta Company.

Cover image: *Historical Guilt*, © Sue Benner, 1990, cotton quilt, 98″ × 94″. Collection of Abrams Properties Limited Partnership, Dallas, Texas.

This book is printed on recycled paper.

THIS TEXT IS DEDICATED to women writers, speakers and thinkers of the past whose diverse voices paved the way insistently *and* quietly; to women today who continue to speak and write to women's issues forcefully *and* gently; and to women of the future whose courageous and unbounded perspectives will continue to touch male and female lives, beliefs, and values in our world.

Preface

This book is a collection of work of various lengths and genres, featuring the voices of mainly contemporary women drawn from diverse socioeconomic classes, ethnic/racial groups, and age groups, covering topics such as the following that are currently on the minds of women:

- What is "women's work"?
- What is "women's nature"?
- After rejecting the patriarchal images of women, what new images do women seek?
- As new images of women emerge, what happens to mother–daughter relationships? Father–daughter relationships?
- What roles are viable and compelling for women today?
- Can women best accomplish the work of reinventing their roles with men or without them?

The book is divided into seven thematic sections: Work; Identity; Making Stereotypes; Breaking Stereotypes; Sexuality, Love, and Commitment; Parents and Children; and Spirituality. Each section contains about a dozen works, which range widely in length, character, and perspective. We have included poems, short stories, and a variety of nonfiction prose pieces in an effort to make the reader's connection with each theme as meaningful as possible. Those prose pieces that are excerpts from longer works all stand on their own. Each reading is preceded by a headnote that provides information about the author and her background.

Some of the authors represented here will be familiar. Others are voices that have not been widely heard, including a number who are not writers by profession. We believe that every woman is affected by the issues touched on in this book, and we have found that many nonprofessional writers express themselves eloquently when writing about these themes. So readers will find that some pieces in the book are less "polished" than others.

The organization of the book is meant to be flexible. The instructor can cover the seven themes in any order desired, or can skip around within different thematic units. The primary market for this book is in introductory women's studies courses, but it could also serve as a reader in composition courses that focus on the experiences of women.

Jim Bull, Tom Broadbent, Pamela Trainer, Margaret Moore, Sondra Glider, Merlyn Holmes, Linda Toy, and the staff at Mayfield deserve special thanks for their patient support and guidance throughout this project. We must also thank Jesse, Mitchell, and Julien Inclán; Richard, Jennifer, and Lara Ballentine; and our friends and colleagues who helped with this manuscript. We would also like to thank the following reviewers for their helpful suggestions: Janice Albert, Las Positas College; Marvin Diogenes, University of Arizona; Susan Gabriel, Southern Illinois University at Edwardsville; Nancy Gish, University of Southern Maine; Jane Hedley, Bryn Mawr College; Susan Miller, University of Utah; Evelyn S. Newlyn, State University of New York, College at Brockport; Frances Freeman Paden, Northwestern University; Claire Pedretti, Berea College; Patricia Taylor, University of Wyoming; and Jane E. Prather, California State University, Northridge.

Contents

Part VII: Spirituality 377

Index of Authors and Titles 411

Diverse Voices of Women

I

Work

The New American Dreamers are setting out on a very different quest for self-realization. They are, in their plans for the future, separating identity from intimacy, saying that they must first figure out who they are and that then and only then will they form a partnership with a man. Among the young women I interviewed, the New American Dreamers stand apart in their intention to make their own way in the world and determine their own destiny prior to forming a significant and lasting intimate relationship.

–RUTH SIDEL, "The New American Dreamers"

Farm women in Africa (and India) are the most overworked humans in the world, working ten to fifteen hours a day at a host of jobs. A typical Zimbabwean woman's day begins at 3:00 A.M. Every day she goes to the river for water, weeds the fields (breastfeeding her baby as she works), chases animals away from crops, pounds grain into flour, prepares meals, and gathers wood (steadily walking farther with these heavy loads because drought and overcutting have depleted fuel wood). She helps her husband cultivate cash crops, processes food (threshes, dries, grinds) and carries it to market. She has weekly tasks like laundering.

–MARILYN FRENCH, "Economic Discrimination"

I love people who harness themselves, an ox to a heavy
cart,
who pull like water buffalo, with massive patience,
who strain in the mud and the muck to move things
forward,
who do what has to be done, again and again.

–MARGE PIERCY, "To Be of Use"

The Secretary Chant

Marge Piercy

Marge Piercy (1936–) is the author of two dozen novels and volumes of poetry, including The Last White Class, *a play co-authored with her husband, Ira Wood. Growing up in inner-city Detroit, Piercy realized she wanted to be a writer at the age of fifteen but says her career "took forever to begin." Although she wanted to publish serious fiction about being a woman, "I broke into print by writing about children and male characters." Piercy wants her writing to be "useful" to women: "To find ourselves spoken for in art gives dignity to our pain, our anger, our lust, our losses."*

My hips are a desk.
From my ears hang
chains of paper clips.
Rubber bands form my hair.
My breasts are wells of mimeograph ink.
My feet bear casters.
Buzz. Click.
My head is a badly organized file.
My head is a switchboard
where crossed lines crackle.
Press my fingers
and in my eyes appear
credit and debit.
Zing. Tinkle.
My navel is a reject button.
From my mouth issue canceled reams.
Swollen, heavy, rectangular
I am about to be delivered
of a baby
Xerox machine.
File me under W
because I wonce
was
a woman.

The New American Dreamers

Ruth Sidel

Ruth Sidel (1933–) lives in Manhattan with her husband, Victor Sidel, and works as a sociologist at Hunter College of the City University of New York. In response to the question of how the women's movement has changed American lives, she wrote Women and Children Last *(1986), an examination of the feminization of poverty.* On Her Own: Growing Up in the Shadow of the American Dream *(1990), from which the following selection is taken, is based on a series of interviews which show, in the words of journalist Deborah Solomon, "that today's young women . . . have absorbed none of the teachings of feminism except the one that has the potential to hurt the most: the one that says you can do it by yourself—alone."*

It's your life. You have to live it yourself. . . . If you work hard enough, you will get there. You must be in control of your life, and then somehow it will all work out.

–ANGELA DAWSON (high-school junior, Southern California)

SHE IS THE PROTOTYPE OF TODAY'S YOUNG WOMAN—confident, outgoing, knowledgeable, involved. She is active in her school, church, or community. She may have a wide circle of friends or simply a few close ones, but she is committed to them and to their friendship. She is sophisticated about the central issues facing young people today—planning for the future, intimacy, sex, drugs, and alcohol—and discusses them seriously, thoughtfully, and forthrightly. She wants to take control of her life and is trying to figure out how to get from where she is to where she wants to go. Above all, she is convinced that if she plans carefully, works hard, and makes the right decisions, she will be a success in her chosen field; have the material goods she desires; in time, marry if she wishes; and, in all probability, have children. She plans, as the expression goes, to "have it all."

She lives in and around the major cities of the United States, in the towns of New England, in the smaller cities of the South and Midwest, and along the West Coast. She comes from an upper-middle-class family, from the middle class, from the working class, and even sometimes from the poor. What is clear is that she has heard the message that women today should be the heroines of their own lives. She looks toward the future, seeing herself as the central character, planning her career, her apartment, her own success story. These young women do not see themselves as playing supporting roles in someone else's life script; it is their own journeys they are planning. They see their lives in terms of *their* aspirations, *their* hopes, *their* dreams.

Beth Conant is a sixteen-year-old high-school junior who lives with her mother and stepfather in an affluent New England college town. She has five brothers, four older and one several years younger. Her mother is a librarian, and her stepfather is a stockbroker. A junior at a top-notch public high school, she hopes to study drama in college, possibly at Yale, "like Meryl Streep." She would like to live and act in England for a time, possibly doing Shakespeare. She hopes to be living in New York by the age of twenty-five, in her own apartment or condo, starting on her acting career while working at another job by which she supports herself. She wants to have "a great life," be "really independent," and have "everything that's mine—crazy furniture, everything my own style."

By the time she's thirty ("that's so boring"), she feels, she will need to be sensible, because soon she will be "tied down." She hopes that by then her career will be "starting to go forth" and that she will be getting good roles. By thirty-five she'll have a child ("probably be married beforehand"), be working in New York and have a house in the country. How will she manage all this? Her husband will share responsibilities. She's not going to be a "supermom." They'll both do child care. He won't do it as a favor; it will be their joint responsibility. Moreover, if she doesn't have the time to give to a child, she won't have one. If necessary, she'll work for a while, then have children, and after that "make one movie a year."

Amy Morrison is a petite, black, fifteen-year-old high-school sophomore who lives in Ohio. Her mother works part-time, and her father works for a local art museum. She plans to go to medical school and hopes to become a surgeon. She doesn't want to marry until she has a good, secure job but indicates that she might be living with someone. She's not sure about having children but says emphatically that she wants to be successful, to make money, to have cars. In fact, originally she wanted to become a doctor "primarily for the money," but now she claims other factors are drawing her to medicine.

Jacqueline Gonzalez is a quiet, self-possessed, nineteen-year-old Mexican-American woman who is a sophomore at a community college in southern California. She describes her father as a "self-employed contractor" and her mother as a "housewife." Jacqueline, the second-youngest of six children, is the first in her family to go to college. Among her four brothers and one sister, only her sister has finished high school. Jacqueline's goal is to go to law school and then to go into private practice. While she sees herself as eventually married with "one or two children," work, professional achievement, and an upper-middle-class life-style are central to her plans for her future.

If in the past, and to a considerable extent still today, women have hoped to find their identity through marriage, have sought to find "validation of . . . [their] uniqueness and importance by being singled out among all other women by a man," the New American Dreamers are setting out on a very different quest for self-realization. They are, in their plans for the future, separating identity from intimacy, saying that they must first figure out who they are and that then and only then will they form a partnership with a man. Among the young women I interviewed, the New American Dreamers stand apart in their intention to make their own way in the world and determine their own destiny prior to forming a significant and lasting intimate relationship.

Young women today do not need to come from upper-middle-class homes such as Beth's or middle-class homes such as Amy's or working-class homes such as Jacqueline's to dream of "the good life." Even young women with several strikes against them see material success as a key prize at the end of the rainbow. Some seem to feel that success is out there for the taking. Generally, the most prestigious, best-paying careers are mentioned; few women of any class mention traditional women's professions such as teaching or nursing. A sixteen-year-old unmarried Arizona mother of a four-and-a-half-month-old baby looks forward to a "professional career either in a bank or with a computer company," a "house that belongs to me," a "nice car," and the ability to buy her son "good clothes." She sees herself in the future as dating but not married. "There is not so much stress on marriage these days," she says.

Yet another young woman, a seventeen-year-old black unmarried mother of an infant, hopes to be a "professional model," have "lots of cash," be "rich," maybe have another child. When asked if a man will be part of the picture, she responds, "I don't know."

An eighteen-year-old Hispanic unmarried mother hopes to "be my own boss" in a large company, have a "beautiful home," send her daughter to "the best schools." She wants, in her words, to "do it, make it, have money."

These young women are bright, thoughtful, personable. And they are quintessentially American:

they believe that with enough hard work they will "make it" in American society. No matter what class they come from, their fantasies are of upward mobility, a comfortable life filled with personal choice and material possessions. The upper-middle-class women fantasize a life even more upper-middle-class; middle-class and working-class women look toward a life of high status in which they have virtually everything they want; and some young women who come from families with significant financial deprivation and numerous other problems dream of a life straight out of "Dallas," "Dynasty," or "L.A. Law." According to one young woman, some of her friends are so determined to be successful that they are "fearful that there will be a nuclear war and that they will die before they have a chance to live their lives. If there is a nuclear war," she explained, "they won't live long enough to be successful."

Young women are our latest true believers. They have bought into the image of a bright future. Many of them see themselves as professional women, dressed in handsome clothes, carrying a briefcase to work, and coming home to a comfortable house or condo, possibly to a loving, caring husband and a couple of well-behaved children. How widespread is the dream? How realistic is it? What is the function of this latest American dream? What about those young women who cling to a more traditional dream? What about those who feel their dreams must be deferred? What about those with no dream at all? And what about those who "share the fantasy," as the Chanel No. 5 perfume advertisement used to say, but have little or no chance of achieving it?

Perhaps the most poignant example of the impossible dream is Simone Baker, a dynamic, bright, eighteen-year-old black woman from Louisiana. Simone's mother is a seamstress who has been off and on welfare over the years, and her father is a drug addict. Simone herself has been addicted to drugs of one kind or another since she was five. She has been in and out of drug-abuse facilities, and although she attended school for many years and was passed from grade to grade, she can barely read and write. When I met her in a drug rehabilitation center, she was struggling to become drug free so that she could join the Job Corps, finish high school, and obtain some vocational training. Her dream of the future is so extraordinary, given her background, that she seems to epitomize the Horatio Alger myth of another era. When asked what she would like her life to be like in the future, Simone replies instantly, her eyes shining: "I want to be a model. I want to have a Jacuzzi. I want to have a *big,* BIG house and a BIG family—three girls and two boys."

"And what about the man?" I ask her.

"He'll be a lawyer. He'll be responsible, hardworking, and sensitive to my feelings. Everything will be fifty-fifty. And he'll take the little boys out to play football and I'll have the girls inside cooking. That would be a dream come true!"

Simone's dream is an incredible mixture of the old and the new—a Dick-and-Jane reader updated. And she's even mouthing the supreme hope of so many women in this age of the therapeutic solution to personal problems—that she'll find a man who is "sensitive" to her "feelings." She has lived a life far from the traditional middle class and yet has the quintessential image of the good life as it has been formulated in the last quarter of the twentieth century. But for Simone, it is virtually an impossible dream. One wishes that that were not so; listening to her, watching her excitement and hope at the mere thought of such a life, one gets caught up and wants desperately for it all to happen. The image is clear: the white house in the suburbs with the brass knocker on the front door, the leaves on the lawn in the fall, the boys playing football with this incredibly wonderful husband/father, and Simone sometimes the successful model, other times at home, cooking with her daughters. But we know how very unlikely it is that this particular dream will come true. And yet, maybe . . .

How have young women come to take on the American Dream as their own? That this is a relatively new dream for women is clear. Until recent years women, for the most part, did not perceive themselves as separate, independent entities with their own needs and agendas. Women fit themselves into other people's lives, molded their needs to fit the needs of others. For the full-time homemaker the day began early enough to enable husband and children to get to work and school on time. Chores had to be done between breakfast and lunch or between lunch and the end of school. Dinnertime was when the man of the house returned from work. When a woman worked outside of the home, her work hours were often those that fit into the schedules of other family members. Her needs were determined by the needs of others, as often her identity rested on her affiliation with them.

What some women seem to be saying now is that

they will form their own identities, develop their own styles, and meet their own needs. They will be the central characters in their stories. They will work at jobs men work at, earn the money men earn; but many of them also plan at the same time to play all the roles women have traditionally played.

What has become clear in talking with young women throughout the country is that many of them are planning for their future in terms of their "public" roles as well as their "domestic" roles, that they are "laying claim to significant and satisfying work . . . as a normal part of their lives and laying claim also to the authority, prestige, power, and salary that . . . [that] work commands." Historically, women have been confined primarily to the "domestic" sphere of life, particularly to child rearing and homemaking, and men, for the most part, have participated in the "public" sphere—that is, in social, economic, and political institutions and forms of association in the broader social structure. This dichotomy between "public" and "domestic" has led to "an asymmetry in the cultural evaluation of male and female that appears to be universal." Margaret Mead noted this asymmetry when she observed that "whatever the arrangements in regard to descent or ownership of property, and even if these formal outward arrangements are reflected in the temperamental relations between the sexes, the prestige values always attach to the activities of men."

In New Guinea, women grow sweet potatoes and men grow yams; yams are the prestige food. In societies where women grow rice, the staple food, and men hunt for meat, meat is the most valued food. Traditionally, the more exclusively male the activity, the more cultural value is attached to it. Because male activities have been valued over female activities and women have become "absorbed primarily in domestic activities because of their role as mothers," women's work of caring has traditionally been devalued. However, as political scientist Joan Tronto has pointed out, it is not simply the dichotomy between the public and the private that results in the devaluation of the female but the immense difference in power between the two spheres. So long as men have a monopoly on the public sphere and it in turn wields great power within society, women, identified with the private sphere, which is seen as relatively powerless, will be devalued.

Since the emergence of the women's movement in the 1960s, women in the U.S. as well as in many other parts of the world have been questioning the traditional asymmetry between men and women, seeking to understand its roots, its causes, and its consequences, and attempting to modify the male monopoly of power. Many strategies have developed toward this end: laws have been passed in an attempt to eliminate discrimination; groups have formed to elect more women to positions of power, those already in power have been urged to appoint more women to administrative roles; dominant, high-status, high-income professions have been pressured to admit more women to their hallowed ranks; and strategies to bring greater equity to male and female salaries have been developed.

Great stress has been placed on raising the consciousness of both women and men concerning this imbalance of power, but particular attention has been devoted to raising the consciousness of women. Discussion about the relative powerlessness of the non-wage-earning "housewife" has been widespread. Books and articles about the impoverishment of the divorced woman, the problems of the displaced homemaker, and the often desperate plight of the single, female head of household have been directed at women. During the 1970s and 1980s, the message suddenly became clear to many women: perhaps they are entitled to play roles formerly reserved for men; perhaps they would enjoy these challenges; perhaps they have something special to offer and can make a difference in the practice of medicine or law or in running the country. Moreover, it became clear that if women want power, prestige, and paychecks similar to those men receive, if they want to lessen the asymmetry between male and female, then perhaps they must enter those spheres traditionally reserved for men. If men grow yams, must women grow yams? If men hunt and women gather, must women purchase a bow and arrow? If men are in the public sphere while women are at home caring for children and doing the laundry, the consensus seems to say that women must enter the public sphere. If men are doctors and lawyers and earn great rewards while women are nurses and teachers and earn meager rewards, then women see what they obviously must do. If men have focused on doing while women have focused on caring, then clearly women must become doers.

It is not sufficient, however, to become a doer in a traditionally female occupation, for, as we know, these occupations are notoriously underpaid and underesteemed. Women must become *real* doers in the arena that counts: they must learn to play hardball, or, as Mary Lou Retton says in her breakfast-cereal advertisements, "eat what the big boys eat." For real power, status, money, and "success," it's law, medicine, and finance—also, possibly, acting, modeling, or working in the media, if one is very lucky.

An illustration of the current emphasis on male-dominated careers as the road to success for young women are the career goals of *Glamour* magazine's "Top Ten College Women '88." One woman hopes to become an astronaut; a second plans to work in the area of public policy, another to be a biologist, another to obtain a degree in business administration, yet another to obtain a degree in acting; and one young woman is currently working in journalism. One college senior is undecided between journalism and law, and the last three are planning to go to law school. These young women, according to *Glamour*, "possess the talents and ambition necessary to shape tomorrow's society." It is noteworthy that none of the women *Glamour* chose to honor are entering any traditionally female occupation or any "helping" profession—not even medicine. Don't nurses, teachers, and social workers "possess the talents and ambition necessary to shape tomorrow's society"? The word has gone out and continues to go out that the way to "make it" in American society and the way to "shape tomorrow's society" is the traditional male route.

Once singled out, these young women play their part in spreading the ideology of the American Dream. Three of the ten honorees appeared on NBC's "Today" show. When asked about the significance of their being chosen, one woman replied without hesitation that if you work hard, you can do whatever you want to do. This statement was greeted by smiles and nods; she had clearly given the right message.

In addition to wanting to break out of the mold of a secondary worker receiving inferior wages and benefits and having little authority or opportunity for advancement, women have been motivated to make real money and to acquire valued skills and some semblance of security because of their relatively recent realization that women, even women with children, may well be forced to care for themselves or, at the very least, to participate in providing for the family unit. Women have come to realize that whether because of divorce (which leaves women on the average 73 percent poorer and men on the average 42 percent richer), childbearing outside of marriage, the inability of many men to earn an adequate "family wage," or their remaining single—either through design or through circumstance—they must be prepared to support themselves and anyone else for whom they feel responsible.

But what of all that caring women used to do—for children, for elderly parents, for sick family members, for the home? What about Sunday dinner, baking chocolate-chip cookies with the kids eating up half the batter, serving Kool-Aid in the backyard on a hot summer day? What about sitting with a child with a painful ear infection until the antibiotic takes effect, going with a four-year-old to nursery school the first week until the child feels comfortable letting you leave, being available when there's an accident at school and your second grader must be rushed to the emergency room? Who's going to do the caring? Who is going to do the caring in a society in which few institutions have been developed to take up the slack, a society in which men have been far more reluctant to become carers than women have been to become doers. Members of the subordinate group may gain significantly in status, in self-image, and in material rewards when they take on the activities and characteristics of the dominant group, but there is little incentive for members of the dominant group to do the reverse.

Above all, how do young women today deal with these questions? How do they feel about doing and caring, about power, prestige, and parenting? What messages is society giving them about the roles they should play, and how are they sorting out these messages?

A key message the New American Dreamers are both receiving and sending is one of optimism—the sense that they can do whatever they want with their lives. Many Americans, of course—not just young people or young women—have a fundamentally optimistic attitude toward the future. Historically, Americans have believed that progress is likely, even inevitable, and that they have the ability to control their own destinies. A poll taken early in 1988 indicates that while the American public was concerned about the nation's future and indeed more pessimistic about "the way things [were] going in the United States" than they had been at any other time since the Carter presidency in the late 1970s, they nonetheless believed that they could "plan and regulate their own lives, even while the national economy and popular culture appear[ed] to be spinning out of control." As one would expect, those with higher incomes and more education are more optimistic than those with less; Republicans are more optimistic than Democrats or Independents; and, significantly, men are more hopeful than women. In looking toward the future, young men clearly dream of "the good life," of upward mobility and their share of material possessions. While young women historically have had far less control over their lives than men, for the past twenty-five years they have been urged to take greater control, both in the workplace and in their private lives, and they have clearly taken the message very much to heart.

Angela Dawson, a sixteen-year-old high-school junior from southern California, sums up the views of the New American Dreamers: "It's your life. You have to live it yourself. You must decide what you want in high school, plan your college education, and from there you can basically get what you want. If you work hard enough, you will get there. You must be in control of your life, and then somehow it will all work out." . . .

This increased commitment on the part of women to enter the "public" sphere and, in many cases, to aim for the most prestigious jobs, to reach for the top, to "go for it," is reflected in other aspects of their lives. One of these is young women's increased participation in athletic activities. A recent survey indicates that among a random sample of girls aged seven to eighteen, 82 percent said that they currently participate in sports. Eighty-seven percent of the parents polled believe that sports are as important for girls as for boys.

Young women clearly have a great deal to gain from intense athletic involvement: the confidence that comes with the development of skills, an understanding of the importance of teamwork, improved body image, and, of course, the friendships that can develop from continuous commitment to and participation in activities one cares about deeply. But perhaps the most important benefit was spelled out by the mother of a teenage female athlete: The "message of sports," she writes, is to "be aggressive . . . Go for the ball. Be intense." It must be noted that in this case it was the athlete's father who continuously counseled her to really "go for it," not to be content to "sit on the bench." The writer notes how girls have been trained for generations to "Be quiet, Be good, Be still . . . not to get dirty" and that being intense is "neither quiet nor good. And it's definitely not pretty." What participation in athletics can teach a young woman, and what she must learn if she is really to be a force in this society, is to not be "afraid to do her best." This is part of what Angela and some of the other young women seem to be saying—they are going to go out there and not be afraid to do their best.

These women have a commitment to career, to material well-being, to success, and to independence. To many of them, an affluent life-style is central to their dreams; they often describe their goals in terms of cars, homes, travel to Europe. In short, they want their piece of the American Dream. Many of them plan eventually to weave marriage and children into the superstructure; some of them are not so sure. But for now their priorities are to figure out who they are, get on with their education, and become successful in their chosen field.

What is new about the dreams of many young women today is not only that they are the central characters in their plans for the future but that they believe they must prepare themselves to go it alone. Young women of all classes talk about the need to be independent. Some quote their mothers and other female relatives who are urging them to organize their lives so that they can take care of themselves. A seventeen-year-old midwestern daughter of divorced parents reports, "My mom tells me I have to be self-secure. I don't want to have to depend on anyone." Another says, "My mother wants me to be happy and she wants me to be able to take care of myself." Yet another: "My grandmother says 'Have your own nest egg.'" Several young women in the Southwest agree. A seventeen-year-old whose parents are divorced: "I want to be independent—financially and emotionally. I want to be stable and independent. I do not want to rely on anyone else," she says emphatically. A twelve-year-old agrees and says her friends talk about the need for women to be able to support themselves and their families. She was five months old when her parents divorced and freely admits she still wishes they would get back together. A sixteen-year-old whose mother is a "housewife" and whose father does "sales-type jobs" but is currently unemployed isn't sure what she wants to do but knows she wants a "decent job" and doesn't want "to end up dependent."

This perception on the part of young women that success is there for the taking, that affluence is a necessary ingredient in any life plan, and that they need to be able to stand on their own can be seen as a coming together of several strands of American thought: the American Dream promises upward mobility to those who plan and work sufficiently hard; the women's movement has taught at least two generations of women that they are entitled to play virtually any roles in society that they are capable of and that they are entitled to reap the appropriate rewards; and the ideology of the Reagan years has both stressed individualism and undermined Americans' belief in the necessity of creating a more humane and equitable environment in which all people can thrive. During the 1980s we have witnessed, I believe, the merging of these three lines of thought against a backdrop of ever-increasing disparities in wealth and well-being between rich and poor, black and white, and ever-increasing emphasis on materialism, often at any cost—what one social critic has called the "empty ostentation and narcissistic culture of the 1980s." Is it any wonder that young women feel they are on their own? The message that they must go it alone is being given to many Americans: the homeless; the hungry; the elderly nursing-home residents; the children who are essentially lost in the foster-care system; the millions who are uninsured for health care and those who do not have access to care because of inadequate or nonexistent services; the numbers of young people receiving inferior education that cannot possibly prepare them for living and working in the next century. Moreover, young women see on a personal level that individuals must be able to care for themselves. They see their divorced parents floundering; they hear the cautionary tales about relying too much on men; they are all too aware of the status and respect given in American society to those who embody the traditional male characteristics of autonomy and power, and know that to protect themselves they must have no less.

The feminist movement did not, of course, set out to bolster and extend to yet another group the ideology of individualism and the American Dream. With its appeal to "sisterhood" and its use of consciousness-raising groups, it set out, rather, on a far more collective course, encouraging women to see themselves not simply as individuals but as part of a long, international struggle for equality. But movements do not exist in a vacuum. The women's movement originated within a class system that drew largely middle- and upper-middle-class adherents and then was in part shaped by their concerns and their needs. It exists today within an individualistic, hierarchical system committed for the most part to private enterprise and profit making. Once it became clear that the movement was not going to disappear, elements of that structure began admitting "the best and the brightest" to their hallowed halls. Leaders of the movement might call for widely available day care, paid parental leave, larger welfare grants, and more money for prenatal care, but what was picked up by the media were the upper-middle-class women in the courtrooms, the board rooms, and the emergency rooms, often putting off marriage and children in order to go for the brass ring of success.

This ideology of independence and individualism can be seen to some degree in all three groups, but it is far more prevalent among the New American Dreamers, and adds significantly to the pressure these young women already feel. They feel pressure to succeed not only for the status and material rewards success bestows but because they recognize the likelihood that they may be the sole support of themselves and their children.

This sense of responsibility, of aloneness, brings a new intensity to the need to be "successful." Many young women see the choices as "making it" or "not making it," being "independent" versus being "dependent." Understood in those terms, the pressure is to work out a way for oneself to live the good life. . . .

Stacy Steinberg, a soft-spoken yet articulate seventeen-year-old high-school junior, whose mother is a school nurse and whose father is an auditor, analyzes the pressures young women feel: "It's so hard to be an adolescent today, and it's only going to get harder. Kids today have to worry about liquor, drugs, sex, *and* their academic work. And your parents want you to do better than they did, but it's harder to do better today than when they were growing up."

She goes on: "Guys have different pressures; they're more into sexual experiences. But it's harder to be a girl. You see models in ads and say, 'I don't look like that; how can I fit into that?' Parents say, 'When you lose a few more pounds, you can get a new outfit.' And the pressure about grades—the girls who cry if they don't do perfectly on a quiz!

"You want to be feminine but independent. What's an independent woman? Someone who if left on her own could fend for herself.

"The world is changing and it's hard to figure out where you belong. I have an anorexic friend; she just wants control over her life. What with competition,

SATs, parents pressuring kids, and divorce, kids need their parents more than ever but they just can't communicate with them."

While the emphasis among the New American Dreamers is on doing, on career, on material rewards, these young women almost always include commitment to family as one of their central concerns. Although they have taken on the goals of high achievement, success, and independence, they have for the most part kept the values of caring for others. They now see a dual responsibility, at work and at home, both public and private. The New American Dreamers may at this time in their lives place their career goals first, but as they look ahead it becomes clear that many fully expect to care for family and children as well.

Alexandra Morgan, a black seventeen-year-old from the Midwest, whose mother is a high-school teacher and whose father is a chemist, hopes to be an oceanographer. She plans to "settle down" after she completes a B.S. and an M.S. in science and oceanography, but only when she finds the right person, one with whom she wants to "share the future." He must be "what I want in a guy"; what is important is "how he carries himself and if he knows what he wants out of life." She plans to have "no more than two children" and worries about "juggling work and coming home to the children—they need to know they are loved." She recalls that her mother always worked but was always there. But her mother had a work life based on the school calendar—Christmas and spring vacations, summers off. How will Alexandra manage to do both? In her plans for the future the doing is clear and concrete; the caring is hazier, harder to imagine.

Wendy Jackson has the dream, too. A twenty-year-old junior from one of the campuses of the University of North Carolina, Wendy is the youngest of three children and comes from a working-class family. Her father, now retired, was a supervisor in a local textile plant, and her mother still works as a winder in another textile plant. Wendy's dream seems in many ways to be at odds with the life she is leading. An undergraduate major in social work, she plans to work with handicapped people, probably as a school social worker. She is also engaged; her fiancé is studying, in her words, "ag ed"—agricultural education—and they plan to live in Raleigh. But Wendy does not see herself marrying until she is at least twenty-six. "The most important thing is independence," she says. "You have to be secure within yourself before making a connection with someone else. If something ever happens, you must be able to stand alone.

"I want to expand, to see things and meet people. I don't want to stay in one place. I don't want to hold back. I want to be released into a new world. I know social work might put me back because of the money; it might not allow me to do the things I want to do. I plan to go on and get an MSW so that I can make more money."

Wendy isn't sure whether she wants children. She does know that she wants to travel and that she wants a different kind of marriage than her mother had. "My father came home and lay on the couch." What kind of relationship does she want? "I'm selfish—call me greedy. I'm not going to come home and wash his clothes. I'd rather not get married than be someone's maid!"

Wendy is on course for a very different life than the one she says she wants. She's studying for a bachelor's degree in social work; as she comments, she is likely to be paid a meager salary and have few opportunities for promotion. Her professional options will improve somewhat with an MSW, but will these opportunities get her where she wants to go? She's engaged at the age of twenty and yet has an image of independence and adventure that seems at odds with the life of a married social worker living in a small city in North Carolina. Wendy's relatively unconventional ideas and dreams seem directly in conflict with her far more conventional life choices. It is almost as though Wendy's hopes for the future were taken from *Ms.* magazine while her real options were rooted in *Good Housekeeping*.

Other young women have this inner drive, this vision of what they want to become that impels them onward when others from similar backgrounds might choose more modest goals. Sandra Curran grew up in New York City, the youngest of four children. Her parents came to this country from Trinidad when Sandra was ten; they have both worked in a hospital for many years—her father as a security guard, her mother as a unit secretary. From the time she was a junior in college, Sandra has had a vision of her future life: she planned to get her master's degree in social work, work a couple of years, and then go on to law school. And she has done exactly that. Along the way she married a young man who is working in computers and also getting his master's degree; she is currently holding down a full-time, extremely demanding job in foster care while attending law school at night. Why is she doing all this? Where does the drive, the impetus come from? Sandra tries to explain:

"I have a picture of a certain life-style that I want. By the time I'm forty I want to be able to enjoy my family, live in the suburbs. I want to work by choice rather than out of necessity.

"Law will enable me to speak out—to advocate for individuals and families. I plan to practice either family or criminal law, and with my MSW and my law degree I can deal with counseling, advocating, and legal issues in a holistic way.

"I just have an image of how I see myself in the future, how I will be comfortable emotionally. I have always had high expectations."

Like many other New American Dreamers, Sandra is clear about how to develop her career but far less clear about how she will manage family and career. As with so many women who are firmly set on their quest, she sees what she must do to get where she wants to be professionally, but while she is also committed to children, to family, and to caring, that aspect of life is less mapped out, more sketchily drawn. One of the characteristics of the New American Dreamers is their focus on what they need to accomplish *before* they become emotionally involved. Their focus is on their professional lives, on doing; caring is part of the picture but less clearly visualized. Nonetheless it is always there, in the background, for though young women understand that they must be active participants in society, they also understand that new arrangements have yet to be worked out to provide the caring that women once provided. The New American Dreamers know that they want to be prepared to take on new roles and responsibilities even as they suspect they will still be expected to perform the old ones as well. . . .

Economic Discrimination

Marilyn French

Marilyn French (1929–   ) was born into a Polish American family in Brooklyn. She married in 1950. After working to put her husband through law school and raising two children, she went to college, completing a Ph.D. at Harvard University in 1972, five years after her divorce. Her best-selling novel, The Women's Room, *was published in 1977. She says that its success "suggested that the world was open to change." Of the many literary conventions the novel broke, French isolates two: It challenged the assumptions that women's work is trivial, and it defeated the premise that men are central to women's lives. The following selection is from* The War Against Women *(1992).*

THE STATISTICS PRESENTED AT THE UNITED NAtions Conference on Women in Copenhagen in 1980 remain true today: women do between two-thirds and three-quarters of the work in the world.[1] They also produce 45 percent of the world's food. But they are still granted only 10 percent of the world's income and 1 percent of the world's property—and part of that 1 percent masks male ownership hidden for tax purposes. (In the United States, property ownership is murky because most people own only a residence, usually placed in the names of both husband and wife. But the U.S. Census Bureau estimates that 16 percent of the property in this country is owned by women in their own right as female heads of household.)[2] And women's situation is worsening because a new world order created by a new global economic system puts men in power everywhere, even in places where women had some voice until recent decades.

The entire world is linked today: few communities exist in isolated autonomy. What links us is economics, world-scale trading. Today, almost everyone is affected by a rise in the price of oil. Droughts and crop failures have more limited impact, yet touch areas far beyond those immediately affected. All states are part of a world market to various degrees controlled by global agencies—the World Bank, the International Monetary Fund, the United Nations. The annual reports of these bodies and of national governments are based on national statistics that claim to represent a country's economic performance. In her book *If Women Counted,* Marilyn Waring explains the significance of such accounts, which with the UNSNA (United Nations System of National Accounts) contain the information the UN uses to assess each nation's yearly contribution and evaluate the success of development programs. These reports are used by aid programs to identify nations most in need of help, by businesses to locate new areas for investment and choose markets, and to guide internal policies.[3]

Everywhere in the world, analyses of these statistics determine what has happened and what should happen in the future. Like a single graph claiming to contain everything important, they guide national and international plans and programs. They do not dictate policy; they are the data on which policies are based. But they are narrow, quantitative, and linear; they are guides only to economic and political exploitation. Omitting more than they include, they cannot guide users to broader social goals like well-being. They reflect not a country's actual production but its *cash-generating* capacities. There are two constants about these statistics: men make the decisions based on them; and what they omit are women, children, and the environment. The current state of the world arises from a system that puts little or no value on peace, preserving natural resources, women's labor, or the unpaid job of reproducing and maintaining human life. As Waring stresses, the system cannot respond to values it refuses to recognize.

At the end of the U.N. Decade for Women in 1985, a report on the state of the world's women concluded that women made some gains in education, health, employment, and politics during the decade, but still bore most responsibility while men had most power. The report stated that 35 percent of married European women work for wages; in Africa, women do 75 percent of the agricultural work over and above their work fetching water and firewood, cleaning, cooking, and tending children; in Malawi, for example, women put in as much work as men raising cotton and doing domestic chores, but also do twice as much work as men growing corn. In Burkina Faso, people lose weight during the rainy season because the women work such long days in the fields they are too exhausted to cook (and evidence suggests it is as hard for a man to prepare his dinner as it is for him to have a baby). In industrialized countries, women work fifty-six hours a week in the home; women in nonindustrial countries spend even more time—besides taking responsibility for procreation.

Women's gigantic task reproducing the human race, supporting and maintaining it, is specifically excluded from both Gross Domestic Product (GDP) and Gross National Product (GNP) statistics. (Gross National Product measures production that generates income *for* a nation's residents; Gross Domestic Product measures production that generates income *within* a country, even if the resources are not owned by its residents. U.N. statistics now use GDP, but the United States continues to favor GNP.)

Women are not counted as part of the labor force because they are not paid for their work, or because men take their wages, or because *their work is not considered work.* Waring offers the example of the Beti people living in the rain forest of southern Cameroon. The Beti practice slash-and-burn agriculture, clearing two new half-acre fields each year and cultivating them for two or three years. Food farmers (women are the farmers in most of Africa) always have four to six fields under cultivation, growing mainly groundnuts, cassava, cocoyams, plantains, and vegetables. Men too farm, but they raise cocoa, a cash crop and major export.

Beti men work seven and a half hours a day. They help the women raise food for an average of less than an hour a day; they work two hours on the cocoa plots, four hours making beer or palm wine or baskets, building or repairing houses, making housing materials or other simple commodities intended for sale, or in part-time wage work. Beti women work *at least* eleven hours a day: five hours raising food, and an extra hour to produce a surplus for city markets; three to four hours to process and cook food for the family, and two hours or more to collect water and firewood, do the washing, tend the children and the sick. Without women's work, the Beti could not live. Yet the International Labor Organization, a U.N. agency, counts the Beti man but not the Beti woman as an "active laborer" because she does not "help . . . the head of the family in his [sic] occupation."

After they won their independence from Western imperialist powers in the mid-twentieth century, many Third World countries, abetted by Western aid agencies and corporations, sponsored projects to "develop" their resources. Most development projects aim at enabling a population to earn cash by selling crops or manufactures for export or to urban national markets. In some countries, land appropriated by colonial powers was redistributed to the people. But it was almost always given only to men, and programs for raising cash crops (intended for market, not subsistence)—which involve instruction, gifts or loans of seeds, fertilizers, and tools—are established for men only. Women in developing countries work harder than men, but because they merely feed society and do not earn cash, their work is valued less than men's—or not at all.

After independence, African states named men "head of household" in census data and planning projects; this alone excluded women from national and international development programs. Men dominate the courts and legal practice, so the legal rights women do possess are rarely enforced. Kenya passed new laws protecting widows' shares in their husbands' estate, but land is still commonly passed to the eldest son. Under apartheid, South African women are disadvantaged by laws confining them to overcrowded reserves, limiting their right to work and own land, and preventing them from moving to cities where they might find opportunities.

Almost all development projects in Africa focus on men. Although women are the farmers in most of Africa, very little help has been channeled to them. Land reform projects transfer land titles to men, which make them eligible for improvement loans and agricultural extension services. Without title to land, women are excluded from these. African women produce not only the food people eat, but most goods for domestic use or trade. Introduction of Western manufactured goods has weakened or ended their economic independence. When the West industrialized, working-class women were hired for factory work; however exploited, they could earn wages that enabled them to escape men's oppressive hold. But as industries spring up in Africa, they do not hire African women for wages or any job that allows them to accumulate capital. All African women get for backbreaking work on farms and providing goods and services in the casual exchange economy is—sometimes—bare survival, their own and their children's. Yet their work subsidizes corporate profits; women's work supports the men working in mines, on cash-crop farms, and in urban industry.

In 1984, an African woman farmer ironically remarked, "This one they call farmer; send in teachers to teach him to farm (while I'm out growing the food); lend him money for tractors and tillers (while I'm out growing the food); promise him fortunes if he'd only raise cotton (while I'm out growing the food). No, I daren't stop working, and I won't abandon that thing I was born for—to make sure my children have food in their bellies."

Farm women in Africa (and India) are the most overworked humans in the world, working ten to fifteen hours a day at a host of jobs. A typical Zimbabwean woman's day begins at 3:00 A.M. Every day she goes to the river for water, weeds the fields (breast-feeding her baby as she works), chases animals away from crops, pounds grain into flour, prepares meals, and gathers wood (steadily walking farther with these heavy loads because drought and overcutting have depleted fuel wood). She helps her husband cultivate cash crops, processes food (threshes, dries, grinds), and carries it to market. She has weekly tasks like laundering. In the Ivory Coast, adult women's workload is twice men's; in Burkina Faso, women do all household work and still spend *82 percent* more time on farm work than men. A Tanzanian man complained, "Water is a big problem *for women.* We can sit here all day waiting for food because there is no woman at home. Always they are going to fetch water."[4] (Emphasis added.)

Women's traditional right to hold land varies from one to another African society, but in practice most women need living husbands to get access to land. Men hold such tight control of land that a woman who cultivates land owned by a husband who works in the city is not allowed to decide what crops to plant. Most Lesotho men work in South African mines, yet their wives need their permission to start a farming operation, hire a sharecropper, or get a loan from a credit union. Because they lack land rights, women cannot get credit. In many places, they cannot even join cooperatives that control credit, transport, and marketing. Nor do they have the right to the income from cash crops, *even if they raise them.*

Producing cash crops often raises family income, yet studies of projects that give men new technology to raise cash crops show that despite increased income, the family eats less and poorer food. Women's and children's nutritional levels fall because the income belongs to the men, who use it to throw "prestige feasts" or buy transistor radios. Men in Cameroon at least pay their children's school fees, but in Kenya, writes Irene Tinker, men gamble, buy liquor, and rent prostitutes, while their families starve—women can no longer raise food for the family because their work and the family land are given over to the men's cash crops.[5] In India, researchers estimate, men spend about 80 percent of their earnings on themselves: motorcycles, radios, watches, television sets, movies, alcohol, and prostitutes. African migrant workers send home a mere 10 percent of their earnings on average; women residents in the hostels in Cape Town roll their eyes at the men's "toys," as they call them—cars in various states of disrepair that clutter up the space around the hostel. In the United States, too, huge numbers of men desert wives and the children they have fathered, spending more on themselves while the family is forced onto welfare.

Studies also show that when women have resources or earn income at all, children's nutritional levels and well-being improve. Indian women, for example, consistently spend 95 percent of their earnings on their children. Indians have a saying: "A penny to a woman is a penny for the family; a penny to a man is a penny for the man." Yet when a Zambian tax code was amended in 1986 to give women half of a child allowance that had formerly gone to men, Zambian men complained women would waste it on "perming their hair, buying makeup and expensive dresses." Yet most Zambian men earn little and appropriate their wives' wages as their property, and most male employers exclude women from wage labor. Such lopsided systems increase male dominance and make it hard for women to negotiate or demand what they need to support themselves and their children. Because men rarely take responsibility for children, the children of the world are at risk.

The most blatantly exploitive form of development is what is called sexploitation or sex-tourism, a new business, tours for men to Third World countries to visit brothels created specially for them, womaned by virtual slaves—girls, often just children, sold into bondage by poor peasant fathers. *Sex-tourism was proposed as a development strategy by international aid agencies.* Maria Mies writes that the sex industry was first planned and supported by the World Bank, the IMF, and the United States Agency for International Development.[6] Thailand, the Philippines, and South Korea are the present centers of Asian sex-tourism. Parties of Japanese businessmen are flown to one of these centers by their companies as a reward. American workers at a construction site in Saudi Arabia, totally fenced off from the culture around them, were flown to Bangkok every two weeks to be serviced by Thai women working in massage parlors. Another part of the sex industry is marriage brokerage: private companies, most in what used to be West Germany, sell Asian or Latin American women as wives, openly advertising them as "submissive, nonemancipated, and docile." Both industries are maintained by a support network of multinational tourist enterprises, hotel chains, airlines, and their subsidiary industries and services.

The global accounting system reveals the profundity of male contempt for the necessary in human life, treating not just women's work but the environment as insignificant. In a damning indictment, Waring describes international environmental policies that directly affect all of us. Consider: economic statistics calculate the value of "undeveloped" rain forest in Brazil at $0. A standing tree offers shade and coolness, prevents erosion, and returns oxygen to the atmosphere. But it has no value in the GDP until it is cut down. Industry has polluted the earth irrevocably; many of us or our children will die from cancers caused by environmental poisoning, or will suffer miscarriage, stillbirth, blindness, organ damage, or insanity. But unless such poisonings become widely known, as at Love Canal or Three Mile Island, such illness is invisible to the UNSNA.

In fact, while common sense dictates that illness should be listed as a debit in national income accounting, medical care and medicines are given *positive* value. Economists say market prices (of medical treatment, in this case) are reflections of actual wants, but there is no way quantitatively to express wants for clean air, safe water, or standing forests. Nor is permanent damage to water, air, or ecosystems included in the accounting. The only item subtracted from the GNP is depreciation on the stock of capital goods—the cost of maintaining stock like nuclear bombs. The cost of cleaning up an ecological disaster is considered an expression of society's "preferences."

The most devastating indication of our values is that while producing and raising children, maintaining families, and preserving the environment count for nothing in global economic accounting, war is treated as productive and valuable. In 1988, the nations of the world spent over $110 for each man, woman, and child on military expenses—overwhelmingly more than on food, water, shelter, health, education, or protecting the ecosystem. Waring explains that militarization can be measured nationally as the share of the GDP devoted to the production of military goods and services or as the military share of a nation's budget. It is measured globally by the military share of global production and the share of international trade occupied by armaments. From 1980 to

1984, world military spending grew from $564 billion to $649 billion (in 1980 prices), a growth rate of over 3.5 percent. Over 5 percent of the production of the world, 27 times more than was spent on overseas development, was spent on the military in 1983, most by industrialized countries. Global military expenditures in 1985 were $900 billion, more than the income of half the human race. Military expenditures surpassed the combined GDP of China, India, and all of sub-Saharan Africa—a sum comparable to the combined GNP of all of Africa and Latin America.

Waring cites an estimate of over 70 million people engaged, directly or indirectly, in military work, work counted as contributing to the GDP of their countries. Military work is counted as a valuable contribution to society; raising children is not. Nor do we value keeping them alive. In the twentieth century alone, the world has fought at least 207 wars that killed 78 million people. And while states glorify the soldiers who fight the wars, most of those killed in them are women and children. In each minute that passes, thirty children die from want of food or inexpensive vaccines; in that same minute, the world's governments spend $1.3 million of wealth produced by the public (between two-thirds and three-quarters of it by women) on military expenditures. This, Waring asserts, is the real war.

A billion human beings go to bed hungry every night of their lives in chronic undernourishment: the majority are women and children. An average of 50,000 people a day die from starvation and the effects of malnutrition: the majority are women and children. Even in rich countries, chronic malnutrition afflicts millions, mainly old people and families headed by unemployed women with dependent children. In the United States, 12 million children are without medical coverage and 5 million teeter on the edge of homelessness. Poor prenatal care in what may be the richest country in the world means, writes economist Sylvia Hewlett, that "a baby born in the shadow of the White House is now more likely to die in the first year of life than a baby born in Costa Rica."[7]

Such problems are commonly viewed as personal—abandoned women are blamed for not being able to hold on to their husbands, for aging, being unattractive, or whatever faults their husbands may claim. But the problem is really systemic: Western society requires women to rear children in the isolated confines of the home. The economic and moral system of the United States requires women to take care of their families without pay, pension plan, or medical insurance of their own. The force of moral opprobrium was (and to some degree is still) exerted on women to force them into this position, backed by rules excluding them from wage work, or confining them to such low-paid jobs that they cannot afford to pay for child care. Even without external pressure, it is very difficult to earn enough to support a family and raise children at the same time. *The system forces mothers into dependency on men.* But neither fathers nor the state are forced to support the women who maintain society. Judges may award divorced women child support or alimony payments, but the majority of men in fact pay little or nothing, and welfare assistance is both demeaning and insufficient. And the system treats older wives whose children are grown, and who may have been out of the work force for thirty or forty years, as owed nothing—despite their years of work and responsibility for others.

This discounting of "women's work"—which is essentially taking care of all of society—has disastrous effects on women in industrial as well as agricultural societies. Women in socialist nations have long maintained that they hold two jobs to men's one. But this is the case in all industrial states—it is just more of a burden in countries lacking food, consumer goods, and labor-saving appliances. Women in rich Western states have the same problems. When they protest, men say "What do women want? They say they want jobs, then decide they want a baby or complain about being overworked. We *told* them it wasn't a tea party out here in the real world." But women are overburdened not by being in the "real world," but by having two jobs. It seems never to occur to men that taking care of themselves and raising their children should be everyone's work, not solely women's. That overworked women have less energy and time for demanding jobs legitimates men in excluding women from them. The circle again.

Transnational corporations hire Third World women to work for low wages in factories, and coopt their men by making them "bosses." Western women workers too are affected by the increasing tendency of business firms to create systems requiring almost no intelligence or skill from (mainly female) workers in order to pay them minimum wages for mindless work that deprives them of any au-

	Median Income
Entire population	$381 per week
All men	445
All women	309
Whites	391
Blacks	306
White men	462
Black men	334
Hispanic men	316
White women	312
Black women	283
Hispanic women	253
Male managers and administrators	667
Male professionals	628
Male technicians	501
Female professionals and mechanics	475
Female executives, administrators, and managers	421

tonomy. And economic analysts predict that in the future most women will be hired only in low-paid jobs.[8]

Men exclude women almost completely from managerial positions.[9] In Bangladesh and Indonesia, women hold 1 percent of such posts. In Norway and Australia, male managers outnumber females by 3 to 1. In the United States, women hold less than one-half of 1 percent of jobs in the highest echelons of corporate managers and only 3 percent of the top five jobs below CEO at all Fortune 1000 companies. Women earn less than 75 percent as much as men doing the same or similar work; they are still 60 percent of the world's illiterates—and these figures are *improvements*.[10] In societies that value primarily money and power, the value of a group is shown by its financial reward. The accompanying table presents a breakdown of figures from the Bureau of Labor Statistics on median income in the United States in 1987, when for the first time women earned 70 percent as much as men.[11] This is after fifteen years of feminist agitation, begun when women earned only 59 percent of male wages. Demands for equal pay for equal work are a mockery when most people remain clustered in segregated jobs: of 504 occupations listed in the 1980 United States Census, 275 were dominated by one sex (by 80 percent or more). And male occupations *always* pay more than female occupations.

Partly because of job segregation, men reach their peak in earnings and prestige between the ages of 45 and 64, but women reach their peak earnings at 44 and decline immediately afterward. The most recent statistics show that in 1989 the median annual income of women between 45 and 54 was $20,466, only 59 percent of the median income of men the same ages, $34,684; and women between 55 and 64 earned 57.7 percent of male wages—$18,727 compared to $32,476. These statistics, drawn from Labor Department, Census Bureau, and other agencies' data, appear in a report by the Older Women's League, which adds that "less than half the wage gap could be explained by differences in education or work experience."[12]

The figures are even more depressing if we factor in race. There has been some convergence in work experience for black and white women, who now join the labor force at an almost identical rate. Black women have increasingly left domestic and service jobs (like janitoring) to join white women in clerical occupations, but they continue to earn less even than white women, and their unemployment rates are twice white women's. Black women are far more likely than white women to live in poverty, because of their lower earning capacity and because black men earn much less, on average, than white men.[13]

Political analysts in the United States, discussing a swing to the right in recent decades, suggest that one factor in this shift is whites' resentment of laws that redress traditional discrimination against people of color. No analysis I have seen links it to an element that became apparent in the same period, a "gender gap" in voting as women increasingly vote as a bloc against conservative candidates. Yet removing barriers to full citizenship for women affects men more intimately than removing them for people of color. Men's motivation to shift to conservativism may well be their opposition to women's increased economic power and political voice. Clearly, both women and people of color are aware of the nature of the battle, even if it is not publicly discussed; both tend to vote for liberal candidates. The "gender gap" is also a "color gap": one could say the gap is between white males and everyone else. But white males remain dominant.

A major force in impelling the swing to the right is the New Right. Marilyn Power describes this group as social revolutionaries whose doctrines center on a return to patriarchal family structure by forcing women back into economic dependency on men and rescinding legal abortion.[14] The New Right, which draws lower-middle-class whites by stressing a free market and (white male) individualism opposed to the state, helped elect the conservative administrations of Ronald Reagan and George Bush.

Reagan and Bush proclaimed ideological agreement with New Right anti-woman policies (under the euphemism "protecting the family") but found them too disruptive to pursue directly. But over the last decade, their administrations undermined the gains made by people of color and women. Reagan's main agenda in office was to restructure the economy to make big capital more profitable and to reestablish the global political and economic dominance of the United States. His administration dealt with economic crisis by making massive cuts in social services, tax cuts favoring the rich and corporations, and undermining labor unions, but increased rather than cut military spending, generating a severe recession. The result was a redistribution of income from the poor working class (many of whom are now homeless indigents) to wealthy individuals and corporations (many of whom have since collapsed under the weight of their own greed): 60 percent of the cuts in federal entitlement programs in fiscal 1982 came from programs for the poor.[15]

Since women were already the bulk of the poor (women and children made up four-fifths of the poorest class in America even before Reagan), they bore the brunt of these cuts—especially women of color. In 1978, one out of five families in the United States was supported and maintained by a single parent (compared with one in nine in 1970), usually a woman. Families of women raising children alone are 5.5 times more likely to be poor than those with a man present; a family raised by a black woman alone is 10.5 times as likely to be poor as the family of a white man.

So these cuts only seemed sex-neutrally directed at "the poor," not at women. They were in fact rooted in patriarchist theory, which is woman-hating. The idea that poverty is a result of human inferiority is rooted in the beliefs that aggressive pursuit of wealth is a characteristic of superior human beings and that economic inequality, stratification of classes, is adaptive, beneficial to the human race. This is essentially to worship domination. Conservatives like Reagan believe that poverty is a result of personal failure and that programs aimed at ameliorating poverty actually increase and perpetuate it by encouraging sloth in the poor. This belief masks an implicit agenda on women, which Power finds most clearly articulated in George Gilder's *Wealth and Poverty,* highly praised by Reagan and his director of the Office of Management and Budget, David Stockman.

Asserting that the keys to success in a capitalist economy are work, family, and faith, Gilder claims the poor are poor because they lack these. Defining "family" as the patriarchal nuclear family with male "head" and economically dependent female "homemaker," he disapproves of women working for wages because their economic power disrupts this "ideal" arrangement and may lead to its collapse. Dismissing the huge numbers of hungry children in this country, Gilder vehemently attacks social programs like Aid to Families with Dependent Children (AFDC) for their supposed effect on *men.* He blasts AFDC for "making optional the male provider role" and demoralizing low-income men who, unmanned, "cuckolded by the compassionate state," tend to leave their families. Families without men are doomed to poverty because women inevitably earn low incomes. By this logic, he would eliminate all options allowing women to live independently of men on the ground that *female wage-earning is responsible for poverty, urban decay, and crime.*

A broader logic would focus on male responsibility—not just in poor men, but those who control most of the country's resources—but blaming the victim is always safe because she can rarely fight back. An equally cruel bit of economic persecution was revealed in a study directed by Ian Ayres, a professor at Northwestern University School of Law. Six people between twenty-four and twenty-eight, college-educated and well dressed, were taught the same script and body language. The testers—one black man, one black woman, one white woman, and three white men—visited ninety car dealerships in Chicago. Despite the fact that a few of the salespeople were black or female, across the board white men were given the best deal on the cars. The people who could most easily afford a car were charged least; those who could least afford one were charged most. The testers found that white women were charged $150 more for a car than white men, black men $400 more than white men, and black women *$900* more than white men.[16]

Notes

1. The estimate of 75 percent comes from Karin Soder, former foreign minister of Sweden, at the Center Party's convention in 1976. Cited by Berit Ås, "The Feminist University," in *Radical Voices: A Decade of Feminist Resistance,* Women's Studies International Forum, ed. Renate D. Klein and Deborah Lynn Steinberg (Elmsford, N.Y.: Pergamon Press, 1989).

2. U.S. Department of Commerce, Bureau of the Census: *Household Wealth and Asset Management: 1988.*

3. Marilyn Waring, *If Women Counted* (San Francisco: Harper & Row, 1988).

4. Statistics and quotations from Jennifer Seymour Whitaker, *How Can Africa Survive?* (New York: Harper & Row, 1988), p. 152.

5. Irene Tinker, "New Technologies for Food-Related Activities: An Equity Strategy," in *Women and Technological Change in Developing Countries,* ed. Roslyn Dauber and Melinda L. Cain (Boulder, Colo.: Westview, 1981).

6. Maria Mies, *Patriarchy and Accumulation on a World Scale: Women in the International Division of Labour* (London: Zed Books, 1986).

7. Hewlett, op. cit.

8. Kenneth B. Noble, "Low-Paying Jobs Foreseen for Most Working Women," *New York Times,* December 12, 1985.

9. Janice Castro, "Get Set: Here They Come!"; Barbara Ehrenreich, "Sorry, Sisters, This Is Not the Revolution," both in *Time,* Special Issue (Fall 1990).

10. The figures in these two paragraphs come from Elaine Sciolino, "UN Finds Widespread Inequality for Women," *New York Times,* June 23, 1985.

11. "Working Women Gained on Men," *New York Times,* February 2, 1988.

12. Tamar Lewin, "Older Women Face Bias in Workplace," *New York Times,* May 11, 1991.

13. Marilyn Power, "Falling Through the 'Safety Net': Women, Economic Crisis, and Reaganomics," *Feminist Studies* 10, 1 (Spring 1984): 31–58.

14. Ibid.

15. Ibid.

16. Cited in *MS.,* January / February 1991.

Feminism Wears a New Suit

A New Decade Brings a New Mood and a New Direction

Nina J. Easton

Nina J. Easton (1958–) was born in Concord, Massachusetts, and received her bachelor's degree in journalism from the University of California at Berkeley. At the age of twenty-four, while working as a staff writer for Ralph Nader's Presidential Accountability Group, she produced Reagan's Ruling Class, *co-authored with Ronald Brownstein. Her own book,* Women Take Charge, *was published in the same year. Since 1988 she has written for the* Los Angeles Times. *In the following article, she examines the paradox that while feminism has been both powerful and effective, "most Americans still view organized feminism with distrust."*

SCENE 1: DOWNTOWN CLEVELAND—SHARON KINsella, dark hair cropped short, dressed in black from shoulder to toe, is hunched over in a chair, telephone jammed in her ear. "OK, let me ask you a couple of questions. Did he touch you?" As the Midwestern secretary on the line answers, smoke from Kinsella's cigaret coils sleepily upward. "Did this happen in front of anyone?"

Kinsella's phone, a mainstay of the help hotline run by the office workers' group 9to5, still hasn't stopped ringing since University of Oklahoma law professor Anita Hill's charges of sexual harassment against Supreme Court nominee Clarence Thomas surfaced in October. Kinsella has always preached a personal-is-political message. Only these days, she's finding a more receptive audience. "OK, so at this point you have an internal complaint filed. Now, you have to keep something in mind when you're dealing with internal structures. Remember who's signing your paycheck."

Scene 2: Coronado Island, San Diego County—Nine hundred women—400 of them state legislators from both major political parties—have just sat down to dinner inside the Grand Hall of the Hotel del Coronado when Anita Hill arrives. The applause builds to a rock-concert roar. One by one, women hike up their skirts and step, in their sensible pumps, onto their seats. By now, they've shed every ounce of dignity. They're waving pink napkins in the air. Some are chanting, "An-i-i-i-ta, An-i-i-i-ta!" Women reach across one another to shake her hand, even just to touch her. "We can't serve dinner at this end of the room," pleads Ruth B. Mandel, director of Rutgers University's Center for the American Woman and Politics, host of this quadrennial conference on women in politics. "Please go back to your tables."

Hill delivers a scholarly but colorful speech on the "beast" of sexual harassment. She should have prepared for a revival meeting. The women clink their glasses and pound the tables. They pick apart the centerpieces, throwing orchids and mums at the podium. As Hill brings her talk to a close, people are shouting, "Run, Anita, run!"

Scene 3: Washington, D.C.—In the Senate caucus room, where days earlier Clarence Thomas' life was paraded before the nation, a female elite of 300 are gathered for lunch. This is the International Women's Forum, a prominent group of executives, scientists and political leaders known for strict decorum and cautious, nonpartisan politics. When Senator Alan K. Simpson, R-Wyoming, the group's noontime speaker, enters the room, he is greeted with hisses. And when he complains that he and his colleagues on the Senate Judiciary Committee were "portrayed as totally insensitive asses" during the Thomas hearings, the response is even less polite: The group explodes into applause, and some women pound the tables. Later, when the group breaks up, there is much debate over whether they had been too rude to the senator.

All of these scenes are notable for one fact: These are women firmly planted in the mainstream of American politics. While some women represented by these groups readily call themselves feminists, many others recoil from the label. Kinsella knows those women firsthand. "A lot of times, callers to the hotline start out by saying, 'I'm not a women's libber, I'm a people's libber, but . . .'" she says.

Few social movements can claim to have so radically, and rapidly, transformed a culture as feminism has America. Aided by an economy that made the two-earner household a prerequisite for the American Dream, the women's movement continues to boast strong public support for its central tenet that women are not second-class citizens—at the office or at home. But ask women if they consider themselves feminists, and most will say no.

For despite a raising of our collective consciousness that made Ms. a courtesy title and put child care on the national agenda, most Americans still view organized feminism with distrust. Substitute the term *feminism* for *women's movement* in public-opinion polls and support plummets. To many, the term *feminist* still evokes images of hairy-legged, humorless extremists who view men as the enemy. In an effort to combat those stereotypes, many feminist leaders have taken aim—at conservatives, at the media, at political leaders, at almost everyone but themselves. By lashing out, they have managed to underscore the militant image that alienated so many Middle American women in the first place.

The Hill-Thomas episode was one of those rare moments when it seemed possible to rekindle a movement that could speak for a broad spectrum of women—not just activists. Although polls showed that the majority of women—like men—ended up supporting Thomas, Hill's treatment at the hands of the all-male Judiciary Committee visibly re-energized a segment of women not normally found on the recruitment rolls of feminist groups.

The breadth of the reaction highlighted a year in which the nation's attention was riveted on women's issues. If anyone in America didn't already understand the nuances of sexual harassment, most learned enough after three days of live TV hearings to steadfastly take sides in the soap opera of Hill vs. Thomas. For anyone who never heard of date rape, the trial of William Kennedy Smith, who was acquitted, provided a televised textbook lesson. And with the Supreme Court on the verge of overturning *Roe vs. Wade,* abortion is back in the media spotlight.

The anger aroused by these events has given feminists their best chance to regain ground lost during the 1980s, to broaden their following and expand a stagnant financial base. Bolstered by opinion polls, feminist leaders predict that 1992 will be the year of the woman candidate. They also expect increased support for legislative battles over workplace issues. And one gain is already locked up: Last year's events were a financial boon to established feminist groups. Direct-mail contributions have swelled by 30 to 50 percent in the months since the Thomas hearings, despite the recession. As any savvy political consultant well knows, popular rage is the fodder of the most lucrative membership drives. And as 1992 opens, women are angry.

For feminist groups, however, staking out a permanent place at the center of American politics is going to take more than direct-mail campaigns. Almost 30 years ago, Betty Friedan's landmark book, "The Feminine Mystique," spoke to women like a next-door neighbor telling it like it is over morning coffee. By the mid-'80s, however, feminist leaders had lost much of that intimate connection—even while American women were enjoying the better jobs and higher pay feminists had fought for.

Membership in groups such as the National Organization for Women waned, bouncing back a few years later when the Supreme Court began chipping away at abortion rights. There had always been questions about whether a movement led by white, college-educated women could represent the interests of the Latina waitress from Arizona, the black textile worker from South Carolina or the white secretary from Ohio. (America's high-income women are three times more likely to call themselves feminists than the country's lowest earners.) But even natural allies—professionals who poured into the workplace and maybe even kept their own names when they got married—seemed to be turning off to feminist groups.

Appealing to the country's middle ground is going to take a more accommodating, pragmatic brand of feminism—one that helps women muddle through the daily conflicts of work and family, not one that constructs "politically correct" road maps of how women should live their lives. Feminists don't build a base with the mainstream by picketing beauty pageants (NOW), criticizing manufacturers of sexy lingerie (author Susan Faludi in feminism's latest Bible, "Backlash"), suing to stop the creation of all-male inner-city schools (NOW again) or implying that staying at home with children is demeaning (the Wellesley College students protesting Barbara Bush's commencement appearance in 1990 because she was a homemaker).

Organized feminism's sometimes overweening emphasis on lesbian issues is also troubling for Middle America. Traditionalists, of course, object on religious or social grounds. But plenty of women who don't consider themselves homophobic worry that the concerns of a small minority are dominating a movement that professes to represent the majority.

But when feminist leaders talk about child care, family leave, job discrimination (from sexual harassment to unequal pay), the women in what former *Savvy* magazine editor Wendy Crisp calls "that great supermarket middle" respond with majority support. Within the family, feminists can't force men to do more of the housekeeping, but they can—and do—press for legislation to improve the collection of child-support payments. The new activist "is not someone who says we need a revolution, we need to take over political power," says Washington public-affairs consultant Joanne Symons. "Rather, they're saying, 'I'm trying to make a living, and now it looks like I need political power to do that.'"

Symons is part of a growing chorus of women who contend that legal equality does not make women the same as men. Women bear children; for the most part they raise children. Plugging women into institutions designed for and by men—without changing the institutional cultures—can be a recipe for failure. Moreover, if we're to believe a growing body of biological and psychological scholarship, women behave differently from men. "It just doesn't connect with people's reality to say that women and men are the same," says Symons.

But downplaying gender differences is precisely what many leading feminists have done for three decades. That's largely because "differences" historically were the legal excuse for discrimination—whether in job legislation or divorce laws. But the sameness question continues to dog the feminist movement. While the proposed Equal Rights Amendment drew broad public support for its economic benefits, it also enabled opponents to conjure up disquieting images of mothers in combat and boys joining the Girl Scouts.

That's not the only quandary facing the movement. Abortion topped the feminist agenda in the 1980s, largely out of a concern that the Supreme Court would enable states to intrude into what most Americans agree is an intensely personal decision. But now some feminist leaders acknowledge that the choice issue has overshadowed others that are equally important. We've been so stuck in only the reproductive-rights movement," says Marie C. Wilson, executive director of the New York-based Ms. Foundation for Women. Some leaders say feminists need to find ways to accommodate the needs of women who choose to have children, as well as those who don't.

Feminism's most immediate obstacle is its public image. The women's movement continues to suffer from a "perception that it is more elitist, more liberal and more upper-class than the mainstream," notes Republican pollster Linda DiVall. An October 1991 Gallup poll found that only about a third of women were willing to accept the "feminist" label. The movement suffers particularly among younger women. One recent poll, conducted by R. H. Bruskin for Whittle Communications, found that only 16 percent of college women "definitely" considered themselves feminists. And Karlyn H. Keene, a public-opinion analyst at the American Enterprise Institute, said she was surprised at the large numbers of young women who used such terms as "man-hater" or "lesbian" when asked to define feminism.

But organizing feminists in the 1990s is more complicated than youth appeal. These days, most women juggling work and family barely have enough time to do the laundry, let alone lick envelopes. "We are isolating ourselves from the women who no longer have leisure time," says Harriett Woods, president of the National Women's Political Caucus. There is also the problem of how to unite such a diverse group. Some veteran feminist leaders joke that American women like to divide society into three genders: men, other women, and themselves.

And what about selling the feminist case to men—at home, at work and in power? With the salaries of women often the only thing keeping families from falling out of the middle class, it's in the interest of many men to support higher pay for women and to make the office more accommodating to families. At the same time, however, the nation's struggling economy makes child care and family leave more difficult legislative fights. And, some say, women may face male colleagues who are wary—even hostile—toward women in the post–Anita Hill era. Those hearings may have added "greater tension" between men and women at work, says Senator Nancy Landon Kassebaum, R-Kansas. "Already, the economic pie is shrinking. Men are feeling threatened, like they're losing jobs to women as women become more aggressive in keeping their own place in the work force."

"I think there's a fear that feminism alienates women from families and communities," says Wilson. "I hope we can find a way to address the question, 'How can you be for women and not against men?' That's where we've gotten our backs to the wall."

Is NOW Out of Touch?

Eleanor Smeal sits in the restaurant of a Washington, D.C., hotel where a press conference given by abortion-rights activists has just wrapped. It's been four years since she stepped down as president of NOW, but her continued influence is palpable—even more so since her Fund for the Feminist Majority received a $10 million grant from Hollywood producer Peg Yorkin last fall. The money will fund a think tank created to put more women into the centers of financial and political power and to help bring the French abortion pill, RU-486, to the United States. Smeal bites into her sweet roll as the question of feminism's image hangs in the air. She fixes a patronizing stare at her interviewer before patiently, flatly, setting the record straight. "Feminism," she states, "has no liabilities. It's a guarantee of support. Why do you think we call ourselves Fund for the Feminist Majority?"

Smeal is a key figure in the segment of the feminist establishment that blames their problems during the 1980s on (1) the Reagan and Bush administrations (2) the rise of the New Right (3) the media. They rely heavily on Faludi's book to make their case. (This well-researched defense of the women's movement by a Pulitzer Prize–winning reporter pins feminism's image troubles largely on the media.)

NOW was founded by Friedan in 1966 to work within the political establishment, and quickly came to be viewed as a more mainstream alternative to the militant groups formed by scores of angry, radical college-age women in consciousness-raising groups. Filing class-action suits, introducing legislation, pressuring federal agencies to enforce the equal-opportunity laws Congress had passed were all high on the group's original agenda. And as Smeal is quick to point out, NOW has always been at the forefront of such workplace issues as child care, flexible working hours, even homemaker benefits. Smeal, herself a former homemaker from Pittsburgh, was a champion of the proposed "Mothers Bill of Rights," modeled after the GI Bill of Rights.

NOW was never a stranger to street tactics. But in the late 1970s and 1980s, leaders like Smeal and Molly Yard helped forge strategies that positioned the organization farther toward the margins—combative and often unwilling to play by the establishment's rules. Legislation on such issues as child care that are watered down to pass an increasingly conservative Congress risk losing NOW's support. Regardless of their support for women's issues, Democratic candidates who misstep face public rebuke. (Witness the group's outcry last fall over Nebraska Senator Bob Kerrey's overheard attempt at a joke about fellow Democratic presidential candidate Jerry Brown and a pair of lesbians.)

The conflict between the modern women's movement and the family isn't surprising, inasmuch as the movement began as a reaction to the 1950s ideal of the woman who stayed at home, in her husband's shadow, raising the children. Anger about men and traditional notions of home life were evident in some of the movement's early slogans: "Women need men like fish need bicycles." Or, "When God created man, She was only joking."

In the 1980s, Friedan served as a kind of friendly

critic of the movement. She wrote in her 1981 book, "The Second Stage," that the movement needed to better address women's roles as wives and mothers, and she criticized leaders for becoming overly concerned with lesbian rights, and for letting anti-male rhetoric dominate their activities.

When NOW's current president, Patricia Ireland, disclosed in December that she is both married and involved in a lesbian relationship, conservative groups immediately seized on this as evidence that NOW remains out of touch. In an interview later with CBS, Ireland said that lesbian rights would remain at the top of NOW's agenda. "We have to get that battle over and done with," she said.

Ireland is a shrewd former commercial lawyer and a savvy political player, recently devising a strategy to directly pressure corporate opponents of parental-leave legislation through public pickets and personal lobbying. Ireland can be pugnacious. She built her reputation inside NOW with on-the-scene tactics to combat anti-abortion protesters blocking health clinics. "When people are pushing on you, when they are bullying you, you have to stand up to them," she says. "You don't win anything by cowering—it only makes them bolder, it only whets their appetite."

A onetime flight attendant as well as an attorney, Ireland says she knows how to reach a wide constituency. "I'm one of those people who can get up and go to a dressy dinner with the judges from Miami," says the former Floridian, who heads to the office in a conservative skirt and blazer, no makeup and a simple pageboy haircut. "But then I'll start talking about lesbian and gay civil rights just to watch them all squirm in their seats."

It's that kind of comment from a feminist leader that makes conservative opponents positively gleeful. But liberal political analysts have other reasons to claim a gap with American voters: They point to the organization's plans to launch a third political party, which awaits approval from NOW's membership in June. By the same token, many Democratic analysts think their party has gone far enough in promoting the feminist agenda. Brian Lunde, a political consultant who formerly served as executive director of the Democratic National Committee, complains that Democratic candidates spend too much time catering to special-interest groups like NOW during the primaries—"pandermonium season" as he calls it. That damages Democratic candidates in the general election, he argues, "where voters say, 'I don't want any special interest in control of my candidate.'"

To Smeal, an architect of the plan for a third party, there's not much choice left. Smeal notes that feminist organizations like NOW have been in the forefront of the effort to make the workplace more responsive to women. But year after year, they've watched legislation get watered down. The Family and Medical Leave Act the House passed last fall, for example, would mandate unpaid leave for employees taking time off for a birth, adoption or to care for an ill family member.

"We'd like paid parental leave," says Smeal, a leader who seems more attuned to the needs of poor working women than to the complaints of corporate managers who can't break through the so-called "glass ceiling" keeping them from advancement.

NOW's leaders are also tired of seeing Democrats—allegedly their allies—fail to override presidential vetoes on legislation aiding women and voting to approve Supreme Court nominees who are virtually certain to overturn abortion rights.

Smeal sees the effort to launch a third party as an opportunity to finally teach men in power not to take the support of women for granted. With rat-a-tat-tat assurance, the former political scientist ticks off all the times in American history that third parties played critical roles in close elections.

NOW's political party, Smeal says, will be "egalitarian. It will have a strong base among minorities. It will address 21st century questions like the environment. It will take as a given the feminist agenda. And it will challenge the Democrats. Mightily."

The Gender Differences Revival

As a historian, Ruth Rosen is trained to look beyond these momentary battles, beyond crude questions of political strategy and public relations. The University of California at Davis professor fixes her sights on the horizons of society, and when she does she sees feminism—whether you like the word or not—as a ubiquitous force in this country. "The women's movement has entered public and private life more deeply (here) than in any other industrial society," she says.

But she also sees a movement that at times has outstripped America's capacity to adapt. The country was not—and arguably still may not be—ready for an Equal Rights Amendment, Rosen says. "You can't have a cultural revolution without society needing pauses," she says.

Faludi's book describes the 1980s as a "backlash" against feminism—by the media, by traditionalists, by men who felt threatened by women's gains. Borrowing Rosen's prism, however, one could view the decade instead as a time when society had to catch up with changes that in the course of only 20 years turned centuries-old traditions of male-female relationships upside down.

In this context, it's not surprising that as the feminist movement bolted rapidly and confidently forward, critics from within its ranks began to express uneasiness about its direction. Friedan kicked off much of that self-examination in "The Second Stage." Author Erica Jong followed five years later with a *Vanity Fair* magazine commentary chiding feminism for not only being "indifferent to the problems of mothers but downright hostile to children and childbearing."

In her 1986 book, "A Lesser Life: The Myth of Women's Liberation in America," economist Sylvia A. Hewlitt wrote that because of their roles as mothers, women need "more than equality with men" to attain equal earning power. "They need job-protected maternity leave, child care, flextime and specially tailored career ladders." In last year's "Prisoners of Men's Dreams," Suzanne Gordon argued that feminism veered off course by encouraging women to strive to be equal in a man's world, rather than changing the masculine marketplace to accommodate life outside of work. Women, she wrote, are confusing equality with male-defined notions of success.

Corporate consultant Felice N. Schwartz was seared by feminists when she wrote in a 1989 *Harvard Business Review* article that for corporations that don't recognize the needs of the family, the turnover rate among women managers can be costly. Her suggestion of one track for "career-primary" women and another for women who desire less demanding jobs while they raise their children—dubbed the "mommy track" by the press—was instantly dismissed by feminists as a dangerous form of "retro-feminism."

As flawed and often vaguely conceived as some elements of these debates are—the mommy track does risk becoming another vehicle for job discrimination—they reflect a range of attempts to grapple with a fact that feminism has done its best to ignore: that biology combined with the social role of motherhood makes women different—not inferior, just different.

Most Western European countries address women's issues in a different way—from the children's perspective. Policy makers there view child rearing as a public concern; European policies typically are gender-neutral. The result is a network of child-care and parental-leave policies vastly more generous than those of the United States.

Increasingly, many U.S. feminist leaders are talking in terms of bolstering the "family" rather than promoting "women's rights," even though the end result may be the same. Like the European models, U.S. legislation such as the Family and Medical Leave Act has been crafted to apply to men and women.

"It doesn't mean Mom can't be Mom," says Judith L. Lichtman, president of the Women's Legal Defense Fund. "But it anticipates that if Dad wants to be an active parent, he has the fabric of social policy and law that permits him to do so."

Wishful thinking by feminists? Although many social observers doubt that family roles will substantially change, Lichtman disagrees. "It may be my grandchildren's children, but it will happen," she insists. "Unless you come up with a social policy for the future that anticipates men's involvement in family life, you will now and forever say that women must carry the dual burdens of worker and caretaker."

Family-Friendly Feminism

Inside the cluttered press gallery of the U.S. Capitol, a whiff of perfume is in the air. Patricia Schroeder, a Democrat representing the 1st District of Colorado in the U.S. House of Representatives, has arrived.

If Smeal represents an older feminism—combative, uncompromising and operating largely outside the traditional political process—Schroeder has emerged as a leader of the new. While Smeal uses such terms as "feminization of power," Schroeder talks about making the workplace more "family-friendly." A member of the House Armed Services and Judiciary committees, she's also among a cadre of lawmakers in Congress—about two dozen from both parties—who consistently needle the White House and its political coterie on women's issues.

Schroeder has drawn the scorn of colleagues by bringing her kids (age 2 and 6 when she was initially elected 19 years ago) into the Capitol. "I had my kids on the floor all the time," she says. "I ran a tab with Yellow Cab, and if we were in late they'd come here for dinner. Colleagues would act like they didn't know who I was, or they'd accuse me of demeaning the job.

"This is the most unfamily-friendly society I've ever seen, and Washington, D.C., is the most unfamily-friendly city in America. You are what you do. You show up with a child anywhere, and they immediately say, 'What's *this?*'"

Schroeder doesn't strike a chord with every woman in America. Her visibility during the Thomas hearings—when she led a group of women lawmakers who stormed over to the Senate to demand full investigation of Hill's charges—drew angry letters, as well as plaudits, from constituents.

But Schroeder draws broad support from women, largely because of her knack for relating political issues to everyday life; in 1987 she briefly considered turning that popularity into a bid for the presidency. Schroeder frequently kicks off speaking engagements before corporate employees with this question: "How many of you would rather call work and say your car broke down than admit that your child or spouse is sick?" When most hands go up, Schroeder drives home her point: "Isn't it interesting that we will tolerate a technology-caring role, but not a human-caring role?" Then she launches into her lobbying campaign for the Family and Medical Leave Act.

Feminist groups are among Schroeder's key allies, and she is gentle in criticizing them. "I think the national organizations have been great ceiling punchers, rather than following up and leveling the playing field," she says. "They've done a good job of opening doors. But we don't have a group organized around the fact that equal does not mean same. Now that you have women in the workplace, why are we not recognizing their care-giver role the way we do in every other society? Women still have to be the care givers, and now the breadwinners too. I think the women's movement needs to step up and speak to that more directly."

In fact, lawmakers such as Schroeder who push women's legislation on Capitol Hill are increasingly relying on supporters outside the feminist establishment. They also look to the professional groups and unions that unite like-minded women inside the workplace. The activist adage that "the personal is political" has become a mantra of these organizations, where it might better be coined as "the politics of business is politics."

Dozens of women's professional organizations have become veterans on Capitol Hill—the American Nurses Association, the American Medical Women's Association, the National Federation of Business and Professional Women, the American Association of University Women, and on and on. In the 1990s, these professional groups—as much as feminist organizations—are defining the terms of the debate in Washington. "These niche groups have a lot of credibility" among members of Congress, says Andrea Camp, a Schroeder aide. Leaders of these groups report that their members were further politicized by the Thomas hearings.

Schroeder's messages that "equal does not mean same" and that "family-friendly" is the watchword of the '90s find a receptive audience among these new feminists. "I've been talking to the nurses, the women in medicine, to women's groups till I'm ready to fall on my ear," she says with feigned exhaustion, before she runs off across the Capitol lawn one November morning to lobby a colleague for his vote on the Family and Medical Leave Act.

A week later, the bill passes—but without enough votes to override a certain presidential veto. Schroeder and her allies, however, will try again. And one day they will probably succeed. The Thomas hearings proved that there are points of unity among millions of women, that they can be moved to action, that their widespread anger can be channeled productively. Reaction to the Thomas hearings gave feminist groups a new sense of their potential.

The future shimmers with opportunity. But now, with more doors open to women, feminism in the '90s must grapple with a new set of issues focusing as much on gender differences as legal equality. How much can family roles be expected to change? Are women ready to give up the historical notion of what it means to be Mom? And if women continue to raise the children—working fewer hours, forgoing promotions—can they ever break through the glass ceiling?

And what about the children? Are they getting the parental attention they need in this time-starved society? Should activists focus on enabling parents to work less, or women to compete more? Should companies be expected to compensate employees—men or women—who spend less time at work and more with their families the same as those who put in longer hours?

There aren't easy answers to any of these questions. Feminism's greatest failure was pretending there were.

Blame It on Feminism

Susan Faludi

Susan Faludi (1960–   ) was raised in New York City. Following her graduation from Harvard, she worked for the Wall Street Journal, *where her story on the leveraged buyout of Safeway won the Pulitzer Prize. Faludi's best-selling book,* Backlash *(1991), was inspired by the national attention given to a 1986 study claiming that after age thirty, a woman's odds for marriage were extremely slim. Speaking to David Sheff, Faludi reports that an effective propaganda movement, a backlash, has arisen to undermine the women's movement—a movement which asks, according to the following selection, that women "be free to define themselves." She believes that "our so-called individualist society is threatened by individuals more than anything else."*

TO BE A WOMAN IN AMERICA AT THE CLOSE OF THE twentieth century—what good fortune. That's what we keep hearing, anyway. The barricades have fallen, politicians assure us. Women have "made it," Madison Avenue cheers. Women's fight for equality has "largely been won," *Time* magazine announces. Enroll at any university, join any law firm, apply for credit at any bank. Women have so many opportunities now, corporate leaders say, that they don't really need opportunity policies. Women are so equal now, lawmakers say, that they no longer need an Equal Rights Amendment. Women have "so much," former president Ronald Reagan says, that the White House no longer needs to appoint them to high office. Even American Express ads are saluting a woman's right to charge it. At last, women have received their full citizenship papers.

And yet . . .

Behind this celebration of the American woman's victory, behind the news, cheerfully and endlessly repeated, that the struggle for women's rights is won, another message flashes: You may be free and equal now, but you have never been more miserable.

This bulletin of despair is posted everywhere—at the newsstand, on the TV set, at the movies, in advertisements and doctors' offices and academic journals. Professional women are suffering "burnout" and succumbing to an "infertility epidemic." Single women are grieving from a "man shortage." The *New York Times* reports: Childless women are "depressed and confused" and their ranks are swelling. *Newsweek* says: Unwed women are "hysterical" and crumbling under a "profound crisis of confidence." The health-advice manuals inform: High-powered career women are stricken with unprecedented outbreaks of "stress-induced disorders," hair loss, bad nerves, alcoholism, and even heart attacks. The psychology books advise: Independent women's loneliness represents "a major mental-health problem today." Even founding feminist Betty Friedan has been spreading the word: She warns that women now suffer from "new problems that have no name."

How can American women be in so much trouble at the same time that they are supposed to be so blessed? If women got what they asked for, what could possibly be the matter now?

The prevailing wisdom of the past decade has supported one, and only one, answer to this riddle: It must be all that equality that's causing all that pain. Women are unhappy precisely because they are free. Women are enslaved by their own liberation. They have grabbed at the gold ring of independence, only to miss the one ring that really matters. They have gained control of their fertility, only to destroy it. They have pursued their own professional dreams—and lost out on romance, the greatest female adventure. "Our generation was the human sacrifice" to the women's movement, writer Elizabeth Mehren contends in a *Time* cover story. Baby-boom women, like her, she says, have been duped by feminism: "We believed the rhetoric." In *Newsweek*, writer Kay Ebeling dubs feminism the "Great Experiment That Failed" and asserts, "Women in my generation, its perpetrators, are the casualties."

In the eighties, publications from the *New York Times* to *Vanity Fair* to *The Nation* have issued a steady stream of indictments against the women's movement, with such headlines as "WHEN FEMINISM FAILED" or "THE AWFUL TRUTH ABOUT WOMEN'S LIB." They hold the campaign for women's equality responsible for nearly every woe besetting women, from depression to meager savings accounts, from teenage suicides to eating disorders to bad complexions. The *Today* show says women's liberation is to blame for bag ladies. A guest columnist in the *Baltimore Sun* even proposes that feminists produced the rise in slasher movies. By making the "violence" of abortion more acceptable, the author reasons, women's-rights activists made it all right to show graphic murders on screen.

At the same time, other outlets of popular culture have been forging the same connection: In Hollywood films, of which *Fatal Attraction* is only the most famous, emancipated women with condominiums of their own slink wild-eyed between bare walls, paying for their liberty with an empty bed, a barren womb. "My biological clock is ticking so loud it keeps me awake at night," Sally Field cries in the film *Surrender*, as, in an all-too-common transformation in the cinema of the eighties, an actress who once played scrappy working heroines is now showcased groveling for a groom. In prime-time television shows, from *thirtysomething* to *Family Man*, single, professional, and feminist women are humiliated, turned into harpies, or hit by nervous breakdowns; the wise ones recant their independent ways by the closing sequence. In popular novels, from Gail Parent's *A Sign of the Eighties* to Stephen King's *Misery*, unwed women shrink to sniveling spinsters or inflate to fire-breathing she-devils; renouncing all aspirations but marriage, they beg for wedding bands from strangers or swing axes at reluctant bachelors. Even Erica Jong's high-flying independent heroine literally crashes by the end of the decade, as the author supplants *Fear of Flying*'s saucy Isadora Wing, an exuberant symbol of female sexual emancipation in the seventies, with an embittered careerist-turned-recovering-"codependent" in *Any Woman's Blues*—a book that is intended, as the narrator bluntly states, "to demonstrate what a dead end the so-called sexual revolution had become and how desperate so-called free women were in the last few years of our decadent epoch."

Popular psychology manuals peddle the same diagnosis for contemporary female distress. "Feminism, having promised her a stronger sense of her own identity, has given her little more than an identity *crisis*," the best-selling advice manual *Being a Woman* asserts. The authors of the era's self-help classic, *Smart Women/Foolish Choices*, proclaim that women's distress was "an unfortunate consequence of feminism" because "it created a myth among women that the apex of self-realization could be achieved only through autonomy, independence, and career."

In the Reagan and Bush years, government officials have needed no prompting to endorse this thesis. Reagan spokeswoman Faith Ryan Whittlesey declared feminism a "straitjacket" for women, in one of the White House's only policy speeches on the status of the American female population—entitled "Radical Feminism in Retreat." The U.S. attorney general's Commission on Pornography even proposed that women's professional advancement might be responsible for rising rape rates: With more women in college and at work now, the commission members reasoned in their report, women just have more opportunities to be raped.

Legal scholars have railed against the "equality trap." Sociologists have claimed that "feminist-inspired" legislative reforms have stripped women of special "protections." Economists have argued that well-paid working women have created a "less stable American family." And demographers, with greatest fanfare, have legitimated the prevailing wisdom with so-called neutral data on sex ratios and fertility trends; they say they actually have the numbers to prove that equality doesn't mix with marriage and motherhood.

Finally, some "liberated" women themselves have joined the lamentations. In *The Cost of Loving: Women and the New Fear of Intimacy,* Megan Marshall, a Harvard-pedigreed writer, asserts that the feminist "Myth of Independence" has turned her generation into unloved and unhappy fast-trackers, "dehumanized" by careers and "uncertain of their gender identity." Other diaries of mad Superwomen charge that "the hard-core feminist viewpoint," as one of them puts it, has relegated educated executive achievers to solitary nights of frozen dinners and closet drinking. The triumph of equality, they report, has merely given women hives, stomach cramps, eye "twitching" disorders, even comas.

But what "equality" are all these authorities talking about?

If American women are so equal, why do they represent two-thirds of all poor adults? Why are more than 70 percent of full-time working women making less than twenty-five thousand dollars a year, nearly double the number of men at that level? Why are they still far more likely than men to live in poor housing, and twice as likely to draw no pension? If women "have it all," then why don't they have the most basic requirements to achieve equality in the work force: unlike that of virtually all other industrialized nations, the U.S. government still has no family-leave and child-care programs.

If women are so "free," why are their reproductive freedoms in greater jeopardy today than a decade earlier? Why, in their own homes, do they still shoulder 70 percent of the household duties—while the only major change in the last fifteen years is that now men *think* they do more around the house? In thirty states, it is still generally legal for husbands to rape their wives; and only ten states have laws mandating arrest for domestic violence—even though battering is the leading cause of injury to women (greater than rapes, muggings, and auto accidents combined).

The word may be that women have been "liberated," but women themselves seem to feel otherwise. Repeatedly in national surveys, majorities of women say they are still far from equality. In poll after poll in the decade, overwhelming majorities of women said they need equal pay and equal job opportunities, they need an Equal Rights Amendment, they need the right to an abortion without government interference, they need a federal law guaranteeing maternity leave, they need decent child-care services. They have none of these. So how exactly have women "won" the war for women's rights?

Seen against this background, the much ballyhooed claim that feminism is responsible for making women miserable becomes absurd—and irrelevant. The afflictions ascribed to feminism, from "the man shortage" to "the infertility epidemic" to "female burnout" to "toxic day care," have had their origins not in the actual conditions of women's lives but rather in a closed system that starts and ends in the media, popular culture, and advertising—an endless feedback loop that perpetuates and exaggerates its own false images of womanhood. And women don't see feminism as their enemy, either. In fact, in national surveys, 75 to 95 percent of women credit the feminist campaign with *improving* their lives, and a similar proportion say that the women's movement should keep pushing for change.

If the many ponderers of the Woman Question really wanted to know what is troubling the American female population, they might have asked their subjects. In public-opinion surveys, women consistently rank their own *inequality,* at work and at home, among their most urgent concerns. Over and over, women complain to pollsters of a lack of economic, not marital, opportunities; they protest that working men, not working women, fail to spend time in the nursery and the kitchen. It is justice for their gender, not wedding rings and bassinets, that women believe to be in desperately short supply.

As the last decade ran its course, the monitors that serve to track slippage in women's status have been working overtime. Government and private surveys are showing that women's already vast representation in the lowliest occupations is rising, their tiny presence in higher-paying trade and craft jobs stalled or backsliding, their minuscule representation in upper management posts stagnant or falling, and their pay dropping in the very occupations where they have made the most "progress."

In national politics, the already small numbers of women in both elective posts and political appointments fell during the eighties. In private life, the average amount that a divorced man paid in child support fell by about 25 percent from the late seventies to the mid-eighties (to a mere $140 a month). And government records chronicled a spectacular rise in sexual violence against women. Reported rapes more than doubled from the early seventies—at nearly twice the rate of all other violent crimes and four times the overall crime rate in the United States.

The truth is that the last decade has seen a powerful counterassault on women's rights, a backlash, an attempt to retract the handful of small and hard-won victories that the feminist movement did manage to win for women. This counterassault is largely insidious: in a kind of pop-culture version of the big lie, it stands the truth boldly on its head and proclaims that the very steps that have elevated women's position have actually led to their downfall.

The backlash is at once sophisticated and banal, deceptively "progressive" and proudly backward. It deploys both the "new" findings of "scientific research" and the dime-store moralism of yesteryear; it turns into media sound bites both the glib pronouncements of pop-psych trend-watchers and the frenzied rhetoric of New Right preachers. The backlash has succeeded in framing virtually the whole issue of women's rights in its own language. Just as Reaganism shifted political discourse far to the right and demonized liberalism, so the backlash convinced the public that women's "liberation" was the true contemporary American scourge—the source of an endless laundry list of personal, social, and economic problems.

But what has made women unhappy in the last decade is not their "equality"—which they don't yet have—but the rising pressure to halt, and even reverse, women's quest for that equality. The "man shortage" and the "infertility epidemic" are not the price of liberation; in fact, they do not even exist. But these chimeras are part of a relentless whittling-down process—much of it amounting to outright propaganda—that has served to stir women's private anxieties and break their political wills. Identifying feminism as women's enemy only furthers the ends of a backlash against women's equality by simultaneously deflecting attention from the backlash's central role and recruiting women to attack their own cause.

Some social observers may well ask whether the current pressures on women actually constitute a backlash—or just a continuation of American society's long-standing resistance to women's equal rights. Certainly hostility to female independence has always been with us. But if fear and loathing of feminism is a sort of perpetual viral condition in our culture, it is not always in an acute stage; its symptoms subside and resurface periodically. And it is these episodes of resurgence, such as the one we face now, that can accurately be termed "backlashes" to women's advancement. If we trace these occurrences in American history, we find such flare-ups are hardly random; they have always been triggered by the perception—accurate or not—that women are making great strides. These outbreaks are backlashes because they have always arisen in reaction to women's "progress," caused not simply by a bedrock of misogyny but by the specific efforts of contemporary women to improve their status, efforts that have been interpreted time and again by men—especially men grappling with real threats to their economic and social well-being on other fronts—as spelling their own masculine doom.

The most recent round of backlash first surfaced in the late seventies on the fringes, among the evangelical Right. By the early eighties, the fundamentalist ideology had shouldered its way into the White House. By the mid-eighties, as resistance to women's rights acquired political and social acceptability, it passed into the popular culture. And in every case, the timing coincided with signs that women were believed to be on the verge of a breakthrough.

Just when women's quest for equal rights seemed closest to achieving its objectives, the backlash struck it down. Just when a "gender gap" at the voting booth surfaced in 1980, and women in politics began to talk of capitalizing on it, the Republican party elevated Ronald Reagan and both political parties began to shunt women's rights off their platforms. Just when support for feminism and the Equal Rights Amendment reached a record high in 1981, the amendment was defeated the following year. Just when women were starting to mobilize against battering and sexual assaults, the federal government cut funding for battered-women's programs, defeated bills to fund shelters, and shut down its Office of Domestic Violence—only two years after opening it in 1979. Just when record numbers of younger women were supporting feminist goals in the mid-eighties (more of them, in fact, than older women) and a majority of all women were calling themselves feminists, the media declared the advent of a younger "postfeminist generation" that supposedly reviled the women's movement. Just when women racked up their largest percentage ever supporting the right to abortion, the U.S. Supreme Court moved toward reconsidering it.

In other words, the antifeminist backlash has been set off not by women's achievement of full equality but by the increased possibility that they might win it. It is a preemptive strike that stops women long before they reach the finish line. "A backlash may be an indication that women really have had an effect," feminist psychiatrist Dr. Jean Baker Miller has written, "but backlashes occur when advances have been small, before changes are sufficient to help many people. . . . It is almost as if the leaders of backlashes use the fear of change as a threat before major change has occurred." In the last decade, some women did make substantial advances before the backlash hit, but millions of others were left behind, stranded. Some women now enjoy the right to legal abortion—but not the forty-four million women, from the indigent to the military worker, who depend on the federal government for their medical care. Some women can now walk into high-paying professional careers—but not the millions still in the typing pools or behind the department-store sales counters. (Contrary to popular myth about the "have-it-all" baby-boom women, the largest percentage of women in this generation remain in office support roles.)

As the backlash has gathered force, it has cut off the few from the many—and the few women who have advanced seek to prove, as a social survival tactic, that they aren't so interested in advancement after all. Some of them parade their defection from the women's movement, while their working-class peers founder and cling to the splintered remains of the feminist cause. While a very few affluent and celebrity women who are showcased in news stories boast about going home to "bake bread," the many working-class women appeal for their economic rights—flocking to unions in record numbers, striking on their own for pay equity, and establishing their own fledgling groups for working-women's rights. In 1986, while 41 percent of upper-income women were claiming in the Gallup poll that they were not feminists, only 26 percent of low-income women were making the same claim.

Women's advances and retreats are generally described in military terms: battles won, battles lost, points and territory gained and surrendered. The metaphor of combat is not without its merits in this context, and, clearly, the same sort of martial accounting and vocabulary is already surfacing here. But by imagining the conflict as two battalions neatly arrayed on either side of the line, we miss the entangled nature, the locked embrace, of a "war" between women and the male culture they inhabit. We miss the reactive nature of a backlash, which, by definition, can exist only in response to another force.

In times when feminism is at a low ebb, women assume the reactive role—privately and, most often, covertly struggling to assert themselves against the dominant cultural tide. But when feminism itself becomes the tide, the opposition doesn't simply go along with the reversal: it digs in its heels, brandishes its fists, builds walls and dams. And its resistance creates countercurrents and treacherous undertows.

The force and furor of the backlash churn beneath the surface, largely invisible to the public eye. On occasion in the last decade, they have burst into view. We have seen New Right politicians condemn women's independence, antiabortion protesters firebomb women's clinics, fundamentalist preachers damn feminists as "whores." Other signs of the backlash's wrath, by their sheer brutality, can push their way into public consciousness for a time—the sharp increase in rape, for example, or the rise in pornography that depicts extreme violence against women.

More subtle indicators in popular culture may receive momentary, and often bemused, media notice, then quickly slip from social awareness: A report, for instance, that the image of women on prime-time TV shows has suddenly degenerated. A survey of mystery fiction finding the numbers of tortured and mutilated female characters mysteriously multiplying. The puzzling news that, as one commentator put it, "so many hit songs have the B word [bitch] to refer to women that some rap music seems to be veering toward rape music." The ascendancy of violently misogynist comics like Andrew Dice Clay, who calls women "pigs" and "sluts," or radio hosts like Rush Limbaugh, whose broadsides against "femi-Nazi" feminists helped make his syndicated program the most popular radio talk show in the nation. Or word that, in 1987, the American Women in Radio and Television couldn't award its annual prize to ads that feature women positively: it could find no ad that qualified.

These phenomena are all related, but that doesn't mean they are somehow coordinated. The backlash is not a conspiracy, with a council dispatching agents from some central control room, nor are the people who serve its ends often aware of their role; some even consider themselves feminists. For the most part, its workings are encoded and internalized, diffuse and chameleonic. Not all of the manifestations of the backlash are of equal weight or significance, either; some are mere ephemera thrown up by a culture machine that is always scrounging for a "fresh" angle. Taken as a whole, however, these codes and cajolings, these whispers and threats and myths, move overwhelmingly in one direction: they try to push women back into their "acceptable" roles—whether as Daddy's girl or fluttery romantic, active nester or passive love object.

Although the backlash is not an organized movement, that doesn't make it any less destructive. In fact, the lack of orchestration, the absence of a single string-puller, only makes it harder to see—and perhaps more effective. A backlash against women's rights succeeds to the degree that it appears *not* to be political, that it appears not to be a struggle at all. It is most powerful when it goes private, when it lodges inside a woman's mind and turns her vision inward, until she imagines the pressure is all in her head, until she begins to enforce the backlash, too—on herself.

In the last decade, the backlash has moved through the culture's secret chambers, traveling through passageways of flattery and fear. Along the way, it has adopted disguises: a mask of mild derision or the painted face of deep "concern." Its lips profess pity for any woman who won't fit the mold, while it tries to clamp the mold around her ears. It pursues a divide-and-conquer strategy: single versus married women, working women versus homemakers, middle versus working class. It manipulates a system of rewards and punishments, elevating women who follow its rules, isolating those who don't. The backlash remarkets old myths about women as new facts and ignores all appeals to reason. Cornered, it denies its own existence, points an accusatory finger at feminism, and burrows deeper underground.

Backlash happens to be the title of a 1947 Hollywood movie in which a man frames his wife for a murder he's committed. The backlash against women's rights works in much the same way: its rhetoric charges feminists with all the crimes it perpetrates. The backlash line blames the women's movement for the "feminization of poverty"—while the backlash's own instigators in Washington have pushed through the budget cuts that have helped impoverish millions of women, have fought pay-equity proposals, and undermined equal-opportunity laws. The backlash line claims the women's movement cares nothing for children's rights—while its own representatives in the capital and state legislatures have blocked one bill after another to improve child care, slashed billions of dollars in aid for children, and relaxed state licensing standards for day-care centers. The backlash line accuses the women's movement of creating a generation of unhappy single and childless women—but its purveyors in the media are the ones guilty of making single and childless women feel like circus freaks.

To blame feminism for women's "lesser life" is to miss its point entirely, which is to win women a wider range of experience. Feminism remains a pretty simple concept, despite repeated—and enormously effective—efforts to dress it up in greasepaint and turn its proponents into gargoyles. As Rebecca West wrote sardonically in 1913, "I myself have never been able to find out precisely what feminism is: I only know that people call me a feminist whenever I express sentiments that differentiate me from a doormat."

The meaning of the word feminism has not really changed since it first appeared in a book review in *The Athenaeum* on April 27, 1895, describing a woman who "has in her the capacity of fighting her way back to independence." It is the basic proposition that, as Nora put it in Ibsen's *A Doll's House* a century ago, "Before everything else I'm a human being." It is the simply worded sign hoisted by a little girl in the 1970 Women's Strike for Equality: "I AM NOT A BARBIE DOLL." Feminism asks the world to recognize at long last that women aren't decorative ornaments, worthy vessels, members of a "special-interest group." They are half (in fact, now more than half) of the national population, and just as deserving of rights and opportunities, just as capable of participating in the world's events, as the other half. Feminism's agenda is basic: It asks that women not be forced to "choose" between public justice and private happiness. It asks that women be free to define themselves—instead of having their identity defined for them, time and again, by their culture and their men.

The fact that these are still such incendiary notions should tell us that American women have a way to go before they enter the promised land of equality.

Housewives Need Their Own Brand of Women's Lib

Leona Nicholas Welch

Leona Nicholas Welch (1942–) was born in Mobile, Alabama, and attended Alabama State University before moving to California. She is married and the mother of six children. After completing her undergraduate education at Mills College, she went on to earn an M.A. from Holy Names College, Oakland. An English teacher at Diablo Valley College, she wrote the following essay when she noticed a development in the women's movement that caused her to ask: "Are women becoming the oppressors of women?" In addressing herself to women she says, "Camaraderie and sisterhood are there—I have no need to exclude men."

Reprinted with permission of the author.

THERE APPEARS TO BE A NERVOUS HUSH ABOUT THE word "housewife" these days. The feminist movement, initiated in the '70s and early '80s, set the tone and the pace for the out-of-the-home woman of America. Career freedom is a triple-plus reality for most women.

But for some—a once-revered majority—the change has created a quiet tension. There is an invisible woman, a silent and nervous minority among us today.

Where have all the housewives gone? I fear many—those who did not choose the business world—are hiding in their closets, suffering unrecognized inferiority complexes. The closet housewife?

A sudden gust of wind, called feminism, has swept many women off their contented course, and these sit hushed and uncertain in the downpour of American role changes, being careful to disagree with no one.

I fear that there is yet a group of women to be heard. These have been summoned out of their homes by the media, feminist leaders, mothers, sisters, aunts and various assortments of well-wishers. These women could succumb to "liberation" if not heard soon.

They have been shown the door, commanded in some instances and cajoled in others to run and get free. They have been offered escape from the drudgery of dishes, laundry, pets, babies and spouse.

They sit hushed, drenching in the rainstorms and wanting very much to be left alone to dry off by themselves—to simply enjoy being who they already are and doing what they already do.

Where have all the choices gone? And why do we have so many contented, still-at-home mothers and wives apologizing for being "just" housewives? And what is freedom, what is liberation anyway?

Some women have chosen to go career all the way. Some (like me) have the best of both worlds, housewifery and career, and love it. Others have decided to remain at home, serving their families as lovingly and diligently as they know how.

Many of these in the latter group find the climate has changed, and though they do not care to change with it, they are uneasy about saying so. These sit silently by, annoyed or fearful. They don't want to rock the boat, or seem anti-woman, weak or foolish, so they suffer the thunderclaps of feminism.

Timidity is at odds with tenacity, and a cold war wages. Tenacity, the new-age liberated woman, goes about asserting her rights to be whom she chooses, while timidity, the "just-a" housewife, longs to be given back her liberty to enjoy who she was all along. And "assertion" is proudly synonymous today with liberation, while "housewife" has become a head-hanging term.

Webster defines the word "oppress" as "to weigh heavily on the mind of; to worry," or "to keep down by the cruel or unjust use of authority." Is there a new oppressor in the house? Definition No. 1 here seems to apply. These women who apologize for being "just" housewives are worried and weighed down, fearful that they might not measure up by new-age terms as real women doing a noble and worthwhile thing with their lives.

It is sad when we swap oppressors and call it liberation because it comes from one like ourselves, when who we love being is not acceptable because something new came along, and so many others said that it was better, and some even insisted that it was better for all. Are women oppressing women?

Can we not all be heard? Oppressed is oppressed, and it doesn't feel any better for one group of women because it comes at the hand (or more accurately, from the mouth) of other women. A rod by any other name, or in any other hand, is still a rod.

I say, let the aproned housewife enjoy her choice as freely and as confidently as the silk-bloused executive enjoys hers. Freedom is as freedom allows.

I'd like to know that no woman ever again needs to sneak into her very own house and silence her vacuum cleaner and mutter embarrassingly, "I'm just a housewife."

Let each woman stake her own claim, and enjoy the respect and nobility that comes with holding the deed. It is time to bring us all in out of the rain. This is true liberation.

A Pink-Collar Worker's Blues

Karen Kenyon

Karen Kenyon (1938–   ) is a freelance writer and poet whose early work appeared in the Newsweek *column "My Turn." Born in Oklahoma City, she received a bachelor's degree from San Diego State University in 1979. Her first book,* Sunshower *(1981), treats the aftermath of her husband Dick's suicide.* Sunshower, *she says, "is not a book about death. It tells the story of coming back from the valley of dying, of letting go and making a choice for living." Left to care for their son, Richard, alone, Kenyon continues to write and to teach writing in the San Diego area. In the following selection, based on her personal experience, she compares the social standing of slaves and secretaries.*

MORE AND MORE WOMEN EVERY DAY ARE GOING out to work. A myth has grown around them: the myth of the "new woman." It celebrates the woman executive. It defines her look (a suit), and her drink (Dewar's or perhaps a fine white wine). It puts her "in charge." But it neglects to say whom she is in charge of—probably some other women.

The world still needs helpers, secretaries and waitresses, and the sad truth is that mostly women fill these serving roles. Today more women hold clerical jobs than ever before (4 million in 1950 and 20 million in 1981). Wherever we look, we see the image of the successful woman executive but, in fact, most women are going out to become secretaries. The current totals: 3 million women in management and 20 million clerical employees. So for the majority of working women—the so-called "pink-collar workers"—liberation from home is no liberation at all.

Recently I took a job as a part-time secretary in a department office of a university. I thought the financial security would be nice (writers never have this) and I needed the sense of community a job can bring. I found there is indeed a sense of community among secretaries. It is, in fact, essential to their emotional survival.

Human Beings

I felt a bit like the author of "Black Like Me," a Caucasian who had his skin darkened by dye and went into the South, where he experienced what it was like to be black. Here I was, "a person," disguised as "a secretary." This move from being a newly published author to being a secretary made it very clear to me that the same people who are regarded as creative human beings in one role will be demeaned and ignored in another.

I was asked one day to make some Xerox invitations to a party, then told I could keep one (not exactly a cordial invitation, I thought). The next day I was asked, "Are you coming to the party?" I brightened and said, "Well, maybe I will." I was then told, "Well, then, would you pick up the pizza and we'll reimburse you."

A friend of mine who is an "administrative assistant" told me about a campus party she attended. She was engaged in a lively, interesting conversation with a faculty wife. The wife then asked my friend, "Are you teaching here?" When my friend replied, "Well, no, actually I'm a secretary," the other woman's jaw dropped. She then said, "Don't worry. Nobody will ever guess."

I heard secretaries making "grateful" remarks like, "They really treat us like human beings here." To be grateful for bottom-line treatment was, I felt, a sorry comment.

We think we have freed our slaves, but we have not. We just call them by a different name. Every time people reach a certain status in life they seem to take pride in the fact that they now have a secretary.

It is a fact that it has to be written very carefully into a job description just what a secretary's duties are, or she will be told to clean off the desk, pick up cleaning and the like. Women in these jobs are often seen as surrogate wives, mothers and servants—even to other women.

Many times, when a secretary makes creative contributions she is not given her due. The work is changed slightly by the person in charge, who takes the credit. Most secretaries live in an area between being too assertive and being too passive. Often a secretary feels she has to think twice before stepping in and correcting the grammar, even when she knows her "superior" can't frame a good sentence.

Envy

When after three months I announced to my coworkers that I was quitting, I was met with kind goodbyes. In some I caught a glimpse of perhaps a gentle envy, not filled with vindictiveness at all, but tinged with some remorse. "I'm just a little jealous that someone is getting out of prison," admitted one woman. "I wish I'd done that years ago," said another.

Their faces remain in my heart. They stand for all the people locked into jobs because they need the money, because they don't know where else to go, afraid there's no place else, because they don't have the confidence or feel they have the chance to do anything else.

I was lucky. I escaped before lethargy or repressed anger or extreme eagerness to please took over. Before I was drawn over the line, seduced by the daily rewards of talk over coffee, exchanged recipes, the photos of family members thumbtacked to the wall near the desk, the occasional lunches to mark birthdays and departures.

I am free now, but so many others are trapped in their carpeted, respectable prisons. The new-woman myth notwithstanding, the true tale of the woman on her own most often ends that way.

As I see it, the slave mentality is alive and well. It manicures its nails. It walks in little pumps on tiny cat feet. It's there every time a secretary says, "Yes, I'll do that. I don't mind" or finds ashtrays for the people who come to talk to someone else. The secretary has often forgotten her own dream. She is too busy helping others to realize theirs.

On Power

Barbara Lazear Ascher

Barbara Lazear Ascher (1946–) was born in Christiansburg, Virginia, and graduated from the Cardozo School of Law in 1979. Her writing career began with a series of essays published in the New York Times *(collected as* Playing After Dark*) and presented in National Public Radio's "Morning Edition." "On Power," included here, reveals the group dynamics that come into play when outsiders try to become insiders. About her sense of mission, Ascher states, "What I care about very much is getting the academic feminism out to women beyond the walls of academe, people like my mother, my grandmother, my aunt. . . . Educated women have always had opportunities. . . . Women who aren't necessarily going to be reading these books have to know they have the right to be free, that they have rights at all."*

WHEN I GRADUATED FROM LAW SCHOOL, I WAS hired by what is known in the business as a Prestigious New York Law Firm. I felt privileged to be associated with talent and money and respectability, to be in a place that promised me four weeks vacation, my own secretary, an office with a window, and, above all, a shot at power. I would not have preferred working for a single practitioner who struggled to pay rent on his windowless, one-room office in the Bronx.

There's a lot to be said for the accouterments of power. Those who asked where I worked immediately assumed, upon being told the name of the firm, that I must have been at the top of my class, an editor of the Law Review and a clerk for a federal judge. I was none of these, but being where the power is frees you from having to explain yourself.

The "outsider's" version of the "insider" is always distorted by the mental glass through which they observe. The outsider tends to think that once inside the power structure the voyage is over, destination reached. No more struggle or strain. But in fact, once you have "arrived," you discover that there are power structures within the power. You may share office space and a central switchboard, but that doesn't mean you are at the controls.

In my firm, the partners (male) took the young associates (also male), resplendent in their red suspenders and newly sported cigars, to lunch, to Dallas, Los Angeles, and Atlanta to meet the clients. The "girl" associates were sent to the library to do research. Actually, they were sent to the library to stay out of trouble.

Soon the clients with whom the associates dined were calling them for advice. These associates were learning how to practice law. Those of us hidden away in the stacks were learning how to be invisible.

A friend at a similar Prestigious New York Law Firm told me that she had tried and failed to enlist the cooperation of the one woman partner. "I suggested that we, the women associates and she, have monthly luncheons to discuss some of the problems we faced. After all, she'd been one of

---

us." But she was no longer "one of us" and feared that if her partners perceived her as an ally of women associates, they might forget that she was, first and foremost, one of "them." She knew that hanging out with weak sisters was no way to safeguard her tentative grasp of success.

Eight years later, when my friend became a partner, she learned that the woman she had approached for help was powerless within the partnership. She was, in the eyes of the men, their token "girl" partner, and power, like beauty, is in the eye of the beholder. She was a lady and that's how she was perceived. How could her mother have known as she trained her daughter for power in the drawing room that what she would want was power in the boardroom?

However, even if hers was a token acceptance, she had entered that heady realm, she was feted around town as "the first woman partner" and she proceeded to follow a pattern not unusual for women who achieve some semblance of power. She refused to reach behind to pull other women along. It was too risky. She might fall backwards. I blush to recall that when, in fourth grade I was the only girl on the boys' baseball team, I joined in their systematic "girl trashing." I enthusiastically participated in disparaging conversations about people who were "just girls." Who threw like girls. Who giggled like girls. Who couldn't whistle through their fingers, burp on command or slide into home plate. Then, all I knew was that my power depended on keeping other girls out. Now, I know about identification with the aggressor.

Not that it makes much difference. There are uncanny similarities between being the only girl on a fourth grade baseball team and the only woman in bigger boys' games. Take, for instance, the response of Harvard Business School's tenured, female professors when their former colleague, Barbara Bund Jackson, filed suit against the school for its refusal to grant her tenure. Nonsense, these women replied to Jackson's charge of a sexist "institutional bias." Not so, they said of her contention that the school sets "impossible standards for female faculty members." Why shouldn't they? Why should Harvard deviate from the accepted wisdom that a man can occasionally goof off and still be perceived as powerful? It's kind of cute, we say. Oh, look, he's got nice human touches, an ability to have fun. How boyish. How charming. Not so for a woman. She who goofs off is a goof-off.

Tenured Harvard professor Regina E. Herzlinger's response to Jackson's claim of discrimination was, "I don't feel there is . . . friction caused by the fact that there are few women on the faculty . . . I don't think there is discrimination on the basis of sex." Of course there isn't friction for those "few women." And Regina'd better keep quiet if she thinks otherwise. Boys don't like girls who turn around and say, "But what about the other girls?" I certainly never invited my friend Linda to play baseball with us, even though she ran like the wind and threw overhand.

But power, who has it and who doesn't, is not limited to the realm of male/female strife. My husband, a physician in practice for many years, volunteers his time, one day a week at a hospital often described with the same breathless reverence as my law firm. This is the place to which ailing shahs and wealthy dowagers come to be healed. The full-time attendings (those with the power) don't like the voluntary attendings (those without the power), and occasionally rise up to divest them of responsibility. How, you might ask, when wise and seasoned physicians are willing to give their time, free of charge, to teach students and treat patients, could there be a complaint? The volunteers are not part of the power structure. And power's particular drive is to grab more for itself, an act which invariably involves stripping others of any.

Recently, some of the voluntary attendings went to the head of their department and informed him, "You make us feel like second-class citizens." He listened, nodded, and assured: "You are second-class citizens."

Irrational, you say? Of course. But whoever thought that the power drive made sense?

In fifth grade, secret clubs were the order of the day. The purpose was, first of all, the secret. A secret name. Secret rules. Secret members. Secret meeting places. The purpose was to exclude, which is the first step in establishing a power base. The second is to create fear in those excluded. Those of us who assembled the group of meanest and most popular children had the run of the playground. We were a force to contend with.

Recently, when I went to choose a puppy from a litter, I was told, "Don't get the Alpha dog, whatever you do!" It seems that, like their ancestors the wolves, each litter has a leader. He or she is the power in the pack, and once the Alpha dog comes to live with your family, you become the pack.

What does the Alpha dog get for his trouble? A certain haughtiness. A certain swagger. What did the Alpha attorneys in my firm get for their power? A certain haughtiness. A certain swagger. And an occasional invitation to the Piping Rock Country Club.

So who cares? We all did. We who sat in the library working on Blue Sky Memos, something my twelve-year-old daughter could have done, given the careful and patronizing instructions we received. We were enraged at being excluded from Making It Big. What we didn't know at the time is that the ones who Make It Big are always watching their backs, but then girls rarely have the opportunity to learn these finer points.

Power sanctions self-centeredness. (It could be argued that that's why girls don't have it—"They're so giving.") It returns you, full circle, to the delicious years of being an infant and toddler when, it seemed, you were the center of the universe. But what is missing at thirty-five, forty, or fifty years of age is the innocence of the infant, the two- or three-year-old. It is a dangerous absence. Self-interest plus muscle power and experience combine to create a being more pervasively harmful than the sandbox bully.

Take, for instance, Manhattan real estate developers. They are currently a favorite target of the less powerful, and are, in some instances, a legitimate target. There are those who use their amassed fortunes to gain political sway by contributing to the campaign funds of elected officials. The elected officials then turn deaf ears to the complaints of less powerful constituents dispossessed from low rent buildings razed to make room for luxury high rises complete with Jacuzzis in every bath.

Donald Trump's song of himself is on the best-seller lists. *Vanity Fair* featured a breathlessly infatuated profile of his wife. Why? Because if you can't be powerful, the next best thing is to fancy yourself on intimate terms with those who are. There is a hunger to know how they make their deals, shop for their children's Christmas presents, stay fresh and alert from five A.M. until Peter Duchin's orchestra plays its last charity ball waltz at midnight. All this, and not a wrinkle in the brow to show for it.

People read about power for the same reason that little girls read *Cinderella,* they want to believe that someday a prince will come to deliver a subject into sovereignty.

One might ask whether adulation of those who are flagrantly self-involved makes any sense when there are thousands of dispossessed sleeping in Grand Central and Pennsylvania Station. It certainly doesn't make mature sense.

But then power is not necessarily in mature hands. It is most often achieved, and clung to by those whose passion for it is fueled by childlike greed and self-interest. What they find, once they have it, is that being the proud possessor of power bears an uncanny similarity to being the two-year-old with the biggest plastic pail and shovel on the beach. It's a life of nervous guardianship.

I left the law because I wasn't motivated to engage in the struggle required to move myself from library to the light of day and lunches with clients. The struggle would have required molding myself in the partners' images, a hard concept for them to visualize since I was female and they were male. It would have been necessary to remember when to speak and when to keep my mouth shut. I would have had to create an asexual aura. I would have had to work very, very hard.

I left the law because that wasn't the power that interested me. Which is not to say that power itself doesn't interest me. I remember the full glory of being the only girl on the boy's baseball team. I remember the total sense of worthlessness that resulted when I grew breasts and the guys banished me from the pitcher's mound to the powerless world of hopscotch. Power is as tantalizing as a hypnotist's swinging pendulum. Power promises that you will never again be stuck with "the girls." Ask Regina Herzlinger. She knows.

I Stand Here Ironing

Tillie Olsen

Tillie Olsen (1913–), the daughter of Jewish-Russian immigrants, was born Tillie Lerner in Omaha, Nebraska. In that same year another Nebraskan, Willa Cather, published "The Bohemian Girl." Whereas Cather, educated and single, wrote reflectively of the pioneer past from New York City, Olsen left high school before graduating, bore five children, and spent twenty years working to earn a living for them. At the age of forty-four, she received a Stegner Fellowship in Creative Writing at Stanford University, publishing her first book, Tell Me a Riddle, *in 1962, six years later. Olsen writes of the struggle of women to realize their creative potential in the face of poverty and indifference. In the following selection, a mother meditates on social forces set against her daughter's youthful spirit.*

I STAND HERE IRONING, AND WHAT YOU ASKED ME moves tormented back and forth with the iron.

"I wish you would manage the time to come in and talk with me about your daughter. I'm sure you can help me understand her. She's a youngster who needs help and whom I'm deeply interested in helping."

"Who needs help." . . . Even if I came, what good would it do? You think because I am her mother I have a key, or that in some way you could use me as a key? She has lived for nineteen years. There is all that life that has happened outside of me, beyond me.

And when is there time to remember, to sift, to weigh, to estimate, to total? I will start and there will be an interruption and I will have to gather it all together again. Or I will become engulfed with all I did or did not do, with what should have been and what cannot be helped.

She was a beautiful baby. The first and only one of our five that was beautiful at birth. You do not guess how new and uneasy her tenancy in her now-loveliness. You did not know her all those years she was thought homely, or see her poring over her baby pictures, making me tell her over and over how beautiful she had been—and would be, I would tell her—and was now, to the seeing eye. But the seeing eyes were few or nonexistent. Including mine.

I nursed her. They feel that's important nowadays. I nursed all the children, but with her, with all the fierce rigidity of first motherhood, I did like the books then said. Though her cries battered me to trembling and my breasts ached with swollenness, I waited till the clock decreed.

Why do I put that first? I do not even know if it matters, or if it explains anything.

She was a beautiful baby. She blew shining bubbles of sound. She loved motion, loved light, loved color and music and textures. She would lie on the floor in her blue overalls patting the surface so hard in ecstasy her hands and feet would blur. She was a miracle to me, but when she was eight months old I had to leave her daytimes with the woman downstairs to whom she was no miracle at all, for I worked or looked for work and for Emily's father, who "could no longer endure" (he wrote in his good-bye note) "sharing want with us."

I was nineteen. It was the pre-relief, pre-WPA world of the depression. I would start running as soon as I got off the streetcar, running up the stairs, the place smelling sour, and awake or asleep to startle awake, when she saw me she would break into a clogged weeping that could not be comforted, a weeping I can hear yet.

After a while I found a job hashing at night so I could be with her days, and it was better. But it came to where I had to bring her to his family and leave her.

It took a long time to raise the money for her fare back. Then she got chicken pox and I had to wait longer. When she finally came, I hardly knew her, walking quick and nervous like her father, looking like her father, thin, and dressed in a shoddy red that yellowed her skin and glared at the pockmarks. All the baby loveliness gone.

She was two. Old enough for nursery school they said, and I did not know then what I know now—the fatigue of the long day, and the lacerations of group life in the kinds of nurseries that are only parking places for children.

Except that it would have made no difference if I had known. It was the only place there was. It was the only way we could be together, the only way I could hold a job.

And even without knowing, I knew. I knew the teacher that was evil because all these years it has curdled into my memory, the little boy hunched in the corner, her rasp, "why aren't you outside, because Alvin hits you? that's no reason, go out, scaredy." I knew Emily hated it even if she did not clutch and implore "don't go Mommy" like the other children, mornings.

She always had a reason why we should stay home. Momma, you look sick. Momma, I feel sick. Momma, the teachers aren't there today, they're sick. Momma, we can't go, there was a fire there last night. Momma, it's a holiday today, no school, they told me.

But never a direct protest, never rebellion. I think of our others in their three-, four-year-oldness—the explosions, the tempers, the denunciations, the demands—and I feel suddenly ill. I put the iron down. What in me demanded that goodness in her? And what was the cost, the cost to her of such goodness?

The old man living in the back once said in his gentle way: "You should smile at Emily more when you look at her." What *was* in my face when I looked at her? I loved her. There were all the acts of love.

It was only with the others I remembered what he said, and it was the face of joy, and not of care or tightness or worry I turned to them—too late for Emily. She does not smile easily, let alone almost always as her brothers and sisters do. Her face is closed and sombre, but when she wants, how fluid. You must have seen it in her pantomimes, you spoke of her rare gift for comedy on the stage that rouses a laughter out of the audience so dear they applaud and applaud and do not want to let her go.

Where does it come from, that comedy? There was none of it in her when she came back to me that second time, after I had had to send her away again. She had a new daddy now to learn to love, and I think perhaps it was a better time.

Except when we left her alone nights, telling ourselves she was old enough.

"Can't you go some other time, Mommy, like tomorrow?" she would ask. "Will it be just a little while you'll be gone? Do you promise?"

The time we came back, the front door open, the clock on the floor in the hall. She rigid awake. "It wasn't just a little while. I didn't cry. Three times I called you, just three times, and then I ran downstairs to open the door so you could come faster. The clock talked loud. I threw it away, it scared me what it talked."

She said the clock talked loud again that night I went to the hospital to have Susan. She was delirious with the fever that comes before red measles, but she was fully conscious all the week I was gone and the week after we were home when she could not come near the new baby or me.

She did not get well. She stayed skeleton thin, not wanting to eat, and night after night she had nightmares. She would call for me, I would rouse from exhaustion to sleepily call back: "You're all right, darling, go to sleep, it's just a dream," and if she still called, in a sterner voice, "now go to sleep, Emily, there's nothing to hurt you." Twice, only twice, when I had to get up for Susan anyhow, I went in to sit with her.

Now when it is too late (as if she would let me hold and comfort her like I do the others) I get up and go to her at once at her moan or restless stirring. "Are you awake, Emily? Can I get you something?" And the answer is always the same: "No, I'm all right, go back to sleep, Mother."

They persuaded me at the clinic to send her away to a convalescent home in the country where "she can have the kind of food and care you can't manage for her, and you'll be free to concentrate on the new baby." They still send children to that place. I see pictures on the society page of sleek young women planning affairs to raise money for it, or dancing at the affairs, or decorating Easter eggs or filling Christmas stockings for the children.

They never have a picture of the children so I do not know if the girls still wear those gigantic red bows and the ravaged looks on the every other Sunday when parents can come to visit "unless otherwise notified"—as we were notified the first six weeks.

Oh it is a handsome place, green lawns and tall trees and fluted flower beds. High up on the balconies of each cottage the children stand, the girls in their red bows and white dresses, the boys in white suits and giant red ties. The parents stand below shrieking up to be heard and the children shriek down to be heard, and between them the invisible wall "Not To Be Contaminated by Parental Germs or Physical Affection."

There was a tiny girl who always stood hand in hand with Emily. Her parents never came. One visit she was gone. "They moved her to Rose Cottage," Emily shouted in explanation. "They don't like you to love anybody here."

She wrote once a week, the labored writing of a seven-year-old. "I am fine. How is the baby. If I write my leter nicly I will have a star. Love." There never was a star. We wrote every other day, letters she could never hold or keep but only hear read—once. "We simply do not have room for children to keep any personal possessions," they patiently explained when we pieced one Sunday's shrieking together to plead how much it would mean to Emily, who loved so to keep things, to be allowed to keep her letters and cards.

Each visit she looked frailer. "She isn't eating," they told us.

(They had runny eggs for breakfast or mush with lumps, Emily said later, I'd hold it in my mouth and not swallow. Nothing ever tasted good, just when they had chicken.)

It took us eight months to get her released home, and only the fact that she gained back so little of her seven lost pounds convinced the social worker.

I used to try to hold and love her after she came back, but her body would stay stiff, and after a while she'd push away. She ate little. Food sickened her, and I think much of life too. Oh she had physical lightness and brightness, twinkling by on skates, bouncing like a ball up and down up and down over the jump rope, skimming over the hill; but these were momentary.

She fretted about her appearance, thin and dark and foreign-looking at a time when every little girl was supposed to look or thought she should look a chubby blonde replica of Shirley Temple. The doorbell sometimes rang for her, but no one seemed to come and play in the house or be a best friend. Maybe because we moved so much.

There was a boy she loved painfully through two school semesters. Months later she told me how she had taken pennies from my purse to buy him candy. "Licorice was his favorite and I brought him some every day, but he still liked Jennifer better'n me. Why, Mommy?" The kind of question for which there is no answer.

School was a worry to her. She was not glib or quick in a world where glibness and quickness were easily confused with ability to learn. To her overworked and exasperated teachers she was an overconscientious "slow learner" who kept trying to catch up and was absent entirely too often.

I let her be absent, though sometimes the illness was imaginary. How different from my nowstrictness about attendance with the others. I wasn't working. We had a new baby, I was home anyhow. Sometimes, after Susan grew old enough, I would keep her home from school, too, to have them all together.

Mostly Emily had asthma, and her breathing, harsh and labored, would fill the house with a curiously tranquil sound. I would bring the two old dresser mirrors and her boxes of collections to her bed. She would select beads and single earrings, bottle tops and shells, dried flowers and pebbles, old postcards and scraps, all sorts of oddments; then she and Susan would play Kingdom, setting up landscapes and furniture, peopling them with action.

Those were the only times of peaceful companionship between her and Susan. I have edged away from it, that poisonous feeling between them, that terrible balancing of hurts and needs I had to do between the two, and did so badly, those earlier years.

Oh there are conflicts between the others too, each

one human, needing, demanding, hurting, taking—but only between Emily and Susan, no, Emily toward Susan that corroding resentment. It seems so obvious on the surface, yet it is not obvious. Susan, the second child, Susan, golden- and curly-haired and chubby, quick and articulate and assured, everything in appearance and manner Emily was not; Susan, not able to resist Emily's precious things, losing or sometimes clumsily breaking them; Susan telling jokes and riddles to company for applause while Emily sat silent (to say to me later: that was *my* riddle, Mother, I told it to Susan); Susan, who for all the five years' difference in age was just a year behind Emily in developing physically.

I am glad for that slow physical development that widened the difference between her and her contemporaries, though she suffered over it. She was too vulnerable for that terrible world of youthful competition, of preening and parading, of constant measuring of yourself against every other, of envy, "If I had that copper hair," "If I had that skin. . . ." She tormented herself enough about not looking like the others, there was enough of the unsureness, the having to be conscious of words before you speak, the constant caring—what are they thinking of me? without having it all magnified by the merciless physical drives.

Ronnie is calling. He is wet and I change him. It is rare there is such a cry now. That time of motherhood is almost behind me when the ear is not one's own but must always be racked and listening for the child cry, the child call. We sit for a while and I hold him, looking out over the city spread in charcoal with its soft aisles of light. "*Shoogily,*" he breathes and curls closer. I carry him back to bed, asleep. *Shoogily.* A funny word, a family word, inherited from Emily, invented by her to say: *comfort.*

In this and other ways she leaves her seal, I say aloud. And startle at my saying it. What do I mean? What did I start to gather together, to try and make coherent? I was at the terrible, growing years. War years. I do not remember them well. I was working, there were four smaller ones now, there was not time for her. She had to help be a mother, and housekeeper, and shopper. She had to set her seal. Mornings of crisis and near hysteria trying to get lunches packed, hair combed, coats and shoes found, everyone to school or Child Care on time, the baby ready for transportation. And always the paper scribbled on by a smaller one, the book looked at by Susan then mislaid, the homework not done. Running out to that huge school where she was one, she was lost, she was a drop; suffering over the unpreparedness, stammering and unsure in her classes.

There was so little time left at night after the kids were bedded down. She would struggle over books, always eating (it was in those years she developed her enormous appetite that is legendary in our family) and I would be ironing, or preparing food for the next day, or writing V-mail to Bill, or tending the baby. Sometimes, to make me laugh, or out of her despair, she would imitate happenings or types at school.

I think I said once: "Why don't you do something like this in the school amateur show?" One morning she phoned me at work, hardly understandable through the weeping: "Mother, I did it. I won, I won; they gave me first prize; they clapped and clapped and wouldn't let me go."

Now suddenly she was Somebody, and as imprisoned in her difference as she had been in anonymity.

She began to be asked to perform at other high schools, even in colleges, then at city and statewide affairs. The first one we went to, I only recognized her that first moment when thin, shy, she almost drowned herself into the curtains. Then: Was this Emily? The control, the command, the convulsing and deadly clowning, the spell, then the roaring, stamping audience, unwilling to let this rare and precious laughter out of their lives.

Afterwards: You ought to do something about her with a gift like that—but without money or knowing how, what does one do? We have left it all to her, and the gift has as often eddied inside, clogged and clotted, as been used and growing.

She is coming. She runs up the stairs two at a time with her light graceful step, and I know she is happy tonight. Whatever it was that occasioned your call did not happen today.

"Aren't you ever going to finish the ironing, Mother? Whistler painted his mother in a rocker. I'd have to paint mine standing over an ironing board." This is one of her communicative nights and she tells me everything and nothing as she fixes herself a plate of food out of the icebox.

She is so lovely. Why did you want me to come in at all? Why were you concerned? She will find her way.

She starts up the stairs to bed. "Don't get me up with the rest in the morning." "But I thought you were having midterms." "Oh, those," she comes back in, kisses me, and says quite lightly, "in a couple of years when we'll all be atom-dead they won't matter a bit."

She has said it before. She *believes* it. But because I have been dredging the past, and all that compounds a human being is so heavy and meaningful in me, I cannot endure it tonight.

I will never total it all. I will never come in to say: She was a child seldom smiled at. Her father left me before she was a year old. I had to work her first six years when there was work, or I sent her home and to his relatives. There were years she had care she hated. She was dark and thin and foreign-looking in a world where the prestige went to blondeness and curly hair and dimples, she was slow where glibness was prized. She was a child of anxious, not proud, love. We were poor and could not afford for her the soil of easy growth. I was a young mother, I was a distracted mother. There were the other children pushing up, demanding. Her younger sister seemed all that she was not. There were years she did not want me to touch her. She kept too much in herself, her life was such she had to keep too much in herself. My wisdom came too late. She has much to her and probably little will come of it. She is a child of her age, of depression, of war, of fear.

Let her be. So all that is in her will not bloom—but in how many does it? There is still enough to live by. Only help her to know—help make it so there is cause for her to know—that she is more than this dress on the ironing board, helpless before the iron.

In the Laundry Room

Alice Childress

Alice Childress (1920–) was born in Charleston, South Carolina, but raised in Harlem. "I was shut out of so much for so long," she says, "I soon began to embrace the low-profile as a way of life, which helped me to develop as a writer." Her best-known work, about teenage heroin addiction, is A Hero Ain't Nothin' But a Sandwich *(1973). She also writes for the theater. Her 1952* Gold Through the Trees *was the first play by an African American woman professionally produced on the American stage. In the following excerpt, written as a dramatic monologue, Mildred tells her friend Marge of the day's main event.*

MARGE . . . SOMETIMES IT SEEMS LIKE THE DEVIL and all his imps are tryin' to wear your soul case out. . . . Sit down, Marge, and act like you got nothin' to do. . . . No, don't make no coffee, just sit. . . .

Today was laundry day and I took Mrs. M . . . 's clothes down to the basement to put them in the automatic machine. In a little while another houseworker comes down—a white woman. She dumps her clothes on the bench and since my bundle is already in the washer I go over to sit down on the bench and happen to brush against her dirty clothes. . . . Well sir! She gives me a kinda sickly grin and snatched her clothes away quick. . . .

Now, you know, Marge, that it was nothin' but the devil in her makin' her snatch that bundle away 'cause she thought I might give her folks gallopin' pellagra or somethin'. Well, honey, you know what the devil in me wanted to do! . . . You are right! . . . My hand was just itchin' to pop her in the mouth, but I remembered how my niece Jean has been tellin' me that *poppin'* people is not the way to solve problems. . . . So I calmed myself and said, "Sister, why did you snatch those things and look so flustered?" She turned red and says, "I was just makin' room for you." Still keepin' calm, I says, "You are a liar." . . . And then she hung her head.

"Sister," I said, "you are a houseworker and I am a houseworker—now will you favor me by answering some questions?" She nodded her head. . . . The first thing I asked her was how much she made for a week's work and, believe it or not, Marge, she earns less than I do and *that ain't easy*. . . . Then I asked her, "Does the woman you work for ask you in a *friendly* way to do extra things that ain't in the bargain and then later on get *demandin'* about it?" . . . She nods, yes. . . . "Tell me, young woman," I went on, "does she cram eight hours of work into five and call it *part time?*" . . . She nods yes again. . . .

Then, Marge, I added, "I am not your enemy, so don't get mad with me just because you ain't free!" . . . Then she speaks up fast, "I am free!" . . .

"All right," I said. "How about me goin' over to your house tonight for supper?" . . . "Oh," she says, "I room with people and I don't think they . . ." I cut her off. . . . "If you're free," I said, "you can pick your own friends without fear."

Wait a minute, Marge, let me tell it now. . . . "How come," I asked her, "the folks I work for are willin' to have me put my hands all over their chopped meat patties and yet ask me to hang my coat in the kitchen closet instead of in the hall with theirs?" . . . By this time, Marge, she looked pure bewildered. . . . "Oh," she said, "it's all so mixed up I don't understand!"

"Well, it'll all get clearer as we go along," I said. . . . "Now when you got to plunge your hands in all them dirty clothes in order to put them in the machine . . . how come you can't see that it's a whole lot safer and makes more sense to put your hand in mine and be friends?" Well, Marge, she took my hand and said, "I want to be friends!"

I was so glad I hadn't popped her, Marge. The good Lord only knows how hard it is to do things the right way and make peace. . . . All right now, let's have the coffee, Marge.

A Business Trip Home

Anna Mass

Translated by Jerzy Kolodziej

Anna Mass (1935—) was born in Moscow, Russia, where she works as a geologist. She is a member of the Writer's Union, an organization which, in 1976, included one woman for every seven men, and ten years later numbered only twelve women in 372 executive positions. In stories like the one included here, she develops the conflict between a woman's personal identity and society's agenda for her. About the role of motherhood in modern Russia, historian Helena Goscilo reports, "Maternity as investment and act of faith possesses a biological, social, and political dimension in the Soviet Union; a woman's reluctance to have children because of professional considerations is tantamount to civic apostasy."

NO ONE WAS MEETING ME. ALL THE SAME, AS THE train slowed by the platform, like many others, I looked out the window, peered into the faces swimming by, and thought, "And what if . . . ?" But this was just a game, an echo of times long past, when from out of the sea of unfamiliar faces my mother's face, searching and excited, would unexpectedly come floating into view, and, experiencing a warm jolt in my chest, I would squeeze my way toward the exit, bumping into everyone with my knapsack.

"Mother!"

She would take a few steps toward me and always uttered the same words:

"Well, at last!"

And even though similar words were uttered by hundreds of people on this and a thousand other platforms all over the globe, these words belonged only to me and to my mother because, after all, how good it was to return *at last* to my mother and father, to become simply a daughter and to relax after many months of geological wanderings.

We would take a cab home, where Father would already be standing on the balcony. With a slight wave, he would run inside the apartment to open the door.

And then I would enter the clean apartment, which seemed unusually large after the cramped quarters of tents. In the entryway I would take off my unbelievably dirty knapsack, and throw my arms around my father, then undertake a tour of my domain. I would note little changes; a new blind in the window, an elegant new oilcloth, a new ceramic vase with a bouquet of fresh gladiolas. . . . Mother and Father would follow on my heels and lovingly examine with *my* eyes the apartment decorated especially for my arrival.

It's so wonderful when something is done especially in honor of your arrival.

In the kitchen my favorite dishes awaited me. Mother certainly knew what I liked. There were pirozhki—long ones stuffed with cabbage and

From *Balancing Acts*. Reprinted by permission of Indiana University Press.

round ones with apples, and roast duck and peaches. Mother and Father planned long and carefully for my arrival; possibly, they even hired someone to clean up and to wash the windows. All so that I would feel cozy and right at home. So that I would say: "How nice it is to be home!" And that very evening I would leave them and all this luxury that had taken so long to prepare, to run off to one of my girlfriends. But they understood and weren't offended.

"Tanechka, your bath is ready!" Mother would announce triumphantly, anticipating with me how I would momentarily throw off my torn tennis shoes, pants, shirt, and faded underwear—the geological hide, so alien to her, which after long months had become molded to my body—and how I would put on a housecoat and at last would turn completely into her daughter Tanechka.

Now this hide would be deposited in a formless heap in a white clothes hamper, and I would crawl into a hot bath—the apogee of my dream of returning. How often when I was out there, during an expedition or in a drenched tent, did I imagine this: the white tile, the white enamel of the tub, the bluish water gently rocking from the running flow, the white gas heater with its blue rows of flames. White and blue, cleanliness and delight.

Afterwards we would all sit at the kitchen table. I'd eat the pirozhki, cut off the most appetizing chunks of duck, stuff myself with juice-covered peaches, and talk and talk about something while my mother and father would listen, opening their eyes wide, shaking their heads, making frightened sounds, and asking questions to clarify some points. But I sensed that they were not so much interested in my adventures—after all, everything was in the past, thank God, and I was with them again—as in looking at me, scrutinizing me, reveling in the fact that I was here, by their sides. In my face and in my intonations—through the thin coating of the new—they would search for the former me, the one they were accustomed to, their own. And I'd do just the opposite as I attempted to emphasize how greatly I'd changed and how much I'd experienced. I talked nonsense and exaggerated. But even in this bragging they saw the former me. And as I chattered away and grew full, I read in their faces such openness, such pure love for me, together with my prattle and my gluttony, that the calm thought would suddenly surface through the excitement of the meeting: "This is happiness."

All that was long ago. My Seriozha will soon be twelve. Now as they see me and my husband off for yet another expedition, the old folks worry not so much for my sake as for their own: Can they hold out until we return? Will they manage with Seriozha? Do they have enough strength? And each time I leave, my heart contracts—will they be there when I return?

Recently they've no longer been meeting me as they did before. No, not like that. Mostly it's been with a feeling of relief: Thank God she's back. Take your child; we've managed to cope, and now we want a break from the responsibility. Now you're in charge.

Without any transition I would plunge into the whirlpool of neglected household chores. I would lug suits and heavy overcoats to the cleaners, wash, cook, and clean. In a word, I would dive headfirst into that world which for the majority of women represents the basis of existence.

In this world there was my son, who, of course, was foremost in my thoughts and cares. It was a pleasant shock to see him for the first time after months of separation, to be astounded at how he had grown, and to hear the altered intonations of his speech. But that's the extent of it. I make attempts to enter his world, but I am less and less able to do so with each passing year.

My husband usually arrives after I do, and his arrival means more household chores for me. With February come the financial report and preparations for a new season of field work. Then we wait impatiently for spring.

I love my work. I love the life in the field. Such a life seems more vivid, more intense, and *more real* than life in a large city with its vanity, thoughts of money, illnesses, the daily need to get something, to wait in lines, and to hurry. In the field, however strange it may sound, I feel more of a woman than in the city, where, tired and loaded down with shopping bags, I return home after work. You can't even call that fatigue, but being overwrought. In the field, now, you can feel fatigue, physical exhaustion. That's another thing altogether.

For some reason, in the city you immediately come down with a cold, or you become indisposed, or irritability sets in. Maybe that's a reaction to a change in life. I don't know. In any case, I'm in constant fear that a year or two will pass, and not only will my old folks not be able to take care of Seriozha, but I will have to stay behind to take care of them.

And now—a letter. Usually Mother wrote the letters and Father would add a few lines at the end. That's why, when I saw Father's handwriting on the envelope, I felt a sense of foreboding. My hands shook as I opened the envelope.

But no, there was no major tragedy. The tone was even quite encouraging. Anyway, my parents always spared me. They were reticent about their illnesses, because they hesitated to interfere with the normal course of my life.

". . . Mother gave us quite a scare a while back," wrote Father. "She felt so bad we simply didn't know what to do. Fortunately there was a doctor among the dacha folk, a marvelous woman, Irina Mikhailovna. She said that Mother had probably suffered a strong attack of stenocardia. She ordered her to stay in bed, brought the necessary medicines, and is giving her the shots herself. Mother feels a lot better now, though she still hasn't gotten up. And it's here that a serious problem has come up. It's the middle of August. Seriozha will have to go to school soon, so it's time to think of moving back to the city. To order the moving van, to pack things up, and so forth. I'm not certain that I can manage all this alone. However, there are kind people in the world, and I hope that everything will get taken care of. . . . As for the rest, everything is fine with us. Seriozha has grown up. He's become unsociable and very independent. In general, he's a fine boy, and Grandmother and I can fault him in nothing. . . .

"In other respects, everything's fine and dandy. . . ." Just like in the song, I thought.

It was an early, sunny morning, already stifling in a typically city way and permeated with smells of asphalt, exhaust fumes, and cigarette smoke. I walked out with the crowd toward the square by the station; a line of people with suitcases, bundles, and children stood waiting there for taxis, which for some reason had formed a long line on the other side of the square and were driving up one by one. Between the line of people and the line of taxis, an angry, excited, sweaty man was rushing about, with a red band on the arm of his tight, short jacket. Something seemed to have set him off early on. Yet, in spite of his frenzied running around, the whole business of seating the citizenry in the taxis was not proceeding any faster. The absurdities of city life were beginning, and suddenly I didn't feel like taking a taxi. I wanted to walk, not all the way home—it was a bit far—but just a stop or two, and then get on the trolley.

As far as anyone was concerned, I hadn't arrived yet. It was as if I existed outside of time and space in these minutes, and I wanted to prolong these moments, to turn off the stopwatch of my life for a little while so that I could take a closer look at myself, at today's self; to focus on myself and only then to continue living.

As I walked, I thought about my two dissimilar lives that were proceeding along parallel lines. From time to time I had to throw a little bridge across to enable me to cross over from one life to the other. In fact, at this very moment I was walking on such a bridge and it was swaying. And I had the sensation that two separate people—not doubles, but totally dissimilar individuals—really ought to merge into one.

I noticed that many women were walking around in long denim skirts. When I left to do field work at the beginning of May, there were only a few skirts like that. I thought to myself now that I would look good in such a skirt and that I would sew one for myself. This thought was a step forward on the swaying bridge, because in *that* life such a thought would simply never occur to me. There were few women there, and the concept "it suits me or doesn't suit me" didn't exist. There, only the person as such was important.

I was struck by the abundance of watermelons in latticed boxes still fastened with hanging locks. I thought, wouldn't it be nice to ship at least one such box there. What a grand occasion that would be for us. And this thought about melons *there* was like a step backward on the precarious bridge.

And so I walked, performing my balancing act outside of time and space. And in this, too, there was yet another of my lives; my very own, unlike anyone else's.

After walking about three stops, I boarded the trolley. The change in my hands felt somehow strange—for several months I hadn't held money at all—and now these two two-kopek pieces seemed a funny convention. Nevertheless, I dropped them into the cashbox and tore off a ticket. And just in time. A ticket inspector was on duty in the trolley. It was a woman, no longer young, with a tired morning face and an unkind, suspicious expression. Her suspiciousness was rewarded with success: she uncovered someone without a ticket. It's possible that he wasn't an evil-intentioned ticketless passenger, this bald citizen in a nice zippered white shirt, wearing glasses and carrying a briefcase. It's also possible that he didn't tear off a ticket from absent-mindedness, or that he lost it, but the face of the woman inspector expressed a vengeful satisfaction as she said to him loudly:

"Let's go!"

Without getting up, he started explaining something quietly; she hovered over him like a crow, tightly gripping the handrails of the neighboring seats as if afraid that he might run away. Or, possibly, she was secretly hoping that he would. Perhaps in this difficult life, which could be read in her face, these skirmishes with ticketless passengers were her only safety valve, the only way she could release the accumulated bitterness of her daily existence.

For some reason I felt sorry for this unappealing inspector, sorrier than for her victim, who was wiping his reddened bald pate with a clean handkerchief.

Without waiting to see the outcome of this duel, I got out and stopped for a moment to breathe in, to absorb the atmosphere of the street so familiar in every detail, down to the cracks in the asphalt. There is the school where I studied and where Seriozha studies now. The mailbox where in my childhood and youth I would drop letters with the sensation that I was performing some sort of magical act. It seemed incredible that my envelope, thumping just audibly against the bottom of the mailbox, would soon find itself in the hands of a distant addressee.

This spring a lawn was put down in the middle of our courtyard, and now the grass has grown in thickly. This little verdant island, in the center of a grey asphalt gulf crowded by cars, produced a pitiful and touching impression.

Maria Fiodorovna, the yardkeeper's wife, was watering the lawn with a hose.

"Greetings, Maria Fiodorovna!" I said.

She raised her head, nodded, and asked:

"Coming from the dacha?"

"Yes," I answered for some reason. Had I said that I'd just flown in from the North Pole, Kamchatka, or the Antarctic, she would have nodded with the same indifference and continued to water the grass. It's only to me now that my appearance in the courtyard seemed a miracle, a return to my native planet, while all these months, day after day, Maria Fiodorovna has been watering the lawn with a hose in just the same way, and what does it matter to her where I've come from?

"The mailwoman brought the pension letter, but none of you were home."

"Thank you, I'll stop by the post office."

I took the stairs up to the fourth floor. Several years ago they installed an elevator in our apartment house. But at the time when I was still being met there was no elevator, and there, far from home, whenever I pictured my return, I would imagine not an elevator but the stairway, with its scratched wooden handrails, and I would hear my mother's quickened breath behind me and see my father on the threshold of the wide-opened door to the apartment.

But now there was only the stairway. I opened the door with my key and walked into the entryway, which wafted to me the stuffy odor of abandoned residences.

I shrugged off my knapsack and walked to the kitchen. In the sink were two unwashed cups with dried tea leaves on the bottom. The refrigerator was turned off, its door held open by a chair. In its empty interior sat a solitary can of beef stew. No, I hadn't dreamed of a miracle, but something quavered painfully within me when I saw this misplaced can, the spot of spilt milk on the oilcloth, and an empty herbal tea box lying on the unwashed linoleum.

Then I walked into my parents' room, where Seriozha's bed also stood—unmade. Seriozha's presence, his carelessness, could be felt strongly here, and I experienced no tender emotion as I looked at the little batteries and instruments scattered in the most inappropriate places. On his desk, among plastic boats, wires, and tacks, lay a school report, also nothing for me to be proud of. I looked at the final grades: "C," "C," "C," "C," "C." . . . And as a little holiday against the background of these grey weekdays, an "A" in history.

"Passed on to the sixth grade." That's something, at least. We ought to get after him more. This "ought to," by the way, has persecuted my husband and me for many years. Empty words. The boy has been brought up by his grandmother and grandfather, who adore him and spoil him terribly.

I caught myself reflecting that I think about Seriozha not as I would about a son, but as I would about a boy in general. In my objectivity I seem to sense indifference, but it is my Seriozha, after all, who touchingly walks around ants so as not to crush them, who cries over a mouse caught in a trap, and who said about a boy who beat him up: "So what? I'm stronger than he is anyway. If I hit him, it'll hurt him." No, it's quite obvious that he doesn't possess any "pugnacious" qualities. On the contrary, he wants to live in a way that doesn't cause the weak any pain.

I opened the door to my room. Time had stopped here at the precise moment when Volodia and I left it, loaded down with knapsacks. Everything remained in the same place it had been at that moment. The bottle of Georgian wine that our friend had brought for a farewell drink. A crumpled piece of paper that had fallen short of the wastebasket and on which Volodia, as was his habit, had made a list of the little things so that we wouldn't forget to take them with us.

But I was especially struck by a little bouquet of lilies of the valley. I remembered buying it before our departure on the corner by the grocery. I vaguely recalled the appearance of the woman from whom I'd bought it, how I'd hurriedly looked for a little vase, didn't find one, and put the flowers in a simple thick glass tumbler. These were the first fresh flowers that had appeared in our apartment after the winter, and maybe that was why this simple little bouquet had seemed so beautiful. I'd inhaled its fragrance with delight.

And so it had stood in a glass all these months, and now they were no longer flowers but mummies of flowers, pitiful, dry little corpses, a symbol of arrested time. I recalled the luxurious gladiolas that used to be bought especially for my return and felt tears welling up in my eyes. I was surprised; I hadn't cried for a long time.

These tears were the final step on the bridge that joined my two lives. I'd entered city life with both feet, and I was immediately seized by a fever of activity.

Calmly now, without those nervous jumps into the past, I turned on the water. While the tub filled, I opened the can of stew, heated it, and ate it straight from the pan. I felt I had successfully plugged myself into the rhythm of a life that was defined by the expression "there isn't any time," into a life that consists of petty, fragmented responsibilities that have to be connected, each linked to the next, so that the eternal engine of household cares won't misfire.

Mother was sitting on the porch reading Dickens. She raised her head as the gate creaked, and an expression of happy incredulity lit up her face,

"Tanechka? How? Where'd you come from?"

"As you see, I've come. Greetings! Not a bad surprise, eh?"

"I mean, we didn't expect you at all! Why so early? Did Volodia come too?"

"No, no, Mom. I haven't come for good. They've let me go for ten days. The head of the expedition put it down as a business trip. Father gave me such a scare with his letter."

"Oh! Only for ten days. . . . But what a treat, anyway! And here I nearly died. . . . Kolia!" she shouted through the half-opened door. "Look who's here! I felt so bad. More than anything, I was afraid to die without seeing you again. And how could I leave your papa? . . . Kolia!" she called him again. And then she complained, "His hearing has gotten worse. He's in there putting the teakettle on. Go and see him."

"In a minute. But where's Seriozha?"

"He went to a friend's to watch television. What a boy! He's wonderful! We'll drink tea in a minute, and you'll tell us about everything. Is Volodia well?"

"Everything's fine with us."

"Well, that's the main thing."

She picked up a cane that was propped against the armchair and, leaning on it, got up heavily. She looked at me and said in a guilty tone:

"Yes, as you see, nowadays I get around with the help of a crutch. What can you do? I've been up only two days. Papa's exhausted."

"Did Seriozha help out at least a bit?"

"Seriozha is a wonderful boy!" she repeated with feeling.

It was as if she were protecting her favorite ahead of time, placing a cushion under our impending quarrels, which I hadn't even thought about yet, but which she obviously already anticipated and had nervously prepared for—and not without foundation, since someone had to be more strict with him.

. . . And here we sit in the kitchen at a table covered with an ancient oilcloth. We're drinking tea, and Father and Mother are asking me questions from both sides, making frightened sounds and opening their eyes wide. I answer something with my mouth full, tell them about something, and I can feel how glad they are that I'm with them, that they can simply look at me, reveling in the mere fact of my presence.

And at those moments I myself am happy. . . .

. . . It was already dusk when I found Seriozha on the banks of a stream. At first I recognized his bicycle, with its torn-off pedal, lying in a pile of other bikes. Then I saw a group of boys squatting around something that was not visible to me beyond their backs. In the middle of them I saw Seriozha concentrating on lighting some matches that were going out quickly. He was so preoccupied that I didn't dare call out to him. I just stood there and watched, feeling a stupid, tender smile on my face. But then he struck several matches at once; the boys crowded even closer around the object that I couldn't see, then quickly moved apart. There was a rather weak, hollow explosion, a bright red flame flashed, and a white rocket rose into the air, leaving a flaming tail behind it. It flew up quite high, then somehow plunged to the side and fell to the ground. The entire company of boys immediately rushed toward it, picked it up off the ground, and started to discuss something loudly, pushing and gesticulating.

"Seriozha!"

Carried away by the conversation, he didn't turn around right away, but some other boys glanced back, and he also looked crossly in my direction. His thoughts were so far away from me at this moment that even when he recognized me he uttered in an interrogative tone, "Mother?" and didn't fling himself toward me, as I'd imagined in my dreams, but turned back toward the boys to hurriedly finish saying something in a businesslike manner. He took the rocket from a boy's hand and only then strode toward me. He didn't dash forward, he didn't rush; he literally strode. Offended, I dropped my arms, which I'd stretched out to him.

"How did you get here?" he asked.

"Quite simply. I got on a train and came. I decided to pay all of you a visit."

"I see," he said. "And on your way here, did you meet anyone?"

"Who was I supposed to meet?"

"Well, you know. . . . I asked some people to come see the launching," he explained obscurely.

My son was not happy to see me. Not at all. My arrival had disturbed his game, and the rhythm of his life in general. It introduced nonfreedom. He had simply become unaccustomed to me.

"Well, and what are you doing here, Seriozha?" I asked the stupid question cheerfully, trying to hide my injured feelings.

He answered:

"Look at this rocket! I made it myself! Did you see how it flies?"

"You really did it yourself?"

"Well, Lioshka helped. And do you know what makes it work? The heads of matches! We stuff them into cartridges made from heart medicine capsules. Grandpa and Grandma give them to me; they've got lots of them. . . . And there you put a wick. You set it on fire and—bang!"

"You know, my dear, that's a good way to lose your eyes. Who gave you permission to take matches?"

"Don't give children matches, they'll take them themselves," he answered, smiling.

"I'm serious, that's not something to play with. Well, besides rockets, what else keeps you busy here?"

. . . My Lord, what a tone! An onlooker might think that a journalist was conducting an interview with a Pioneer from some school. Yet there, out in the field, I mentally carried on such interesting conversations with him. I told him about all sorts of things that happened and sang geologists' songs for him. . . . What is the matter with me? It's as if I were all tied up. But that's because he feels shy with me and answers my journalistic questions thoroughly and hopelessly, as if he were answering a question at school for which—he's sure ahead of time—he is bound to get an unsatisfactory grade.

"Well, . . . I do a lot of things. . . . We're getting ready to string a telephone from Liosha's dacha to ours. They're selling them in the village store. We go there on our bikes to get matches. . . . Well, and for groceries, too. . . . It costs twelve-fifty. We've already got six rubles."

"Where did you get the money?"

"We earned it ourselves. We hired out to paint some people's fence for twelve rubles. Later we divided it. Lioshka got six rubles and I got six. Except that I lost mine. . . ."

"Lost it?! Like always. . . ."

"It wasn't my fault! It was Lioshka! I had them in a coin purse in a pocket of my shorts. We went out in a boat . . . and Lioshka started rocking the boat, and my shorts fell in the water. . . . I fished them out, but the coin purse sank. . . . And so did the watch. . . . Afterwards we dove and dove. . . ."

"There you have it!" I said. "That's just like you. And I said to your grandfather, 'Don't buy him a watch, it's too early.' And of course, you've lost it! It's simply amazing how anyone could be such a muddler! But then, you only get 'Cs' in your courses. . . ."

"That's enough!" he shouted with tears in his voice. "It's started! She's back!"

. . . What in the world is this? . . .

He marched scowling beside me, walking his bike. I saw that he would like to jump on his bicycle and speed along the streets of the dacha settlement with his former freedom, now lost so unexpectedly and inopportunely.

"Do you know what I've brought you?" I asked in a conciliatory tone. "A collection of minerals. Some of our people went to Kamchatka, and I got them to give you some. There's quartz with little veins of gold."

"Really?" he said stiffly. Then, assuming my conciliatory tone, he asked with interest, "Is it real gold?"

"Of course it's real. And they also gave me two starfish for you. You remember you asked for them?"

"Are they pretty? What color?"

"White. When they dry out they turn white."

"And did you bring me bell-bottoms, by any chance?"

"What? . . ."

"Bell-bottom trousers."

"N-no. . . ."

"Will you get them?" he asked, and something unspoken flashed across his face. Maybe it was apprehension that I'd get "wound up" again or make fun of his request.

"Fine . . . but why?"

"Because all the boys have them, and I don't."

Our conversation was like a talk between diplomats representing two powers in a state of temporary truce. We spoke carefully, now and then reaching sharp corners and cautiously walking around them.

"And how's the camera?" I asked. "Is it still working?"

"Almost," he said after a pause. "The shutter got jammed. Lioshka and I took it apart a little bit. . . . But we'll put it together!"

He shot me a frightened glance. What an absolute fool I am.

"What took you so long? We were getting worried."

On the table are slices of watermelon and a cake. Around it sit Mother and Father and a youngish woman with a knot of greying hair. A blood pressure monitor lies next to her on a stool. It's Irina Mikhailovna, the doctor.

"Here's our daughter!" Mother says proudly.

Irina Mikhailovna and I shake hands. What a nice smile she has. I feel a surge of gratitude toward this woman who didn't leave my old folks in dire straits.

"Your mother's pressure is almost ideal," she says to me. "See what positive emotions will do!"

"Have another piece of cake, Irina Mikhailovna!" invites Mother. "Tanechka brought it. Seriozha! Tanechka! Hurry up, sit down! Seriozha, you were dying for some watermelon. Your mother brought some!"

We eat the watermelon and launch into a conversation about the benefits of watermelon, about how harmful cake is for the elderly, about blood pressure, and about how nice the sour cream is in the local store. Although I am completely indifferent to all these subjects, I feel good because my old folks are enjoying themselves. They're beaming. The family is at the table. We're having a peaceful conversation. There's plenty of everything. We all like one another. What more do you need for happiness?

I make my bed on the veranda. Seriozha and I are sitting on the fold-up bed examining rocks.

"That's a spar!" he says. "And that's quartzite. It's even prettier than quartz."

We look at the starfish.

"How hard they are," says Seriozha. "They look like little octopuses. Look how the tentacle has bent. Do they attack people in the sea?"

"Oh, come now. They're small."

"I feel sorry for them," he says. "They were swimming around happily. . . . Is there a sea where you work?"

"No. But next year we may be going to the Okhotsk Sea."

"If only I could. . . ."

"When you grow up we'll take you with us."

"How much do I have to grow?"

"A lot."

I yawn. My eyes are gluing shut. I'm tired after spending the night on the road.

"I think I'll go to sleep, Seriozha."

"Can I stay up and read?"

"Go ahead. What are you reading?"

"*The Three Musketeers*. Have you read it?"

"Of course!"

"And which of the musketeers did you like most?" he asks.

"D'Artagnan, of course."

"Well, I liked Athos. I don't especially like D'Artagnan."

"Why? He's handsome . . . brave. . . ."

"Yes, he's brave. But just look. He fell in love with Constance, but they abducted her. Anyone else would have rushed to find her, but he didn't even look for her. He fell in love with Milady. And when he found out that she'd betrayed him, he fell in love with her servant. That's what I don't like. I couldn't behave that way. Mom! Do you know her name?"

"Whose?" I resurfaced from my sleep.

"Milady's servant's?"

"No . . . I don't remember. . . ."

"Her name's Kitty," he says with an expression as if he were intimating a secret. And he falls silent as if expecting some question.

. . . But I feel so good lying on the clean sheet under a warm camel's-hair blanket. I remember my sleeping bag and the tent, the crackling of wood in a small iron stove . . . and Volodia sitting beside it on a sawed-off stump, the reddish reflections of the fire in his bearded face. . . . I start dividing into two again, but that's because I'm falling asleep.

And that's all the time I had with him that evening. But it wasn't even an evening, only a half-hour before bedtime. I had a lot of things to take care of. After all, I was on a business trip. As I was leaving, Volodia had said, "If everything's more or less in order, try not to delay. The amount of work we have—you yourself know. . . ." Of course I knew, and that was yet another reason I hurried.

In the morning I went to town. I had to convince those in charge to speed up the shipment of two gravimeters, and I had to run a number of other errands. I also had to clean the apartment, order the van for the move, and buy Seriozha a school uniform, shoes for the fall, shirts, and underwear, as well as notebooks and other minor school supplies.

As I approached the village, I suddenly saw Seriozha. He was pushing his bicycle by the handlebars. Walking beside him was a girl. They were coming toward me, and with a purely feminine, jealous curiosity I studied the girl from afar. She was taller than Seriozha and looked older. Slim and long-legged, she wore a short dark-blue skirt and a blue boy's shirt. The boy's shirt emphasized her budding femininity. Her light, almost straw-colored hair reached down to her shoulders. She was very pretty, and, to tell the truth, my poor Seriozha didn't look all that good beside her.

Suddenly he recognized me. He gave a confused, embarrassed smile, then frowned, trying to assume an unconcerned expression. But I could see that he was constrained by his shyness and that he was afraid. Yes, that wasn't shyness, but quite ordinary fear on his face. He was afraid that I'd come out with yet another tactless remark, and his fear was not without foundation. It's precisely with your own child that you most often lose your sense of tact. You always think that they're too young. Most probably you don't even think at all, but just blurt out whatever comes into your head.

I answered him with a cheerful, understanding smile. I almost winked at him.

"Hi, there! How are things at home? In order?"

"Seem to be."

"Had lunch yet?"

"Not yet."

The girl looked at me with interest and without the slightest embarrassment. I waved to them and continued walking. I badly wanted to turn around and take another look at my son walking with a girl, almost a young woman. A staggering sight! As far as I knew he'd been horribly shy with girls since the first grade.

Mother and Father were sitting on the porch. They seemed to have been sitting there like that the whole time I was rushing around in the city. They were waiting for me.

The three of us had lunch together. Seriozha hadn't shown up. At lunch I mentioned that I'd met him with a girl.

"A tall blonde?" asked my mother. "That's Katia, Irina Mikhailovna's granddaughter. A delightful creature. But she's older. She's fourteen."

Katia . . . Kitty. . . .

The last evening, when the suitcases were already packed, I asked him:

"You didn't forget the starfish?"

"I don't have them anymore," he answered, "I gave them to someone."

He was silent and added:

"Are you going to yell at me?"

"No. . . . Why should I? . . . They're yours. Whom did you give them to, if it's not a secret?"

"It's a secret," he answered.

In the morning when everything was ready for departure—the things loaded, and Mother sitting in the cab of the truck—Seriozha suddenly disappeared. That is, he'd disappeared earlier, but we became aware of it only at the last minute. I ran off to look for him, but where? I rushed angrily around the village. And suddenly I saw him.

"Are you in your right mind?" I shouted. "We're waiting for you, worrying. I'm running around like an idiot."

He wore the expression of a person struck down by grief. I said no more.

We were sitting on our things in the truck, and as it roared into a turn, two people on bicycles came alongside and passed us. A dark-haired boy in a bright-red jersey and a girl with light, almost straw-colored hair down to her shoulders. Seriozha followed them with his eyes and turned away.

The truck drove out onto the highway. We were sitting on a sofa, facing the traffic. I wanted to comfort Seriozha, but how? What did I know about him? He has his secrets, which he has no desire to share with the woman sitting next to him, this so-called mother who lives two parallel lives and knows nothing, nothing about that unique, that most important life which she herself once created and which now has become alien to her.

. . . In old age we are hurt by the ingratitude of our children. But what is it that they should be grateful for? What did we sacrifice for them? Did we deny ourselves anything as far as they were concerned? On the contrary, we constantly try to fix it so that our children don't disturb us, don't deprive us of our well-deserved rest. We chase them away or yell at them if their interests run counter to ours. Under the guise of educating them, we push them aside, and we're relieved to be rid of them for a time. So then, why should we be offended when, upon reaching adulthood, they start avoiding us? Or talk back to us in words they didn't dare use when they were little? Or pay us back in kind? We give people back what we get from them.

. . . Well, that seems to be all.

"What a treat," says Mother. "What would we do without you? How nicely you've fixed everything up, even the gladiolas. . . ."

And here again is the platform of the train station. The little bridge rocks, one more step, then another . . . and there, on the shore, will remain an exhausted, nervous creature bearing my first and last name, while I return home. But where am I to hide from the bitterness, the shame I feel for that woman? No, for this woman. . . . I bear my shame, my helplessness, and like a heavy burden, they bend my back.

To Be of Use

Marge Piercy

Marge Piercy (1936–   ) says of her poetry, "Usually the voice of the poems is mine. . . . The experiences, however, are not always mine. . . . I imagine that I speak for a constituency, living and dead, and that I give utterance to energy, experience, insight, words flowing from many lives." Sara Blackburn, New York Times *Book Review contributing critic, writes that Piercy's work addresses "lost identity and desperation which, once recognized as common experience, has sparked the rage and solidarity of the women's liberation movement."*

The people I love the best
jump into work head first
without dallying in the shallows
and swim off with sure strokes almost out of sight.
They seem to become natives of that element,
the black sleek heads of seals
bouncing like half-submerged balls.

I love people who harness themselves, an ox to a heavy cart,
who pull like water buffalo, with massive patience,
who strain in the mud and the muck to move things forward,
who do what has to be done, again and again.

I want to be with people who submerge
in the task, who go into the fields to harvest
and work in a row and pass the bags along,
who are not parlor generals and field deserters
but move in a common rhythm
when the food must come in or the fire be put out.

The work of the world is common as mud.
Botched, it smears the hands, crumbles to dust.
But the thing worth doing well done

---

has a shape that satisfies, clean and evident.
Greek amphoras for wine or oil,
Hopi vases that held corn, are put in museums
but you know they were made to be used.
The pitcher cries for water to carry
and a person for work that is real.

II

Identity

I can't afford to look back, and I can't figure out how to look forward. In both directions, I may see a Medusa, and I already feel the danger of being turned into stone. Betwixt and between, I am stuck and time is stuck within me. Time used to open out, serene, shimmering with promise. If I wanted to hold a moment still, it was because I wanted to expand it, to get its fill. Now, time has no dimension, no extension backward or forward. I arrest the past, and I hold myself stiffly against the future; I want to stop the flow.

–Eva Hoffman, *Lost in Translation*

But female fat is the subject of public passion, and women feel guilty about female fat, because we implicitly recognize that under the myth, women's bodies are not our own but society's, and that thinness is not a private aesthetic, but hunger a social concession exacted by the community. A cultural fixation on female thinness is not an obsession about female beauty but an obsession about female obedience.

–Naomi Wolf, "Hunger"

once I hated the likes of me
and looked for me in everyone else
now I see and love what I see
in love with me as I see myself

–Leona Nicholas Welch, "A Private Affair"

Empty Bowl

Rebecca Randall

Rebecca Randall (1961–   ) was born in San Francisco. She earned her B.A. (1985) from the California State University at Stanislaus and her master's degree (1987) from San Francisco State University. She teaches English at Diablo Valley College in California. Married to a writer of children's books, she and her husband are the parents of two boys. It was when she began teaching, especially in a program for re-entry women, that she awakened to the domination of the literary canon by men. Now, she seeks women writers to speak to the students in today's classrooms. In "Empty Bowl" she describes a woman's changing sense of self.

My children left a bowl
outside yesterday.
I found it in a pile of fallen leaves,
three lone
unpopped corn kernels and an ant
at the bottom.
I picked up the bowl
and rested the rim
against my chest,
running one hand
under its cool metal lip.

Your touch, days ago, reminded
me of feeling—
reminded me of me.
My skin
is me.
Through me,
I feel pleasure, feel
the beat of life.
Your hand told me I was still there,

---

listening,
pulsing,
waking.
Waiting.
I am connected—
nerves to nerves,
brain to heart.
I ached with life.
I was who I am.

Yet, later, cold,
tired,
angry,
thinking,
Feeling the forlorn slopes
of the empty bowl,
running fingers
down its aluminum sides,
I wondered
how I could find myself again.

Lost in Translation

Eva Hoffman

Eva Hoffman (1945–   ) was born Ewa *in Krakow, Poland. Her name was changed by a high-handed teacher after her immigration to Canada in 1959.* Lost in Translation *(1989), an excerpt of which follows, is her autobiographical account of the experience of assimilation: "I have been driven to writing by the condition of exile, and by the intense relationship to the English language which resulted from it—a relationship which has involved both an alienation from language and a desire to possess it." Hoffman's Ph.D. is from Harvard University. She has served as an editor at the* New York Times *since 1980 and currently edits the Book Review section.*

"DEAR BASIA," I WRITE, "I AM SITTING AT A WINdow looking out on a garden in which there is a cherry tree, an apple tree, and bushes of roses now in bloom. The roses are smaller and wilder here, but imagine! All this in the middle of a city. And tomorrow I am going to a party. There are parties here all the time, and my social life is, you might say, blooming." I am repeating a ritual performed by countless immigrants who have sent letters back home meant to impress and convince their friends and relatives—and probably even themselves—that their lives have changed for the better. I am lying. But I am also trying to fend off my nostalgia. I couldn't repudiate the past even if I wanted to, but what can I do with it here, where it doesn't exist? After a while, I begin to push the images of memory down, away from consciousness, below emotion. Relegated to an internal darkness, they increase the area of darkness within me, and they return in the dark, in my dreams. I dream of Cracow perpetually, winding my way through familiar-unfamiliar streets, looking for a way home. I almost get there, repeatedly; almost, but not quite, and I wake up with the city so close that I can breathe it in.

I can't afford to look back, and I can't figure out how to look forward. In both directions, I may see a Medusa, and I already feel the danger of being turned into stone. Betwixt and between, I am stuck and time is stuck within me. Time used to open out, serene, shimmering with promise. If I wanted to hold a moment still, it was because I wanted to expand it, to get its fill. Now, time has no dimension, no extension backward or forward. I arrest the past, and I hold myself stiffly against the future; I want to stop the flow. As a punishment, I exist in the stasis of a perpetual present, that other side of "living in the present," which is not eternity but a prison. I can't throw a bridge between the present and the past, and therefore I can't make time move.

The car is full of my new friends, or at least the crowd that has more or less accepted me as one of their own, the odd "greener" tag-along. They're as lively as a group of puppies, jostling each other with sharp elbows, crawling over each other to change seats, and expressing their well-being and amiability by trying to outshout each other. It's Saturday night, or rather Saturday Night, and party spirits are obligatory. We're on our way to the local White Spot, an early Canadian version of McDonald's, where we'll engage in the barbarous—as far as I'm concerned—rite of the "drive-in." This activity of sitting in your car in a large parking lot, and having sloppy, big hamburgers brought to you on a tray, accompanied by greasy french fries bounding out of their cardboard containers, mustard, spilly catsup, and sickly smelling relish, seems to fill these peers of mine with warm, monkeyish, groupy comfort. It fills me with a finicky distaste. I feel my lips tighten into an unaccustomed thinness—which, in turn, fills me with a small dislike for myself.

"Come on, foreign student, cheer up," one of the boys sporting a flowery Hawaiian shirt and a crew cut tells me, poking me in the ribs good-naturedly. "What's the matter, don't you like it here?" So as the car caroms off, I try to get in the mood. I try to giggle coyly as the girls exchange insinuating glances—though usually my titter comes a telling second too late. I try to join in the general hilarity, as somebody tells the latest elephant joke. Then—it's always a mistake to try too hard—I decide to show my goodwill by telling a joke myself. Finding some interruption in which to insert my uncertain voice, I launch into a translation of some slightly off-color anecdote I'd heard my father tell in Polish, no doubt hoping to get points for being risqué as well as a good sport. But as I hear my choked-up voice straining to assert itself, as I hear myself missing every beat and rhythm that would say "funny" and "punch line," I feel a hot flush of embarrassment. I come to a lame ending. There's a silence. "I suppose that's supposed to be funny," somebody says. I recede into the car seat.

Ah, the humiliation, the misery of failing to amuse! The incident is as rankling to my amour propre as being told I'm graceless or ugly. Telling a joke is like doing a linguistic pirouette. If you fall flat, it means not only that you don't have the wherewithal to do it well but also that you have misjudged your own skill, that you are fool enough to undertake something you can't finish—and that lack of self-control or self-knowledge is a lack of grace.

But these days, it takes all my will to impose any control on the words that emerge from me. I have to form entire sentences before uttering them; otherwise, I too easily get lost in the middle. My speech, I sense, sounds monotonous, deliberate, heavy—an aural mask that doesn't become me or express me at all. This willed self-control is the opposite of real mastery, which comes from a trust in your own verbal powers and allows for a free streaming of speech, for those bursts of spontaneity, the quickness of response that can rise into pleasure and overflow in humor. Laughter is the lightning rod of play, the eroticism of conversation; for now, I've lost the ability to make the sparks fly.

I've never been prim before, but that's how I am seen by my new peers. I don't try to tell jokes too often, I don't know the slang, I have no cool repartee. I love language too much to maul its beats, and my pride is too quick to risk the incomprehension that greets such forays. I become a very serious young person, missing the registers of wit and irony in my speech, though my mind sees ironies everywhere.

If primness is a small recoil of distaste at things that give others simple and hearty pleasure, then prim is what I'm really becoming. Although I'm not brave enough or hermit enough to stay home by myself every night, I'm a pretend teenager among the real stuff. There's too much in this car I don't like; I don't like the blue eye shadow on Cindy's eyelids, or the grease on Chuck's hair, or the way the car zooms off with a screech and then slows down as everyone plays we're-afraid-of-the-policeman. I don't like the way they laugh. I don't care for their "ugly" jokes, or their five-hundred-pound canary jokes, or their pickle jokes, or their elephant jokes either. And most of all, I hate having to pretend.

Perhaps the extra knot that strangles my voice is rage. I am enraged at the false persona I'm being stuffed into, as into some clumsy and overblown astronaut suit. I'm enraged at my adolescent friends because they can't see through the guise, can't recognize the light-footed dancer I really am. They only see this elephantine creature who too often sounds as if she's making pronouncements.

It will take years before I pick and choose, from the Babel of American language, the style of wit that fits. It will take years of practice before its nuances and patterns snap smartly into the synapses of my brain so they can generate verbal electricity. It will take years of observing the discreet sufferings of the corporate classes before I understand the equally discreet charm of *New Yorker* cartoons.

For now, when I come across a *New Yorker* issue, I stare at the drawings of well-heeled people expressing some dissatisfaction with their condition as yet another demonstration of the weirdness all around me. "What's funny about that?" my mother asks in puzzlement. "I don't know," I answer, and we both shrug and shake our heads. And, as the car veers through Vancouver's neatly shrubberied and sparsely populated streets, I know that, among my other faculties, I've lost my sense of humor. I am not about to convert my adolescent friends to anti-Russian jokes. I swallow my injury, and giggle falsely at the five-hundred-pound canary.

Happy as larks, we lurch toward the White Spot.

If you had stayed there, your hair would have been straight, and you would have worn a barrette on one side.

But maybe by now you would have grown it into a ponytail? Like the ones you saw on those sexy faces in the magazine you used to read?

I don't know. You would have been fifteen by now. Different from thirteen.

You would be going to the movies with Zbyszek, and maybe to a café after, where you would meet a group of friends and talk late into the night.

But maybe you would be having problems with Mother and Father. They wouldn't like your staying out late.

That would have been fun. Normal. Oh God, to be a young person trying to get away from her parents.

But you can't do that. You have to take care of them. Besides, with whom would you go out here? One of these churlish boys who play spin the bottle? You've become more serious than you used to be.

What jokes are your friends in Cracow exchanging? I can't imagine. What's Basia doing? Maybe she's beginning to act. Doing exactly what she wanted. She must be having fun.

But you might have become more serious even there.

Possible.

But you would have been different, very different.

No question.

And you prefer her, the Cracow Ewa.

Yes, I prefer her. But I can't be her. I'm losing track of her. In a few years, I'll have no idea what her hairdo would have been like.

But she's more real, anyway.

Yes, she's the real one.

For my birthday, Penny gives me a diary, complete with a little lock and key to keep what I write from the eyes of all intruders. It is that little lock—the visible symbol of the privacy in which the diary is meant to exist—that creates my dilemma. If I am indeed to write something entirely for myself, in what language do I write? Several times, I open the diary and close it again. I can't decide. Writing in Polish at this point would be a little like resorting to Latin or ancient Greek—an eccentric thing to do in a diary, in which you're supposed to set down your most immediate experiences and unpremeditated thoughts in the most unmediated language. Polish is becoming a dead language, the language of the untranslatable past. But writing for nobody's eyes in English? That's like doing a school exercise, or performing in front of yourself, a slightly perverse act of self-voyeurism.

Because I have to choose something, I finally choose English. If I'm to write about the present, I have to write in the language of the present, even if it's not the language of the self. As a result, the diary becomes surely one of the more impersonal exercises of that sort produced by an adolescent girl. These are no sentimental effusions of rejected love, eruptions of familial anger, or consoling broodings about death. English is not the language of such emotions. Instead, I set down my reflections on the ugliness of wrestling; on the elegance of Mozart, and on how Dostoyevsky puts me in mind of El Greco. I write down Thoughts. I Write.

There is a certain pathos to this naïve snobbery, for the diary is an earnest attempt to create a part of my persona that I imagine I would have grown into in Polish. In the solitude of this most private act, I write, in my public language, in order to update what might have been my other self. The diary is about me and not about me at all. But on one level, it allows me to make the first jump. I learn English through writing, and, in turn, writing gives me a written self. Refracted through the double distance of English and writing, this self—my English self—becomes oddly objective; more than anything, it perceives. It exists more easily in the abstract sphere of thoughts and observations than in the world. For a while, this impersonal self, this cultural negative capability, becomes the truest thing about me. When I write, I have a real existence that is proper to the activity of writing—an existence that takes place midway between me and the sphere of artifice, art, pure language. This language is beginning to invent another me. However, I discover something odd. It seems that when I write (or, for that matter, think) in English, I am unable to use the word "I." I do not go as far as the schizophrenic "she"—but I am driven, as by a compulsion, to the double, the Siamese-twin "you."

My voice is doing funny things. It does not seem to emerge from the same parts of my body as before. It comes out from somewhere in my throat, tight, thin, and mat—a voice without the modulations, dips, and rises that it had before, when it went from my stomach all the way through my head. There is, of course, the constraint and the self-consciousness of an accent that I hear but cannot control. Some of my high school peers accuse me of putting it on in order to appear more "interesting." In fact, I'd do anything to get rid of it, and when I'm alone, I practice sounds for which my speech organs have no intuitions, such as "th" (I do this by putting my tongue between my teeth) and "a," which is longer and more open in Polish (by shaping my mouth into a sort of arrested grin). It is simple words like "cat" or "tap" that give me the most trouble, because they have no context of other syllables, and so people often misunderstand them. Whenever I can, I do awkward little swerves to avoid them, or pause and try to say them very clearly. Still, when people—like salesladies—hear me speak without being prepared to listen carefully, they often don't understand me the first time around. "Girls' shoes," I say, and the "girls'" comes out as a sort of scramble. "Girls' shoes," I repeat, willing the syllable to form itself properly, and the saleslady usually smiles nicely, and sends my mother and me to the right part of the store. I say "Thank you" with a sweet smile, feeling as if I'm both claiming an unfair special privilege and being unfairly patronized.

It's as important to me to speak well as to play a piece of music without mistakes. Hearing English distorted grates on me like chalk screeching on a blackboard, like all things botched and badly done, like all forms of gracelessness. The odd thing is that I know what is correct, fluent, good, long before I can execute it. The English spoken by our Polish acquaintances strikes me as jagged and thick, and I know that I shouldn't imitate it. I'm turned off by the intonations I hear on the TV sitcoms—by the expectation of laughter, like a dog's tail wagging in supplication, built into the actors' pauses, and by the curtailed, cutoff rhythms. I like the way Penny speaks, with an easy flow and a pleasure in giving words a fleshly fullness; I like what I hear in some movies; and once the Old Vic comes to Vancouver to perform *Macbeth,* and though I can hardly understand the particular words, I am riveted by the tones of sureness and command that mold the actors' speech into such majestic periods.

Sociolinguists might say that I receive these language messages as class signals, that I associate the sounds of correctness with the social status of the speaker. In part, this is undoubtedly true. The class-linked notion that I transfer wholesale from Poland is that belonging to a "better" class of people is absolutely dependent on speaking a "better" language. And in my situation especially, I know that language will be a crucial instrument, that I can overcome the stigma of my marginality, the weight of presumption against me, only if the reassuringly right sounds come out of my mouth.

Yes, speech is a class signifier. But I think that in hearing these varieties of speech around me, I'm sensitized to something else as well—something that is a matter of aesthetics, and even of psychological health. Apparently, skilled chefs can tell whether a dish from some foreign cuisine is well cooked even if they have never tasted it and don't know the genre of cooking it belongs to. There seem to be some deep-structure qualities—consistency, proportions of ingredients, smoothness of blending—that indicate culinary achievement to these educated eaters' taste buds. So each language has its own distinctive music, and even if one doesn't know its separate components, one can pretty quickly recognize the propriety of the patterns in which the components are put together, their harmonies and discords. Perhaps the crucial element that strikes the ear in listening to living speech is the degree of the speaker's self-assurance and control.

As I listen to people speaking that foreign tongue, English, I can hear when they stumble or repeat the same phrases too many times, when their sentences trail off aimlessly—or, on the contrary, when their phrases have vigor and roundness, when they have the space and the breath to give a flourish at the end of a sentence, or make just the right pause before coming to a dramatic point. I can tell, in other words, the degree of their ease or disease, the extent of authority that shapes the rhythms of their speech. That authority—in whatever dialect, in whatever variant of the mainstream language—seems to me to be something we all desire. It's not that we all want to speak the King's English, but whether we speak Appalachian or Harlem English, or Cockney, or Jamaican Creole, we want to be at home in our tongue. We want to be able to give voice accurately and fully to ourselves and our sense of the world. John Fowles, in one of his stories in *The Ebony Tower,* has a young man cruelly violate an elderly writer and his manuscripts because the legacy of language has not been passed on to the youthful vandal properly. This seems to me an entirely credible premise. Linguistic dispossession is a sufficient motive for violence, for it is close to the dispossession of one's self. Blind rage, helpless rage is rage that has no words—rage that overwhelms one with darkness. And if one is perpetually without words, if one exists in the entropy of inarticulateness, that condition itself is bound to be an enraging frustration. In my New York apartment, I listen almost nightly to fights that erupt like brushfire on the street below—and in their escalating fury of repetitious phrases ("Don't do this to me, man, you fucking bastard, I'll fucking kill you"), I hear not the pleasures of macho toughness but an infuriated beating against wordlessness, against the incapacity to make oneself understood, seen. Anger can be borne—it can even be satisfying—if it can gather into words and explode in a storm, or a rapier-sharp attack. But without this means of ventilation, it only turns back inward, building and swirling like a head of steam—building to an impotent, murderous rage. If all therapy is speaking therapy—a talking cure—then perhaps all neurosis is a speech dis-ease.

My parents, sister, and I have formed ourselves into an assembly line leading from the back alley through the garden and into our basement, where we are depositing an odd collection of items. There is a ratty couch with its stuffing half pulled out, a vacuum cleaner, a stained mattress, some heavy pieces of metal whose provenance is unclear. The objects are dusty, awkward, heavy; but worst of all, they bring with them the onus and burden of demotion. Having to lug such stuff is not a nice, middle-class occupation.

My parents have managed to gather a down payment on a "small stucco house," as it was advertised in the paper—I've combed through such ads repeatedly, trying to decode the nuances of wood and old English manses, and, yes, stucco—and we are now installed in this minimally furnished cell of the American Dream, which also functions as the location of a rudimentary business. Rudimentary, but laden with hope. Lots of the people we've met started out just this way—peddling junk. The very name of this occupation chafes me with its bare roughness. But in the community in which we've found ourselves, "junk" has come to acquire a certain compelling ring. For some people, scrap metal has literally turned to gold, and then into spacious homes with thick wall-to-wall rugs. Mr. Landauer still owns a big junkyard from which he draws fat profits. Besides, if, like my father, you have no money, no language, and no accredited profession, what exactly do you turn your hand to? This basic form of exchange in which the Great Chain of Business begins and ends is a logical way to start out for an immigrant who is starting out with nothing. So my father has acquired a small truck—a rickety, much-used vehicle whose shaking and rattling are an inescapable accompaniment to our first immigrant years, and on which I'll later learn how to drive—and in this noisy contraption, he goes off for the day to unknown destinations from which he brings home this medley discard of suburban life. These items, in our version of free enterprise, then get carried into our basement, from where we try to sell them for sums less small than what my father paid for them.

The whole thing is indeed basic, so much so that I keep looking for a hidden trick. In fact, the transaction is stunningly simple, but its every step is, for my parents, fraught with tension for the stunningly simple reason that our survival quite literally depends on it. We have come to Canada at an odd time—between waves of emigration, when there seem to be no support systems to ease the "newcomers'" first steps. We are on our own, and the most obvious elements of every exchange present themselves as hurdles to be deciphered and mastered. There is, for example, the matter of placing an ad in the paper. For me, this is an entirely new idea.

▪ ▪ ▪

But being "an immigrant," I begin to learn, is considered a sort of location in itself—and sometimes a highly advantageous one at that. In uneventful Vancouver, I'm enough of a curiosity that I too enjoy the fifteen minutes of fame so often accorded to Eastern European exotics before they are replaced by a new batch. The local newspaper takes me up as a sort of pet, printing my picture when I give a concert at the

Jewish Community Center and soliciting my views when I come back from a bus trip to the United Nations, on which I've been sent after winning a speech contest. They want to know my opinions of the various cities I've been in, and I have no hesitation about offering them. "New York is the real capital of the United States," I readily opine. "Washington just has the government. It doesn't have the excitement." I take such attention blithely for granted, so I'm not too bowled over when a local radio pontificator, after meeting me in a group of high school students, tells me he would like to hear my opinion on anything at all; for this purpose, he'll lend me one of the fifteen-minute spots that bring him fame with weekly regularity. At this point in my initiation into the English language, I have an active vocabulary of about six hundred words, but it doesn't occur to me that I should mince any of them. I want to tell Canadians about how boring they are. "Canada is the dullest country in the world," I write in the notes for my speech, "because it is the most conformist." People may pretend to have liberal beliefs, I go on, but really they are an unadventurous lot who never dare to sidestep bourgeois conventions. With the hauteur that can only spring from fourteen-year-old innocence, I take these observations to be self-evident, because they are mine. And it doesn't occur to me, of course, that my audience might be offended at being read such stern lessons; after all, I'm simply telling the truth.

▪ ▪ ▪

My mother says I'm becoming "English." This hurts me, because I know she means I'm becoming cold. I'm no colder than I've ever been, but I'm learning to be less demonstrative. I learn this from a teacher who, after contemplating the gesticulations with which I help myself describe the digestive system of a frog, tells me to "sit on my hands and then try talking." I learn my new reserve from people who take a step back when we talk, because I'm standing too close, crowding them. Cultural distances are different, I later learn in a sociology class, but I know it already. I learn restraint from Penny, who looks offended when I shake her by the arm in excitement, as if my gesture had been one of aggression instead of friendliness. I learn it from a girl who pulls away when I hook my arm through hers as we walk down the street—this movement of friendly intimacy is an embarrassment to her.

I learn also that certain kinds of truth are impolite. One shouldn't criticize the person one is with, at least not directly. You shouldn't say, "You are wrong about that"—though you may say, "On the other hand, there is that to consider." You shouldn't say, "This doesn't look good on you," though you may say, "I like you better in that other outfit." I learn to tone down my sharpness, to do a more careful conversational minuet.

Perhaps my mother is right, after all; perhaps I'm becoming colder. After a while, emotion follows action, response grows warmer or cooler according to gesture. I'm more careful about what I say, how loud I laugh, whether I give vent to grief. The storminess of emotion prevailing in our family is in excess of the normal here, and the unwritten rules for the normal have their osmotic effect.

Because I'm not heard, I feel I'm not seen. My words often seem to baffle others. They are inappropriate, or forced, or just plain incomprehensible. People look at me with puzzlement; they mumble something in response—something that doesn't hit home. Anyway, the back and forth of conversation is different here. People often don't answer each other. But the mat look in their eyes as they listen to me cancels my face, flattens my features. The mobility of my face comes from the mobility of the words coming to the surface and the feelings that drive them. Its vividness is sparked by the locking of an answering gaze, by the quickness of understanding. But now I can't feel how my face lights up from inside; I don't receive from others the reflected movement of its expressions, its living speech. People look past me as we speak. What do I look like, here? Imperceptible, I think; impalpable, neutral, faceless.

"When I think of love, I think of running with someone through a sunny meadow, holding hands," Penny says dreamily, rolling over on her bed.

"Sunny?" I say, surprised. "When I think of love, I think of a dark forest that you go into by a narrow path." What I really think about, of course, is Marek, but that's too delicate a matter to talk about with this new friend. Penny and I are lying on two single beds in her pink-and-white bedroom, where I've come for an overnight visit—that luxurious benefit of big houses and private rooms. We're dressed in our nighties, and are talking in that pleasant dozy, irresponsible state in which you can speak slowly and utter your deepest thoughts.

"You know what Larry said to me today?" Penny says, now sounding a little kittenish.

"What?"

"He said, 'Kid, you'd be good on a desert island.'"

▪ ▪ ▪

On one of my overnight visits, our conversation takes an entirely different turn. When the lights are out and I am about to go to sleep, she begins crying softly.

"What is it?" I ask her.

After a long pause, Penny begins to tell me, in a small and pained voice, about her older sister, Janet, who had tried to kill herself, to end her own life.

"But why?" I ask, disbelieving. This comfortable house, this atmosphere of prosy, daily concerns, seems like an utterly incongruous setting for a young girl's attempted suicide.

"Oh," Penny says, "it's my mother. She doesn't really like her. They have fights all the time. Janet has a terrible inferiority complex. I mean, my mother is a good egg, but she is so horrible to Janet . . ."

"That's terrible," I say, utterly at a loss for anything more. A good egg? But she has driven her daughter to this, by not treating her well enough? It doesn't add up, not in my cosmos, and it is only after I come across many more gothic secrets, smoldering in the sensible interiors of these intact suburban households, that I begin to get inklings of what may ail their inhabitants, of the strangled suffering that can be bred within them. For now, I haven't yet learned how to read the surfaces either of Penny's face or of lives like hers well enough to see what's behind them, to discern the paradoxes inherent in their very smoothness.

The Scrapbook of Katherine Mansfield

1905–13

Katherine Mansfield

Katherine Mansfield (1888–1923) was born in Wellington, New Zealand. She moved to London to attend college in 1903, married in 1909 but soon became pregnant by another man, events which inform her first collection of stories, In a German Pension *(1911). Also in 1911 she met editor John Middleton Murry, whom she married in 1918. Their life together included an intense friendship with D. H. Lawrence and his wife, Frieda (reflected in Lawrence's* Women in Love*), as well as the publication of Mansfield's work in Murry's periodicals. According to novelist and biographer Margaret Drabble, "Her stories were the first in English to show the influence of Chekhov, whom she greatly admired." After Mansfield died of tuberculosis at the age of thirty-four, her husband continued to publish her miscellaneous writing in collections like* The Scrapbook of Katherine Mansfield *(1939), from which the following selections are taken.*

About Pat

In the days of our childhood we lived in a great old rambling house planted lonesomely in the midst of huge gardens, orchards and paddocks. We had few toys, but—far better—plenty of good strong mud and a flight of concrete steps that grew hot in the heat of the sun and became dreams of ovens.

The feeling of making a mud pie with all due seriousness is one of the most delicious feelings that we experience; you sit with your mixture in the doll's saucepan, or if it is soup, in the doll's wash-hand basin, and stir and stir, and thicken and "whip," and become more deliciously grimy each minute; whilst the sense of utter wickedness you have if it happens to be on clean pinafore days thrills me to this hour.

Well I remember one occasion when we made pies with real flour, stole some water from the dish by the dog's kennel, baked them and ate them.

Very soon after, three crushed, subdued little girls wended their way quietly up to bed, and the blind was pulled down.

At that period our old Irish gardener was our hero. His name was Patrick Sheehan. On Sunday he wore gloves with real "kid backs," and a tie-pin made out of a boar's tusk. Every morning I went across to the feed-room where he cleaned Father's boots, and always at a certain stage of the proceedings, I would say, "Oh please, Pat, don't!" He invariably replied that "nothing else at all gave them such a fine gloss." He used to hoist me up on to the table, and recount long tales of the Dukes of Ireland whom he had seen and even conversed with. We were most proud of our gardener having rubbed shoulders with Ireland's aristocracy, and in the evening when Pat was at tea in the kitchen we would steal out and beg him to show us the manners of the people in Ireland. Standing in a row, hand in hand, we would watch while Pat put some salt on his knife, tapped it off with his fork, the little finger of his right hand well curled, in a manner which seemed to us ingenious enough for the first Lords of the land.

Pat was never very fond of me. I am afraid he did not think my character at all desirable. I professed no joy in having a bird in a cage; and one day committed the unpardonable offence of picking a pumpkin flower. He never recovered from the shock occasioned by that last act of barbarism. I can see him now, whenever I came near, nodding his head and saying, "Well now to think! It might have become the finest vegetable of the season, and given us food for weeks."

Pat's birthdays occurred with alarming frequency. We always gave him the same presents—three sticks of Juno tobacco and three cakes of hoky-poky. The presentation took place in the back-yard, and he sang us a wonderful Irish song, of which we never guessed any more than the phrase, "I threw up me hat." It seemed to be the one definite remark throughout.

He considered it a duty to propose to each cook who came to the house, making them the offer of himself, the gloves with the "kid backs," and the boar-tusk tie-pin whenever the occasion demanded. They never by any chance accepted him, and I am sure that he never expected them to do so.

Every afternoon he used to brush his old brown bowler hat, harness the mare and start for town, and every evening when he had come home it was my delight to wait till he had unharnessed the mare, then to be lifted on to her back, and start at a jogging trot through the big white gates, down the quiet road and into the paddock. There I waited until Pat came swinging along with the milk pails.

On those late evenings he had wonderful stories to tell of a little old man no bigger than his thumb with a hat as high as the barbed-wire fence, who in the night crept out of the creek, climbed up the blue-gum tree, picked some leaves from the topmost branches, and then crept down again.

"You see," Pat would say, his dear weather-beaten face as grave as possible, "it's from blue gums that you get eucalyptus, and the old man suffered from cold, living in such dampness."

On those evenings, too, I had my first lessons in the mysterious art of milking, but try as I would I could never obtain more than a teacupful. On several occasions the ignominy of this reduced me to tears, but Pat would say, "You see, she's such a keen old cow is Daisy. Having had children of her own, she knows how much you ought to have, and how much more would give you indigestion." I was always much comforted. Pat had a wonderfully young heart. He entered into our pleasures with as much zest as we did ourselves. I played a game which had no end and no beginning, but was called "Beyond the Blue Mountains." The scene was generally placed near the rhubarb beds, and Pat officiated as the villain, the hero, and even the villainess, with unfailing charm.

Sometimes, to make it more real, we had lunch together, sitting on the wheel-barrow turned upside down, and sharing the slice of German sausage and a bath-bun with loaf sugar on it.

On Sunday mornings Pat, in the full glory of a clean shirt and corduroy trousers, took us for a walk in the great pine plantation.

He, childishly, used to collect gum and carry it in a corner of his handkerchief. For years afterwards I believed that those trees just grew for the old witches of the woods, who used their needles in making the big, big umbrella over our heads, and all the dresses of the flowers, basting their nice, fine, blue-sky calico with the gum thoughtfully provided for them. . . .

When we left that house in the country and went to live in town, Pat left us to try his luck in the gold-fields. We parted with bitter tears. He presented each of my sisters with a goldfinch and me with a pair of white china vases cheerfully embroidered with forget-me-nots and pink roses. His parting advice to us was to look after ourselves in this world and never to pick the flowers out of the vegetable garden because we liked the colour.

From that day to this I have never heard of him.

(1905)

The Grandmother

Underneath the cherry trees
The grandmother in her lilac printed gown
Carried Little Brother in her arms.
A wind, no older than Little Brother,
Shook the branches of the cherry trees
So that the blossom snowed on her hair
And on her faded lilac gown
And all over Little Brother.
I said "May I see?"

She bent down and lifted a corner of his shawl.
He was fast asleep,
But his mouth moved as if he were kissing.
"Beautiful!" said the grandmother, nodding and
smiling.
But my lips quivered,
And looking into her kind face
I wanted to be in the place of Little Brother,
To put my arms round her neck
And kiss the two tears that shone in her eyes.

(1909)

Along the Gray's Inn Road

Over an opaque sky grey clouds moving heavily like the wings of tired birds. Wind blowing: in the naked light buildings and people appear suddenly grotesque—too sharply modelled, maliciously tweaked into being.

A little procession wending its way up the Gray's Inn Road. In front, a man between the shafts of a handbarrow that creaks under the weight of a piano-organ and two bundles. The man is small and greenish brown, head lolling forward, face covered with sweat. The piano-organ is bright red, with a blue and gold "dancing picture" on either side. The bundle is a woman. You see only a black mackintosh topped with a sailor hat; the little bundle she holds has chalk-white legs and yellow boots dangling from the loose ends of the shawl. Followed by two small boys, who walk with short steps, staring intensely at the ground, as though afraid of stumbling over their feet.

No word is spoken; they never raise their eyes. And this silence and preoccupation gives to their progress a strange dignity.

They are like pilgrims straining forward to Nowhere, dragging, and holding to, and following after that bright red, triumphant thing with the blue and gold "dancing picture" on either side.

(1910)

Texas Women: True Grit and All the Rest

Molly Ivins

Molly Ivins (1944–   ) moved to Texas, the state of her birth, following her formal education at Smith College and the Columbia School of Journalism. Her "Humor" column for Ms. *provided an opportunity to comment on Texas politics, which she describes as "the finest form of free entertainment ever invented." Her writing, admired by Texas governor Ann Richards, has been collected under the title* Molly Ivins Can't Say That, Can She? *(1991). In the following description of the condition of women in Texas, she comments, "Having a sense of humor about men is not a luxury here; it's a necessity."*

THEY USED TO SAY THAT TEXAS WAS HELL ON women and horses—I don't know why they stopped. Surely not because much of the citizenry has had its consciousness raised, as they say in the jargon of the women's movement, on the issue of sexism. Just a few months ago one of our state representatives felt moved to compare women and horses—it was the similarity he wanted to emphasize. Of course some Texas legislator can be found to say any fool thing, but this guy's comments met with general agreement from his colleagues. One can always dismiss the entire Legislature as a particularly deplorable set of Texans, but as Sen. Carl Parker observes, if you took all the fools out of the Lege, it wouldn't be a representative body anymore.

I should confess that I've always been more of an observer than a participant in Texas Womanhood: the spirit was willing but I was declared ineligible on grounds of size early. You can't be six feet tall and cute, both. I think I was first named captain of the basketball team when I was four and that's what I've been ever since. I spent my girlhood as a Clydesdale among thoroughbreds. I clopped along amongst them cheerfully, admiring their grace, but the strange training rituals they went through left me secretly relieved that no one would ever expect me to step on a racetrack. I think it is quite possible to grow up in Texas as an utter failure in flirting, gentility, cheerleading, sex-pottery, and manipulation and still be without any permanent scars. Except one. We'd all rather be blonde.

Please understand I'm not whining when I point out that Texas sexism is of an especially rank and noxious variety—this is more a Texas brag. It is my belief that it is virulence of Texas sexism that accounts for the strength of Texas women. It's what we have to overcome that makes us formidable survivors, say I with some complacency.

As has been noted elsewhere, there are several strains of Texan culture: They are all rotten for women. There is the Southern belle nonsense of our Confederate heritage, that little-woman-on-a-pedestal, flirtatious, "you're so cute when you're mad," Scarlett O'Hara myth that leads, quite naturally, to the equally pernicious legend of the Iron Magnolia. Then there's the machismo of our Latin heritage, which affects not only our Chicana sisters, but has been integrated into Texas culture quite as thoroughly as barbecue, rodeo, and Tex-Mex food.

Next up is the pervasive good-ol'-boyism of the *Redneckus texensis,* that remarkable tribe that has made the pickup truck with the gun rack across the back window and the beer cans flying out the window a synonym for Texans worldwide. Country music is a good place to investigate and find reflected the attitudes of kickers toward women (never ask what a kicker kicks). It's your basic, familiar virgin/whore dichotomy—either your "Good-Hearted Woman" or "Your Cheatin' Heart," with the emphasis on the honky-tonk angels. Nor is the jock idolatry that permeates the state helpful to our gender: Football is not a game here, it's a matter of blood and death. Woman's role in the state's national game is limited, significantly, to cheerleading. In this regard, I can say with great confidence that Texas changeth not—the hopelessly intense, heartbreaking longing with which most Texas girls will want to be cheerleader can be observed at every high school, every September.*

Last but not least in the litany of cultures that help make the lives of Texas women so challenging is the legacy of the frontier—not the frontier that Texas women lived on, but the one John Wayne lived on. Anyone who knows the real history of the frontier knows it is a saga of the strength of women. They worked as hard as men, they fought as hard as men, they suffered as much as men. But in the cowboy movies that most contemporary Texans grew up on, the big, strong man always protects "the little lady" or "the gals" from whatever peril threatens. Such nonsense. Mary Ann Goodnight was often left alone at the JA Ranch near the Palo Duro Canyon. One day in 1877, a cowboy rode into her camp with three chickens in a sack as a present for her. He naturally expected her to cook and eat the fowl, but Goodnight kept them as pets. She wrote in her diary, "No one can ever know how much company they were." Life for farm and ranch wives didn't improve much over the next 100 years. Ruth White raised nine children on a farm near High, Texas, in the 1920s and thirties. She used to say, "Everything on this farm is either hungry or heavy."

All of these strains lead to a form of sexism so deeply ingrained in the culture that it's often difficult to distinguish the disgusting from the outrageous or the offensive from the amusing. One not infrequently sees cars or trucks sporting the bumper sticker HAVE FUN—BEAT THE HELL OUT OF SOMEONE YOU LOVE. Another is: IF YOU LOVE SOMETHING, SET IT FREE. IF IT DOESN'T COME BACK, TRACK IT DOWN AND KILL IT. I once heard a legislator order a lobbyist, "Get me two sweathogs for tonight." At a benefit "roast" for the battered women's shelter in El Paso early in 1985, a couple of the male politicians told rape jokes to amuse the crowd. Most Texas sexism is not intended to be offensive—it's entirely unconscious. A colleague of mine was touring the new death chamber in Huntsville last year with a group of other reporters. Their guide called to warn those inside they were coming through, saying, "I'm coming over with eight reporters and one woman." Stuff like that happens to you four or five times a day for long enough, it will wear you down some.

Other forms of the phenomenon are, of course, less delightsome. Women everywhere are victims of violence with depressing regularity. Texas is a more violent place than most of the rest of America, for reasons having to do with guns, machismo, frontier traditions, and the heterogeneous population. While the law theoretically applies to male and female alike, by unspoken convention, a man who offs his wife or girlfriend is seldom charged with murder one: we wind up filed under the misnomer manslaughter.

That's the bad news for Texas women—the good news is that all this adversity has certainly made us a bodacious bunch of overcomers. And rather pleasant as a group, I always think, since having a sense of humor about men is not a luxury here; it's a necessity. The feminists often carry on about the importance of role models and how little girls need positive role models. When I was a kid, my choice of Texas role models went from Ma Ferguson to the Kilgore Rangerettes. Of course I wanted to be a Rangerette: Ever seen a picture of Ma? Not that we haven't got real women heroes, of course, just that we were never taught anything about them. You used to have to take Texas history two or three times in order to get a high

*In February 1991, a woman in Channelview, Texas, was indicted for plotting the murder of the mother of her own daughter's chief rival for the cheerleading squad.

school diploma in this state: The Yellow Rose of Texas and Belle Starr were the only women in our history books. Kaye Northcott notes that all the big cities in the state have men's last names—Houston, Austin, Dallas. All women got was some small towns called after their front names: Alice, Electra, Marfa. This is probably because, as Eleanor Brackenridge of San Antonio (1837–1924) so elegantly put it, "Foolish modesty lags behind while brazen impudence goes forth and eats the pudding." Brackenridge did her part to correct the lag by founding the Texas Woman Suffrage Association in 1913.

It is astonishing how recently Texas women have achieved equal legal rights. I guess you could say we made steady progress even before we could vote—the state did raise the age of consent for a woman from 7 to 10 in 1890—but it went a little smoother after we got some say in it. Until June 26, 1918, all Texans could vote except "idiots, imbeciles, aliens, the insane and women." The battle over woman's suffrage in Texas was long and fierce. Contempt and ridicule were the favored weapons against women. Women earned the right to vote through years of struggle; the precious victory was not something handed to us by generous men. From that struggle emerged a generation of Texas women whose political skills and leadership abilities have affected Texas politics for decades. Even so, Texas women were not permitted to serve on juries until 1954. As late as 1969, married women did not have full property rights. And until 1972, under Article 1220 of the Texas Penal Code, a man could murder his wife and her lover if he found them "in a compromising position" and get away with it as "justifiable homicide." Women, you understand, did not have equal shooting rights. Although Texas was one of the first states to ratify the Equal Rights Amendment, which has been part of the Texas Constitution since 1972, we continue to work for fairer laws concerning problems such as divorce, rape, child custody, and access to credit.

Texas women are just as divided by race, class, age, and educational level as are other varieties of human beings. There's a pat description of "what every Texas woman wants" that varies a bit from city to city, but the formula that Dallas females have been labeled with goes something like this: "Be a Pi Phi at Texas or SMU, marry a man who'll buy you a house in Highland Park, hold the wedding at Highland Park Methodist (flowers by Kendall Bailey), join the Junior League, send the kids to St. Mark's and Hockaday in the winter and Camps Longhorn and Waldemar in the summer, plus cotillion lessons at the Dallas Country Club, have an unlimited charge account at Neiman's as a birthright but buy almost all your clothes at Highland Park Village from Harold's or the Polo Shop, get your hair done at Paul Neinast's or Lou's and drive a Jeep Wagoneer for carpooling and a Mercedes for fun." There is a kicker equivalent of this scenario that starts, "Every Texas girl's dream is a double-wide in a Lubbock trailer park. . . ." But I personally believe it is unwise ever to be funny at the expense of kicker women. I once met a kicker lady who was wearing a blouse of such a vivid pink you could close your eyes and still see the color; this confection was perked up with some big rhinestone buttons and a lot of ruffles across an impressive bosom. "My," said I, "where did you get that blouse?" She gave me a level look and drawled, "Honey, it come from mah coutouri-ay, Jay Cee Penn-ay." And if that ain't class, you *can* kiss my grits.

To my partisan eye, it seems that Texas women are more animated and friendly than those from, say, Nebraska. I suspect this comes from early training: Girls in Texas high schools are expected to walk through the halls smiling and saying "Hi" to everyone they meet. Being enthusiastic is bred into us, as is a certain amount of obligatory social hypocrisy stemming from the Southern tradition of manners, which does rather tend to emphasize pleasantness more than honesty in social situations. Many Texas women have an odd greeting call—when they haven't seen a good friend for a long time, the first glimpse will provoke the cry, "Oooooooo—honey, how good to see yew again!" It sounds sort of like the "Soooooey, pig" call.

Mostly Texas women are tough in some very fundamental ways. Not unfeminine, nor necessarily unladylike, just tough. It may be possible for a little girl to grow to womanhood in this state entirely sheltered from the rampant sexism all around her—but it's damned difficult. The result is that Texas women tend to know how to cope. We can cope with put-downs and come-ons, with preachers and hustlers, with drunks and cowboys. And when it's all over, if we stick together and work, we'll come out better than the sister who's buried in a grave near Marble Falls under a stone that says, "Rudolph Richter, 1822–1915, and Wife."

Texas Celebrates, 1986

The Color of Friendship

Teresa Moore

Teresa Moore (1962–   ) was born in Danville, Virginia, a textile and tobacco town of 45,000 people. The oldest of six children, she was raised by her mother and grandmother after the death of her father. Her B.A. (1985) is from Princeton University. She also attended the UC Berkeley School of Journalism on a Regents' Scholarship. While working as a staff writer for the San Francisco Chronicle, *Moore wrote this piece about events at Mills College, a private women's college in nearby Oakland. Moore says that she "looks at race relations through the eyes of the post–Civil Rights generation," and says, "Feminism has been racially divided for years. It's time black feminists and white feminists were integrated."*

Students and faculty of color at Mills college are outraged over the appointment of a white woman as the school's new provost and dean of faculty. They argue that this woman does not have enough experience dealing with minorities and that a white will not be responsive to their needs. On a campus with almost one-third minority students and only one tenure-track person of color, some declare that this appointment is a powerful sign of the administration's indifference to racial issues.

I hadn't been paying much attention to this uproar—which echoes controversies at San Jose State University, the University of California at Berkeley and the San Francisco Unified School District—until a couple weeks ago when I heard a black student and a black professor from Mills express their frustration with the choice on a radio call-in show. A name I hadn't heard in years caught my ear: The new appointee was Faith Gabelnick, my old professor from the University of Maryland.

Eleven years ago I was one of a handful of black students in the General Honors program there in College Park. Even though I was a National Merit Scholar, some campus office persisted in sending me the same offers of tutoring sessions that they seemed to send to every black and Latino student—regardless of grade-point average. My black dormmates proudly showed me off to their friends. "This is Teresa, the honors student," they said. "She's a real brainiac." The first few times I entered the Honors Lounge, one of the white or Asian students hanging out there asked me if I was lost. After a while, I stopped going in there—except for my weekly seminar with Faith, who was then co-chair of the honors program.

Faith was busy—besides running the honors program and teaching, she was raising children—but she always had time to listen to me. We talked about books, feminism, race, my grandfather's death. I remember telling her how I hated the pack mentality that seemed to prevail in my dorm, the whole hall going to dinner at the same time—whether you were hungry at 4:30 or not. We talked about how a person could enjoy company but still need vast amounts of time alone. When I decided to transfer to Princeton, I used her as a sounding board. A couple of years later, when I took time off from my studies at Princeton, she tried to help me find a job. But it would be unfair to suggest that Faith was my only anchor. There were other administrators and professors who reached out to me, people named Gerald and Robert and John.

It saddens me to think that now that Faith has been chosen for the Mills post, there are people on that campus who will resent her and avoid her because she does not match their racial profile. Compassion and energy are neither race- nor gender-linked traits.

I agree with the Mills women that it is important to have people of color in positions of influence. For one thing, I think the mere presence of a powerful person of color can raise the consciousness of a mostly white administration; it is harder (though not impossible) to forget or ignore minorities when one of us is sitting at the table.

Faculty and leaders of color are essential to the survival of any place where people study and learn. Mills College is now 29 percent minority, a number that is likely to grow as the state's minority population soars. If the academy is to remain vital and relevant, it must respond to the society that serves it.

Women of color at Mills say they are sick and tired of having to explain themselves to their white teachers, counselors and classmates. I hear that. From my own college days, I can recall white girls asking me why I didn't wash my hair every day and why I didn't have to shave my legs and why my skin got darker in the sun and how do you make corn-rows and why didn't I have them? This sort of thing doesn't end in college. Nowadays I'm asked why are black men so violent and why can't blacks be thrifty and prosperous like Asians and why are blacks getting all the great jobs and how do you make dreadlocks and why don't I have them?

White people are used to thinking of themselves as unique and individual, but more often than not they tend to see the rest of us as representatives of whole alien, abnormal groups. This is why Mills needs *lots* of people of color in charge: so that eventually, everyone can have a chance to be seen as an individual and not merely as a token or exception. Had there been many black honors students at the University of Maryland, people might have seen me as a regular person and not some kind of circus freak.

The sad truth is that as much as I would hope that another woman or minority would be in my corner, life has taught me not to count on it. More than once I have watched female professors neglect female students and go out of their way to help males. Along with other minority students, I was once assigned to the same minority faculty adviser. Although this man worked hard to help people find jobs and scholarships, his inappropriate overtures angered and embarrassed many female students and soured the classroom atmosphere for men and women.

On the other hand, at Princeton, Cecelia Drewry, a black dean, eased my transfer to that campus by talking me through my worries and welcoming me into her home. But so did Susan Hollander, a white dean, who, one snowy January Saturday, introduced me to the Metropolitan Museum of Art.

Yet for the most part, the people outside my family who have done the most to help me are almost all white men. They have written letters of recommendation and letters of introduction. They have pulled strings and broken rules for me. They have found me scholarships and lent me money. They have turned over their car keys and house keys and given me the run of their Rolodexes. The best of them have made me believe that I can do anything. Not once has any of them ever made me feel compromised or patronized.

There is a reason white men have played a crucial role in my education and career: There are simply more of them in power. The surprise is that these guys who represent my demographic opposites have been so supportive. They haven't just been able; they've been willing.

The point is: Scumbags and saints come in all colors and both sexes.

Last spring I attended a party for a young black woman who had just graduated from a prestigious law school. Almost all of the guests were women, and the party was hosted by one of her professors and his wife. A large white man, he is an influential legal scholar who enjoys campus notoriety for breaking people's bones on the basketball court. The graduate and a group of female classmates made national news last year when they published a study of how sexual bias hindered female students seeking law clerkships. The professor and the new graduate laughed when they reminisced about how they came to know each other: He was impressed that she had the audacity to sit in the front row of his lecture listening to a Walkman.

Looking at them, I couldn't help but remember the time I made one of my professors, a World War II Marine fighter pilot, cry. When I told this white man that school was making me crazy and I was taking time off, he sat and wept with me. He invited me to move in with him and his wife. He told me that I was acting like one of those Marines who turned their planes at the last minute, afraid to drop their bombs. When none of this moved me to stay in school, he lent me a new edition of the Norton anthology of British literature and told me he expected me to return it the following year. I still have his books, but I also have my degree.

A generation ago, these alliances would have been unlikely, if not impossible. Today, they seem like healthy signs that growth and common ground are possible across race and gender lines.

I look forward to the day when the racial and gender composition of classrooms, newsrooms, boardrooms, hospitals, courtrooms and public offices mirror the country we live in. But while we are moving toward that day, we should work with what we have. In a perfect world, many of my teachers, counselors and editors would be sympathetic black women who would instinctively understand my concerns and always have my welfare at heart. In the real world, though, I've discovered allies and advocates in all sorts of unexpected places. Now that Faith Gabelnick is coming to Mills, I hope that young women of color will be able to look at her and see a human being. I know that's what she saw when she looked at me.

Hunger

Naomi Wolf

Naomi Wolf was born in San Francisco in 1963. A graduate of Yale and a Rhodes scholar, Wolf developed the idea of The Beauty Myth *(1992) while working on a thesis at New College, Oxford. Her argument is that "the patriarchy, and its agents, the film makers and magazine editors of both sexes . . . , impose unattainable images of beauty as a way of keeping women in their places." Although critics are divided on the depth of her research, Germaine Greer has called the book "the most important feminist publication since* The Female Eunuch.*" The subject of the following excerpt is anorexia.*

"Hunger," pp. 179–217 from *The Beauty Myth* by Naomi Wolf.

I saw the best minds of my generation destroyed by madness, starving. . . .

—Allen Ginsberg, "Howl"

There is a disease spreading. It taps on the shoulder America's firstborn sons, its best and brightest. At its touch, they turn away from food. Their bones swell out from receding flesh. Shadows invade their faces. They walk slowly, with the effort of old men. A white spittle forms on their lips. They can swallow only pellets of bread, and a little thin milk. First tens, then hundreds, then thousands, until, among the most affluent families, one young son in five is stricken. Many are hospitalized, many die.

The boys of the ghetto die young, and America has lived with that. But these boys are the golden ones to whom the reins of the world are to be lightly tossed: the captain of the Princeton football team, the head of the Berkeley debating club, the editor of the *Harvard Crimson*. Then a quarter of the Dartmouth rugby team falls ill; then a third of the initiates of Yale's secret societies. The heirs, the cream, the fresh delegates to the nation's forum selectively waste away.

The American disease spreads eastward. It strikes young men at the Sorbonne, in London's Inns of Court, in the administration of The Hague, in the Bourse, in the offices of *Die Zeit*, in the universities of Edinburgh and Tübingen and Salamanca. They grow thin and still more thin. They can hardly speak aloud. They lose their libido, and can no longer make the effort to joke or argue. When they run or swim, they look appalling: buttocks collapsed, tailbones protruding, knees knocked together, ribs splayed in a shelf that stretches their papery skin. There is no medical reason.

The disease mutates again. Across America, it becomes apparent that for every well-born living skeleton there are at least three other young men, also bright lights, who do something just as strange. Once they have swallowed their steaks and Rhine wine, they hide away, to thrust their fingers down their throats and spew out all the nourishment in them. They wander back into Maury's or "21," shaking and pale. Eventually they arrange their lives so they can spend hours each day hunched over like that, their highly trained minds telescoped around two shameful holes: mouth, toilet; toilet, mouth.

Meanwhile, people are waiting for them to take up their places: assistantships at *The New York Times,* seats on the stock exchange, clerkships with federal judges. Speeches need to be written and briefs researched among the clangor of gavels and the whir of fax machines. What is happening to the fine young men, in their brush cuts and khaki trousers? It hurts to look at them. At the expense-account lunches, they hide their medallions of veal under lettuce leaves. Secretly they purge. They vomit after matriculation banquets and after tailgate parties at the Game. The men's room in the Oyster Bar reeks with it. One in five, on the campuses that speak their own names proudest.

How would America react to the mass self-immolation by hunger of its favorite sons? How would Western Europe absorb the export of such a disease? One would expect an emergency response: crisis task forces convened in congressional hearing rooms, unscheduled alumni meetings, the best experts money can hire, cover stories in newsmagazines, a flurry of editorials, blame and counterblame, bulletins, warnings, symptoms, updates; an epidemic blazoned in boldface red. The sons of privilege *are* the future; the future is committing suicide.

Of course, this is actually happening right now, only with a gender difference. The institutions that shelter and promote these diseases are hibernating. The public conscience is fast asleep. Young women are dying from institutional catatonia: four hundred dollars a term from the college endowment for the women's center to teach "self-help"; fifty to buy a noontime talk from a visiting clinician. The world is not coming to an end because the cherished child in five who "chooses" to die slowly is a girl. And she is merely doing too well what she is expected to do very well in the best of times.

Up to one tenth of all young American women, up to one fifth of women students in the United States, are locked into one-woman hunger camps. When they fall, there are no memorial services, no intervention through awareness programs, no formal message from their schools and colleges that the society prefers its young women to eat and thrive rather than sicken and die. Flags are not lowered in recognition of the fact that in every black-robed ceremonial marches a fifth column of death's-heads.

Virginia Woolf in *A Room of One's Own* had a vision that someday young women would have access to the rich forbidden libraries of the men's colleges, their sunken lawns, their vellum, the claret light. She believed that would give young women a mental freedom that must have seemed all the sweeter from where she imagined it: the wrong side of the beadle's staff that had driven her away from the library because she was female. Now young women have pushed past the staff that barred Woolf's way. Striding across the grassy quadrangles that she could only write about, they are halted by an immaterial barrier she did not foresee. Their minds are proving well able; their bodies self-destruct.

When she envisaged a future for young women in the universities, Woolf's prescience faltered only from insufficient cynicism. Without it one could hardly conceive of the modern solution of the recently all-male schools and colleges to the problem of women: They admitted their minds, and let their bodies go. Young women learned that they could not live inside those gates and also inside their bodies.

The weight-loss cult recruits women from an early age, and eating diseases are the cult's bequest. Anorexia and bulimia are female maladies: From 90 to 95 percent of anorexics and bulimics are women. America, which has the greatest number of women who have made it into the male sphere, also leads the world with female anorexia. Women's magazines report that there are up to a million American anorexics, but the American Anorexia and Bulimia Association states that anorexia and bulimia strike a million American women *every year;* 30,000, it reports, also become emetic abusers.

Each year, according to the association, 150,000 American women die of anorexia. If so, every twelve months there are 17,024 more deaths in the United States alone than the total number of deaths from AIDS tabulated by the World Health Organization in 177 countries and territories from the beginning of the epidemic until the end of 1988; if so, more die of anorexia in the United States each year than died in ten years of civil war in Beirut. Beirut has long been front-page news. As criminally neglectful as media coverage of the AIDS epidemic has been, it still dwarfs that of anorexia; so it appears that the bedrock question—why must Western women go hungry—is one too dangerous to ask even in the face of a death toll such as this.

Joan Jacobs Brumberg in *Fasting Girls: The Emergence of Anorexia Nervosa as a Modern Disease* puts the number of anorexics at 5 to 10 percent of all American girls and women. On some college campuses, she believes, one woman student in five is anorexic. The number of women with the disease has increased dramatically throughout the Western world starting twenty years ago. Dr. Charles A. Murkovsky of Gracie Square Hospital in New York City, an eating diseases specialist, says that 20 percent of American college women binge and purge on a regular basis. Kim Chernin in *The Hungry Self* suggests that at least half the women on campuses in the United States suffer at some time from bulimia or anorexia. Roberta Pollack Seid in *Never Too Thin* agrees with the 5- to 10-percent figure for anorexia among young American women, adding that up to six times that figure on campuses are bulimic. If we take the high end of the figures, it means that of ten young American women in college, two will be anorexic and six will be bulimic; only two will be well. The norm, then, for young, middle-class American women, is to be a sufferer from some form of the eating disease.

The disease is a deadly one. Brumberg reports that 5 to 15 percent of hospitalized anorexics die in treatment, giving the disease one of the highest fatality rates for a mental illness. *The New York Times* cites the same fatality rate. Researcher L.K.G. Hsu gives a death rate of up to 19 percent. Forty to 50 percent of anorexics never recover completely, a worse rate of recovery from starvation than the 66 percent recovery rate for famine victims hospitalized in the war-torn Netherlands in 1944–45.

The medical effects of anorexia include hypothermia, edema, hypotension, bradycardia (impaired heartbeat), lanugo (growth of body hair), infertility, and death. The medical effects of bulimia include dehydration, electrolyte imbalance, epileptic seizure, abnormal heart rhythm, and death. When the two are combined, they can result in tooth erosion, hiatal hernia, abraded esophagus, kidney failure, osteoporosis, and death. Medical literature is starting to report that babies and children underfed by weight-conscious mothers are suffering from stunted growth, delayed puberty, and failure to thrive.

It is spreading to other industrialized nations: The United Kingdom now has 3.5 million anorexics or bulimics (95 percent of them female), with 6,000 new cases yearly. Another study of adolescent British girls alone shows that 1 percent are now anorexic. According to the women's press, at least 50 percent of British women suffer from disordered eating. Hilde Bruch states that in the last generation, larger patient groups have been reported in publications in Russia, Australia, Sweden, and Italy as well as Great Britain and the United States. Sweden's rate is now 1 to 2 percent of teenage girls, with the same percentage of women over sixteen being bulimic. The rate for the Netherlands is 1 to 2 percent; of Italian teenagers also, 1 percent suffer from anorexia or bulimia (95 percent of them female), a rise of 400 percent in ten years. That is just the beginning for Western Europe and Japan, since the figures resemble numbers for the United States ten years ago, and since the rate is rising, as it did in America, exponentially. The anorexic patient herself is *thinner* now than were previous generations of patients. Anorexia followed the familiar beauty myth pattern of movement: It began as a middle-class disease in the United States and has spread eastward as well as down the social ladder.

Some women's magazines report that 60 percent of American women have serious trouble eating. The majority of middle-class women in the United States, it appears, suffer a version of anorexia or bulimia; but if anorexia is defined as a compulsive fear of and fixation upon food, perhaps most Western women can be called, twenty years into the backlash, mental anorexics.

What happened? Why now? The first obvious clue is the progressive chiseling away of the Iron Maiden's body over this century of female emancipation, in reaction to it. Until seventy-five years ago in the male artistic tradition of the West, women's natural amplitude was their beauty; representations of the female nude reveled in women's lush fertility. Various distributions of sexual fat were emphasized according to fashion—big, ripe bellies from the fifteenth to the seventeenth centuries, plump faces and shoulders in the early nineteenth, progressively generous dimpled buttocks and thighs until the twentieth—but never, until women's emancipation entered law, this absolute negation of the female state that fashion historian Ann Hollander in *Seeing Through Clothes* characterizes, from the point of view of any age but our own, as "the look of sickness, the look of poverty, and the look of nervous exhaustion."

Dieting and thinness began to be female preoccupations when Western women received the vote around 1920; between 1918 and 1925, "the rapidity with which the new, linear form replaced the more curvaceous one is startling." In the regressive 1950s, women's natural fullness could be briefly enjoyed once more because their minds were occupied in domestic seclusion. But when women came en masse into male spheres, that pleasure had to be overridden by an urgent social expedient that would make women's bodies into the prisons that their homes no longer were.

A generation ago, the average model weighed 8 percent less than the average American woman, whereas today she weighs 23 percent less. Twiggy appeared in the pages of *Vogue* in 1965, simultaneous with the advent of the Pill, to cancel out its most radical implications. Like many beauty-myth symbols, she was double-edged, suggesting to women the freedom from the constraint of reproduction of earlier generations (since female fat is categorically understood by the subconscious as fertile sexuality), while reassuring men with her suggestion of female weakness, asexuality, and hunger. Her thinness, now commonplace, was shocking at the time; even *Vogue* introduced the model with anxiety: "'Twiggy' is called Twiggy because she looks as though a strong gale would snap her in two and dash her to the ground . . . Twiggy is of such a meagre constitution that other models stare at her. Her legs look as though she has not had enough milk as a baby and her face has that expression one feels Londoners wore in the blitz." The fashion writer's language is revealing: Undernurtured, subject to being overpowered by a strong wind, her expression the daze of the besieged, what better symbol to reassure an establishment faced with women who were soon to march tens of thousands strong down Fifth Avenue?

In the twenty years after the start of the second wave of the women's movement, the weight of Miss Americas plummeted, and the average weight of Playboy Playmates dropped from 11 percent below the national average in 1970 to 17 percent below it in eight years. Model Aimee Liu in her autobiography claims that many models are anorexic; she herself continued to model as an anorexic. Of dancers, 38 percent show anorexic behavior. The average model, dancer, or actress is thinner than 95 percent of the female population. The Iron Maiden put the shape of a near skeleton and the texture of men's musculature where the shape and feel of a woman used to be, and the small elite corps of women whose bodies are used to reproduce the Iron Maiden often become diseased themselves in order to do so.

As a result, a 1985 survey says, 90 percent of respondents think they weigh too much. On any day, 25 percent of women are on diets, with 50 percent finishing, breaking, or starting one. This self-hatred was generated rapidly, coinciding with the women's movement: Between 1966 and 1969, two studies showed, the number of high school girls who thought they were too fat had risen from 50 to 80 percent. Though heiresses to the gains of the women's movement, their daughters are, in terms of this distress, no better off: In a recent study of high school girls, 53 percent were unhappy with their bodies by age thirteen; by age eighteen and over, 78 percent were dissatisfied. The hunger cult has won a major victory against women's fight for equality if the evidence of the 1984 *Glamour* survey of thirty-three thousand women is representative: 75 percent of those aged eighteen to thirty-five believed they were fat, while only 25 percent were medically overweight (the same percentage as men); 45 percent of the *underweight* women thought they were too fat. But more heartbreaking in terms of the way in which the myth is running to ground hopes for women's advancement and gratification, the *Glamour* respondents chose losing ten to fifteen pounds above success in work or in love as their most desired goal.

Those ten to fifteen pounds, which have become a fulcrum, if these figures are indicative, of most Western women's sense of self, are the medium of what I call the One Stone Solution. One stone, the British measurement of fourteen pounds, is roughly what stands between the 50 percent of women who are not overweight who believe they are and their ideal self. That one stone, once lost, puts these women well below the weight that is natural to them, and beautiful, if we saw with eyes unconstrained by the Iron Maiden. But the body quickly restores itself, and the cycle of gain and loss begins, with its train of torment and its risk of disease, becoming a fixation of the woman's consciousness. The inevitable cycles of failure ensured by the One Stone Solution create and continually reinforce in women our uniquely modern neurosis. This great weight-shift bestowed on women, just when we were free to begin to forget them, new versions of low self-esteem, loss of control, and sexual shame. It is a genuinely elegant fulfillment of a collective wish: By simply dropping the official weight one stone below most women's natural level, and redefining a woman's womanly shape as by definition "too fat," a wave of self-hatred swept over First World women, a reactionary psychology was perfected, and a major industry was born. It suavely countered the historical groundswell of female success with a mass conviction of female failure, a failure defined as implicit in womanhood itself.

The proof that the One Stone Solution is political lies in what women feel when they eat "too much": guilt. Why should guilt be the operative emotion, and female fat be a moral issue articulated with words like good and bad? If our culture's fixation on female fatness or thinness were about sex, it would be a private issue between a woman and her lover; if it were about health, between a woman and herself. Public debate would be far more hysterically focused on male fat than on female, since more men (40 percent) are medically overweight than women (32 percent) and too much fat is far more dangerous for men than for women. In fact, "there is very little evidence to support the claim that fatness causes poor health among women. . . . The results of recent studies have suggested that women may in fact live longer and be generally healthier if they weigh ten to fifteen percent *above* the life-insurance figures *and* they refrain from dieting," asserts *Radiance;* when poor health is correlated to fatness in women, it is due to chronic dieting and the emotional stress of self-hatred. The National Institutes of Health studies that linked obesity to heart disease and stroke were based on male subjects; when a study of females was finally published in 1990, it showed that weight made only a fraction of the difference for women that it made for men. The film *The Famine Within* cites a sixteen-country study that fails to correlate fatness to ill health. Female fat is not in itself unhealthy.

But female fat is the subject of public passion, and women feel guilty about female fat, because we implicitly recognize that under the myth, women's bodies are not our own but society's, and that thinness is not a private aesthetic, but hunger a social concession exacted by the community. A cultural fixation on female thinness is not an obsession about female beauty but an obsession about female obedience. Women's dieting has become what Yale psychologist Judith Rodin calls a "normative obsession," a never-ending passion play given international coverage out of all proportion to the health risks associated with obesity, and using emotive language that does not figure even in discussions of alcohol or tobacco abuse. The nations seize with compulsive attention on this melodrama because women and men understand that it is not about cholesterol or heart rate or the disruption of a line of tailoring, but about how much social freedom women are going to get away with or concede. The media's convulsive analysis of the endless saga of female fat and the battle to vanquish it are actually bulletins of the sex war: what women are gaining or losing in it, and how fast.

The great weight shift must be understood as one of the major historical developments of the century, a direct solution to the dangers posed by the women's movement and economic and reproductive freedom. Dieting is the most potent political sedative in women's history; a quietly mad population is a tractable one. Researchers S. C. Wooley and O. W. Wooley confirmed what most women know too well—that concern with weight leads to "a virtual collapse of self-esteem and sense of effectiveness." Researchers J. Polivy and C. P. Herman found that "prolonged and periodic caloric restriction" resulted in a distinctive personality whose traits are "passivity, anxiety and emotionality."

It is those traits, and not thinness for its own sake, that the dominant culture wants to create in the private sense of self of recently liberated women in order to cancel out the dangers of their liberation.

Women's advances had begun to give them the opposite traits—high self-esteem, a sense of effectiveness, activity, courage, and clarity of mind. "Prolonged and periodic caloric restriction" is a means to take the teeth out of this revolution. The great weight shift and its One Stone Solution followed the rebirth of feminism so that women just reaching for power would become weak, preoccupied, and, as it evolved, mentally ill in useful ways and in astonishing proportions. To understand how the gaunt toughness of the Iron Maiden has managed spectacularly to roll back women's advances toward equality, we have to see that what is really at stake is not fashion or beauty or sex, but a struggle over political hegemony that has become—for women, who are often unaware of the real issues behind our predicament—one of life and death.

Theories abound to explain anorexia, bulimia, and the modern thinning of the feminine. Ann Hollander proposes that the shift from portraiture to moving images made thinness suggestive of motion and speed. Susie Orbach in *Fat Is a Feminist Issue* "reads" women's fat as a statement to the mother about separation and dependence; she sees in the mother "a terrible ambivalence about feeding and nurturing" her daughter. Kim Chernin in *The Obsession* gives a psychoanalytic reading of fear of fat as based on infantile rage against the all-powerful mother, and sees food as the primordial breast, the "lost world" of female abundance that we must recover "if we are to understand the heartland of our obsession with the female body. . . . We can understand how," Chernin writes, "in a frenzy of terror and dread, [a man] might be tempted to spin out fashionable images of [a woman] that tell her implicitly that she is unacceptable . . . when she is large." In *The Hungry Self,* Chernin interprets bulimia as a religious rite of passage. Joan Jacobs Brumberg sees food as a symbolic language, anorexia as a cry of confusion in a world of too many choices, and "the appetite as voice": "young women searching for an idiom in which to say things about themselves focused on food and styles of eating." Rudolph Bell in *Holy Anorexia* relates the disease to the religious impulses of medieval nuns, seeing starvation as purification.

Theories such as these are enlightening within a private context; but they do not go far enough. Women do not eat or starve only in a succession of private relationships, but within a public social order that has a material vested interest in their troubles with eating. Individual men don't "spin out fashionable images" (indeed, research keeps proving that they are warm to women's real shapes and unmoved by the Iron Maiden); multinational corporations do that. The many theories about women's food crises have stressed private psychology *to the neglect of* public policy, looking at women's shapes to see how they express a conflict about their society rather than looking at how their society makes use of a manufactured conflict with women's shapes. Many other theories have focused on women's reaction to the thin ideal, but have not asserted that the thin ideal is *proactive,* a preemptive strike.

We need to reexamine all the terms again, then, in the light of a public agenda. What, first, is food? Certainly, within the context of the intimate family, food is love, and memory, and language. But in the public realm, food is status and honor.

Food is the primal symbol of social worth. Whom a society values, it feeds well. The piled plate, the choicest cut, say: We think you're worth this much of the tribe's resources. Samoan women, who are held in high esteem, exaggerate how much they eat on feast days. Publicly apportioning food is about determining power relations, and sharing it is about cementing social equality: When men break bread together, or toast the queen, or slaughter for one another the fatted calf, they've become equals and then allies. The word *companion* comes from the Latin for "with" and "bread"—those who break bread together.

But under the beauty myth, now that all women's eating is a public issue, our portions testify to and reinforce our sense of social inferiority. If women cannot eat the same food as men, we cannot experience equal status in the community. As long as women are asked to bring a self-denying mentality to the communal table, it will never be round, men and women seated together; but the same traditional hierarchical dais, with a folding table for women at the foot.

In the current epidemic of rich Western women who cannot "choose" to eat, we see the continuation of an older, poorer tradition of women's relation to food. Modern Western female dieting descends from a long history. Women have always had to eat differently from men: less and worse. In Hellenistic Rome, reports classicist Sarah B. Pomeroy, boys were rationed sixteen measures of meal to twelve measures allotted to girls. In medieval France, according to historian John Boswell, women received two thirds of the grain allocated to men. Throughout history, when there is only so much to eat, women get little, or none: A common explanation among anthropologists for female infanticide is that food shortage provokes it. According to UN publications, where hunger goes, women meet it first: In Bangladesh and Botswana, female infants die more frequently than male, and girls are more often malnourished, because they are given smaller portions. In Turkey, India, Pakistan, North Africa, and the Middle East, men get the lion's share of what food there is, regardless of women's caloric needs. "It is not the caloric value of work which is represented in the patterns of food consumption" of men in relation to women in North Africa, "nor is it a question of physiological needs. . . . Rather these patterns tend to guarantee priority rights to the 'important' members of society, that is, adult men." In Morocco, if women are guests, "they will swear they have eaten already" or that they are not hungry. "Small girls soon learn to offer their share to visitors, to refuse meat and deny hunger." A North African woman described by anthropologist Vanessa Mahler assured her fellow diners that "she preferred bones to meat." Men, however, Mahler reports, "are supposed to be exempt from facing scarcity which is shared out among women and children."

"Third World countries provide examples of undernourished female and well-nourished male children, where what food there is goes to the boys of the family," a UN report testifies. Two thirds of women in Asia, half of all women in Africa, and a sixth of Latin American women are anemic—through lack of food. Fifty percent more Nepali women than men go blind from lack of food. Cross-culturally, men receive hot meals, more protein, and the first helpings of a dish, while women eat the cooling leftovers, often having to use deceit and cunning to get enough to eat. "Moreover, what food they do receive is consistently less nutritious."

This pattern is not restricted to the Third World: Most Western women alive today can recall versions of it at their mothers' or grandmothers' table: British miners' wives eating the grease-soaked bread left over after their husbands had eaten the meat; Italian and Jewish wives taking the part of the bird no one else would want.

These patterns of behavior are standard in the affluent West today, perpetuated by the culture of female caloric self-deprivation. A generation ago, the justification for this traditional apportioning shifted: Women still went without, ate leftovers, hoarded food, used deceit to get it—but blamed themselves. Our mothers still exiled themselves from the family circle that was eating cake with silver cutlery off Wedgwood china, and we would come upon them in the kitchen, furtively devouring the remains. The traditional pattern was cloaked in modern shame, but otherwise changed little. Weight control became its rationale once natural inferiority went out of fashion.

The affluent West is merely carrying on this traditional apportioning. Researchers found that parents in the United States urged boys to eat, regardless of their weight, while they did so with daughters only if they were relatively thin. In a sample of babies of both sexes, 99 percent of the boys were breast-fed, but only 66 percent of the girls, who were given 50 percent less time to feed. "Thus," writes Susie Orbach, "daughters are often fed less well, less attentively and less sensitively than they need." Women do not feel entitled to enough food because they have been taught to go with less than they need since birth, in a tradition passed down through an endless line of mothers; the public role of "honored guest" is new to us, and the culture is telling us through the ideology of caloric restriction that we are not welcome finally to occupy it.

What, then, is fat? Fat is portrayed in the literature of the myth as expendable female filth; virtually cancerous matter, an inert or treacherous infiltration into the body of nauseating bulk waste. The demonic characterizations of a simple body substance do not arise from its physical properties but from old-fashioned misogyny, for above all fat is female; it is the medium and regulator of female sexual characteristics.

Cross-culturally, from birth, girls have 10–15 percent more fat than boys. At puberty, male fat-to-muscle ratio decreases as the female ratio increases. The increased fat ratio in adolescent girls is the medium for sexual maturation and fertility. The average healthy twenty-year-old female is made of 28.7 percent body fat. By middle age, women cross-culturally are 38 percent body fat: This is, contrary to the rhetoric of the myth, "not unique to the industrialized advanced Western nations. They are norms characteristic of the female of the species." A moderately active woman's caloric needs, again in contradiction to a central tenet of the myth, are only 250 calories less than a moderately active man's (2,250 to 2,500), or two ounces of cheese. Weight gain with age is also normal cross-culturally for both sexes. The body is evidently programmed to weigh a certain amount, which weight the body defends.

Fat is sexual in women; Victorians called it affectionately their "silken layer." The leanness of the Iron Maiden impairs female sexuality. One fifth of women who exercise to shape their bodies have menstrual irregularities and diminished fertility. The body of the model, remember, is 22 to 23 percent leaner than that of the average woman; the average woman wants to be as lean as the model; infertility and hormone imbalance are common among women whose fat-to-lean ratio falls below 22 percent. Hormonal imbalances promote ovarian and endometrial cancer and osteoporosis. Fat tissues store sex hormones, so low fat reserves are linked with weak estrogens and low levels of all the other important sex hormones, as well as with inactive ovaries. Rose E. Frisch in *Scientific American* refers to the fatness of Stone Age fertility figures, saying that "this historical linking of fatness and fertility actually makes biological sense" since fat regulates reproduction. Underweight women double their risk of low-birthweight babies.

Fat is not just fertility in women, but desire. Researchers at Michael Reese Hospital in Chicago found that plumper women desired sex more often than thinner women. On scales of erotic excitability and readiness, they outscored thin women by a factor of almost two to one. To ask women to become unnaturally thin is to ask them to relinquish their sexuality: "Studies consistently show that with dietary deprivation, sexual interests dissipate." Subjects of one experiment stopped masturbating or having sexual fantasies at 1,700 calories a day, 500 more than the Beverly Hills Diet. Starvation affects the endocrine glands; amenorrhea and delayed puberty are common features in starving women and girls; starved men lose their libido and become impotent, sometimes developing breasts. Loyola University's Sexual Dysfunction Clinic reports that weight-loss disorders have a far worse effect on female sexuality than do weight-gaining disorders; the heavier women were eager for courtship and sex, while anorexics "were so concerned with their bodies that they had fewer sexual fantasies, fewer dates, and less desire for sex." The *New England Journal of Medicine* reports that intense exercisers lose interest in sex. Joan Jacobs Brumberg agrees that "clinical materials suggest an absence of sexual activity on the part of anorexics." Pleasure in sex, Mette Bergstrom writes, "is rare for a bulimic because of a strong body hatred." "The evidence seems to suggest," writes Roberta Pollack Seid, "and common sense would confirm, that a hungry, undernourished animal is less, not more, interested in the pleasures of the flesh."

What, finally, is dieting? "Dieting," and, in Great Britain, "slimming," are trivializing words for what is in fact self-inflicted semistarvation. In India, one of the poorest countries in the world, the very poorest women eat 1,400 calories a day, or 600 more than a Western woman on the Hilton Head Diet. "Quite simply," writes Seid, dieters "are reacting the way victims of semi-starvation react . . . semi-starvation, even if caused by self-imposed diets, produces startlingly similar effects on all human beings."

The range of repulsive and pathetic behaviors exhibited by women touched by food diseases is portrayed as quintessentially feminine, proof positive of women's irrationality (replacing the conviction of menstrual irrationality that had to be abandoned when women were needed for the full-time work force). In a classic study done at the University of Minnesota, thirty-six volunteers were placed on an extended low-calorie diet and "the psychological, behavioral and physical effects were carefully documented." The subjects were young and healthy, showing "high levels of ego strength, emotional stability, and good intellectual ability." They "began a six-month period . . . in which their food intake was reduced by half—a typical weight reduction technique for women.

"After losing approximately 25% of their original body weight, pervasive effects of semistarvation were seen." The subjects "became increasingly preoccupied with food and eating, to the extent that they ruminated obsessively about meals and food, collected recipes and cookbooks, and showed abnormal food rituals, such as excessively slow eating and hoarding of food related objects." Then, the majority "suffered some form of emotional disturbance as a result of semistarvation, including depression, hypochondriasis, hysteria, angry outbursts, and, in some cases, psychotic levels of disorganization." Then, they "lost their ability to function in work and social contexts, due to apathy, reduced energy and alertness, social isolation, and decreased sexual interest." Finally, "within weeks of reducing their food intake," they "reported relentless hunger, as well as powerful urges to break dietary rules. Some succumbed to eating binges, followed by vomiting and feelings of self-reproach. Ravenous hunger persisted, even following large meals during refeeding." Some of the subjects "found themselves eating continuously, while others engaged in uncontrollable cycles of gorging and vomiting." The volunteers "became terrified of going outside the experiment environment where they would be tempted by the foods they had agreed not to eat . . . when they did succumb, they made hysterical, half-crazed confessions." They became irritable, tense, fatigued, and full of vague complaints. "Like fugitives, [they] could not shed the feeling they were being shadowed by a sinister force." For some, doctors eventually had to prescribe tranquilizers.

The subjects were a group of completely normal healthy college men.

During the great famine that began in May 1940 during the German occupation of the Netherlands, the Dutch authorities maintained rations at between 600 and 1,600 calories a day, or what they characterized as the level of semistarvation. The worst sufferers were defined as starving when they had lost 25 percent of their body weight, and were given precious supplements. Photos taken of clothed starving

Dutch women are striking for how preternaturally modern they look.

At 600–1,600 calories daily, the Dutch suffered semistarvation; the Diet Centers' diet is fixed at 1,600 calories. When they had lost 25 percent of their body weight, the Dutch were given crisis food supplementation. The average healthy woman has to lose almost exactly as much to fit the Iron Maiden. In the Lodz Ghetto in 1941, besieged Jews were allotted starvation rations of 500–1,200 calories a day. At Treblinka, 900 calories was scientifically determined to be the minimum necessary to sustain human functioning. At "the nation's top weight-loss clinics," where "patients" are treated for up to a year, the rations are the same.

The psychological effects of self-inflicted semistarvation are identical to those of involuntary semistarvation. By 1980 more and more researchers were acknowledging the considerable emotional and physical consequences of chronic dieting, including "symptoms such as irritability, poor concentration, anxiety, depression, apathy, lability of mood, fatigue and social isolation." Magnus Pyke, describing the Dutch famine, writes that "starvation is known to affect people's minds and these people in Holland became mentally listless, apathetic and constantly obsessed with thoughts of food." Bruch notes that with involuntary progressive semistarvation, "there is a coarsening of emotions, sensitivity and other human traits." Robert Jay Lifton found that World War II victims of starvation "experienced feelings of guilt over having done something bad for which they are now being punished, and dreams and fantasies of food of every kind in limitless amounts." Starving destroys individuality; "anorexic patients," like others who starve, asserts Hilde Bruch, "exhibited remarkably uniform behavior and emotional patterns until they gained some weight." "Food deprivation," Roberta Pollack Seid sums it up, "triggers food obsessions for both physical and psychological reasons. . . . undernourishment produces lassitude, depression and irritability. Body metabolism slows down. . . . And hunger drives the hungry person to obsess about food." The psychological terror of hunger is cross-cultural: Orphans adopted from poor countries cannot control their compulsion to smuggle and hide food, sometimes even after living for years in a secure environment.

Authoritative evidence is mounting that eating diseases are caused mainly by dieting. Ilana Attie and J. Brooks-Gunn quote investigators who found "chronic, restrained eating" to "constitute a cumulative stress of such magnitude that dieting itself may be 'a sufficient condition for the development of anorexia nervosa or bulimia.'" Roberta Pollack Seid reaches the same conclusion. "Ironically, dieting . . . itself may provoke obsessive behaviour and binge-eating. It may indeed *cause* both eating disorders and obesity itself." Sustained caloric deprivation appears to be a severe shock to the body that it remembers with destructive consequences. Seid writes that "women's problems with food seem to stem . . . from their effort to get an ultra-lean body. . . . The only way 95% can get it is by putting themselves on deprivatory diets." Attie and Brooks-Gunn concur: "Much of the behavior thought to cause anorexia nervosa and bulimia may actually be a consequence of starvation. . . . The normal weight dieter who diets to look and feel thin also is vulnerable to disturbed emotional, cognitive and behavioral patterns by virtue of the constant stress of trying to stay below the body's 'natural' or biologically regulated weight." Dieting and fashionable thinness make women seriously unwell.

Now, if female fat is sexuality and reproductive power; if food is honor; if dieting is semistarvation; if women have to lose 23 percent of their body weight to fit the Iron Maiden and chronic psychological disruption sets in at a body weight loss of 25 percent; if semistarvation is physically and psychologically debilitating, and female strength, sexuality, and self-respect pose the threats explored earlier against the vested interests of society; if women's journalism is sponsored by a $33-billion industry whose capital is made out of the political fear of women; then we can understand why the Iron Maiden is so thin. The thin "ideal" is not beautiful aesthetically; she is beautiful as a political solution.

The compulsion to imitate her is not something trivial that women choose freely to do to ourselves. It is something serious being done to us to safeguard political power. Seen in this light, it is inconceivable that women would not have to be compelled to grow thin at this point in our history.

The ideology of semistarvation undoes feminism; what happens to women's bodies happens to our minds. If women's bodies are and have always been wrong whereas men's are right, then women are wrong and men are right. Where feminism taught women to put a higher value on ourselves, hunger teaches us how to erode our self-esteem. If a woman can be made to say, "I hate my fat thighs," it is a way she has been made to hate femaleness. The more financially independent, in control of events, educated and sexually autonomous women become in the world, the more impoverished, out of control, foolish, and sexually insecure we are asked to feel in our bodies.

Hunger makes women feel poor and think poor. A wealthy woman on a diet feels physically at the mercy of a scarcity economy; the rare woman who makes $100,000 a year has a bodily income of 1,000 calories a day. Hunger makes successful women feel like failures: An architect learns that her work crumbles; a politician who oversees a long-range vision is returned to the details, to add up every bite; a woman who can afford to travel can't "afford" rich foreign foods. It undermines each experience of control, economic security, and leadership that women have had only a generation to learn to enjoy. Those who were so recently freed to think beyond the basics are driven, with this psychology, back to the feminine mental yoke of economic dependence: fixation on getting sustenance and safety. Virginia Woolf believed that "one cannot think well, sleep well, love well if one has not dined well." "The lamp in the spine does not light on beef and prunes," she wrote, contrasting the dispiriting food of poverty, of the hard-pressed women's colleges with that of the rich men's colleges, the "soles sunk in a deep dish, over which the college cook has spread a counterpane of the whitest cream." Now that some women at last have achieved the equivalent of £500 a year and a room of their own, it is back once more to four ounces of boiled beef and three unsweetened prunes, and the unlit lamp.

The anorexic may begin her journey defiant, but from the point of view of a male-dominated society, she ends up as the perfect woman. She is weak, sexless, and voiceless, and can only with difficulty focus on a world beyond her plate. The woman has been killed off in her. She is almost not there. Seeing her like this, unwomaned, it makes crystalline sense that a half-conscious but virulent mass movement of the imagination created the vital lie of skeletal female beauty. A future in which industrialized nations are peopled with anorexia-driven women is one of few conceivable that would save the current distribution of wealth and power from the claims made on it by women's struggle for equality.

For theorists of anorexia to focus on the individual woman, even within her family, misses the tactical heart of this struggle. Economic and political retaliation against female appetite is far stronger at this point than family dynamics.

This can no longer be explained as a private issue. If suddenly 60 to 80 percent of college women can't eat, it's hard to believe that suddenly 60 to 80 percent of their families are dysfunctional in this particular way. There is a disease in the air; its cause was generated with intent; and young women are catching it.

Just as the thin Iron Maiden is not actually beautiful, anorexia, bulimia, even compulsive eating, symbolically understood, are not actually diseases. They *begin,* as Susie Orbach notes, as sane and mentally healthy responses to an insane social reality: that most women can feel good about themselves only in a state of permanent semistarvation. The anorexic refuses to let the official cycle master her: By starving, she masters it. A bulimic may recognize the madness of the hunger cult, its built-in defeat, its denial of pleasure. A mentally healthy person will resist having to choose between food and sexuality—sexuality being bought, today, by maintenance of the official body. By vomiting, she gets around the masochistic choice. Eating diseases are often interpreted as symptomatic of a neurotic need for control. But surely it is a sign of mental health to try to control something that is trying to control you, especially if you are a lone young woman and it is a massive industry fueled by the needs of an entire determined world order. Self-defense is the right plea when it comes to eating disasters; not insanity. Self-defense bears no stigma, whereas madness is a shame.

Victorian female hysteria, mysterious at the time, makes sense now that we see it in the light of the social pressures of sexual self-denial and incarceration in the home. Anorexia should be as simple to understand. What hysteria was to the nineteenth-century fetish of the asexual woman locked in the home, anorexia is to the late-twentieth-century fetish of the hungry woman.

Anorexia is spreading because it works. Not only does it solve the dilemma of the young woman faced with the hunger cult, it also protects her from street harassment and sexual coercion; construction workers leave walking skeletons alone. Having no fat means having no breasts, thighs, hips, or ass, which for once means not having asked for it. Women's magazines tell women they *can* control their bodies; but women's experiences of sexual harassment make them feel they *cannot* control what their bodies are said to provoke. Our culture gives a young woman only two dreams in which to imagine her body, like a coin with two faces: one pornographic, the other anorexic; the first for nighttime, the second for day—the one, supposedly, for men and the other for other women. She does not have the choice to refuse to toss it—nor, yet, to demand a better dream. The anorexic body is sexually safer to inhabit than the pornographic.

At the same time, it works for male-dominated institutions by processing women smoothly, unwomaned, into positions closer to power. It is "trickling down" to women of all social classes from elitist schools and universities because that is where women are getting too close to authority. There, it is emblematic of how hunger checkmates power in any woman's life: Hundreds of thousands of well-educated young women, living and studying at the fulcrum of cultural influence, are causing no trouble. The anorexic woman student, like the anti-Semitic Jew and the self-hating black, fits in. She is politically castrate, with exactly enough energy to do her schoolwork, neatly and completely, and to run around the indoor track in eternal circles. She has no energy to get angry or get organized, to chase sex, to yell through a bullhorn, asking for money for night buses or for women's studies programs or to know where all the women professors are. Administering a coed class half full of mentally anorexic women is an experience distinct from that of administering a class half full of healthy, confident young women. The woman in these women canceled out, it is closer to the administration of young men only, which was how things were comfortably managed before.

For women to stay at the official extreme of the weight spectrum requires 95 percent of us to infantilize or rigidify to some degree our mental lives. The beauty of thinness lies not in what it does to the body but to the mind, since *it is not female thinness that is prized, but female hunger, with thinness merely symptomatic.* Hunger attractively narrows the focus of a mind that has "let itself go." Babies cannot feed themselves; invalids and the orthodox require special diets. Dieting makes women think of ourselves as sick, religious babies. Only this new mystique could prove strong and deep-reaching enough to take on the work given up by domestic isolation and enforced chastity. "Natural" is a word that is rightly challenged. But if there is a most natural urge, it is to satisfy hunger. If there is a natural female shape, it is the one in which women are sexual and fertile and *not always thinking about it.* To maintain hunger where food is available, as Western women are doing, is to submit to a life state as unnatural as anything with which the species has come up yet. It is more bizarre than cannibalism.

Dieting is the essence of contemporary femininity. Denying oneself food is seen as good in a woman, bad in a man. For women, the Austin (Texas) Stress Clinic found, "dieting concern" was strongly related to "positive feminine traits"; for men, food restraint was related to "socially undesirable femininity." Where the feminine woman of the Feminine Mystique denied herself gratification in the world, the current successful and "mature" model of femininity submits to a life of self-denial in her body.

But this hallmark of enviable adjustment has as little innate validity as the earlier one. It too is based upon a vital lie. Where "immature" women in the 1950s wanted clitoral orgasms while "mature" ones passively yielded, today oral desire is interpreted in a similar sexual code. It is considered immature for women to eat heartily, since they're told they risk their sexuality; they are seen as mature if they starve, promised to win sexuality that way. In the 1970s, when clitoral pleasure was reclaimed, many women must have wondered how they had lived in an atmosphere that denied it. In the 1980s women were forced to deny their tongues and mouths and lips and bellies. In the 1990s, if women can reclaim the pleasure of appetite, we may wonder what possessed us during the long, mean, pointless years of hunger. Women's self-denial where food is concerned is represented today as good for her mate and even better for herself. Beyond the beauty myth, feminine hunger will look as obviously destructive to the well-being of women and their loved ones as their earlier enforced suffocation in the home looks to us from here.

Sex, food, and flesh; it is only political ideology—not health, not men's desires, not any law of loveliness—that keeps women from believing we can have all three. Young women believe what they have no memory to question, that they may not have sex, food, and flesh in any abundance; that those three terms cancel each other out.

Dead Easy

It is dead easy to become an anorexic. When I was twelve I went to visit an older, voluptuous cousin. "I try," she said, to explain the deep-breathing exercises she did before bedtime, "to visualize my belly as something I can love and accept and live with." Still compact in a one-piece kid's body, I was alarmed to think that womanhood involved breaking apart into pieces that floated around, since my cousin seemed to be trying to hold herself together by a feat of concentration. It was not a comforting thought. The buds of my breasts hurt already. As she did her exercises, I leafed through a copy of *Cosmopolitan,* which had an article demonstrating to women how to undress and pose and move in bed with their partners so as to disguise their fatness.

My cousin looked me over. "Do you know how much you weigh?" No, I told her. "Why don't you just hop on the scale?" I could feel how much my cousin wished to inhabit a simple, slight twelve-year-old body. That could only mean, I thought, that when I was a woman, I would want to get out of my own body into some little kid's.

A year later, while bent over the drinking fountain in the hall of my junior high school, Bobby Werner, whom I hardly knew, gave me a hard poke in the soft part of my stomach, just below the navel. It would be a decade before I would remember that he was the class fat boy.

That evening I let the juice of the lamb chop congeal on my plate. I could see viscous nodules of fat, a charred outer edge of yellow matter, cooling from liquid to solid, marked USDA CHOICE in edible blue dye. The center bone, serrated, had been cloven with a powerful rotary blade. I felt a new feeling, a nausea wicked with the pleasure of loathing. Rising hungry from the table, a jet of self-righteousness lit up under my esophagus, intoxicating me. All night long I inhaled it.

The next day I passed the small notepad kept by the dishwasher. I knew what it said, though it was my mother's and private: "½ grpfruit. Blk. coff. 4 Wheat Thins. 1 Popsicle." A black scrawl: "*binge.*" I wanted to tear it up. Some memoir.

I had no more patience for the trivial confessions of women. I could taste from my mouth that my body had entered ketosis, imbalanced electrolytes—good. The girl stood on the burning deck. I put the dishes in the sink with a crash of declaration.

At thirteen, I was taking in the caloric equivalent of the food energy available to the famine victims of the siege of Paris. I did my schoolwork diligently and kept quiet in the classroom. I was a wind-up obedience toy. Not a teacher or principal or guidance counselor confronted me with an objection to my evident deportation in stages from the land of the living.

There were many starving girls in my junior high school, and every one was a teacher's paragon. We were allowed to come and go, racking up gold stars, as our hair fell out in fistfuls and the pads flattened behind the sockets of our eyes. When our eyeballs moved, we felt the resistance. They allowed us to haul our bones around the swinging rope in gym class, where nothing but the force of an exhausted will stood between the ceiling, to which we clung with hands so wasted the jute seemed to abrade the cartilage itself, and the polished wooden floor thirty-five feet below.

An alien voice took mine over. I have never been so soft-spoken. It lost expression and timbre and sank to a monotone, a dull murmur the opposite of strident. My teachers approved of me. They saw nothing wrong with what I was doing, and I could swear they looked straight at me. My school had stopped dissecting alleycats, since it was considered inhumane. There was no interference in my self-directed science experiment: to find out just how little food could keep a human body alive.

The dreams I could muster were none of the adolescent visions that boys have, or free and healthy girls; no fantasies of sex or escape, rebellion or future success. All the space I had for dreaming was taken up by food. When I lay on my bed, in that posture of adolescent reverie, I could find no comfort. My bones pressed sharply into the mattress. My ribs were hooks and my spine a dull blade and my hunger a heavy shield, all I had to stave off the trivialities that would attach themselves like parasites to my body the minute it made a misstep into the world of women. My doctor put his hand on my stomach and said he could feel my spine. I turned an eye cold with loathing on women who evidently lacked the mettle to suffer as I was suffering.

I made a drawing: myself, small, small, curled in a sort of burrow, surrounded by nesting materials, with a store of nuts and raisins, protected. This smallness and hiddenness was what I craved at the time of life when Stephen Dedalus longed to burst like a meteor on the world. What did that drawing mean? It was not a longing to return to the womb, but to return to my body. I was not longing to be safe from the choices of the world, but from the obligation to enter into a combat in which I could only believe if I forgot all about myself, and submitted to starting again dumber, like someone hit hard on the back of the head.

I'd have to forget they were my friends and believe they were really my enemies: the other playground gamblers of jacks, my fellow thieves of Pepsi-flavored lip gloss: Gemma and Stacey and Kim, who used to stand beside me in a row in the dark master bedroom, staring into the mirror. Our chins lit up from below by a candle, we chanted, scared rigid, *We're not afraid of Bloody Mary.* I knew that if I let myself fall forward into time, I would never be able to stand like that again: shoulder to shoulder before the one mirror, with the ghoul on the far side of the glass; nothing in ourselves, nothing in each other.

Adolescent starvation was, for me, a prolonged reluctance to be born into woman if that meant assuming a station of beauty. Children resist being baffled with convention, and often see social madness in full dimensions. In seventh grade, we knew what was coming, and we all went berserk with cogent fear; not a normal craziness of adolescence, but panic at what unnaturally loomed. Like a life-sized game of Mother May I, we knew that beauty was going to say, "Freeze," and wherever we were, that would be it.

"We learned the truth at seventeen," mourned a song that was popular that year, "that love was meant for beauty queens." We traded new bathing suits, and ruined them, and swore we wouldn't forgive the borrower. When Gemma and Kim mooned at Stacey's Polaroid, Kim said, "Oh, don't worry about the picture, you were closer to the camera." Gemma twisted her neck in front of the mirror, looking for the horrible truth, while Kim wondered how her mother's words came out of her own brain.

Confiding Julie, the first to get breasts, was cynical by Thanksgiving. Since no one else looked like the class slut, she was given the position, and she soon capitulated. She bleached her hair with Sun In, and started to mess around with boys who played in garage rock bands. Marianne, because she had long legs and a stem neck, rushed from school to her pliés at the barre, her hair in a bun, her head held high, to arch and sweep and bow toward the mirror until night fell. Cara delivered her audition piece flat, but since she had a wheat-colored rope of braid that brushed her waist, she would be Titania in the school play. Emily, blunt-nosed and loud, could outact Cara in her sleep; when she saw the cast list she turned silently to her best friend, who handed her a box of milk chocolate creams. Tall, strong, bony Evvy watched Elise try out her maddening dimple. She cornered her outside class to ask her if she thought she was cute. Elise said yes, and Evvy threw a pipette of acid, stolen from the biology lab, in her face. Dodie hated her tight black hair that wouldn't grow. She crept up behind blond Karen in home ec class and hacked out a fistful with pinking shears. Even Karen understood that it wasn't personal.

The things we saw women doing for beauty looked crazy. I wanted to travel, but I saw that beauty led women in circles. My mother, a beautiful woman, got too little of the pleasures that I could understand. I saw that her beauty hurt her: teeth-gritting abstinence at celebration dinners, fury on the scale, angry rubdowns, self-accusing photographs posted over the refrigerator. She'd won—why wasn't that enough? It would be nice to be beautiful like her, I figured, sure; but nothing about it seemed nice enough to make up for that endless degradation.

Anorexia was the only way I could see to keep the dignity in my body that I had had as a kid, and that I would lose as a woman. It was the only choice that really looked like one: By refusing to put on a woman's body and receive a rating, I chose not to have all my future choices confined to little things, and not to have the choices made for me, on the basis of something meaningless to me, in the larger things. But as time went on, my choices grew smaller and smaller. Beef bouillon or hot water with lemon? The bouillon had twenty calories—I'd take the water. The lemon had four; I could live without it. Just.

Now, when I can bring myself to think of that time at all—another blackout, by beauty, of the cities of memory—my sadness can't shake off the rage that follows it close behind. To whom do I petition for that lost year? How many inches in height did I lose from having calcium withheld from my bones, their osteoblasts struggling without nourishment to multiply? How many years sooner will a brittle spine bend my neck down? In the Kafkaesque departments of this bureau of hunger, which charged me guilty for a crime no more specific than inhabiting a female body, what door do I knock upon? Who is obliged to make reparations to me for the thought abandoned, the energy never found, the explorations never considered?

Who owes me for the year-long occupation of a mind at the time of its most urgent growth?

In our interpretation of the damages done by the beauty myth, it is not yet possible to lay blame anywhere but on oneself. I can say finally, for myself at least: at thirteen, to starve half to death? Not guilty. Not that child. There is certainly a charge of guilt to be made, long overdue. But it doesn't belong to me. It belongs somewhere, and to something, else.

The youngest victims, from earliest childhood, learn to starve and vomit from the overwhelmingly powerful message of our culture, which I found no amount of parental love and support strong enough to override. I knew my parents wanted me not to starve because they loved me; but their love contradicted the message of the larger world, which wanted me to starve in order to love me. It is the larger world's messages, young women know, to which they will have to listen if they are to leave their parents' protection. I kept a wetted finger up to the winds of that larger world: Too thin yet? I was asking it. What about now? No? Now?

The larger world never gives girls the message that their bodies are valuable simply because they are inside them. Until our culture tells young girls that they are welcome in any shape—that women are valuable to it with or without the excuse of "beauty"—girls will continue to starve. And institutional messages then reward young women's education in hunger. But when the lesson has been taken too dangerously to heart, they ignore the consequences, reinforcing the disease. Anorexics want to be saved; but they cannot trust individual counselors, family members, or friends; that is too uncertain. They are walking question marks challenging—pleading—with schools, universities, and the other mouthpieces that transmit what is culturally acceptable in women, to tell them unequivocally: This is intolerable. This is unacceptable. We don't starve women here. We value women. By turning an indifferent eye to the ravages of the backlash among their young women, schools and universities are killing off America's daughters; and Europe is learning to do the same to its own. You don't need to die to count as a casualty. An anorexic cannot properly be called alive. To be anorexic is to keep a close daily tally of a slow death; to be a member of the walking undead.

Since institutions are treating this epidemic as one of those embarrassing feminine things imported into the cloister like tampon dispensers or commoner's gowns worn over skirts, there is no formal mourning. Women students are kept from openly recognizing what they privately know is going on around them. They are not permitted to claim this epidemic as real, and deadly, and taking place beside and inside them. So they have to repress horrifying knowledge, or trivialize it, or blame the sufferer. Another one sickens. Another disappears. Another one bites the dust.

In college, we never had a chance to mourn for Sally. Dressed like a tatty rag doll, in faded ginghams and eyelet lace, she wore a peacock feather in an old hat. She kept her round kwashiorkor belly politely hidden and her vicious intelligence sheathed, but she was able to shred an argument into so much cotton wool and negligently hold up a conclusion sharp as quartz. Her small voice would come to a flat halt and her lips press whitely together. At parties she'd lean back her flossy head, so much too big for her body, to get the leverage to bang it again and again into the nearest wall; her brain loosened for comfort, she would dance like a Halloween creepie, waving her disjointed limbs. It was a campus set piece: "Play something good for Sally to dance to."

She left suddenly. Her roommates had to pack her things up after her: the postage scales for weighing the day's half bread roll; the fifteen-pound hand weights; the essay of devastating clarity left on her desk half-finished.

When I was told her strength had run out, I remembered one bright blue afternoon in autumn, when a group of students came out of a classroom, arguing, high on words. She dropped her books with a crash. Flinging back her shoulders, from which her sweater hung letting in great pockets of icy air, she turned in a slow pirouette, and leaped right up into the knot of the group. A boy caught her before she fell, and offered her to me, wriggling like a troublesome baby.

I held her between my forearms without strain. She'd made it. She had escaped gravity. Her limbs were as light as hollow birch branches, the scrolls of their bark whole, but the marrow crumbled, the sap gone brittle. I folded her up easily, because there was nothing to her.

Bundles of twigs, bones in worn-soled Nikes, slapping forward into a relentless weather; the young women cast shadows of Javanese stick-puppets, huge-headed, disappearing in a sideways light. Dry-mouthed like the old, unsteady, they head home on swollen knees while it is still morning.

Nothing justifies comparison with the Holocaust; but when confronted with a vast number of emaciated bodies starved not by nature but by men, one must notice a certain resemblance. The starving body cannot know it is middle-class. The imprisoned body cannot tell that it is considered free. The experience of living in a severely anorexic body, even if that body is housed in an affluent suburb, is the experience of a body living in Bergen-Belsen—if we imagine for the Belsen inmate a 40-percent chance of imprisonment forever and a 15-percent chance of death. These experiences are closer to one another than either is to that of a middle-class body that is not in prison in the affluent First World. Though I am trying to avoid the imagery of death camps, it returns. These young women weigh no more than the bodies documented in the archives of what is legitimately called Hell. They have, at their sickest, no more to eat; and they have no choice. For an unknown reason that must be physiological, at a certain point in their starvation they lose the ability to stop starving, the choice to eat. Finally—as is seldom acknowledged—they are hungry; I was hungry every conscious moment; I was hungry in my sleep.

Women must claim anorexia as political damage done to us by a social order that considers our destruction insignificant because of what we are—less. We should identify it as Jews identify the death camps, as homosexuals identify AIDS: as a disgrace that is not our own, but that of an inhumane social order.

Anorexia is a prison camp. One fifth of well-educated American young women are inmates. Susie Orbach compared anorexia to the hunger strikes of political prisoners, particularly the suffragists. But the time for metaphors is behind us. To be anorexic or bulimic *is* to be a political prisoner.

The Third Wave: Frozen in Motion

If we look at most young women's inert relationship to feminism, we can see that with anorexia and bulimia, the beauty myth is winning its offensive. Where are the women activists of the new generation, the fresh blood to infuse energy into second-wave burnout and exhaustion? Why are so many so quiet? On campuses, up to a fifth of them are so quiet because they are starving to death. Starving people are notorious for a lack of organizational enthusiasm. Roughly another 50 percent are overcome with a time-devouring and shameful addiction to puking their guts out in the latrines of the major centers of higher learning. The same young women who would seem to be its heiresses are not taking up the banner of the women's movement for perhaps no more profound reason than that many of them are too physically ill to do much more than cope with immediate personal demands. And on a mental level, the epidemic of eating disorders may affect women of this generation in such a way as to make feminism seem viscerally unconvincing: Being a woman is evidently nothing to be up in arms about; it makes you hungry, weak, and sick.

Beyond this are other succession problems generated by the myth. Young women inherited twenty years of the propagandizing caricature of the Ugly Feminist, so—"I'm feminine, not a feminist," says a college senior in a *Time* magazine report; "I picture a feminist as someone who is masculine and doesn't shave her legs." Too many young women do not realize that others pictured "a feminist" in that way so that they would be sure to respond as this one does. Others, alarmingly, blame the women's movement for the beauty backlash against it—"Kathryn," a twenty-five-year-old quoted by Sylvia Ann Hewlett, describes a party at her law firm: "I often resent . . . the way women's liberation has increased the expectations of men": Twenty years ago, she complains, a young male lawyer would want to arrive with "a drop-dead blonde" on his arm, whereas today he and his colleagues compete to escort the highest achiever—"the only catch was that these yuppie women had to look every bit as glamorous as the drop-dead blondes of the past." Finally, the myth seeks to discourage all young women from identifying with earlier feminists—simply because these are older women. Men grant themselves tradition to hand down through the generations; women are permitted only fashion which each season renders obsolete. Under that construct, the link between generations of women is weakened by definition: What came before is rarely held up for admiration as history or heritage, but derided by fashion's rigid rule as embarrassingly démodé.

To share a meal with a young woman of the present generation, you have to be prepared to witness signs of grave illness. You ignore her frantic scanning of the menu, the meticulous way she scrapes the sauce. If she drinks five glasses of water and sucks and chews the ice, you mustn't comment. You look away if she starts to ferret a breadstick into her pocket, and ignore her reckless agitation at the appearance of the pastry tray, her long shame-faced absence after the meal, before the coffee. "Are you okay?" "I'm *fine.*" How dare you ask.

When you share the bill, you haven't shared a meal. The always renewed debate that young people of each generation take for granted, about how to change the world to suit their vision, is not going to be renewed for women over a table such as this. The pastry cart comes first; its gilt handles tower over you, blocking out the landscape. The world will have to wait. That's how it works.

There is no villain lurking by the cash register. No visible enemy has done this to you two; there's only your waiter, and the block-print tablecloths, the blackboard with the daily menu, the ice bucket full of melting cubes, the discreet hallway that leads to the bathroom with its sliding bolt. Evil, said Hannah Arendt, is banal. But the work is done anyway, and it looks as if it has been done by your own hands. You claim your coats and step outside and part ways, having talked nothing new whatever into life.

Young girls and women are seriously weakened by inheriting the general fallout of two decades of the beauty myth's backlash. But other factors compound these pressures on young women so intensely that the surprise is not how many do have eating diseases, but that any at all do not.

Girls and young women are also starving because the women's movement changed educational institutions and the workplace enough to make them admit women, but not yet enough to change the maleness of power itself. Women in "coeducational" schools and colleges are still isolated from one another, and admitted as men manqué. Women's studies are kept on the margins of the curriculum, and fewer than 5 percent of professors are women; the worldview taught young women is male. The pressure on them is to conform themselves to the masculine atmosphere. Separated from their mothers, young women on campus have few older role models who are not male; how can they learn how to love their bodies? The main images of women given them to admire and emulate are not of impressive, wise older women, but of girls their own age or younger, who are not respected for their minds. Physically, these universities are ordered for men or unwomaned women. They are overhung with oil portraits of men; engraved with the rolling names of men; designed, like the Yale Club in New York, which for twenty years after women were admitted had no women's changing room, for men. They are not lit for women who want to escape rape; at Yale, campus police maps showing the most dangerous street corners for rape were allegedly kept from the student body so as not to alarm parents. The colleges are only marginally concerned with the things that happen to women's bodies that do not happen to the bodies of the men. Women students sense this institutional wish that the problems of their female bodies would just fade away; responding, the bodies themselves fade away.

Added to this isolation and lack of recognition is the unprecedented level of expectation placed on ambitious young women. Older women, in some ways, explored the best of both gender roles: They grew up as women and fought their way into the masculine work force. They learned to affirm the values of women and master the work of men. They are doubly strong. Young women have been doubly weakened: Raised to compete like men in rigid male-model institutions, they must also maintain to the last detail an impeccable femininity. Gender roles, for this generation of women, did not harmonize so much as double: Young women today are expected to act like "real men" and look like "real women." Fathers transferred to daughters the expectations of achievement once reserved for sons; but the burden to be a beauty, inherited from the mothers, was not lightened in response.

Ceremonies of achievement play out this conflict: Meant to initiate young people into a new level of power or expertise, those ceremonies summon an unfeminine emotion—pride. But with each rite of passage through these institutions, payment is exacted from the young woman in the form of "beauty"; placating and flattering to men in power, it is required at these times as proof that she does not mean anything too serious by winning this diploma or this promotion. On one hand, here again the powerful stress the beauty myth so as to neutralize the achievement of the women involved; on the other, women do homage to the myth at such moments in request for its protection, a talisman that will let them get to the next stage unpunished.

In the 1950s, "domesticity" was what mitigated these moments of achievement. As a Listerine ad put it: "What was the diploma compared to those precious sparkling rings Babs and Beth were wearing?" Today "beauty" does the same work: "Only fifteen days until Becky's graduation. I want her to be proud of me too. . . . Alba makes your diet a sweet success." In a Johnnie Walker ad, it takes two high-fashion models to muse that "he thinks it's fine for me to make more than he does." *The New York Times* cites a woman whose boyfriend gave her breast implants for completing her doctorate. A current trend in the United States is for graduating daughters to get breast implant surgery while boys get the traditional grand tour of Europe. The most brilliant female students on campus are often the closest to full starvation. Women are having breast surgery, liposuction, rhinoplasty, not only as rewards for attaining power—doctorates, inheritances, bat mitzvahs—they are also having these things, and being asked to have them, as antidotes for their having attained this power.

This sacrificial impulse is religious, to propitiate the gods before undertaking the next stage of a journey. And the gods are thirsty; they are asking to be propitiated. "Boys, that's all," said the administrator preparing Rhodes Scholarship interviewees at Yale. "Girls, please stay a few moments for pointers on clothes, posture, and makeup." At the interview luncheon, when boys were asked, "How do you plan to save the world from itself?" a girl was asked, "How do you manage to keep your lovely figure?"

Achievement ceremonies are revealing about the need of the powerful to punish women through beauty, since the tension of having to repress alarm at female achievement is unusually formalized in them. Beauty myth insults tend to be blurted out at them like death jokes at a funeral. Memories of these achievement ceremonies are supposed to last like Polaroid snapshots that gel into permanent colors, souvenirs to keep of a hard race run; but for girls and young women, the myth keeps those colors always liquid so that, with a word, they can be smeared into the uniform shades of mud.

At my college graduation, the commencement speaker, Dick Cavett—who had been a "brother" of the university president in an all-male secret society—was confronted by two thousand young female Yale graduates in mortarboards and academic gowns, and offered them this story: When he was at Yale there were no women. The women went to Vassar. There, they had nude photographs taken in gym class to check their posture. Some of the photos ended up in the pornography black market in New Haven. The punch line: The photos found no buyers.

Whether or not the slur was deliberate, it was still effective: We may have been Elis but we would still not make pornography worth his buying. Today, three thousand men of the class of 1984 are sure they are graduates of that university, remembering commencement as they are meant to: proudly. But many of the two thousand women, when they can think of that day at all, recall the feelings of the powerless: exclusion and shame and impotent, complicit silence. We could not make a scene, as it was our parents' great day for which they had traveled long distances; neither could they, out of the same concern for us.

The sun steamed through the rain, the microphone crackled, the mud churned, we sat still, all wrong, under our hot polyester gowns. The speaker had transposed us for a moment out of the gentle quadrangle, where we had been led to believe we were cherished, and into the tawdry district four blocks away where stolen photographs of our naked bodies would find no buyers. Waiting for the parchment that honored our minds, we were returned with reluctant confusion to our bodies, which we had just been told were worthless. Unable to sit still for the rest of the speeches unless we split our minds, being applauded, from our bodies, being derided, we did so. We wanted the honor, we deserved it. The honor and derision came at the same time from the same podium. We shifted in our seats.

We paid the price asked of us. With moments like that to live through, the unreal-sounding statistics of young women's eating diseases begin to come clear. A split like that makes one nauseous. The pride of four years' hard work and struggle was snatched back from us at the moment we reached for it, and returned to us fouled. There was the taste of someone else's bile in our mouths.

The pressure of beauty pornography and the pressures of achievement combine to strike young women where they are most vulnerable: in their exploration of their sexuality in relation to their sense of their own worth. Beauty pornography makes an eating disease seem inevitable, even desirable, if a young woman is to consider herself sexual and valuable: Robin Lakoff and Raquel Scherr in *Face Value* found in 1984 that "among college women, 'modern' definitions of beauty—health, energy, self-confidence"—prevailed. "The bad news" is that they all had "only one overriding concern: the shape and weight of their bodies. They all wanted to lose 5–25 pounds, even though most [were] not remotely overweight. They went into great detail about every flaw in their anatomies, and told of the great disgust they felt every time they looked in the mirror." The "great disgust" they feel comes from learning the rigid conventions of beauty pornography before they learn their own sexual value; in such an atmosphere, eating diseases make perfect sense.

The Anorexic/Pornographic Generation

When women of different ages do have the rare opportunity to talk, the gap between older women and those of the anorexic/pornographic generations causes grave mistranslations. "This is what I say to get their attention," says Betty Friedan of her college audiences.

> *"How many of you have ever worn a girdle?" And they laugh. Then I say . . . "It used to be that being a woman in the United States meant that . . . you encased your flesh in rigid plastic casing that made it difficult to breathe and difficult to move, but you weren't supposed to notice that. You didn't ask why you wore the girdle, and you weren't supposed to notice red welts on your belly when you took it off at night." And then I say, "How can I expect you to know what it felt like when you have never worn anything under your blue jeans except panty hose, or little bikinis?" That gets to them. Then I explain how far we've come, where we are now, and why they have to start saying, "I am a feminist."*

For many young women in Friedan's audience, the girdle is made of their own flesh. They can't take it off at night. The "little bikinis" have not brought this generation heedless bodily freedom; they have become props that superimpose upon the young women chic pseudosexual scenarios that place new limits on what they can think, how they can move, and what they can eat. The backlash does to young women's minds, so much more free, potentially, than any ever before, what corsets and girdles and gates on universities no longer can. The post-1960 daughter sees more images of impossibly "beautiful" women engaged in "sexual" posturing in one day than her mother saw throughout adolescence: She needs to be shown more if she is to know her place. By saturation in imagery, the potential explosiveness of this generation is safely defused.

Young women born after 1960 have been made ill enough from having seen little representation of sexuality apart from beauty pornography. But they are not as ill as the generation who were children in the 1970s; those even younger women are sick almost to death. And the daughters of the eighties?

"Preadolescent dieting has increased 'exponentially' in recent years. . . . We know that dieting is rampant in the fourth and fifth grades," reports Vivian Meehan, president of the National Association of Anorexia Nervosa and Associated Disorders. In a survey of 494 middle-class schoolgirls in San Francisco, more than half described themselves as overweight, while only 15 percent were so by medical standards. Thirty-one percent of nine-year-olds thought they were too fat, and 81 percent of the ten-year-olds were dieters. A 1989 article in *The New York Times,* titled "Babes in Makeup Land," describes a new marketing drive of cosmetics for little girls, six-year-olds "painted to the hilt"; one doll, Li'l Miss Makeup, "resembles a girl that's 5 or 6 years old" who, when cold water is painted on, "springs eyebrows, colored eyelids, fingernails, tinted lips and a heart-shaped beauty mark."

These little girls, born around the time of Ronald Reagan's first election, are showing third-generation mutations from the beauty backlash against the women's movement. They are born with a congenital deformity: They lack childhoods. This generation will have even more trouble with life in the body than do daughters of the 1960s and 1970s. Born to compete, they will from their earliest memories associate femaleness with deprivation. Hunger is already being eroticized for today's little girls as an entry into adult sexuality. For a contemporary seven-year-old, to climb onto a scale and to exclaim with horror is as much a ritual of femininity, inextricable from the promise of sexual gratification, as my generation's posing provocatively on high heels in front of mirrors, and of my mother's generation dressing dolls in white satin. If they start dieting at seven and don't have sex until their mid-teens, it will already be too late: They will have spent over half their lives learning masochism in preparation for sexual gratification. They will have had little chance to build up memories of erotic life in the Edenic, undivided, pleasure-seeking, satisfied child's body. They will be learning masochism as they learn sexuality, and will enter a long, insecure adolescence, besieged by further messages of beauty as masochism, unprotected by the integrity of a sexual core innocent of pain.

Off the Road

The protection of chaperons left behind, the protection of sexual integrity not yet fully claimed, young women are vulnerable in brand-new ways. They do have greater leeway to move unaccompanied through the world than ever before; but that, ironically, has created still another new use for eating disorders.

The old claustrophobia has a new irritant, more chafing than ever. The young girl knows, more than her mother could at her age, what it is she is missing; she has had a taste. In Christina Rossetti's poem "Goblin Market," one sister, who did not taste forbidden fruit, stayed whole. The other took one sip of sweetness and found it addictive. She needed more, she needed to glut herself, or she would waste away.

The threat of sexual danger makes the girl's body a landscape on which she must project the outer world that now closes in. This house arrest of adolescence brings dreams of quest and exploration to a barren awakening. Marrakesh, Malabar, the Spice Islands, fantasies of discovery collapse, and she learns to put a dot of highlighter in the center of her upper lip. Her adventures must be restricted to those in which she can safely be looked at, because the really good adventures will expose her to being looked at to disastrous effect. Where her male peers go On the Road, she and the golden shackle of her "beauty" have to turn off it.

As an adolescent, she realizes with mounting horror that they were not kidding: For her to walk alone will be a fraught activity forever. Anorexia, bulimia, and exercise fixations work off and numb the frustration of the claustrophobia that accompanies the girl's grieving realization that the wide world she had imagined, and just inherited, is shut down to her by the threat of sexual violence.

If she were to eat, she would have energy; but adolescence is arranged for the safe venting of masculine steam. From athletic events to sexual conquests to a moody walk in the woods, boys have outlets for that agitation of waiting to fly. But if a girl has her full measure of wanderlust, libido, and curiosity, she is in a bad way. With ample stores of sugar to set off the buzz for intellectual exploration, starch to convert into restlessness in her elongating legs, fat to fuel her sexual curiosity, and the fearlessness born from a lack of concern over where her next meal will come from—she will get in trouble.

What if she doesn't worry about her body and eats enough for all the growing she has to do? She might rip her stockings and slam-dance on a forged ID to the Pogues, and walk home barefoot, holding her shoes, alone at dawn; she might baby-sit in a battered-women's shelter one night a month; she might skateboard down Lombard Street with its seven hairpin turns, or fall in love with her best friend and do something about it, or lose herself for hours gazing into test tubes with her hair a mess, or climb a promontory with the girls and get drunk at the top, or sit down when the Pledge of Allegiance says stand, or hop a freight train, or take lovers without telling her last name, or run away to sea. She might revel in all the freedoms that seem so trivial to those who could take them for granted; she might dream seriously the dreams that seem so obvious to those who grew up with them really available. Who knows what she would do? Who knows what it would feel like?

But if she *is not careful* she will end up: raped, pregnant, impossible to control, or merely what is now called fat. The teenage girl knows this. Everyone is telling her to be careful. She learns that making her body into her landscape to tame is preferable to any kind of wildness.

Dieting is being careful, and checking into a hunger camp offers the ultimate in care.

Judging the Beauty Judges

Gloria Steinem

Gloria Steinem (1934–) was born in Toledo, Ohio. Although celebrated as the co-founder of Ms. *magazine in 1968, her initial work was academic and political. A Chester Bowles Scholarship following her graduation from Smith College in 1956 took her to India where she wrote for the Indian government. Returning to New York, Steinem worked as a reporter until her 1969 coverage of the abortion issue showed her that "men valued me only to the extent that I imitated them." Her first collection of essays,* Outrageous Acts and Everyday Rebellions *(1982), was dedicated to her mother, Ruth Nuneviller Steinem, "who performed the miracle of loving others even when she could not love herself." The following essay is from the more recent* Revolution from Within *(1992).*

Just one. I wish I'd been prettier.

–Eleanor Roosevelt (When asked if she had any regrets about her life)

Any man with $42 million looks exactly like Clark Gable.

–Don King (When asked about Mike Tyson)

Society's standards of physical perfection seem immutable and "right." Our bodies seem variable and "wrong." But once we see the machinery behind the facade of perfection, society turns out to be, like the Wizard of Oz, a frightened little man behind a curtain. We can change him. Indeed, we *are* him. Consider these examples:

- In poor and agricultural countries, plumpness is so much a part of the "feminine" ideal that thin women are often seen as unsensual or poor childbearing risks, and young girls may be prepared for courtship by an especially rich diet. Similarly, a wife's girth is considered such a tribute to her husband's wealth that rich men have been known to force-feed their wives in order to possess proper status symbols. In rich and industrialized countries, the ideal "feminine" body is so thin that on any given day, most women are dieting, just ending a diet, or on the verge of starting one.
- Thin was not always desirable in this country. When North America was poorer and the goal was to populate the frontier, large families were the ideal, and so were large, voluptuous breasts and hips. After the frontier closed and manufacturing became the main source of wealth, the national preference for buxom women like Lillian ("Diamond Lil") Russell changed, too. The ideal breast and hip size diminished during the suffragist movement and World War I, stayed small during the 1920s craze for the flat-chested flapper, increased again when the

---

bosomy look made a modified comeback in escapist Hollywood movies during the Depression, shrank again in the 1940s when women went to work in defense plants, and returned complete with waist cinchers and padded bras after World War II, when women were supposed to replenish the population. Once that need had been met, however, the Marilyn Monroe curves of the 1950s gave way to the Jackie Kennedy look of the 1960s, and its apotheosis, the androgynous Twiggy.

- There is one "feminine" trait shared by all of the styles preferred in all of the above-mentioned eras, whether in Europe, North America, or the Third World: weakness. Rich cultures may prefer thin women and poor cultures may prefer fat ones—because as far as possessions go (and women *are* still possessions) whatever is rarest confers the most status—but all patriarchal cultures idealize, sexualize, and generally prefer weak women. Even women laborers who must be strong are often made to envy and imitate the fragile, delicate appearance of women of the upper classes. Only rebellions that come from women ourselves seem to mitigate this idealization of weakness. Nineteenth-century feminists protested the wasp-waisted look that forced women into corsets, fainting spells, and pulmonary problems, and put women on bicycles and the tennis court instead. Modern feminists protest the you-can't-be-too-thin cult, encourage sports and muscle-building, and stress access to nontraditional jobs, even combat. But strength is not part of any "femininity" that male-supremacist systems encourage.
- Since men's bodies are valued more as instruments of power than of attraction, men are much less likely to be judged by their appearance. If a man wins at money-making, sports, war, and so on, that's what counts. Nonetheless, ideals of "masculine" appearance do change with caste, class, and the kind of behavior society wants. For instance, the high heels and powdered wigs of French courtiers, the long nails of Chinese mandarins, the foppish fashions that came and went in the upper classes of this country, all proudly announced a distance from physical labor. In an age when most work is done at desks, however, male muscles have become a luxury that announces leisure, discipline, sexuality, and fitness. Some young men have begun to experiment with steroids, and older ones with muscle implants.
- Hierarchies of skin color and racial features are sad testimonies to racism's power to undermine self-esteem, and thus to maintain a racial status quo. Not only are women of color subject to white ideals of beauty—from Caucasian models in Japanese fashion magazines to the blond ideal in the mostly nonblond United States—but within the African-American community here, inside India, Brazil, and anywhere else that racial oppression and colonialism have run deep, the ruling class's valuation of appearance is internalized to the extent that it is often hard to reject, even when the reasons for it are clear. Only increased power on the part of the "wrong" color group can change these externally imposed ideals. African-American novelist Ralph Ellison was one of the first to comment on the relationship between power and appearance when he suggested in the early 1960s that white kids would eventually imitate black appearance. At the time he was laughed at, but that's exactly what happened with Afro hairstyles, dress, dance, music, rap, and other parts of black culture—a clear departure from the days of slavery when straight hair and white skin were worshiped. Globally, movements for independence and racial pride are making more and more people see black (as well as brown, red, and yellow) as beautiful.
- Clothes and body ornamentation follow the same political rules as male strength and female weakness. Female versions restrict the body, and male versions allow freedom of movement. Thus, in Ethiopia or other areas of Africa, and some parts of Asia, women are adorned with neck rings and heavy soldered-on metal anklets that inhibit movement, and the gap-toothed look considered beautiful is achieved by extracting a few crucial teeth—not incidentally those necessary to chew meat, thus leaving the limited protein supply for the men. Male decoration is usually confined to body painting, ornamental scarring, or clay that shapes the hair; nothing that restricts nutrition or mobility. In Moslem areas of the world, women are often required to wear a *chador,* a full-body veil first seen on the wives of upper-class men, and then on poorer women to whom it was presented as a symbol of protection, status, and, more recently, na-

tionalism. Like versions of the painfully bound "lotus feet" of upper-class Chinese women—a lifelong torture that was eroticized as beautiful and made a precondition of marriage—women's marks of beauty involve restrictions of freedom, and often pain and health deprivation as well. In the West, the difference is one of degree, not kind: little girls learn passivity from having to stay neat and clean, and helplessness from dresses that button in the back, while grown-up women limp along on spike heels and are hobbled by tight skirts. By contrast, even the most vain of "masculine" fashions allows freedom and comfort of movement. As Phil Donahue puts it: "Men may do some silly things, but you won't catch them walking in a snowstorm with a cute little hole at the end of their shoe."

- Perhaps the most universal of gender-related beauty standards has to do with age. Obviously, youth in women is considered more beautiful wherever their primary importance is as sex objects and childbearers—which means everywhere except in those cultures where age is venerated so much that even women benefit. But even in such youth-worshiping lands as this one, some women have begun to carve out their own power, with the result that we now see two things happening. The age limit of beauty is moving up (think of Cher, Goldie Hawn, and many others over forty, or Sophia Loren, Tina Turner, Jane Fonda, Cicely Tyson, and others over fifty, in a film industry that once discarded stars at thirty); but meanwhile, some men are resorting in a kind of backlash to child-women (think of teenage models and actresses, "kiddie porn," and twelve-year-old prostitutes).

Sex isn't the only reason for valuing youth in women. With age comes authority, and beauty standards are often a way of getting rid of women just as they are attaining real power. Thus, while more women have become visible as television newscasters, they are also much younger than their male counterparts and subject to much stricter appearance requirements. Men on television remain acceptable about twenty years longer. When men *are* held to youthful physical standards, however, these standards serve the same function as they do with women—they enable well-paid, more experienced workers to be replaced by lower-salaried, less experienced ones. But the double standard is still obvious: women age, but men mature.

Those examples are just the tip of an iceberg that spreads out wide and deep beneath the surface of our culture. We need to take the politics of beauty seriously because it affects every part of our lives, from our vision of who can be powerful to the comfort of our feet and the freedom of our hair. As Alice Walker has written, "Oppressed Hair Puts a Ceiling on the Brain."

Once we look behind the curtain and see that the Wizard of Oz is just a scared society—that beauty standards change with what society wants or fears—we see that beauty is less about looks than about behavior. For women, the behavior is more sexual and reproductive, and for men, it's more economic and productive. Though we are supposed to think that standards of beauty conform to an objective aesthetic handed down from history or the heavens—which is how society shirks the blame for creating them and makes us feel intrinsically wrong for not conforming to them—they are capricious, perishable standards that people made and people can unmake.

With this concept in mind, we can thread our way through confusing imperatives and cultural differences. Once we get a grip on an understanding that, for males or females, *standards of beauty are really about what society wants us to do or not to do,* then we can affect them by taking power into our own hands and altering the way we behave. Indeed, ideas of beauty are regularly turned upside down from one culture to the next, from one era to the next: behind the *form* of what is considered beautiful, there is always the *function* of what is considered acceptable to do. Thus, before we accept a standard of beauty for ourselves, we can ask, "Do I really like the behavior it symbolizes?"

If we could be taught in school about the politicization of beauty, it would help to create a healthier diversity in the United States, where a majority of black children still choose white dolls (sometimes even saying that black dolls are "dirty")[1] and seven-year-old little girls of normal weight think they are "too fat."[2] There has been some change. The ever-popular Barbie doll now comes in different skin colors and with an optional astronaut suit, but she still has the equivalent of a thirty-six-inch bust and an eighteen-inch waist, legs so long they are deformed, and itty-bitty feet that are impossible to stand on.[3]* The ultimate purpose is to help each child know that he or she is beautiful in a unique way, and that means placing the power to decide what is beautiful *within ourselves,* not in some all-powerful "they" out there. It means deciding what behavior is healthy and what bodily expression is appropriate, comfortable, celebratory, or joyous, *for us.* What's at stake is no less than the ability to see the beauty of our authentic selves.

Our health may be at stake, too. In *The Beauty Myth,* a smart and angry exposé of the ways in which beauty standards coerce women into changing themselves to fit the world, instead of vice versa, Naomi Wolf likens this pressure to conform to the medieval instrument of torture known as the Iron Maiden: a body-shaped casket that slowly starved or quickly impaled the unlucky prisoner locked within. On its cover was painted the face and body of a beautiful young woman.[4]

Consider the disease of anorexia, in which people—over 90 percent of them young females—starve themselves into thinness and may literally die for an ideal of perfection. "Anorexia nervosa" was named and identified as a disease by Western physicians in the 1870s;[5] and both Eastern and Western history are full of accounts, even personal diaries, of teenage girls who starved themselves in the name of a god or devotion to a saint, thus rebelling against arranged marriages and other forms of female bondage with the only thing within their power: their own bodies. This obsession with starving themselves into a perfect, permanently adolescent body had the same sorts of goals then as it does now: controlling and putting off their destiny as females.

In this country alone, according to the American Anorexia and Bulimia Association, about 150,000 females die of anorexia each year—and they're often the female version of "the best and the brightest": intelligent and sensitive young women who want to use their talents, yet are still in an economic class and culture that pressure women to be decorative and "perfect." As Naomi Wolf asks on behalf of her contemporaries, "How would America react to the mass self-immolation by hunger of its favorite sons?"[6]

Because the average weight of teenagers is going down, thus leaving less margin for safety, the lethal potential of anorexia and other starving diseases is increasing. In other rich, industrialized bastions of the thinness cult, the Iron Maiden's victims are increasing, too. In England, Japan, and many areas of Western Europe, eating disorders are about as prevalent as they were in this country ten years ago—and catching up fast.

Plastic surgery for questionable or obviously unhealthy reasons is becoming an epidemic, and the average age of patients is getting ever younger. In the U.S., 87 percent of all those who have undergone plastic surgery are females. Though some of this disproportion is attributable to the childhood sexual abuse that causes more women than men to "blame" their bodies and try to change them,[7] much of it comes straight from the double standard of beauty. (And, of course, the sexualization of very young women by the beauty myth connects those two causes.) A few of these cosmetic assaults have been reduced by feminist-inspired changes in the idea of what a female body should look like—for instance, some young girls thought to be "too tall" were once subjected to the surgical removal of leg-bone sections or to growth-arresting estrogen treatments—but many more are on the increase, from breast implants to jaw wirings for the purpose of ensuring weight loss.

Some of the Iron Maiden's most lethal punishments are alternatives to eating, especially smoking, which is perceived (and marketed) as an aid to being thin. Young women are the only group in the United States among whom smoking is actually on the increase, and the reason most often given is a desire to lose weight or a fear of gaining weight if they quit—motives that cigarette ads exploit by depicting slender and beautiful women, and by using words like *slim* and *thin* in their brand names. Since it would be difficult not to be aware of the danger of smoking, many women are valuing thinness over life itself.

Of course, the Iron Maiden was an equal-opportunity torture device, and many men are also trapped by its rigid standards of appearance—though not to the extent women are. The equivalent for men is the Iron Man, powerful, strong, and handsome: a symbol designed to keep almost all men trying vainly to measure up. In the United States, for instance, the average male height is five nine, yet the ideal goes right on being six feet and over. To take the average of many studies, 70 to 90 percent of all males

*The late Jack Ryan, designer of the Barbie doll and Chatty Cathy for Mattel, Inc., also helped to design the Sparrow and Hawk missiles for Raytheon, a major military manufacturer. He was once married to Zsa Zsa Gabor. (Obituary, *New York Times,* August 21, 1991.)

would like to change something about their appearance, a third would consider cosmetic surgery, and more than half don't like how they look naked—perhaps a result of the cruel emphasis on penis size. Since men's bodies are more instruments of power than ornaments, their behavior and expressions are more the focus of control than their appearance. Of the four intonation levels of voice commonly used in daily speech, for instance, both men and women are capable of speaking in them all; yet men almost never use the highest one, thus limiting their own expressiveness in order to avoid sounding in the least "feminine."[8] Men are discouraged not only from crying, but even from smiling too much. In the military, sports, and other areas of "masculine" power, smiling may be seen as a sign of ingratiation and weakness.

Conversely, women, as well as male members of discriminated-against races, often have to adopt pasted-on smiles, lest they be seen as not sufficiently eager to please, or even threatening. It's a phenomenon that spreads from slavery and class subservience to the female variety of "smiling" jobs in which body control is a requirement, or to the man in the street who feels the right to demand, "Why-aren't-you-smiling-honey?"

If even our bodies—their health, their freedom, their adornment, their uses—are not our own, what is?

It's a question that men of color have asked in many anticolonial movements, from Gandhi in British India to Steve Biko, who founded the Black Consciousness Movement in South Africa—a message of autonomy and self-respect for which, even in 1977, he was imprisoned and beaten to death. Blacks with the self-esteem to look to themselves for a sense of what was beautiful and proud were too threatening to the white minority regime.[9]

It's a question that women in every country are asking as they defy customs and laws that control female bodies for sex and reproduction; a control sometimes instituted by men of a different race to limit reproduction, and sometimes by men of their own race to force reproduction. Whether an older woman is going under the knife for cosmetic surgery because she fears losing her husband, or a younger one is forced to undergo a clitoridectomy because she is not marriageable without it (in many parts of the world, cutting out the clitoris is done at about eight, usually brutally and without anesthetic, as a traumatic lesson in social ownership and the excision of sexual will), females rarely own their own bodies.[10] In the United States, too, a woman may be told she is too fat for a job, be kicked off the airwaves for being too old, be reduced by economic need to selling her body for sex or surrogate motherhood, be forced to seek approval from the state for an abortion because she is too young, suffer the common body invasion of rape and be blamed for inviting the crime by the very fact of having a female body, and be constrained in a thousand other ways. The basic message is the same: A woman's power is not supposed to extend as far as her own skin. Which is why, as Adrienne Rich wrote at the end of *Of Woman Born,* "The repossession by women of our bodies will bring far more essential change to human society than the seizing of the means of production by workers."

It's a question that women who love women and men who love men are also asking when they overturn homophobic, pronatalist punishments that subject the most private uses of our bodies to the most public laws, or when they agitate for the right to be affectionate with each other at high school proms and anywhere else that heterosexual couples are. They are struggling against a bias so extreme that in the United States almost half of gays have experienced violent attacks from strangers, peers, or their own families—and are six times more likely to attempt suicide than their heterosexual counterparts—even while they are still adolescents.[11] Now in the era of AIDS, the unfair stigma of "carrying" a disease is a danger both to self and to self-esteem.

It's a question that many men of supposedly powerful groups are asking, too, when they challenge everything from laws on the length of their hair to the largely unnecessary rite of circumcision;[12] from standards of height to hierarchies based on muscles, prowess at sports, and ability to fight each other; from an assumption that they must be willing to die for state-approved purposes to one that they will kill for them.

The answer to the question of who owns our bodies lies in establishing the legal, moral, and social principle of bodily integrity, so that each person controls the universe within our skins. It lies in getting rid of both the Iron Maiden and the Iron Man so we can have choice, not compulsion; more beauty in our lives, not less; pleasure, not constraint. In Naomi Wolf's imagery, we are changing the self-consciousness of a spotlight *on* the body for the self-confidence of a light radiating *from* the body.

That's the shift of paradigm here: Instead of a light that is directed at us by others, a light that shines from within.

To embody this contrast in a more familiar way, I often think of Margaret Mead and Eleanor Roosevelt. Both were brilliant and beloved, both had a lasting impact on their times, and neither was beautiful by conventional standards. In fact, both were often ridiculed for the way they looked. Yet Margaret grew up confidently and as far removed from the Iron Maiden's influence as any young girl could, while Eleanor was made to feel she should fit its constraints. A mother who was a great beauty herself, a debutante upbringing, and a socially correct, flesh-denying grandmother had seen to that. From earliest childhood, Margaret simply convinced people she was beautiful by being so magnetic, sensual, and entirely herself that even men who most disdained "a lady intellectual" fell under her spell. She lived an adventurous and satisfying life with three husbands and many lovers, both women and men, and succeeded in her work partly because she was secure enough to empathize with the sexualities of different cultures. Margaret Mead simply refused to let the Iron Maiden rule, and was gloriously herself. I used to see her in my New York neighborhood, stalking along with her big, forked walking stick, coming to a beauty parlor on my corner to have her hair done each week; as unself-conscious about this female ritual as about her country walking stick in the city.

Eleanor grew up feeling shy and gawky, too tall and out of place, simultaneously disdaining her mother as superficial and reproaching herself for not measuring up to her great beauty. ("My mother," Blanche Wiesen Cook quotes Eleanor as saying at the beginning of her long-awaited biography, "was the most beautiful woman I ever saw."[13]) After the early deaths of her mother and her adored, handsome, womanizing father, Eleanor tried vainly to fit her tall and angular body into the ladylike image her grandmother taught, and even forced her voice to a higher register, thus giving it the odd crackling sound that was to be so ridiculed by her critics. After she had married her charming and politically ambitious cousin Franklin, she struggled with both her own shyness and her overbearing mother-in-law. Later, when Eleanor discovered Franklin's long-term affair with a "prettier" woman (who would not be the last), she was humiliated, undone, as if she had been betrayed by both her husband and her father at the same time, for they were in that way so much alike. From photographs taken during this period, Blanche Cook theorizes that Eleanor may have become anorexic; certainly, her frequent inability to keep food down in times of emotional conflict is well documented in her letters.

Though she rose above these betrayals, her restricted upbringing, and her own shyness to become one of the most compassionate and humane leaders of her time—and though one hopes for her sake that she did have the affairs with a man and perhaps a woman friend or two that her letters and photographs hint at—Eleanor Roosevelt's triumphant and world-respected later years were still haunted by an uncertain, unpretty girl of the past.

It would have been unworthy of Margaret Mead's life if she had ended it with the regret for not being "prettier." It was unworthy of Eleanor's life, too.

It would also be unworthy of yours or mine.

Notes

1. In 1947, psychologists Kenneth B. and Mamie Clark conducted a classic study of black children ages three to seven in Massachusetts and Arkansas. Two thirds of them picked white dolls when given a choice of four, two black and two white. It was such poignant evidence of low self-esteem among black children that it was cited in the 1954 Supreme Court decision mandating school desegregation. Forty years later, however, a Connecticut study using Cabbage Patch dolls, identical except for color, produced the same sad result—65 percent of black children chose white dolls—as did another study in Trinidad. As one of these two later studies found, only when self-esteem was bolstered by praising children who selected the black doll was the preference for the white dolls reversed. See proceedings of the American Psychological Association meeting, New York City, 1987. Also reported in *Time*, September 14, 1987, p. 74.

2. Study in *Pediatrics* as reported in *New York Times*, February 11, 1988.

3. Cathy Meredig, a Minneapolis engineer, has created the Happy To Be Me doll, with realistic measurements, as an alternative fantasy/fashion doll. "I want to offer girls a healthier body image," as she explained in August 1991 about her Self-Esteem Toy Corporation. At this writing, it's too soon to know whether her entry can compete with the giant Mattel Corporation, which manufactures Barbie.

4. This insight is developed by Naomi Wolf in *The Beauty Myth: How Images of Beauty Are Used Against Women*, New York, William Morrow, 1991, p. 17.

5. Joan Jacobs Brumberg, *Fasting Girls: The Emergence of Anorexia Nervosa as a Modern Disease,* Cambridge, Massachusetts: Harvard University Press, 1988, p. 3.

6. Wolf, *The Beauty Myth,* p. 182. Wolf's anger at the ignoring of this problem that is destroying some of the most talented women of her generation has produced an effective chapter, "Hunger," that anyone who doubts the seriousness of eating disorders should read; pp. 179–217.

7. Dr. Elizabeth Morgan, the Washington, D.C., plastic surgeon best known for having gone to jail rather than disclose her daughter's whereabouts to a sexually abusing father, had previously done research showing that women addicted to multiple plastic surgeries were also often trying to punish their bodies for "attracting" incestuous abuse.

8. Gloria Steinem, "Men and Women Talking," *Outrageous Acts and Everyday Rebellions,* New York: Holt, Rinehart and Winston, 1983, pp. 176–190.

9. For one account of the life of Stephen Biko and the messages of the Black Consciousness Movement, see *Biko* by Donald Woods, New York: Henry Holt, 1987.

10. Clitoridectomies and often infibulation—the removal of the entire clitoris and the labia, plus joining the scraped sides of the vulva so they grow together in a chastity belt of flesh that must be ripped open and resewn for every insemination and birth—are practiced in large areas of the Middle East, Africa, and some other parts of the world by some groups of Moslems, Coptic Christians, indigenous tribal religions, Catholics and Protestants, and Fellasha, an Ethiopian Jewish sect. In England and in the United States, clitoridectomies were sometimes performed as treatment for masturbation, sexual "deviance," or prostitution. Robin Morgan and Gloria Steinem, "The International Crime of Genital Mutilation," *Outrageous Acts and Everyday Rebellions,* pp. 292–300.

11. R. Harding, "Gay Youth Six Times More Likely to Commit Suicide," *The Washington Blade,* May 16, 1986, p. 1. For information on gay adolescents, both problems and helpful programs, contact The Hetrick-Martin Institute, 401 West Street, New York, New York 10014.

12. The highest medical estimate of males who need circumcision due to the tightness of the foreskin is 10 percent. No increased cleanliness has been proved, and there is considerable testimony that circumcision toughens the tip of the penis and reduces sexual pleasure. It seems to be largely a symbolic testimony of allegiance to a patriarchal god.

13. Blanche Wiesen Cook, *Eleanor Roosevelt,* New York: Viking Press, 1992. The first of two volumes.

The Body Minimal

Wendy Wasserstein

Wendy Wasserstein (1950–   ), born in Brooklyn, is described at age thirty-eight as "the preeminent theatrical chronicler of the momentous changes in the lives of women over the last generation" (Current Biography Yearbook, *1988). A graduate of Mount Holyoke, she collaborated with Christopher Durang when they were students together at the Yale University School of Drama* (When Dinah Shore Ruled the Earth, *1975, a spoof of beauty contests).* The Heidi Chronicles *(1988) looks back at the women's movement through the eyes of Heidi Holland, an art history professor. The following selection, "The Body Minimal," appeared in her essay collection* Bachelor Girls *(1990).*

THIS IS WRITTEN FOR RAQUEL, MORGAN, JANE, Joan, Linda, and Victoria. I want to thank them for helping me enter thirty, approach forty, and commit to a healthier, more vital fifty. Without their guidance, concern, and inspiration, I would never have realized that I've devoted my life to a unique and easy-to-follow diet and exercise plan:

The Body Minimal

The secret to The Body Minimal plan is *Minimal.* Remember that! Choice causes stress and anxiety and, therefore, overeating and exhaustion. Simply by following the Minimal food and exercise regimen, you eliminate decision-making.

The Body Minimal is not a fad. It is a way of life. There are no pills, no powders, no yo-yo aftermaths—just a few Minimal daily suggestions.

Morning

The morning meal *must* include rest and a newspaper. When you wake up, look at the clock and then pull the covers back over your head. This stretching action of pulling up the covers begins the daily exercise regimen.

After three or four good blanket-stretches, get up and wander around your house or apartment to the kitchen. Brew a cup of coffee, bend to reach for the newspaper that's been delivered to your door, and wander back into the bedroom. Wandering is safer than jogging in the park, and you can do it at any time in the privacy of your own home.

Feel free to have a croissant with butter and preserves for breakfast, but *never* a *pain au chocolat.* Chocolate for breakfast means unnecessary calories, and it might also leave a difficult stain in the bed.

Rest in the midmorning. This can be accomplished at home by never getting out of bed, or, with a few minor adjustments, in the office. Simply ask your office mates about their careers, personal lives, and any planned adulteries. Just by listening to gossip, you will take your mind off the passing Danish trolley.

An added tip for the morning: Always use a dial phone. Touchtone doesn't exercise the fingers and promote circulation like a good old-fashioned dial phone.

Lunch

We now enter problem area number one: lunch.

Lunch is often anticipated as the highlight of the day until dinner. But why not skip it? Go shopping instead. Especially good places to shop are malls or department stores with chocolate or cookie outlets. The calories burned by chewing and digesting truffles or macadamia chocolate-chunks while wandering through Calvin Klein size fours are considerable. Be careful, however, not to handle the sale merchandise without a napkin, as these items are not returnable.

Now, aren't you glad you didn't have the *pain au chocolat* for breakfast and worked off the sweets at lunch instead!

Afternoon

Teatime—time for a pick-me-up from the daily routine. Once more we are confronted with alternatives. Out comes the dreaded Danish trolley again. (Perhaps just one, to avoid another chat with the office mates.) Out comes the after-school Oreo treat. (If the kids can have it, shouldn't you demonstrate your affection by having one, too?) On comes "Another World." (Wouldn't the Frame family want you to share in their kaffeeklatsch while they discuss yesterday's marriage, bankruptcy, and teen-age fratricide?)

Teatime is precisely the time to think Minimal. Conflict is imposing itself, but the answer is simple: Teatime is the time to join a health club.

Be very clear about this! I am only saying to *join.* The effort expended in getting to the Club La Racquette and writing a check gives you a bonus of at least 200 calories that can be counted toward a late-night snack. And consider the investment of future calories you'll burn by opening your mailbox and carrying the weekly fliers for squash meets as well as the regular renewal notices. Followers of the Body Minimal plan have joined more than one thousand health clubs a year without ever having had to change out of their street clothes. It's fun, it's expensive, but it's never strenuous.

For variety, teatime is also a good time to join weight-loss programs, to buy hardcover workout plans, or to rent exercise videos at your local video shop. Carrying workout books and videocassettes can tone muscles as efficiently as jogging with weights. Again, I must emphasize that it is the effort involved in the preliminary exploration that is the most challenging and physically stimulating. The follow-through is routine.

Dinner

After a vigorous day of resting, doing dial-phone isometrics, and writing checks to health clubs comes your reward—dinner.

Now, I said the plan is Minimal; I never said it doesn't involve discipline. Just at the dinner hour comes the day's most stringent requirement: You *must* take a taxi to dinner.

Finding a taxi at rush hour involves leaping across the street, signaling rhythmically with an extended arm, and facing a hostile contretemps with fellow Body Minimalists. This is aerobics—pressing the heart to its limits! Moreover, the taxi ride itself will inevitably involve jolts over potholes, the irritation of a confused destination, and even a conversation in a foreign language. Riding the bus, taking the subway, or walking could never provide this much physical exertion.

At dinner, be sure to fill up on hors d'oeuvres and cocktails. This will leave little room for the main course. Besides, the natural oil found in the martini olive will help to replenish the skin. When dining out, you should scour the restaurant's menu for dishes unappealing to your particular palate. This way you'll be certain to leave a healthy portion of the meal on your plate. For example, vegetarians on the Body Minimal plan might enjoy a night out at Gallagher's Steak House.

We've arrived at the point where neophyte Minimalists often say: "This was Minimal so far, but what do I do about dessert? Do I get my 200-calorie bonus now?" The Body Minimal is a health and diet plan, and, as in any other health and diet plan, the secret to dessert is: *Think fruit.* Lemon mousse has fewer calories than chocolate mousse. Apple pie has fewer calories than Boston cream pie. Strawberry sundaes have a higher water content than hot fudge sundaes—and water is vital to fitness. The Body Minimal is at all times a *total* fitness regimen.

Evening

After-dinner snacking is an inalienable right. Eminent physicians and miniseries stars have suggested various Band-Aid solutions—snacking on carrots, sunflower seeds, and unbuttered, unsalted popcorn, for example. Anyone who has tried snacking on carrots, sunflower seeds, and unbuttered, unsalted popcorn suggests leaving the house.

Leaving the house, however, can lead us into temptation. At the movies: buttered, salted popcorn and ice-cream bonbons. At baseball games: hot dogs and Cracker Jacks. At Broadway shows: sugary orange drinks and three-pound Chunky bars.

But science marches on. A growing number of Body Minimalists have discovered an anti-snacking breakthrough. When they opt to leave the house, they attend the noncommercial theater. The concession stand at a good Off-Off-Broadway play or New Wave dance concert serves granola cookies, bananas, black coffee, and cider. The cost is usually $1.50 to $3.00 per item—and don't forget that contributions to the arts are tax-deductible!

Nighttime

The day is almost ended, but desire knows no timetable. In the wee hours comes the constant refrain, "Don't I deserve a reward, a treat, a consolation prize for all my discipline and willpower?" Mrs. Marvin Finn of Englewood Cliffs, New Jersey, writes: "It's midnight—when do I get my bonus? What if I just split a little something with my husband? It's not his fault I had to modify my behavior. Don't I get to relax?"

Mrs. Finn, you do get to relax. Take a bath. And be sure to use nondigestible hair and skin products. Body Minimalists have saved thousands of calories by avoiding shampoos that contain avocado, beer, or honey.

Never go to sleep on a full stomach. If it's bedtime and you're still digesting, try watching TV to stay awake. Late-night television also offers challenging local slimnastics programs. Just changing the channel manually, instead of lounging with a remote control, tones the thigh muscles. And this is an activity you can share by alternating with your partner.

Additional

The Body Minimal is the only minimal program that can change your life. To enroll in your FREE introductory session, call 24 hours a day, 7 days a week: 1-800-MINIMAL. Or mail this essay.

Warning: Consult a physician before beginning any dietary plan. The Surgeon General has determined that The Body Minimal may be hazardous to your health.

New Frontier

Jane Fonda

Jane Fonda (1937–) was born in New York City, the daughter of Henry Fonda. After sampling college, she worked as a model and an actress, activities which took her to France. Her political awakening began when she witnessed the 1968 student uprising in Paris. Fonda has succeeded as an actress (Academy Awards for Klute *and* Coming Home*) and as a shaper of opinion (her film company, IPC, has successfully "made message movies in an entertaining way"). Her* Workout Book *(1979), dedicated to her daughter, was on the* New York Times' *best-seller list for two years. The following selection from* Women Coming of Age *(1984) was written with Mignon McCarthy.*

We who are older have nothing to lose! We have everything to gain by living dangerously! We can be the risk-takers, daring to challenge and change systems, policies, lifestyles, ourselves.

–MAGGIE KUHN, Founder, Gray Panthers

TO BE A MIDLIFE WOMAN IN OUR SOCIETY IS, IN many respects, to be a pioneer. The middle years of life for women represent virtually uncharted territory—and it is those of us now in or approaching midlife who will draft its maps. We have to clear a path through the debris of outworn yet still harmful myths that obscure the real promise of this new period in our lives.

Few of us have anyone to point the way. None of the women who peopled my earlier life shed any positive light on what was to come at this later stage. My mother chose to take her own life when she was younger than I am now. Her doctor told me that among the many phantoms shadowing her world was the fear of youth's passing. Your mothers, like mine, may have also come upon these years fearfully. Perhaps they were uncertain of the tools needed in this new phase, which may have seemed to them the far edge of life.

We are the transition generation.

Those of us in midlife today are at the heart of a major redefinition of "middle age" as the women before us have known it. For those who will follow us, our daughters and their generation, the middle years will be fundamentally transformed. What has been a dreaded and shunned phase of life will become for them a highly valued and productive time. For us, in the epicenter of this change, a massive shift in our notion of midlife is already repositioning this period from its former place near life's end to one vitally at life's center.

When does midlife begin—at forty, at forty-five? Does it end at sixty, at sixty-five? Such numbers seem so arbitrary, so inadequate to account for all the variations experienced by individual people. And early midlife is clearly very different from later midlife. Mindful of these limitations, I have come to think of midlife as a diverse span of three decades—fifteen years on either side of menopause, which generally occurs around the age of fifty. I include ages thirty-five to thirty-nine because our bodies do begin to change even as early as thirty. These changes may not be visible in our early thirties, but if we can acknowledge them we will allow ourselves time to prepare, to ease ourselves more comfortably into the next stage.

But, oh, what cries of protest we hear from younger women who rebel at the thought that they can be considered middle-aged! And no wonder. Our society is not kind to women as we grow older. We've been prized for our ability to reproduce and for a sexual attractiveness based on youth. Hence, we've faced double trouble when, reaching midlife, we leave both youthful and fertile years behind. We've found ourselves to be healthy survivors in a culture that rejects us and that does not want our full participation.

The Myths

Our generation inherits a whole mythology of aging that prescribes an early obsolescence for women, heaving us over the hill at forty, removing us from the flowing mainstream of life. We are to have no worthwhile contribution to make to our society. We are to believe it's too late to fulfill or to reshape our life's goals, whatever they may be. We are led to expect an inevitable and swift decline in our physical, psychological, and intellectual well-being which means becoming unhealthy, emotionally bereft, and mentally dull.

With this kind of future before her, a woman's fear of aging begins early. I've seen it close to home among the young girls who come to the children's camp Tom and I have run for the past eight years. Last summer when I said my age aloud amidst a group of campers, for example, several of the teenagers winced and whispered to me that I shouldn't let on how old I was because I didn't *look* forty-six. Of course, they viewed their advice as complimentary. I was tempted to respond with an updated version of Gloria Steinem's now-famous retort, "*This* is what forty-six looks like!"

It saddened me that these young women already viewed midlife as something to hide from, believing they were at that moment in the best years of their lives. Yet, most of us probably wouldn't want to go back now to those earlier years. We prefer where we are today. I like being able to look back—at twenty-five-cent movies with newsreels, a world free of fast-food chains, an era with no TV when people actually talked to one another, a time when we respected and trusted our country's leadership and no child ever wondered if there would be a tomorrow.

I wouldn't want to give up these memories. Nor would I want to relinquish all I've learned along the way in exchange for being young again. By midlife, most of us know ourselves better, like ourselves better, understand our bodies and what pleases us better. We're more self-confident and less dependent on the approval of others. We're less inhibited and potentially feel ourselves to be more exciting sexual partners—and we seek that in others. But, my, isn't it a well-kept secret? And it will remain so as long as we unwittingly buy into society's negative attitudes, leaving the young ones no distant future to look forward to.

Often, the fear of being discarded for "younger models" in our jobs and in our relationships with men pressures us into denying our age—not only to others but to ourselves as well. But when we take up the exhausting burden of denying our age, we are also denying who we are. To the extent we succeed in passing as younger, we abandon where we've been. We rob ourselves of genuine pride in the years we've really lived. And we separate ourselves from the women who may show signs of aging more quickly, at a time when closeness with other women can give us strength, solace and validation. Our lives end up consisting of three phases: being young, *pretending* to be young, and old age. The whole rich middle period is lost. As an actress, I can tell you Act Three can be pretty shaky when Act Two is missing.

A Double Standard

For a man, the middle years are his prime, a time when he is more likely to be at the peak of his career. His self-worth and his sexuality derive from his full participation in life. These are not tied to the state of his physical being or, more narrowly, to his reproductive organs as they are for us. His attractiveness is not in question. His sexuality is above suspicion.

While a woman's face, like her body, is valued as long as it remains smooth and unchanging, a man's lines are the product of experience. The changes in his appearance become *additions* to who he is as a person, whereas those same changes in us become *liabil-*

ities. Paul Newman gets silver hair and becomes distinguished. I get gray hair and am told I'd best dye it. My pal Redford gets furrows and character lines. I get wrinkles and crow's feet. It ain't fair!

Cultural Missing Persons

For me, as a film actress, middle age holds a special set of challenges and anxieties. What I have to offer in my work is not at all separate from me, as would be the case if my talents lay in some other field like sculpting or medicine or management. My creative "product" is my very self—the characters and emotions I create with my body, my face, my eyes, my hands. What you see is what you get. This puts me in a precarious position at age forty-six, since until quite recently American producers and writers have seemed to think that American audiences don't want to see a woman with wrinkles, at least not in a leading screen role where she might be required to be sexual and dynamic and where her character would be pivotal.

In the world of movies and television, the most important image-making institutions of our society, active, strong, independent midlife women have been virtually invisible. We've been cultural missing persons. The Screen Actor's Guild (SAG) helped to document this after a ten-year study in the 1970s of prime time and children's weekend television programming: positive portrayals of women begin to disappear from television as women reach forty. The presence of powerful, sophisticated, sexy men over forty, on the other hand, begins to increase. Most women on TV are *under thirty;* most men *over thirty-five!* (How often do we see an older man paired with an older woman?) Our absence in the media only serves to deepen an already ominous view of aging in the minds of our children and ourselves. The heaviest TV-viewers, SAG found, are the most likely to believe that women become old very early in life and to think there are few older persons in general in our society! On television, SAG concluded, "A man is for all seasons, but a woman only for spring."

Well, I'm autumn and I'm mad! Several options are open to me. I can retire. Or, I can attempt to maintain the image of "an attractive woman in her late thirties"—I get offered a lot of those. Or I can own up to the fact that I don't really want to go backwards. I'm not interested in playing younger women even if I *could* be made to look that age. I would find it constricting to have to bring myself back to my thirties. I want to play *my own age,* with everything that means. I'm interested in the character of women who are where I am now.

Those of us who are midlife actresses have to forge new identities, and at the same time convince those same writers and directors, the ones who see only pre–thirty-five, that there are *a lot* of midlife women out there who would flock to see good films about women of their age.

Fortunately, many of us who are mature actresses have already become producers. This increases the likelihood that we will be the first generation of actresses to give a cultural face and voice to midlife women, correcting society's blind spot, proclaiming via the mass media, the creator of the popular consciousness, that there does indeed exist a vibrant, sensual, appealing, *lined* woman's face between the prettiness of youth and the special beauty and character of a woman in her seventies and eighties.

Turning Points

All of the myths and misperceptions about middle-aged women in this society are on a collision course with new realities. Some may already be familiar to you:

- There are more of us than ever before.
- We're entering the middle years physically stronger than ever before.
- And all of this is occurring at the same time that women of all ages are reexamining their place in society and discovering the real potentials that exist for them.

Growing Strong

We have reached a period of unprecedented transformation in our society. We are moving from a culture of mostly young people to one whose majority consists of midlife and older people. There are also more women than men. Consider these points:

1. People born during the baby boom following World War II are now entering their middle years. *Forty million* of them are women.
2. Because young people are having fewer babies, the middle-aged represent a larger and larger *pro-*

portion of our society. Midlife women alone are approaching a remarkable 20 percent of the *entire* population, giving us the potential for enormous influence in the marketplace, in politics, and in society as a whole—far into the twenty-first century.

3. Midlife and older people, with women in the majority, are not only the largest, but the *fastest growing* segment of American society. This flourishing group will represent over 50 percent of the population by the turn of the century.
4. In this country a woman born in 1900 was expected to live to be about forty-seven, the age I am now. At that time, life's midpoint was less than age twenty-five. The lives of most of us then would have ended *during* our reproductive years. Today, the average woman is expected to live to age seventy-eight, the average man seventy-one—an increase of thirty years for most of us!
5. Because of improved nutrition, sanitation and health care, people are living longer everywhere. The aging of the American population is only part of a global phenomenon that will mean a *doubling* of the number of people over sixty worldwide in just twenty years.
6. Excellent health is now possible well into our old age. Many of the chronic diseases and physical disabilities we now encounter when we survive into our later years are *not* the inevitable companions of aging and are for the most part *preventable.*
7. Although we still do not know why women continue to outlive men, we do know that we have longer, healthier lives. We must challenge the cultural assumption that we're supposed to become old around the midpoint of our lives.

Not so long ago, the outer limit of middle age was considered to be around fifty, coinciding with the average age of menopause. Now, midlife is commonly thought of as a much longer time period—extending years beyond menopause. And menopause, while still a central event, is no longer the single determining factor it once was. It takes its place alongside the other equally powerful dimensions of a woman's midlife, which now spans the last of the childbearing years and the beginning of the postreproductive years.

Most of us will have one-third of our lives left to live after menopause.

This fact, among others, is shaking up the tradition we're heir to—of womanhood based foremost on fertility and motherhood. Our childbearing years make up *less than half* of our life span and the years we actually spend with children at home much, much less than that. This new reality should enable a woman to see herself whole, not defined solely by her uterus or by her relationship to children or to a partner. An expanded midlife may mean expanded identities as well.

Changing Roles, New Risks

Like many of you, I grew up in the 1950s, a time of very prescribed and limited roles for women. The "feminine mystique" was at its peak after World War II when many of our generation married. We learned an idealized version of family life in this decade of togetherness and "Momism," neither of which necessarily translated into the real joys of mothering or true family closeness.

Though women, in fact, began increasingly to work outside the home, we were supposed to be perfect mothers and dedicated homemakers—exclusively. Marriage was to be the pivotal, preeminent event in a woman's life. I recall a sense of being out of it as I approached the end of my sophomore year in college when, unlike so many of my friends, I had no engagement ring on my finger and no subscription to *Bride's* magazine. I was frequently a bridesmaid at the weddings of my friends and, though a wiser inner voice told me to wait, I often feared I'd be doomed to a lonely life on the fringe, with little chance of winning the security, normalcy and other expected rewards of marriage.

In those days, if we prepared at all for our futures, it was only for the first half of our lives. We were raised as though life stopped at forty, after which everything was somehow just an incomprehensible blur. We thought a lot about getting married, but not a lot about what happened after that. The roles of wife and mother, of which we had only a vague but glorified notion, were to last for life. And the concept of women influencing their society was totally foreign. For me at least, the idea that a woman could change anything was limited to diapers, linens and the furniture arrangement.

I'll wager most of us assumed that by our early forties we would own our own homes, send our husbands off to work every morning, and be helping our daughters or daughters-in-law through their first pregnancies. But now, through massive transformations in the family and marriage, only the exception fits this mold of lifelong wifehood and motherhood—though the stereotype understandably persists in our minds as the norm. Today only one family in six fits our long-held concept of the American nuclear family—a working, breadwinning father and a full-time homemaking mother, raising two or more children.

Now, *well over half* of women in midlife work outside the home and more of us are supporting our families, with or without partners. More of us are also facing a greater part of our lives on our own—one out of four midlife women is single. Many of us who married early will have divorced or separated by the time we enter our midlife—one out of three marriages, at the least, now ends in divorce. Some of us will experience the death of our partner as we move toward the later years. And some of us will delay marrying until midlife or decide not to marry at all. Whatever the circumstances, being single in midlife is an increasingly commonplace and accepted way of life.

These new patterns of marriage and singlehood bring new patterns of mothering too. More women are arriving at midlife as single mothers raising their children alone—most with fragile financial resources, 30 percent with incomes *below* the poverty line. Women are also having their children later, which means a longer period of mothering in midlife. Women like myself who waited until their thirties to have children will still be raising them in midlife. I will probably be in my early fifties before my first child leaves home. My maternal grandmother already had teenaged grandchildren at that age.

Just decades ago, women expected their lives to be very much like those of their friends and contemporaries. Now, given the assemblage of paths before us, we're infinitely more diverse, as varied as the colors of leaves in autumn. I see this in the many midlife women I talk with across the country—like Doris, a forty-year-old woman from Cleveland who told me, "I've been working since I was twenty and never felt I could afford to take time off till now to have a child. I'm about to have my first." Or Mary, a never-married single woman in her mid-thirties, about to make a major move in careers and also to buy her own home in Los Angeles. "I never thought it would happen this way," she said. "But I've saved up and finally am about to realize the dream of having my own place." Or my friend Susan in New York, a woman in her fifties who has just become a new grandmother and also recently launched a new business as an art dealer. "I decided to turn my apartment into a gallery for women's paintings. I love being on my own."

We are not who we were prepared to be in the 1950s—neither is the world the one we expected. "We're becoming the men we always wanted to marry," says my friend Steinem. A broader vision of what it means to be a woman in this society is taking form—just look, on the political frontier, to the history-making nomination of a woman, Congresswoman Geraldine Ferraro, for Vice President of the United States. The notion of a woman's place will never be the same.

Nothing has prepared us for the profound potential in these immense changes. And nothing has prepared us for the possible pain that may be inflicted by the reshaping of the traditional contours of marriage and family. Nevertheless, we're emerging at midlife strengthened, with a new sense of ourselves.

We are learning that developing new roles within and outside of marriage, beyond the strictures of the "feminine mystique," may be good for us—critical to both our psychological and physical health. "The more women become involved away from the household," says the National Institute on Aging, "the better they are doing." Our entry into the world of work, outside the home, is perhaps among the most important elements of our changing status and our changing well-being.

Nine-to-Five

It was women over thirty-five who broke the barriers against married women working outside the home when they entered the paid work force in large numbers during the Second World War. Since that time, midlife women have played an increasingly important role in the American economy. Now nearly 60 percent of us are employed and half of all women who work outside the home are in their middle and later years.

Work has become a large, important part of our lives. Most of us will spend at least *thirty years* in the paid labor force—longer by far than we spend raising our children, longer than we may spend in our marriages. Even with interruptions of our paid employment due to childraising responsibilities, a woman's overall money-earning work life will average only ten years less than a man's. It requires the same planning and care as any other central aspect of our lives—and the determination to succeed in spite of obstacles.

The myths we encounter as women in midlife follow us into our work lives. Still commonplace, for example, is the erroneous belief that achievement and productivity, so fundamental to a man's sense of well-being and happiness, are for us not so important. A midlife woman's work outside the home has been perceived as "busywork" to compensate for too much time on her hands, even though, as for men, the *overriding* reason most of us enter the work force is economic. We've been encouraged not to take our jobs seriously as careers or as life goals, but rather to view them as superfluous transitory activities. We've been taught to conspire against ourselves by developing blind spots when it comes to recognizing our own very real accomplishments in the world of work—outside *or* inside the home.

These harmful misperceptions translate to more tangible difficulties when women try to enter or re-enter the job market during their middle years. As early as thirty-five, a woman is likely to meet up with the Dracula Complex of business—the need for fresh, that is, young, blood. In spite of existing age discrimination laws, this tendency permeates hiring *and* promotion practices, telling us that as workers, we're already old. Midlife women, like all working women, also remain a cheap labor pool for business—last hired in good economic times and first fired in hard times—concentrated in dead-end occupations, such as clerical and service work that traditionally offers only the lowest pay. According to the U.S. Department of Commerce, a midlife woman still earns *less* than her male counterpart in a comparable job with comparable experience even when she's taken no time out to raise children. True to the double standard, a man's salary stays on an upward slope throughout his life while a woman's slides downward, and the two levels never even intersect because he starts out higher. A young woman who begins her work life making 76 cents to a man's dollar will end it as an older woman making 53 cents to his dollar—*barely over half of what her male equivalent earns.*

Getting Better

Yet, notwithstanding the continuing barriers to real equal-employment opportunities, midlife women are in the work force to stay. Our increasing presence and contribution in the economic arena will better fortify us to change the negative working conditions for women and ultimately for men as well. And working outside the home appears to be beneficial to our overall well-being. It was expected that exposure to the stress of the workplace would be harmful, but the reverse has been the case for women. Since the 1960s, for example, our rate of heart disease, the most notorious of stress-related illnesses, has *decreased* rather than increased, even though our numbers in the paid labor force are higher than ever.

In a small Massachusetts town called Framingham, nearly half the population has been involved for decades in one of the most unique ongoing heart studies in the country. A group of midlife women were followed for a period of ten years to observe the health effects of working. The study found that women who had worked outside their homes for more than half their adult lives were *not* significantly more likely to develop heart disease than women who worked inside the home. The report went further. If any vulnerability to stress in the workplace does exist for midlife women, it appears to lie not in working itself but rather in the *kinds* of work women do. The clerical and sales worker was found to be subject to the most stress of all midlife women working outside the home—not the professional white-collar or even blue-collar worker who might have greater relative freedom of movement or responsibility. The clerical worker who also had children at home was the most likely of all to develop a stress-related problem. Juggling job, housekeeping, the mothering responsibilities more often than not remains the woman's problem alone rather than one shared with a partner, an employer, or policymaker. Our country's criminal negligence in the area of child care leaves the working mother doing double duty—and probably overtime—to make sure bills are paid and food is on the table.

Amazingly, with all these pressures, employed women in general are still more likely to report their health as excellent or good. Women who are exclusively homemakers, on the other hand, seem to experience more chronic illnesses like allergies, asthma, ulcers, and diabetes. All of the evidence so far says we're getting better as our spheres of activity and self-determination enlarge.

According to several important studies, there has also been an unprecedented increase over the last thirty years in the psychological well-being of midlife women. In 1975 the National Center for Health Statistics reported extraordinary improvements in the mental health of women over forty, compared with an earlier study in 1960. In another example, the Midtown Manhattan Study of midlife women in New York back in the 1950s reported over 20 percent as "psychologically impaired." Remarkably, the same research repeated twenty years later in the 1970s found only 8 percent with psychological difficulties. (During this same time, the mental health problems of men remained unchanged at 9 percent.)

This is good news! Previously, serious depression was considered to be part and parcel of women's growing older. Now this frightening specter is lifting. Of course, some midlife women still experience depression, as women may at any time of life. We spoke about this with therapist Randi Gunther, a woman in her forties who also sees many women of our age in her practice. Dr. Gunther believes that depression in midlife occurs when a woman begins to feel acutely the *limits* in her life, especially in regard to the traditional roles. We may feel an important sense of satisfaction and mastery in the private realm of motherhood and marriage, she explained, "but there's so much of us left over after what the expectation is that women don't know where to go with who they are."

Abiding by what she thought was her part in the social contract, the woman who has chosen the traditional route exclusively is apt to experience a great deal of difficulty when her children leave home, or when her marriage is no longer intact—or both. A woman who has singlemindedly devoted herself to mothering, for example, is more likely to feel deeply bereft at the departure of her children during midlife—left with what, regrettably, has been called "the empty nest." With her life's sole anchor gone, this woman may feel completely adrift, without direction. Rather than experiencing this transition positively, with the important task of nurturing completed and the possibility emerging of new, more mature relationships with her children, family and friends, she feels at a dead end, with no confidence that she can begin to define her future. At any age, what the traditional homemaker may share with the clerical working mother is the heightened vulnerability that comes from a lack of power or from the hurtful limits of their assigned roles.

> *It's not responsibility that kills, it's the lack of control. The driver isn't under as much pressure as the passengers.*
>
> –ESTELLE RAMEY, M.D., Professor of Physiology and Biophysics, Georgetown University Medical School

Everything is telling us that breaking the boundaries of these old limits, when possible, and taking charge of our lives is in our best interest. As one role contracts, another may expand. And the new risks bring with them new rewards, giving us a strong degree of protection against the myths of aging that have assigned impossible, unsatisfying scripts to mature women and—ultimately—to mature men as well.

Ours is the first generation of women to be better prepared for midlife. Our consciousness about ourselves is changing. We've got the numbers, the health, and the knowledge to make us better able to meet whatever difficulties this phase may bring. We're in a stronger position than ever to seize its many opportunities as well—daring to fail, daring to excel. Our actions, like stones tossed into a pond, will ripple to every inlet of society. As we shape our own futures, positively, so do we help to transform the experience that is midlife.

Movie Love

Complete Reviews 1988–1991

Pauline Kael

Pauline Kael (1919–   ) was born in Petaluma, California, and attended the University of California at Berkeley, 1936–40. She has reviewed movies for fifty years, half of that time writing for The New Yorker *(1968–91). Her reviews have been collected into several volumes,* I Lost It at the Movies *being the first (1965). Kael says movies are "our national theater." She has been praised for "her unique grasp of movies both as business and as social institutions." Writing in the* Library Journal, *Gary Corey observes, "Kael's reviews are a total turn-on. . . . She allows us to share her excitement and confusion in coming to terms with the movies; and she not only makes us defend our opinions and sharpen our perceptions, she also deepens our enthusiasm."*

Gorillas in the Mist

As the anthropologist Dian Fossey, in *Gorillas in the Mist,* Sigourney Weaver storms into a large hotel restaurant in central Africa, stalks the length of the room, delivers a strident tongue-lashing to a Dutch zoo broker who's having lunch with his friends, and, cursing loudly, makes her exit—all the while carrying a good-sized baby gorilla in her arms, holding it tenderly, with awe. Weaver's physical strength alone is inspiring in this movie, and there's a new freedom in her acting. She's so vivid that you immediately feel Dian Fossey's will and drive. Weaver's Dian is ecstatic when she steps off the plane in Africa, and she's enraptured when she's perched high up on a mountain, crouched down opposite a giant gorilla, mimicking his language and gestures from the inside—trying to think the way he does. Weaver is something to see. What happens between her and the animals is really happening (or, at least, appears to be), and there's joy in it. It makes everything else—all the acted-out passion and heroism and melodrama of Dian Fossey's eighteen years on her mountain—seem tired.

Partly, the picture is disappointing because it's overscaled at the start. When Dian enters a huge, crowded lecture hall in Louisville, Kentucky, in 1966, where Dr. Louis Leakey (Iain Cuthbertson) is saying that there are two big adventures left—space and who we are and what made us that way—we're prepared for a whopping epic. *Gorillas* doesn't fulfill the promise of that opening: we never see Dian learn much of anything about primates or about our origins. Instead, we see her arrive in Africa, form an emotional attachment to a gorilla family, and cut herself off more and more from people, until she's a fiercely maternal harridan who can't work with anyone. By then, Weaver's jaw juts out stubbornly; in her mania, Dian becomes apelike. Yet when she thinks of happy times with her favorites, her face is transformed. She blooms. Weaver acts the way she's built—she's monumental.

The director, Michael Apted, and the screenwriter, Anna Hamilton Phelan, want us, I think, to see the movie as a triumphant woman-and-gorillas love story. They probably want us to be inspired by Dian Fossey as an activist heroine—a woman who made a difference. (A title at the close tells us that she saved the mountain gorillas from extinction.) But they didn't find a way to fit this inspirational idea into their account of Dian Fossey's becoming convinced that she was the only one who knew how to protect the gorillas, and operating like a half-crazed terrorist. (In her later years, she probably damaged her cause.)

The movie is quite watchable; it's never sluggish or outright stupid. And it has its high romantic moment—the time a tough old silverback gorilla puts his hand in Dian's hand. A photographer (Bryan Brown) sent out by *National Geographic,* which is also financing her work, gets the pictures. (Shortly afterward, Dian and the photograher make love.) There's an authentic piece of drama, too, even if it's somewhat muffled: The photographer works out a plan whereby he and Dian can spend six months a year at her station in Rwanda and six months in other places—he on assignment, she doing primate research—and she refuses and sends him packing. It isn't research she cares about; it's her gorilla family. After he has left, she huddles among the gorillas, in the rain.

Yet the movie seems to belong to the past of movies rather than to the modern era. When Dian arrives in the Congo, she spends six weeks tracking gorillas, and then, when she and her head tracker, Sembagare (John Omirah Miluwi), see them for the first time, the cinematographer, John Seale, comes up with the glorious gorillas-in-the-mist vision that's called for. But before you can suck in your breath, music is poured on, signifying lyrical exaltation. (The credit reads "Original music by Maurice Jarre." Hah!) When civil war erupts in the Congo, and Dian argues with the soldiers who are telling her to get out of the country, we're given a dose of agitation music. Miluwi, who's actually a climber and part of the Mt. Kenya rescue team, gives an affecting, quiet performance, but he's used as a symbolic dignified, loyal native who knows right from wrong. And when Dian sets up camp on the other side of the border, in Rwanda, there are cuts to the tracker's worried reactions whenever she displays her ruthlessness—terrifying a Batwa Pygmy child to get information from him, or setting fire to the Pygmy poachers' huts. These shots are like inserts that have been recycled from a forties epic. Despite its subject, the movie can't be taken seriously. It's a feminist version of King Kong—now it's the gorillas who do the screaming.

October 17, 1988

Working Girl

The first ten minutes of Mike Nichols' *Working Girl* are laid in very deftly, preparing us for a bouncy, updated version of the Cinderella comedies that Ginger Rogers made in the thirties between her musicals with Fred Astaire. Tess McGill (Melanie Griffith), a poor but enterprising girl from Staten Island, fights off the sleazoid bosses and struggles to break through the educational-background barriers and climb from Wall Street secretary to executive. But the Cinderella feeling must all still be in Nichols' head; the emotion has been relegated to an idea, and a rather grim idea, at that. We're supposed to be cheered by watching Tess become part of the establishment: she makes it into the world of mergers and acquisitions. Her victory is certified when she's ensconced in a cubicle high up in a skyscraper; on the soundtrack, Carly Simon and a women's choir sing exultantly. No, there's no irony—only fatuity.

Lest we get the wrong idea, the picture makes it clear that the victory is only for a sweet, feminine girl like Tess—not for anybody forceful or butch. The villain is Tess's sneaky, upper-crust boss, played by Sigourney Weaver: she doesn't just try to steal Tess's big, career-making radio-network idea; she's also unwomanly. At first, Weaver is a confident, entertaining cartoon of moneyed egomania; she's a genuinely game actress, eager to be funny. But then the picture demeans her, by making her a ludicrous witch who can't hang on to her guy or her job. (It even demeans her in small, gross ways: when she's in the hospital, doctors try to look under her nightie.) Weaver looks stranded in the last part of the movie. The director seems to have abdicated, and the staging is so broad you can't tell whether satire is intended or just dumb jokes; even with sharp editing, nothing has any edge.

Is this really the work of the Mike Nichols who is said to be a miracle man with actors? Tall, skinny-legged Melanie Griffith is warm and, yes, down to earth and very appealing, and she has funny bits all the way through. She carries what there is of the picture. But her funky (and infinitely preferable) performances in De Palma's *Body Double* and Jonathan Demme's *Something Wild* are the skeletons rattling in this picture's closet. The subtext of *Working Girl* is that Mike Nichols is trying to let a little bit of tackiness into a big-budget movie—a little bit of John Waters and *Something Wild*. It must have been the funky Melanie that this picture with its double-entendre title was meant to be about. But Nichols may be afraid of swinging the door open, and so Melanie Griffith is ostensibly used for "vulnerability." This is the kind of star performance in which the heroine's misty eyes and soft-focus smiles are supposed to turn our brains to jelly. Since Tess keeps beating her head against a wall trying to succeed, it wouldn't be inappropriate for her to look bleary and depressed. But the moviemakers try to conceal Griffith's being out of condition. The camera goes lyrical; it babies her, making her a cuddlebug, and showing us her firm, round haunches while pretending it isn't doing what it's doing. (One of the things it's doing is catching her in black garter belts, push-up bra, and bikini panties; there's even a peeky porno tease when she bustles about cleaning Weaver's house while wearing undies.) As the investment-banker hero, Harrison Ford tries for the casualness of a big-time smoothie, and he has some style, but, whether because of what he's attempting or because of the director's listlessness, the film's pacing slackens just when he appears. Ford does manage to be diverting in moments that have nothing to do with the tinny plot: a scene where Tess has passed out and he makes small talk in her direction, and, later, a scene when he gets a food delivery at the door and goes back to Tess in bed, whistling "If I Only Had a Brain." (He suggests a man who keeps himself amused.)

The picture does better by some of the players in minor roles: Joan Cusack (of the euphoric grin) as Tess's happy, rowdy best friend; Kevin Spacey as a coke-snorting arbitrageur who's an irrepressible lech; and Nora Dunn as the office suckup and priss. But Nichols must have a cummerbund around his head: the directing is constricted—there's no visual inventiveness or spontaneity. And in his hands the script (by Kevin Wade) has no conviction: the lines have a lot of surprise, but the situations (and digressions) are moldy. After Tess gives up her tattooed Staten Island boyfriend (Alec Baldwin), she returns and has more scenes with him—as if the tattoos hadn't already told us everything. When Tess and her investment man get overheated by a deal they've got going, and rush from a business meeting to their big sex scene, the movie pokes only the mildest fun at them. The plot hinges on Tess's making an impression on a fatherly tycoon (Philip Bosco), who materializes out of an earlier era of movies; this dear old geezer sees that justice is meted out to everyone. Yet the way the wedding of the tycoon's daughter is set up suggests that he lives among twerps and has spawned a bumpkin. There's a classic piece of inept plotting: the last-minute introduction of a disk jockey who's the linchpin of the network deal. It's as if somebody ran onto the stage waving a telegram just as the curtain came down on his head.

This Cinderella story seems to have been concocted by people at the top of the skyscraper who have no fellow-feeling for losers. The film makes the point that Tess, like the other working-class secretaries, tries to get attention and does exactly the wrong thing: she puts on so much makeup she looks like a brainless bimbo, and then she wonders why the Ivy League graduates get jobs over her. The secretaries wear their hair scooped up high in front and hanging down around their shoulders, and it's all teased and whipped and snarled. Another director might have shown us how pretty they are in their purple and green and blue eyeshadow and dishevelled Marie-Antoinette hairdos, but Nichols has them looking like procuresses. The discrimination against them should be by the blind Ivy League bosses; here it's by the blind director.

January 9, 1989

Miss Firecracker

The playwright Beth Henley is a fey, witty observer, with a knack for impish parody. But her themes are sometimes poetic—she wants us to feel exalted—and she's not a poet. She doesn't transform her material; the transformation process goes no further than turning everything into slightly fermented local color. Set in Yazoo City, Mississippi, *Miss Firecracker*—she adapted it from her 1984 play, *The Miss Firecracker Contest*—is a farce about Southern eccentrics that's at the same time (and here's the death knell) a loving tribute to the indomitability of screwed-up, lonely dreamers.

Holly Hunter is the waif Carnelle, who was orphaned at eight and raised with her classier cousins Elain (Mary Steenburgen) and Delmount (Tim Robbins). After tall, willowy Elain married a wealthy Atlanta businessman and Delmount went away, Carnelle stayed on alone in the big, decaying family mansion. Yazoo City isn't rich in opportunities for Carnelle; she works the gutsucker machine on the assembly line of a catfish-packing plant. She has just one rhapsodic memory: it's of the time, back in 1972, when she watched the triumphal big parade featuring her idol Elain, who had won the Fourth of July beauty pageant—the Miss Firecracker Contest. Carnelle isn't considered much to look at, and her effort to gain acceptance by hopping into bed with local boys has already got her the title Miss Hot Tamale, but she thinks that if she can just win this year's contest (it's the last year she'll be eligible) she'll be respected, and she'll be able to leave town "in a blaze of glory." The movie is about what Carnelle goes through for the chance of winning (and, yes, how she discovers true values).

The contest is a rambunctious "This Is Your Life" freak show. The patrician Elain returns home; she's been asked to deliver the keynote speech. Delmount, a dilettantish aspiring poet-philosopher, has just been released from the asylum that Elain had him committed to; he comes back to try to sell the tumbledown house. And he is soon charmed by Popeye (Alfre Woodard), the black seamstress who's working on the shiny outfit for Carnelle to wear in the talent competition. (To the tune of "The Star-Spangled Banner," Carnelle marches, tap-dances, does cartwheels, and twirls a red-white-and-blue wooden rifle—all pretty much simultaneously.)

Thomas Schlamme, directing his first feature, has tried for vividness, and it should be acknowledged that the movie is never plain boring. But its comic pathos and Southern-gothic cuteness can grate on you. Almost everything to do with Carnelle's dream is like some quaint form of torture—it's as if somebody behind you were whacking you on the head and saying "Isn't this priceless?" in one ear and "Doesn't this girl have gumption!" in the other. Henley overindividualizes the characters; you get the feeling that a whole summertime seminar of creative-writing students has gone to work on each one of them, punching them up. Then Schlamme directs the actors to brighten them up even more. Holly Hunter initiated the role of Carnelle on the stage, and she gives it a determinedly virtuosic stage performance; she cries and smiles almost as much as Luise Rainer did, and Rainer wasn't feisty. Schlamme compounds this folly with closeups of Hunter acting full tilt. Probably from the best of motives—admiration of Hunter's talent—he force-feeds us Carnelle's desperation, her courage, and her heartbreaking pint-size gallantry. So it's just about impossible to laugh at her.

But even if he didn't—even if he brought the emotions down a few shades—the material still might not work, because there is something off in Henley's technique. In some aberrant way (which can work on the stage), her writing is all exposition; everything is told to us, and it all feels like anecdotes that are already set from previous tellings—that are finished. Henley is too meticulous a student of playwriting: she positions all the skeletons in the funky closets and prepares us for each thing that happens—Carnelle and Elain enter amid a flutter of briefing papers.

Mary Steenburgen, with her calm, deliberate way of talking, isn't bad. At first, she seems to be overdoing Elain's flower-of-Southern-womanhood diction and her self-adoring meanness, but then, as the picture goes on, Elain's twanging pseudo graciousness becomes more effective. You listen to the elegant trickiness of the line readings; since Elain the coquette is a false identity that was confirmed when she won the Miss Firecracker contest, Steenburgen is probably justified in keeping us aware of the gears grinding. (But Elain could have been made funnier; we don't need to see that the actress "understands" the character.) Some of the other performers provide texture in the background: Ann Wedgeworth and Trey Wilson as the contest officials who sing during the swimsuit competition; Angela Turner as the blond contestant who delivers the Scarlett O'Hara "As God is my witness!" monologue.

But the only element that really makes the movie worth seeing is Tim Robbins' droll, courtly Delmount. When I first saw Robbins in a starring role, he was playing the prim civil-rights worker in *Five Corners;* he was good, all right, but I thought it was a case of sensational casting—I didn't see how he could play anything else. I assumed that the stiffness and the idealist's bulging, bumpy forehead and the squinched-up pug face were the only way he could look. Then, as the flirty, baby-faced rookie pitcher in *Bull Durham,* he showed that he could use his six-foot-four frame for slapstick. And as the "video visionary" in (the generally negligible) *Tapeheads* he had an agreeable loose humor. (When he and John Cusack danced together on a roof, the scene recalled the relaxed teamwork of the Laurel and Hardy dances.) But Robbins' Delmount suggests that he could be a major actor.

He has the gift of looking just right for each of his roles, and he has a puckish commanding presence here (though Delmount can't command, because he's a creature of impulses: he never thinks anything out). The role is a baroque contraption, and that's what Henley is good at; she has a wonderfully silly talent—Delmount even suffers from gothic nightmares. Robbins gives the movie some richness; he gives it scenes that flow, that spill over. He uses his full height here, and his sweaty hair, curling from the humidity, provides him with an aureole. Delmount, the misfit prince with a dinky ponytail, has Southern grace and formality along with a wild, infantile sense of fun. When he's quarrelling with his sister Elain—and especially when they swing into a ballroom dance—they have a tingling love-hate intimacy, something voluptuous that they take for granted. As Elain, Steenburgen plays off Robbins with a cool, lofty satisfaction; they're marvellous together. Delmount is completely different in his lovestruck scenes with Alfre Woodard's Popeye: grinning and boyish, he's her heartthrob. The two of them are so nuttily harmonious they're like Shakespearean clown-lovers, or Papageno and Papagena—they're spellbound. I wouldn't have guessed that Woodard (who has played so many put-upon, suffering women) had this kind of lightness in her. The role is a caricature, but so, of course, are most of the other roles (underneath their awful rounding). What makes Woodard's Popeye stand out is that, with a black actress playing the part (it was written in the play as white), Popeye becomes a black caricature. There's naughtiness in the performance: Woodard's rapt gaze evokes memories of Butterfly McQueen at her dizziest.

Tim Robbins brings some comic poetry into the movie. When Delmount is bawling himself out for his own pretentiousness, or watching the pageant and sucking on a little pipe, he makes you feel that behind his sneaky, demon eyes he's thinking thoughts no character in a movie has ever thought before. And he's stimulated by them.

May 29, 1989

The Little Mermaid

Hans Christian Andersen's tear-stained *The Little Mermaid* is peerlessly mythic. It's the closest thing women have to a feminine Faust story. The Little Mermaid gives up her lovely voice—her means of expression—in exchange for legs, so she'll be able to walk on land and attract the man she loves. If she can win him in marriage, she will gain an immortal soul; if she can't, she'll be foam on the sea.

I didn't expect the new Disney *The Little Mermaid* to be Faust, but after reading the reviews ("everything an animated feature should be," "reclaims the movie house as a dream palace," and so on) I expected to see something more than a bland reworking of old Disney fairy tales, featuring a teen-age tootsie in a flirty seashell bra. This is a technologically sophisticated cartoon with just about all the simpering old Disney values in place. (The Faust theme acquires a wholesome family sub-theme.) The film does have a cheerful calypso number ("Under the Sea"), and the color is bright—at least, until the mermaid goes on land, when everything seems to dull out.

Are we trying to put kids into some sort of moral-aesthetic safe house? Parents seem desperate for harmless family entertainment. Probably they don't mind this movie's being vapid, because the whole family can share it, and no one is offended. We're caught in a culture warp. Our children are flushed with pleasure when we read them *Where the Wild Things Are* or Roald Dahl's sinister stories. Kids are ecstatic watching videos of *The Secret of NIMH* and *The Dark Crystal.* Yet here comes the press telling us that *The Little Mermaid* is "due for immortality." People are made to feel that this stale pastry is what they should be taking their kids to, that it's art for children. And when they see the movie they may believe it, because this *Mermaid* is just a slightly updated version of what their parents took them to. They've been imprinted with Disney-style kitsch.

December 11, 1989

Postcards from the Edge

Meryl Streep just about always seems miscast. (She makes a career out of seeming to overcome being miscast.) In *Postcards from the Edge,* she's witty and resourceful, yet every expression is eerily off, not quite human. When she sings in a country-and-Western style, she's note-perfect, but it's like a diva singing jazz—you don't believe it. Streep has a genius for mimicry: she's imitating a country-and-Western singer singing. These were my musings to a friend, who put it more simply: "She's an android." Yes, and it's Streep's android quality that gives *Postcards* whatever interest it has.

This tale of a sorrowful, wisecracking starlet whose brassy, boozing former-star mother (Shirley MacLaine) started her on sleeping pills when she was nine is camp without the zest of camp. It's camp played borderline straight—a druggy-Cinderella movie about an unformed girl who has to go past despair to find herself. The director, Mike Nichols, is a parodist who feigns sincerity, and his tone keeps slipping around. What's clear is that we're meant to adore the daughter, who is wounded by her mother's cheap competitiveness. Nichols wants us to be entralled by the daughter's radiant face, her refinement, her honesty. He keeps the camera on Streep as if to prove that he can make her a popular big star—a new Crawford or Bette Davis. (She remains distant, emotionally atonal.)

When the novel that the movie is based on—Carrie Fisher's semi-autobiographical account of her life as drug-addicted Hollywood royalty—was published, in 1987, Fisher told the *Times* that she hadn't wanted to write the kind of book about star parents (hers are Debbie Reynolds and Eddie Fisher) that makes the child a victim. And she didn't play that game. But it's the game the movie plays. The script (which Carrie Fisher wrote, with Nichols' uncredited collaboration) has some funny, barbed lines, but, like everything else in the movie, they're shaped to show the daughter's self-deprecating courage and her superiority to the people she lives among. Streep's Suzanne Vale is a noble victim. She's also a talented singer, in contrast with her musical-comedy-star mother, who belts out Stephen Sondheim's "I'm Still Here" Vegas style, without a trace of musicality. Nichols directs Shirley MacLaine to overdo the mother's self-preoccupation; it's a blast-off performance—she's playing the stale essence of old show biz. Yet MacLaine has a reality that Streep doesn't have. The cartoon mother is meant to make a gut connection with the audience.

The tacky, bright-colored movie is watchable in the same way that Nichols' last film, *Working Girl,* was. Once again, there are a lot of people to look at. Dennis Quaid, who plays the predatory lech that Suzanne falls for, is photographed in profile, so that he seems to be nothing but a big nose. He gives a forced, overwrought performance, and his core speech in which he reveals what a pig he is, is played off Streep's sensitive face. The virtuous characters are just as extreme: Richard Dreyfuss is pure niceness as the doctor who courts Suzanne, and Gene Hackman is a stern but fair movie director—a man of weight and authority who serves as a father figure to her. Hackman manages to give his lines a personal rhythm—he makes his scenes halfway credible.

Two women in the cast draw the audience to them: Robin Bartlett, as Suzanne's roommate in a drug-rehab program, and the striking Annette Bening, in the role of an actress who has been cast as a lowdown hooker. (For a few seconds, Bening is so alive she seems to run off with *Postcards.*) Streep does well with the ballad made famous by Ray Charles, "You Don't Know Me," and she does one tiny thing that gives you pleasure: in a slapstick routine, she hangs on to a ledge at the top of a tall building and lifts her hands in a lovely shrug.

The camp intensity that Nichols gives this new-fangled, near-plotless version of a woman's picture is what makes it play. (It's this confident showiness that made *Working Girl* play better than his earlier *Heartburn.*) You see how many obstacles Suzanne faces, and you watch her (like the Working Girl) overcoming them. Nichols loads the scenes with banal revelations—"insights." The mother is seen as competing with the daughter, but the daughter is never seen as competing with the mother. *Postcards* is like *Mildred Pierce* told from Ann Blyth's point of view. It's also a variation of *Now, Voyager:* Suzanne Vale is first cousin to Bette Davis's Charlotte Vale, who escapes her repressive mother by going to a rest home. In the new therapeutic terrain, the ditzy mother and the smart-ass daughter get to know themselves (and each other) better. They're both troupers, and when the detoxified daughter hits the comeback trail the mother cheers for her. The movie reneges on everything it has said it was about, and it even provides the heroine with a fine, upstanding man waiting in the wings. Nichols doesn't go all the way with camp except in a hospital scene where the mother is shorn of her wig and photographed mercilessly without makeup; for a minute, Nichols tops the humiliation scene in *Mr. Skeffington* (when pieces of Bette Davis's curly coiffure fall on the dance floor). Even here Nichols is slippery. The scene is presented as sympathy for the shrivelled old lady, and admiration of her tough spirit.

There's a deep jadedness in this picture (and in *Working Girl*) that can pass for sophistication. Nichols appeals to the narcissism of show-biz insiders and to the would-be insider in the rest of us. The assumption of *Postcards* is the assumption of the tabloids: that all any of us really want is to be movie stars, and we despise the ordinary Joes who aren't rich. The movie brings out the part of us that feels bitchily superior to our own lives. If Nichols were up front about what he was doing, we might enjoy his pissing on the rnings of squares, but *Postcards* is jadedness pretending warm goodwill. There's an element of the gracious host in Nichols: he keeps retreating into taste.

The key scene is the Hollywood party where Shirley MacLaine's hairless old trouper in her red wig barks "I'm Still Here" and flashes her undies. The party guests love her style, and even the daughter, watching her, marvels. Nichols is saying, "You may be appalled, but the whole culture loves this stuff, and maybe I do, too." At the end, he's got Streep belting. Glamour and contempt are all mixed up in Nichols' work. He's acclaimed for being hip to the Zeitgeist.

October 22, 1990

Boys and Girls

Alice Munro

Alice Munro (1931–   ) was born in Ontario, Canada, and received her bachelor's degree from the University of Western Ontario. She writes about female characters and their quest for recognition and autonomy. Reviewers have noted that "her voice is unmistakably Ontarian in its lack of emphasis, its sly humor, and willingness to live with a mystery." Of Munro's style, Joyce Carol Oates says, "We know we are in the presence of an art that works to conceal itself, in order to celebrate its subject." The following selection is from Dance of the Happy Shades, *which won the Governor General's Award for Fiction in 1968.*

MY FATHER WAS A FOX FARMER. THAT IS, HE RAISED silver foxes, in pens; and in the fall and early winter, when their fur was prime, he killed them and skinned them and sold their pelts to the Hudson's Bay Company or the Montreal Fur Traders. These companies supplied us with heroic calendars to hang, one on each side of the kitchen door. Against a background of cold blue sky and black pine forests and treacherous northern rivers, plumed adventurers planted the flags of England or of France; magnificent savages bent their backs to the portage.

For several weeks before Christmas, my father worked after supper in the cellar of our house. The cellar was whitewashed, and lit by a hundred-watt bulb over the worktable. My brother Laird and I sat on the top step and watched. My father removed the pelt inside-out from the body of the fox, which looked surprisingly small, mean and rat-like, deprived of its arrogant weight of fur. The naked, slippery bodies were collected in a sack and buried at the dump. One time the hired man, Henry Bailey, had taken a swipe at me with this sack, saying, "Christmas present!" My mother thought that was not funny. In fact she disliked the whole pelting operation—that was what the killing, skinning, and preparation of the furs was called—and wished it did not have to take place in the house. There was the smell. After the pelt had been stretched inside-out on a long board my father scraped away delicately, removing the little clotted webs of blood vessels, the bubbles of fat; the smell of blood and animal fat, with the strong primitive odor of the fox itself, penetrated all parts of the house. I found it reassuringly seasonal, like the smell of oranges and pine needles.

Henry Bailey suffered from bronchial troubles. He would cough and cough until his narrow face turned scarlet, and his light blue, derisive eyes filled up with tears; then he took the lid off the stove, and, standing well back, shot out a great clot of phlegm—hsss—straight into the heart of the flames. We admired him for this performance and for his ability to make his stomach growl at will, and for his laughter, which was full of high whistlings and gurglings and involved the whole faulty machinery of his chest. It was sometimes hard to tell what he was laughing at, and always possible that it might be us.

After we had been sent to bed we could still smell fox and still hear Henry's laugh, but these things, reminders of the warm, safe, brightly lit downstairs world, seemed lost and diminished, floating on the stale cold air upstairs. We were afraid at night in the winter. We were not afraid of *outside* though this was the time of year when snowdrifts curled around our house like sleeping whales and the wind harassed us all night, coming up from the buried fields, the frozen swamp, with its old bugbear chorus of threats and misery. We were afraid of *inside,* the room where we slept. At this time the upstairs of our house was not finished. A brick chimney went up one wall. In the middle of the floor was a square hole, with a wooden railing around it; that was where the stairs came up. On the other side of the stairwell were the things that nobody had any use for any more—a soldiery roll of linoleum, standing on end, a wicker baby carriage, a fern basket, china jugs and basins with cracks in them, a picture of the Battle of Balaclava, very sad to look at. I had told Laird, as soon as he was old enough to understand such things, that bats and skeletons lived over there; whenever a man escaped from the county jail, twenty miles away, I imagined that he had somehow let himself in the window and was hiding behind the linoleum. But we had rules to keep us safe. When the light was on, we were safe as long as we did not step off the square of worn carpet which defined our bedroom-space; when the light was off no place was safe but the beds themselves. I had to turn out the light kneeling on the end of my bed, and stretching as far as I could to reach the cord.

In the dark we lay on our beds, our narrow life rafts, and fixed our eyes on the faint light coming up the stairwell, and sang songs. Laird sang "Jingle Bells," which he would sing any time, whether it was Christmas or not, and I sang "Danny Boy." I loved the sound of my own voice, frail and supplicating, rising in the dark. We could make out the tall frosted shapes of the windows now, gloomy and white. When I came to the part, *When I am dead, as dead I well may be*—a fit of shivering caused not by the cold sheets but by pleasurable emotion almost silenced me. *You'll kneel and say, an Ave there above me*—What was an Ave? Every day I forgot to find out.

Laird went straight from singing to sleep. I could hear his long, satisfied, bubbly breaths. Now for the time that remained to me, the most perfectly private and perhaps the best time of the whole day, I arranged myself tightly under the covers and went on with one of the stories I was telling myself from night to night. These stories were about myself, when I had grown a little older; they took place in a world that was recognizably mine, yet one that presented opportunities for courage, boldness and self-sacrifice, as mine never did. I rescued people from a bombed building (it discouraged me that the real war had gone on so far away from Jubilee). I shot two rabid wolves who were menacing the schoolyard (the teachers cowered terrified at my back). I rode a fine horse spiritedly down the main street of Jubilee, acknowledging the townspeople's gratitude for some yet-to-be-worked-out piece of heroism (nobody ever rode a horse there, except King Billy in the Orangemen's Day parade). There was always riding and shooting in these stories, though I had only been on a horse twice—bareback because we did not own a saddle—and the second time I had slid right around and dropped under the horse's feet; it had stepped placidly over me. I really was learning to shoot, but I could not hit anything yet, not even tin cans on fence posts.

Alive, the foxes inhabited a world my father made for them. It was surrounded by a high guard fence, like a medieval town, with a gate that was padlocked at night. Along the streets of this town were ranged large, sturdy pens. Each of them had a real door that a man could go through, a wooden ramp along the wire, for the foxes to run up and down on, and a kennel—something like a clothes chest with airholes—where they slept and stayed in winter and had their young. There were feeding and watering dishes attached to the wire in such a way that they could be emptied and cleaned from the outside. The dishes were made of old tin cans, and the ramps and kennels of odds and ends of old lumber. Everything was tidy and ingenious; my father was tirelessly inventive and his favorite book in the world was Robinson Crusoe. He had fitted a tin drum on a wheelbarrow, for bringing water down to the pens. This was my job in summer, when the foxes had to have water twice a day. Between nine and ten o'clock in the morning, and again after supper, I filled the drum at the pump and trundled it down through the barnyard to the pens, where I parked it, and filled my watering can and went along the streets. Laird came too, with his little cream and green gardening can, filled too full and knocking against his legs and slopping water on his canvas shoes. I had the real watering can, my father's, though I could only carry it three-quarters full.

The foxes all had names, which were printed on a tin plate and hung beside their doors. They were not named when they were born, but when they survived the first year's pelting and were added to the breeding stock. Those my father had named were called names like Prince, Bob, Wally and Betty. Those I had named were called Star or Turk, or Maureen or Diana. Laird named one Maud after a hired girl we had when he was little, one Harold after a boy at school, and one Mexico, he did not say why.

Naming them did not make pets out of them, or anything like it. Nobody but my father ever went into the pens, and he had twice had blood-poisoning from bites. When I was bringing them their water they prowled up and down on the paths they had made inside their pens, barking seldom—they saved that for nighttime, when they might get up a chorus of community frenzy—but always watching me, their eyes burning, clear gold, in their pointed, malevolent faces. They were beautiful for their delicate legs and heavy, aristocratic tails and the bright fur sprinkled on dark down their backs—which gave them their name—but especially for their faces, drawn exquisitely sharp in pure hostility, and their golden eyes.

Besides carrying water I helped my father when he cut the long grass, and the lamb's quarter and flowering money-musk, that grew between the pens. He cut with the scythe and I raked into piles. Then he took a pitchfork and threw fresh-cut grass all over the top of the pens, to keep the foxes cooler and shade their coats, which were browned by too much sun. My father did not talk to me unless it was about the job we were doing. In this he was quite different from my mother, who, if she was feeling cheerful, would tell me all sorts of things—the name of a dog she had had when she was a little girl, the name of boys she had gone out with later on when she was grown up, and what certain dresses of hers had looked like—she could not imagine now what had become of them. Whatever thoughts and stories my father had were private, and I was shy of him and would never ask him questions. Nevertheless I worked willingly under his eyes, and with a feeling of pride. One time a feed salesman came down into the pens to talk to him and my father said, "Like to have you meet my new hired man." I turned away and raked furiously, red in the face with pleasure.

"Could of fooled me," said the salesman. "I thought it was only a girl."

After the grass was cut, it seemed suddenly much later in the year. I walked on stubble in the earlier evening, aware of the reddening skies, the entering silences, of fall. When I wheeled the tank out of the gate and put the padlock on, it was almost dark. One night at this time I saw my mother and father standing talking on the little rise of ground we called the gangway, in front of the barn. My father had just come from the meathouse; he had his stiff bloody apron on, and a pail of cut-up meat in his hand.

It was an odd thing to see my mother down at the barn. She did not often come out of the house unless it was to do something—hang out the wash or dig potatoes in the garden. She looked out of place, with her bare lumpy legs, not touched by the sun, her apron still on and damp across the stomach from the supper dishes. Her hair was tied up in a kerchief, wisps of it falling out. She would tie her hair up like this in the morning, saying she did not have time to do it properly, and it would stay tied up all day. It was true, too; she really did not have time. These days our back porch was piled with baskets of peaches and grapes and pears, bought in town, and onions and tomatoes and cucumbers grown at home, all waiting to be made into jelly and jam and preserves, pickles and chili sauce. In the kitchen there was a fire in the stove all day, jars clinked in boiling water, sometimes a cheesecloth bag was strung on a pole between two chairs straining blue-black grape pulp for jelly. I was given jobs to do and I would sit at the table peeling peaches that had been soaked in the hot water, or cutting up onions, my eyes smarting and streaming. As soon as I was done I ran out of the house, trying to get out of earshot before my mother thought of what she wanted me to do next. I hated the hot dark kitchen in summer, the green blinds and the flypapers, the same old oilcloth table and wavy mirror and bumpy linoleum. My mother was too tired and preoccupied to talk to me, she had no heart to tell about the Normal School Graduation Dance; sweat trickled over her face and she was always counting under her breath, pointing at jars, dumping cups of sugar. It seemed to me that work in the house was endless, dreary and peculiarly depressing; work done out of doors, and in my father's service, was ritualistically important.

I wheeled the tank up to the barn, where it was kept, and I heard my mother saying, "Wait till Laird gets a little bigger, then you'll have a real help."

What my father said I did not hear. I was pleased by the way he stood listening, politely as he would to a salesman or a stranger, but with an air of wanting to get on with his real work. I felt my mother had no business down here and I wanted him to feel the same way. What did she mean about Laird? He was no help to anybody. Where was he now? Swinging himself sick on the swing, going around in circles, or trying to catch caterpillars. He never once stayed with me till I was finished.

"And then I can use her more in the house," I heard my mother say. She had a dead-quiet, regretful way of talking about me that always made me uneasy. "I just get my back turned and she runs off. It's not like I had a girl in the family at all."

I went and sat on a feed bag in the corner of the barn, not wanting to appear when this conversation was going on. My mother, I felt, was not to be trusted. She was kinder than my father and more easily fooled, but you could not depend on her, and the real reasons for the things she said and did were not to be known. She loved me, and she sat up late at night making a dress of the difficult style I wanted, for me to wear when school started, but she was also my enemy. She was always plotting. She was plotting now to get me to stay in the house more, although she knew I hated it (*because* she knew I hated it) and keep me from working for my father. It seemed to me she would do this simply out of perversity, and to try her power. It did not occur to me that she could be lonely, or jealous. No grown-up could be; they were too fortunate. I sat and kicked my heels monotonously against a feed bag, raising dust, and did not come out till she was gone.

At any rate, I did not expect my father to pay any attention to what she said. Who could imagine Laird doing my work—Laird remembering the padlock and cleaning out the watering dishes with a leaf on the end of a stick, or even wheeling the tank without it tumbling over? It showed how little my mother knew about the way things really were.

I have forgotten to say what the foxes were fed. My father's bloody apron reminded me. They were fed horsemeat. At this time most farmers still kept horses, and when a horse got too old to work, or broke a leg or got down and would not get up, as they sometimes did, the owner would call my father, and he and Henry went out to the farm in the truck. Usually they shot and butchered the horse there, paying the farmer from five to twelve dollars. If they had already too much meat on hand, they would bring the horse back alive, and keep it for a few days or weeks in our stable, until the meat was needed. After the war the farmers were buying tractors and gradually getting rid of horses altogether, so it sometimes happened that we got a good healthy horse, that there was just no use for any more. If this happened in the winter we might keep the horse in our stable till spring, for we had plenty of hay and if there was a lot of snow—and the plow did not always get our road cleared—it was convenient to be able to go to town with a horse and cutter.

The winter I was eleven years old we had two horses in the stable. We did not know what names they had had before, so we called them Mack and Flora. Mack was an old black workhorse, sooty and indifferent. Flora was a sorrel mare, a driver. We took them both out in the cutter. Mack was slow and easy to handle. Flora was given to fits of violent alarm, veering at cars and even at other horses, but we loved her speed and high-stepping, her general air of gallantry and abandon. On Saturdays we went down to the stable and as soon as we opened the door on its cosy, animal-smelling darkness Flora threw up her head, rolled her eyes, whinnied despairingly and pulled herself through a crisis of nerves on the spot. It was not safe to go into her stall; she would kick.

This winter also I began to hear a great deal more on the theme my mother had sounded when she had been talking in front of the barn. I no longer felt safe. It seemed that in the minds of people around me there was a steady undercurrent of thought, not to be deflected, on this one subject. The word *girl* had formerly seemed to me innocent and unburdened, like the word *child;* now it appeared that it was no such thing. A girl was not, as I had supposed, simply what I was; it was what I had to become. It was a definition, always touched with emphasis, with reproach and disappointment. Also it was a joke on me. Once Laird and I were fighting, and for the first time ever I had to use all my strength against him; even so, he caught and pinned my arm for a moment, really hurting me. Henry saw this, and laughed, saying, "Oh, that there Laird's gonna show you, one of these days!" Laird was getting a lot bigger. But I was getting bigger too.

My grandmother came to stay with us for a few weeks and I heard other things. "Girls don't slam doors like that." "Girls keep their knees together when they sit down." And worse still, when I asked some questions, "That's none of girls' business." I continued to slam the doors and sit as awkwardly as possible, thinking that by such measures I kept myself free.

When spring came, the horses were let out in the barnyard. Mack stood against the barn wall trying to scratch his neck and haunches, but Flora trotted up and down and reared at the fences, clattering her hooves against the rails. Snowdrifts dwindled quickly, revealing the hard gray and brown earth, the familiar rise and fall of the ground, plain and bare after the fantastic landscape of winter. There was a great feeling of opening-out, of release. We just wore rubbers now, over our shoes; our feet felt ridiculously light. One Saturday we went out to the stable and found all the doors open, letting in the unaccustomed sunlight and fresh air. Henry was there, just idling around looking at his collection of calendars which were tacked up behind the stalls in a part of the stable my mother had probably never seen.

"Come to say goodbye to your old friend Mack?" Henry said. "Here, you give him a taste of oats." He poured some oats into Laird's cupped hands and Laird went to feed Mack. Mack's teeth were in bad shape. He ate very slowly, patiently shifting the oats around in his mouth, trying to find a stump of a molar to grind it on. "Poor old Mack," said Henry mournfully. "When a horse's teeth's gone, he's gone. That's about the way."

"Are you going to shoot him today?" I said. Mack and Flora had been in the stable so long I had almost forgotten they were going to be shot.

Henry didn't answer me. Instead he started to sing in a high, trembly, mocking-sorrowful voice, *Oh, there's no more work, for poor Uncle Ned, he's gone where the good darkies go.* Mack's thick, blackish tongue worked diligently at Laird's hand. I went out before the song was ended and sat down on the gangway.

I had never seen them shoot a horse, but I knew where it was done. Last summer Laird and I had come upon a horse's entrails before they were buried. We had thought it was a big black snake, coiled up in the sun. That was around in the field that ran up beside the barn. I thought that if we went inside the barn, and found a wide crack or a knothole to look through, we would be able to see them do it. It was not something I wanted to see; just the same, if a thing really happened, it was better to see it, and know.

My father came down from the house, carrying the gun.

"What are you doing here?" he said.

"Nothing."

"Go on up and play around the house."

He sent Laird out of the stable. I said to Laird, "Do you want to see them shoot Mack?" and without waiting for an answer led him around to the front door of the barn, opened it carefully, and went in. "Be quiet or they'll hear us," I said. We could hear Henry and my father talking in the stable, then the heavy, shuffling steps of Mack being backed out of his stall.

In the loft it was cold and dark. Thin, crisscrossed beams of sunlight fell through the cracks. The hay was low. It was a rolling country, hills and hollows, slipping under our feet. About four feet up was a beam going around the walls. We piled hay up in one corner and I boosted Laird up and hoisted myself. The beam was not very wide; we crept along it with our hands flat on the barn walls. There were plenty of knotholes, and I found one that gave me the view I wanted—a corner of the barnyard, the gate, part of the field. Laird did not have a knothole and began to complain.

I showed him a widened crack between two boards. "Be quiet and wait. If they hear you you'll get us in trouble."

My father came in sight carrying the gun. Henry was leading Mack by the halter. He dropped it and took out his cigarette papers and tobacco; he rolled cigarettes for my father and himself. While this was going on Mack nosed around in the old, dead grass along the fence. Then my father opened the gate and they took Mack through. Henry led Mack away from the path to a patch of ground and they talked together, not loud enough for us to hear. Mack again began searching for a mouthful of fresh grass, which was not to be found. My father walked away in a straight line, and stopped short at a distance which seemed to suit him. Henry was walking away from Mack too, but sideways, still negligently holding on to the halter. My father raised the gun and Mack looked up as if he had noticed something and my father shot him.

Mack did not collapse at once but swayed, lurched sideways and fell, first on his side; then he rolled over on his back and, amazingly, kicked his legs for a few seconds in the air. At this Henry laughed, as if Mack had done a trick for him. Laird, who had drawn a long, groaning breath of surprise when the shot was fired, said out loud, "He's not dead." And it seemed to me it might be true. But his legs stopped, he rolled on his side again, his muscles quivered and sank. The two men walked over and looked at him in a businesslike way; they bent down and examined his forehead where the bullet had gone in, and now I saw his blood on the brown grass.

"Now they just skin him and cut him up," I said. "Let's go." My legs were a little shaky and I jumped gratefully down into the hay. "Now you've seen how they shoot a horse," I said in a congratulatory way, as if I had seen it many times before. "Let's see if any barn cat's had kittens in the hay." Laird jumped. He seemed young and obedient again. Suddenly I remembered how, when he was little, I had brought him into the barn and told him to climb the ladder to the top beam. That was in the spring, too, when the hay was low. I had done it out of a need for excitement, a desire for something to happen so that I could tell about it. He was wearing a little bulky brown and white checked coat, made down from one of mine. He went all the way up just as I told him, and sat down on the top beam with the hay far below him on one side, and the barn floor and some old machinery on the other. Then I ran screaming to my father, "Laird's up on the top beam!" My father came, my mother came, my father went up the ladder talking very quietly and brought Laird down under his arm, at which my mother leaned against the ladder and began to cry. They said to me, "Why weren't you watching him?" but nobody ever knew the truth. Laird did not know enough to tell. But whenever I saw the brown and white checked coat hanging in the closet, or at the bottom of the rag bag, which was where it ended up, I felt a weight in my stomach, the sadness of unexorcised guilt.

I looked at Laird, who did not even remember this, and I did not like the look on his thin, winter-pale face. His expression was not frightened or upset, but remote, concentrating. "Listen," I said, in an unusually bright and friendly voice, "you aren't going to tell, are you?"

"No," he said absently.

"Promise."

"Promise," he said. I grabbed the hand behind his back to make sure he was not crossing his fingers. Even so, he might have a nightmare; it might come out that way. I decided I had better work hard to get all thoughts of what he had seen out of his mind—which, it seemed to me, could not hold very many things at a time. I got some money I had saved and that afternoon we went into Jubilee and saw a show, with Judy Canova, at which we both laughed a great deal. After that I thought it would be all right.

Two weeks later I knew they were going to shoot Flora. I knew from the night before, when I heard my mother ask if the hay was holding out all right, and my father said, "Well, after tomorrow there'll just be the cow, and we should be able to put her out to grass in another week." So I knew it was Flora's turn in the morning.

This time I didn't think of watching it. That was something to see just one time. I had not thought about it very often since, but sometimes when I was busy, working at school, or standing in front of the mirror combing my hair and wondering if I would be pretty when I grew up, the whole scene would flash into my mind: I would see the easy, practiced way my father raised the gun, and hear Henry laughing when Mack kicked his legs in the air. I did not have any great feeling of horror or opposition, such as a city child might have had; I was too used to seeing the death of animals as a necessity by which we lived. Yet I felt a little ashamed, and there was a new wariness, a sense of holding-off, in my attitude to my father and his work.

It was a fine day, and we were going around the yard picking up tree branches that had been torn off in winter storms. This was something we had been told to do and also we wanted to use them to make a teepee. We heard Flora whinny, and then my father's voice and Henry's shouting, and we ran down to the barnyard to see what was going on.

The stable door was open. Henry had just brought Flora out, and she had broken away from him. She was running free in the barnyard, from one end to the other. We climbed up on the fence. It was exciting to see her running, whinnying, going up on her hind legs, prancing and threatening like a horse in a Western movie, an unbroken ranch horse, though she was just an old driver, an old sorrel mare. My father and Henry ran after her and tried to grab the dangling halter. They tried to work her into a corner, and they had almost succeeded when she made a run between them, wild-eyed, and disappeared around the corner of the barn. We heard the rails clatter down as she got over the fence, and Henry yelled, "She's into the field now!"

That meant she was in the long L-shaped field that ran up by the house. If she got around the center, heading toward the lane, the gate was open; the truck had been driven into the field this morning. My father shouted to me, because I was on the other side of the fence, nearest the lane, "Go shut the gate!"

I could run very fast. I ran across the garden, past the tree where our swing was hung, and jumped across a ditch into the lane. There was the open gate. She had not got out, I could not see her up on the road; she must have run to the other end of the field. The gate was heavy. I lifted it out of the gravel and carried it across the roadway. I had it halfway across when she came in sight, galloping straight toward me. There was just time to get the chain on. Laird came scrambling through the ditch to help me.

Instead of shutting the gate, I opened it as wide as I could. I did not make any decision to do this, it was just what I did. Flora never slowed down; she galloped straight past me, and Laird jumped up and down, yelling, "Shut it, shut it!" even after it was too late. My father and Henry appeared in the field a moment too late to see what I had done. They only saw Flora heading for the township road. They would think I had not got there in time.

They did not waste any time asking about it. They went back to the barn and got the gun and the knives they used, and put these in the truck; then they turned the truck around and came bouncing up the field toward us. Laird called to them, "Let me go too, let me go too!" and Henry stopped the truck and they took him in. I shut the gate after they were all gone.

I supposed Laird would tell. I wondered what would happen to me. I had never disobeyed my father before, and I could not understand why I had done it. Flora would not really get away. They would catch up with her in the truck. Or if they did not catch her this morning somebody would see her and telephone us this afternoon or tomorrow. There was no wild country here for her to run to, only farms. What was more, my father had paid for her, we needed the meat to feed the foxes, we needed the foxes to make our living. All I had done was make more work for my father who worked hard enough already. And when my father found out about it he was not going to trust me any more; he would know that I was not entirely on his side. I was on Flora's side, and that made me no use to anybody, not even to her. Just the same, I did not regret it; when she came running at me and I held the gate open, that was the only thing I could do.

I went back to the house, and my mother said, "What's all the commotion?" I told her that Flora had kicked down the fence and got away. "Your poor father," she said, "now he'll have to go chasing over the countryside. Well, there isn't any use planning dinner before one." She put up the ironing board. I wanted to tell her, but thought better of it and went upstairs and sat on my bed.

Lately I had been trying to make my part of the room fancy, spreading the bed with old lace curtains, and fixing myself a dressing table with some leftovers of cretonne for a skirt. I planned to put up some kind of barricade between my bed and Laird's, to keep my section separate from his. In the sunlight, the lace curtains were just dusty rags. We did not sing at night any more. One night when I was singing Laird said, "You sound silly," and I went right on but the next night I did not start. There was not so much need to anyway, we were no longer afraid. We knew it was just old furniture over there, old jumble and confusion. We did not keep to the rules. I still stayed awake after Laird was asleep and told myself stories, but even in these stories something different was happening, mysterious alterations took place. A story might start off in the old way, with a spectacular danger, a fire or wild animals, and for a while I might rescue people; then things would change around, and instead, somebody would be rescuing me. It might be a boy from our class at school, or even Mr. Campbell, our teacher, who tickled girls under the arms. And at this point the story concerned itself at great length with what I looked like—how long my hair was, and what kind of dress I had on; by the time I had these details worked out the real excitement of the story was lost.

It was later than one o'clock when the truck came back. The tarpaulin was over the back, which meant there was meat in it. My mother had to heat dinner up all over again. Henry and my father had changed from their bloody overalls into ordinary working overalls in the barn, and they washed their arms and necks and faces at the sink, and splashed water on their hair and combed it. Laird lifted his arm to show off a streak of blood. "We shot old Flora," he said, "and cut her up in fifty pieces."

"Well I don't want to hear about it," my mother said. "And don't come to my table like that."

My father made him go and wash the blood off.

We sat down and my father said grace and Henry pasted his chewing gum on the end of his fork, the way he always did; when he took it off he would have us admire the pattern. We began to pass the bowls of steaming, overcooked vegetables. Laird looked across the table at me and said proudly, distinctly, "Anyway it was her fault Flora got away."

"What?" my father said.

"She could of shut the gate and she didn't. She just open' it up and Flora run out."

"Is that right?" my father said.

Everybody at the table was looking at me. I nodded, swallowing food with great difficulty. To my shame, tears flooded my eyes.

My father made a curt sound of disgust. "What did you do that for?"

I did not answer. I put down my fork and waited to be sent from the table, still not looking up.

But this did not happen. For some time nobody said anything, then Laird said matter-of-factly, "She's crying."

"Never mind," my father said. He spoke with resignation, even good humor, the words which absolved and dismissed me for good. "She's only a girl," he said.

I didn't protest that, even in my heart. Maybe it was true.

The Feeder

Maria Bruno

Maria Bruno (1948–   ) was born into an Italian neighborhood in Detroit, Michigan, but grew up in the suburb of Birmingham where the public school encouraged her to write. She is a graduate of Michigan State University: B.A. (1970), M.A. in creative writing (1981), and Ph.D. (1986). In the 80s, she discovered the writing of Alix Shulman, Lisa Alther, and Marge Piercy. Editor Linda Wagner-Martin tells us that, in writing "The Feeder," Bruno drew upon a real-life situation in which the abused wife did eventually leave her husband. The story describes a macho sexual and economic force that Wagner-Martin finds "malignant."

THAT SUMMER DAY ALMA WINTERS CAME TO lunch, I noticed she had lost weight. She had lost the fullness of her breasts, the pinkish flesh of her cheeks, and could have been a small boy sitting there, instead of a grown woman playing with the food on her plate. Her once fiercely platinum hair was a faded brown, cropped close to her head with rigid sprouts standing upright at her crown and temples. Her gray eyes seemed much larger than I ever remembered, glass marbles fixed in a dull yellowed skin. Alma did not look at me as she arranged the meal into forced geometric designs on her plate. There was a sense of primordial ritual as she played with the food, separating it into squares and triangles with the tines of her fork, then pushing the food together into a larger rectangle. It was only after several minutes of this ceremonial rite that she took a bite. She showed no measure of enjoyment in her food, which could have been tasteless stones, the way she labored to swallow. Periodically she would lay down her fork, reach for her water goblet, and take measured mechanical sips, her lips never leaving the rim of the glass.

I felt like a cow next to her. My breasts were round and full from nursing my daughter Jenny, and David had joked just that morning that my arms and legs were getting to look like baby sea whales. I felt misshapen, a flesh balloon, sweat trickling down my inner thighs, making my print shift stick to my skin. I smelled of cooking grease and soured milk. I was uncomfortable in the late summer heat. Alma was cool and composed.

Jenny, who was seated in her highchair, squirmed momentarily and threw a large pasty noodle on the floor. She whined and I knew she wanted my breast. I lifted her out of the highchair, wiped the tomato sauce away from her face with a napkin, and opened the top button of my dress. Jenny maneuvered herself into a comfortable position, letting her smooth cheek disappear into the soft white breast, her lips blowing little fish kisses until she reached the nipple. Alma did not look up. She rearranged the food on her plate.

"It's too bad David can't be home for lunch,"

"The Feeder" reprinted from *Women's Studies Newsletter*, Spring 1985.

I said, shifting Jenny deeper into my arm for more leverage. "He would have loved to have seen you."

"Oh really?" she asked, taking a small even bite of the noodle.

"But then, I'm kind of glad we had this time to talk alone."

Alma neatly wiped her mouth with the cloth napkin, appearing to be finished, even though a great deal of food was left on her plate. I noticed fine strands of brown hair growing above her lip, alien shadows to this formerly very feminine creature.

"So," I paused, "when did you begin losing all this weight?"

"Oh, it's all come about gradually," she answered.

The breast milk from my untended breast seeped through the fabric of my dress. I was embarrassed, and shifted Jenny, who at nine months seemed too big and cumbersome to nurse. She eagerly reached for the swollen nipple of my other breast, while I wiped myself with a cloth diaper that I carried on my shoulder.

"I've been losing weight for a while now," Alma continued, placing her silverware on her plate and pushing the plate forward. "Every time I look in the mirror, I see fat. It seems my stomach is an inevitable fate." She pinched a thin line of skin where her stomach should have been through the fabric of her tailored blouse. "You know, I don't even have my periods any more. I love it."

"Alma, I'm worried about you."

"Don't be."

"How does Cal feel about this?"

"Oh Calvin. He's been a bit of a brute. But let's not talk about me, please."

And so I launched into a self-conscious monologue about my life, my life with baby, my life with David. The night feedings, the diapers, the baby edging herself around the coffee table like a plump duck, giggling and cooing one moment, engaged in a tirade the next. I talked at considerable length about my body, all round and sagging, laced with white ribbons of stretch marks, and how the heat made me feel like a swollen pear, all thick and ripe and miserable. I talked about David and the business, how he liked his shirts ironed, that he liked his phone messages written neatly in ink, and how he wrote me a little note every morning before he left for work, "Sylvia, stick to your diet." And then I talked of the baby again, the La Leche League, the parenting group meetings, how zinc oxide is better for diaper rash than anything commercial on the market, how I intended to nurse Jenny until she was two years old even though my mother-in-law thought the whole idea disgusting. And it struck me as I spoke that I had no idea what language I spoke before this Baby Talk. What could I have possibly thought or said before there was a David or a Jenny? My head was filled with every movement that Jenny made, every monosyllable that she uttered, every new and startling skill she mastered. And when I did not speak of Jenny, it was David and his business, David and his needs, his desires for the family. I vaguely remember a young woman, with long black hair and black eyes, a literature major at a small university, who romped in a woolen turtleneck and faded blue jeans, carried a Greek woven bag she had bought in Europe, laced leather sandals up her calves, who met friends in dark campus taverns, political rallies, and in the dormitory rooms late at night. I vaguely remember her speaking, but the language and tools of speech are alien to me now, and the faces and names of her cohorts are impossible to remember. And this woman adopted a new language, and spoke to a woman who politely listened, but who did not share the language either.

Alma once had told me she had graduated from Stephens College in Missouri when Stephens was a finishing school devoted solely to preparing each young woman for a life with a successful man. Alma had jokingly mentioned once there was a mini-course in "the art of pouring tea" and she laughed, "the art of wearing gloves." She had been waiting for Calvin when he came along, she said. She was attracted to his angular frame and Nordic coloring, and she was bored with Stephens and her courses, and she fell for him so passionately that she forgot who she was and why she had ever gone to college in the first place. She quit Stephens her junior year and married Cal in a large ceremony somewhere out East.

I managed to finish college, but I fell hard for David, much like Alma did for Cal. David told me he didn't usually like literature majors because he found them flighty and unpredictable, but he thought he could handle me and mold me into the perfect wife. I remember tossing back my black hair and laughing at that remark, telling him, this abrasive young man I had only known for two weeks, that you can only mold gelatin and cheese, neither of which I remotely resembled. He roared at that one, and later he told me he had decided that night he wanted to marry me.

Something about the anger in my eyes intrigued him.

As I rambled on, Alma sat composed, smooth like carved marble, smiling a thin line of a smile, her hands, a small child's hands, folded neatly in her lap. Jenny was asleep at my breast.

After Alma had left, and I had put Jenny in her crib, I remembered back to the time when I had first met Alma. It was the night she and her husband Cal had thrown a celebration party honoring his new partnership with my husband, David. She was much rounder then, her face a soft pink, her blonde hair like a child's doll, and she was open, receptive, not the frigid mannequin that measured every move, every bite of food. She laughed appreciatively at everything her husband said that night, as if his words were golden, or god inspired, and she sat with her tea, her lacquered nails tapping delicately on the porcelain cup, smiling, giggling, winking at the other guests. I remembered the earrings and the fine golden chains that dangled from her neck and fell into the crevice of her then fuller breasts. She dressed flamboyantly, in odd-glittered colors, and men crowded around her. These same men often congratulated Cal on how lucky he was to find such a fine hostess and a good wife, and the other wives in the room envied her, myself included, because she was many things we were not. I hadn't had Jenny yet, and I sat at the dinner table, my pregnant belly resting in folds, straining in a slanted position, my puffed legs sprawled beneath me. David kept laying his hand on my stomach saying things like "That better be my cake baking in this oven," and he patted my stretched flesh, as if I wasn't even there, merely a receptacle for some precious cargo. Alma laughed heartily at David's humor, along with the other men at the table who spat and choked and roared, and I sat back, grinning, pretending I enjoyed all this attention. I remembered at one point the baby gave a strong kick and David raised his hand with an almost religious gesticulation and shouted, "Goddamn, it's going to be a first-string linebacker, sure as hell." I remember sipping my mineral water, amidst the laughing, and wondered what exactly a first-string linebacker did.

Alma sought me out later in the evening. "I'm so glad our husbands are going to be partners. We're going to be fast friends, I can tell. I want to hear all about your baby." And before I had a chance to respond, she had flittered away, off to Cal's side, crawling into the folds of his arms, and he steadied her, positioned her, and her form became fluid as she melted into a cool liquid in his grasp.

Several months had passed after that summer lunch with Alma, and I did not think much about her. I was engrossed with Jenny and the house, and my diet, which was David's pet obsession as well as mine. David had devised a curious regimen he had found in an old Air Force manual. He had written down my instructions neatly on a legal pad, detailing the precise amount of sit-ups, leg lifts, arm twirls that I was to do each day. By each category, there was a box to be checked each time the prescribed exercises were completed. Every morning, next to his "Daily Notes for Sylvia" ("Don't touch that Jamoca Almond Fudge ice cream, Syl, I'll check the level when I get home"), he left the annoying Air Force regimen, with a newly sharpened pencil laid next to it. I often greeted the note with a half-eaten banana or toasted bagel hanging from my mouth, and in an act of silent defiance, I checked the little squares perfunctorily as I dipped my finger into the Jamoca Almond Fudge.

I decided to have Alma over for lunch again in November. She arrived promptly, dressed in a roomy t-shirt that swallowed her boyish frame. Her hair was shorter, swept back above her ears, and she had lost more weight. She seemed to be in even more control, her posture rigid, almost military, her hands tight and folded in her lap, the purplish veins transparent, like frozen rivers in her flesh. I stared at her face, the skin still yellowed, but now deep grey circles swelled around the eyes, and her smile, much tighter, stretched like a violet string across her face. I had fixed something rich and pasty, I wanted to fatten her up, but she no longer bothered to lift the food to her mouth. She neatly separated it and let it converge again with each mechanical movement of her fork.

"Alma," I began, "is it possible that you could have lost more weight? You really didn't need to." I saw in her form the frozen pictures of war and famine that lay like a sheet of cellophane over my consciousness.

"When I look into the mirror all I see is fat. It's funny, but I find I can live quite nicely on some meat broth and a sliver of fruit."

"But that's not enough, Alma. You need more."

"No, you're wrong," she shook her head. "I need nothing. I'm in complete control now."

"What do you mean you're in control?"

"My body is my own."

"Has Cal said anything about this to you?"

She laughed, and said nothing for a moment, then straightened herself in the chair. "Oh he forces me to eat. He pinches the food between his fingers and forces it into my mouth. I swallow it alright, but I throw it up later." She laughed again. "You think I'm crazy, don't you?"

"No, I don't think that," I answered. "But you and Cal were always so close."

"Oh really? Is that what you thought?" I heard the faint stirrings of Jenny in the upstairs bedroom. She's probably hungry, I thought, and my breasts ached. "I think that's the baby, Sylvia," Alma said, and stood to leave.

"Alma, please stay. You just got here. Have dessert. I made it special."

"Sylvia, please don't worry about me."

"How can I help you?"

"You can't."

I noticed the bruise as she was putting on her overcoat. It lay under her arm, large, circular, the deep purple of a summer plum.

"Alma!" She jerked, I must have startled her. "What happened to you?" I heard Jenny wailing in the upstairs bedroom. My attention shifted in the direction of the bedroom door, then back to Alma, who was quickly buttoning up her overcoat.

"Oh, that. A gift from Calvin. He had a bad day at work."

She lifted the woolen hood over her head, opened the door, and walked rigidly into the brutal wind. I felt a chill as the wind crept into the open weave of my sweater. I folded my arms across my chest and hid my hands under each arm. I closed the door behind her and stood for a moment ignoring the persistent cries of my child.

"She's the joke of the office," David said that night at dinner. "Mort Kreiners calls her 'Alma from Auschwitz.'"

"That's so sick," I said. "I can't believe you can even repeat that."

"Alma used to be some broad," he continued, "Cal was considered lucky going home to that every night. Mort says you couldn't pay him to lay her now."

"Mort Kreiners is an asshole."

"Mort Kreiners sold three houses last week."

"How can you defend him?"

"Like I said, he sold three houses last week."

"Anyway, I tried to get her to eat. I made lasagne. She just played with it. Wouldn't take a bite."

"I figure if you can't get her to eat, no one can," he smirked, patting the meat of my thighs. "You're always feeding everyone, including yourself." He reached for his coffee, and swirled the black brew with his spoon. He smiled. "Did you do your leg lifts today?"

"I didn't have time." He let that one slip in, I thought, he's a real professional, him and his little calculated doses of disapproval. I had covered my advancing weight that winter with oversized sweaters and pants, and had been careful to keep my arms covered and my legs hidden under large towels after a shower, and then safely lost under a lounging gown. Even though Jenny had several teeth and was increasingly mobile, I was still nursing her and my breasts were still huge and swollen and laced with purple veins. That's it I thought. No more nursing, Jenny, you're going cold turkey tomorrow. No more feeding off of Momma.

"I think Cal has been hitting Alma and I'm worried," I said, looking for some type of reaction in David's face. I folded my hands across my breasts hoping to minimize my misshapen body.

"He says he has to get tough with her to make her eat. It's none of your business, Syl. Now drop it." He got up from the table and turned, "Cal is my friend, my partner, and we get along fine. Just drop all of this."

I took David's advice, letting it go, hoping Alma could resolve what was troubling her on her own, after all, she herself said I couldn't help her. Months later in the spring, when I had all but forgotten about Alma, and David ceased to even mention her in conversation, I became absorbed with Jenny and her expanding vocabulary. I wrote down every new word she acquired and the day she uttered it into a little journal I had been keeping since her birth. Her newest phrase was "I want, I want," and she followed me around the house playfully reiterating her new sentence. David had left a note for me one morning in the spring, and instead of his usual "Stick to your diet, Syl!", there was a set of terse instructions: "Get a hold of Alma Winters. Invite her and Cal to dinner tonight. I'll explain later."

Alma was distant on the phone, and responded in short, brittle sentences: "Yes. That will be fine. We can make it. Thank you. Goodbye." Her voice was a bizarre parody of one of those computer toys that respond verbally to a child's persistent finger punches. I heard a grey undercurrent of pain, not the whinings of a hungry child that I was so used to responding to, but the low, hollow moans of the wounded. Her voice made me think of that morning when I lay in bed, startled by the imperiled quakings of a small bird trapped in our roof that the workman had finished repairing the day before. It was a sparrow or a Brewers blackbird, which often nests in the soffits and gutters of the neighborhood homes. I stared at the sloped ceiling, directing my attention to where the bird had been entombed between the rafters. The scratchings became more frantic as I envisioned the bird flapping its fragile wings in the darkness, in blind panic, buffeted only by the freshly laid insulation. I threw off my covers and stood on the mattress.

"What are you doing Sylvia?" David had asked, turning in a half sleep. I lifted my fingertips and grazed the ceiling.

"There's a bird trapped in the ceiling. Can't you hear him?"

"He'll die soon. Let it go."

"Can't we get it out?"

"Now, how are we going to get it out, Syl? We just paid eight hundred dollars to have the roof fixed, and you want to save some damn bird?"

"I can't stand listening to it die."

"Then go downstairs and fix me some coffee."

"How can you stand it, David?"

"It's easy," he had answered, sitting up in bed. He turned on the radio.

The dinner party was Cal's idea. He had hoped that if Alma was around familiar faces, she might eat. He admitted to David she was losing more weight, that he had found her vomiting several more times in the bathroom, and that he had to get physical with her. He had to watch her constantly now, following her to the bathroom and having to force-feed her in the mornings before he went to work and at night when he got home. He thought it was time to involve a doctor, but Alma had refused.

The dinner surprisingly went well. Alma made a visible effort to eat, not toying with the food, but actually scooping large amounts of food onto her fork and shoving them into her mouth. David and Cal made a deliberate attempt to not watch Alma, and were engaged in a raucous retelling of some more office antics of Mort Kreiners. He had, so they said, deliberately spilled coffee on Miss Kendall's bosom, in hopes of getting to wipe it away with his pocket handkerchief. Miss Kendall, the secretary, was noticeably upset when old Mort dropped his handkerchief down her cleavage and proceeded to retrieve it. David recounted that "Her jugs were just a jiggling" at the sight of Kreiners' hand, and she poured another cup of coffee on his three-piece pinstripe. I often wondered how a man I could be married to could defend a man who had such an open contempt for women. It seemed to me that David and Cal, and all men for that matter, had a fierce camaraderie, impenetrable, a shared, personal knowledge, fraternity, partnership, that excluded women. It is a code, an unspoken devotion. I felt jealous of Cal and David and Mort, much like I felt in high school when I saw the male athletes on a football or basketball squad hug each other after a win, or pat each other on the rump, or fiercely defend each other on the field, while I enviously sat in the stands, surrounded by the other girls, yearning for that type of camaraderie. The girls would cheer and wave at the men hoping for some form of recognition or male attention. But we were all separate entities, failing to acknowledge each other, only interested in extrapolating a small fragment of this male fraternity.

Alma asked for seconds of the dessert after finishing two helpings of the main course, and Cal smiled appreciatively at me. David nodded. She smiled and took large chunks of the cheesecake onto her fork and dropped them into her mouth. I reached for a piece of the cheesecake for myself, hoping that David was so lost in his reverie with Cal that he would not notice, but, as if on cue, he tapped my elbow with the prongs of his fork and whispered so Cal and Alma could almost certainly hear, "Not tonight, Darling, you've had enough as it is." So I continued to minister the meal, monitoring everyone's plate, standing, then sitting, treating each portion of food as a personal gift to the taker.

After coffee, Alma excused herself and left the table. Calvin gave me a sour, pleading look, so I offered to walk her up to the bathroom using the excuse that I wanted to check on Jenny. David winked at me, letting me know I had done the right thing.

I stood by the closed bathroom door. I heard the low guttural sounds, the heavings, the moans, and then the sudden flush of the toilet. I wondered if I should knock, and then the door opened. Alma stood in the doorway, not surprised to see me at all, her dull hair matted and wet, fresh yellow balls of sweat beading her forehead and the pronounced hair above her lip. "Please don't tell Cal, Sylvia." I felt as if we shared a small closet, suffocating in the dark, acrid smell of vomit, and I felt the sad, sick walls of enclosure. She lifted her sweater and showed me several side strips of surgical tape wrapped around her emaciated body. "He did this," she announced, and headed down the stairs, her form distinctly masculine in nature. Her body was propelled by some ethereal energy, giving her strength, and as she disappeared down the stairway, I knew I would say nothing.

Alma called three weeks later, her voice was different, not the clipped military sentences, but a series of unpunctuated fragments. She asked to see me. It was urgent. I remembered a doctor's appointment I had made that day for Jenny's inoculations, and the promise to pick up David's pinstripe at the cleaners, and my luncheon meeting with David's mother. "Yes, Alma. Please come. I'll be waiting here for you."

I suddenly felt the same fear I did the night I stood in the imaginary closet, the stale air that hung low around me, the feeling of hopeless enclosure. Jenny had tripped over a line of toys in front of her and held out her arms for solace, a green plastic frog lodged in one hand, the other tugging at the fabric of my shirt, pleading to nurse. I walked into the kitchen and poured her a cup of juice, she tagging behind me, at first resisting the cup, still tugging at the cloth of my shirt. "No, Jen, you use a cup now. Momma has no more milk."

Ten minutes later Alma stood in the doorway in a pair of denims and a bloodied white shirt. There was a large untended bruise, split and bleeding on her forehead. I ushered her in, her frail body quaking, her hands, like strings of bones, convulsing. She bit into her shaking hand, making small indentations in the skin, trying by the self-induced pain, to steady herself. She composed herself, transfixed by the tiny dots that filled with blood and steamed the hollows of her skin. "Let me take care of that cut, Alma. Please." I sat her in the living room and then ran for some disinfectant and some bandages. When I returned, Jenny was yelling, "Hurt, Momma, hurt!" Shaking, I spilled the bright orange Mercurochrome over the wound. Jenny pummeled my legs, disturbed at my behavior, tugged demandingly at my slacks, and then sat curiously to watch the bright spectacle, the Mercurochrome spreading like ink on white paper, creating a Rorschach abstract on Alma's face. I took some tissue out of my pocket and gently wiped away the excess, placed some soft gauze over the wound, finishing with two strips of adhesive tape.

"I thought I was strong enough to kill him," she began. "I worked at being strong . . . in control . . . I thought I could do it this time, this time . . . I waited so long for just the right time . . . I thought I had the power . . . I had the power . . ."

"Alma, what are you saying?" I grabbed her fists that were wound tight like hoarded string.

"I thought he couldn't touch me anymore . . . I thought my body was my own . . . I felt strong . . . did everything, everything right . . ."

"Alma . . ."

"But oh oh that bastard that bastard he walks in on me in the bathroom I had to had to vomit that toast he made me eat that morning and he walked in that bastard and he grabbed me and he still can beat me he still can hurt me and it still hurts still hurts and I thought I had the power to make it stop. I yelled I was going to leave him and he said 'You skinny bitch, I'll kill you yet.'"

"Alma, please, calm down, slow down."

Her trembling ceased and I wrapped my arms around her. Jenny, surprised by the sudden silence, edged into our circle, and with a surge of compassion that young children often intuitively display, reached for both of us. We sat there a very long time, arms entwined, heads together, eyes closed, listening to the ancient rhythm of our blood. And in this human huddle, we shared a secret knowledge, a silent, undying bond, a communion that only females can share.

Later in the day, David walked into the kitchen and found Alma, quiet and contemplative, sitting at the kitchen table warming her hands around a cup of tea. Jenny was in her highchair fingerpainting with a jello salad, tossing bits of strawberry gelatin onto the linoleum floor. David grabbed me by the arm and led me outside to the living room.

"Get her out of here, Sylvia," he said.

"She's hurt, David. She needs help."

"Cal said she got hysterical this morning, trying to puke her breakfast into the toilet. He says he's having her committed."

"He's the one that should be committed. He's an animal."

"Can't you see she's fucking nuts?" he yelled, and then more quietly, "Listen honey. She's his wife. This is his business. You're my wife, and I want you to get her out of here."

"I can't."

"He's my friend, Sylvia. He's my partner. This is his mess. I'm calling him." He picked up the phone and began to dial.

"David, please, don't."

"Do what I say Sylvia. Get your daughter, clean up that fucking mess she's made in there, and then start dinner. I'm not coming home to this kind of thing. I mean it!"

I walked into the kitchen, went over to Jenny, and lifted her from the highchair and wiped her face and hands with a dishrag. I looked at the bowl of jello on the floor and the little strawberry hills that peppered the tiles. I looked up at Alma, whose flushed and bruised face registered nothing. She sipped her tea. "Come on, Alma. We're going." She looked up. "Come on, I'm getting you out of here. David is calling Cal. He'll be here soon." She didn't move. I felt as if my chest was exploding. My anger was so rich, so deep, surging like volcanic lava, a grit that burned my throat, enflamed my voice. God, I thought. It's not only Alma that had to get out of there.

As we drove off, all three of us in the front seat, huddled together again, as soldiers do in combat trenches, I looked through the rearview mirror to see David in the driveway, yelling, I suppose, my name. As we pulled further and further away, I saw our roof, still neatly repaired, and I thought of that lost sparrow, entombed in the darkness, shrouded with its broken wings.

A White Man's Word

Debra Swallow

Debra Swallow (1954–) was born in South Dakota into the Oglala tribe. She has attended Oglala Community College and lives in Manderson, South Dakota. Her story "A White Man's Word" is reprinted from A Gathering of Spirit: A Collection by North American Indian Women *(1988), edited by Beth Brant. This story explores the vocabulary of ethnic ridicule from the viewpoint of a young Lakota woman.*

THE SCREEN DOOR SLAMMED SHUT, AND I JUST knew eighty flies came in. Then I heard wailing and gibberish and ran to see who it was. My nine-year-old son was running toward me with blood, tears and dirty sweat trickling off his chin, making my knees go weak.

"What happened? Who did this to you?" I asked, kneeling to wipe his round face with a cool, damp cloth.

"I got in a fight, Mom. Mom, what's a half-breed?"

I felt like my blood stopped running, and I closed my eyes to kill my tears, my mind opening up a day I'd almost forgotten.

I opened my eyes to see how under-water looked, and a sting like cactus tips closed them fast. Surfacing, I looked across the pool for my friend. The water shimmered turquoise blue, reflecting nothing but the painted concrete bottom and rectangles of green light from the roof. Forty or fifty pale faces and arms bobbed and floated above the water, but no sign of my friend's brown, familiar face.

"Maybe it's time to go," I thought and swam to the closest edge. Feeling the rough, slimy cement on the palms of my hands, I hauled myself out of the water. Unsure of my footing, I walked slowly toward the shower rooms.

Screams, giggles and little-girl conversation filled the room, along with spraying, splashing and draining water. Stooping to peek under the first shower stall, I saw two white feet and moved on to the second door. Also two white feet. Next door, four white feet. I could feel myself starting to shiver now and my breath felt trapped in my chest. "What if they left me? I don't know anybody here," I thought.

My friend and her mom took me with them to Rushville to swim. My first time alone away from my family, and here I was, scared among white people—the only Indian in sight.

I decided to just kind of stand around in the shower room. I knew she wasn't in the pool, so she had to come here, where our clothes were. Trying to be as unnoticeable as possible, I leaned against a cool, wet wall and watched the white girls in the room, curious because I'd never been around any before.

"My dad bought me a brand-new bike and it has a blue daisy basket on the handlebars," one girl whined to her friend. "Well, I already knew that, but did you know my dad bought me a new bed and it has a canopy on it!" she whined back in a sing-song voice. The two girls were probably eight years old like me, but both were chubby with blonde ringlets and painted toenails.

Spacing out their words, I was thinking about the bike Dad made my sister and me. He made it from all different parts he found at the trash pile, and it looked funny and rusty, but it worked real well. Daddy also made us a pair of stilts, a playhouse and a pogo stick, which all our friends wanted to play with. I knew my dad was better than theirs, he BUILT stuff for us.

I noticed the first girl was dressed now, and while waiting for her friend to finish, she pulled out a whole handful of red licorice and chewed on one while her friend jabbered, every once in a while glancing at me, not knowing my tongue ached to taste just one mouthful of her licorice. Every time she looked at me, I wanted to evaporate. I had on a borrowed swimsuit a size too big, dull and old-fashioned compared to the bright-colored flower or print-covered two-pieces all the other girls wore. My hair hung down my back, straight and thick and dark.

The first girl said, "Look, this Indian is staring at us," and glared at me with icy blue eyes, her nose pointing to the ceiling. The second girl said, "Oh, she don't know what we're saying anyhow. Dirty Indians don't know anything." Her friend said, "I don't think she's really a real Indian. My dad says some of them are half-breeds. So she's not *all* dirty."

"Only half-dirty," her friend said, and they giggled together and laughed at me.

My face felt hot and my arms were heavy as I walked carefully across the wet, slippery floor towards them. I noticed from far away that the room's noises started to fade.

I grabbed one of them by her hair and threw her away, wrapped my arm around the other one's neck and wrestled her down, and sitting on her, I kept punching her till her friend grabbed me. I stood up, and jerking away, I tripped her, landing her by her friend. They were both still crying and screaming on the floor when I walked out, carrying my bundle of clothes under my arm.

Standing outside in the shade of the pool building, I was really scared. There was someone yelling, "Debi! Debi!" but I wouldn't look. Somehow I thought they found out my name and were going to do something to me. But it was my friend's mom; she and my friend went for popsicles and just got back. I ran to their car and told them what I did, so my friend's mom went in after the clothes my friend left in the shower room and we headed back for home.

Safe once again with my family, I told Mom and Dad I got in a fight.

"Daddy, what's a half-breed?" I asked him.

The house got quiet, the only sound was the wind. Daddy looked at me and his eyes were sad.

"My girl, you're an Indian. The way of living is Indian. Lakota."

I said, "Yes, but what is a half-breed?"

"A white man's word," is what he said. "It's just a white man's word."

Now, eighteen years later, I was wiping blood from my son's face, and his question made my body shake with anger, sadness, frustration and hatred. Opening my eyes, I answered, "You're Lakota, son. The way of living is Indian. You're Lakota." He looked at me with black eyes shining with tears he now refused to shed, and asked me again what a half-breed was.

"A white man's word," is what I said. "It's just a white man's word."

Woman with Kite

Chitra Divakaruni

Chitra Divakaruni (1956–   ) was born in Calcutta, India, and grew up speaking both English and Bengali. She received a B.A. from Presidency College in Calcutta; her Ph.D. (1985) is from the University of California at Berkeley. Her writing career began in 1987 with the publication of Dark Like a River *(Writers Workshop Press, Calcutta), which was followed by* The Reason for Nasturtiums *(1990). She lives in California with her husband and young son. A poet and teacher of English, she co-directs the annual National Creative Writing Conference at Foothill College. She wrote the following poem when she observed that very little writing about women describes them at play.*

Meadow of crabgrass, faded dandelions,
querulous child-voices. She takes
from her son's disgruntled hands the spool
of a kite that will not fly. Pulls
on the heavy string, ground-glass rough
between her thumb and finger. Feels the kite,
translucent purple square, rise
in a resistant arc, flapping
against the wind. Kicks off her *chappals,*
tucks up her *kurta* so she can
run with it, light
flecking off her hair as when she was
sexless-young. Up, up

past the puff-cheeked clouds, she
follows it, her eyes slit-smiling
at the sun. She has forgotten
her tugging children, their *give me,*
give me wails. She sprints
backwards, sure-footed, she cannot
fall, connected to the air, she
is flying, the wind blows through her, takes

her red *dupatta,* mark of marriage.
And she laughs like a woman
should never laugh

so the two widows on the park bench
stare and huddle their white-veiled heads
to gossip-whisper. The children
have fallen, breathless,
in the grass behind. She
laughs like wild water, shaking
her braids loose, she laughs
like a fire, the spool a blur
between her hands, the string
unraveling all the way
to release it into space, her life,
into its bright, weightless orbit.

A Private Affair

Leona Nicholas Welch

Leona Nicholas Welch (1942–   ) was born in Mobile, Alabama, and now lives with her husband and children in Richmond, California. She has written in many forms, including plays. Her work "Hands in the Mirror," published in Centerstage: 21 Black Contemporary Plays, *celebrates the role of old black women in seven poems meant to be danced as well as recited. The following poem was first published in* Black Gibraltar *(1971). Of her life, she says, "I have been able to become the three things I always wanted to be: teacher, mother, writer."*

me alone
alone with me
no one else
me by myself
    learning
    thinking
    reflecting on me
no one else
me by myself

once I hated the likes of me
and looked for me in everyone else
now I see and love what I see
in love with me as I see myself

III

Making Stereotypes

He slipped his hands through the break in the blanket and found her hips, rested his hands on their notches and drew her against him. Like the pause between lightning and thunder, he allowed a hesitation before tilting his head for another kiss.

She took part primly, with her arms wedged against this chest, her body canted back at the waist. After a stretch of persuasion which bore no results, he retreated and they stood facing each other in the half-embrace.

"You want to enjoy it, don't you?" . . .

–LaVyrle Spencer, *Forgiving*

So the fateful marriage occurs, the mingling of the sweetly naive and the dastardly unlit. When Bluebeard leaves on his journey, the young woman does not realize that even though she is exhorted to do anything she wishes—except that one thing—she is living less, rather than living more. Many women have literally lived the Bluebeard tale. They marry while they are yet naive about predators, and they choose someone who is destructive to their lives. They are determined to "cure" that person with love. They are in some way "playing house." One could say they have spent much time saying, "His beard isn't really so blue."

–Clarissa Pinkola Estés, *Women Who Run With the Wolves*

By the time they are seventeen, many young women have surrendered their ambitions to a growing need for affection, and their autonomy to an emotional dependence on the approval and good will of others. The spell is cast, and the promise of "beauty"—of being desirable—lulls the young woman into an existential limbo where everything is measured by the expectation of the one who is to come. Sleeping Beauty is not idle, however—she is busy living out the Pygmalion script (the male version of the myth), allowing herself to be sculpted, shaved, painted, plastered, pushed aside, pedestaled, pounded into a lifelike Galatea, the perfect fulfillment of a man's fantasies. At seventeen the young woman is well on her way to being a "formula female."

–MADONNA KOLBENSCHLAG, *Kiss Sleeping Beauty Good-Bye*

Biting the Hand

Rebecca Radner

Rebecca Radner (1940–) was born in Chicago. Twenty years after moving to California in 1963, she received her M.A. in creative writing from San Francisco State University. In the 70s she began to write poetry and has been published in journals such as the Harvard Review, *the* Iowa Review, *the* New England Review, *and the* Berkeley Poet's Co-op. *Radner is represented in this collection by two of her early poems. She says of "Biting the Hand," "That was an amazingly angry period—I was furious with everything and everyone, including myself. Sometimes that's necessary, for a while, creatively speaking."*

I was a trader on the stock exchange
beautifully dressed, with plastic bags on my feet
a bag lady at the stock exchange
I didn't know what to do, no one could tell me
the market was crashing, Gotterdammerung, holy chaos
so I figured, buy or sell, it didn't matter
action was everything
although merely a dream, it presented,
don't you think, a good attitude for daily occasions

take an ordinary sixteen-year-old foot
slide it into a silver high-heeled sandal
stand on it
the foot feels funny
tell it to be quiet, that's how it ought to feel
dance for hours on feet anesthetized by hope
don't limp for days

I had a terrible dream
one more doctor-lover, one more forced operation
the last time, he dressed me in white & cut out a piece of my cunt
this time, he had to fix my mouth, my throat, my stomach
because I was wounded as a child

---

by a man, by daddy-lover
could not speak, sing, or digest my life
trust me, my doctor said, I'll fix it
above the mask, his face was white & fearful

I had more terrible dreams about my daddy-lover
in various disguises
take my word for it, they were gruesome
I won't bore you with them
all women have bad dreams about men
about shrink-lovers, priest-lovers, CEO-lovers
no doubt men dream about nurse-lovers,
stewardess-lovers, dental hygienist-lovers
oh, the erotic punch of sexual stereotypes
there's nothing like it
I'm sick of it, poisoned, I want to spit it out
spit it back, back where it came from
even before daddy-lover
you didn't think I was this angry, did you
thought I'd settle for a little mild irony, as usual
which has gotten me this far, no farther

now my intention is to bitch, carry on,
&, as they say, ventilate
that is, make a big fuss
just as we were always told not to do
because, if we did, men wouldn't like us
we should have been so lucky

now I know they've been conned just as surely as I have
we're all in this together, etcetera
but, putting it mildly, I can't always feel it
what can I say, guys, I'm sorry
but not very
just don't come any closer
& in time I may regain my composure
though it looks increasingly doubtful

I learned very early what to do
my daddy taught me
I was a quick study

though not naturally gifted
all you need is a little faith in the system
& a lot of terror

it's time for a break
some quiet screaming

I wake from another nightmare
my teeth ache from grinding, clenching
back to soft food tomorrow
nursery food, they once called it
why should I be the one who can't chew, can't bite
in his eighties, all his teeth were pulled
despite false ones, he could still bite, my daddy-lover
he bit anything that came too close
& not much did

after my divorce, men told me
"I'm not your ex-husband,
please don't confuse us"
had they known more, they might have said
"I'm not your daddy, either"
I'd have said, "what do you mean?"
"what are you talking about?"
"huh?"

we're told these things take time
they're not kidding

take an ordinary forty-year-old foot
cram it in a silver high-heeled sandal
try to stand on it
the foot feels godawful
the foot screams to high heaven
both of them scream
try to reason with the feet
tell them they look lovely
no, they scream, stupid, stupid
watch them kick
take off the sandals
put on a pair of old Nikes

now, you say, are you happy, you dumb feet
they snarl at you, they aren't even grateful

I had a wonderful dream
I was back in the stock exchange, in the lobby
but without my plastic bags
oh, this time I was totally elegant
if one didn't look too close
I left my briefcase on a chair
two men came & sat on it
the exchange was about to open, I had to go make money, or lose it
who cares, action is everything
I asked the men for my briefcase
"oh, honey," they said, "what's your rush?
come & have a drink"
"the exchange is opening," I said, "I have to be there"
"aw, babe," they said, "you're too cute to worry about money"
"hey, assholes, give me my stuff," I said, & they did
I rushed off to buy, sell, whatever
I still didn't know what to do
except create even more chaos
no one's noticed

the smell of pipe tobacco
& fresh evening newsprint
the Campbell Soup Twins in the SatEvePost
for me to see the pictures, after daddy read it
brushing my teeth, bedtime, nightmares

I'd like to end on an upbeat note
I could tell you how I dreamed a group of lost women found a jar,
& opened it, & it was full of courage
I really dreamed that, just the other morning
but we all know that's too easy
realistically as well as aesthetically
these things take time
courage couldn't hurt, it's all how you define it
a good nasty bite
a little screaming
some holy chaos

Forgiving

LaVyrle Spencer

LaVyrle Spencer (1943–) was born in Brownerville, Minnesota, where she attended high school and married at age eighteen. She worked as a seamstress and an instructional aide before publishing the first of her sixteen titles. An award-winning writer of historical romance, she guides her writing by two rules learned from a tenth-grade English teacher: "a moment of tension requires an economy of words," and "what you take out is as important as what you put in." The setting of the following excerpt is Deadwood, Dakota Territory, 1876.

HE GRIPPED HER ARMS AND DREW HER TO HER FEET. "That's bullshit, Sarah, and you know it." His head lowered and their mouths joined—his opened, hers closed. He waited, but she would not relent and allow herself to kiss him back. In time he lifted his head.

"I'm in no hurry," he whispered. "Take your time deciding."

He returned to his preoccupation with her lips, wetting them languidly with his tongue, undeterred by her tightly crossed arms and her refusal to comply. He was very adept, very patient, very convincing.

She trembled and tightened her grip on the blanket.

Lifting his head, he remained close, kneading her shoulders through the thick wrap of wool while her wide eyes fixed upon his: light pricks of contact in the darkness.

He slipped his hands through the break in the blanket and found her hips, rested his hands on their notches and drew her against him. Like the pause between lightning and thunder, he allowed a hesitation before tilting his head for another kiss.

She took part primly, with her arms wedged against his chest, her body canted back at the waist. After a stretch of persuasion which bore no results, he retreated and they stood facing each other in the half-embrace.

"You want to enjoy it, don't you?" He lifted his hand to stroke the hair from her temple, and she shivered. "Let yourself . . ." In slowest motion he kissed her eyelids, her cheek, earlobe, the underside of her jaw, stealing her wariness, setting her heart a-hurry. He kissed her mouth once more, spreading the flavor of smoke upon her tongue, bringing the texture of silk where his mustache rode her skin. His hands slipped behind her, low, where her nightgown lay full and loose, made faint movements that sent it whispering across her skin like a curtain across a sill. He spread his hands wide and brought her flush against him.

With a despairing cry she conceded, flowing to him like a breaker to a shore, throwing her arms up and veiling them both with the blanket. Their warm, full lengths joined and he held her in place without moving, their hearts beating crazily.

She had not known simply standing so against another could make mockery of all one believed. Again a sound formed in her throat, trapped, fearful. From outside came the dying peal of the last chime. It seemed to ring within her body and shimmer outward to all the surfaces he embraced.

• • •

"What I mean to say is, do you have any feelings for me?"

She stopped stitching. Her eyes remained downcast. The needle moved on.

"I've always had feelings for you, Robert."

"Then would you . . ." He reached over and covered her right hand to stop it. "Would you look at me, Addie?"

She wouldn't. He waited several seconds, but she wouldn't. He left his chair, removing the work from her hands, placing it on the table before going down on one knee beside her chair. He took both her hands and looked up at her beautiful, pale face.

"Addie, I came here today to tell you I love you. I've loved you for so long. I don't remember a time when it wasn't true."

She lifted her beloved green eyes. They were brimming.

"You do?"

"Yes. And I want to marry you."

She swallowed once, trying very hard to hold her tears in check. "Oh Robert," she whispered, "what took you so long?"

Their reunion was swift and fierce. He caught her hard against him, so hard the impact sent her tears spilling. Her arms doubled around his neck and for a moment they merely clung, their eyes closed, his bearded cheek pressed against her pale jaw. At length he drew back and lifted his face to kiss her, kneeling yet with his trousers lost in the folds of her white apron. She held his face in both her hands, forgetting she still wore the thimble on one of them. What a long, long, long-awaited kiss, flavored of coffee and geranium vegetal, open and wet and tempered by all those years, and all that history that had brought them to this moment of truth. When the kiss ended he laid his face against her apron bib and breathed, "Oh Addie, I love you so much. I've been so miserable these last three weeks."

"So have I." She continued caressing the back of his head, his neck, his shoulders, while he pressed kisses wherever his lips touched her starched clothing. "I thought I'd have to marry him to finally get you to realize you loved me."

"You've known it?" He drew back to see her eyes.

She nodded, stroking his hair back from his temples, the expression in her eyes loving and uncomplicated for one of the first times in their lives. "For quite some time."

"Noah gave me a good talking-to yesterday. He told me I was going to lose you if I didn't pull my head out of the sand."

"Hooray for Noah," she replied softly.

They kissed once more, Robert still kneeling while Addie's palms covered his silken beard. They tasted each other shallow and deep, letting time drift by unheeded. When the kiss ended he remained for a while with his forehead against her chin, her left hand softly skimming his shoulders while he held her right and discovered the thimble still on it.

He sat back and looked down at it, fitting and refitting the thimble on the tip of her finger.

Finally he looked up into her eyes. "You haven't said you love me."

"But I do."

"I want to hear you say it."

"Oh Robert, in all my life I've never loved another man but you."

"Then you'll marry me?"

"Of course."

"Even though Birtle Matheson will have to perform the ceremony?"

"Even though."

"He won't like it."

"He knew all along how I felt about you. I told him the very first day he took me out walking that I loved you."

"You did?"

She nodded, lifting one hand to sculpt the hair above his right ear, following its contour with her fingertips while his face was lifted to receive the love in her gaze.

"We've come through some hell to get here, haven't we, Addie?"

"That's all over now." She kissed him as if to promise only heaven ahead, leaning down and slanting her mouth over his, running her palms over the scratchy new wool covering his back. He rose, drawing her to her feet, fitting their hips together and holding her close while his head tipped and their open mouths joined. He made a sound, throaty and passionate, an ode to the end of their separateness while he locked her ever tighter to his mouth and body.

The thimble dropped to the floor. Ruler shot out from beside the stove and batted it against a chair leg while above her the man and woman went on kissing. On and on the thimble rolled—across the bare floor, against a mop board, across the floor again—creating the only sound in the otherwise quiet room.

Bluebeard

Clarissa Pinkola Estés

Clarissa Pinkola Estés (1943–   ), born of Mexican parents, was adopted and raised by a Hungarian family in Michiana, Illinois. Following the awarding of her Ph.D., she became a Jungian analyst and director of the C. G. Jung Center in Denver, Colorado. In 1989 she began to record a collection of folk tales that she had gathered as a legacy for her two daughters. This project, which grew into nine audiotapes, became the basis of Women Who Run With the Wolves *(1992), from which the following excerpt is taken. Patricia King writes, "Estés, along with Camille Paglia, contends there really is a feminine nature to be celebrated and not reasoned away."*

THIS PREDATORY POTENTATE[1] SHOWS UP TIME after time in women's dreams. It erupts in the midst of their most soulful and meaningful plans. It severs the woman from her intuitive nature. When its cutting work is done, it leaves the woman deadened in feeling, feeling frail to advance her life; her ideas and dreams lay at her feet drained of animation.

Bluebeard is a story of such a matter. In North America, the best known Bluebeard versions are the French and the German.[2] But I prefer this old version in which the French and the Slavic have been mingled. It is close to the one given to me by my Aunt Kathé (pronounced "Katie"), who lived in Csíbrak near Dombovar in Hungary. Among the cadre of farmwomen tellers, the Bluebeard tale is begun with an anecdote about someone who knew someone who knew someone who had seen the grisly proof of Bluebeard's demise. And so we begin.

There is a hank of beard which is kept at the convent of the white nuns in the far mountains. How it came to the convent no one knows. Some say it was the nuns who buried what was left of his body, for no one else would touch it. Why the nuns would keep such a relic is unknown, but it is true. My friend's friend has seen it with her own eyes. She says the beard is blue, indigo-colored to be exact. It is as blue as the dark ice in the lake, as blue as the shadow of a hole at night. This beard was once worn by one who they say was a failed magician, a giant man with an eye for women, a man known by the name of Bluebeard.

'Twas said he courted three sisters at the same time. But they were frightened of his beard with its odd blue cast, and so they hid when he called. In an effort to convince them of his geniality he invited them on an outing in the forest. He arrived leading horses arrayed in bells and crimson ribbons. He set the sisters and their mother upon the horses and off they cantered into the forest. There they had a most wonderful day riding, and their dogs ran beside and ahead. Later they stopped beneath a giant tree and Bluebeard regaled them with stories and fed them dainty treats.

The sisters began to think, "Well, perhaps this man Bluebeard is not so bad after all."

They returned home all a-chatter about how interesting the day had been, and did they not have a good time? Yet, the two older sisters' suspicions and fears returned and they vowed not to see Bluebeard again. But the youngest sister thought if a man could be that charming, then perhaps he was not so bad. The more she talked to herself, the less awful he seemed, and also the less blue his beard.

So when Bluebeard asked for her hand in marriage, she accepted. She had given his proposal great thought and felt she was to marry a very elegant man. Marry they did, and after, rode off to his castle in the woods.

One day he came to her and said, "I must go away for a time. Invite your family here if you like. You may ride in the woods, charge the cooks to set a feast, you may do anything you like, anything your heart desires. In fact, here is my ring of keys. You may open any and every door to the storerooms, the money rooms, any door in the castle; but this little tiny key, the one with the scrollwork on top, do not use."

His bride replied, "Yes, I will do as you ask. It all sounds very fine. So, go, my dear husband, and do not have a worry and come back soon." And so off he rode and she stayed.

Her sisters came to visit and they were, as all souls are, very curious about what the Master had said was to be done while he was away. The young wife gaily told them.

"He said we may do anything we desire and enter any room we wish, except one. But I don't know which one it is. I just have a key and I don't know which door it fits."

The sisters decided to make a game of finding which key fit which door. The castle was three stories high, with a hundred doors in each wing, and as there were many keys on the ring, they crept from door to door having an immensely good time throwing open each door. Behind one door were the kitchen stores, behind another the money stores. All manner of holdings were behind the doors and everything seemed more wonderful all the time. At last, having seen all these marvels, they came finally to the cellar and, at the end of the corridor, a blank wall.

They puzzled over the last key, the one with the little scrollwork on top. "Maybe this key doesn't fit anything at all." As they said this, they heard an odd sound—"errrrrrrrrrrr." They peeked around the corner, and—lo and behold!—there was a small door just closing. When they tried to open it again, it was firmly locked. One cried, "Sister, sister, bring your key. Surely this is the door for that mysterious little key."

Without a thought one of the sisters put the key in the door and turned it. The lock scolded, the door swung open, but it was so dark inside they could not see.

"Sister, sister, bring a candle." So a candle was lit and held into the room and all three women screamed at once, for in the room was a mire of blood and the blackened bones of corpses were flung about and skulls were stacked in corners like pyramids of apples.

They slammed the door shut, shook the key out of the lock, and leaned against one another gasping, breasts heaving. My God! My God!

The wife looked down at the key and saw it was stained with blood. Horrified, she used the skirt of her gown to wipe it clean, but the blood prevailed. "Oh, no!" she cried. Each sister took the tiny key in her hands and tried to make it as it once was, but the blood remained.

The wife hid the tiny key in her pocket and ran to the cook's kitchen. When she arrived, her white dress was stained red from pocket to hem, for the key was slowly weeping drops of dark red blood. She ordered the cook, "Quick, give me some horsehair." She scoured the key, but it would not stop bleeding. Drop after drop of pure red blood issued from the tiny key.

She took the key outdoors, and from the oven she pressed ashes onto it, and scrubbed some more. She held it to the heat to sear it. She laid cobweb over it to staunch the flow, but nothing could make the weeping blood subside.

"Oh, what am I to do?" she cried. "I know, I'll put the little key away. I'll put it in the wardrobe. I'll close the door. This is a bad dream. All will be aright." And this she did do.

Her husband came home the very next morning and he strode into the castle calling for his wife. "Well? How was it while I was away?"

"It was very fine, sir."

"And how are my storerooms?" he rumbled.

"Very fine, sir."

"How are my money rooms?" he growled.

"The money rooms are very fine also, sir."

"So everything is good, wife?"

"Yes, everything is good."

"Well," he whispered, "then you'd best return my keys."

Within a glance he saw a key was missing. "Where is the smallest key?"

"I . . . I lost it. Yes, I lost it. I was out riding and the key ring fell down and I must have lost a key."

"What have you done with it, woman?"

"I . . . I . . . don't remember."

"Don't lie to me! Tell me what you did with that key!"

He put his hand to her face as if to caress her cheek, but instead seized her hair. "You infidel!" he snarled, and threw her to the floor. "You've been into the room, haven't you?"

He threw open her wardrobe and the little key on the top shelf had bled blood red down all the beautiful silks of her gowns hanging there.

"Now it's your turn, my lady," he screamed, and dragged her down the hall and into the cellar till they were before the terrible door. Bluebeard merely looked at the door with his fiery eyes and the door opened for him. There lay the skeletons of all his previous wives.

"And now!!!" he roared, but she caught hold of the door frame and would not let go. She pleaded for her life, "Please! Please, allow me to compose myself and prepare for my death. Give me but a quarter hour before you take my life so I can make my peace with God."

"All right," he snarled, "you have but a quarter of an hour, but be ready."

The wife raced up the stairs to her chamber and posted her sisters on the castle ramparts. She knelt to pray, but instead called out to her sisters.

"Sisters, sisters! Do you see our brothers coming?"

"We see nothing, nothing on the open plains."

Every few moments she cried up to the ramparts, "Sisters, sisters! Do you see our brothers coming?"

"We see a whirlwind, perhaps a dust devil in the distance."

Meanwhile Bluebeard roared for his wife to come to the cellar so he could behead her.

Again she called out, "Sisters, sisters! Do you see our brothers coming?"

Bluebeard shouted for his wife again and began to clomp up the stone steps.

Her sisters cried out, "Yes! We see them! Our brothers are here and they have just entered the castle."

Bluebeard strode down the hall toward his wife's chamber. "I am coming to get you," he bellowed. His footfalls were dense; the rocks in the hallway came loose, the sand from the mortar poured onto the floor.

As Bluebeard lumbered into her chamber with his hands outstretched to seize her, her brothers on horseback galloped down the castle hallway and charged into her room as well. There they routed Bluebeard out onto the parapet. There and then, with swords, they advanced upon him, striking and slashing, cutting and whipping, beating Bluebeard down to the ground, killing him at last and leaving for the buzzards his blood and gristle.

The Natural Predator of the Psyche

Developing a relationship with the wildish nature is an essential part of women's individuation. In order to execute this, a woman must go into the dark, but at the same time she must not be irreparably trapped, captured, or killed on her way there or back.

The Bluebeard story is about that captor, the dark man who inhabits all women's psyches, the innate predator. He is a specific and incontrovertible force which must be memorized and restrained. To restrain the natural predator[3] of the psyche it is necessary for women to remain in possession of all their instinctual powers. Some of these are insight, intuition, endurance, tenacious loving, keen sensing, far vision, acute hearing, singing over the dead, intuitive healing, and tending to their own creative fires.

In psychological interpretation we call on all aspects of the fairy tale to help us represent the drama within a single woman's psyche. Bluebeard represents a deeply reclusive complex which lurks at the edge of all women's lives, watching, waiting for an opportunity to oppose her. Although it may symbolize itself similarly or differently in men's psyches, it is the ancient and contemporary foe of both genders.

It is difficult to completely comprehend the Bluebeardian force, for it is innate, meaning indigenous to all humans from birth forward, and in that sense is without conscious origin. Yet I believe we have a hint of how its nature developed in the preconscious of humans, for in the story, Bluebeard is called "a failed magician." In this occupation he is related to other fairy tales which also portray the malignant predator of the psyche as a rather normative-looking but immeasurably destructive mage.

Using this description as an archetypal shard, we compare it to what we know of failed sorcery or failed spiritual power in mytho-history. The Greek Icarus flew too close to the sun and his waxen wings melted, catapulting him to earth. The Zuni myth "The Boy and the Eagle" tells of a boy who would have become a member of the eagle kingdom but for thinking he could break the rules of Death. As he soared through the sky his borrowed eagle coat was torn from him and he fell to his doom. In Christian myth, Lucifer claimed equality with Yahweh and was driven down to the underworld. In folklore there are any number of sorcerers' apprentices who foolishly dared to venture beyond their actual skill levels, or attempted to contravene Nature. They were punished by injury and cataclysm.

As we examine these leitmotifs, we see the predators in them desire superiority and power over others. They carry a kind of psychological inflation wherein the entity wishes to be loftier than, as big as, and equal to The Ineffable, which traditionally distributes and controls the mysterious forces of Nature, including the systems of Life and Death and the rules of human nature, and so forth.

In myth and story we find that the consequence for an entity attempting to break, bend, or alter the operating mode of The Ineffable is to be chastened, either by having to endure diminished ability in the world of mystery and magic—such as apprentices who are no longer allowed to practice—or lonely exile from the land of the Gods, or a similar loss of grace and power through bumbling, crippling, or death.

If we can understand the Bluebeard as being the internal representative of the entire myth of such an outcast, we then may also be able to comprehend the deep and inexplicable loneliness which sometimes washes over him (us) because he experiences a continuous exile from redemption.

The problem with Bluebeard in the fairy tale is that rather than empowering the light of the young feminine forces of the psyche, he is instead filled with hatred and desires to kill the lights of the psyche. It is not hard to imagine that in such a malignant formation there is trapped one who once wished for surpassing light and fell from Grace because of it. We can understand why thereafter the exiled one maintains a heartless pursuit of the light of others. We can imagine that it hopes that if it could gather enough soul(s) to itself, it could make a blaze of light that would finally rescind its darkness and repair its loneliness.

In this sense we have at the beginning of the tale a formidable being in its unredeemed aspect. Yet this fact is one of the central truths the youngest sister in the tale must acknowledge, that all women must acknowledge—that both within and without, there is a force which will act in opposition to the instincts of the natural Self, and that that malignant force *is what it is.* Though we might have mercy upon it, our first actions must be to recognize it, to protect ourselves from its devastations, and ultimately to deprive it of its murderous energy.

All creatures must learn that there exist predators. Without this knowing, a woman will be unable to negotiate safely within her own forest without being devoured. To understand the predator is to become a mature animal who is not vulnerable out of naïveté, inexperience, or foolishness.

Like a shrewd tracker, Bluebeard senses the youngest daughter is interested in him, that is, willing to be prey. He asks for her in marriage and in a moment of youthful exuberance, which is often a combination of folly, pleasure, happiness, and sexual intrigue, she says yes. What woman does not recognize this scenario?

Naive Women as Prey

The youngest sister, the most undeveloped sister, plays out the very human story of the naive woman. She will be captured temporarily by her own inner stalker. Yet, she will out in the end, wiser, stronger, and recognizing the wily predator of her own psyche on sight.

The psychological story underlying the tale also applies to the older woman who has not yet completely learned to recognize the innate predator. Perhaps she has begun the process over and over again but, lacking guidance and support, has not yet finished with it.

This is why teaching stories are so nourishing; they provide initiatory maps so even work which has hit a snag can be completed. The Bluebeard story is usable by all women, regardless of whether they are very young and just learning about the predator, or whether they have been hounded and harassed by it for decades and are at last readying for a final and decisive battle with it.

The youngest sister represents a creative potential

within the psyche. A something that is going toward exuberant and fissioning life. But there is a detour as she agrees to become the prize of a vicious man because her instincts to notice and do otherwise are not intact.

Psychologically, young girls and young boys are as though asleep about the fact that they themselves are prey. Although sometimes it seems life would be much easier and much less painful if all humans were born totally awake, they are not. We are all born *anlagen,* like the potential at the center of a cell: in biology the *anlage* is the part of a cell characterized as "that which will become." Within the anlage is the primal substance which in time will develop, causing us to become a complete someone.

So our lives as women are ones of quickening the anlage. The Bluebeard tale speaks to the awakening and education of this psychic center, this glowing cell. In service of this education, the youngest sister agrees to marry a force which she believes to be very elegant. The fairy-tale marriage represents a new status being sought, a new layer of the psyche about to be unfurled.

However, the young wife has fooled herself. Initially she felt fearful of Bluebeard. She was wary. However, a little pleasure out in the woods causes her to overrule her intuition. Almost all women have had this experience at least once. As a result she persuades herself that Bluebeard is not dangerous, but only idiosyncratic and eccentric. Oh, how silly. Why am I so put off by that little old blue beard? Her wildish nature, however, has already sniffed out the situation and knows the blue-bearded man is lethal, but the naive psyche disallows this inner knowing.

This error of judgment is almost routine in a woman so young that her alarm systems are not yet developed. She is like an orphan wolf pup who rolls and plays in the clearing, heedless of the ninety-pound bobcat approaching from the shadows. In the case of the older woman who is so cut away from the wild that she can barely hear the inner warnings, she too proceeds, smiling naively.

You might well wonder if all this could be avoided. As in the animal world, a young girl learns to see the predator via her mother's and father's teachings. Without parents' loving guidance she will certainly be prey early on. In hindsight, almost all of us have, at least once, experienced a compelling idea or semi-dazzling person crawling in through our windows at night and catching us off guard. Even though they're wearing a ski mask, have a knife between their teeth, and a sack of money slung over their shoulder, we believe them when they tell us they're in the banking business.

However, even with wise mothering and fathering, the young female may, especially beginning about age twelve, be seduced away from her own truth by peer groups, cultural forces, or psychic pressures, and so begins a rather reckless risk-taking in order to find out for herself. When I work with older teenage girls who are convinced that the world is good if they only work it right, it always makes me feel like an old gray-haired dog. I want to put my paws over my eyes and groan, for I see what they do not see, and I know, especially if they're willful and feisty, that they're going to insist on becoming involved with the predator at least once before they are shocked awake.

At the beginning of our lives our feminine viewpoint is very naive, meaning that emotional understanding of the covert is very faint. But this is where we all begin as females. We are naive and we talk ourselves into some very confusing situations. To be uninitiated in the ways of these matters means that we are in a time of our life when we are vulnerable to seeing only the overt.

Among wolves, when the bitch leaves her pups to go hunting, the young ones try to follow her out of the den and down the path. She snarls at them, lunges at them, and scares the bejeezus out of them till they run slipping and sliding back to the den. Their mother knows her pups don't yet know how to weigh and assess other creatures. They don't know who is a predator and who is not. But in time she will teach them, both harshly and well.

Like wolf pups, women need a similar initiation, one which teaches that the inner and outer worlds are not always happy-go-lucky places. Many women do not even have the basic teaching about predators that a wolf mother gives her pups, such as: if it's threatening and bigger than you, flee; if it's weaker, see what you want to do; if it's sick, leave it alone; if it has quills, poison, fangs, or razor claws, back up and go in the other direction; if it smells nice but is wrapped around metal jaws, walk on by.

The youngest sister in the story is not only naive about her own mental processes, and totally ignorant about the murdering aspect of her own psyche, but is also able to be lured by pleasures of the ego. And why not? We all want everything to be wonderful. Every woman wants to sit upon a horse dressed in bells and go riding off through the boundless green and sensual forest. All humans want to attain early Paradise here on earth. The problem is that ego desires to feel wonderful but a yen for the paradisical, when combined with naïveté, makes us not fulfilled, but food for the predator.

This acquiescence to marrying the monster is actually decided when girls are very young, usually before five years of age. They are taught to not see, and instead to "make pretty" all manner of grotesqueries whether they are lovely or not. This training is why the youngest sister can say, "Hmmm, his beard isn't really *that* blue." This early training to "be nice" causes women to override their intuitions. In that sense, they are actually purposefully taught to submit to the predator. Imagine a wolf mother teaching her young to "be nice" in the face of an angry ferret or a wily diamondback rattler.

In the tale, even the mother colludes. She goes on the picnic, "goes along for the ride." She doesn't say a word of caution to any of her daughters. One might say the biological mother or the internal mother is asleep or naive herself, as is often the case in very young girls, or in unmothered women.

Interestingly, in the tale, the older sisters demonstrate some consciousness when they say they do not like Bluebeard even though he has just entertained and regaled them in a very romantic and paradisical manner. There is a sense in the story that some aspects of the psyche, represented by the older sisters, are a little more developed in insight, that they have "knowing" which warns against romanticizing the predator. The initiated woman pays attention to the older sisters' voices in the psyche; they warn her away from danger. The uninitiated woman does not pay attention; she is as yet too identified with naïveté.

Say, for instance, a naive woman keeps making poor choices in a mate. Somewhere in her mind she knows this pattern is fruitless, that she should stop and follow a different value. She often even knows how to proceed. But there is something compelling, a sort of Bluebeardian mesmerization, about continuing the destructive pattern. In most cases, the woman feels if she just holds on to the old pattern a little longer, why surely the paradisical feeling she seeks will appear in the next heartbeat.

At another extreme, a woman involved in a chemical addiction most definitely has at the back of her mind a set of older sisters who are saying, "No! No way! This is bad for the mind and bad for the body. We refuse to continue." But the desire to find Paradise draws the woman into the marriage to Bluebeard, the drug dealer of psychic highs.

Whatever dilemma a woman finds herself in, the voices of the older sisters in her psyche continue to urge her to consciousness and to be wise in her choices. They represent those voices in the back of the mind that whisper the truths that a woman may wish to avoid for they end her fantasy of Paradise Found.

So the fateful marriage occurs, the mingling of the sweetly naive and the dastardly unlit. When Bluebeard leaves on his journey, the young woman does not realize that even though she is exhorted to do anything she wishes—except that one thing—she is living less, rather than living more. Many women have literally lived the Bluebeard tale. They marry while they are yet naive about predators, and they choose someone who is destructive to their lives. They are determined to "cure" that person with love. They are in some way "playing house." One could say they have spent much time saying, "His beard isn't really so blue."

Eventually a woman thus captured will see her hopes for a decent life for herself and her children diminish more and more. It is to be hoped that she will finally open the door to the room where all the destruction of her life lies. While it may be the woman's actual mate who denigrates and dismantles her life, the innate predator within her own psyche concurs. As long as a woman is forced into believing she is powerless and/or is trained to not consciously register what she knows to be true, the feminine impulses and gifts of her psyche continue to be killed off.

When the youthful spirit marries the predator, she is captured or restrained during a time in her life that was meant to be an unfoldment. Instead of living freely, she begins to live falsely. The deceitful promise of the predator is that the woman will become a queen in some way, when in fact her murder is being planned. There is a way out of all of this, but one must have a key.

Notes

1. The natural predator appears in fairy tales personified as robber, animal groom, rapist, thug, and sometimes as evil woman of various stripe. Women's dream images closely follow the distribution pattern of natural predator in female

protagonist fairy tales. Deleterious relationships, abusive authority figures, and negative cultural prescriptions influence dream and folkloric images as much as or more so than one's own innate archetypal patterning, the latter referred to by Jung as archetypal nodes inherent in each person's psyche. The tale properly belongs to the "meeting the Life and Death force" rather than the "meeting the witch" category.

2. There are published versions in the collections of Jakob and Wilhelm Grimm, Charles Perrault, Henri Pourrat, and others. There are oral versions existent throughout Asia and Mesoamerica as well.

3. In folklore, mythos, and dreams, the natural predator almost always has a predator or stalker of itself as well. It is the battle between these two that finally brings about a change or a balance. When it does not, or when no other goodly antagonist arises, the story is most often called a horror story. The lack of a positive force that is successfully antithetical to the negative predator strikes the deepest fear into the hearts of humans.

Too, in day to day life, there are plenty of light-stealers and consciousness-killers afoot. In the main, a predatory person misappropriates a woman's creative juice, taking it for their own pleasure or use, leaving her whitened and wondering what happened, while they themselves somehow grow more rosy and hearty. The predatory person desires that a woman not heed her instincts lest she perceive that a siphon has been attached to her mind, her imagination, her heart, her sexuality, or whatever else.

The pattern of surrendering one's core life may have begun in childhood, fostered by caretakers who wanted the child's gifts and loveliness to augment the caretaker's own emptiness and hunger. To be trained thusly gives enormous power to the innate predator and sets one out to be prey for others. Until one's instincts are put back in proper order, a woman so raised is exceedingly vulnerable to being overwhelmed by the unspoken and devastating psychic needs of others. Generally, a woman with good instincts knows the predator is insinuated nearby when she finds herself involved in a relationship or situation that causes her life to become smaller rather than larger.

Necessary Losses

Judith Viorst

Judith Viorst (1931–) was born in Newark, New Jersey, and received her B.A. from Rutgers University in 1952. Married to writer Milton Viorst, she attributes her sense of confidence to her husband's support, especially early in her career. Her three sons have inspired much of her writing for children, as in The Tenth Good Thing About Barney *(1971). Famous as a columnist and writer of light verse, Viorst credits her study at the Washington Psychoanalytic Institute for changing her direction since 1981.* Necessary Losses, *which grew out of that period of study, examines the painful separations we must all undergo.*

When you meet a human being, the first distinction you make is "male or female?"

–Sigmund Freud

Our infantile omnipotence—our dizzy, delicious, little-kid sense of power—crows that we can do and have and be anything. Sibling rivals and parents that we can never never possess notify us that no, this is not true. So does our discovery, at eighteen or so months of age, that girls and boys are different from each other. And whatever else this discovery of the anatomical differences may do, it will certainly instruct us in sex-linked limits.

For we cannot become both sexes although—it's been claimed—our wish to do so may be "one of the deepest tendencies in human nature." We cannot, like Virginia Woolf's transmutable hero/heroine Orlando, be a man and then a woman and sometimes both. Through our built-in bisexuality and our capacity for empathy we can experience some of the opposite sex's experiences. And through broader definitions of what it means to be a woman or a man we can expand our own sex's experience, too. But we also will have to recognize that neither sex is complete, that there are some limitations upon our potential, and that our gender identity, with all of its juices and joys, must shape itself to these limits—to this loss.

I am saying that the mere fact of our inhabiting a male or female body importantly defines—and confines—our experience.

I am saying that—close as we are—my husband and sons are psychologically different from me in ways that women—any women—are not.

I am saying with Freud that no one can see us—nor can we see them—divorced from the "male" or "female" designation.

I am saying that sex-linked limits on our "anything's possible" omnipotentiality is yet another necessary loss.

It is argued that sex-linked limits have been culturally produced. It is argued that sex-linked limits are innate. What gender-identity studies seem to strongly suggest, however, is that—from the moment of birth—both boys and girls are so clearly treated as boys or as girls, that even very early displays of "masculine" or "feminine" behavior cannot be detached from environmental influences.

For parents make a distinction between boys and girls.

They have different ways of holding boys and girls.

They have different expectations for boys and girls.

And as their children imitate and identify with their attitudes and activities, they encourage or discourage them, depending on whether or not they are boys or girls.

Are there, in actual fact, *real* sex-linked limits? Is there an inborn male or female psychology? And is there any possible way of exploring such tricky questions unbiased by culture, upbringing or sexual politics?

Here are the answers, for instance, that I received from three feminist writers when I asked if they thought men and women differed innately.

Novelist Lois Gould replied: "Women menstruate, lactate and procreate; men inseminate. All our other differences come from trying to build civilizations around those primitive talents—as if they were the only ones we had."

And journalist Gloria Steinem replied: "For ninety-five percent of life there are more differences between any two women or between any two men that there are between males and females as groups."

And novelist-poet Erica Jong replied: "The only difference between men and women is that women are able to create new little human beings in their bodies while simultaneously writing books, driving tractors, working in offices, planting crops—in general, doing everything men do."

Sigmund Freud would have answered the question differently.

Indeed, he went on record as saying that women are more masochistic, narcissistic, jealous and envious than men, and also less moral. He saw these qualities as the inevitable consequences of the anatomical differences between the sexes—the result of the fact (fact?) that the original sexuality of the little girl is masculine in character, that her clitoris is merely an undeveloped penis and that she correctly perceives herself as nothing more than a defective boy. It is the girl's perception of herself as a mutilated male that irrevocably damages her self-esteem, leading to resentments and attempts at reparation which produce all the subsequent defects in her character.

Well, as his friends say, who can be right about everything?

For in the years since this was written, science has established that while genetic sex is determined at fertilization by our chromosomes (XX for girls; XY for boys), all mammals, including humans, *regardless of their genetic sex,* start out female in nature and in structure. This female state persists until the production, some time later in fetal life, of male hormones. It is only with the appearance of these hormones, at the right time and in the right amount, that anatomical maleness and post-natal masculinity become possible.

While this may not tell us much about the psychology of femaleness and maleness, it does put a permanent crimp in Freud's phallocentricity. For, far from little girls starting out as incomplete little boys, in the beginning all human beings are female.

Despite his phallocentricity, however, Freud was smart enough to note at the time that his comments on the nature of women were "certainly incomplete and fragmentary."

He also said: "If you want to know more about femininity, enquire from your own experiences of life, or turn to the poets, or wait until science can give you deeper and more coherent information."

• • •

Even in the mid-1980s, at an Eastern liberal-elite private school where the mothers of students are doctors and lawyers and government officials and the students themselves are full of feminist rhetoric, there are echoes of the Cinderella Complex. One of the teachers, who gives a course in human behavior to the high school seniors, told me that he has asked them, for the last several years, where they expect to see themselves at age thirty. The answers, he said, are consistently the same. Both boys and girls expect that the girls will be bearing and rearing children, while also engaged in some interesting *part-time* work. And although the boys express a desire to have a great deal of freedom at that age, the girls routinely place the boys in successful *full-time* jobs, supporting their families.

Now it surely is true that a great many women live with a someday-my-prince-will-take-care-of-me fantasy. It is true that the way girls are raised may help explain why. But we also need to consider that the source of female dependence may run deeper than the customs of early child care. And we also need to remember that dependence isn't always a dirty word.

For female dependence appears to be less a wish to be protected than a wish to be part of a web of human relationships, a wish not only to get—but to give—loving care. To need other people to help and console you, to share the good times and bad, to say "I understand," to be on your side—*and also to need the reverse, to need to be needed*—may lie at the heart of women's very identity. Dependence on such connections might be described as "mature dependence." It also means, however, that identity—for women—has more to do with intimacy than with separateness.

In a series of elegant studies, psychologist Carol Gilligan found that while male self-definitions emphasized individual achievement over attachment, women repeatedly defined themselves within a context of responsible caring relationships. Indeed, she notes that "male and female voices typically speak of the importance of different truths, the former of the role of separation as it defines and empowers the self, the latter of the ongoing process of attachment that creates and sustains the human community." It is only because we live in a world where maturity is equated with autonomy, argues Gilligan, that women's concern with relationships appears to be a weakness instead of a strength.

Perhaps it is both.

Claire, an aspiring physician, finds essential meaning in attachment. "By yourself, there is little sense to things," she says. "It is like the sound of one hand clapping. . . . You have to love someone else, because while you may not like them, you are inseparable from them. In a way, it is like loving your right hand. *They are part of you;* that other person is part of that giant collection of people that you are connected to."

But then there is Helen who, talking about the end of a relationship, reveals the risks inherent in intimacy. "What I had to learn . . . ," she says, "wasn't only that I had a Self that could survive it when Tony and I broke up; but that I had a Self *at all!* I wasn't honestly sure that, when we two were separate, there would be anything there that was *me.*"

Freud once observed that "we are never so defenseless against suffering as when we love, never so helplessly unhappy as when we have lost our loved object or its love." Women will find these words particularly true. For women, far more often than men, succumb to that suffering known as depression when important love relationships are through. The logic thus seems to be that women's dependence on intimacy makes them, if not the weaker sex, the more vulnerable one.

By the end of the oedipal phase we have acquired a richer, more complicated sense of what it means to be masculine or feminine. The resolution of our triangular conflicts helps shape what kind of woman or man we will be. Girls strengthen their feminine identification, hoping someday to marry a man like their father. Boys strengthen their masculine identification, hoping someday to marry a woman like mom. In the process, all of us more clearly learn what we cannot have or be. "Daddy, I love you!" a four-year-old says with a most erotic look. "I think I'll marry a man when I grow up." But that four-year-old is a boy and he will learn that the mommy he also dearly loves is the more standard model for objects of sexual longings.

While our gender identity shapes itself around our same-sex parent, we identify with our other parent too. And in middle-class America here near the end of the twentieth century, the ways one can be male or female are wide, wide open. Nevertheless we have bodies whose parts will forevermore be different from each other. And, as we travel the road of psychosexual development, we will take different forks—one for girls and another for boys. As heterosexual humans we identify and love in accordance with gender patterns and possibilities. But it is how we perceive our limits that determines if our anatomy is our destiny.

For surely some sex-linked limits do exist. And surely we may perceive them as a loss. But a recognition of limits need not oppose—*indeed it may be a requirement for*—the creative development of our potentiality.

"The potter who works with clay recognizes the limitations of his material," writes Margaret Mead; "he must temper it with a given amount of sand, glaze it thus, keep it at such and such a temperature, fire it at such a heat. But by recognizing the limitations of his material he does not limit the beauty of the shape that his artist's hand, grown wise in a tradition, informed by his own special vision of the world, can impose upon that clay."

She is saying that freedom begins when we acknowledge what is possible—and what is not.

She is saying that if we come to know the nature of our clay, we can impose our destiny on anatomy.

Sleeping Beauty at Seventeen

Madonna Kolbenschlag

Madonna Kolbenschlag (1935–) was born in Cleveland, Ohio, and studied for her doctorate at the University of Notre Dame, where she was appointed assistant professor of American Studies in 1973. She is known internationally as a speaker on women's development and spirituality, and has served (1983–87) as fellow at the Woodstock Theological Center in Washington, D.C. Her lifelong interest in folklore and fairy tales as embodiments of cultural values is shown in this excerpt.

WHERE DOES IT ALL BEGIN? IT BEGINS WITH THE fantasies of a young man or woman about their unborn child. Parental projections begin to affect the unborn female long before she becomes a reality in the lives of her parents. Unborn children, particularly the first-born, are usually sexualized in our fantasies in the dominant, or male gender. Pregnancy guides and doctors talk about "him." (Books on infant care will concede an occasional "her.") More importantly, Mom and Dad have already begun the subtle "behavior modification" of their child through sex roles. Parents fantasize that their child will be "great"—will exceed their own capabilities, will magnify them in essence and act. The dream is inevitably cast in the male gender for the fantasy is that of the hero, and only males fit the mythic pattern of the hero. Unless consciously reversed, it is the boy baby that dominates the imagination of prospective parents.

Parents also relate differently to each child, depending on its sex. One father will relate to his daughter in a very different way than another father relates to his little girl, and so some will claim that there is no stereotypical programming involved. The crucial effect, however, is the fact that no matter how the father relates to his daughters, he will usually relate to his sons differently. Likewise, the mother. From the beginning, everything shouts *vive la difference* to the young child.

Ultimately, it is a destructive differentiation. It is the beginning of the "spell" cast on the young female, the onset of the gradual contraction of the world her imagination is allowed to live in, of the roles she is allowed to aspire to. She will be given dolls and "cooed" to more; her brother will have cars for toys and will enjoy more physical roughhouse. Later, when she asks for an erector set or a football, she might be coaxed into "wanting" something else. When she skins her knee or bumps her head, she will probably enjoy more soothing, protective assurances. She will be expected to be cleaner than little boys and certainly more manageable. She may, however, be more unmanageable *because of* these expectations. Scarlett O'Hara is a classic, if uncommon, example of this phenomenon in its adult form:

> *I'm tired of everlastingly being unnatural and never doing anything I want to do. I'm tired of acting like I don't eat more than a bird and walking when I want to run, and saying I feel faint after a waltz, when I could dance for two days and never get tired. I'm tired of saying "how wonderful you are" to fool men who haven't got one-half the sense I've got, and I'm tired of pretending I don't know anything, so men can tell me things and feel important while they're doing it.*[1]

Later on and with increasing intensity the cultural milieu and peer pressure will inhibit the little girl, discouraging her from being too assertive or too individualistic. She will learn the art of "fading into the wallpaper." Peer pressure and cultural attitudes will shape the little boy in the opposite direction, encouraging him to be competitive, aggressive and individualistic—even to the point of exhibitionism. In general, little boys receive much more opportunity for solving problems and modifying their environment.

The play activities of children reinforce these social expectations. Boys engage more often in physical activities—testing their limits constantly. Girls play, on the whole, more sedentary games—games that often prefigure the social role they will play in the future. Boys construct and contact, girls read and relate. And increasingly, children do neither—they watch TV, imitate and identify with the role models they see there.

Boys, however, are generally given much more exposure to team sports than girls. Through team sports they develop a capacity for "bonding" and a competitive resilience that is relatively lacking in girls. Among mature women this often manifests itself in an evident lack of capacity for female "bonding," in emotional inadequacy in competitive situations, in a tendency to overrelate to authority figures, in an unconscious fear of success and resentment of it in other women.

The assertiveness and independence factor in the young female is muted even further by the schooling years. Since most teachers at the elementary and high school level are white middle-class females, they tend to reinforce feminine or conforming behavior in the educational situation. Absorption and regurgitation of facts is commonly rewarded: questioning, objecting, arguing, conjecturing on alternative possibilities is, at best, uncultivated—at worst, discouraged and even punished. This atmosphere leaves most boys, who have been socialized to independent behavior since infancy, at a disadvantage. The schooling process inevitably categorizes females as "achievers" in their first twelve years of school. But with their entry into the collegiate arena, where debate and disagreement are exercised vigorously, women are at a disadvantage. Female deficiency in independent thinking is compounded by the emotional programming that has convinced the young woman, consciously or unconsciously, that demonstrating such skill is unfeminine. And, lest we forget, her teachers (who will be predominantly male in the better colleges and universities) have also been programmed with this expectation.

There's an old teacher's anecdote that demonstrates the truth of the matter very bluntly. It goes something like this:

> *The difference between teaching an all-boys class and an all-girls class is that when you enter a class of boys and say "Good morning," half the hands shoot up demanding to know what you mean by "good," and the other half what you mean by "morning." When you say "Good morning" to a class of girls, they all write it down in their notebooks . . .*

Of more critical significance is the fact that the developmental pattern of girls is less consistent than that of boys. Many young girls who exhibit active, creative and competitive traits in childhood drop these behavior patterns during adolescence and assume more feminine interests. At the same time, they show a rapid increase during early school years of withdrawal from challenging, problematic situations, and the IQ levels of achieving girls do not increase through the school years as do those of boys.

The "tomboy" phase, which often precedes puberty, is, for many young girls, the last eruption of individuated personality before the fall into "beauty" and the inevitable "sleep" of the female psyche. Very few, if any, boys ever wish they were girls. But many young girls share the fantasy of wanting to be boys. By middle childhood a preference for masculine roles appears in many young girls, along with varying degrees of disenchantment with the condition of being female. The tomboy temporarily transcends this condition and enjoys the best of both worlds—she is not measured by the same competitive peer-stature as her brothers, yet she enjoys the freedom of role experimentation, of aggression and engagement with reality, of daring and spontaneity. She gains a sense of self-determination, of comradeship, of control over her surroundings. For a brief moment, perhaps, in her life span, she is the warrior-maiden-adventurer—the archetypal androgyne. Soon, a part of her will be sacrificed. Psychologists have called it "animus," poets have called it "the left hand." Always, the metaphor signifies the same thing. It is a euphemism for the suppression of the capacity for self-actualization and transcendence. Dory Previn's song "Left Hand Lost" is a kind of lament for this lost wholeness, a dream of creative personhood:

> . . . sometimes
> i get so low so low
> sometimes
> i get so depressed
> as though i lost
> a part of me that loved me
> the part that knew me best . . .
> my right hand fills the china teacups
> and needlepoints with old maid aunts
> my right hand clings to rosary beads
> and waters dying plants
> but it's never painted a picture
> nor run for president
> my left hand
> might have done these things
> if its roots
> had not been bent
> a sculptor
> a poet
> it might have been
> instead of a useless thing
> to decorate with bangles and bracelets
> and my mother's wedding ring[2]

There is no experience comparable to the tomboy phase for prepubertal males. Boys are, in fact, not as free to express cross-sex preferences, and girls have much more latitude to indulge in a spectrum of male activities. Because the masculine role is dominant and associated with superior status, deviation from it by males is less tolerated. Girls, on the other hand, belong to a class of "outsiders," a group that has inferior status in the cultural paradigm. Like members of minority groups, they often show greater adeptness in role changes and are more psychologically free to experiment. While this elasticity diminishes greatly after puberty, nevertheless the fact that "it is more important for a boy to be all boy than for a girl to be all girl" remains constant throughout the life span.

By the same token, there is no male equivalent for "Daddy's little girl," and the female child is destined from her earliest years to learn how to exist for others. Although every little girl is endowed with her own motive and psychic force, she is soon equipped with two kinds of persona, to be tried on, occasionally worn, held in readiness for the future. She will specialize in one of the roles, or perhaps interchange both, later when she is a "woman." One persona is that of *the desirable object*. This role will school her in the art of cosmetic allurement, seductive mannerism and the sublimation of straightforward assertion. If she is well-disciplined in the role, it will leave her with a compulsive need for exclusive adulation. Her capacity for developing a healthy self-concept and strong peer relations will be crippled for life.

The second persona in the little girl's repertoire is that of the desire to *live for another*. This role will school her in self-forgetfulness, service and sacrifice, in nurturing rather than initiating behaviors. Above all, it will teach her to "sleep"—to wait, forever if necessary, for the expected *other* who will make her life meaningful and fulfilled. She will give up everything when the expected one comes, even the right of creating her own self. Whether it is a husband, a religion or a revolution, she is ready to live outside of herself, to abdicate from responsibility for herself in favor of something or someone else.

With the onset of puberty the feminine role becomes an imperative—the rehearsal is at an end, the real-life drama begins. The personae or masks that the young girl experimented with are now donned permanently. The creative, self-actualizing potential recedes gradually as the young woman is enveloped in preoccupations with her complexion, her popularity and her boyfriends (or lack of them). A dimension of her personality has been anesthetized, perhaps forever.

At this critical turning point in the young girl's

life, the educational environment often exerts a crucial influence. Most junior and senior high schools are, in fact, mausoleums of the past. The whole process and organization of the school system tends to reinforce stereotypical norms and sex-role expectations, whether it is the teacher, the textbook, the curriculum or the peer stratification of the learning environment. Single-sex private schools can modify these effects somewhat, particularly in respect to the experience of "bonding" and achievement motivation, but a too premature and prolonged experience of this kind of environment can have diminishing returns—especially in terms of cross-sex socialization and academic competition. Moreover, a young girl might be at a disadvantage in merging from a female-dominated nurturing environment into the more impersonal milieu of social pluralism and corporate competition.

I learned the truth at seventeen
That love was meant for beauty queens
and high school girls with clear-skinned smiles
who married young, and then retired

The valentines I never knew
The Friday night charades of youth
were spent on one more beautiful
At seventeen, I learned the truth

–Janis Ian, "At Seventeen"

By the time they are seventeen, many young women have surrendered their ambitions to a growing need for affection, and their autonomy to an emotional dependence on the approval and good will of others. The spell is cast, and the promise of "beauty"—of being desirable—lulls the young woman into an existential limbo where everything is measured by the expectation of the one who is to come. Sleeping Beauty is not idle, however—she is busy living out the Pygmalion script (the male version of the myth), allowing herself to be sculpted, shaved, painted, plastered, pushed aside, pedestaled, pounded into a lifelike Galatea, the perfect fulfillment of a man's fantasies. At seventeen the young woman is well on her way to being a "formula female."

Notes

1. Margaret Mitchell, *Gone with the Wind* (New York: Macmillan Co., 1945), p. 79.
2. Dory Previn, "Left Hand Lost," from album *Mary C. Brown and the Hollywood Sign,* United Artists, 1972.

The Habit of Loving

Barbara Lazear Ascher

Barbara Lazear Ascher (1946–) was born in Christiansburg, Virginia, and attended Bennington College and the Cardozo School of Law. The Habit of Loving *(1989) is her second essay collection. About the essay form itself, Ascher says, "It's very satisfying to have a small space in which to tell what it was you wanted to tell. You get to the point right away instead of having to drag it out and slowly reveal it." Writing for the* New York Times *has taught her that "if you really dare to be deeply personal in your writing, you will find what is deeply personal is in fact the most universal."*

Frogs Eat Butterflies.
Snakes Eat Frogs.
Hogs Eat Snakes.
Men Eat Hogs

—Wallace Stevens

Girls, they say, are afraid of bugs, and so my husband kills the spider.

"Not with a Kleenex!" I warn him. "Use a box. With Kleenex you'll feel the crunch."

Of course roaches are worse. With a roach, no matter how large the weapon, you will hear the carapace collapse. You will feel the slow reluctant give. I leave the room before contact.

"I ain't afraid of no bug!" I protested at ten, imitating the local lingo and longing for the company of boys. I yearned for their acceptance, for entry into their muddy games, their fits and starts, giggles, kicking, rolling, hitting. Their life force. Their freedom. They offered escape from tea parties for dolls. From a dusty, still, indoor life. Relief for legs and arms that felt like elastic bands stretched to the snapping point. I longed to be propelled into their adventures, expeditions to haunted houses, overnights, and campfires.

"Oh, yeah?" said Sean with his hands behind his back. "If you like bugs so much, how about this one." His fingers were suddenly beneath my nose. He dangled the daddy longlegs before me as if it were a Christmas ornament. I smiled. My feet went cold. I stood my ground. He pulled off the legs one by one.

Such malice was fueled by his primitive sense of truth: Girls are afraid of bugs and boys are afraid of girls.

Thus the threshold guardians of the male barricades were in place: daddy longlegs, centipedes, beetles, and things unnamed squirming beneath logs.

Reptiles were less effective tools of terror, even though we were warned that playing with toads would give us warts. David was proof of that: A collector of toads, he had brown, lumpy hands to show for it. I was willing to risk such a fate in order to hold a toad or salamander or frog.

I mastered the technique of taking them alive. Lie flat. Breathe as you imagine the grass breathes. Move as you imagine the earth moves. You've got all day. You've got all of childhood to make your way, flat on your belly to the edge of the pond, to a lily pad that supports a sleeping frog. The glistening green of ponds and frogs urges you on.

There have been few victories in my life as triumphant as the hand that closes, not on itself, but on the throbbing surprise of a frog. We both open our eyes at the same time, stare, and breathe hard. We've each made a plunge for life, and this time I'm the winner. Belly down and breathless, staring into bulging eyes.

As I was on the edge of ponds, so the life of boys was on the edge of danger. Their talk was of copperheads, bears, and ominous things lurking in swamp and forest. They were attracted to these dark depths, to that which was beyond the sight of girls. If they held us in fear, they held us at bay.

We waited in the sunlight. We stood waiting to be scared. Shrieking before there was reason to shriek. Living in fear of the sudden appearance of something with many legs fighting for its life. Such a wild display quickened the heart and made one run for one's life. Or away from it.

The Superwoman Syndrome

Marjorie Hansen Shaevitz

Marjorie Hansen Shaevitz (1943–   ) was born in Fresno, California, and received a B.A. from Fresno State College in 1964 and an M.A. from Stanford University in 1967. With her husband, Morton H. Shaevitz, she is the co-author of Making It Together as a Two-Career Couple *(1980). Both her work for the University of California and her private practice have focused on helping women make transitions without falling into the Superwoman trap. She says, "I work, in association with my husband, assisting couples to deal more effectively with marital issues, dual-career stresses, and other family system problems."*

I BELIEVE THE SUPERWOMAN SYNDROME HAS DEVELOPED as a result of both historical and contemporary forces, leading us to push ourselves to do and be everything. Until you know what is causing you to act like a Superwoman, you won't be able to stop being so upset. And until you can stop feeling so upset, you won't be able to stop acting like a Superwoman. It is a well-known fact that one's ability to act effectively increases with greater understanding of a situation. So let's take a look at this Superwoman situation.

The Most Important Force Is Our Socialization*

The most powerful force determining our Superwoman status has to do with being brought up as a girl in this culture. In academic circles this process of raising children is called socialization. Socialization is "the process whereby a person [especially a child] acquires sensitivity to social stimuli [especially the pressures and obligations of group life] and learns to get along with, and to behave like, others in his group or culture. . . ."[2] Essentially, socialization lets us know what our

*For hundreds of years researchers have been looking at the nature/nurture controversy—that is, whether such things as intelligence, personality, and aptitudes are a result of our genetic predisposition (what we inherit) or of socialization (how we are influenced by the environment). This has been of particular concern to individuals studying the differences between men and women. Most of this chapter has to do with socialization factors. Let me summarize what John and Georgene Seward[1] say about the biological differences between boys and girls:

1. Girls have better verbal skills; boys have better spatial skills.
2. Girls tend to approach things in general ways; boys in analytical ways.
3. Girls are less active than boys.
4. Girls are less aggressive than boys.
5. Girls take fewer risks than do boys.

culture considers proper ways to think, behave, talk, feel, relate to others, and deal with situations.

Before the early seventies, how parents raised girls and boys seemed straightforward. Few, if any, questioned the traditional model of raising girls to be housewives and mothers and raising boys to be breadwinners. From the child's earliest months, parents and grandparents laid the groundwork for these predetermined sex roles to be played out later. Most parents employed both conscious and unconscious techniques for making their girls "girllike" or their boys "boylike." Parental socialization was then reinforced at school and in movies, magazines, newspapers, and books—by the whole of our culture.

Of course, in the eighties virtually everyone recognizes that by giving girls dolls and giving boys trucks one can influence adult behavior and thought.

It has been only in the past few years that social scientists have alerted us to the differences in socialization that men and women have experienced. Because men and women were raised *differently,* they react, think, behave, talk, argue, and deal with situations very *differently.*

By examining the differences between men and women, you will better understand yourself and your behavior; but, even more important, you will also understand some of the conflicts, misunderstandings, and interpersonal difficulties between the sexes.

The twin goals of traditional socialization were for a girl *to become a wife, mother, and homemaker,* and for a boy *to become a successful breadwinner.*

The behaviors we encouraged in girls were supposed to ready them for their future home and family roles. Likewise, the way we raised boys prepared them for the male work world.

What Parents Told Boys and Girls

How did we encourage girls to be good wives and mothers? Above all, *females were raised to be relationship- and people-oriented.* They were supposed to be *other-* rather than *self-*oriented. Here are some of the parental messages women received:

- *"Be nice!"*
- *"Be helpful; above all, don't be selfish."*
- *"Help people feel good about themselves."*
- *"Don't show tension—relieve it."*
- *"Be collaborative, not competitive."*
- *"Be warm, loving, nurturing."*
- *"Be compliant, accepting, understanding."*
- *"Don't say no; it's not nice."*
- *"Don't bother people; if you want something, do it or get it yourself."*

For comparison, let's take a look at some of the messages that boys were given:

- *"Be strong!"*
- *"Don't be helpful; someone might get an edge on you."*
- *"Argue, swear, show tension; it will keep the other guy on guard."*
- *"Be competitive, even combative; nice guys never win."*
- *"Take care of yourself; don't think the other guy is going to take care of you!"*
- *"Figure out what you want and go after it."*
- *"Don't do it if someone else can do it for you."*

Unlike men, women have been trained to be psychologically "there" twenty-four hours a day for their spouses and children.[3] Many women report that they rarely take their minds off their families. Even when they work outside the home, they think loving thoughts about their children, wonder what they are doing, and worry about them. They also report thinking about their husbands, making plans to do nice things for them, or wondering how they are. One patient of mine said she felt like she had an internal beeper that kept her always "on call."

Females have been trained to perform a mental-health function for their spouses that often is not reciprocated.[4] Women traditionally have been very available to their husbands for emotional support, encouragement, and help. Without even thinking about it, they provide an ear, an arm . . . whatever is required for as long as it is required. A University of Michigan study reported that women supply to their husbands twice as much emotional support as they receive.[5] Needless to say, some women feel they never get back what they give, and they're right. At least now we understand why.

Girls have been taught to be keepers of family tradition and ties; boys have not. Who remembers Aunt Minnie's birthday? Who sets up family gatherings? Who buys the Christmas presents? Who sends cards and gifts and flowers to acknowledge important occasions? You know who!

Girls were trained to want and need intimacy in a relationship from courtship to the end of time. Boys are trained to desire moments of intimacy, especially during courtship, but not continuously. This important difference in women and men often results in great conflict. At the end of a long working day, a working woman will still want to connect emotionally with her partner, to talk and to share. However, many a man wants to come home, withdraw, relax, be left alone to his newspaper or TV news, or his computer, because for him, the most important part of his day is over.

Girls were told to "take care" of everybody but themselves; therefore, as adults, they have difficulty asking for help or delegating tasks. Boys were told to take care of themselves and, as adults, do not have as much difficulty in asking or delegating. Most women don't think twice about doing whatever needs to be done. Unlike their husbands, who don't hesitate to accept assistance, women somehow feel that it is wrong to ask. Often, they can't even form the words. When they do, their requests are filled with qualifiers, such as "Would you please"; "If it isn't too much trouble"; "When you have the time"; or, "Oh, never mind, it really isn't that important."

Girls were taught not to express negative feelings. Because it was so important to be *nice,* girls were not to be argumentative, attacking, rejecting, oppositional, or challenging. Boys, on the other hand, were encouraged to be all these things. After all, how could they possibly expect to take care of themselves out in that cruel, competitive work world without these defenses?

Young women were taught to express themselves by being proper, personal, open, emotional, self-disclosing, reactive, indirect, and manipulative. Men were taught that opposition must be shown up or put down, deference must be exacted, directness and solutions are preferable, and face must be saved. (The trouble is that women find these male behaviors confusing at the least, frightening and threatening at the most.)

Girls were taught to be sensitive to nonverbal cues. As a result, women "read" their parents, teachers, girl friends, and, most important, the men in their lives. But men are much less sensitive than women to nonverbal cues.

Everything in a girl's socialization and training was designed around the expectation that she would someday be a mother.[6] Little or no training was given to boys for their future father roles, save their contributions as providers for their families.

In addition to providing her husband and children emotional support, a woman was also prepared by traditional socialization to take care of the family household needs. As a result of observing our mothers and being trained by them, we have emerged with internalized values, images, and feelings about appropriate behaviors and techniques for the household. Similarly, men also have internalized values, images, and feelings about the household; but theirs are based on what they saw their fathers do, and not do, in the home.

Notes

1. John P. and Georgene H. Seward, *Sex Differences* (Lexington, Mass.: Lexington Books, 1980).

2. Horace B. and Eva Champney English, *A Comprehensive Dictionary of Psychological and Psychoanalytical Terms* (New York: David McKay, 1958), 508.

3. Jessie Bernard, *The Female World* (New York: Free Press, 1981).

4. Ibid.

5. Ibid.

6. Ibid.

Names and Labels

Madeleine L'Engle

Madeleine L'Engle (1918–) was born in New York City into a family of artistic achievement. An only child, she suffered in the war between her parents over how she was to be raised. Forced to attend a Swiss school she disliked, L'Engle says that she learned to concentrate there, if only to shut out the "alien atmosphere" and, as a result, "can write anywhere." While raising her own children, she tried to give up writing but found that she could not. Although L'Engle's writing career spans forty years, her most rewarded effort is A Wrinkle in Time, *published by Farrar-Straus in 1963. Themes of family love coupled with moral responsibility are prominent in her work. The following selection is from* Walking on Water: Reflections on Faith and Art *(1980).*

Reprinted from *Walking on Water* by Madeleine L'Engle, © 1980 by Crosswicks. Used by permission of Harold Shaw Publishers, Wheaton, IL.

THE WORLD WANTS TO SHOVE US INTO WHAT IT CONSIDERS the appropriate pigeon-hole. I do not like to be labelled as a "Christian children's writer," because I fear that this will shove me even further into the pigeon-hole which began to be prepared for me when *A Wrinkle in Time* won the Newbery medal. If I am so labelled, then the implication is that I am to be read only by children, and Christian children at that. Though the chief reason that *Wrinkle* was rejected for over two years and by thirty-odd publishers was because it is a difficult book for many adults, the decision was made to market it as a children's book; it won a medal for children's books. Therefore, I am a children's writer, and that is all I'm allowed to be.

But I'm a writer. That's enough of a definition. (I infinitely prefer to say that I am a Christian than to mention any denomination, for such pigeonholing is fragmenting, in religion as in art.) So. I am a Christian. I am a writer. When I am grappling with ideas which are radical enough to upset grown-ups, then I am likely to put these ideas into a story which will be marketed for children, because children understand what their parents have rejected and forgotten. Because I am a struggling human being, trying to make sense out of the meaninglessness of much of life in this century and daily searching for revelatory truth in Scripture, it's highly unlikely that I'll ever want to write novels of pessimism or porno, no matter how realistic my work. But I don't want to be shut in, labelled, the key turned, so that I am not able to grow and develop, as a Christian, as a writer. I want that freedom which is a large part of the Christian promise; and I don't want any kind of label to diminish that freedom. It is sad and ironic to have to admit that it does.

To write a story is an act of Naming; in reading about a protagonist I can grow along with, I myself am more named. And we live in a world which would reduce us to our social security numbers. Area codes, zip codes, credit card codes, all take precedence over our names. Our signatures already mean so little that it wouldn't be a surprise if, by the year 2000, we, like prisoners, are known only by our numbers.

But that is not how it was meant to be. Coleridge writes,

> *The Jews would not willingly tread upon the smallest piece of paper in their way, but took it up; for possibly, said they, the name of God may be upon it. Though there was a little superstition in this, yet truly there is nothing but good religion in it, if we apply it to man. Trample not on any; there may be some work of grace there, that thou knowest not of. The name of God may be written upon that soul thou treadest on; it may be a soul that Christ thought so much of as to give his precious blood for it; therefore, despise it not.*

The name of God is so aweful, so unpronounceable, that it has never been used by any of his creatures. Indeed, it is said that if, inadvertently, the great and terrible name of God should be spoken, the universe would explode. The letters JHWH are a jumble of Hebrew consonants, and a better translation than Jehovah is *The Lord.*

But we, the creatures, are named, and our names are part of our wholeness. It used to be a moment of great importance when someone said, "Oh, don't call me Mrs. X. Call me Anne—or Katherine. Alex or John. My name is a gift which I offer to you."

Now the name is taken automatically—grabbed away. On television programs, the interviewer immediately calls whoever he is interviewing—head of state, composer, scientist—by the first name.

I love the rare moments when I am permitted to offer my name to someone. And I love the letters which I begin "Dear Madeleine," because the writers feel that I have already given the gift of the name through the books. And I remember times when I have been given a name—and to be given a name is an act of intimacy as powerful as any act of love.

Reflections on the History of Women

Elizabeth Janeway

Elizabeth Janeway (1913–) was born in Brooklyn and educated at Swarthmore and Barnard Colleges (B.A. 1935). Although her recent work is nonfiction, she began her career as a novelist, producing seven novels that examine women's place in family groups. During the 60s, she turned to lecturing and social criticism. Her interest in the women's movement led to Man's World, Woman's Place *(1971), which examines the paradox of the power of dependent women. The following selection, taken from* Between Myth and Morning: Women Awakening *(1974), sheds light on her assertion that there is "*no special *women's history."*

AMERICAN WOMEN ARE NOT THE ONLY PEOPLE IN the world who manage to lose track of themselves, but we do seem to mislay the past in a singularly absentminded fashion. A century ago, observers as different as Mark Twain and Henry James noticed that our identities appeared to fit loosely and be readily subject to change. In part, this is because we are Americans, geographically and socially mobile, fellow countrymen of the Henry Ford who said, "History is bunk." In part, it is because we are women, people whose lives are recurrently jolted away from continuity. Look at our personal histories, and you will find old scars of passage from one state of being to another: tomboy to junior miss; drum majorette to sociology student; art historian to computer programmer; candidate for an M.A. to harried wife-and-mother; priestess of the Feminine Mystique to divorcée; housewife to financial analyst; and older woman who has suffered the feared and fracturing shift from busy middle life to lonely, widowed age.

Acquaintance with change has some positive advantages. These transitions should, and often do, keep alive our capacity to adjust to new circumstances and to learn new rules and roles. Women are less surprised than men when they find that they do not control their lives. They have less pride invested in setting up and maintaining a consistent image of themselves to front the outside world. They are, in fact, less apt to be engaged directly with the outside world. The dooms pronounced on them by Sigmund Freud and Erik Erikson still exert force: "Anatomy is destiny." "Women are concerned with inner space, with family and child-rearing." Challenged as these dicta have been, they remain at least partially true as current, demonstrable fact. It will take more time than we have yet lived to reduce them to the level of superstition toward which they are tending. Women can't help but know that they live in a changing world. The very fashions of dress, which even nuns are now allowed to follow, tell them so.

In the abstract, then, this ability to accept

change can be seen as healthy, as a responsive adjustment which contributes to survival. But when we say this, we are at once raising the question of *who is it that survives;* of what core within us remains the same in a world of change. Certainly some of the energy of the current liberation movement derives from the urge among women to find more secure identities, the need to know who and what they have been in the past, in order to see themselves as participants with a stake in the present and a valid grasp on the future. Every emerging social group wants a history, rather as every aspirant nineteenth-century merchant wanted ancestors, roots and a coat of arms. Snobs can laugh but, in fact, a sense of one's own connection to the past, of one's continuity of being, is as much needed for healthy survival as one's ability to accept change. Particularly is this true for the sex which has been told for centuries by parents, prelates and philosophers that the traditional role of its members is to live for others and find their identities in personal relationships. To live in response to others is to live a life which is necessarily fragmented and ephemeral.

These reflections are called forth by the opportunity to take a long look at the social image of women in the last several generations, that period which hovers somewhere between hearsay and history. The first thing one discovers is that the scholarly historians who deride the idea of a special history of women are quite correct. Women have not been trend-setters, activists or protagonists in the drama of great events. If they turn up in the middle of some climactic scene, they are likely to have got there by the accident of marriage or, occasionally, of birth. Women monarchs have inherited power under laws made by men, not laid hands on it themselves, and rare indeed has been any influence their rule has had on the lives of other women *as* women. The history of women has not been made within their own ranks but has followed from external, male-initiated processes. Like their personal lives, women's history is fragmented, interrupted; a shadow history of human beings whose existence has been shaped by the efforts and the demands of others.

Even as subordinates, women have not formed a distinct group or class whose development can be treated coherently as, for example, black history can. Though women's activities have been circumscribed, the background of their lives has always been enormously diverse. They have been queens and slaves and prostitutes, ladies and laborers, poets and procurers. True, none has been president, few if any have been pornographers. They have rarely headed major industrial firms, conducted symphonies, functioned as trial lawyers or orthopedic surgeons. In top-level politics they are scarce on the ground. Once again, these limits are determined by external enforced conventions. Women's history must therefore deal less with what they have done than with what they have been allowed to do. Within the limits permitted, women have done everything, lived lives of variety and activity. They have simply behaved like human beings; and have, therefore, *no* special women's history. What is special is not their own plans and deeds but, rather, the roles, expectations and interpretations that have been projected onto them.

The paradoxical result is that any useful history of women has to be a history of what has been thought about them. It is the *image* of woman, originating in men's eyes, that alone gives her a special group identity. Which is not to say that women don't often accept such an identity—accept it whether they approve of it, resent it or (as today) see it as a unifying force, a challenge against which an attack can be mounted. The Women's Movement, indeed, is seizing on the old, demeaning image of women, the old submissive identity, in order to escape from it by overthrowing it. It is a kind of outsize palace revolution which is taking place; and those who are startled or put off by the anger the Movement activists voice might reflect on the frustration implicit in the situation of a group whose very identities have been forged by others, so that a woman's ego can hardly be trusted until it is reclaimed and made over. That will have happened on the day when women see themselves, and are seen, as human beings who happened to have been born with female sex; but it has not happened yet. The present and the recent past still bear out Simone de Beauvoir's admirable description: women are regarded as "object," misunderstood as "other" and dealt with as "the second sex."

Just the same, if we look at a compendium of popular attitudes toward women over the past century, we find much reason to hope that more realistic estimates of women's abilities are replacing the superstitions of the past. Like annals and archives, journalism can offer a pertinent and revealing selection of news items, essays, reports and advertising appeals having to do with women. Back in the 1860's, for example, the drafting of men to fight opened new opportunities for women. True, a Victorian smog of condescension and contempt soon descended again; but from the 1890's on, we can trace a sort of social case history of woman-as-she-is-seen which does document a growing, if uneven, advance toward personal dignity, autonomy and freedom of choice. These are chronicles of change, source material for the historian of ideas—or, perhaps better, of myth.

For one can't really sort out these articles and items in terms of factual news stories on the one hand and opinion pieces on the other. Opinion and news are thoroughly mixed up together, and what turns out to be most illuminating is often the taken-for-granted background, or even the tone of voice. A news item reporting the successful elopement of young Miss Double and her fiancé, Mr. Wirth (pursued across Central Park by angry Mr. Double père), is a cheerful enough anecdote of young love. But it is also bread-and-butter evidence, worthy of Lévi-Strauss, that marriageable young girls were considered by their parents to be objects of barter just seventy years ago. Indeed, the patriarchal approach of men in general to women in general is a clear indication that women were habitually thought of then as being never quite grown-up. The authority of the father descended to the husband so that a kind of paternal sway was continued inside marriage; and the mode of address to women by such figures of authority as the writers of editorials apes the affectionate, rather waggish tone of the stage father. What we are witnessing in the background of what seem to be simply news developments (Carrie Nation arrested. Growing interest in athletics for women.) is the assumption and tacit assertion that women engaged in any activities outside the home are not to be taken seriously. We are being shown not only the limits of woman's place but also the means by which the limits were then enforced. That was seldom done by argument. Instead, it was continually suggested that *women weren't worth arguing with.* The effect was to devalue woman's experience, weakening her sense of identity and her ability to hold to her convictions.

In short, the fight for women's rights has always involved more than a struggle for tangible goals like equal pay, equal opportunity, the vote itself. It has been a fight for the very right to fight, to assert one's demands, to declare that one's ambitions and needs are as important as those of men. I emphasize this point because it illuminates the purpose of those consciousness-raising groups which puzzle many people, both men and women. Why, it is asked, do women need to come together and tell each other their troubles? Aren't they just indulging in self-pity and airing emotions which should really be private? But sharing experience is a declaration of the right to judge events and emotions by one's own lights instead of by received opinion. How distorting to women the received opinions of the recent past were is well documented in this collection. A good example is a turn-of-the-century discussion among several men of women's literary interests. Do they read books at all? Don't they simply parrot the judgments put forward in reviews? No, is the reply, they do read; for they think that they may pick up ideas and information which will make them more attractive to men. And, of course, some of them are lonely. One is reminded of the caricatures of Jews *Der Stürmer* printed in the 1930's and, chillingly, that both attitudes were eminently respectable.

To be fair, such views were in contention even at the time and not only by women. An editorial writer speculates that women may well turn away from the cultivation of higher values like literature, music and art because a concern for culture will "only unfit them for living with the dullards they marry." A few years later novelist Ellen Glasgow declares that "real women," human and articulate, are beginning to appear in fiction and drive out the stereotypes of the last century. But as late as 1913 we find that any serious discussion of women's work is apt to deal with—household management! Which turns out to mean the proper instructions to, and supervision of, a staff of servants, whose numbers may be twenty-five to forty in a "large establishment" or the "typical" six.

Part of the interest of such a chronicle, then, is that it introduces us to a varnished world and does so in contemporary terms. It is very hard not to look at the past through our own hang-ups and psychic scars. To many, the early years of the century seem a haven of comfort and certainty. To others they are surrounded by an aura of nostalgic glamour. To a few they are remembered as years of deprivation and strife. But they are seldom seen without some bias of emotion. Well, here they are as they were. We can see what we have lost, and that much of it is well lost; not only the rigidly defined sex roles but also the hierarchy of class. So important was "position" that many progressive causes are reported on simply as the activities of "leading clubwomen" who interested themselves in do-gooding.

At the same time, the stark facts of life appear, as

in the report of an energetic young woman who spent a year moving from city to city to discover what jobs were open to inexperienced girls and what wages were offered. In Chicago a department store will pay beginners $5 a week, and mother's helpers are offered as little as $10 a month. In New York addressing envelopes brings $1 per thousand and a worker can soon manage to make $1.25 a day. Skill pays. Experienced stenographers ask for $15 to $18 a week in the ads placed at about this period. But what can we say to "Wanted: A little girl handy with the needle to learn fancy work. $2.50 to begin."? Or to the study of tuberculosis rates among textile workers, two and a quarter to five times those of women in other occupations? Such details underline the fact that pre–World War I America, like Disraeli's England, was made up of two nations, the "Haves" and the "Have-nots."

Intellectually, however, change was already under way in the pre–World War I years. Questions that have continued to engage the attention of women in their drive toward equality show up astonishingly early. In the two years 1905 and 1906 we find the brilliant theoretician of women's rights Charlotte Gilman noting (forty years before de Beauvoir) how women, seen as objects, take their standards and self-images from men; how social change has isolated them from the world of work until their contribution to the mainstream of life has dwindled to a point where the world could practically run without them, except for their services as domestic and industrial drudges. Susan B. Anthony discusses what women's unpaid work within marriage entitles them to after divorce. An Iowa couple (both, be it noted, veterans of earlier marriages) agrees on a detailed marriage contract, defining their roles, limiting the number of children they will have, providing for a division of money and setting a term at which they will review their life together and decide whether to renew their agreement or not. Elsie Clews Parson seriously sets forth the advantages of trial marriage. Here is the philosophic background of the suffrage movement.

Again, with the advent of World War I, we see how the need for women as workers paralleled their advance toward getting the vote. Unenthusiastic at first, President Wilson ended by presenting woman suffrage to Congress as a vital war measure. In 1918 women were being urged to go into war industry in order to free men to fight; or, more accurately, to be drafted. Jobs were being opened to women in order to force men out, for one aspect of the War between the Sexes not often noted is its manipulative use by the State and the Establishment.

With the 1920's we are in the era of the "emancipated" woman. She had the vote, of course. She also had short hair and lipstick—sermons were preached on this topic. But though we tend to think of her as a Fitzgerald flapper, or as Zelda herself, the meaning of emancipation was wider than simple citizenship in the Jazz Generation. Thus, young women with jobs didn't have to marry the first man who asked them. Most of them were still in "women's jobs," but there were not only women doctors and lawyers listed in the 1920 census, but also women architects, engineers, dentists, opticians and taxi drivers. There were also protests over inequities of jobs and wages. And there was a hard-fought battle, paralleling the current struggle for the right to abortion, over birth control. In a very real way the 1920's forecast the 1970's in the range of issues which questioned old ways and pointed up social change.

The Depression years of the 1930's produced contradictory tugs on women's status. Frances Perkins sat as Secretary of Labor in Franklin Roosevelt's cabinet, but massive male unemployment brought forth demands that married women be dismissed from jobs in order to spread work, and the National Recovery Administration put an official stamp on lower minimum wages for women workers. Another war changed this, drew women back into industry in the 1940's and for the first time in American history into the armed forces on a par with men. With the 1950's another swing of opinion persuaded many women that home was where they belonged. Young girls married earlier than ever and the baby boom began the population explosion. But, as we all remember, "Togetherness" of the 1950's began to come apart in the 1960's. This was not simply the effect of another change of mind. In spite of low wages and the restriction of women to subordinate, nonexecutive jobs, their participation in the labor force was steadily rising. Much of the affluence of the prosperous 1960's was due to the rising number of working wives and mothers. When the new Women's Movement got under way, millions of women knew from their own experience that "equal rights for women" was a phrase but not a fact.

In his memoir *Speak Memory,* Vladimir Nabokov recalls how reading Hegel on historical development via thesis, antithesis and synthesis brought home to him "the essential spirality of all things in time." History is not a linear process, in which syllogisms are posited, proven and left behind. It is a matter of human emotions, beliefs and behavior challenged by new demands, rising reluctantly (and only sometimes successfully) to meet them, falling back and then, if need be, returning to cope again with unappeased pressures. The Women's Movement began as an unfocused and almost inarticulate search for a more honorable and worthy life. It was shaped by external restrictions, some of them economic, some of them social, some psychological. It fell from time to time into absurdity, but seldom into absurdity approaching the majestic, pompous nonsense with which the status quo condemned it; take, for example, the 1909 interview with *Ladies' Home Journal* editor Edward W. Bok on the question of woman suffrage. Most women, he assured the *Times* interviewer, were *opposed* to receiving the vote, would not use it, were busy at home. Just so, psychology professor Joseph Adelson of the University of Michigan wrote in March 1972 that the Women's Liberation Movement was receiving support from only 3 percent of women interviewed and provoked in most "an attitude somewhere between irritation and indifference." So, though things have changed some, they have not changed all that much. The image of women still includes the belief that women are not capable of knowing what's good for them!

If every nation gets the government it deserves, every generation writes the history which corresponds with its view of the world. No one conceived that a record of the doings of women might be interesting or important until the old sex roles came into question. If, one day, sex roles blur so that women are fully integrated into mainstream activities, a history of women will cease to be significant. Historiography, that is, is nearly as transitory as historical events. Even so, the record of how women were thought of, what behavior was deemed proper to them, what doors were shut, and how sanctions were applied against the violation of assigned roles—these data will always be important. They explain the attitudes of the past, and the present is built on such attitudes. Their value is permanent, just because they supply a chronicle of what was thought and not an interpretation of it. Historians return to source material long after they have ceased to read earlier historians.

For all of us, historians and laymen, men and women, the reproduction of past certainties which have lost their plausibility and persuasiveness is always useful. "I beseech you, in the bowels of Christ," wrote Oliver Cromwell to the Elders of the Church of Scotland, "think it possible that you may be mistaken." Every cocksure ideologue needs to hear such an injunction once in a while. The men and women who lived out recent changes of role and relationship discovered for themselves how they were mistaken and sometimes, thank heaven, how they were right; right in their convictions and right also in their questioning. The most valuable thing we learn from the past (and I think sometimes the only thing) is that we may be mistaken. No certainty should be immune from questioning; and when the questioning springs from and is supported by experience, certainties will shift. There can be no better illustration of *this* certainty—that change occurs—than the annals of woman's changing role.

Sexual Personae

The Cancelled Preface

Camille Paglia

Camille Paglia (1947–   ) was born in Endicott, New York, and educated at Yale University. She reports that she spent her youth in the library, reading and rereading the story of Amelia Earhart, whom she describes as "an image of everything a woman should be. . . . She is woman alone. Not woman hand holding in a group and whining about men. Woman alone!" Her principal work, Sexual Personae *(1990), investigates literature from the time of the Greeks, looking at "power relationships and the use of personae in scenes of psychic combat." Paglia is a controversial figure among feminists. Lillian Faderman writes of her, "As infuriating as Paglia often is, one must be awed by her vast energy, erudition and wit."*

HERE ARE MY CONCLUSIONS, AFTER A LIFETIME of observation and reflection. Maleness at its hormonal extreme is an angry, ruthless density of self, motivated by a principle of "attack" (cf. "roid rage," produced in male bodybuilders by anabolic steroids). Femaleness at its hormonal extreme is first an acute sensitivity of response, literally thin-skinned (a hormonal effect in women), and secondly a stability, composure, and self-containment, a slowness approaching the sultry. Biologically, the male is impelled toward restless movement; his moral danger is brutishness. Biologically, the female is impelled toward waiting, *expectancy;* her moral danger is stasis. Androgen agitates; estrogen tranquilizes—hence the drowsiness and "glow" of pregnancy. Most of us inhabit not polar extremes but a constantly shifting great middle. However, a preponderance of gray does not disprove the existence of black and white. Sexual geography, our body image, alters our perception of the world. Man is contoured for invasion, while woman remains *the hidden,* a cave of archaic darkness. No legislation or grievance committee can change these eternal facts.

Thus, despite my deviant and rebellious beginnings, I have been led by my studies to reaffirm the most archaic myths about male and female. I aim to recover the truth in sexual stereotypes. Was woman's ancient mystery really only a male mirage? As a woman, I am a mystery to myself. In this book, I accept and celebrate woman's fabled incarnation of mystery and glamour, which man cannot rival except in hierarchic intensifications of kingship and godhead. Woman is at the heart of my myth-system, as she is in Harold Bloom's. Bloom wrote on the manuscript of my dissertation: "Woman is born of woman. But man is born of woman and never recovers from that fact." Possibly because of my Italian heritage, I am partial to the mystical idea of the mother. Paternal or communal proxies can never supplant the magic unity of mother and child, begun in the nine-months' dialogue of the womb.

But woman's maternal fate, from which I made an Amazonian swerve, has a darker side. From puberty to menopause, women are hormonally mired in the liquid realm to which this book gives the peculiar name the "chthonian swamp," my symbol for unregenerate nature. Pregnant or premenstrual, the female body is slowed or even immobilized by edemic engorgement, a Dionysian dowry. Women with water signs prominent in their astrological charts know what I'm talking about. The chthonian swamp, my mythic equivalent to the dread Black Forest of Northern European fairy tales, is perhaps a racial memory of the malarial Pontine Marshes of central Italy, which were finally reclaimed by Mussolini. But ultimately it is the oceanic matrix, the primal soup from which evolution inched forward and into which woman plunges month by month, in the marine obscurity of her hormonal cycle.

Equality of opportunity, a crucial political ideal that all must support, should not be confused with sexual similitude, which remains a wishful fiction. Some past tests (never entirely reliable) suggested that female intelligence occupies the broad median of the spectrum and that women do not reach the heights and depths of men, who may be genius or moron. This rings true to me. I do not believe that the historical absence of great women composers, mathematicians, and philosophers is entirely due to social factors, that is, to woman's lack of access to education and mentoring. Note, for example, in this liberated age, the rarity of world-class female chess masters. Chess shops and parks all over the world are filled with men, not women. Obsessed computer hackers are mostly male. Even sex crimes and mass murders demonstrate the greater conceptualism of men, who have a monopoly on fetishism and perversion.

I suspect men are able to "think cold"; that is, they can detach logic from emotion, in ways that may be creative but also inhumane. However, though men may be deep, mentally they are slow. Compared to women, they are poor at the rapid absorption of verbal data. Narration of complex social incidents is hopelessly impeded by male auditors, who require backtracking, repetition, and endless clarification. Women, on the other hand, can communicate even by sentence fragments: "Did he know that she saw that he—?" "Yes, absolutely!" "Oh, no! And did they—?" "Yes, right then!" This giddy telegraphy is the daily demotic of female intuition, another myth I happily defend. Women finish each other's sentences in the same way that nuns, roommates, and sorority sisters end up menstruating together—a phenomenon that even Madonna, on the road with her backup singers, has complained of. Women are in league with each other, a secret conspiracy of hearts and pheromones.

My odd point of view from the disputed borderline between the sexes began in childhood. I was an early mummer of sexual personae. Halloween was my pagan high holy day. My ingenious parents sewed and constructed splendid costumes to my specifications. At four, I was Alice, in homage to Lewis Carroll's two books, my all-time favorites. After that, my personae were transsexual: at five, Robin Hood; at six, the toreador from *Carmen;* at seven, a Roman soldier; at eight, Napoleon; at nine, Hamlet. Long before the women's movement, I was making eccentric nonconformist gestures.

Jung says every man has a repressed female self, the anima, and every woman a repressed male self, the animus. In my case, it was the anima that took longer to emerge, for the animus was never repressed. I remember my fifth-grade teacher making me stay after school because of some shoving and wrangling—I was always fighting with boys to be first in line. Furious, she pushed a dictionary toward me and made me look up the word *aggressive,* which I did, hot tears of shame rolling down my cheeks. Colorful incidents abound, such as when, as a graduate student shopping in Liggett's drugstore at Yale, I broke my umbrella over the head of a rash molester. From childhood to the present day, I have considered it my task to challenge, by word and deed, the public standards for female behavior.

Misdiagnosing the Body

Premenstrual Syndrome, Postmenstrual Syndrome, and Other Normal "Diseases"

Carol Tavris

Carol Tavris (1939?–) received her Ph.D. in social psychology from the University of Michigan. She began her publishing career in the 70s, working with the magazine Psychology Today *and editing the collection of papers entitled* Everywoman's Emotional Well Being *(1977). She has published twice with Carole Wade, co-authoring* The Longest War: Sex Differences in Perspective *(1977) and* The Mismeasure of Women *(1992). In the following selection, Tavris reviews the criteria by which we "read" men's and women's states of mind. With reference to current psychological research, she asks: Are we using a female standard to interpret the feelings of men?*

Conversation overheard in a Hollywood casting office, between a man and a woman angry at being kept waiting by a female casting director:

MAN: "It must be her time of the month."

WOMAN: "And how do we explain the rudeness of male casting directors?"

IN 1975, WHEN I WAS WORKING FOR *PSYCHOLOGY Today* magazine, we ran a short article called "A Person Who Menstruates Is Unfit to Be a Mother." The author maintained that women are hypertense and anxious for the week before menstruation, moody and incapacitated for the week of menstruation, and utterly exhausted for the week after menstruation. How, then, could the complex care of children, which requires stamina, intelligence, and several advanced degrees, be entrusted to persons who are erratic and unreliable three weeks out of the month?

This essay poked delighted fun at the then-common argument that women's abilities are limited by their physiology. Edgar Berman, Hubert Humphrey's personal physician, had recently declared that women's "raging hormonal influences" made them unfit for political office. The Canadian anthropologist Lionel Tiger had publicly worried that female hormones were ruining women's entire intellectual lives: "An American girl writing her Graduate Record Examinations over a two-day period or a week-long set of finals during the premenstruum," he wrote, apparently with a straight face, "begins with a disadvantage which almost certainly condemns her to no higher than a second-class grade. A whole career in the educational system can be unfairly jeopardized because of this phenomenon."[1]

So all of the second-class female students I knew were heartened by the burst of new research in the 1970s that was rapidly debunking many old myths and preconceptions about women's alleged physical limitations. Raging-hormone theories were on the way out, as research showed again and again that women were just as able as men to work, play, think, sing, pass exams, and otherwise carry on, even when they were menstruating, premenstruating, postmenstruating, and nonmenstruating.

It was too good to last, and it didn't. Today we are witnessing a rebirth of the belief in the unruly female body. A U.S. District Judge, hearing a recent sex discrimination case, commented that women "have a monthly problem which upsets them emotionally, and we all know that."[2] Every week another story appears about how women's hormones affect women's personalities and behaviors, another research finding about sex differences in hormones and anatomy. On a basis of a single small study, "Female Sex Hormone Is Tied to Ability to Perform Tasks" was a front-page news story coast-to-coast, although no headline appeared to announce, as a much larger study found, "Male Sex Hormone Is Tied to Antisocial Behavior and Crime."

Hormone studies are part of an ongoing tidal wave of biological research in general, and much of this research has benefited women. Women should know that the physiological changes of the menstrual cycle vary enormously, that *normal* women range from having no pain or discomfort to having considerable though temporary pain. It is important for women to know that morning sickness during pregnancy is entirely a hormonal matter, and not, as a male physician once said to a friend of mine, "a woman's way of saying she doesn't want to be pregnant." It is important for women to know that hot flashes and vaginal dryness during menopause are likewise due to temporary hormonal changes, not to a neurotic loss of femininity or sexual inhibitions.

In short, it is beneficial and empowering for women to understand the normal changes of their bodies, and not to have their feelings dismissed as psychosomatic whining. A friend of mine told me that she felt depressed when she stopped breastfeeding her daughter, and, being a psychotherapist, she immediately reached for a psychological explanation. "I thought my depression must signal a pathological inability to 'let go' of my daughter," she said, "until I mentioned my feelings to my female pediatrician. She said, 'Oh, sure, that depression is due to the hormonal adjustment. It'll be gone in a few days.'"

But while there are many dangers to the overpsychologizing of normal biological processes, as my friend learned, there are also dangers of reducing all of our feelings, problems, and conflicts to them. Everywhere we look today, we find that the normal changes of menstruation and menopause are increasingly being regarded as diseases, problems, and causes of women's emotional woes and practical difficulties. In particular, biomedical researchers have taken a set of bodily changes that are normal to women over the menstrual cycle, packaged them into a "Premenstrual Syndrome," and sold them back to women as a disorder, a problem that needs treatment and attention. Of course, the only thing worse for women than menstruating is not menstruating. When women cease having the monthly "disease" of PMS, they suffer the "disease" of Menopausal Estrogen Deficiency.

The biological mismeasurement of women's bodies poses many emotional and intellectual conflicts for women, who are caught between defending their reproductive differences from men and asserting their intellectual equality and competence. The story of "premenstrual syndrome" highlights this conflict perfectly. Research on the menstrual cycle was long overdue, as it were, and feminist scholars had to press for research funds and scientific attention to be given to a bodily process that only women experience. Many women themselves have responded positively to the language of PMS, feeling validated at last by the attention being paid to menstrual changes. But the enthusiastic support for PMS masks the more important fact that the menstrual cycle does not affect a healthy woman's ability to do what she needs to do. It also diverts public attention from other matters, such as the effects of hormones on men and the fact that men's and women's moods and physical symptoms are more alike than different.

The public and scientific fascination with PMS and allied "normal disorders" of the female reproductive system is, in turn, part of a larger medical zeitgeist, reflected in the continuing effort to reduce all human problems and emotions to the correct gene, neurotransmitter, hormone, or disease. I'm getting very grumpy about this. I must be premenstrual.

The Manufacture of "PMS"

Let's start by trying to identify the problem. A small percentage of women report having particularly difficult emotional symptoms associated with the premenstrual phase. Some describe severe Jekyll-and-Hyde-like personality changes that recur cyclically and predictably. In my lifetime of knowing hundreds of women, I have never met such a Jekyll-and-Hyde-like female. But there is something compelling about the testimony of women themselves and of researchers who have observed their behavior clinically. A woman in one study described herself this way:

> *Something seems to snap in my head. I go from a normal state of mind to anger, when I'm really nasty. Usually I'm very even tempered, but in these times it is as if someone else, not me, is doing all this, and it is very frightening.*[3]

A larger percentage of women describe premenstrual mood changes, notably depression and irritability, that they swear occur as predictably as ragweed in spring. "Unbeknownst to me, my husband kept track of my irritability days in his office diary," one friend reports, "and he could predict like clockwork when I was within a week of my period."

Which group has the premenstrual syndrome? The Jekyll-and-Hyde phenomenon reflects an abnormality in degree, kind, and severity of symptoms. But many researchers, the media, and women themselves now confuse mood changes that are abnormal and occur in *few* women with mood changes that are normal for *all* women—and, as it turns out, for all men, too.

This confusion is apparent in virtually all contemporary discussions of PMS in the media. Most of the media today regard PMS as if it were a clearly defined disorder that most, if not all, women "suffer." For example, *Science News* called it "the monthly menace," and the *Orange County Register* called it "an internal earthquake." An article in *Psychology Today* began: "Premenstrual Syndrome (PMS) remains as baffling to researchers as it is troublesome to women." *Troublesome?* To *all* women, as implied? The article turns out to be about a study of 188 nursing students and tea factory workers in China. In the tea factory, "almost 80% suffered from PMS." *Suffered?* "Overall, nearly 74% rated their symptoms as mild, 24% as moderate and 3% said they were severe." In other words, for 97 percent of the women the symptoms of this "syndrome" were no big deal.

Likewise, an article in the *Baltimore Sun*, headlined "Why PMS Triggers Hunger," begins by asking "Why is it so hard to diet when you're suffering from premenstrual syndrome?" (There we are "suffering" again.) The answer turns out to have nothing at all to do with PMS, or, for that matter, with suffering. According to the research, women feel hungrier in the few days before menstruation because their metabolism has increased. This is normal, the article states: "Your body is working as it should, building up the uterine lining . . ." Working as it should? Then why am I suffering from a syndrome?

It's easy to understand the media's confusion, because the list of symptoms thought to characterize "PMS" doesn't leave much out. One popular paperback book offers a "complete checklist" of physical, behavioral, and emotional changes, including weight gain, eye diseases, asthma, nausea, blurred vision, skin disorders and lesions, joint pains, headaches, backaches, general pains, epilepsy, cold sweats and hot flashes, sleeplessness, forgetfulness, confusion, impaired judgment, accidents, difficulty concentrating, lowered school or work performance, lethargy, decreased efficiency, drinking or eating too much, mood swings, crying and depression, anxiety, restlessness, tension, irritability, and loss of sex drive.[4] That's just for starters. Other alleged symptoms include allergies, alcoholism, anemia, low self-esteem, problems with identity, and cravings for chocolate. Some physicians have specified as many as *150* different symptoms.

Mercy! With so many symptoms, accounting for most of the possible range of human experience, who wouldn't have "PMS"? Obviously, the more symptoms that are listed, the more likely that someone will have them, at least sometimes. This likelihood is increased in checklists that include mutually contradictory symptoms (such as "was less interested in sex" *and* "was more sexually active," or "had less energy" *and* "couldn't sit still") and the entire range of negative emotions ("irritable or angry," "sad or lonely," "anxious or nervous").[5] On these lists, there is no way you can't have some symptoms.

Because researchers themselves don't agree on whether they are talking about a problem that a few women experience or that all women experience, estimates of the prevalence of the syndrome range from 5 percent (women who are severely incapacitated) to 95 percent (the number of women who will experience, as one article put it, "one or more PMS symptoms sometime in their lives"). In one typical conference on "PMS—an important and widespread problem," sponsored by England's Royal Society of Medicine Services, participating physicians tried to determine the scope of the "widespread problem." One thought it affected "between 20% and 40% of women at some stage in their lives." Another said that "a very large proportion of women are aware of cyclical physical and mood changes, but probably fewer than 5% of them are sufficiently moved by these symptoms to seek medical help." A third said that "Probably all women at some time in their lives have disturbing premenstrual symptoms . . . [but only] 5–10% of women have clear-cut PMS."[6]

It's heartening to know, I suppose, how many experts are worried about the cost to the economy of all those millions and millions of sick women whose premenstrual symptoms keep them from doing whatever work they do. One newspaper reported that "PMS-related absenteeism is estimated to have cost industry $5 billion in 1979 . . . not counting women who are working but who aren't functioning as well because of PMS." A physician writing in the *Wall Street Journal* estimated that "the illness [of PMS] costs U.S. industry 8% of its total wage bill."[7] This is no wonder, because so many PMS symptoms interfere with a woman's ability to work: she suffers from "confusion," "has trouble concentrating," and is "forgetful," "uncoordinated," and "inefficient." Some PMS guidebooks advise women to turn to routine tasks at that time of the month, and leave the really hard thinking work to later. Most of the women I know couldn't afford this luxury.

In short, everywhere you look, you find agreement that PMS is a real disorder, a disease. There's a widespread sickness among women! Up to half of all women are sick every month! Nearly all of us are sick sometimes! We're slowing down the economy! How fortunate that men are running things!

Luckily, help is at hand, because PMS cures are a thriving business. Across the country, nutritionists, psychologists, nurses, physicians, and writers are promoting books, tapes, and seminars. (One typical tape, "PMS: A positive program to gain control," promises to help all those uncontrollable premenstrual women get hold of themselves.) Physicians are setting up PMS Medical Groups, some funded by drug companies, for the specific treatment of premenstrual syndrome and, according to the promotion letter of one such center, its "disabling psychological symptoms [including] depression, mood swings, irritability, confusion, agoraphobia, panic attacks and alcoholism."[8] Many products have appeared to help women manage all these disabling symptoms. Good old Midol, "the menstrual specialist™," now offers Midol PMS, "the premenstrual specialist™." A product redundantly called "prēmsyn PMS" consists of "premenstrual syndrome caplets" which the sufferer is to "take at the first sign of PMS." These products consist of acetaminophen (an aspirin substitute, used in Tylenol), pamabrom (a diuretic), and pyrilamine maleate (a common ingredient in all pain relievers).

Natural remedies for PMS are equally popular. The health and nutrition magazines have jumped on the PMS bandwagon uncritically, offering medical, psychological, and homeopathic treatments for their confused, depressed premenstrual readers who are phobically stuck at home, drinking too much and shouting at the children. Health magazines have frequent news notes and features on PMS. "It *is* true that few women feel at their best during PMS," one item proclaimed, with no evidence for this assertion whatsoever; it went on to describe a study of sixty "PMS sufferers" who benefited from Vitamin E. Another report, titled "New Study Strengthens Link Between Caffeine and PMS," acknowledged that the "causes of PMS are not completely understood" and that "a cause-and-effect relationship between caffeine and PMS has not been firmly established." Nevertheless the article recommended that women stop drinking coffee and tea when they are premenstrual.[9]

In a nutrition magazine called *Delicious!*, the infelicitously named Jeffrey Bland, described as a "nutritional biochemist," advises women on how to "Break the cycle of monthly discomfort." Bland thinks that Judy Garland, Mary Todd Lincoln, and Queen Victoria were all victims of PMS—a rather cavalier reduction of their complicated and difficult lives to the menstrual cycle. (Retrospective diagnoses of famous people are easy, after all, since the "sufferers" can't object.) Undeterred by the lack of scientific validity regarding the variety and prevalence of symptoms, Bland has divided PMS into four subclasses and somehow calculated the alleged proportions of "PMS sufferers" in each one, offering the appropriate nutritional treatments for each. "PMS C" types, for example (for "craving"), should take Vitamin B-6, zinc, and vitamin C to control their "cravings" for sweets or salty foods.[10] Other *Delicious!* remedies include anemone pulsatilla, which may "relieve symptoms of weepiness and emotional sensitivity." Headlines in nutrition newsletters and magazines tell the story:

- "Premenstrual syndrome: coping with the enigma" (*Mayo Clinic Nutrition Letter*)
- "Pasta and potatoes prescribed for PMS" (*the Edell Health Letter*)
- "Oh! those menstrual blues: how to fight back" (*Teen Magazine*)
- "Nutrient therapy relieves pain of PMS" (*Better Nutrition*)
- "PMS? Let 'em eat carbs" (*Vegetarian Times*)

Perhaps these nutritionists should read *Cooking Light* magazine, which admitted that "No scientific evidence shows that any food, nutritional supplement, vitamin, or mineral effectively combats PMS." It couldn't resist adding, however, that "Many women are able to control their symptoms of premenstrual syndrome with proper diet, stress management, and regular exercise."[11] Jeffrey Bland, for one, agrees. Exercise, diet, and stress-reduction programs "may help many women reach their potential," he writes patronizingly, "—every day." So would a good job.

How did women manage before they knew they had a premenstrual syndrome? The story of how we got from then to now is an illuminating tale, for the idea that menstruation is a debilitating condition that makes women unfit for work has its own cycle: It comes and goes in phase with women's participation in the labor market.

In 1931, a gynecologist named Robert T. Frank created the term "Premenstrual Tension" in an article he published in *The Archives of Neurology and Psychiatry*. "The group of women to whom I refer," wrote Frank, "especially complain of a feeling of indescribable tension from ten to seven days preceding menstruation which, in most instances, continues until the time that the menstrual flow occurs. These patients complain of unrest, irritability, 'like jumping out of their skin' and a desire to find relief by foolish and ill considered actions."[12] Frank was concerned about the consequences of these ill-considered actions in the work force, because "employers of labor," he said, must "make provision for the temporary care of their employees," and some women suffer such severe symptoms that a couple of days of bed rest are necessary.

Before we evaluate what Frank was saying, let us consider when he was saying it. "It strikes me as exceedingly significant," observes anthropologist Emily Martin, "that Frank was writing immediately after the Depression, at a time when the gains women had made in the paid labor market because of World War I were slipping away."[13] It strikes me as significant, too, especially after reading Martin's account of how research findings about menstruation change over time, corresponding to women's role in the work force. At the start of World War II, for example, studies suddenly found that menstruation and "premenstrual tension" were not problems for working women. One researcher, who wrote in 1934 that menstruation was debilitating, changed her mind after the war began: "Any activity that may be performed with impunity at other times," she wrote in 1944, "may be performed with equal impunity during menstruation."[14]

But after World War II, the news changed again. The real mover and shaker on behalf of PMS was Katharina Dalton, a British physician, who throughout the 1950s wrote articles on the dangers of menstruation: "Effect of Menstruation on Schoolgirls' Weekly Work," "Menstruation and Crime," "Menstruation and Accidents," "Menstruation and Acute Psychiatric Illness," "The Influence of Mother's Menstruation on Her Child." Reading these articles is enough to make you agree that a person who menstruates is unfit to be a mother.

In the early 1950s, Dalton and a colleague coined the term "premenstrual syndrome" (to include all those women who had more symptoms than simply premenstrual tension), and in 1964 she published a book, *The Premenstrual Syndrome*.[15] The term stuck like lint. In the ensuing decades, PMS became an increasingly hot research topic, as I learned by doing a computer search.

As the accompanying table shows, research on PMS erupted in the 1970s, a decade when, as Martin observes, "women had made greater incursions into the paid work force for the first time without the aid of a major war."[16] The growing emphasis on PMS, she argues, fits the pattern of recent history: When women's participation in the labor force is seen as a threat instead of a necessity, menstruation becomes a liability.

The table tells another story as well: the coopting of "PMS" by biomedical researchers. Mary Brown Parlee, a psychologist who has been conducting

Number of articles in medical and psychological journals on "PMS," Premenstrual Syndrome, and Premenstrual Tension, 1964 through 1989. (This list omits other menstrual-cycle research that did not use these terms or categories.)

	Number of Articles in:	
Years	*Medical Journals*	*Psychological Journals*
1964	1	—
1965	16	—
1966–1967	67	8
1968–1969	84	9
1970–1971	74	5
1972–1973	87	9
1974–1975	114	16
1976–1977	146	20
1978–1979	128	16
1980–1981	148	25
1982–1983	187	36
1984–1985	218	77
1986–1987	260	107
1988–1989	305	120

excellent menstrual-cycle research for many years, observes that psychologists who were studying menstruation tended to focus on normal menstrual cycles. The big money, the big grants, increasingly went to the biomedical researchers, on the assumption that PMS was a disease or a physiological abnormality that was best studied by radioimmunoassays of gonadal hormones and by other new weapons in the medical arsenal.[17]

The move toward the medicalization of PMS was and is actively supported by drug companies, Parlee observes, which stand to make a great deal of money if every menstruating woman would take a few pills every month. Drug companies sponsor research conferences and "medical education" seminars on PMS, events, she says, "for which they actively and effectively seek media coverage."[18] It is to the drug companies' interest, she adds, if physicians and the public confuse the small minority of women who have premenstrual or menstrual problems with the majority who have normal, undrugworthy menstrual cycles.

Because of this confusion, researchers are now reduced to speaking of "clearcut" or "true" PMS to distinguish the small group of women who have severe premenstrual symptoms from those who have normal menstrual changes—and from those who have other disorders. In studies of women who come in or are referred for treatment for PMS and who keep a daily diary of their symptoms over several cycles, three groups emerge: women who have significant premenstrual symptoms but no psychological problems; a group whose major problem is depression, and whose depressive symptoms are aggravated by menstruation; and a group that proves not to have premenstrual problems although they believe they do. Women with a history of emotional disorders are overrepresented in the latter two categories.[19]

By 1987, PMS was enshrined as an official psychiatric disorder in the reference manual of the American Psychiatric Association, *The Diagnostic and Statistical Manual of Mental Disorders,* where it is called Late Luteal Phase Dysphoric Disorder, or LLPDD. LLPDD is supposed to apply to premenstrual symptoms that are severe enough to "seriously interfere with work or with usual social activities or relationships with others."[20] Even for women who have severe symptoms that are unrelated to existing emotional disorders, it is bizarre, and many researchers think detestable, to have such a diagnosis in a manual of *mental disorders.* If LLPDD is a medical condition, why is a psychiatric diagnosis necessary? Thyroid abnormalities cause mood and behavior changes, but we don't consider these physiologically based changes a psychiatric disorder. And if LLPDD reflects a psychological problem, such as depression, why is a medical diagnosis of "late luteal phase dysphoric disorder" necessary? We might draw an analogy to a man who suffers from chronic anxiety. Several times a month, he plays racquetball, an exercise that raises his heartbeat and sets off an anxiety attack. The man's problem is anxiety, not racquetball; he does not have Post-Exercising Syndrome.

Because of the evidence of sloppy research and confusion over the prevalence, diversity, and nature of premenstrual changes, LLPDD was relegated to an appendix in the manual, in a section of diagnoses needing "further study." Nevertheless, there it sits, a convenient label for physicians and psychiatrists to use in diagnosing patients and in turn receiving insurance compensation.[21]

In the early 1970s, Parlee published a major review of the research that had been done to date on the effects of the menstrual cycle. She put "PMS" in quotation marks, in order to denote it as an odd or unusual concept that "was purportedly scientific but was not supported by data." In a recent speech she described what happened:

> *A copy editor took out all the quotation marks, and with them the meaning I wanted to establish. I lost—was silenced—then in my effort to shape in a small way the scientific discourse about PMS. The processes through which "PMS" has come to mean what it does today are too powerful, too internally and mutually self-sustaining, for that meaning to be affected by the results of good science. . . . People—women, researchers, the media, drug company representatives—now use the term PMS as if it had a clearly understood and shared meaning; the only question is how to help women who "have" it. Thus PMS has become real. The quotation marks have been removed.*[22]

Many institutions and individuals now benefit from the concept of PMS. Biomedical researchers, medical schools, and drug companies profit financially. Gynecologists, many of whom have closed their obstetrical services because of malpractice insurance costs, have lost a traditional source of income and are turning to new patient groups and new diagnoses for replenishment. Many psychiatrists have shifted from conducting long-term psychotherapy to prescribing short-term (repeatable) drug treatments. Indeed, obstetricians and psychiatrists are already engaged in turf wars over who is best suited to diagnose and treat all those women with premenstrual symptoms.

But the success of PMS is not entirely a conspiracy of big institutions, although, as Parlee says, if PMS didn't exist as a "psychologically disturbing, socially disruptive, biologically caused disease" they would have needed to invent it. (They did.) We must also ask why so many women have responded so favorably to the term and use it so freely. Parlee suggests that "the language of 'PMS' is a means by which many women can have their experiences of psychological distress, or actions they do not understand, validated as 'real' and taken seriously."[23] In that sense the language of PMS is empowering for women, she believes, because it gives a medical and social reality to experiences that were previously ignored, trivialized, or misunderstood.

Like all psychological diagnoses, then, PMS cuts two ways: It validates women, but it also stigmatizes them. Psychiatrist Leslie Hartley Gise directs a PMS program at Mt. Sinai Hospital in New York, yet she too is worried about the stigmatizing effects of making PMS a psychiatric diagnosis. "If even the rumor that Michael Dukakis had undergone treatment for depression could be held against him," Gise told an interviewer, "think of what a PMS diagnosis would mean for a woman seeking public office."[24] We've come full circle. The ghost of Edgar Berman must be smiling.

Notes

1. Lionel Tiger, "Male Dominance? Yes, Alas. A Sexist Plot? No," *The New York Times Magazine,* October 25, 1970, pp. 35–37ff.

2. *Los Angeles Times,* May 10, 1990. This is the same judge, A. Andrew Hauk, whom we met in Chapter 3 giving a woman a reduced sentence for the crime of robbery.

3. Woman interviewed by Emily Martin, 1987, p. 132.

4. Judy Lever and Michael G. Brush, *Pre-menstrual Tension* (New York: Bantam, 1981).

5. For example, see "A Nightly Checklist for PMS," *American Health,* December 1989, p. 58.

6. The debate on nature and prevalence of "PMS" symptoms is in Fisher, 1987, pp. 1–2.

7. Cited in Peele, 1989, p. 141, and in Golub, 1988.

8. From an (undated) publicity letter to health professionals written by Joseph T. Martorano, M.D., Director of the "P.M.S. Medical Group: A Center for the Treatment of Premenstrual Syndrome" in New York. The letter announces that "PMS MEDICAL GROUP has been effectively treating thousands of women." That's a lot of sick women.

9. News item on Vitamin E, "The Oil of Relief," *American Health,* April 1988; on caffeine, "A Cuppa Trouble?", October 1989.

10. Jeffrey Bland, "Break the Cycle of Monthly Discomfort," *Delicious!,* March 1988, pp. 10–12.

11. "Relief for PMS Symptoms," *Cooking Light,* March/April 1988, p. 19.

12. Frank, 1931, p. 1054. On the concern of employers, p. 1053.

13. Martin, 1987, p. 118.

14. G. H. Seward's 1944 paper, "Psychological Effects of the Menstrual Cycle on Women Workers," quoted in Martin, 1987, p. 120.

15. Actually, Greene and Dalton introduced the term "premenstrual syndrome" in 1953, as an improvement over Frank's "premenstrual tension"; they wanted, they said, "to prevent missing the diagnosis when tension was absent or

overshadowed by a more serious complaint." While acknowledging that "PMS covers a wide spectrum from normality to gross abnormality," Dalton nevertheless argues that "PMS does exist and has only one definition: it is a syndrome needing treatment." (Dalton, 1987, p. 135).

16. Martin, 1987, p. 120. See also Laws, 1983, who argues that the emphasis on PMS was a direct response to the challenges of feminism; and Anne Fausto-Sterling (1985), among the first to sound the alarm against the growing PMS bandwagon.

17. Mary Brown Parlee, "The Science and Politics of PMS Research." Invited address presented at the annual meeting of the Association for Women in Psychology, Newport, R.I., 1989. See also Parlee, 1987.

18. Parlee, 1989. (See Note 17.)

19. See for example DeJong et al., 1985; Hammarback and Backstrom, 1989.

20. American Psychiatric Association, 1987, p. 369.

21. There is considerable confusion, among researchers and clinicians, as to whether PMS and LLPDD are the same or even related phenomena. Some researchers consider LLPDD to be a subset of the more severe symptoms of PMS; others think that PMS simply refers to normal menstrual changes, whereas LLPDD is a distinct disorder; others think the two labels refer to the same phenomenon. In practice, however, most of the studies attempting to confirm LLPDD as a diagnostic category use the same measures as studies of PMS do; and they lack criteria for degree of symptom severity, let alone criteria of "interference with work or relationships."

22. Parlee, 1989. (See Note 17.) The original paper she is referring to is Parlee, 1973.

23. Ibid.

24. Quoted in Lynn Payer, "Hell Week," *Ms.*, March 1989, pp. 28–31. Quote on p. 28.

The Women's Century

Francine du Plessix Gray

Francine du Plessix Gray (1930–) was born in the French Embassy in Warsaw, Poland, the daughter of Tatiana Jacovieff and Bertrand du Plessix, a French diplomat who was to distinguish himself as a Resistance hero. (In 1983, while researching her award-winning article on Klaus Barbie, she learned how her father died.) French and Russian were her first languages. She was brought to the United States in 1941 at the age of eleven and educated at several colleges, receiving a B.A. from Barnard College in 1952. She draws upon her immigrant experience in her book Soviet Women: Walking the Tightrope *(1990), from which the following selection is taken.*

THE HEROINE OF ONE OF THE MOST POPULAR WORKS of Soviet fiction of the past decades, Natalya Baranskaya's novella *Nedelya Kak Nedelya* ("A Week Like Any Other")[1] is a young scientist so harassed by the double burden of career and motherhood that she constantly feels guilty of being a failure at both. The most commonly repeated verbs in this text are "run" and "fly."

Like many working mothers, the heroine, Olga, lives over an hour away from work, in a new district of the Moscow periphery where there are as yet no stores; she runs into her laboratory on Monday mornings, often late because of some crisis with her children, interpreting every look or word from her superiors as a reprimand; after work she runs and flies from bus stops to trolley stops to subway stops to sparsely stocked grocery stores, her arms laden with groceries, often stumbling, scraping her knees. Yet this is a privileged life. Olga and her husband are research scientists with advanced university degrees. Olga shares a laboratory—where her job is to test polymer materials—with eight women colleagues who live in states of "constant anxiety, eternal rushing, fear" somewhat akin to hers.

Written in the form of one week's diary entries, "A Week Like Any Other," the angriest woman-centered text published in the U.S.S.R. since 1930, expresses with unsurpassed poignancy the nightmares of Soviet women's daily life: Food shortages; eternal queues; indifferent doctors hastily attending children who constantly get ill from sloppily run nursery schools; a dearth of the most basic household implements or services; passive husbands buried in TV or newspapers who never lift a finger to help out.

At the office, as she fills out a government-issued "Questionnaire for Women" which asks her how many hours she spends on "leisure," Olga sardonically muses: "What nonsense. Leisure. Personally, my sport is running." The next question puts our heroine into a state of panic: She must count the days of work she's skipped for reasons of illness—hers, her family's. There are only fourteen days of paid sick leave a year, and she's

---

absented herself for seventy-eight whole days because of the colds her children constantly catch at the day care center. As her colleagues chat sardonically over the questionnaire, Olga asks a subversive question: "What exactly does the concept of 'a real Soviet woman' entail?"

Olga's mornings are a particular nightmare. The children are two and four, her husband helps but grudgingly to get them washed, fed, dressed in the many layers needed in a Moscow winter. "It is five past seven and I am running, of course . . ." Throughout this narrative, one senses that the most precious part of Olga's life, outside of her beloved children, is the daily support of the women in her work collective. They take turns shopping for each other, sacrificing their lunch hour to buy communal kilos of butter, bologna, bread, liters of milk. The pressure of a woman friend's hand across Olga's cheek is the week's only reassurance, its only soothing moment.

In the evenings, if there has been a late meeting at the lab, Olga runs back toward the subway and bus stops, flies across empty lots, runs up the stairs to find her hungry children ruining their appetites by munching bread while her husband remains buried in technical journals. After dinner, while he continues reading, Olga does the dishes, washes and mends her children's and husband's laundry, prepares their clothes for the morning, sweeps the kitchen. In constant terror of the 6 A.M. alarm clock, she is seldom in bed before midnight, and must often get up during the night to soothe a child made sick by the nursery school diet.

Olga's husband, Dima, does take out the garbage.

It has been years since the couple have "been" anywhere together—a film, a ballet, even a café. It is intimated that although they "love" each other and seldom quarrel, their life is so harassed that sexual contact occurs but rarely.

Olga belongs to that new generation of Soviet women who cannot count on *babushkas* to take care of their children; their mothers are too busy with their own careers.

At work Olga is in constant anxiety of being fired.

"Am I that good a mother?" she also worries as she runs homeward from subways to trolley stops. If she forgets to alert her husband about a late conference she finds an angry spouse, children weeping again with tiredness and hunger, or made ill by the supper their father has hastily prepared.

When the longed-for Saturday morning finally comes around, Olga, promising research scientist at a distinguished laboratory, makes five days' worth of soup, dusts, scrubs floors, does the week's heavy laundry, puts up dry fruit compote, grinds meat for hamburgers, sends her children out with their father for their only fresh air of the week, irons, sews, has her weekly shampoo.

Throughout these days Olga has kept reminding herself that she's a luckier woman than most—luckier than her colleague Shura, whose husband is a drunkard; or her colleague Lyusa, who was abandoned by a married man late in her pregnancy. Still, on Saturday night there are harsh words exchanged between the spouses because Dima considers it his privilege to read while Olga continues working. After dinner she breaks down into tears during the children's weekly bath, slaps them unfairly for some small misdemeanor.

"I'm tired, do you understand? Tired!" Olga shouts out. "The undone work keeps growing!" She breaks down and sobs. "My youth is passing . . ."

Her crying fit keeps growing, Dima puts her to bed like a child as their babies howl about them, brings her a cup of tea. But later that night Olga and Dima resume their argument. Why, with two careers, do they have barely enough money to make ends meet . . . half of their salary is spent on food. . . . How to solve their dilemma . . .

Dima's suggestion is similar to many being currently proposed by Soviet husbands: Olga should stop working and stay home to take care of the family—what with all the "sick" days she takes off she earns next to nothing anyhow.

But Olga is appalled by the suggestion: "You want to shut me in here for the whole year! How could we live on your salary!" Dima replies that if he could be freed of "his share of domestic chores" he could earn more.

"All this boring stuff is for me alone," she exclaims, pointing to the kitchen mess, "and the only interesting things are for you!" What about Olga's five years of graduate study, her dissertation, her professional standing? At week's end, the couple are as harassed by the burdens of everyday life, their marriage is more tense than it was at week's beginning.

Olga's nightmarish week is hauntingly close to the plight of women deplored by Lenin in 1919, when he wrote:

"Woman . . . continues to be a *domestic slave,* because *petty housework* crushes, stultifies, and degrades her, chains her to the kitchen and the nursery, and she wastes her labor on barbarously unproductive, petty, nerve-racking, and crushing drudgery."

Olga's plight is surely not what Lenin had in mind for Soviet women when he wrote, in the same essay:

"The real *emancipation of women,* real communism, will begin only where and when an all-out struggle begins . . . against this petty housekeeping."[2] (The italics are Lenin's.)

I met many Olgas during the past year—in Riga, Leningrad, Moscow, Tbilisi, Tashkent, Irkutsk—as I traveled throughout the U.S.S.R. as the guest of a generous Moscow publisher, Progress. Progress assigned one of its editors to be my guide throughout my Soviet journey, the wondrously warm, generous, and cultivated Nonna Ionovna Volenko. Like all Soviet publishers, Progress is under the jurisdiction of a government publishing committee, *Goskomizdat,*[3] which has a branch in all of the U.S.S.R.'s major cities. Thus the local *Goskomizdat* of each region we visited could assign one of its employees to be our local guide; and it made appointments for us with women of various professions—doctors, lawyers, teachers, journalists, psychologists, factory workers—while leaving us free to speak with any other citizen who wished to open her heart to us.

Throughout the weeks of our travels together, as Nonna and I shared hotel rooms, meals, grueling night flights, and a growing friendship, we heard women complain about the double burdens of home and career in a mood of candor, bitterness, and frequent anger made possible only by Gorbachev's *glasnost.* In this nation where over 92 percent of women are fully employed, and comprise 51 percent of the nation's work force, the word we heard most frequently was *peregruzhennost',* "overburdening." It is the same word one sees in all Soviet elevators, warning passengers of the perils of overloading the vehicle with one passenger too much.

Few communal fates are more ironic than that of contemporary Soviet women. For upon the Revolution of 1917, the Bolshevik regime became the first government in history to declare women's emancipation as one of its primary goals, and to inscribe it into its constitution. Laws ensuring equal pay for equal work—akin to our doomed Equal Rights Amendment—were instantly effected. And women's right (if not their obligation) to work became central to Soviet notions of citizenship. According to Engels and Lenin, women's full participation in the labor force, and the communal households that must replace the nuclear family, would put an end to the "open or disguised domestic enslavement" (Friedrich Engels' words) imposed on them since time immemorial. The Soviet founding fathers also predicted that the overthrow of capitalism would automatically effect a radical change of male attitudes that would assure women full equality at home and at the workplace.

Yet after the first fifteen years of Soviet rule, it became evident that the Leninist ideal of freeing women from the fetters of wedlock, diapers, and saucepans was still a distant Utopia; that the government was not able or willing to implement any communalizing of household tasks, or of effecting that "radical reeducation" of the male psyche promised in 1917. In retrospect, it is also evident that the U.S.S.R.'s commitment to women's equal employment has never been ideological; it has been based, rather, on pragmatic, demographic factors—rapid economic growth, labor shortages, and a frequent deficit in the male population.

In a country as phenomenally backward as the Soviet Union, female labor, from the onset of the first Bolshevik government, was considered essential to the speedy industrialization process central to the country's survival. Stalin's Five Year Plan of 1928, and the tragic loss of men's lives caused by succeeding historical events, incited the state to mobilize still vaster amounts of women into the work force: It is now estimated that some 40 million men died in the process of coercive collectivization, in World War II and in Stalin's purges.

The Stalin years also brought a startling reversal of all earlier Bolshevik ideals concerning women and family structure. In the 1930s, the legal abortions and liberal divorce laws originally legislated under Lenin were repealed or severely curtailed. As Stalin's regime realized that rapid industrialization, contrary to original expectations, did need the discipline of family life, there arose a cult of motherhood quite as intense as it had been under the czars. The state evolved a vast hierarchy of rewards glorifying fertility—Motherhood Medals, Order of the Glory of Motherhood, Mother Heroines (ten children or more).

Divorce and abortion laws were liberalized again after Stalin's death. And in the succeeding decades severe social flaws—dire scarcities of food and housing, an enduring tradition of male chauvinism, increasingly ineffectual social services—consistently thwarted the government's appeal for larger families.

Thus since the early 1960s, the Soviet leadership has been confronted by a perhaps insolvable dilemma: It needs woman as both producer and reproducer. It is faced with impending labor shortages, a dramatic increase of divorces, and an alarming decline of births in those European parts of Russia where its major industries are clustered (a shortage of 1.7 million industrial workers is forecast for the year 2000).[4] It is thus encouraging more women than ever to work full time; but in order to salvage its future labor force, it is simultaneously demanding an increasing amount of offspring—preferably three per family—from a nation of women so harassed that they are more and more reluctant to bring up more than one child.

Ironically, the government's propaganda for larger families has helped to heighten women's awareness of their second-class citizenship. Citizens such as the archetypal Olga of "A Week Like Any Other" have become increasingly conscious of the paper equality offered them, of their segregation to poorly paid sectors of the economy, and of the sex-role stereotyping that causes their poor promotion records.

For in the past decade the average female worker, although slightly better educated than her male counterpart, earned only two thirds of the average male income—a proportion close to those of the last prerevolutionary years. Nearly half of Soviet women are employed in unskilled manual labor or low-skilled industrial work.[5] They comprise, for instance, 98 percent of the nation's janitors and street cleaners, 90 percent of conveyor belt operators, one third of railroad workers, over two thirds of highway construction crews and of warehouse workers—much of it heavy physical labor that can be extremely harmful to women's reproductive systems.[6] As for that fast-declining population still employed in agriculture, a whopping 85 percent of the mechanized operations are run by men, leaving women to perform a major part of the more arduous manual work.

The higher professions are equally unbalanced: Over 80 percent of school teachers are women, yet they comprise only about one third of school principals. Some 77 percent of doctors are women, but 52 percent of hospital administrators are men, who remain in charge of formulating all national health policy. The inequity is even more striking among engineers and skilled technical workers, 70 percent of whom are women: In those fields, women only constitute 6 percent of work collectives' leadership, from section chief to enterprise manager.[7]

This inequity prevails even though the quality of women's work is unanimously admitted to be better than men's. Upon my very first week of researching this book I heard one of the chief editors of my Moscow publishing house state his preference for women employees. "If I have to choose between a man or a woman for a *middle-level* editorial position," he said (he emphasized those two words), "in nine cases out of ten I'll choose the woman. How much more careful, responsible, punctual, neat, conscientious, they are in their work!"

I would repeatedly hear these flattering attributes concerning the working habits of the "Fair Sex"—a phrase still traditional to Soviet men, now used ironically by women to stress their growing discontent.

"Our women work well out of a sense of duty, even if the task bores them," says physicist Ivar Knets, the rector of Riga's Polytechnic Institute, who has spent two years in the United States on exchange fellowships. "Whereas Soviet men have a shorter attention span, keep changing lines of work out of restlessness, will only work decently if they feel the immediate usefulness of their labor."

His fellow Rigan Monika Zile, editor of Latvia's largest women's magazine, believes that the quality of Soviet men's work is too often undermined by their lack of self-esteem.

"In any working situation men need far more compliments than women do," she says. "They must be constantly reassured, constantly thanked for what they're doing. We must evolve some way to boost the morale of our male workers, perhaps on the model of the Japanese managers, who handle morale brilliantly. Somewhat like the Japanese, our women are motivated by their pride in their work rather than by their level of material achievement, which is the way it should be." (Soviets often refer to women workers as "our Japanese" because of the meticulous, self-assured diligence of their work patterns; I have also heard it said that one of the aims of *perestroika* is to motivate men to work as well as women.)

Yet however esteemed their work habits, women remain clustered in positions of lower wages and lesser power because they are viewed as an unstable work force: Due to childbearing and the need to care for their children when they are ill, they have a high rate of absenteeism. In any branch of skilled work, male employers are wary of the loss of research knowledge caused by such absences.

These imbalances of power in a nation founded on

the principle of sexual equality cannot be solely attributed to patriarchal attitudes. In analyzing Soviet women's absence from the higher echelons of politics and labor, Western feminists have tended to put too much blame on men's sexist biases. Soviet women are the first to admit that their numerous material hardships, such as the daily stint of standing in long queues for the family's evening meal, rob them of the spiritual and physical energy to strive for positions of greater power. And in the *glasnost* era they often note, with a touch of irony and pride, that in view of the totalitarianism and moral debacle of past Soviet regimes (only recently disclosed to them) their skeptical reticence toward political power may have been prophetic.

"Politics always struck me and my women friends as something deeply unethical, as dirty work," says Olga Lipovskaya, a young Leningrad mother who supports her family by working as a night watchman in a factory. "We've always sensed that personal goals were more important."

"From earliest youth women have far greater distrust then men of political slogans, of all political activities," says Leningrad fashion designer Aleksandra Sokolova. "that's because we've got sharper minds."

Politics seems to be equally distrusted by women of the "working class," as industrial workers are still habitually (and admiringly) designated. I once asked a Moscow factory worker why, in her opinion, women, in any average year, have formed less than 5 percent of the Central Committee.[8] (Only two women, Yekaterina Furtseva, and, as of 1988, Aleksandra Biryukova, have ever been a member of the all-powerful Politburo.)

"Thank God there are so few of us on the Central Committee," she quipped. "Let the guys fight it out up there with their power games, why should we bother with such junk?"

By the early 1980s, at the end of those Brezhnev years now referred to as *Zastoi*, "the Great Stagnancy," the heroic tolerance of Soviet working women was showing signs of wear. They had begun to use the ironic phrase "We have *too much* equality." To many of them, equality had begun to mean the equal right to carry hundred-pound sacks of grain or bricks, weight loads that often infringe on the thirty-pound limit defined by the state for women workers. Meanwhile, many of the social structures and services which enabled their mothers and grandmothers to pursue careers, and which had once made the Soviet Union a showcase welfare state—free medical care, preschool centers, government family benefits, parental help—had degenerated beyond recognition.

The *babushkas* who helped to rear a generation of youngsters in the first Soviet decades have begun to be an extinct species, for the mothers of most young women are themselves hard at work. An increasing amount of young mothers are therefore jeopardizing income and careers to stay home with their children for three years or more in order to keep them out of poorly run government crèches. There have been numerous reports, from such institutions, of corrupt *nyanyas*—day-care workers—who adulterate the little ones' milk with water, and mix bread into their meat rations in order to take the food home; of centers so carelessly run that the youngsters frequently get lice and other skin diseases; of centers so understaffed that their supervisors keep windows open throughout the coldest days, deliberately inducing respiratory infections in order that more children might stay home. For throughout the Soviet Union, the dearth of day care centers is such that some 3 million youngsters are wait-listed for them.

In the past two years, when Gorbachev's *glasnost* began truly to flower, and ravaged the seventy-year-old myth of a Perfect Society, many women have become vociferous in their complaints against such social flaws. My friend Olga Voronina, a philosopher, points to the appalling disparity between Soviet women's arduous schedules and the relative freedom of their men. The average working mother, she notes, spends a staggering forty hours a week on shopping, food preparation, housecleaning, and laundry. The corresponding amount of time spent by men on domestic tasks amounts to less than five hours, most of it devoted to shopping.[9]

"We still apply the old stereotype of the all-capable and resilient [Soviet] woman," historian Anna Pankratova recently wrote in the popular weekly *Moscow News*. "Yes, she *can* do everything, but she *doesn't want to any more*."[10] "Everything has been proclaimed, but all still has to be obtained," another protester writes in the same newspaper, comparing Soviet women's so-called emancipation to "Atlases putting all their load on the shoulders of caryatids." A sociological tool seldom used before the Gorbachev era—public opinion polling—shows that even though the working mother still enjoys far greater prestige in the eyes of her children and husband, and the term *khozyaika*, "homemaker," remains very derogatory, one out of five Soviet women would willingly give up work if they could so afford.

Karl Marx liked to quote the words of the French Utopian socialist Charles Fourier: "Social progress can be measured accurately according to the social status of the fair sex."[11] Due to their arduous double shift, and to the lack of any national tradition of collective action since 1917, women have little opportunity to lobby for the fulfillment of this particular Marxist ideal. They are also hindered from cohesive action, to this day, by their government's censure of any "feminist" movement that would function outside of Party control (such an activity is still branded as "bourgeois deviation"), and by their curious lack of solidarity.

For in our decade, the deep, loyal friendships for which Russians have been fabled seem to have waned among women. There is a striking lack of trust among females—a result, perhaps, of the scarcity of men that has prevailed since World War II, women's abiding sense of competing for the precious male. Most professional women, even in a society of traditional Moslem roots like Tashkent's, will admit that there are few members of their own sex, beyond their mother or grandmother, on whom they can rely; their most trusted confidants seem to be men, "platonic friends" who are usually members of the same work collective.

"We simply don't have enough energy left to have friendships outside of the workplace, we have no time to pick up the phone and communicate our grief and weariness to a sister soul," a school teacher in Leningrad told me. "In such solitude, with such a heavy professional and domestic work load, how do you expect us to fight for women's rights as you do in Chicago?"

One of the most poignant outcries I heard against Soviet women's "double shift" came from a young mother of two who is a program producer at the government television station in Riga, Latvia. In the company of four of her colleagues and of my traveling companion Nonna Volenko, we had again been discussing Soviet women's central complaint—the overburdening duties of career, housekeeping, and child-rearing summed up by the constantly recurring phrase *trudnosti byta*, "the hardships of everyday life." Who is more lonely *within* marriage, I'd asked her, men or women?

"Women are far, far lonelier," the television executive said with bitterness. "Look here, I come home, I'm exhausted. I feel lonely because I'm so exhausted that I can't and don't want to love any one, I only want to rest, they all just bother me, all my womanly instincts have been drained out of me . . .

"I'm too tired to love!" she exclaimed on the brink of tears.

A vehement chorus of agreement, and of anger toward men, rose from her colleagues. "Of course, when *they* come home they can all rest, they have nothing else to do, or else they pretend to tinker about the house again. . . ." The group went on to agree that "no man we know is capable of washing his own plate."

And yet many women I've talked to prefer to remain exhausted, to continue complaining, and to keep their husbands out of the kitchen, where "it is not their place to be." As nineteenth-century Russian literature evidences, women's suffering as redemptive force is a central theme of Russian culture. And many contemporary women admit that their tradition of heroic self-sacrifice is a form of power play, a way of retaining their aura and their status.

"Of course we're grossly overburdened," a factory worker in Siberia told me. "But we're so used to it we wouldn't give it up for the world. We take such *pride* in surviving it."

Notes

1. Natalya Baranskaya, "A Week Like Any Other," *The Massachusetts Review*, Autumn 1974.

2. V. I. Lenin, *A Great Beginning*, excerpted in *Not by Politics Alone, the Other Lenin*, edited by Tamara Deutscher (Westport, Conn.: L. Hill, 1973).

3. The official translation of *Goskomizdat* is "State Committee of the U.S.S.R. for Publishing, Printing, and Book Trade."

4. *Novoye Vremya*, July 1987.

5. Olga Voronina, "Zhenshchina V Muzhskom Obshchestve," in *Sotsiologicheskaia Publitsistika*, no. 2, 1988.

6. Ibid.

7. E. B. Gruzdeva and E. S. Chertikhina, *Soviet Sociology*, Winter 1987–88. See also Mary Buckley, "Women in the Soviet Union," *Feminist Review*, 1981.

8. Gail Warshowsky Lapidus, "Occupational Segregation and Public Policy: A Comparative Analysis of American and Soviet Patterns," *Signs*, Summer 1976.

9. Voronina, "Zhenshchina."

10. *Moskovskie Novosti*, "Angry Women Demand Change," June 15, 1988.

11. Quoted in *Moskovskie Novosti*, "On the Women's Problem," August 21–28, 1988.

Fool's Fire

Bernadette Vaughan

Bernadette Vaughan (1935–   ) was born in Reading, England, and taken to France and French West Africa (now Senegal) as a young child. She returned to England in 1941 and lived there for twenty years before coming to the United States in 1961. She has worked as an actress with the American Conservatory Theater and the Inner Stage. Vaughan comments on the condition of American women that "they are not permitted to grow old." Writing for the Berkeley Monthly *and the Kensington Ladies Erotica Society, she agrees with Chilean author Isabel Allende that "writers should remain exiles." "Women," Vaughan adds, "are the most abandoned of exiles."*

I HAVE ALWAYS WANTED TO BE NORMAL. MY mother, accustomed to being yanked into outer psychic space with scant warning by the whims of her parachute-size soul, was a firm believer in the power of outward appearances. She was sure that if you looked right you could fool all the people all the time.

Somewhat understandably, then, I always gave normality an appearance. This was just fine when I was very young and cared for by a doting nursemaid: tremendous amounts of time were spent on the way I looked. We lived a charmed colonial life, my sisters and I, in what was then French West Africa: the three adorably-dressed little girls of a debonair Englishman and his chic, vivacious French wife.

But then, as Jacques Brel says, the wars came down. The old order changed abruptly. After a precipitous flight from our life of dubious ease I found myself in blitzed, blazing England, a pupil in a convent school run by a French order of largely Irish nuns. My mother, traumatized beyond repair, turned with increasing fervor to her turbulent inner visions. Reflecting her internal deterioration, her punctilious elegance flipped to its dark side and she embraced dishevellment with the same energy she had applied to expressions of high style. Gripped by obsessions and fetishes, a nomad lost in her own troubled landscape, she had only her frayed silk turbans, her Coty *Chypre* scent and her enormous snakeskin handbag, stuffed with photographs, birth certificates and house deeds, to reassure her of her lost place in the world's eyes.

Commensurate with her decline, my desire for normality increased. I did not know then that this was to be my life's preoccupation. All I knew was that I yearned to count as my friends the girls whose mothers baked sad, damp, wartime cakes and went to Women's Institute meetings wearing small hats hung blamelessly with bunches of cherries. I wanted to be like their daughters, cherished girls whose Viyella uniform blouses stayed clean all day long; whose shiny hair was braided and tied with satin bows that never fell off or turned

Reprinted with permission of the author.

to string; whose homework was handed in unblemished by ink, or jam, or bacon fat or tears. These were the girls the nuns loved and praised. Their school clothes at the end of term were as pristine, as crisp and fresh, as they were on the first day. We wore uniforms made of wool serge, tussore silk, velours and panama straw. Now, considering these extravagances, I shiver to think of the sacrifices made by merchant seamen plowing through U-Boat haunted waters to satisfy the vanity of our fee-paying parents.

Instead, however, I found myself gravitating toward friendships with the eccentric misfits among my contemporaries—rangy, unkempt girls who read voraciously, loathed field hockey and wept noisily at the first intonement of Mother Superior's dread precursor to punishment: "Ah, glory be to God, 'tis a *bold* girl ye are!" Among them, stockings ran, milk dripped, hair ribbons shredded and ink relentlessly saturated every expensive texture. By the end of the term I was a moral and sartorial mess: stained, scuffed and shamed.

All I wanted was to be *normal.* I kept trying, but there came a point in the process when I perceived that my goal was unusually elusive. Perhaps I was trying too hard? Or too prematurely—perhaps normality would happen, miraculously (and certainly I believed in miracles) when I reached A Certain Age? Come to think of it, perhaps that was what was meant when people, usually men, spoke with averted eyes about "women of A Certain Age." Perhaps I didn't have to do anything, simply wait. Perhaps a little patience was in order.

So I waited for it to happen to me. I went to college, and dated Pakistanis bound for the Diplomatic Corps and English atheists with working class accents, avoiding the well-bred young barristers and stock brokers I understood to be my salvation. In those days, as they waited for marriage, women took jobs as secretaries and perfected the techniques of subservience and behind-the-scenes power brokerage that would be their mainstays in a life of career domestication. But I wanted to write. "Be a writer's secretary," said my mother, and I did, arriving each morning for work at a secluded enclave off Piccadilly just in time to be unnerved by Graham Greene's haunted stare from his doorstep as I let myself in to his neighbor's apartments across the courtyard.

My career as handmaid to the literary rich and famous was brief. My employer was a recent and zealous convert to Catholicism; I was an avowed apostate. We quarrelled irreparably about St. Therese of Lisieux and I went to work in public relations.

My arrival in the United States was the result of impulse; once here I married my psychotherapist. My first child was born by the Lamaze method while every other woman in the hospital was either anesthetized or groggily mumbling "Is it a boy or a girl?" I nursed my babies when breast-feeding was considered pornographic; when my second child was born I rose from the delivery table and walked back to my room, fulfilling my promise to the obstetrician, who wanted to make the point to the hospital—from which he was almost fired for reckless endangerment—that childbirth is a natural process, not a debilitating disease, and if God had wanted us wheeled out of delivery rooms He would have given us rubber tires.

After divorcing my husband, urgency set in. I needed a place to be, work to do. As an environment, what could be less normal than a thickly forested hillside in upstate Pennsylvania? I had two small children to raise. I'd go West to find normality, to San Francisco, perhaps the Haight. The children spent the summer with their father and I drove out to the coast with a gambler friend and without a spare wheel. As for work, what better than the stage? I enrolled at the American Conservatory Theatre, sent for my children and involved us all in an alternative, parent-participatory school that held classes in the Panhandle and at the beach.

And still I waited. Perhaps when I was forty, I told myself, I would be normal. Right now things did not look too hopeful, but *some day soon* it would happen. I knew what it would look like, too. My hair would suddenly become manageable. My legs would become long and slender. I would not screech: "Oh my God, *no!*" on hearing less than welcome news; I would say the right thing, always, like Jim's aunt in "A Child's Christmas in Wales." My children, far from disowning me in airports, zoos and other public places, would glow with pride and say: "That's my mom! Isn't she wonderful?"

Oh, I could see it all. The only question was: *When would it happen?*

Forty came and went and my life remained largely the same—that is, inevitably taking turns for the extreme. All around me, lives were being brought under control. My friends (like myself single parents who had spent the seventies perched on the knife-edge of personal or financial disaster) emerged from the era's maelstrom of shared cars, food, time and emotions as Ph.D.s and C.E.O.s and real-estate moguls. They gave up experimenting, frequented expensive hair salons and had their colors done. I went to England and reconciled with my family. "Zany elegance," said my Sloane Ranger sister fondly, watching me unpack my wardrobe. "You don't change, darling."

Back in this country, my remarriage signalled brightly that normality might be at hand (my husband is a physician and I have noticed that, viewed from afar, in a fog and lit from behind, doctors' wives in my age group appear to have a handle on it). The reception—my idea—was a picnic under the California redwoods in the first sopping wet week of January. Meanwhile, my stage career was taking a turn for the bizarre: I was deriving far greater satisfaction and drawing more attention playing absurdist grotesques than I was from the classics and drawing room comedies I saw as my natural professional *milieu.* My audition for the Queen in "Hamlet"—a summer Shakespeare festival—brought me to the attention of the director of a tandem production. He thought I would be perfect for the part of the Player King in "Rozencrantz and Guildenstern Are Dead."

It was time to pause and reconsider. Did the rest of the world know something I did not? Things were not going according to plan, and time was running short.

Then my agent took me in hand. I should know, she said, that I looked *abnormally* (the familiar word, familiarly italicized) young for the age group to which I chronologically belonged. I should *normalize* my appearance somewhat: throw away the feather boa, pension off the velvet boots; weave some grey into my hair. Think middle-aged rather than ageless and for God's sake, try to be more—well, *normal.*

She's right, I thought. The hell with it. This *fuego fatuo* has been eluding me for more than half a century. It's time to deploy some primitive forces. What this quest needs is the modern equivalent of the jawbone of an ass, something to help me corner it, club it senseless, wear it like a pelt and let the power rub off. And I went straight to the hair salon without making an appointment. A glowing-eyed girl of twenty or so was assigned my stylist. Her name was Sara; she watched as I leafed crossly through one of those glossy coffee table books on haute hair couture. Some photographs of the spikes, glitter and eccentric asymmetries of punk hairwork appeared. Immediately I stopped turning the pages. Oh, damn and blast—I *liked* these looks! I liked their iconoclasm, their self-mockery, their sly, sparkling mischief. They were emblems of some vital, sublime connectedness, like a jester's cap and bells. Suddenly, I was terribly tired.

"You'd look great with one of those," said Sara. "Everyone's wrong about them—they're not for kids at all. They're too knowing. They're for women who've lived and who know themselves. Your age, my mom's age. Want to try one? We could paint some streaks in after, gold, pink. Nothing you couldn't shampoo out if you didn't like it. What do you think?"

What did I think? I thought this was one of those crystalline moments of perfection that Ingmar Bergman talked about in "Cries and Whispers." I thought this infant should be next in line for Pope. This babe, this most recent suckling, had opened her mouth and in her wisdom affirmed the direction of my life. I saw what I had been missing for all these years: normality is not tantalizingly *out there,* somewhere, a commodity reserved for the world's elite, available only to the lucky few. It's here, within, making its presence felt as joyous, compassionate self-acceptance, waiting for the signal to work its transformational magic. And suddenly, decisively, something that I had always believed in but had incorporated only in a vague and intellectual way moved in and took up residence in my consciousness: an unassailable acceptance of the value, the moral necessity, of variety in the elegant, universal design. (It was what a friend used to call "a Thomas Treherne attack." They tend to happen at unexpected and often inopportune moments, since my response to epiphanies is speechlessness).

Sitting back, I looked in the mirror. Some words I had read somewhere scrolled across my mind: "I must learn to love the fool in me . . . who feels too much, talks too much, takes too many chances, wins sometimes and loses often, lacks self-control, loves and hates, hurts and gets hurt, promises and breaks promises, laughs and cries. It alone protects me against the utterly self-controlled, masterful tyrant whom I also harbor and who would rob me of humanity, aliveness, humility and dignity, but for my fool."*

"Go right ahead," I said to the tall child with the scissors, standing behind my chair. Plainly, she would do better than most as Secretary General of the UN but right now she was waiting to bring order to some local chaos. "Whatever it takes. Pink *and* gold, if the spirit moves you. Just don't make me look normal."

*Theodore Isaac Rubin: "Thoughts from a Psychoanalyst's Notebook."

"Take Off the Red Shoes"

Rebecca Radner

Rebecca Radner (1940–) was born in Chicago. At present she lives in San Francisco, where she writes poetry and reviews books for publications such as the San Francisco Chronicle. *A Buddhist practitioner, she is drawn to feminism but does not believe in* isms. *The following poem alludes to the 1948 film* The Red Shoes, *itself based on a story by Hans Christian Andersen. In the movie, a young ballerina (Moira Shearer) is destroyed by the choice she must make between her love for dance and her attraction to a possessive young composer.*

"Take off the red shoes"
she cried dying
in the movie
but in the story
they simply cut
off her feet & the shoes
danced away

    I fear I'll lose
    everything for love &
    I did once I did

        Giselle Swan
Lake Coppélia Love
leading inescapably
    to death One white feather
fluttering to the stage

from the wings we could see
the ballerinas sweating
Greasepaint Satin shoes
worn out in an evening Stiffened
skirts wilted
        We could hear
the hard pointes of slippers

---

thunking on the resined stage
    & on the stage
each swan in turn bent
Spun & Died

the older girls had calloused
knotty feet Long hair pinned
back Wide scared eyes

    her feet danced
    away without her
    After a while
    she died

when I did get toe
shoes they were of course
pink with long satin ribbons
& hard blocked toes In time
the fronts of my narrow feet
broadened The toes
bent & sometimes bled
    Petits battements
at the barre *Tours chaînés*
across the floor Studying
mirrors Trying
harder ("your second toe's
too long") Rebellion of maimed
feet Take off the frayed
shoes Wrap
them in tissue
        Last year I tried on
the toe shoes of a young
girl Once around
the room was all
I could stand

    I saw the movie seven
    times Red-haired
    & chic she dances
    Does a *grand jeté* off the bridge
    before the approaching train
    "Take off
    the red shoes"

my husband said "you can't
cross the room without
bumping into something How could
you have danced"

I dance at night
while he watches TV
I divorce him
I dance in my one-
room apartment
At parties With men
Sprain my ankle
Break it Tear
the ligaments Stop
dancing Start
Barefoot Careful
Alone

we've never danced
together I know
how it would be
You'd lead &
I'd let you What
have I learned

One way or another Pain
Repentance & Death Her whitened soul
ascends to heaven where
she will never dance again

but first she whispers "take
off the red
shoes" which demanded more
than she was willing
in the end to give Demanded
she give herself
herself

I am ten years old
I have perfect
feet I have not begun
to imagine you I am waiting
for my red shoes

IV

Breaking Stereotypes

But at the same time may I remind you that there have been at least two colleges for women in existence in England since the year 1866; that after the year 1880 a married woman was allowed by law to possess her own property; and that in 1919—which is a whole nine years ago—she was given a vote? May I also remind you that the most of the professions have been open to you for close on ten years now?

–Virginia Woolf, *A Room of One's Own*

In another factory in Easton, Pa., Cassidy inspects sportswear, and her life as a working mother, for flaws. "I think you can work and be a good mother," said the 42-year-old mother of two. "We're doing it. When people compliment you that they're nice children, then I think you've been a terrific mother."

–Susan Chira, "Women say goodbye to life of June Cleaver"

Until very recently, the choice to be or not to be a mother was virtually unavailable to most women; even today, the possibility of choice remains everywhere in jeopardy. This elemental loss of control over her body affects every woman's right to shape the imagery and insights of her own being. We speak of women as "nonmothers" or "childless"; we do not speak of "nonfathers" or "childless men."

–Adrienne Rich, *Motherhood in Bondage*

Superwoman

Anne Petker Dickau

Anne Petker Dickau (1953–   ) was born in Fowler, California, and grew up among Mennonites in Bakersfield. She prepared for her career as an elementary school teacher through the program in education at California State University, Los Angeles. Currently, she lives in Minnesota with her husband and two children. About her writing, she says that Sue Bender's book Plain and Simple *had the effect of crystallizing for her the message that a woman can't do it all, but if she will focus and get her life in order, she can do what's important to her. In the poem "Superwoman" (1991), Dickau imagines a magazine image which taunts her with the illusion that "you can have it all."*

I crumpled Superwoman up in my hands and threw her away,
But another appeared again on the next page,
Sensuous and commanding.
Blinded, yet inspired,
I flew up, reaching toward perfection.
The cape, once in flight, fluttered helplessly behind
    my unveiled eyes.
Exhaustion, Tears, and Defeat
Surrounded my steady descent toward reality.

A crumpled Superwoman gazed back at me thru paper eyes.
A fictional heroine born of
My dreams, the Movement, and life's demands.
She was doomed from the beginning,
Yet her myth struggled to survive.
Both of us could not be.
So, since I was real and she was not,
I killed her.

A New Life Plan for Women

Betty Friedan

Betty Friedan (1921–   ) was born in Peoria, Illinois, received her B.A. in psychology from Smith College in 1947, and continued to study at the University of California at Berkeley and the Esalen Institute. She became a freelance writer after her marriage and the birth of her children. In The Feminine Mystique *(1963), from which the following excerpt is taken, she explored what had become of the gains for women during the early twentieth century and World War II. Why, Friedan asked, did the 50s find women back in the kitchen? In 1966 she founded and became the first president of the National Organization of Women (NOW).* The Second Stage *(1981) discusses the women's movement twenty years later.*

"Easy enough to say," the woman inside the housewife's trap remarks, "but what can I do, alone in the house, with the children yelling and the laundry to sort and no grandmother to baby-sit?" It is easier to live through someone else than to become complete yourself. The freedom to lead and plan your own life is frightening if you have never faced it before. It is frightening when a woman finally realizes that there is no answer to the question "who am I" except the voice inside herself. She may spend years on the analyst's couch, working out her "adjustment to the feminine role," her blocks to "fulfillment as a wife and mother." And still the voice inside her may say, "That's not it." Even the best psychoanalyst can only give her the courage to listen to her own voice. When society asks so little of women, every woman has to listen to her own inner voice to find her identity in this changing world. She must create, out of her own needs and abilities, a new life plan, fitting in the love and children and home that have defined femininity in the past with the work toward a greater purpose that shapes the future.

To face the problem is not to solve it. But once a woman faces it, as women are doing today all over America without much help from the experts, once she asks herself "What do I want to do?" she begins to find her own answers. Once she begins to see through the delusions of the feminine mystique—and realizes that neither her husband nor her children, nor the things in her house, nor sex, nor being like all the other women, can give her a self—she often finds the solution much easier than she anticipated.

Of the many women I talked to in the suburbs and cities, some were just beginning to face the problem, others were well on their way to solving it, and for still others it was no longer a problem.

▪ ▪ ▪

The only way for a woman, as for a man, to find herself, to know herself as a person, is by creative

---

work of her own. There is no other way. But a job, any job, is not the answer—in fact, it can be part of the trap. Women who do not look for jobs equal to their actual capacity, who do not let themselves develop the lifetime interests and goals which require serious education and training, who take a job at twenty or forty to "help out at home" or just to kill extra time, are walking, almost as surely as the ones who stay inside the housewife trap, to a nonexistent future.

If a job is to be the way out of the trap for a woman, it must be a job that she can take seriously as part of a life plan, work in which she can grow as part of society. Suburban communities, particularly the new communities where social, cultural, educational, political, and recreational patterns are not as yet firmly established, offer numerous opportunities for the able, intelligent woman. But such work is not necessarily a "job." In Westchester, on Long Island, in the Philadelphia suburbs, women have started mental-health clinics, art centers, day camps. In big cities and small towns, women all the way from New England to California have pioneered new movements in politics and education. Even if this work was not thought of as "job" or "career," it was often so important to the various communities that professionals are now being paid for doing it.

In some suburbs and communities there is now little work left for the nonprofessional that requires intelligence—except for the few positions of leadership which most women, these days, lack the independence, the strength, the self-confidence to take. If the community has a high proportion of educated women, there simply are not enough such posts to go around. As a result, community work often expands in a kind of self-serving structure of committees and red tape, in the purest sense of Parkinson's law, until its real purpose seems to be just to keep women busy. Such busywork is not satisfying to mature women, nor does it help the immature to grow. This is not to say that being a den mother, or serving on a PTA committee, or organizing a covered-dish supper is not useful work; for a woman of intelligence and ability, it is simply not enough.

One woman I interviewed had involved herself in an endless whirl of worthwhile community activities. But they led in no direction for her own future, nor did they truly utilize her exceptional intelligence. Indeed, her intelligence seemed to deteriorate; she suffered the problem that has no name with increasing severity until she took the first step toward a serious commitment. Today she is a "master teacher," a serene wife and mother.

■ ■ ■

The picture of the happy housewife doing creative work at home—painting, sculpting, writing—is one of the semi-delusions of the feminine mystique. There are men and women who can do it; but when a man works at home, his wife keeps the children strictly out of the way, or else. It is not so easy for a woman; if she is serious about her work she often must find some place away from home to do it, or risk becoming an ogre to her children in her impatient demands for privacy. Her attention is divided and her concentration interrupted, on the job and as a mother. A no-nonsense nine-to-five job, with a clear division between professional work and housework, requires much less discipline and is usually less lonely. Some of the stimulation and the new friendships that come from being part of the professional world can be lost by the woman who tries to fit her career into the physical confines of her housewife life.

A woman must say "no" to the feminine mystique very clearly indeed to sustain the discipline and effort that any professional commitment requires. For the mystique is no mere intellectual construct. A great many people have, or think they have, a vested interest in "Occupation: housewife." However long it may take for women's magazines, sociologists, educators, and psychoanalysts to correct the mistakes that perpetuate the feminine mystique, a woman must deal with them now, in the prejudices, mistaken fears, and unnecessary dilemmas voiced by her husband; her friends and neighbors; perhaps her minister, priest, or rabbi; or her child's kindergarten teacher; or the well-meaning social worker at the guidance clinic; or her own innocent little children. But resistance, from whatever source, is better seen for what it is.

■ ■ ■

The problem that has no name—which is simply the fact that American women are kept from growing to their full human capacities—is taking a far greater toll on the physical and mental health of our country than any known disease. Consider the high incidence of emotional breakdown of women in the "role crises" of their twenties and thirties; the alcoholism and suicides in their forties and fifties; the housewives' monopolization of all doctors' time. Consider the prevalence of teenage marriages, the growing rate of illegitimate pregnancies, and even more seriously, the pathology of mother–child symbiosis. Consider the alarming passivity of American teenagers. If we continue to produce millions of young mothers who stop their growth and education short of identity, without a strong core of human values to pass on to their children, we are committing, quite simply, genocide, starting with the mass burial of American women and ending with the progressive dehumanization of their sons and daughters.

These problems cannot be solved by medicine, or even by psychotherapy. We need a drastic reshaping of the cultural image of femininity that will permit women to reach maturity, identity, completeness of self, without conflict with sexual fulfillment. A massive attempt must be made by educators and parents—and ministers, magazine editors, manipulators, guidance counselors—to stop the early-marriage movement, stop girls from growing up wanting to be "just a housewife," stop it by insisting, with the same attention from childhood on that parents and educators give to boys, that girls develop the resources of self, goals that will permit them to find their own identity.

▪ ▪ ▪

The key to the trap is, of course, education. The feminine mystique has made higher education for women seem suspect, unnecessary and even dangerous. But I think that education, and only education, has saved, and can continue to save, American women from the greater dangers of the feminine mystique.

The Female Eunuch

Germaine Greer

Germaine Greer (1939–) was born in Australia, graduated from the Universities of Melbourne and Sydney, and received her doctorate, in Renaissance studies, from Cambridge University. With the publication of The Female Eunuch *in 1969 and its release in the United States in 1971, she became an international feminist figure. Called in 1979 to the Graduate Faculty of Modern Letters at the University of Tulsa, Oklahoma, she directed the Tulsa Center for the Study of Women's Literature until 1982. Greer believes that women will be stronger when they learn to talk to their mothers, when they find a way to love them and "purge the fear and resentment" of the debilitating socialization their mothers force upon them.*

THE WOMEN WHO ARE MOST CONSCIOUS OF THE disabilities which afflict women are those who are educated to the point of demanding and deserving the same kind of advancement as men. In the higher educational establishments in which women are segregated there is a curious air of constipated revolt. Most women teachers are not married and do not have any very significant intercourse with the opposite sex. Their students sometimes suspect them of sexual relationships with each other, and certainly there is an intensity in their personal relationships which would argue some degree of thwarted attraction or affection, although I would maintain that the extreme repressions practiced by such women on themselves in other respects indicate impotence in this regard. When a group of girl students presented a rather churlishly expressed list of grievances to the principal of a women's college in which I had the misfortune to be immured for a whole year before I could escape, she and her cronies clung together in her Hollywood-interior lodge, refusing to deal with the matters expressed in the petition, except to complain that they had wanted us to be so happy and we had *hurt* them. It is a kind of female rebellion to eschew cosmetics and the business of attraction, and some of these establishment rebels certainly cultivated respectable slatternliness to an impressive degree. Gentility went by the board as well. One such eminent lady, whose bloated form in a red knitted bathing suit had been known to drive every vestige of color from a male don's cheek, was famous for farting and belching at table, and I once saw her put a meringue which she had shot on to the floor back on her plate and eat it with complete unconcern. Rather than concede some sort of genetic imbalance in these gifted women I should claim that their braying voices and shattering footsteps were deliberate reactions against feminine murmuring and pussyfooting. They were helped by the existence of an acceptable British stereotype of the aristocratic countrywoman, who is a good sport and more capable with a plough or a snaffle bit than many a man. Only a small proportion of the girls in their

---

charge emulated them, for most of them were still coming through the last stages of puberty, and developing along more orthodox feminine lines despite their mistresses' attempts to keep them playing hockey and beating the men's marks at the end of the year.

Such unremarkable and unconscious forms of rebellion against the feminine role are old and ineffectual. If we were to compare the high incidence of positive homosexuality as well as effeteness and epicenity among male inhabitants of the establishments of higher learning we might discern a valid reaction against the male stereotype of brawn and insensitivity, but as long as the situation remains unrationalized it has little significance except as a personal motivation or a partial factor in neurosis. Rationalization has begun, however, and it was first practiced by women from this class, the most privileged of their sex. The history of suffragettism and its survival until our own day is beyond the scope of this book, although it is remarkable how many of today's militant women can remember some extraordinary old lady who sought (in vain) to plant the seeds of rebellion in their minds. From time to time wonderfully vivid old women appear on TV, or are written up in obituaries in *The Times,* to remind us not only of the continuity of the movement but of the tactical address and joyful courage of petticoated, corseted and hatted gentlewomen of a lifetime ago. The progress since their times has not been uniform: women's clothes have fluctuated between the loose and unrestricting and the voluminous and pinching, the novelette heroine has been plucky and good-humored, and then once more sexy and languishing. The beginning of the second feminist wave, of which this book must be considered a part, was Betty Friedan's research into the post-war sexual sell which got American women out of the factories and back into their homes. Mrs. Friedan is a *summa cum laude* graduate of Smith College and held a research fellowship in psychology at Berkeley, a professional woman of considerable reputation and attainments. What she discovered during the five years that she worked on her book has led to her forming the most influential of the women's groups in America, the National Organization of Women, which now has a membership of more than three thousand and branches in many cities. Somewhere on the way she shed the husband to whom she dedicated her book. Her movement is the only one to achieve any degree of recognition from the political establishment. When NOW was formed it was read into the Congressional record; it provides most of the motivation and the personnel for the numerous women's groups and committees which now figure in various Congressional bodies. Clearly, what Mrs. Friedan suggests cannot be at all radical. Her whole case rests upon the frustration suffered by the educated woman who falls for the Freudian notion that physiology is destiny. For Mrs. Friedan sexuality seems to mean motherhood, an argument which other feminist groups also seem to be misled by, so that in rejecting the normative sex role of women they are forced to stress nonsexual aspects of a woman's destiny at the expense of her libido, a mistake which will have serious consequences. She represents the cream of American middle-class womanhood, and what she wants for them is equality of opportunity within the status quo, free admission to the world of the ulcer and the coronary. She has continued the campaign for the passage of the Equal Rights Amendment, which was begun in 1923, and for the repeal of the abortion laws on the most subtle grounds, arguing that they are unconstitutional as breaches of privacy, limitations on free speech and so forth. She feels that the problems of housewives' neuroses will be solved when they are socialized, encouraged to look beyond the kitchen to the community.[1] So far she has succeeded in "forcing" the *New York Times* to increase its reputation for fairmindedness and freedom from male chauvinism by desegregating the Want Ads. Of course she could not desegregate the jobs: the immediate result of that tactic was that more qualified women wasted more time and energy reading about, applying for, and being rejected from jobs they had no chance of getting in the first place. As long as even female employers continue to prefer male employees, such token reforms will have only negative results. NOW also boycotted Colgate-Palmolive in a protest against job discrimination, although they have never leveled an attack of any significance against the whole ludicrous cosmetic industry, when the same worthless ingredients make up all the preparations from the cheapest to the most fabulously expensive, and female insecurity is cultivated by degrading advertising so that these mucky preparations can be sold more quickly than ever. NOW also raided a bar in the Plaza Hotel where women were not admitted except at certain times of the day, and then only if accompanied by a male.

It was not long before intelligent members of

NOW realized that their aims were too limited and their tactics too genteel. One of the more interesting women to emerge in the movement is Ti-Grace Atkinson, a leader of the most radical and most elite women's group, the Feminists—A Political Organization to Annihilate Sex Roles. This is a closed group of propaganda-makers who are trying to develop the notion of a leaderless society in which the convention of Love ("the response of the victim to the rapist"), the proprietary relationship of marriage, and even uterine pregnancy will no longer prevail. Their pronouncements are characteristically gnomic and rigorous; to the average confused female they must seem terrifying. They have characterized men as the enemy, and, as long as men continue to enact their roles as misconceived and perpetuated by themselves and women, they are undoubtedly right. Nevertheless it is not true that to have a revolution you need a revolutionary theory: they might well find that a theory devised by minds diseased by the system will not be able to avail itself of the facts of a changing situation. It is dangerous to eschew sex as a revolutionary tactic because it is inauthentic and enslaving in the terms in which it is now possible, when sex is the principal confrontation in which new values can be worked out. Men are the enemy in much the same way that some crazed boy in uniform was the enemy of another like him in most respects except the uniform. One possible tactic is to try to get the uniforms off.

■ ■ ■

A much more naïve attempt to prove that the struggle of women against oppression was a part of the class struggle had been made as early as 1954, by Evelyn Reed, in the October Discussion Bulletin of the Socialist Workers' Party, in which she attempts to prove that sex rivalry and the emergence of women as sexual objects were the results exclusively of bourgeois capitalism. She invoked the notion of a primitive society free from any form of sex exploitation or property or rivalry, where cosmetics were used simply as a means of identification, describing the propaganda machine of femininity as the deliberate sinister ploy of money-hungry capitalists in the nineteenth century expanded to gargantuan limits in the twentieth. The basic trend of the argument is probably correct, but she is so patently arguing from her convictions to her evidence, none of which has any source that she quotes, that the most sympathetic reader is alienated, unless, presumably, he has no way of knowing better. In 1969 her contributions to the woman question were all issued in a pamphlet called *Problems of Women's Liberation: A Marxist Approach*. Her arguments are couched in typical Marxist doctrinaire terminology, buttressed by phony anthropology and poor scholarship. The cover features a reproduction of a figure on an Attic vase, misidentified as a "goddess symbol of the matriarchy" when it is actually a graceful Bacchante with thyrsus and dead wildcat. Evelyn Reed would have been horrified if she had realized that her work was decorated with the symbol of hippiedom and drug culture, flowing hair, snake diadem and all. There is a symbolism in the error: there is certainly more hope for women in Marcuse than in Marx. The booklet[2] is unusually well-distributed and may be influential, which is in some ways a pity, for much time will be wasted debating invalid conclusions. Juliet Mitchell's article is much better argued and much more scrupulous.

There are many other women's liberation movements now operating in America, from the university chapters, which count twenty-five as a large turnout and remain local manifestations dealing with their own problems, to groups like the Red Stockings, formed when they were jeered by the men at the anti-inaugural demonstration in Washington, who concentrate on consciousness-raising in the Marcusian sense, to the October 17 movement of which Anne Koedt and Shulamith Firestone are members, to Cell 55, to Abby Rockefeller's Boston-based Women's Liberation movement, whose conference last summer was attended by five hundred women who got up at 10 o'clock on a Sunday morning to watch a karate demonstration (Rockefeller and Roxanne Dunbar have green belts), to the Congress to Unite Women (which sadly only marshaled five hundred women). The movement is endlessly divided and dividing but this may be taken as a sign of life, if not power.

In England Women's Liberation workshops are appearing in the suburban haunts of the educated housewife, and in the universities. There is no great coherence in their theory and no particular imagination or efficiency to be observed in their methods. The Tufnell Park Liberation workshop produced a paper called *Shrew* which is badly distributed. After five phonecalls to try and secure back numbers I gave up. When these worthy ladies appeared at the Miss World contest with their banners saying "We are not sexual objects" (a proposition that no one seemed inclined to deny) they were horrified to find that girls from the Warwick University movement were chanting and dancing around the police. They begged them to desist because it was so unladylike and their image was already so shabby, and when the next issue of *Shrew* appeared it contained an official lamentation about the demeanor of these strange women, assuming in pity for their uncouthness that they were Coventry housewives with four children apiece, the very people the women liberators were anxious to help! In fact, the Coventry chapter is one of the few which are attended by working-class women who tell the privileged girls how it is, a tendency which could well be followed by other privileged women who have not so far learned to demand anything but the vacuous notion of "equal opportunity."[3]

Nevertheless, despite chaos and misconception, the new feminism grows apace. The new Feminist Theater, sponsored by Red Stockings, fills the Village Gate in New York. Although few women are misled by the red herring of learning male violence as a revolutionary tactic or practicing celibacy, wives and mothers did march round the Hudson Street alimony jail with posters announcing that they didn't want alimony. As Gloria Steinem remarked, the growth of the liberation movement has "happened not so much by organization as contagion."[4] The actual movement extends farther and deeper than the underground organization whose publications are disseminated by the N.E.F.P. and Agitprop, and even wider than Mrs. Friedan's female establishment. An anti-female-liberation motion was overwhelmingly defeated by a predominantly male audience at a university debate that I spoke at lately, when a similar debate five years ago, although argued much better than this, was roundly defeated. When I addressed a very mixed and uneccentric audience at an adult education center on Teesside the week before, soft-spoken nervous women spoke in front of their husbands about the most subversive ideas. Nurses are misbehaving, the teachers are on strike, skirts are all imaginable levels, bras are not being bought, abortions are being demanded . . . rebellion is gathering steam and may yet become revolution.

Notes

1. Betty Friedan, *The Feminine Mystique* (New York, 1963).

2. Evelyn Reed, *Problems of Women's Liberation: A Marxist Approach* (New York, 1969).

3. Mention ought also to be made of the N.J.A.C.C. and Midge McKenzie's Feminists, who produced the mimeographed *Harpies Bizarre.* Women's Liberation Workshop has now expanded to thirteen groups, while another group in Nottingham puts out a duplicated sheet called *Socialist Woman,* and another at Bristol, *Enough Is Enough.* A conference at Oxford, February to March, 1970, drew five hundred participants, along with four hundred children and fifty menfolk.

4. Gloria Steinem, "The City Politic," *New York,* March 10, 1969.

Letters of a Woman Homesteader

Proving Up

Elinore Pruitt Stewart

Elinore Pruitt Stewart (1878–19??) grew up in Denver, Colorado, one of six children who had to raise themselves after their parents died. When her marriage ended with the death of her husband, Mr. Rupert, she took her daughter to Wyoming where she filed for land under the Homestead Act. In 1910 she married her next-door neighbor, Mr. Stewart. Her letters to her friend Mrs. Coney in Denver tell the story of her life as a widow and homesteader. She postponed telling her friend of her marriage for many months, finally confessing, "I was afraid you would think I didn't need your friendship and would desert me." Indeed, she continued, other women friends had already done so.

October 14, 1911.

DEAR MRS. CONEY,—

I think you must be expecting an answer to your letter by now, so I will try to answer as many of your questions as I remember. Your letter has been mislaid. We have been very much rushed all this week. We had the thresher crew two days. I was busy cooking for them two days before they came, and have been busy ever since cleaning up after them. Clyde has taken the thresher on up the valley to thresh for the neighbors, and all the men have gone along, so the children and I are alone. No, I shall not lose my land, although it will be over two years before I can get a deed to it. The five years in which I am required to "prove up" will have passed by then. I could n't have held my homestead if Clyde had also been proving up, but he had accomplished that years ago and has his deed, so I am allowed my homestead. Also I have not yet used my desert right, so I am still entitled to one hundred and sixty acres more. I shall file on that much some day when I have sufficient money of my own earning. The law requires a cash payment of twenty-five cents per acre at the filing, and one dollar more per acre when final proof is made. I should not have married if Clyde had not promised I should meet all my land difficulties unaided. I wanted the fun and the experience. For that reason I want to earn every cent that goes into my own land and improvements myself. Sometimes I almost have a brainstorm wondering how I am going to do it, but I know I shall succeed; other women have succeeded. I know of several who are now where they can laugh at past trials. Do you know?—I am a firm believer in laughter. I am real superstitious about it. I think if Bad Luck came along, he would take to his heels if some one laughed right loudly.

I think Jerrine must be born for the law. She always threshes out questions that arise, to her own satisfaction, if to no one else's. She prayed for a long time for her brother; also she prayed for some puppies. The puppies came, but we did n't let her know they were here until they were able to walk. One morning she saw them following their mother, so she danced for joy. When her little brother came she was plainly disappointed. "Mamma," she said, "did God really make the baby?" "Yes, dear." "Then He has n't treated us fairly, and I should like to know why. The puppies could walk when He finished them; the calves can, too. The pigs can, and the colt, and even the chickens. What is the use of giving us a half-finished baby? He has no hair, and no teeth; he can't walk or talk, nor do anything else but squall and sleep."

After many days she got the question settled. She began right where she left off. "I know, Mamma, why God gave us such a half-finished baby; so he could learn our ways, and no one else's, since he must live with us, and so we could learn to love him. Every time I stand beside his buggy he laughs and then I love him, but I don't love Stella nor Marvin because they laugh. So that is why." Perhaps that is the reason.

Zebbie's kinsfolk have come and taken him back to Yell County. I should not be surprised if he never returned. The Lanes and the Pattersons leave shortly for Idaho, where "our Bobbie" has made some large investments.

I hope to hear from you soon and that you are enjoying every minute. With much love,

Your friend,

ELINORE STEWART.

Argonauta

Anne Morrow Lindbergh

Anne Morrow Lindbergh (1906–   ), born in New Jersey, is the child of Elizabeth Cutter, poet, children's writer, and acting president of Smith College, and Dwight Whitney Morrow, businessman and ambassador. Thrust into the world of celebrity by her marriage to aviator Charles Lindbergh in 1929, which was followed by the kidnapping and murder of their first son in 1932, her accomplishment of writing both in private and for the public is even more noteworthy. In 1963 Betty Friedan wrote, "Every woman has to listen to her own inner voice to find her identity in this changing world." Lindbergh, in Gift from the Sea *(1955), had already written, "Woman must come of age by herself."*

THERE ARE IN THE BEACH-WORLD CERTAIN RARE creatures, the "Argonauta" (Paper Nautilus), who are not fastened to their shell at all. It is actually a cradle for the young, held in the arms of the mother argonaut who floats with it to the surface, where the eggs hatch and the young swim away. Then the mother argonaut leaves her shell and starts another life. I am fascinated by this image of the argonaut, whose temporary dwelling I have seen only as the treasure of a specialist's collection. Almost transparent, delicately fluted like a Greek column, this narcissus-white snail shell is feather light as some coracle of ancient times, ready to set sail across unknown seas. It was named, the book tells me, for the fabled ships of Jason that went in search of the Golden Fleece. Sailors consider these shells a sign of fair weather and favorable winds.

Lovely shell, lovely image—I am tempted to play with it in my mind. Is this the symbol for another stage in relationships? Can we middle-aged argonauts when we outgrow the oyster bed, look forward to the freedom of the nautilus who has left its shell for the open seas? But what does the open sea hold for us? We cannot believe that the second half of life promises "fair weather and favorable winds." What golden fleece is there for the middle-aged?

In speaking of the argonauta one might as well admit one has left the usual shell collections. A double-sunrise shell, an oyster bed—these are common knowledge to most of us. We recognize them; we know about them; they are part of our daily life and the lives of others around us. But with this rare and delicate vessel, we have left the well-tracked beaches of proven facts and experiences. We are adventuring in the chartless seas of imagination.

Is the golden fleece that awaits us some kind of new freedom for growth? And in this new freedom, is there any place for a relationship? I believe there is, after the oyster bed, an opportunity for the best relationship of all: not a limited, mutually exclusive one, like the sunrise shell; and not a functional, dependent one, as in the oyster bed; but the meeting of two whole fully developed

---

people as persons. It would be, to borrow a definition of the Scottish philosopher, MacMurray, a fully personal relationship, that is, "a type of relationship into which people enter as persons with the whole of themselves." "Personal relationships," he goes on to explain, ". . . have no ulterior motive. They are not based on particular interests. They do not serve partial and limited ends. Their value lies entirely in themselves and for the same reason transcends all other values. And that is because they are relations of persons as persons." This relationship of "persons as persons" was prophetically hinted at by the German poet, Rilke, almost fifty years ago. He foresaw a great change in the relationships between men and women, which he hoped in the future would no longer follow the traditional patterns of submission and domination or of possession and competition. He described a state in which there would be space and freedom for growth, and in which each partner would be the means of releasing the other. "A relation," he concludes, "that is meant to be of one human being to another, . . . And this more human love (that will fulfill itself, infinitely considerate and gentle, and good and clear in binding and releasing) will resemble that which we are with struggle and endeavor preparing, the love that consists in this, that two solitudes protect and touch and greet each other."

But this new relationship of persons as persons, this more human love, this two solitudes conception is not something that comes easily. It must have grown, like all firm-rooted growth, slowly. It perhaps can only follow a long development in the history of human civilization and individually in each human being's life. Such a stage in life, it would seem to me, must come not as a gift or a lucky accident, but as part of an evolutionary process, an achievement which could only follow certain important developments in each partner.

It cannot be reached until woman—individually and as a sex—has herself come of age, a maturing process we are witnessing today. In this undertaking she must work alone and cannot count on much help from the outsider, eager as he may be in pointing out the way. There are many signs of interest in the new woman today, chiefly in the form of mechanistic studies of her as a female animal. Of course it is necessary and helpful for woman to understand and accept her sexual needs and habits but it is only one side of a very complex problem. One cannot expect statistics on her physical reactions to add much knowledge or nourishment to her inner life, to her basic relation to herself, or to her long postponed hope and right, as a human being, to be creative in other ways besides the purely physical one.

Woman must come of age by herself. This is the essence of "coming of age"—to learn how to stand alone. She must learn not to depend on another, nor to feel she must prove her strength by competing with another. In the past, she has swung between these two opposite poles of dependence and competition, of Victorianism and Feminism. Both extremes throw her off balance; neither is the center, the true center of being a whole woman. She must find her true center alone. She must become whole. She must, it seems to me, as a prelude to any "two solitudes" relationship, follow the advice of the poet to become "world to oneself for another's sake."

In fact, I wonder if both man and woman must not accomplish this heroic feat. Must not man also become world to himself? Must he not also expand the neglected sides of his personality; the art of inward looking that he has seldom had time for in his active outward-going life; the personal relationships which he has not had as much chance to enjoy; the so-called feminine qualities, aesthetic, emotional, cultural and spiritual, which he has been too rushed to fully develop. Perhaps both men and women in America may hunger, in our material, outward, active, masculine culture, for the supposedly feminine qualities of heart, mind and spirit—qualities which are actually neither masculine nor feminine, but simply human qualities that have been neglected. It is growth along these lines that will make us whole, and will enable the individual to become world to himself.

And this greater wholeness in each person, this being "world to oneself," does this not mean greater self-sufficiency and therefore, inevitably, greater separation between man and woman? With growth, it is true, comes differentiation and separation, in the sense that the unity of the tree-trunk differentiates as it grows and spreads into limbs, branches, and leaves. But the tree is still one, and its different and separate parts contribute to one another. The two separate worlds or the two solitudes will surely have more to give each other than when each was a meager half.

No Name Woman

Maxine Hong Kingston

Maxine Hong Kingston (1940–   ), born in Stockton, California, received her B.A. in English from the University of California at Berkeley in 1962 and married Earll Kingston that same year. In 1976 her first book, The Woman Warrior, *won the National Book Critics' Circle Award. Although her subject matter is the experience of her Chinese family in America, she finds the issue of being a representative ethnic writer "very bothersome." Because her parents neither speak nor read English, she believes that they have no accurate sense of her work. According to Arturo Islas, "At the end of* The Woman Warrior, *the resolution that takes place between the mother and daughter is linked to the feminist issue of breaking female silence."*

"YOU MUST NOT TELL ANYONE," MY MOTHER SAID, "what I am about to tell you. In China your father had a sister who killed herself. She jumped into the family well. We say that your father has all brothers because it is as if she had never been born.

"In 1924 just a few days after our village celebrated seventeen hurry-up weddings—to make sure that every young man who went 'out on the road' would responsibly come home—your father and his brothers and your grandfather and his brothers and your aunt's new husband sailed for America, the Gold Mountain. It was your grandfather's last trip. Those lucky enough to get contracts waved good-bye from the decks. They fed and guarded the stowaways and helped them off in Cuba, New York, Bali, Hawaii. 'We'll meet in California next year,' they said. All of them sent money home.

"I remember looking at your aunt one day when she and I were dressing; I had not noticed before that she had such a protruding melon of a stomach. But I did not think, 'She's pregnant,' until she began to look like other pregnant women, her shirt pulling and the white tops of her black pants showing. She could not have been pregnant, you see, because her husband had been gone for years. No one said anything. We did not discuss it. In early summer she was ready to have the child, long after the time when it could have been possible.

"The village had also been counting. On the night the baby was to be born the villagers raided our house. Some were crying. Like a great saw, teeth strung with lights, files of people walked zigzag across our land, tearing the rice. Their lanterns doubled in the disturbed black water, which drained away through the broken bunds. As the villagers closed in, we could see that some of them, probably men and women we knew well, wore white masks. The people with long hair hung it over their faces. Women with short hair made it stand up on end. Some had tied white bands around their foreheads, arms, and legs.

"At first they threw mud and rocks at the

house. Then they threw eggs and began slaughtering our stock. We could hear the animals scream their deaths—the roosters, the pigs, a last great roar from the ox. Familiar wild heads flared in our night windows; the villagers encircled us. Some of the faces stopped to peer at us, their eyes rushing like searchlights. The hands flattened against the panes, framed heads, and left red prints.

"The villagers broke in the front and the back doors at the same time, even though we had not locked the doors against them. Their knives dripped with the blood of our animals. They smeared blood on the doors and walls. One woman swung a chicken, whose throat she had slit, splattering blood in red arcs about her. We stood together in the middle of our house, in the family hall with the pictures and tables of the ancestors around us, and looked straight ahead.

"At the time the house had only two wings. When the men came back, we would build two more to enclose our courtyard and a third one to begin a second courtyard. The villagers pushed through both wings, even your grandparents' rooms, to find your aunt's, which was also mine until the men returned. From this room a new wing for one of the younger families would grow. They ripped up her clothes and shoes and broke her combs, grinding them underfoot. They tore her work from the loom. They scattered the cooking fire and rolled the new weaving in it. We could hear them in the kitchen breaking our bowls and banging the pots. They overturned the great waist-high earthenware jugs; duck eggs, pickled fruits, vegetables burst out and mixed in acrid torrents. The old woman from the next field swept a broom through the air and loosed the spirits-of-the-broom over our heads. 'Pig.' 'Ghost.' 'Pig,' they sobbed and scolded while they ruined our house.

"When they left, they took sugar and oranges to bless themselves. They cut pieces from the dead animals. Some of them took bowls that were not broken and clothes that were not torn. Afterward we swept up the rice and sewed it back up into sacks. But the smells from the spilled preserves lasted. Your aunt gave birth in the pigsty that night. The next morning when I went for the water, I found her and the baby plugging up the family well.

"Don't let your father know that I told you. He denies her. Now that you have started to menstruate, what happened to her could happen to you. Don't humiliate us. You wouldn't like to be forgotten as if you had never been born. The villagers are watchful."

Whenever she had to warn us about life, my mother told stories that ran like this one, a story to grow up on. She tested our strength to establish realities. Those in the emigrant generations who could not reassert brute survival died young and far from home. Those of us in the first American generations have had to figure out how the invisible world the emigrants built around our childhoods fit in solid America.

The emigrants confused the gods by diverting their curses, misleading them with crooked streets and false names. They must try to confuse their offspring as well, who, I suppose, threaten them in similar ways—always trying to get things straight, always trying to name the unspeakable. The Chinese I know hide their names; sojourners take new names when their lives change and guard their real names with silence.

Chinese-Americans, when you try to understand what things in you are Chinese, how do you separate what is peculiar to childhood, to poverty, insanities, one family, your mother who marked your growing with stories, from what is Chinese? What is Chinese tradition and what is the movies?

If I want to learn what clothes my aunt wore, whether flashy or ordinary, I would have to begin, "Remember Father's drowned-in-the-well sister?" I cannot ask that. My mother has told me once and for all the useful parts. She will add nothing unless powered by Necessity, a riverbank that guides her life. She plants vegetable gardens rather than lawns; she carries the odd-shaped tomatoes home from the fields and eats food left for the gods.

Whenever we did frivolous things, we used up energy; we flew high kites. We children came up off the ground over the melting cones our parents brought home from work and the American movie on New Year's Day—*Oh, You Beautiful Doll* with Betty Grable one year, and *She Wore a Yellow Ribbon* with John Wayne another year. After the one carnival ride each, we paid in guilt; our tired father counted his change on the dark walk home.

Adultery is extravagance. Could people who hatch their own chicks and eat the embryos and the heads for delicacies and boil the feet in vinegar for party food, leaving only the gravel, eating even the gizzard lining—could such people engender a prodigal aunt? To be a woman, to have a daughter in starvation time was a waste enough. My aunt could not have been the lone romantic who gave up everything for sex. Women in the old China did not choose. Some man had commanded her to lie with him and be his secret evil. I wonder whether he masked himself when he joined the raid on her family.

Perhaps she encountered him in the fields or on the mountain where the daughters-in-law collected fuel. Or perhaps he first noticed her in the marketplace. He was not a stranger because the village housed no strangers. She had to have dealings with him other than sex. Perhaps he worked an adjoining field, or he sold her the cloth for the dress she sewed and wore. His demand must have surprised, then terrified her. She obeyed him; she always did as she was told.

When the family found a young man in the next village to be her husband, she stood tractably beside the best rooster, his proxy, and promised before they met that she would be his forever. She was lucky that he was her age and she would be the first wife, an advantage secure now. The night she first saw him, he had sex with her. Then he left for America. She had almost forgotten what he looked like. When she tried to envision him, she only saw the black and white face in the group photograph the men had had taken before leaving.

The other man was not, after all, much different from her husband. They both gave orders: she followed. "If you tell your family, I'll beat you. I'll kill you. Be here again next week." No one talked sex, ever. And she might have separated the rapes from the rest of living if only she did not have to buy her oil from him or gather wood in the same forest. I want her fear to have lasted just as long as rape lasted so that the fear could have been contained. No drawn-out fear. But women at sex hazarded birth and hence lifetimes. The fear did not stop but permeated everywhere. She told the man, "I think I'm pregnant." He organized the raid against her.

On nights when my mother and father talked about their life back home, sometimes they mentioned an "outcast table" whose business they still seemed to be settling, their voices tight. In a commensal[1] tradition, where food is precious, the powerful older people made wrongdoers eat alone. Instead of letting them start separate new lives like the Japanese, who could become samurais and geishas, the Chinese family, faces averted but eyes glowering sideways, hung on to the offenders and fed them leftovers. My aunt must have lived in the same house as my parents and eaten at an outcast table. My mother spoke about the raid as if she had seen it, when she and my aunt, a daughter-in-law to a different household, should not have been living together at all. Daughters-in-law lived with their husbands' parents, not their own; a synonym for marriage in Chinese is "taking a daughter-in-law." Her husband's parents could have sold her, mortgaged her, stoned her. But they had sent her back to her own mother and father, a mysterious act hinting at disgraces not told me. Perhaps they had thrown her out to deflect the avengers.

She was the only daughter; her four brothers went with her father, husband, and uncles "out on the road" and for some years became western men. When the goods were divided among the family, three of the brothers took land, and the youngest, my father, chose an education. After my grandparents gave their daughter away to her husband's family, they had dispensed all the adventure and all the property. They expected her alone to keep the traditional ways, which her brothers, now among the barbarians, could fumble without detection. The heavy, deep-rooted women were to maintain the past against the flood, safe for returning. But the rare urge west had fixed upon our family, and so my aunt crossed boundaries not delineated in space.

The work of preservation demands that the feelings playing about in one's guts not be turned into action. Just watch their passing like cherry blossoms. But perhaps my aunt, my forerunner, caught in a slow life, let dreams grow and fade and after some months or years went toward what persisted. Fear at the enormities of the forbidden kept her desires delicate, wire and bone. She looked at a man because she liked the way the hair was tucked behind his ears, or she liked the question-mark line of a long torso curving at the shoulder and straight at the hip. For warm eyes or a soft voice or a slow walk—that's all—a few hairs, a line, a brightness, a sound, a pace, she gave up family. She offered us up for a charm that vanished with tiredness, a pigtail that didn't toss when the wind died. Why, the wrong lighting could erase the dearest thing about him.

It could very well have been, however, that my aunt did not take subtle enjoyment of her friend, but, a wild woman, kept rollicking company. Imagining her free with sex doesn't fit, though. I don't know any women like that, or men either. Unless I see her life branching into mine, she gives me no ancestral help.

To sustain her being in love, she often worked at

herself in the mirror, guessing at the colors and shapes that would interest him, changing them frequently in order to hit on the right combination. She wanted him to look back.

On a farm near the sea, a woman who tended her appearance reaped a reputation for eccentricity. All the married women blunt-cut their hair in flaps about their ears or pulled it back in tight buns. No nonsense. Neither style blew easily into heart-catching tangles. And at their weddings they displayed themselves in their long hair for the last time. "It brushed the backs of my knees," my mother tells me. "It was braided, and even so, it brushed the backs of my knees."

At the mirror my aunt combed individuality into her bob. A bun could have been contrived to escape into black streamers blowing in the wind or in quiet wisps about her face, but only the older women in our picture album wear buns. She brushed her hair back from her forehead, tucking the flaps behind her ears. She looped a piece of thread, knotted into a circle between her index fingers and thumbs, and ran the double strand across her forehead. When she closed her fingers as if she were making a pair of shadow geese bite, the string twisted together catching the little hairs. Then she pulled the thread away from her skin, ripping the hairs out neatly, her eyes watering from the needles of pain. Opening her fingers, she cleaned the thread, then rolled it along her hairline and the tops of her eyebrows. My mother did the same to me and my sisters and herself. I used to believe that the expression "caught by the short hairs" meant a captive held with a depilatory string. It especially hurt at the temples, but my mother said we were lucky we didn't have to have our feet bound when we were seven. Sisters used to sit on their beds and cry together, she said, as their mothers or their slave removed the bandages for a few minutes each night and let the blood gush back into their veins. I hope that the man my aunt loved appreciated a smooth brow, that he wasn't just a tits-and-ass man.

Once my aunt found a freckle on her chin, at a spot that the almanac said predestined her for unhappiness. She dug it out with a hot needle and washed the wound with peroxide.

More attention to her looks than these pullings of hairs and pickings at spots would have caused gossip among the villagers. They owned work clothes and good clothes, and they wore good clothes for feasting the new seasons. But since a woman combing her hair hexes beginnings, my aunt rarely found an occasion to look her best. Women looked like great sea snails—the corded wood, babies, and laundry they carried were the whorls on their backs. The Chinese did not admire a bent back; goddesses and warriors stood straight. Still there must have been a marvelous freeing of beauty when a worker laid down her burden and stretched and arched.

Such commonplace loveliness, however, was not enough for my aunt. She dreamed of a lover for the fifteen days of New Year's, the time for families to exchange visits, money, and food. She plied her secret comb. And sure enough she cursed the year, the family, the village, and herself.

Even as her hair lured her imminent lover, many other men looked at her. Uncles, cousins, nephews, brothers would have looked, too, had they been home between journeys. Perhaps they had already been restraining their curiosity, and they left, fearful that their glances, like a field of nesting birds, might be startled and caught. Poverty hurt, and that was their first reason for leaving. But another, final reason for leaving the crowded house was the never-said.

She may have been unusually beloved, the precious only daughter, spoiled and mirror gazing because of the affection the family lavished on her. When her husband left, they welcomed the chance to take her back from the in-laws; she could live like the little daughter for just a while longer. There are stories that my grandfather was different from other people, "crazy ever since the little Jap bayoneted him in the head." He used to put his naked penis on the dinner table, laughing. And one day he brought home a baby girl, wrapped up inside his brown western-style greatcoat. He had traded one of his sons, probably my father, the youngest, for her. My grandmother made him trade back. When he finally got a daughter of his own, he doted on her. They must have all loved her, except perhaps my father, the only brother who never went back to China, having once been traded for a girl.

Brothers and sisters, newly men and women, had to efface their sexual color and present plain miens.[2] Disturbing hair and eyes, a smile like no other, threatened the ideal of five generations living under one roof. To focus blurs, people shouted face to face and yelled from room to room. The immigrants I know have loud voices, unmodulated to American tones even after years away from the village where they called their friendships out across the fields. I have not been able to stop my mother's screams in public libraries or over telephones. Walking erect (knees straight, toes pointed forward, not pigeon-toed, which is Chinese-feminine) and speaking in an inaudible voice, I have tried to turn myself American-feminine. Chinese communication was loud, public. Only sick people had to whisper. But at the dinner table, where the family members came nearest one another, no one could talk, not the outcasts nor any eaters. Every word that falls from the mouth is a coin lost. Silently they gave and accepted food with both hands. A preoccupied child who took his bowl with one hand got a sideways glare. A complete moment of total attention is due everyone alike. Children and lovers have no singularity here, but my aunt used a secret voice, a separate attentiveness.

She kept the man's name to herself throughout her labor and dying; she did not accuse him that he be punished with her. To save her inseminator's name she gave silent birth.

He may have been somebody in her own household, but intercourse with a man outside the family would have been no less abhorrent. All the village were kinsmen, and the titles shouted in loud country voices never let kinship be forgotten. Any man within visiting distance would have been neutralized as a lover—"brother," "younger brother," "older brother"—one hundred and fifteen relationship titles. Parents researched birth charts probably not so much to assure good fortune as to circumvent incest in a population that has but one hundred surnames. Everybody has eight million relatives. How useless then sexual mannerisms, how dangerous.

As if it came from an atavism[3] deeper than fear, I used to add "brother" silently to boys' names. It hexed the boys, who would or would not ask me to dance, and made them less scary and as familiar and deserving of benevolence as girls.

But, of course, I hexed myself also—no dates. I should have stood up, both arms waving, and shouted out across libraries, "Hey, you! Love me back." I had no idea, though, how to make attraction selective, how to control its direction and magnitude. If I made myself American-pretty so that the five or six Chinese boys in the class fell in love with me, everyone else—the Caucasian, Negro, and Japanese boys—would too. Sisterliness, dignified and honorable, made much more sense.

Attraction eludes control so stubbornly that whole societies designed to organize relationships among people cannot keep order, not even when they bind people to one another from childhood and raise them together. Among the very poor and the wealthy, brothers married their adopted sisters, like doves. Our family allowed some romance, paying adult brides' prices and providing dowries so that their sons and daughters could marry strangers. Marriage promises to turn strangers into friendly relatives—a nation of siblings.

In the village structure, spirits shimmered among the live creatures, balanced and held in equilibrium by time and land. But one human being flaring up into violence could open up a black hole, a maelstrom that pulled in the sky. The frightened villagers, who depended on one another to maintain the real, went to my aunt to show her a personal, physical representation of the break she had made in the "roundness." Misallying couples snapped off the future, which was to be embodied in true offspring. The villagers punished her for acting as if she could have a private life, secret and apart from them.

If my aunt had betrayed the family at a time of large grain yields and peace, when many boys were born, and wings were being built on many houses, perhaps she might have escaped such severe punishment. But the men—hungry, greedy, tired of planting in dry soil, cuckolded—had had to leave the village in order to send food-money home. There were ghost plagues, bandit plagues, wars with the Japanese, floods. My Chinese brother and sister had died of an unknown sickness. Adultery, perhaps only a mistake during good times, became a crime when the village needed food.

The round moon cakes and round doorways, the round tables of graduated size that fit one roundness inside another, round windows and rice bowls—these talismans had lost their power to warn this family of the law: a family must be whole, faithfully keeping the descent line by having sons to feed the old and the dead, who in turn look after the family. The villagers came to show my aunt and her lover-in-hiding a broken house. The villagers were speeding up the circling of events because she was too short-sighted to see that her infidelity had already harmed the village, that waves of consequences would return unpredictably, sometimes in disguise, as now, to hurt her. This roundness had to be made coin-sized so that she would see its circumference: punish her at the birth of her baby. Awaken her to the inexorable. People who refused fatalism because they could invent small resources insisted on culpability. Deny accidents and wrest fault from the stars.

After the villagers left, their lanterns now scattering in various directions toward home, the family broke their silence and cursed her. "Aiaa, we're going to die. Death is coming. Death is coming. Look what you've done. You've killed us. Ghost! Dead ghost! Ghost! You've never been born." She ran out into the fields, far enough from the house so that she could no longer hear their voices, and pressed herself against the earth, her own land no more. When she felt the birth coming, she thought that she had been hurt. Her body seized together. "They've hurt me too much," she thought. "This is gall, and it will kill me." With forehead and knees against the earth, her body convulsed and then relaxed. She turned on her back, lay on the ground. The black well of sky and stars went out and out and out forever; her body and her complexity seemed to disappear. She was one of the stars, a bright dot in blackness, without home, without a companion, in eternal cold and silence. And agoraphobia rose in her, speeding higher and higher, bigger and bigger; she would not be able to contain it; there would be no end to fear.

Flayed, unprotected against space, she felt pain return, focusing her body. This pain chilled her—a cold, steady kind of surface pain. Inside, spasmodically, the other pain, the pain of the child, heated her. For hours she lay on the ground, alternately body and space. Sometimes a vision of normal comfort obliterated reality: she saw the family in the evening gambling at the dinner table, the young people massaging their elders' backs. She saw them congratulating one another, high joy on the mornings the rice shoots came up. When these pictures burst, the stars drew yet further apart. Black space opened.

She got to her feet to fight better and remembered that old-fashioned women gave birth in their pigsties to fool the jealous, pain-dealing gods, who do not snatch piglets. Before the next spasms could stop her, she ran to the pigsty, each step a rushing out into emptiness. She climbed over the fence and knelt in the dirt. It was good to have a fence enclosing her, a tribal person alone.

Laboring, this woman who had carried her child as a foreign growth that sickened her every day, expelled it at last. She reached down to touch the hot, wet, moving mass, surely smaller than anything human, and could feel that it was human after all—fingers, toes, nails, nose. She pulled it up on to her belly, and it lay curled there, butt in the air, feet precisely tucked one under the other. She opened her loose shirt and buttoned the child inside. After resting, it squirmed and thrashed and she pushed it up to her breast. It turned its head this way and that until it found her nipple. There, it made little snuffling noises. She clenched her teeth at its preciousness, lovely as a young calf, a piglet, a little dog.

She may have gone to the pigsty as a last act of responsibility: she would protect this child as she had protected its father. It would look after her soul, leaving supplies on her grave. But how would this tiny child without family find her grave when there would be no marker for her anywhere, neither in the earth nor the family hall? No one would give her a family hall name. She had taken the child with her into the wastes. At its birth the two of them had felt the same raw pain of separation, a wound that only the family pressing tight could close. A child with no descent line would not soften her life but only trail after her, ghost-like, begging her to give it purpose. At dawn the villagers on their way to the fields would stand around the fence and look.

Full of milk, the little ghost slept. When it awoke, she hardened her breasts against the milk that crying loosens. Toward morning she picked up the baby and walked to the well.

Carrying the baby to the well shows loving. Otherwise abandon it. Turn its face into the mud. Mothers who love their children take them along. It was probably a girl; there is some hope of forgiveness for boys.

"Don't tell anyone you had an aunt. Your father does not want to hear her name. She has never been born." I have believed that sex was unspeakable and words so strong and fathers so frail that "aunt" would do my father mysterious harm. I have thought that my family, having settled among immigrants who had also been their neighbors in the ancestral land, needed to clean their name, and a wrong word would incite the kinspeople even here. But there is more to this silence: they want me to participate in her punishment. And I have.

In the twenty years since I heard this story I have not asked for details nor said my aunt's name; I do not know it. People who can comfort the dead can also chase after them to hurt them further—a reverse ancestor worship. The real punishment was not the raid swiftly inflicted by the villagers, but the family's deliberately forgetting her. Her betrayal so maddened them, they saw to it that she would suffer forever, even after death. Always hungry, always needing, she would have to beg food from other ghosts, snatch and steal it from those whose living descendants give them gifts. She would have to fight the ghosts massed at crossroads for the buns a few thoughtful citizens leave to decoy her away from village and home so that the ancestral spirits could feast unharassed. At peace, they could act like gods, not ghosts, their descent lines providing them with paper suits and dresses, spirit money, paper houses, paper automobiles, chicken, meat, and rice into eternity—essences delivered up in smoke and flames, steam and incense rising from each rice bowl. In an attempt to make the Chinese care for people outside the family, Chairman Mao encourages us now to give our paper replicas to the spirits of outstanding soldiers and workers, no matter whose ancestors they may be. My aunt remains forever hungry. Goods are not distributed evenly among the dead.

My aunt haunts me—her ghost drawn to me because now, after fifty years of neglect, I alone devote pages of paper to her, though not origamied into houses and clothes. I do not think she always means me well. I am telling on her, and she was a spite suicide, drowning herself in the drinking water. The Chinese are always very frightened of the drowned one, whose weeping ghost, wet hair hanging and skin bloated, waits silently by the water to pull down a substitute.

Notes

1. Eating at the same table; sharing meals as table companions. [Eds.]

2. Appearances. [Eds.]

3. The reappearance of a characteristic after a long absence. [Eds.]

A Room of One's Own

Virginia Woolf

Virginia Woolf (1882–1941), born at Hyde Park Gate, London, England, was educated at home by both parents while her brothers attended school and university. Following their father's death in 1904, she and her siblings moved to Bloomsbury where they formed the nucleus of the Bloomsbury Group, whose members hastened the development of Britain's art and literature by rejecting the artistic and social restrictions of Victorian society. In 1912 she married Leonard Woolf. As a writer, she produced letters, diaries, reviews, short stories, and novels, as well as her famous extended essay on women's subjugation and the development of women's writing in England, A Room of One's Own *(1929), from which the following excerpt is taken. In this work, and in her novel* Orlando *(1928), Woolf explores the possibility of freedom from gender in the concept of the androgynous mind.*

EVEN SO, THE VERY FIRST SENTENCE THAT I WOULD write here, I said, crossing over to the writing-table and taking up the page headed Women and Fiction, is that it is fatal for any one who writes to think of their sex. It is fatal to be a man or woman pure and simple; one must be woman-manly or man-womanly. It is fatal for a woman to lay the least stress on any grievance; to plead even with justice any cause; in any way to speak consciously as a woman. And fatal is no figure of speech; for anything written with that conscious bias is doomed to death. It ceases to be fertilised. Brilliant and effective, powerful and masterly, as it may appear for a day or two, it must wither at nightfall; it cannot grow in the minds of others. Some collaboration has to take place in the mind between the woman and the man before the act of creation can be accomplished. Some marriage of opposites has to be consummated. The whole of the mind must lie wide open if we are to get the sense that the writer is communicating his experience with perfect fullness. There must be freedom and there must be peace. Not a wheel must grate, not a light glimmer. The curtains must be close drawn. The writer, I thought, once his experience is over, must lie back and let his mind celebrate its nuptials in darkness. He must not look or question what is being done. Rather, he must pluck the petals from a rose or watch the swans float calmly down the river. And I saw again the current which took the boat and the undergraduate and the dead leaves; and the taxi took the man and the woman, I thought, seeing them come together across the street, and the current swept them away, I thought, hearing far off the roar of London's traffic, into that tremendous stream.

Here, then, Mary Beton ceases to speak. She has told you how she reached the conclusion—the prosaic conclusion—that it is necessary to have five hundred a year and a room with a lock on the door if you are to write fiction or poetry. She has tried to lay bare the thoughts and impressions that led her to think this. She has asked you to follow her flying into the arms of a Beadle, lunching here, dining there, drawing pictures in the British Museum, taking books from the shelf, looking out of the window. While she has been doing all these things, you no doubt have been observing her failings and foibles and deciding what effect they have had on her opinions. You have been contradicting her and making whatever additions and deductions seem good to you. That is all as it should be, for in a question like this truth is only to be had by laying together many varieties of error. And I will end now in my own person by anticipating two criticisms, so obvious that you can hardly fail to make them.

No opinion has been expressed, you may say, upon the comparative merits of the sexes even as writers. That was done purposely, because, even if the time had come for such a valuation—and it is far more important at the moment to know how much money women had and how many rooms than to theorise about their capacities—even if the time had come I do not believe that gifts, whether of mind or character, can be weighed like sugar and butter, not even in Cambridge, where they are so adept at putting people into classes and fixing caps on their heads and letters after their names. I do not believe that even the Table of Precedency which you will find in Whitaker's *Almanac* represents a final order of values, or that there is any sound reason to suppose that a Commander of the Bath will ultimately walk in to dinner behind a Master in Lunacy. All this pitting of sex against sex, of quality against quality; all this claiming of superiority and imputing of inferiority, belong to the private-school stage of human existence where there are "sides," and it is necessary for one side to beat another side, and of the utmost importance to walk up to a platform and receive from the hands of the Headmaster himself a highly ornamental pot. As people mature they cease to believe in sides or in Headmasters or in highly ornamental pots. At any rate, where books are concerned, it is notoriously difficult to fix labels of merit in such a way that they do not come off. Are not reviews of current literature a perpetual illustration of the difficulty of judgment? "This great book," "this worthless book," the same book is called by both names. Praise and blame alike mean nothing. No, delightful as the pastime of measuring may be, it is the most futile of all occupations, and to submit to the decrees of the measurers the most servile of attitudes. So long as you write what you wish to write, that is all that matters; and whether it matters for ages or only for hours, nobody can say. But to sacrifice a hair of the head of your vision, a shade of its colour, in deference to some Headmaster with a silver pot in his hand or to some professor with a measuring-rod up his sleeve, is the most abject treachery, and the sacrifice of wealth and chastity which used to be said to be the greatest of human disasters, a mere flea-bite in comparison.

Next I think that you may object that in all this I have made too much of the importance of material things. Even allowing a generous margin for symbolism, that five hundred a year stands for the power to contemplate, that a lock on the door means the power to think for oneself, still you may say that the mind should rise above such things; and that great poets have often been poor men. Let me then quote to you the words of your own Professor of Literature, who knows better than I do what goes to the making of a poet. Sir Arthur Quiller-Couch writes:[1]

"What are the great poetical names of the last hundred years or so? Coleridge, Wordsworth, Byron, Shelley, Landor, Keats, Tennyson, Browning, Arnold, Morris, Rossetti, Swinburne—we may stop there. Of these, all but Keats, Browning, Rossetti were University men; and of these three, Keats, who died young, cut off in his prime, was the only one not fairly well to do. It may seem a brutal thing to say, and it is a sad thing to say: but, as a matter of hard fact, the theory that poetical genius bloweth where it listeth, and equally in poor and rich, holds little truth. As a matter of hard fact, nine out of those twelve were University men: which means that somehow or other they procured the means to get the best education England can give. As a matter of hard fact, of the remaining three you know that Browning was well to do, and I challenge you that, if he had not been well to do, he would no more have attained to write *Saul* or *The Ring and the Book* than Ruskin would have attained to writing *Modern Painters* if his father had not dealt prosperously in business. Rossetti had a small private income; and, moreover, he painted. There remains but Keats; whom Atropos slew young, as she slew John Clare in a mad-house, and James Thomson by the laudanum he took to drug disappointment. These are dreadful facts, but let us face them. It is—however dishonouring to us as a nation—certain that, by some fault in our commonwealth, the poor poet has not in these days, nor has had for two hundred years, a dog's chance. Believe me—and I have spent a great part of ten years in watching some three hundred and twenty elementary schools—we may prate of democracy, but actually, a poor child in England has little more hope than had the son of an Athenian slave to be emancipated into that intellectual freedom of which great writings are born."

Nobody could put the point more plainly. "The poor poet has not in these days, nor has had for two hundred years, a dog's chance . . . a poor child in England has little more hope than had the son of an Athenian slave to be emancipated into that intellectual freedom of which great writings are born." That is it. Intellectual freedom depends upon material things. Poetry depends upon intellectual freedom. And women have always been poor, not for two hundred years merely, but from the beginning of time. Women have had less intellectual freedom than the sons of Athenian slaves. Women, then, have not had a dog's chance of writing poetry. That is why I have laid so much stress on money and a room of one's own. However, thanks to the toils of those obscure women in the past, of whom I wish we knew more, thanks, curiously enough, to two wars, the Crimean which let Florence Nightingale out of her drawing-room, and the European War which opened the doors to the average woman some sixty years later, these evils are in the way to be bettered. Otherwise you would not be here tonight, and your chance of earning five hundred pounds a year, precarious as I am afraid that it still is, would be minute in the extreme.

Still, you may object, why do you attach so much importance to this writing of books by women when, according to you, it requires so much effort, leads perhaps to the murder of one's aunts, will make one almost certainly late for luncheon, and may bring one into very grave disputes with certain very good fellows? My motives, let me admit, are partly selfish. Like most uneducated Englishwomen, I like reading—I like reading books in the bulk. Lately my diet has become a trifle monotonous; history is too much about wars; biography too much about great men; poetry has shown, I think, a tendency to sterility, and fiction—but I have sufficiently exposed my disabilities as a critic of modern fiction and will say no more about it. Therefore I would ask you to write all kinds of books, hesitating at no subject however trivial or however vast. By hook or by crook, I hope that you will possess yourselves of money enough to travel and to idle, to contemplate the future or the past of the world, to dream over books and loiter at street corners and let the line of thought dip deep into the stream. For I am by no means confining you to fiction. If you would please me—and there are thousands like me—you would write books of travel and adventure, and research and scholarship, and history and biography, and criticism and philosophy and science. By so doing you will certainly profit the art of fiction. For books have a way of influencing each other. Fiction will be much the better for standing cheek by jowl with poetry and philosophy. Moreover, if you consider any great figure of the past, like Sappho, like the Lady Murasaki, like Emily Brontë, you will find that she is an inheritor as well as an originator, and has come into existence because women have come to have the habit of writing naturally; so that even as a prelude to poetry such activity on your part would be invaluable.

But when I look back through these notes and criticise my own train of thought as I made them, I find that my motives were not altogether selfish. There runs through these comments and discursions the conviction—or is it the instinct?—that good books are desirable and that good writers, even if they show every variety of human depravity, are still good human beings. Thus when I ask you to write more books I am urging you to do what will be for your good and for the good of the world at large. How to justify this instinct or belief I do not know, for philosophic words, if one has not been educated at a university, are apt to play one false. What is meant by "reality"? It would seem to be something very erratic, very undependable—now to be found in a dusty road, now in a scrap of newspaper in the street, now in a daffodil in the sun. It lights up a group in a room and stamps some casual saying. It overwhelms one walking home beneath the stars and makes the silent world more real than the world of speech—and then there it is again in an omnibus in the uproar of Piccadilly. Sometimes, too, it seems to dwell in shapes too far away for us to discern what their nature is. But whatever it touches, it fixes and makes permanent. That is what remains over when the skin of the day has been cast into the hedge; that is what is left of past time and of our loves and hates. Now the writer, as I think, has the chance to live more than other people in the presence of this reality. It is his business to find it and collect it and communicate it to the rest of us. So at least I infer from reading *Lear* or *Emma* or *La Recherche du Temps Perdu.* For the reading of these books seems to perform a curious couching operation on the senses; one sees more intensely afterwards;

the world seems bared of its covering and given an intenser life. Those are the enviable people who live at enmity with unreality; and those are the pitiable who are knocked on the head by the thing done without knowing or caring. So that when I ask you to earn money and have a room of your own, I am asking you to live in the presence of reality, an invigorating life, it would appear, whether one can impart it or not.

Here I would stop, but the pressure of convention decrees that every speech must end with a peroration. And a peroration addressed to women should have something, you will agree, particularly exalting and ennobling about it. I should implore you to remember your responsibilities, to be higher, more spiritual; I should remind you how much depends upon you, and what an influence you can exert upon the future. But those exhortations can safely, I think, be left to the other sex, who will put them, and indeed have put them, with far greater eloquence that I can compass. When I rummage in my own mind I find no noble sentiments about being companions and equals and influencing the world to higher ends. I find myself saying briefly and prosaically that it is much more important to be oneself than anything else. Do not dream of influencing other people, I would say, if I knew how to make it sound exalted. Think of things in themselves.

And again I am reminded by dipping into newspapers and novels and biographies that when a woman speaks to women she should have something very unpleasant up her sleeve. Women are hard on women. Women dislike women. Women—but are you not sick to death of the word? I can assure you that I am. Let us agree, then, that a paper read by a woman to women should end with something particularly disagreeable.

But how does it go? What can I think of? The truth is, I often like women. I like their unconventionality. I like their subtlety. I like their anonymity. I like—but I must not run on in this way. That cupboard there,—you say it holds clean table-napkins only; but what if Sir Archibald Bodkin were concealed among them? Let me then adopt a sterner tone. Have I, in the preceding words, conveyed to you sufficiently the warnings and reprobation of mankind? I have told you the very low opinion in which you were held by Mr. Oscar Browning. I have indicated what Napoleon once thought of you and what Mussolini thinks now. Then, in case any of you aspire to fiction, I have copied out for your benefit the advice of the critic about courageously acknowledging the limitations of your sex. I have referred to Professor X and given prominence to his statement that women are intellectually, morally and physically inferior to men. I have handed on all that has come my way without going in search of it, and here is a final warning—from Mr. John Langdon Davies.[2] Mr. John Langdon Davies warns women "that when children cease to be altogether desirable, women cease to be altogether necessary." I hope you will make a note of it.

How can I further encourage you to go about the business of life? Young women, I would say, and please attend, for the peroration is beginning, you are, in my opinion, disgracefully ignorant. You have never made a discovery of any sort of importance. You have never shaken an empire or led an army into battle. The plays of Shakespeare are not by you, and you have never introduced a barbarous race to the blessings of civilisation. What is your excuse? It is all very well for you to say, pointing to the streets and squares and forests of the globe swarming with black and white and coffee-coloured inhabitants, all busily engaged in traffic and enterprise and love-making, we have had other work on our hands. Without our doing, those seas would be unsailed and those fertile lands a desert. We have borne and bred and washed and taught, perhaps to the age of six or seven years, the one thousand six hundred and twenty-three million human beings who are, according to statistics, at present in existence, and that, allowing that some had help, takes time.

There is truth in what you say—I will not deny it. But at the same time may I remind you that there have been at least two colleges for women in existence in England since the year 1866; that after the year 1880 a married woman was allowed by law to possess her own property; and that in 1919—which is a whole nine years ago—she was given a vote? May I also remind you that the most of the professions have been open to you for close on ten years now? When you reflect upon these immense privileges and the length of time during which they have been enjoyed, and the fact that there must be at this moment some two thousand women capable of earning over five hundred a year in one way or another, you will agree that the excuse of lack of opportunity, training, encouragement, leisure and money no longer holds good. Moreover, the economists are telling us that Mrs. Seton has had too many children. You must, of course, go on bearing children, but, so they say, in twos and threes, not in tens and twelves.

Thus, with some time on your hands and with some book learning in your brains—you have had enough of the other kind, and are sent to college partly, I suspect, to be uneducated—surely you should embark upon another stage of your very long, very laborious and highly obscure career. A thousand pens are ready to suggest what you should do and what effect you will have. My own suggestion is a little fantastic, I admit; I prefer, therefore, to put it in the form of fiction.

I told you in the course of this paper that Shakespeare had a sister; but do not look for her in Sir Sidney Lee's life of the poet. She died young—alas, she never wrote a word. She lies buried where the omnibuses now stop, opposite the Elephant and Castle. Now my belief is that this poet who never wrote a word and was buried at the crossroads still lives. She lives in you and in me, and in many other women who are not here tonight, for they are washing up the dishes and putting the children to bed. But she lives; for great poets do not die; they are continuing presences; they need only the opportunity to walk among us in the flesh. This opportunity, as I think, is now coming within your power to give her. For my belief is that if we live another century or so—I am talking of the common life which is the real life and not of the little separate lives which we live as individuals—and have five hundred a year each of us and rooms of our own; if we have the habit of freedom and the courage to write exactly what we think; if we escape a little from the common sitting-room and see human beings not always in their relation to each other but in relation to reality; and the sky, too, and the trees or whatever it may be in themselves; if we look past Milton's bogey, for no human being should shut out the view; if we face the fact, for it is a fact, that there is no arm to cling to, but that we go alone and that our relation is to the world of reality and not only to the world of men and women, then the opportunity will come and the dead poet who was Shakespeare's sister will put on the body which she has so often laid down. Drawing her life from the lives of the unknown who were her forerunners, as her brother did before her, she will be born. As for her coming without that preparation, without that effort on our part, without that determination that when she is born again she shall find it possible to live and write her poetry, that we cannot expect, for that would be impossible. But I maintain that she would come if we worked for her, and that so to work, even in poverty and obscurity, is worthwhile.

Notes

1. *The Art of Writing,* by Sir Arthur Quiller-Couch.
2. *A Short History of Women,* by John Langdon Davies.

Women Say Goodbye to Life of June Cleaver

Susan Chira

Susan Chira (1958–) was born in Manhattan and grew up in Rye, New York. As an undergraduate, she was reporter, editor, and then president of the Harvard Crimson *before graduating summa cum laude in 1980. A history and East Asian studies major, she joined the* New York Times *in 1981 and corresponded for the* Times *in Tokyo from 1984 to 1989. Currently, she has returned to the United States and lives in Manhattan with her husband, Michael Shapiro, and their son while continuing to report on the field of education and review for the* Times. *She also contributed the "Introduction" to Shapiro's book on South Korea,* The Shadow in the Sun *(1990).*

FREMONT, Mich.—The American mother—that self-sacrificing, self-effacing, cookie-baking icon—has been shoved into the center of a political morality play, one where stick-figure mothers battle in a debate that does not begin to suggest the complexity, diversity and confusion of being a mother in 1992.

Instead of Marilyn Quayle and Hillary Clinton, those caricatures of stay-at-home and working mothers, talk to Toni Rumsey, who cried when her first child was born and she realized she would have to keep her factory job at Gerber Baby Foods in Fremont, Mich., or face living in a trailer.

Or Stacy Murdock, who watches every penny on her farm in Murray, Ky., because her family's income dropped by more than half when she quit teaching, unable to bear leaving her children.

Or Nancy Cassidy, a garment worker in Easton, Pa., who loves to work and believes her children are the better for it.

These mothers are haunted by the ghost of the mythical 1950s television mother—one that most women today cannot be, even if they want to.

Caught between a fictional ideal, changing expectations of women's roles and the reality that many mothers now work because they must, women around the country are groping for a new definition of the good mother.

The old images linger, but they fit fewer people's lives. Motherhood in America has undergone a breathtaking transformation in little more than 30 years, propelled by shrinking wages of husbands and changing social attitudes.

In 1960, 20 percent of mothers with children under 6 years old were in the labor force; by last year, that had swelled to 58 percent, with most of them working full time. Twenty-nine percent of all American families are now headed by one parent.

Some more affluent women choose to work for self-fulfillment, and some who started out that way found that they could not afford to leave their jobs as the economy soured.

Whether or not a conservative backlash movement is trying to shame women into staying at home, more and more mothers see work as a financial and personal necessity.

Small wonder, then, that Republican strategists quickly folded their family values banner when they found the reality of motherhood in this election year at odds with campaign slogans.

With politicians in both parties now courting middle America, many of these same working-class women have been forced to take jobs outside the home, often monotonous and regimented ones at low wages that may not allow them to buy help with child care and housecleaning.

As interviews with more than 30 mothers around the country show, politicians have waded into one of the most wrenching issues of American life.

"I never feel like I'm a full mom," said Rumsey, a 34-year-old mother of two who checks Gerber's baby food for shards of glass and signs of spoilage from 7 a.m. to 3 p.m.

"I make the cookies, the homemade costumes for Halloween. I volunteer for everything to make up to them for not being here. When I do all that, I make myself so tired that they lose a happy cheerful mom and then I'm cheating them again. It's hard when you were raised with Donna Reed and the Beav's mom."

In another factory in Easton, Pa., Cassidy inspects sportswear, and her life as a working mother, for flaws. "I think you can work and be a good mother," said the 42-year-old mother of two. "We're doing it. When people compliment you that they're nice children, then I think you've been a terrific mother."

Some women have found that they could not be good mothers in the old sense because working has become so important to their identities. These women say they know in their hearts that being at home all day does not automatically make a good mother.

"You can be there without being there," said Cheryl Moorefield, a labor nurse in Winston-Salem, N.C., who has two children.

Yet ask most women their image of a good mother, and the old verities come tumbling forth.

"A mother doesn't have a right to be tired or sick," said Deborah Gray, a 38-year-old mother of six whose shift can run 12 hours a day during the busy summer season at Heinz's pickling plant in Holland, Mich. "A mother must be available no matter what. A mother is a person that can perform miracles."

It is precisely because convictions about what kind of mother is best run so strong and deep that family values became such an explosive issue.

Despite all the talk about fathers' becoming more involved with children, it is mothers who remain at the center of this debate.

Most women interviewed said they were worried about the future of the family, but many said the debate, at least as conducted by politicians, seemed irrelevant.

"Family values is a cheap way out," Rumsey said. "We all believe in family morals and values. I'm not going to put down what you're doing and don't put me down for what I'm trying to do."

Motherhood in Bondage

Adrienne Rich

Adrienne Rich (1929–) was born in Baltimore, Maryland, received her bachelor's degree from Radcliffe College in 1951, and is currently on the faculty of the Department of English at Stanford University. A prolific writer, she has published twenty-five titles of poetry, prose, and plays. After winning the Yale Series of Younger Poets award in 1951, her writing voice underwent a transformation between 1954 and 1962 as she let go of traditional, masculine forms. Calling poetry an "almost natural women's form," she says, "I wrote very short poems in the fifties because I had to write while the children were napping, between chores."

EVERY GREAT NEW MOVEMENT IN HUMAN CONsciousness arouses both hope and terror. The understanding that male–female relationships have been founded on the status of the female as the property of the male, or of male-dominated institutions, continues to be difficult for both women and men. It is painful to acknowledge that our identity has been dictated and diminished by others, or that we have let our identity depend on the diminishment and exploitation of other humans. This idea still meets with the resistance that has always risen when unsanctioned, long-stifled realities begin to stir and assert themselves.

Resistance may take many forms. Protective deafness—the inability to hear what is actually being said—is one. Trivialization is another: the reduction of a troubling new complexity to a caricature, or a clinical phenomenon. A literary critic, reviewing two recent anthologies of women's poetry, declares that "the notion that the world has been put together exclusively by men, and solely for their own benefit, and that they have conspired together for generations to discriminate against their mothers and sisters, wives and daughters, lovers and friends, is a neurosis for which we do not yet have a name." It is striking that, even in his denial, this writer can describe women only as appendages to men.

In her history of birth control in America, the Marxist historian Linda Gordon writes, "For women . . . heterosexual relations are always intense, frightening, high-risk situations which ought, if a woman has any sense of self-preservation, to be carefully calculated."[1] The power politics of the relations between the sexes, long unexplored, is still a charged issue. To raise it is to cut to the core of power relations throughout society, to break down irreparably the screens of mystification between "private life" and "public affairs."

But even more central a nerve is exposed when motherhood is analyzed as a political institution. This institution—which affects each woman's personal experience—is visible in the male dispensation of birth control and abortion; the guardianship of men over children in the courts and the educational system; the subservience, through most of history, of women and children to the patriarchal father; the economic dominance of the father over the family; the usurpation of the birth process by a male medical establishment. The subjectivity of the fathers (who are also sons) has prescribed how, when, and even where women should conceive, bear, nourish, and indoctrinate their children. The experience of motherhood by women—both mothers and daughters—is only beginning to be described by women themselves.

Until very recently, the choice to be or not to be a mother was virtually unavailable to most women; even today, the possibility of choice remains everywhere in jeopardy. This elemental loss of control over her body affects every woman's right to shape the imagery and insights of her own being. We speak of women as "nonmothers" or "childless"; we do not speak of "nonfathers" or "childless men." Motherhood is admirable, however, only so long as mother and child are attached to a legal father: Motherhood out of wedlock, or under the welfare system, or lesbian motherhood, are harassed, humiliated, or neglected. In the 1970s in the United States, with 26 million children of wage-earning mothers, 8 million in female-headed households, the late nineteenth-century stereotype of the "mother at home" is still assumed as the norm—a "norm" that has, outside of a small middle-class minority, never existed.

In trying to distinguish the two strands: motherhood as *experience,* one possible and profound experience for women, and motherhood as enforced identity and as political *institution,* I myself only slowly began to grasp the centrality of the institution, and how it connects with the dread of difference that infects all societies. Under that institution, all women are seen primarily as mothers; all mothers are expected to experience motherhood unambivalently and in accordance with patriarchal values; and the "nonmothering" woman is seen as deviant.

Since the "deviant" is outside the law, and "abnormal," the pressure on all women to assent to the "mothering" role is intense. To speak of maternal ambivalence; to examine the passionate conflicts and ambiguities of the mother–daughter relationship, and the role of the mother in indoctrinating her daughters to subservience and her sons to dominance; to identify the guilt mothers are made to feel for societal failures beyond their control; to acknowledge that a lesbian can be a mother and a mother a lesbian, contrary to popular stereotypes; to question the dictating by powerful men as to how women, especially the poor and nonwhite, shall use their bodies, or the indoctrination of women toward a one-sided emotional nurturing of men, is to challenge deeply embedded phobias and prejudices.

Such themes anger and terrify, precisely because they touch us at the quick of human existence. But to flee them, or trivialize them, to leave the emotions they arouse in us unexamined, is to flee both ourselves and the dawning hope that women *and* men may one day experience forms of love and parenthood, identity and community that will not be drenched in lies, secrets, and silence.

Note

1. Linda Gordon, *Woman's Body, Woman's Right: A Social History of Birth Control in America* (New York: Viking Grossman, 1976).

Exit the Frog Prince

Madonna Kolbenschlag

Madonna Kolbenschlag (1935–) was born in Cleveland, Ohio, and studied for her doctorate at the University of Notre Dame. From 1980 to 1985 she worked as a legislative aide and research analyst in the United States House of Representatives, work which informs her 1988 book, Lost in the Land of Oz. *In the following selection, the "Epilogue" to* Kiss Sleeping Beauty Goodbye *(© 1988 Harper-Collins), she imagines a transformed fairy-tale Princess addressing the Prince who must also experience transformation. Even while the newly awakened Beauty calls for an end to the traditional roles of men and women, she acknowledges "the subtle ways in which I seduce you into being the traditional male."*

Dearest Prince,

I have not quite decided whether I should leave you. I know you are confused and anxious. You keep looking at me with that "whatever-happened-to-the-princess-I-married" look. Your confusion is understandable. In the past few months, years, I have literally self-destructed. Disintegrated my false self, in order to reassemble my true self. Your self, unfortunately, is tailor-made for that old, false self. You are accustomed to playing "hero"; suddenly you're a "heavy."

Like many other men, you have difficulty seeing yourself as an oppressor because you have difficulty seeing yourself as a member of a class. Men regard themselves as individuals and look to their own motives to justify or reprove their behavior. They suppress their symbolic role in an apolitical illusion of personal innocence: "I have never discriminated against women or bullied them, so why should I be accused?" They are blind to their participation in sustaining oppressive arrangements in human relations. They have accepted the way things are, and in that acceptance is an act of complicity—regardless of their own personal motives. Their individualistic view inevitably seduces them into interpreting efforts to redress the situation of women—"affirmative action" plans, etc.—as threats to their own individual rights. The hue and cry about "reverse discrimination" is a pathetic wail of self-centeredness as the last lifeboats on the *Titanic* are loaded.

In working through my own liberation I have experienced much anger and a great deal of fear. But I am beginning to emerge on the other side of that, now. I can begin to look beyond myself to be concerned in a new way about others. My anger has changed to anguish—anguish especially about you. In so many ways, your situation is worse than mine. Your self-deception is deeper and more profound.

I know you instinctively regard the "woman problem" as a question of giving them time and space enough to "catch up" with men. You don't see yourself as having a problem, too. White, middle-class American males always think that everything is someone else's problem—the blacks have a problem, women have a problem, chicanos have a problem. You don't recognize your own socialized masculinity as a problem, as the root of all the other problems.

In a sense everyone's liberation depends on the liberation of white males, precisely because they have the power to prevent women and minorities from seeking a broader range of alternatives if they do not play the game by the rules of the masculine value system. Unless you can admit that you *are* the problem and begin the task of liberating yourself and dismantling the male-ordered system, many so-called "liberated" women will be seduced into a patriarchal, elitist, one-dimensional, masculine role. We will simply have a new set of "half-persons" who happen to be female.

In many ways, you are more fragile than I. I know if I leave you, it will crush you beyond anything I will suffer. By being a good wife, mother, mistress, servant, handmaid, Girl Friday—and little else—I've made you all the more dependent on me for your sense of well-being. The impression of autonomy that you project to others is a well-practiced reflex. But you are not a truly free person. The heteronomy I struggle with binds me primarily to persons and to the demands they make on me. The heteronomy you have to exorcise is more abstract, insidious and pervasive. Independence will not necessarily free you to the extent that it will free me. I had to recognize that I had no being of my own. You have to recognize the extent to which your being is dependent on affirmation by women and by your "inferiors." Your dominance, your assumption of the natural superiority of the male sex, is really an attempt to guarantee the continued presence of those on whom you depend for your identity as a male.

As women, we are constantly made aware of our immanence, of our contingency, of the social and biological parameters that circumscribe our being—we need few reminders of what it means to be female. Men, on the other hand, enjoy a more individuated transcending role. Thus, their awareness of their masculinity—in a patriarchal society—requires the recognition and confirmation of their supremacy. One can't be a Chief unless there are Indians who provide evidence of it, willingly or unwillingly.

The masculine role is at the same time more restrictive, more abstract and more artificial than the feminine role. Liberating yourself from it will perhaps be more difficult than my exodus from the feminine mystique. Girls grow up with a greater exposure to a same-sex parental model than boys. In the relative absence of his father and care-taking male models for direct imitation, a boy absorbs a culturally rather than concretely defined masculine role: from his mother and teachers, from his peers, from television and other sources of conventional stereotypes. Thus, the role is more abstract and more demanding, more total and more distorted. Deviations from it are more critical; dilemmas abound. Being a man demands independent, aggressive, physically active, ambitious behavior. Educational and societal values tend to be more feminine, emphasizing politeness, obedience, passivity, cleanliness, etc. These double-binds increase as a boy changes into a man, intensifying inner stress and conflict.

Growing up male exacts a terrible price, ultimately requiring capitulation to the absolute heteronomy of the masculine ideal.

As a conditioned male you must undergo a mutilation of spirit that amputates some of your deepest human capacities. Feelings are perhaps the most serious threat to the masculine ideal. You are expected to play the role of the independent strong achiever, always in control, always deliberate, calculated. You are expected to be task-oriented, undistracted by personal matters. You are expected to repress any responses that might impede your efficiency in achieving your goals. And so you listen neither to your feelings, nor to your body. You do not sense the approach of illness or register the whispers of your own mind. You often do not hear what others are trying to say; you translate non-verbal messages poorly. Your belief in your own self-sufficiency makes you resistant to the idea of seeking help from someone else. Physically and emotionally, you ignore the pain that signals your innermost desire for health and growth. Not surprising that some psychologists compare the behavior of many men to that of autistic children: the characteristic fear of being touched, of expressing feelings, of relating intimately, with a compensating fixation on inanimate objects.

Sometimes you show very little respect for words; you are impatient with the process of communication and reflection. Your muteness and your silence are often testimony to your worship of will and action. You say you thrive on competition. I'm not so sure. All I know is, it drives you to do things you wouldn't do if you were in your right mind. Sometimes you even compete with your own kids.

In subtle ways you consistently invalidate the experience, the tasks of women. You play the "professional" and demand freedom from simple human tasks—at the cost of your humanity. You hide from life through "specialization." You want your work to be an escalator to success with as few deviations as possible. Oh, I envy your confidence in yourself. But I know it's only skin-deep. You're sure of yourself in the few roles—jobs you've mastered. Left without them, you collapse like a jellyfish in a heap of inadequacy. You haven't learned the art of living. You wear a public face easily, but you're very insecure in intimate situations. You know what mask, what language to use when, but you're out of sync with your inner self.

I would like to free you of your compulsive workaholism, your "breadwinner" fixation. But I can't share that load unless you relieve me of some of the burden of homemaking and child rearing. Can you learn to work less, earn less, spend more time with the kids—and be happy? If you can't, then I can't be happy either. Can you stop measuring yourself by the size of your paycheck?

I want to be an equal partner with you in supporting our home and in building a world. I think I should work, but I don't want to betray myself in "liberating" myself into the marketplace. I know I have to learn how to cope with competition. But I don't want to be infected with it, as you are. If my professional advancement is going to depend on conforming to the male model of achievement (compulsive-accretive production, narrow specialization, manipulation of data, the ability to walk over others on the way up, "chutzpah" and hustling, a cool and stoic demeanor), then I would be a fool to remake myself in your image.

Your institutions are like your automobiles—extensions of your ego. So pervaded by the masculine consciousness that they have become lethal instruments, harmful to all forms of human life. Your hospitals, schools, universities, governments and churches are all corporations, factories. All in bondage to the idea of male supremacy, that might makes right and wealth dictates policy, where workers are excluded from ownership and decision making, and profit becomes synonymous with survival. Most of your institutions are still modeled on the plantation—a few privileged white-male professionals supported by a huge substructure of underpaid, underprivileged, largely female labor force.

When I work in these institutions, I have to endure high visibility as a woman and low visibility as a professional and as a person. My comments are frequently ignored at committee or board meetings. But if you make the same proposal a few minutes later, it's accepted enthusiastically. You are conditioned to notice my face, figure, clothes, manner, but have very little talent for observing and judging capacity. In fact, you are exceptionally stupid when it comes to making judgments about women. Probably because you prefer to surround yourself with "safe" types who will not attempt to challenge or change anything. The fact that they often turn out to be incompetent or lacking in conviction seems to have escaped you.

I'm tired of cloaking my competence with a veneer of coyness—so as not to castrate my male peers. I'm tired of having to let you win—whether it's in checkers or politics. Do I have to spend my entire life coddling male egos? (High school and college were a prolonged ordeal of this kind of dishonesty.) When are you going to recognize your paranoia of competent, assertive women for what it is? An infantile reflex against Mom. *Look* at me: I'm not your mother, your older sister, your baby sister, your first-grade teacher, your servant, or your pet—I'm your *peer.* I'm a *person.*

I'm tired of lobbying for shared responsibility, equal pay, promotions and job opportunities. Women have always wanted these things, unless they've been brainwashed beyond repair. We won't get these things, however, until men realize that *they* have to give up something—power, advantage—in order for us to be equal. Until you promote women's liberation, there won't be any. It isn't going to happen by natural evolution—your present position is too comfortable. You play the "anointed" role, as if authority always had to be given to the oldest son. It might be easier to take if you simply acknowledged the lust for power and the insecurity that underlies your need to be in charge. But you keep referring your status to some fundamental principle of cosmic order, or worse yet, as "God's plan for the human species." The possibilities of human destiny, human structures and human relationships are infinitely more varied than this. Stand back and let the future unfold.

But let us not be naïve. The mere presence of women in new jobs, in management positions—in greater numbers—is not necessarily going to make a difference. Misogyny and patriarchy run deep, in women as well as men. Much more fundamental changes in social structures are needed if human persons are to develop to their full spiritual maturity.

The look on your face tells me I am guilty, too. Yes, I hate myself for the subtle ways in which I seduce you into being a traditional male—how do we unlearn these old scripts? How can I begin to show you that your personhood means more to me than your masculinity? Will the world around us still convince you otherwise?

I am torn between my resentment of your protective paternalism and the real need I have of the security of your love, your help and your confidence in me. But please, no more Pygmalion postures. I'm trying to reclaim my responsibility for myself, for my own growth and maturity. If I fail, I fail. On the other hand, I don't like being ignored either. You find it easy to promote, help and encourage—to nurture—other men. But you leave women to their own devices. Your distance forces me to work twice as hard to prove myself.

In countless ways we need each other as models for change. But I don't want to be what you are, and you wouldn't want to be what I have been. Can we become something new together?

I am perturbed by your isolation from other men. Oh, you maintain a certain easy acceptance of each other. You can always depend on your cronies for assistance, commiseration. But you have no really intimate male friends, one or two "soul friends," to whom you could open your heart. Am I the only one you can achieve that kind of intimacy with? That's too much for one person to have to provide.

You seem unwilling to admit the presence of "love" in your relationships with other men. Although I suppose if you did, I might instinctively reflect jealousy or suspicion—I've been conditioned too.

I'd like to have some friendships with other men that don't necessarily involve sex. I know I'm capable of this kind of relationship, but I can't seem to find many men who are. Most of them assume that sex is the terminal point of all relationships. And then there's the problem of your possessiveness and jealousy.

I worry about your influence on our children, on the young people we care for. You treat the boys so differently from the girls. Your hyperanxiety about your son is already affecting him. If you were around more, perhaps your daughter would be better off too.

All of these anxieties and frustrations have brought me to a point of decision about you. My own *anger* and *depression* finally forced me to transform my life. What will it take to transform yours? Is *rejection* the only way to open your eyes? Do I have to leave you, abandon you to your self-serving universe? If we go our separate ways, there will be pain and loss. The tapestry of relationships that we have woven with our lives will be rent. If we remain together, we may succumb to the bribes of our old way of life and be diminished that much more. Either way there is risk.

Change will no doubt be more precarious for you than for me. It will be a more lonely, more alienated path. In shedding the husk of your reflected masculine glory, you will discover what many women already know—what it means to be a no-thing. Women in the process of a consciousness breakthrough usually experience rage and frustration. Our behavior is often overtly anti-male. Men undergoing the same process will experience more of a feeling of loss. Anger and resolve motivate a woman to sustain her changed consciousness and evolve new relationship patterns. As she withdraws from male hegemony she will often discover the support and encouragement of other women who will reach out to her in her struggle. You, on the other hand, are likely to suffer the loss, not only of the women to whom you can no longer relate in the old way, but also the loss of your male buddies—because you have betrayed the masculine code. You will be alone, you will be tempted to revert to the old patriarchal and macho scenarios. You have everything to lose by continuing the struggle; I have everything to lose by giving it up.

I want you to know that I understand what is at stake for you. I want you to know that I can support you in that death and rebirth process—it is the price of reclaiming your humanity and your own soul. I can be your companion. My conversion to feminism is an unfinished, incomplete experience unless it leads to your liberation. We can walk beside each other and support each other. We need not be spouses—in fact, it might be better if we weren't. Believe me when I say that I want you to be different (in spite of the fact that I sometimes behave instinctively to the contrary). If I give up my princess ways, will you give up your princedom?

I know I will have to steel myself to accept the consequences. If you begin to take on more responsibility for home and children, I will have to sacrifice some of my matriarchal prerogatives there. If you begin to shed the "team" mystique at work, take a stand on sensitive issues, work fewer hours, I will have to bear with the consequences in loss of promotions, lower pay, job changes, whatever may come. I'll have to bear with insecurity and loss of status without putting guilt on you. You'll have to stop putting guilt on me for abandoning the "imperial motherhood" role in the home and the Girl Friday role in the office.

Perhaps the most difficult change of all will be admitting that neither of us can be all things to the other. If we are married, we will have to allow others to be a part of our lives, individually and together. We will need more than other supportive couples, mirror images of our own dyad. I will need women and men as friends; you will need men and women as friends.

We have to be committed to this transformation. These changes will come slowly and painfully. We will have to bear with different rhythms of growth in each other. We will have to persevere in them in spite of the pressures of society. We will have to explode and upset our life together, occasionally, in order to find new ways to keep ourselves growing. This commitment to each other's liberation and growth should be our best reason for being together. If that is not a part of our continuing compact, then even if I love you, I *must* leave you.

You came into my life once and awakened me from sleep, rescued me from servitude, led me through the forest safely. I can do nothing less for you. Can we walk out of the fairy tale into the future together?

With love and hope,

Sleeping Beauty,
Snow White
Cinderella,
Goldilocks and
Beauty

Hazel Tells LaVerne

Katharyn Howd Machan

Katharyn Howd Machan (1952–) lived in Woodbury, Connecticut, until she was thirteen years old. Her degrees are from the College of St. Rose in Albany, New York (B.A.), the University of Iowa (M.A. in English literature), and Northwestern University (Ph.D. in performance studies). She teaches in the Writing Program at Ithaca College, where she has also directed the Feminist Writing Workshops (1984–88). Her most recent publication is The Kitchen of Your Dreams, *which won the 1992 Goodman Award. Following her remarriage, she gave up the name Katharyn Aal and took her husband's name Howd for her middle name, restoring her Czech family name, Machan, as her surname.*

last night
im cleanin out my
howard johnsons ladies room
when all of a sudden
up pops this frog
musta come from the sewer
swimmin aroun an tryin ta
climb up the sida the bowl
so i goes ta flushm down
but sohelpmegod he starts talkin
bout a golden ball
an how i can be a princess
me a princess
well my mouth drops
all the way to the floor
an he says
kiss me just kiss me
once on the nose
well i screams
ya little green pervert
an i hitsm with my mop
an has ta flush
the toilet down three times
me
a princess

Reprinted with permission of the author.

V

Sexuality, Love, and Commitment

Men and women speak different languages of love, but in psychotherapy, research, and popular lore, the female language has become the dominant one. Women appear to be better than men at intimacy because intimacy is defined as what women do: Talk, express feelings, and disclose personal concerns. Intimacy is rarely defined as sharing activities, being helpful, doing useful work, or enjoying companionable silence. Because of this bias, men rarely get credit for the kinds of loving actions that are more typical of them.

–CAROL TAVRIS, "The Feminizing of Love"

Danu opened Her eyes to the sight of dark green sprouts on the soft triangle below Her navel. Gingerly, She fingered these spiky curling firs and then delighted Herself when they didn't fall away. More sprang up, in the valleys under Her arms and on the lush three-sided range between Her legs, until those sweet places were most forested with trees.

–CAROLYN MCVICKAR EDWARDS,
"The Gift of Rhythm and Blood"

So I hobble down a hall
of disappointments past where
your darkness and my darkness have
had intercourse with each other.
Why have I wasted my life
in anger, thinking I could have more
than what is glimpsed in recognition?
I will let go, as we must
let go of an angel called
back to heaven; I will not hold
her glittering robe, but let it
drift above me until I see
the last shred of evidence.

–TOI DERRICOTTE, "The Promise"

Open Window

Janet Hamill

Janet Hamill (1945–) was born in Jersey City, New Jersey, where she grew up as "a good Irish Catholic working-class kid." At Glassboro State College she received her undergraduate training—and met her lifelong friend and fellow poet, Patti Smith. As a writer, she has been most heavily influenced by French and Spanish surrealist authors: Octavio Paz, Carlos Fuentes, Gabriel García Márquez. Her poems have been published under the title The Temple *and, most recently,* Nostalgia of the Infinite *(1992), a collection inspired by the work of the surrealist painter de Chirico. "Open Window" makes reference to the "open window" paintings of Matisse. Hamill lives with her husband in Middleton, New York.*

The air is cool. coming
with the tourmaline sea
into my symphonic interior
caresses. both yours
and the breeze's lingering
longer days of dazzling
light. flood the room
above the Avenue of Palms

a bed with the imprint
of your body on it. sugar
almonds on a silver tray
posing as if for a painting
before a moorish screen
four goldfish swim in a bowl
on fire. my skin is blushing
pink. like a battle of roses

after a bath. the charged
idleness accompanying your
absence wraps around me. in
the silk of a white kimono

Reprinted from *Deep Down*, edited by Laura Chester, 1988.

in the frame of the open
window. I can see my buoyant
heart. sailing the Mediter-
ranean with a wind caught
under its wings

The Feminizing of Love

Carol Tavris

Carol Tavris (1939?–   ) received her Ph.D. from the University of Michigan. She joined the staff of Psychology Today *in 1969 and became a senior editor in the 70s. She and her husband, Ronan O'Casey, live in the Los Angeles area where she works as a writer, lecturer, and teacher of psychology at UCLA. She is a fellow of the American Psychological Association and the author of* Anger—the Misunderstood Emotion *(1982). In this selection from* The Mismeasure of Women *(1992), she discusses reasons why "many women and men end up misreading one another's messages of love, affection, and despair."*

Dear Abby: Another St. Valentine's Day has come and gone without flowers, candy or any kind of a valentine from my husband. I'm 25 and he is 26, and we've been married for three years. I'd have been thrilled if he had brought me a flower—or even handed me a valentine—but he ignored the day completely. . . . He's a super guy, hard-working and decent, so maybe I shouldn't complain. But it sure would have felt great to have been remembered on St. Valentine's Day. Any suggestions?[1]

–NOBODY'S VALENTINE

"NOBODY'S VALENTINE" IS IN GOOD COMPANY, BUT I wonder whether she would be consoled to know that 85 percent of all valentine cards are purchased by women.[2] This is a fascinating statistic. Why aren't more men buying valentines? And why do so many women want them so much?

"Nobody's Valentine" is the target audience for countless books and articles that offer to help women learn to understand, manage, or change men and get them to be more "loving," at least as women define loving—by revealing their feelings. The cover line on an issue of *Self* magazine is typical: Right after "Breakthrough! The easiest diet!" and "6 Steps to a GREAT BODY!" is "*Get him to talk—tonight.*"

Of course, for all the women who are asking, "Why won't he talk to me? Why won't he say he loves me?" there is a corresponding number of men who are complaining, "Why doesn't she shut up? Why does she keep needing reassurance that I love her?" Many women say that their greatest wish for their marriages is that their husbands be more intimate, better at communication. "If only my husband would tell me what he is thinking," they say, "everything would be perfect." For their part, men say, "If only she were happy, if only she would stop complaining, everything would be fine. She expects me to read her mind and know why she is unhappy; I'm truly baffled by what she says she wants."

Underlying these reciprocal complaints is the real problem: that men and women tend to define intimacy and express love differently. For many men, love is action: doing things for the other person. For many women, love is talking: acknowledging the immediate feeling of the other person's adorableness.

For example, psychotherapist Richard Driscoll, in *The Binds That Tie,* describes the following scene: A wife, Paula, asks her husband, Don, if he "really" loves her. Don tries to give her an honest answer: "'I know I want to be married to you. I am satisfied to go to work every morning, because I know that I am supporting you and that you are there for me. I would never want to leave you, and I would never want you to leave me. Is that what you mean by love?' This answer leaves her unsatisfied. 'But why can't you say you *love* me?'" Yet, as Driscoll points out, Don did in fact say he loved her, but in his own words rather than in her words.

Paula did not see this, says Driscoll, because "she thinks of love as a feeling" and "he thinks of it as a commitment to being with a woman and working to provide for her."[3] This is one reason, he believes, that many men are reluctant to say "I love you," at least with the frequency women do. Repeating this phrase daily or on demand from a woman, says Driscoll, "sounds stupid to them. After it has been said once, these gents argue, there's no reason to repeat it over and over like a trained seal yapping on cue from a handler."[4]

Here is another husband, participating with his wife in a study of love. He says:

> *What does she want? Proof? She's got it, hasn't she? Would I be knocking myself out to get things for her—like to keep up this house—if I didn't love her? Why does a man do things like that if not because he loves his wife and kids? I swear, I can't figure what she wants.*

But his wife says:

> *It is not enough that he supports us and takes care of us. I appreciate that, but I want him to share things with me. I need for him to tell me his feelings.*[5]

What men *do,* every day of their lives, simply doesn't feel like love to this wife, to Driscoll's client Paula, and to Nobody's Valentine, who knows but discounts the fact that her husband is "hard-working and decent."

The resulting misunderstandings between couples occur daily in countless households. In one study, seven couples recorded their activities and marital satisfaction for several days.[6] Every day, they noted down how often the spouse did a helpful chore, like cooking a good meal or repairing a faucet; how often the spouse expressed affection; and how satisfied they were feeling with the marriage. The wives thought their marital relations were best on days when their husbands had verbally expressed affection to them, regardless of what the husbands *did.* But the husbands' degree of satisfaction depended on their wives' deeds, not on their affectionate words!

The researchers then directed the husbands to step up the frequency of expressions of love toward their wives, and asked the wives to keep track of any such demonstrations they noticed. After a while, they called up the husbands whose wives said there had been no change, and asked them why they had not complied with instructions. One husband replied huffily that he certainly had complied . . . by washing his wife's car. The husband thought that was a perfectly good way to express his love for her, but she, of course, hadn't a clue.

The doing-versus-talking distinction in the emotional styles of males and females begins in childhood, when boys tend to develop what psychologists call "side-by-side" relationships, in which intimacy means sharing the same activity—sports, games, watching a movie or sports event together, bantering and joking. Girls tend to prefer "face-to-face" relationships, in which intimacy means revealing ideas and emotions in a heart-to-heart exchange. As adults, women may have a tough time understanding that for many men a "shared intimate activity" can be something as banal as watching TV or being in the same room together doing different things. Words are irrelevant, even superfluous. As a woman I interviewed said:

> *My husband and I have a custom of reading the papers and having coffee together every morning. He loves to listen to music in the background, so the radio is usually on. I don't like the music especially—I'd rather have quiet—but I know how much he does. One morning, though, the radio was annoying me, so I got up to read the paper in the other room. My husband protested immediately—"Where are you going?" I said I was leaving so he could enjoy his concert. "Never mind the music," he said, rather crossly, "come back here and I'll turn it off." His tone made me feel cranky,*

until I realized what he was really saying—he'd rather share the morning with me than with the radio.

This woman is fortunate that she got his message. Being together comfortably is the soul of intimacy to him.

For most women, in contrast, intimacy rests on talk—both "deep talk" about significant feelings and worries and "small talk" about daily events. Without it, many women feel like unwatered plants; they wither. So do their relationships. A common refrain in the explanations divorced women give for the failure of their marriages is "lack of communication." A bad marriage, they say, is by definition one in which there is "no talking."[7]

Moreover, women demand a particular kind of talk. When men talk to each other or to women, they tend to discuss relatively impersonal matters, such as cars, sports, work, and politics. When they reveal anything about themselves, it tends to be their strengths and achievements. Women like to talk about personal matters, such as their feelings and relationships; they are willing, often eager, to reveal weaknesses and fears. When a woman is worried, the first thing she does is call a friend to discuss it. When a man is worried, the first thing he does is distract himself by watching TV, playing racquetball, or drinking with his buddies.

In short, some of the basic functions of talk are different for men and women. For many men, the purpose of talking about feelings and problems is to solve them; for many women, the purpose of talking is to talk—simply to share the feeling. When women report the benefits of intimate conversation, they list relief from stress, feeling better, and self-improvement. The benefits that men report are more constructive, such as getting advice or help in solving problems. Thus, when a woman describes her worries, fears, or anger about a problem, she is often seeking confirmation of her *feeling;* the man interprets her talk as a request for *help.*[8]

In her book *You Just Don't Understand,* Deborah Tannen describes the story of a woman, Eve, who had had a lump removed from her breast. Eve tells her sister, a woman friend, and her husband, Mark, how upsetting it was to undergo the operation, and how unhappy she is with the stitches and the changed contour of her breast. The sister says, "I know. When I had my operation I felt the same way." The friend says, "I know. It's like your body has been violated." But Mark says, "You can have plastic surgery to cover up the scar and restore the shape of your breast." Mark's comment makes Eve feel hurt and angry; she thinks it means he is disgusted with how she looks. But of course he thinks *she* is disgusted with the way she looks and he wants to be helpful. "Eve wanted the gift of understanding," Tannen observes, "but Mark gave her the gift of advice. He was taking the role of problem solver, whereas she simply wanted confirmation for her feelings."[9]

Men and women speak different languages of love, but in psychotherapy, research, and popular lore, the female language has become the dominant one. Women appear to be better than men at intimacy because intimacy is defined as what women do: talk, express feelings, and disclose personal concerns. Intimacy is rarely defined as sharing activities, being helpful, doing useful work, or enjoying companionable silence. Because of this bias, men rarely get credit for the kinds of loving actions that are more typical of them.

"Part of the reason that men seem so much less loving than women," argues Francesca Cancian, a sociologist and author of *Love in America,* "is that men's behavior is measured with a feminine ruler."[10] Many social scientists, she shows, use what she calls "a feminized definition of love" in their research: For instance, they label practical activities and helping the spouse as "instrumental behavior" and expressing feelings as "affectionate behavior." This distinction, she observes, thereby denies the affectionate aspect of practical help.

Yet most men are more likely than women to agree with statements like "When she needs help I help her" and "She would rather spend her time with me than with anyone else" as evidence of the love in their relationships. Many men define "commitment" not as constant reassurances of love, but as the daily work they do to support their families. "Many working-class women agree with men that a man's job is something he does out of love for his family," Cancian observes. "But middle-class women and social scientists rarely recognize men's practical help as a form of love."[11]

To observe this bias in action, consider the following test of "intimacy maturity" in marriage. A team of psychologists evaluates couples according to five components of intimacy: orientation to the other person and to the relationship; caring and concern; sexuality; commitment; and communication. On each dimension, a person is scored as being at one of three levels of maturity: from egocentric and self-serving at the low end to most mature at the high end. "Most mature" reflects "an ability to integrate conflicting needs, cope with frustrations, and value the partner for his or her unique qualities."[12]

Although the five elements of intimacy are different, all of them, including sexuality, are evaluated primarily according to the couples' *feelings* and how well the couples express themselves. People who describe their sex lives only in terms of frequency or variety are being "self-focused," and get a low score. Couples get a high score on sexuality for, among other things, "*talking freely* about the sexual relationship with the partner" and placing "a high value *on the expression of tenderness.*"

The communication component of intimacy, according to the researchers, involves "self-disclosure, initiating, listening, and responding." Egocentric communicators "usually focus exclusively on concrete issues and matters external to the relationship"—who will get the car repaired, what's for dinner, and when the plumber will get here. They place a low value on communicating and usually have "very poor communication skills." (The traditional, hard-working husband married to Nobody's Valentine would get a low score.) People at the most mature level, say the researchers, "*express a very high value on communicating in their relationships.* . . . There is usually evidence of a commitment to *making time to talk,* despite busy schedules and other obstacles, as well as an ability to resolve conflicts meaningfully" (my emphasis).[13] Sounds like a marriage of psychologists to me.

I do not disagree entirely with the researchers' measurement of intimacy; as a woman, I find it perfectly normal. But I wish to highlight the bias inherent in it—to see what it leaves out. The psychologists' equation of "most mature" with "most verbally expressive" represents a validation of the female standard of intimacy and almost entirely excludes the male standard. Their definition of maturity rests entirely on psychological qualities rather than on *behavior.* What about all the men and women who reliably support their families, who put the wishes of other family members ahead of their own preferences, or who act in a moral and considerate way when conflicts arise? Such individuals are surely being mature and loving, even if they are not articulate or do not value "communication."

Moreover, the researchers did not ask the husbands and wives how *they* defined intimacy; they imposed their own complex definition on the couples, just as Masters and Johnson imposed their notion of the normal sexual response cycle on their volunteers. As one result, they failed to sympathize with the fact that sexuality is part of the masculine language of love. They dismiss "frequency and variety" as criteria for sexual intimacy, yet many men express their deepest affections this way.

For instance, Cancian describes an interview with a twenty-nine-year-old carpenter who said that after sex he feels especially close to his wife, that he feels then that they are truly a family: "I don't talk to her very often, I guess, but somehow I feel we have really communicated after we have made love."[14] Many women, of course, want to feel that they have "really communicated"—that is to say, communicated in words—*before* making love. If the tables were turned, Cancian suggests, and sexual behavior were regarded as an expression, indeed a definition, of love the way talking about feelings currently is, it would appear that men want love more than women do.

When men do speak for themselves, their styles of intimacy are as effective as women's in producing feelings of emotional closeness and meaningful connection. Psychologist Scott Swain conducted a study in which he defined intimacy as any action in a friendship "that connotes a positive and mutual sense of meaning and importance to the participants." The participants, not the observers, got to define what intimacy meant to them, and "any action" would do. One young man said that his most intimate experiences with other men consisted of "a lot of outdoor-type things—fishing, hunting, Tom-Sawyer-type things."[15]

Swain's interviews reveal how different male intimacy is from the female standard. Men use the degree of comfort and relaxation they feel with other men as an index of closeness, says Swain. One interviewee explained that he was "more relaxed around guys. You don't have to watch what you say. . . . I wouldn't be careful I shouldn't say something like this, or I shouldn't do this. That's because with the guys, they're just like you."[16] When asked to recall a "meaningful" time with men friends, another young man said:

> *The fun things come to mind. We rented a VCR and some movies and watched those, and just all the laugh-*

ing together comes to mind as most memorable. As to the most meaningful, those also come pretty close to being the most meaningful, because there was just total relaxation, there. That I felt no need to worry. There's no need to worry about anyone making conversation. The conversation will come. And we can laugh at each other, and you can laugh at yourself, which is handy.[17]

When they were asked to describe the "most meaningful occasion spent with a same-sex friend," the men mentioned twenty-six events, of which twenty were spent in "an activity other than talking"—fishing, playing guitars, diving, drinking, weightlifting, winning a court case, being with a close friend whose sister had died. "Can't think of just one thing that stood out in my mind," one man said. "It was more like a push-pull type thing. Like I'd pull him through things and he'd pull me through things."[18]

Several men said that intimacy with women friends is "just talking"; the talk that women like is, to them, "the lighter side of things." For many men, actions speak louder than words and carry greater value for the friendship, as they do in love relationships. They do not need to say to each other, "I like you"; being invited to a game or another activity *means* "I like you." (Many parents try to teach their daughters this fact about boys, explaining that if a boy puts a frog in a girl's lunchbox, it means he likes her. Girls find this hard to believe.) Men convey affection to one another, adds Swain, with "physical gestures, laughing at jokes, doing one another favors, keeping in touch, 'doing stuff,' teasing, and just being around friends."[19]

Of all these expressions of affection and closeness, perhaps the one that women tend to understand least is men's language of teasing and "joking around." Here, for example, is an exchange between a worried mother and Dr. Joyce Brothers:

Dear Dr. Brothers: Our 14-year-old son loves to tease his young sister. While he has a lively sense of humor, she often doesn't appreciate it, and this becomes the cause of some really unpleasant quarrels. Is there anything we can do about this?

Joyce Brothers, being a woman and a psychologist, uses a female yardstick to measure this boy's behavior:

Teasing often is not simple harmless fun. It can be a way of masking hostility, a kind of hit-and-run attack. . . . Ask your son how he'd like it if he were constantly the butt of jokes or if these same tricks were played on him. . . . Discourage the "teasing" and try to get your son to explore what's behind it.[20]

Notice that the direction of the intervention here is to change the boy's way into the girl's way. Joyce Brothers does not advise the parents, "Discourage your daughter's humorlessness and try to get her to explore the reasons she takes her brother's teasing so seriously." The son *does* know what it's like to be the butt of jokes, because that is how boys and men express many of their feelings to one another. Girls and women keep looking for the meaning "behind" the jokes, a doomed enterprise that makes women seem, to men, overly literal and humorless. To many women, like Joyce Brothers, it is obvious that the boy's teasing is hostile and demeaning. To many men, it is just as obvious that the boy's teasing is his way of being affectionate while also being appropriately masculine.

Men use jokes, teasing, and "horsing around" as ways of creating bonds of camaraderie and in-group knowledge. Jokes communicate affection (and other feelings) indirectly, so no one can accuse the speaker of being wimpy or soft; they protect the speaker from the risk of rejection (or counterattack) that a straightforward remark might evoke. One of my husband's golfing friends, on hearing that my husband's son would be playing with them that day, said, "That's good; I hope he's a better player than you are." It's the kind of teasing remark that few women would say to a female friend—it would be regarded as a hurtful put-down—but my husband laughed and knew it to mean "I enjoy golfing with you and like you very much, even if you do beat me more often than I like."

Among men friends, Swain concludes, joking "camouflages the hidden agenda of closeness." Most men recognize the hidden agenda, but many women do not. In Swain's study, for example, one man had learned to waterski from his best friend. He had trouble getting the knack of it, but by joking the friend removed competitive pressure and worries about failure:

We were just able to make jokes about it, and we laughed at each other all day. And it finally worked out. I mean it was great for me to be that frustrated and that up-tight about it and know the only thing he was going to do was laugh at me.[21]

Of course, men also use jokes to create distance and to express anger or contempt; women who encroach on traditionally male territory do not mistake the hostility behind the sexist put-downs that they are expected to tolerate with "good humor." But the ambiguity in much of male teasing is the reason that jokes are such a good disguise for love and attachment: The speaker can always claim the listener didn't understand his intention. Most males become fluent in joke-speak and its many meanings by adolescence. They know that "What a jerk!," coming from a friend when they fall off a bicycle, conveys amused affection, but the same remark from a passing stranger is an act of hostility.

Just as many people often overlook or misinterpret men's expressions of love, they often overlook or misinterpret men's expressions of distress when they lose love. The pressures that bar men from the direct revelation of their feelings are especially powerful when the feelings imply vulnerability or weakness, as do the emotions of grief, sadness, fear, loneliness, or anxiety. One unhappy consequence of male emotional silence is the mistaken impression that most men lack these feelings and are harder-hearted than women. By not understanding men's expressions of grief, many psychologists and lay people infer that there is something wrong with men because they seem not to feel anything after divorce, loss, or the death of a loved one.

This mistake figures prominently in the diagnosis of depression in men. Women are more likely than men to talk about feeling depressed (in both mild and extreme cases), to seek help for depression, and to be diagnosed as being clinically depressed. Much of the difference in depression rates has to do with the greater likelihood that women will experience abuse, discrimination, and dead-end work.[22] But some of the difference in rates is more apparent than real: Many men fail to be recognized or diagnosed as depressed because, as with love, *what women do when they are depressed constitutes the norm on which the criteria for depression are based.* In clinical research and psychotherapy, most of the measurements of depression and distress are measured on typically female reactions such as crying, staying in bed, talking about one's unhappiness and misery, and developing eating disorders. Because many men do not express grief this way, it is easy to infer that men suffer less than women when relationships are in trouble, or even that men are incapable of love.

Catherine Riessman is one researcher who came to question the female norm for depression after she had interviewed a large number of wives and husbands about their divorces. The men and women spoke at length about their pain, anguish, and loneliness, but in entirely different ways. The men were suffering as much as the women, Riessman learned, but they didn't *say* so. They did not report the usual symptoms of depression, because these are not, she explains, the "culturally approved idioms for men."[23] Thus, in response to straightforward questions, most of the men said they felt sad "some or a little of the time" and that they felt depressed or lonely "none of the time."

Instead, Riessman found, the men expressed grief in ways that are stereotypically masculine, that they have a vocabulary for, that they can reveal without conflict or shame—"frantic work," heavy drinking, driving crazily, singing sentimental songs. Many of the men had low scores on standard depression scales, yet their lives were in shambles. They described a potpourri of symptoms: trouble concentrating at work; difficulties on the job; extreme restlessness and hyperactivity; and numerous physical ailments and stress symptoms. One man confessed that for four months after his separation he "threw up every morning"—but no, no, he wasn't actually "depressed." Another expressed no feelings of sadness, helplessness, or vulnerability, but in the six months since his divorce he had racked up a long list of criminal charges.

All of these signs of distress have one thing in common, says Riessman: "the distancing of the self from feelings of sadness."[24] A few men, asserting that they felt no pain whatsoever, even had scores of *zero* on the depression scale. "I can't put it into words," many men said of their emotions, while describing lives of desperation and chaos. One man, Rick, tried to explain his feelings this way:

I was running sort of like wide open, 90 miles an hour down a dead-end street, as the song goes . . . yeah I started drinking much more just because it was something to do. . . . And uh I was monumentally unhappy, I did not *want her to leave, which I discovered after she left, you know. But there's lots of songs about that too you know so [laughs] what can you do.*[25]

Rick goes on to describe the sad songs—"maudlin sorts of things in a country vein"—that he wrote after his separation. But you won't find "writing maudlin sorts of songs" or "running sort of like wide open" on any set of criteria for depression.

Rick's narrative of the aftermath of his divorce, Riessman shows, is very different from what most women would say. It contains many metaphors of pressure: "something's got to give," "running wide open," "driving faster," "just pushing it"—images, she observes, that are "in sharp contrast to the overt images of emptiness, loss, and vulnerability and behaviors like crying that are more consistent with depression in women's talk."[26] Rick constantly apologizes for not having the right word, for not being able to explain himself exactly; he borrows images and feelings from songs.

Even Rick's way of speaking differs from a woman's: "He rushes through his account of his emotions," Riessman explains, "not dwelling on the topic as the women tend to do in their accounts. The language also suggests a fear of loss of control—he is on the edge of disorganization, and whatever restraints that usually contain his strong feelings are breaking down. Whether the issue is overwhelming anger or the sorrow of loss, the prevailing image is of running from it." If he gets too close to identifying an emotion, he runs: "Rick states a feeling, backs off from it, restates it, and backs off again, in repeated cycles," says Riessman.[27]

This typical male pattern of coping with loss—run from it, separate yourself from it, escape from it in activity or drugs—is already apparent in childhood and adolescence, once you know where to look. In a study of the emotional experiences of several hundred schoolchildren, Janice Stapley and Jeannette Haviland concluded, as Riessman had, that depression scales are biased "toward measuring deviation from normal female emotional experience" and do not contain questions that would be "sensitive to male emotional experience."[28] For boys, depression presents itself in such deviations from the male norm as being unable to relax with friends and not being interested in sports or "riding around"! Boys were more likely than girls to deny ever having emotional reactions and to avoid telling others how they were feeling. For instance, when asked to *recall* whether they felt sad, disgusted, guilty, or afraid in the last month, most of the boys said no, they hadn't. But when they kept a daily record of their feelings, they reported having them all.

Men's unwillingness and inability to articulate their griefs may take two extreme forms. When driven to despair, some men can find no middle course between violence and withdrawal. Read any newspaper story of a man who has run amok and killed his family, and what will it invariably say in the fourth paragraph? "John Jones's wife, Mary, had just filed for divorce" or "Friends said that Smith had been despondent ever since his wife left him." Look at this list of the factors that most strongly predict the likelihood of a man killing his wife: the use of drugs or alcohol; strong cultural pressures to save face; previous threats of suicide or vengeance; *recent deep depression; recent failed love relationship;* and *recently separated from family unit.*[29] Almost all of these factors are related to loss of a loved one, since depression often follows separation and many men act out that depression by abusing drugs and alcohol.

The other extreme response takes the form of a total emotional shutdown. Psychotherapist Ronald Taffel believes that many severely depressed men retreat behind a façade of stony silence in their families, but that neither they nor their families recognize the symptoms. Taffel writes of his own father:

In the middle of the night I would find him there. Alone at the kitchen table, he sat bent over a book or the daily newspaper. "What's the matter, Daddy?" I would ask, already knowing what the answer would be. "Oh, it's nothing, Ronnie. I just have something on my mind, so I couldn't sleep." He'd look up at me, the glasses magnifying some expression in his eyes I wasn't able to name. "Don't worry," he would say. "Go back to bed and I'll see you in the morning." The next morning there would be a noticeable pall over the house.[30]

Taffel has studied 125 men, almost none of whom said they were depressed. "Only 14 percent would have received a formal diagnosis of depression," he observes. "But the partners of 62 percent of them described mood difficulties in the men serious enough to color the atmosphere of the entire household. There is a gloomy undertow in these homes, just below the surface of everyday life. Whether the men passively disappear into the woodwork or shake the foundations of the house with their agitation, they share one characteristic—they cannot regulate their own moods . . . and they depend on their partners and children to do so for them."[31]

And so it is that many women and men end up misreading one another's messages of love, affection, and despair. The feminization of love has its counterpart in the masculinization of silence: To the extent that women are encouraged to talk about their emotions, men are in general expected to remain controlled and silent about theirs. Many men are caught in a conflict between the demands for silence that the world makes of them and the demands for talk the woman makes on them. The world usually wins, which is why Nobody's Valentine doesn't get her card.

Notes

1. "Dear Abby," *Los Angeles Times,* March 14, 1990, p. E3.
2. This statistic is from Harper's Index, *Harper's* magazine, February 1991, p. 19. The Index cited Hallmark Cards.
3. Driscoll, 1991, p. 61.
4. Ibid., p. 62.
5. This couple is quoted in Cancian, 1987, p. 76.
6. Wills, Weiss, and Patterson, 1974.
7. Riessman, 1990, p. 97.
8. On the different functions of talk: See Lakoff, 1990; Maltz and Borker, 1982; McConnell-Ginet, 1983; Tannen, 1990.
9. Tannen, 1990, pp. 49–50.
10. Cancian, 1987, p. 74. Joseph Pleck, 1981, also argues that men enjoy and need their family relationships more than they get credit for.
11. Ibid., p. 76.
12. White et al., 1986, p. 155.
13. Ibid., p. 156.
14. Quoted in Cancian, 1987, p. 77.
15. Swain, 1989, p. 72. "Tom-Sawyer-type things," p. 74.
16. Ibid., p. 75.
17. Ibid.
18. Ibid., p. 77.
19. Ibid., p. 80.
20. *Los Angeles Times,* January 28, 1991, p. C3.
21. Swain, 1989, p. 82.
22. For a review of the research on women and depression, see McGrath et al., 1990.
23. Riessman, 1990, pp. 156–157.
24. Ibid., p. 153.
25. Ibid., p. 144.
26. Ibid., p. 145.
27. Ibid.
28. Stapley and Haviland, 1989, p. 307.
29. This list of predictors is from police psychologist Theodore Blau, who was interviewed by Robert Trotter for "Psychologist With a Badge," *Psychology Today,* November 1987, p. 26.
30. Ronald Taffel, "The Politics of Mood," *The Family Therapy Networker,* September/October 1990, pp. 49–53, 72. Quote, p. 49.
31. Ibid., p. 51.

The Gift of Rhythm and Blood

Carolyn McVickar Edwards

Carolyn McVickar Edwards (1954–) grew up in Southern California after being born in Carmel. At eighteen she moved to Berkeley to attend the University of California. She received a B.A. in arts management in 1982. Growing up in a Fundamentalist Christian setting had acquainted her with Bible stories. As an adult she began to feel a need to undo the "God, God, God" and fill that space with stories of the Goddess. The Storyteller's Goddess *(1991) was written over a period of six years while she worked as a secretary. She likes the following story because "there aren't many stories about the origin of menstruation."*

Danu (DAN-oo)—The Earth (Ireland)

Despite increasing industrialization, today's Ireland is famed for her still-told stories of fairy mounds and little people in the grass. Today's tales are Earth-respecting remnants of the sagas of human-sized, magically powered queens, kings, heroes, and heroines that preceded them. These stories, in turn, recapitulate the even older tales when Goddesses and Gods, representing the powers of Earth, Water, Fire, and Air, peopled the world. The tellers of those ancient stories called themselves the Tuatha De Danaan, or the "Tribe of the Goddess Danu."

The Irish Danu, Danuna, or Dana shared Her name with forms of the Great Mother in cultures around the world, such as the Danes and the biblical Danites (called "serpents" by writers of the Old Testament). The Russians called Her Dennitsa (see the story of the Zoryas); the classical Greeks named Her Danae; the Hebrews Dinah; and the Babylonians called Her Danu or Dunnu.

Although the ancient Tuatha De Danaan named the Earth Goddess as the very source of their lives, Danu is rarely mentioned by today's authors trying to piece together the myths from that time. Instead, most stories told today emphasize the role of Dagdu, the Sun God. A traveler to County Meath in Ireland can, for example, visit Newgrange, a beautifully preserved tomb built in the form of an underground temple in 3000 B.C.E.—or five hundred years before the erection of the pyramids. The entrance stones are inscribed with giant spirals, and the damp, cool passageway to the center is now rigged electrically to expose spirals and inverted triangles etched on the inner walls. The guide also uses an electric light to reenact the nearly miraculous once-a-year flooding of the dark center (through the window in the roof) with the light of the rising Sun on the morning of the Winter Solstice. The sense of being in a womblike place is overwhelming. The literature provided to Newgrange visitors, however, fails to note this obvious reality. Instead, it first praises the high degree of architectural, engineering, and artistic skill displayed by this ancient crop-raising people and carefully notes the measurements and placement of roofbox, chambers, great circle, and surrounding standing stones of the Great Mound. The pamphlet's author then declares that Newgrange is a monument to "no less a personage than the chief of all the gods," Dagdu the Sun.

I wrote the story of Danu the Earth after a moving visit to this underground temple. Unlike the pamphlet's author, I had to ask myself why a people would build a monument to the Sun inside the Earth in such a way as to take the light of the Sun into its depths for only minutes each year.

I was further inspired by my visit to the bowels of Dublin's museum in which are gathered a dozen or so of what curators call "sheila-na-gigs." Sheila-na-gigs are stone figures of squatting women displaying their sometimes red-stained vulvas. As late as the Middle Ages, these figures were carved above church entryways. Both the churches and their startling guardians were built by medieval Goddess-worshiping villagers in the process of capitulating to the Christian religion.

Danu, I have no doubt, was a figure much like the far more modern sheila-na-gigs, who almost certainly represented the womb and tomb as the single point at which meet life and death in the Cycle of the Great Mother.

In Danu's story, I hope to spiral through time to the very center of our own stories. It is the story of Danu's filling the world with Her rhythm, that She might surge always in the blood tides of our bodies and hearts.

At the beginning of the beginning, the Goddess Danu glittered tiny as a fairy in the mists. You'd scarce have seen Her, even had you been there, for the swirl of milky gray about Her gossamer self. But Danu was there, sure as we're here: a glistening globe of possibility at the start of it all.

It was Danu's dreamtime then. Asleep, Her thoughts quivered and swelled. Awake, She held Her face in Her hands, wondering and humming, lost in Her own stillness. It may well have been the dreams that caused the growing. The dreams trickled at first and then flooded in the pearly dark place between sleeping and waking, where time is like water and nothing is impossible. But whether it came from the dreaming or something else, Danu the Goddess grew. Oh, it surprised Her how She grew!

It was Her legs at first. She extended them to relieve their aching and splayed Her toes. Somehow those spread toes came to hold whole bays between their peninsular lengths, and Her limbs stretched lopingly long. Hard and round and luscious they'd become—with knees and thighs fair like mountains, they were so huge. Her arms shot from their sockets and came to end in gigantic slender-fingered hands in which She could suddenly see the streams and creeks of veins. The once plump little wrists took on the definition of hills—and, oh! the down of Her forearms resembled meadows more than anything. Her neck, too, had lost its cushion and got a swivel to match the capacity of Her stride.

How shy this Danu, how astounded! How full of Her change She was, once wee as an idea and now enormous as the world. She had flitted once, effortlessly. Now Her movements felt tremendous and heavy. Danu mused, twirling absently a tuft of hair behind Her ear. Then She heaved Herself into the sleep of exhaustion, only to wake to even more growing.

Danu opened Her eyes to the sight of dark green sprouts on the soft triangle below Her navel. Gingerly, She fingered these spiky curling firs and then delighted Herself when they didn't fall away. More sprang up, in the valleys under Her arms and on the lush three-sided range between Her legs, until those sweet places were most forested with trees.

And then, before She slept again, Danu's breasts grew. Gone were the days when She could arch Her chest and describe a smooth bridge between belly and neck! Now that arch was soft and spilling as twin mountains tipped by ranunculi and grazed by sheep! Danu touched a ranunculus and bit Her lower lip in Her teeth.

When Danu plunged again into sleep, She dreamed this time of a great ball of fire in the sky that splintered the mists around Her as the music of a pipe and drum fill a silence. When She awoke, Her haunches felt sure and deep and She found a river of blood flowing between Her legs. Danu tasted the rosy wetness in wonder and turned Her eyes to the sky. Immediately She was sugared with a yellow warmth, and the skin of Her shoulders expanded with pleasure.

"You're My dream!" She cried out, and Her eyes glinted in the light.

"I'm Your dream," a voice agreed. "I am Dagdu the Sun."

Danu cast down Her eyes, and Her smile dazzled when She turned them up again. "Do stay, Dagdu the Sun," said Danu the Earth. "I can't tell You how good You feel!"

"Oh, I will stay, lovely green, brown, and red Lady!" said the voice. "I will stay."

Danu sighed and turned over. Dagdu the Sun broke all the way through the mists and beat down on the body of the Goddess. She fell asleep there in the heat. Who knows how long She slept, but when She awoke this time, Dagdu was gone. Danu sat up and caught up the back of Her hair in Her hand. She looked at the silvery clouds and remembered Dagdu's delicious warmth. Then She looked down and put Her hand on the place where the river of blood had come. How soft and good it felt there! The wetness lay in a pool beside Her, but it had ceased to flow. She moved Her hand up to the wings of Her pelvis and then dipped them again to the cave between Her legs. For surely that's what She felt: a deep, wet cavern that nestled in the protection of the two mountains of Her bones.

How pleased Danu was to see Her Dagdu again! For in His absence, She'd begun to think of Him that way—as Her Dagdu, Her wonderful Sun whose light would shine especially for Her delight. Not far from the truth, either, that way of thinking, for it happened that Dagdu Himself came to think never so clearly as when He imagined His Danu and felt never so free as when He held Her in His arms. For that's what became of the friendship of Earth and Sun. They talked to each other; they traced each other's noses and bit each other's palms. They made each other shout with laughter. One day Danu told Dagdu about the dark, secret place under Her forests. Dagdu's voice was tender when He asked if He could look inside.

It was Dagdu who told Her about the smooth, round globe at the back of Her cave that changed again and again from pale mauve to the color of wine. For Danu did finally invite Dagdu to flood Her dark with His light, and it was once in a reverie that followed a time when They had held each other in this way that Danu had Her dream of making animals and people. She awoke flushed and intense with excitement. Dagdu kissed the ridge of Her cheek when She told Him and plucked away the damp tendril of hair that clung to Her forehead. "It's a wonderful dream," He said.

On the evening of the day Danu followed Her dream and formed animals and people of the soft Earth of Her breasts and the pool of blood beside Her, Dagdu told Her that She'd never looked so beautiful. "When You pursed Your lips up like that and set the people moving with Your breath! Hmmmm! The scent of You, Danu! You are amazing," He said, and nestled His head in Her neck. The sky grew soft and pink around that comely couple while They watched the animals mew and burrow for cover and the humans sing tunes and smear their mouths purple with currants.

Perhaps an eon passed before Danu and Dagdu had the argument. Couples will argue, you know, much as they may also please each other, for they are not one but two beings and so they are bound to see and feel things differently. But isn't it true that the argument that makes one so cross at the time can, not so much later, be the inspiration for wonderful change? It was certainly that way with the argument of Danu and Dagdu, for out of Their misunderstanding came the very rhythm of our world.

Danu had been dreaming again, asleep in Dagdu's embrace. She jerked awake suddenly one night, shaking with the cracked pieces of a nightmare inside Her.

"Dagdu!" Danu's voice was sharp.

"Hmmmm." Dagdu's voice was dim with sleep.

"Dagdu. I dreamed that My people forget Me." The God heard the pellets of fear in Danu's voice. He lay His finger on Her lips and made hushing noises while He rocked Her against Him.

Danu may have returned to sleep, but She spoke urgently again about the dream in the morning. Dagdu was languid and toyed with Her little finger as She talked. "What was it, darling?" He said.

Danu couldn't remember the images. She just knew it was a terrible feeling of dread She had and this knowing that Her people had forgotten Her.

"Darling, they're not going to forget You!" Dagdu said soothingly. "You *made* them, honey. They can't forget."

"I can't explain it," said Danu. "But it was as if the people—I think there were thousands of them—as if they thought I were dead, but I was really alive. it was horrible." Danu turned Her head away.

Dagdu curled four of Her fingers around one of His own. "Danu, they can't forget either of Us," He said. His voice was teasing. "They certainly can't forget *Me*, anyway. I'm much too hot and warm, and I feel too good."

Danu snatched Her hand away. Now Dagdu had meant, I'm sure, to nuzzle Her with His teasing and relax Her with His caresses. However, Dagdu had the handicap of not having dreamed Danu's dream, and Danu's averted head prevented Her from seeing the playful sympathy on Dagdu's face. She heard only the lightness of His mood in contrast to Her own despair, and She was furious.

A black wind came up and the Goddess stayed alone for a long time. She wept and She slept. She screamed and She dreamed. She felt the curve and the flatness of Herself. She watched Her blood river come and go. She spoke aloud and unraveled the meaning and horror of that nightmare about a kind of aloneness not healing and full of truth like this one, but dangerous and a lie.

Slowly there grew in Danu a plan, details blurred at first. But came the day when it was clear and simple as if She'd known it all along.

First She reached inside the cave of Herself and drew out the globe that Dagdu had told Her waxed and waned with a cycle He said seemed to match Her desire to lie in His arms. She gazed at it creamy and gray in Her palm and remembered the uninterrupted mists of Her beginnings. Then She hung it in the sky and called it Moon.

Next Danu called to Her all the people that had breasts and valleys like Her own. Like Herself, She told them, they would bleed, in rhythm with Her Moon, rivers between their legs so that they and those who love them might ever remember Her. Like Herself, they would find refuge and joy in both the light and the dark.

The people were thrilled with Danu's plan. In their village, they made a temple like Danu's cave with long narrow windows to welcome Dagdu's light. They drew on the walls there the story of the ebb and flow of the blood river by counting its days with careful marks. They pecked its clock with circular spirals on giant stones. They painted red the door of Her sacred triangle to mark the place from which all had come and to which they would return.

Danu, too, was filled with peace. Maybe you can imagine that speechless shyness with which She reopened Her friendship with Dagdu. How the words tumbled when the shyness melted. And how much They had to tell about what each had learned in the time of solitude and introspection. Time passed and They repeated the cycle again and again. It was true, They agreed. Never did They feel so verdant, so radiant, as when They came together again after the renewal of separation.

And so it was with Danu's humans. Never did the world throb so rightly as when the people remembered to sing in the cave of their Goddess and to dance in the light of their God. Ever through time has circled this remembering, even in the days when the people, as Danu once dreamed, are so close to forgetting Her. But Her wonderful plan, born in the contemplation of Her terror, prevents forgetting. For in the bodies of Danu's women flows Her river, and in Her sky moves Her Moon. And so for women, and all those who love them, the Goddess lives. Tiny as a fairy in the mists, perhaps, or gigantic as the world. She lives.

The Female World of Love and Ritual

Relations Between Women in Nineteenth-Century America

Carroll Smith-Rosenberg

Carroll Smith-Rosenberg (1936–) was born in New York City and received her bachelor's degree from Connecticut College and her Ph.D. from Columbia University. She is a professor of humanities and director of the women's studies program at the University of Pennsylvania. In the introduction to her first book, Religion and the Rise of the American City *(1971), she thanks her parents for encouraging her to become "a lady historian." In the twenty years following, she has been a Rockefeller Fellow and a Radcliffe Fellow, a Guggenheim Fellow, a fellow at the Institute for Advanced Studies at Princeton and at the Rockefeller Center at Bellagio, Italy. Poet and professor of English Sandra Gilbert says, "Carroll Smith-Rosenberg is one of our most intelligent and imaginative feminist historians."*

THE FEMALE FRIENDSHIP OF THE NINETEENTH CENTURY, the long-lived, intimate, loving friendship between two women, is an excellent example of the type of historical phenomena which most historians know something about, which few have thought much about, and which virtually no one has written about.[1] It is one aspect of the female experience which consciously or unconsciously we have chosen to ignore. Yet an abundance of manuscript evidence suggests that eighteenth- and nineteenth-century women routinely formed emotional ties with other women. Such deeply felt, same-sex friendships were casually accepted in American society. Indeed, from at least the late eighteenth through the mid-nineteenth century, a female world of varied and yet highly structured relationships appears to have been an essential aspect of American society. These relationships ranged from the supportive love of sisters, through the enthusiasms of adolescent girls, to sensual avowals of love by mature women. It was a world in which men made but a shadowy appearance.[2]

Defining and analyzing same-sex relationships involves the historian in deeply problematical questions of method and interpretation. This is especially true since historians, influenced by Freud's libidinal theory, have discussed these relationships almost exclusively within the context of individual psychosexual developments or, to be more explicit, psychopathology.[3] Seeing same-sex relationships in terms of a dichotomy between normal and abnormal, they have sought the origins of such apparent deviance in childhood or adolescent trauma and detected the symptoms of "latent" homosexuality in the lives of both those who later became "overtly" homosexual and those who did not. Yet theories concerning the nature and origins of same-sex relationships are frequently contradictory or based on questionable or arbitrary data. In recent years such hypotheses have been subjected to criticism both from within and without the psychological professions. Historians who seek to work within a psychological framework, therefore, are faced with two hard questions: Do sound psychodynamic theories concerning the nature and origins of same-sex relationships exist? If so, does the historical datum exist which would permit the use of such dynamic models?

I would like to suggest an alternative approach to female friendships—one which would view them within a cultural and social setting rather than from an exclusively individual psychosexual perspective. Only by thus altering our approach will we be in the position to evaluate the appropriateness of particular dynamic interpretations. Intimate friendships between men and men and women and women existed in a larger world of social relations and social values. To interpret such friendships more fully they must be related to the structure of the American family and to the nature of sex-role divisions and of male–female relations both within the family and in society generally. The female friendship must not be seen in isolation; it must be analyzed as one aspect of women's overall relations with one another. The ties between mothers and daughters, sisters, female cousins and friends, at all stages of the female life cycle constitute the most suggestive framework for the historian to begin an analysis of intimacy and affection between women. Such an analysis would not only emphasize general cultural patterns rather than the internal dynamics of a particular family or childhood; it would shift the focus of the study from a concern with deviance to that of defining configurations of legitimate behavioral norms and options.[4]

This analysis will be based upon the correspondence and diaries of women and men in thirty-five families between the 1760s and the 1880s. These families, though limited in number, represented a broad range of the American middle class, from hard-pressed pioneer families and orphaned girls to daughters of the intellectual and social elite. It includes families from most geographic regions, rural and urban, and a spectrum of Protestant denominations ranging from Mormon to orthodox Quaker. Although scarcely a comprehensive sample of America's increasingly heterogeneous population, it does, I believe, reflect accurately the literate middle class to which the historian working with letters and diaries is necessarily bound. It has involved an analysis of many thousands of letters written to women friends, kin, husbands, brothers, and children at every period of life from adolescence to old age. Some collections encompass virtually entire life spans; one contains over 100,000 letters as well as diaries and account books. It is my contention that an analysis of women's private letters and diaries which were never intended to be published permits the historian to explore a very private world of emotional realities central both to women's lives and to the middle-class family in nineteenth-century America.[5]

The question of female friendships is peculiarly elusive; we know so little or perhaps have forgotten so much. An intriguing and almost alien form of human relationship, they flourished in a different social structure and amidst different sexual norms. Before attempting to reconstruct their social setting, therefore, it might be best first to describe two not atypical friendships. These two friendships, intense, loving, and openly avowed, began during the women's adolescence and, despite subsequent marriages and geographic separation, continued throughout their lives. For nearly half a century these women played a central emotional role in each other's lives, writing time and again of their love and of the pain of separation. Paradoxically to twentieth-century minds, their love appears to have been both sensual and platonic.

Sarah Butler Wister first met Jeannie Field Musgrove while vacationing with her family at Stockbridge, Massachusetts, in the summer of 1849.[6] Jeannie was then sixteen, Sarah fourteen. During two subsequent years spent together in boarding school, they formed a deep and intimate friendship. Sarah began to keep a bouquet of flowers before Jeannie's portrait and wrote complaining of the intensity and anguish of her affection.[7] Both young women assumed nom de plumes, Jeannie a female name, Sarah a male one; they would use these secret names into old age.[8] They frequently commented on the nature of their affection: "If the day should come," Sarah wrote Jeannie in the spring of 1861, "when you failed me either through your fault or my own, I would forswear all human friendship, thenceforth." A few months later Jeannie commented: "Gratitude is a word I should never use toward you. It is perhaps a misfortune of such intimacy and love that it makes one regard all kindness as a matter of course, as one has always found it, as natural as the embrace in meeting."[9]

Sarah's marriage altered neither the frequency of

their correspondence nor their desire to be together. In 1864, when twenty-nine, married, and a mother, Sarah wrote to Jeannie: "I shall be entirely alone [this coming week]. I can give you no idea how desperately I shall want you. . . ." After one such visit Jeannie, then a spinster in New York, echoed Sarah's longing: "Dear darling Sarah! How I love you & how happy I have been! You are the joy of my life. . . . I cannot tell you how much happiness you gave me, nor how constantly it is all in my thoughts. . . . My darling how I long for the time when I shall see you. . . ." After another visit Jeannie wrote: "I want you to tell me in your next letter, to assure me, that I am your dearest. . . . I do not doubt you, & I am not jealous but I long to hear you say it once more & it seems already a long time since your voice fell on my ear. So just fill a quarter page with caresses & expressions of endearment. Your silly Angelina." Jeannie ended one letter: "Goodbye dearest, dearest lover—ever your own Angelina." And another, "I will go to bed . . . [though] I could write all night—A thousand kisses—I love you with my whole soul—your Angelina."

When Jeannie finally married in 1870 at the age of thirty-seven, Sarah underwent a period of extreme anxiety. Two days before Jeannie's marriage Sarah, then in London, wrote desperately: "Dearest darling—How incessantly have I thought of you these eight days—all today—the entire uncertainty, the distance, the long silence—are all new features in my separation from you, grevious to be borne. . . . Oh Jeannie. I have thought & thought & yearned over you these two days. Are you married I wonder? My dearest love to you wherever and *who*ever you are."[10] Like many other women in this collection of thirty-five families, marriage brought Sarah and Jeannie physical separation; it did not cause emotional distance. Although at first they may have wondered how marriage would affect their relationship, their affection remained unabated throughout their lives, underscored by their loneliness and their desire to be together.[11]

During the same years that Jeannie and Sarah wrote of their love and need for each other, two slightly younger women began a similar odyssey of love, dependence and—ultimately—physical, though not emotional, separation. Molly and Helena met in 1868 while both attended the Cooper Institute School of Design for Women in New York City. For several years these young women studied and explored the city together, visited each other's families, and formed part of a social network of other artistic young women. Gradually, over the years, their initial friendship deepened into a close intimate bond which continued throughout their lives. The tone in the letters which Molly wrote to Helena changed over these years from "My dear Helena," and signed "your attached friend," to "My dearest Helena," "My Dearest," "My Beloved," and signed "Thine always" or "thine Molly."[12]

The letters they wrote to each other during these first five years permit us to reconstruct something of their relationship together. As Molly wrote in one early letter:

> *I have not said to you in so many or so few words that I was happy with you during those few so incredibly short weeks but surely you do not need words to tell you what you must know. Those two or three days so dark without, so bright with firelight and contentment within I shall always remember as proof that, for a time, at least—I fancy for quite a long time—we might be sufficient for each other. We know that we can amuse each other for many idle hours together and now we know that we can also work together. And that means much, don't you think so?*

She ended: "I shall return in a few days. Imagine yourself kissed many times by one who loved you so dearly."

The intensity and even physical nature of Molly's love was echoed in many of the letters she wrote during the next few years, as, for instance in this short thank-you note for a small present: "Imagine yourself kissed a dozen times my darling. Perhaps it is well for you that we are far apart. You might find my thanks so expressed rather overpowering. I have that delightful feeling that it doesn't matter much what I say or how I say it, since we shall meet so soon and forget in that moment that we were ever separated. . . . I shall see you soon and be content."[13]

At the end of the fifth year, however, several crises occurred. The relationship, at least in its intense form, ended, though Molly and Helena continued an intimate and complex relationship for the next half-century. The exact nature of these crises is not completely clear, but it seems to have involved Molly's decision not to live with Helena, as they had originally planned, but to remain at home because of parental insistence. Molly was now in her late twenties.

Helena responded with anger and Molly became frantic at the thought that Helena would break off their relationship. Though she wrote distraught letters and made despairing attempts to see Helena, the relationship never regained its former ardor—possibly because Molly had a male suitor.[14] Within six months Helena had decided to marry a man who was, coincidentally, Molly's friend and publisher. Two years later Molly herself finally married. The letters toward the end of this period discuss the transition both women made to having male lovers—Molly spending much time reassuring Helena, who seemed depressed about the end of their relationship and with her forthcoming marriage.[15]

It is clearly difficult from a distance of 100 years and from a post-Freudian cultural perspective to decipher the complexities of Molly and Helena's relationship. Certainly Molly and Helena were lovers—emotionally if not physically. The emotional intensity and pathos of their love becomes apparent in several letters Molly wrote Helena during their crisis: "I wanted so to put my arms round my girl of all the girls in the world and tell her . . . I love her as wives do love their husbands, as *friends* who have taken each other for life—and believe in her as I believe in my God. . . . If I didn't love you do you suppose I'd care about anything or have ridiculous notions and panics and behave like an old fool who ought to know better. I'm going to hang on to your skirts. . . . You can't get away from [my] love." Or as she wrote after Helena's decision to marry: "You know dear Helena, I really was in love with you. It was a passion such as I had never known until I saw you. I don't think it was the noblest way to love you." The theme of intense female love was one Molly again expressed in a letter she wrote to the man Helena was to marry: "Do you know sir, that until you came along I believe that she loved me almost as girls love their lovers. *I know I loved her so.* Don't you wonder that I can stand the sight of you." This was in a letter congratulating them on their forthcoming marriage.[16]

The essential question is not whether these women had genital contact and can therefore be defined as heterosexual or homosexual. The twentieth-century tendency to view human love and sexuality within a dichotomized universe of deviance and normality, genitality and platonic love, is alien to the emotions and attitudes of the nineteenth century and fundamentally distorts the nature of these women's emotional interaction. These letters are significant because they force us to place such female love in a particular historical context. There is every indication that these four women, their husbands and families—all eminently respectable and socially conservative—considered such love both socially acceptable and fully compatible with heterosexual marriage. Emotionally and cognitively, their heterosocial and their homosocial worlds were complementary.

One could argue, on the other hand, that these letters were but an example of the romantic rhetoric with which the nineteenth century surrounded the concept of friendship. Yet they possess an emotional intensity and a sensual and physical explicitness that is difficult to dismiss. Jeannie longed to hold Sarah in her arms; Molly mourned her physical isolation from Helena. Molly's love and devotion to Helena, the emotions that bound Jeannie and Sarah together, while perhaps a phenomenon of nineteenth-century society were not the less real for their Victorian origins. A survey of the correspondence and diaries of eighteenth- and nineteenth-century women indicates that Molly, Jeannie, and Sarah represented one very real behavioral and emotional option socially available to nineteenth-century women.

This is not to argue that individual needs, personalities, and family dynamics did not have a significant role in determining the nature of particular relationships. But the scholar must ask if it is historically possible and, if possible, important, to study the intensely individual aspects of psychosexual dynamics. Is it not the historian's first task to explore the social structure and the world view which made intense and sometimes sensual female love both a possible and an acceptable emotional option? From such a social perspective a new and quite different series of questions suggests itself. What emotional function did such female love serve? What was its place within the hetero- and homosocial worlds which women jointly inhabited? Did a spectrum of love-object choices exist in the nineteenth century across which some individuals, at least, were capable of moving? Without attempting to answer these questions it will be difficult to understand either nineteenth-century sexuality or the nineteenth-century family.

Several factors in American society between the mid-eighteenth and the mid-nineteenth centuries may well have permitted women to form a variety of close emotional relationships with other women. American society was characterized in large part by rigid gender-role differentiation within the family and within society as a whole, leading to the emotional segregation of women and men. The roles of daughter and mother shaded imperceptibly and ineluctably into each other, while the biological realities of frequent pregnancies, childbirth, nursing, and menopause bound women together in physical and emotional intimacy. It was within just such a social framework, I would argue, that a specifically female world did indeed develop, a world built around a generic and unself-conscious pattern of single-sex or homosocial networks. These supportive networks were institutionalized in social conventions or rituals which accompanied virtually every important event in a woman's life, from birth to death. Such female relationships were frequently supported and paralleled by severe social restrictions on intimacy between young men and women. Within such a world of emotional richness and complexity devotion to and love of other women became a plausible and socially accepted form of human interaction.

An abundance of printed and manuscript sources exists to support such a hypothesis. Etiquette books, advice books on child rearing, religious sermons, guides to young men and young women, medical texts, and school curricula all suggest that late eighteenth- and most nineteenth-century Americans assumed the existence of a world composed of distinctly male and female spheres, spheres determined by the immutable laws of God and nature.[17] The unpublished letters and diaries of Americans during this same period concur, detailing the existence of sexually segregated worlds inhabited by human beings with different values, expectations, and personalities. Contacts between men and women frequently partook of a formality and stiffness quite alien to twentieth-century America and which today we tend to define as "Victorian." Women, however, did not form an isolated and oppressed subcategory in male society. Their letters and diaries indicate that women's sphere had an essential integrity and dignity that grew out of women's shared experiences and mutual affection and that, despite the profound changes which affected American social structure and institutions between the 1760s and the 1870s, retained a constancy and predictability. The ways in which women thought of and interacted with each other remained unchanged. Continuity, not discontinuity, characterized this female world. Molly Hallock's and Jeannie Fields's words, emotions, and experiences have direct parallels in the 1760s and the 1790s.[18] There are indications in contemporary sociological and psychological literature that female closeness and support networks have continued into the twentieth century—not only among ethnic and working-class groups but even among the middle class.[19]

Most eighteenth- and nineteenth-century women lived within a world bounded by home, church, and the institution of visiting—that endless trooping of women to each others' homes for social purposes. It was a world inhabited by children and by other women.[20] Women helped each other with domestic chores and in times of sickness, sorrow, or trouble. Entire days, even weeks, might be spent almost exclusively with other women.[21] Urban and town women could devote virtually every day to visits, teas, or shopping trips with other women. Rural women developed a pattern of more extended visits that lasted weeks and sometimes months, at times even dislodging husbands from their beds and bedrooms so that dear friends might spend every hour of every day together.[22] When husbands traveled, wives routinely moved in with other women, invited women friends to teas and suppers, sat together sharing and comparing the letters they had received from other close women friends. Secrets were exchanged and cherished, and the husband's return at times viewed with some ambivalence.[23]

Summer vacations were frequently organized to permit old friends to meet at water spas or share a country home. In 1848, for example, a young matron wrote cheerfully to her husband about the delightful time she was having with five close women friends whom she had invited to spend the summer with her; he remained at home alone to face the heat of Philadelphia and a cholera epidemic.[24] Some ninety years earlier, two young Quaker girls commented upon the vacation their aunt had taken alone with another woman; their remarks were openly envious and tell us something of the emotional quality of these friendships: "I hear Aunt is gone with the Friend and wont be back for two weeks, fine times indeed I think the old friends had, taking their pleasure about the country . . . and have the advantage of that fine woman's conversation and instruction, while we poor young girls must spend all spring at home. . . . What a disappointment that we are not together. . . ."[25]

Friends did not form isolated dyads but were normally part of highly integrated networks. Knowing each other, perhaps related to each other, they played a central role in holding communities and kin systems together. Especially when families became geographically mobile women's long visits to each other and their frequent letters filled with discussions of marriages and births, illness and deaths, descriptions of growing children, and reminiscences of times and people past provided an important sense of continuity in a rapidly changing society.[26] Central to this female world was an inner core of kin. The ties between sisters, first cousins, aunts, and nieces provided the underlying structure upon which groups of friends and their network of female relatives clustered. Although most of the women within this sample would appear to be living within isolated nuclear families, the emotional ties between nonresidential kin were deep and binding and provided one of the fundamental existential realities of women's lives.[27] Twenty years after Parke Lewis Butler moved with her husband to Louisiana, she sent her two daughters back to Virginia to attend school, live with their grandmother and aunt, and be integrated back into Virginia society.[28] The constant letters between Maria Inskeep and Fanny Hampton, sisters separated in their early twenties when Maria moved with her husband from New Jersey to Louisiana, held their families together, making it possible for their daughters to feel a part of their cousins' network of friends and interests.[29] The Ripley daughters, growing up in western Massachusetts in the early 1800s, spent months each year with their mother's sister and her family in distant Boston; these female cousins and their network of friends exchanged gossip-filled letters and gradually formed deeply loving and dependent ties.[30]

Women frequently spent their days within the social confines of such extended families. Sisters-in-law visited each other and, in some families, seemed to spend more time with each other than with their husbands. First cousins cared for each others' babies—for weeks or even months in times of sickness or childbirth. Sisters helped each other with housework, shopped and sewed for each other. Geographic separation was borne with difficulty. A sister's absence for even a week or two could cause loneliness and depression and would be bridged by frequent letters. Sibling rivalry was hardly unknown, but with separation or illness the theme of deep affection and dependency reemerged.[31]

Sisterly bonds continued across a lifetime. In her old age a rural Quaker matron, Martha Jefferis, wrote to her daughter Anne concerning her own half-sister, Phoebe: "In sister Phoebe I have a real friend—she studies my comfort and waits on me like a child. . . . She is exceedingly kind and this to all other homes (set aside yours) I would prefer—it is next to being with a daughter." Phoebe's own letters confirmed Martha's evaluation of her feelings. "Thou knowest my dear sister," Phoebe wrote, "there is no one . . . that exactly feels [for] thee as I do, for I think without boasting I can truly say that my desire is for thee."[32]

Such women, whether friends or relatives, assumed an emotional centrality in each others' lives. In their diaries and letters they wrote of the joy and contentment they felt in each others' company, their sense of isolation and despair when apart. The regularity of their correspondence underlines the sincerity of their words. Women named their daughters after one another and sought to integrate dear friends into their lives after marriage.[33] As one young bride wrote to an old friend shortly after her marriage: "I want to see you and talk with you and feel that we are united by the same bonds of sympathy and congeniality as ever."[34] After years of friendship one aging woman wrote of another: "Time cannot destroy the fascination of her manner . . . her voice is music to the ear. . . ."[35] Women made elaborate presents for each other, ranging from the Quakers' frugal pies and breads to painted velvet bags and phantom bouquets.[36] When a friend died, their grief was deeply felt. Martha Jefferis was unable to write to her daughter for three weeks because of the sorrow she felt at the death of a dear friend. Such distress was not unusual. A generation earlier a young Massachusetts farm woman filled pages of her diary with her grief at the death of her "dearest friend" and transcribed the letters of condolence other women sent her. She marked the anniversary of Rachel's death each year in her diary, contrasting her faithfulness with that of Rachel's husband who had soon remarried.[37]

These female friendships served a number of emotional functions. Within this secure and empathetic world women could share sorrows, anxieties, and joys, confident that other women had experienced similar emotions. One mid-nineteenth-century rural matron in a letter to her daughter discussed this particular aspect of women's friendships: "To have such a friend as thyself to look to and sympathize with her—and enter into all her little needs and in whose bosom she could with freedom pour forth her joys and sorrows—such a friend would very much relieve the tedium of many a wearisome hour. . . ." A generation later Molly more informally underscored the importance of this same function in a letter to Helena: "Suppose I come down . . . [and] spend Sunday with you quietly," she wrote Helena, " . . . that means talking all the time until you are relieved of all your latest troubles, and I of mine. . . ."[38] These were frequently troubles that apparently no man could understand. When Anne Jefferis Sheppard was first married, she and her older sister Edith (who then lived with Anne) wrote in detail to their mother of the severe depression and anxiety which they experienced. Moses Sheppard, Anne's husband, added cheerful postscripts to the sisters' letters—which he had clearly not read—remarking on Anne's and Edith's contentment. Theirs was an emotional world to which he had little access.[39]

This was, as well, a female world in which hostility and criticism of other women were discouraged, and thus a milieu in which women could develop a sense of inner security and self-esteem. As one young woman wrote to her mother's longtime friend: "I cannot sufficiently thank you for the kind unvaried affection & indulgence you have ever shown and expressed both by words and actions for me. . . . Happy would it be did all the world view me as you do, through the medium of kindness and forbearance."[40] They valued each other. Women, who had little status or power in the larger world of male concerns, possessed status and power in the lives and worlds of other women.[41]

An intimate mother-daughter relationship lay at the heart of this female world. The diaries and letters of both mothers and daughters attest to their closeness and mutual emotional dependency. Daughters routinely discussed their mothers' health and activities with their own friends, expressed anxiety in cases of their mother's ill health and concern for her cares.[42] Expressions of hostility which we would today consider routine on the part of both mothers and daughters seem to have been uncommon indeed. On the contrary, this sample of families indicates that the normal relationship between mother and daughter was one of sympathy and understanding.[43] Only sickness or great geographic distance was allowed to cause extended separation. When marriage did result in such separation, both viewed the distance between them with distress.[44] Something of this sympathy and love between mothers and daughters is evident in a letter Sarah Alden Ripley, at age sixty-nine, wrote her youngest and recently married daughter: "You do not know how much I miss you, not only when I struggle in and out of my mortal envelop and pump my nightly potation and no longer pour into your sympathizing ear my senile gossip, but all the day I muse away, since the sound of your voice no longer rouses me to sympathy with your joys or sorrows. . . . You cannot know how much I miss your affectionate demonstrations."[45] A dozen aging mothers in this sample of over thirty families echoed her sentiments.

Central to these mother-daughter relations is what might be described as an apprenticeship system. In those families where the daughter followed the mother into a life of traditional domesticity, mothers and other older women carefully trained daughters in the arts of housewifery and motherhood. Such training undoubtedly occurred throughout a girl's childhood but became more systematized, almost ritualistic, in the years following the end of her formal education and before her marriage. At this time a girl either returned home from boarding school or no longer divided her time between home and school. Rather, she devoted her energies on two tasks: mastering new domestic skills and participating in the visiting and social activities necessary to finding a husband. Under the careful supervision of their mothers and of older female relatives, such late-adolescent girls temporarily took over the household management from their mothers, tended their young nieces and nephews, and helped in childbirth, nursing, and weaning. Such experiences tied the generations together in shared skills and emotional interaction.[46]

Daughters were born into a female world. Their mother's life expectations and sympathetic network of friends and relations were among the first realities in the life of the developing child. As long as the mother's domestic role remained relatively stable and few viable alternatives competed with it, daughters tended to accept their mother's world and to turn automatically to other women for support and intimacy. It was within this closed and intimate female world that the young girl grew toward womanhood.

One could speculate at length concerning the absence of that mother-daughter hostility today considered almost inevitable to an adolescent's struggle for autonomy and self-identity. It is possible that taboos against female aggression and hostility were sufficiently strong to repress even that between mothers and their adolescent daughters. Yet these letters seem so alive and the interest of daughters in their mothers' affairs so vital and genuine that it is difficult to interpret their closeness exclusively in terms of repression and denial. The functional bonds that held mothers and daughters together in a world that permitted few alternatives to domesticity might well have created a source of mutuality and trust absent in societies where greater options were available for daughters than for mothers. Furthermore, the extended female network—a daughter's close ties with her own older sisters, cousins, and aunts—may well have permitted a diffusion and a relaxation of mother-daughter identification and so have aided a daughter in her struggle for identity and autonomy. None of these explanations are mutually exclusive; all may well have interacted to produce the degree of empathy evident in those letters and diaries.

At some point in adolescence, the young girl began to move outside the matrix of her mother's support group to develop a network of her own. Among the middle class, at least, this transition toward what was at the same time both a limited autonomy and a repetition of her mother's life seemed to have most frequently coincided with a girl's going to school. Indeed education appears to have played a crucial role in the lives of most of the families in this study. Attending school for a few months, for a year, or longer, was common even among daughters of relatively poor families, while middle-class girls routinely spent at least a year in boarding school.[47] These school years ordinarily marked a girl's first separation from home. They served to wean the daughter from her home, to train her in the essential social graces, and, ultimately, to help introduce her into the marriage market. It was not infrequently a trying emotional experience for both mother and daughter.[48]

In this process of leaving one home and adjusting to another, the mother's friends and relatives played a key transitional role. Such older women routinely accepted the role of foster mother; they supervised the young girl's deportment, monitored her health and introduced her to their own network of female friends and kin.[49] Not infrequently women, friends from their own school years, arranged to send their daughters to the same school so that the girls might form bonds paralleling those their mothers had made. For years Molly and Helena wrote of their daughters' meeting and worried over each others' children. When Molly finally brought her daughter east to school, their first act on reaching New York was to meet Helena and her daughters. Elizabeth Bordley Gibson virtually adopted the daughters of her school chum, Eleanor Custis Lewis. The Lewis daughters soon began to write Elizabeth Gibson letters with the salutation "Dearest Mama." Eleuthera DuPont, attending boarding school in Philadelphia at roughly the same time as the Lewis girls, developed a parallel relationship with her mother's friend, Elizabeth McKie Smith. Eleuthera went to the same school and became a close friend of the Smith girls and eventually married their first cousin. During this period she routinely called Mrs. Smith "Mother." Indeed Eleuthera so internalized the sense of having two mothers that she casually wrote her sisters of her "Mamma's" visits at her "mother's" house—that is at Mrs. Smith's.[50]

Even more important to this process of maturation than their mother's friends were the female friends young women made at school. Young girls helped each other overcome homesickness and endure the crises of adolescence. They gossiped about beaux, incorporated each other into their own kinship systems, and attended and gave teas and balls together. Older girls in boarding school "adopted" younger ones, who called them "Mother."[51] Dear friends might indeed continue this pattern of adoption and mothering throughout their lives; one woman might routinely assume the nurturing role of pseudomother, the other the dependency role of daughter. The pseudomother performed for the other woman all the services which we normally associate with mothers; she went to absurd lengths to purchase items her "daughter" could have obtained from other sources, gave advice and functioned as an idealized figure in her "daughter's" imagination. Helena played such a role for Molly, as did Sarah for Jeannie. Elizabeth Bordley Gibson bought almost all Eleanor Parke Custis Lewis's necessities—from shoes and corset covers to bedding and harp strings—and sent them from Philadelphia to Virginia, a procedure that sometimes took months. Eleanor frequently asked Elizabeth to take back her purchases, have them redone, and argue with shopkeepers about prices. These were favors automatically asked and complied with. Anne Jefferis Sheppard made the analogy very explicitly in a letter to her own mother written shortly after Anne's marriage, when she was feeling depressed about their separation: "Mary Paulen is truly kind, almost acts the part of a mother and trys to aid and *comfort me,* and also to *lighten my new cares.*"[52]

A comparison of the references to men and women in these young women's letters is striking. Boys were obviously indispensable to the elaborate courtship ritual girls engaged in. In these teenage letters and diaries, however, boys appear distant and warded off—an effect produced both by the girls' sense of bonding and by a highly developed and deprecatory whimsy. Girls joked among themselves about the conceit, poor looks or affectations of suitors. Rarely, especially in the eighteenth and early nineteenth centuries, were favorable remarks exchanged. Indeed, while hostility and criticism of other women were so rare as to seem almost tabooed, young women permitted themselves to express a great deal of hostility toward peer-group men.[53] When unacceptable suitors appeared, girls might even band together to harass them. When one such unfortunate came to court Sophie DuPont she hid in her room, first sending her sister Eleuthera to entertain him and then dispatching a number of urgent notes to her neighboring sister-in-law, cousins, and a visiting friend who all came to Sophie's support. A wild female romp ensued, ending only when Sophie banged into a door, lacerated her nose, and retired, with her female cohorts, to bed. Her brother and the presumably disconcerted suitor were left alone. These were not the antics of teenagers but of women in their early and mid-twenties.[54]

Even if young men were acceptable suitors, girls referred to them formally and obliquely: "The last week I received the unexpected intelligence of the arrival of a friend in Boston," Sarah Ripley wrote in her diary of the young man to whom she had been engaged for years and whom she would shortly marry. Harriet Manigault assiduously kept a lively and gossipy diary during the three years preceding her marriage, yet did not once comment upon her own engagement nor indeed make any personal references to her fiancé—who was never identified as such but always referred to as Mr. Wilcox.[55] The point is not that these young women were hostile to young men. Far from it; they sought marriage and domesticity. Yet in these letters and diaries men appear as an other or out group, segregated into different schools, supported by their own male network of friends and kin, socialized to different behavior, and coached to a proper formality in courtship behavior. As a consequence, relations between young women and men frequently lacked the spontaneity and emotional intimacy that characterized the young girls' ties to each other.

Indeed, in sharp contrast to their distant relations with boys, young women's relations with each other were close, often frolicsome, and surprisingly long lasting and devoted. They wrote secret missives to each other, spent long solitary days with each other, curled up together in bed at night to whisper fantasies and secrets.[56] In 1862 one young woman in her early twenties described one such scene to an absent friend: "I have sat up to midnight listening to the confidences of Constance Kinney, whose heart was opened by that most charming of all situations, a seat on a bedside late at night, when all the household are asleep & only oneself & one's confidante survive in wakefulness. So she has told me all her loves and tried to get some confidences in return but being five or six years older than she, I know better. . . ."[57] Elizabeth Bordley and Nelly Parke Custis, teenagers in Philadelphia in the 1790s, routinely secreted themselves until late each night in Nelly's attic, where they each wrote a novel about the other.[58] Quite a few young women kept diaries, and it was a sign of special friendship to show their diaries to each other. The emotional quality of such exchanges emerges from the comments of one young girl who grew up along the Ohio frontier:

> *Sisters CW and RT keep diaries & allow me the inestimable pleasure of reading them and in turn they see mine—but O shame covers my face when I think of it; theirs is so much better than mine, that every time. Then I think well now* I will *burn mine but upon second thought it would deprive me the pleasure of reading theirs, for I esteem it a very great privilege indeed, as well as very improving, as we lay our hearts open to each other, it heightens our love & helps to cherish & keep alive that sweet soothing friendship and endears us to each other by that soft attraction.*[59]

Girls routinely slept together, kissed and hugged each other. Indeed, while waltzing with young men scandalized the otherwise flighty and highly fashionable Harriet Manigault, she considered waltzing with other young women not only acceptable but pleasant.[60]

Marriage followed adolescence. With increasing frequency in the nineteenth century, marriage involved a girl's traumatic removal from her mother and her mother's network. It involved, as well, adjustment to a husband, who, because he was male came to marriage with both a different world view and vastly different experiences. Not surprisingly, marriage was an event surrounded with supportive, almost ritualistic, practices. (Weddings are one of the last female rituals remaining in twentieth-century America.) Young women routinely spent the months preceding their marriage almost exclusively with other women—at neighborhood sewing bees and quilting parties or in a round of visits to geographically distant friends and relatives. Ostensibly they went to receive assistance in the practical preparations for their new home—sewing and quilting a trousseau and linen—but of equal importance, they appear to have gained emotional support and reassurance. Sarah Ripley spent over a month with friends and relatives in Boston and Hingham before her wedding; Nelly Custis Lewis exchanged visits with her aunts and first cousins throughout Virginia.[61] Anne Jefferis, who married with some hesitation, spent virtually half a year in endless visiting with cousins, aunts, and friends. Despite their reassurance and support, however, she would not marry Moses Sheppard until her sister Edith and her cousin Rebecca moved into the groom's home, met his friends, and explored his personality.[62] The wedding did not take place until Edith wrote to Anne: "I can say in truth I am entirely willing thou shouldst follow him even away in the Jersey sands believing if thou are not happy in thy future home it will not be any fault on his part. . . ."[63]

Sisters, cousins, and friends frequently accompanied newlyweds on their wedding night and wedding trip, which often involved additional family visiting. Such extensive visits presumably served to wean the daughter from her family of origin. As such they often contained a note of ambivalence. Nelly Custis, for example, reported homesickness and loneliness on her wedding trip. "I left my Beloved and revered Grandmamma with sincere regret," she wrote Elizabeth Bordley. "It was sometime before I could feel reconciled to traveling without her." Perhaps they also functioned to reassure the young woman herself, and her friends and kin, that though marriage might alter it would not destroy old bonds of intimacy and familiarity.[64]

Married life, too, was structured about a host of female rituals. Childbirth, especially the birth of the first child, became virtually a *rite de passage*, with a lengthy seclusion of the woman before and after delivery, severe restrictions on her activities, and finally a dramatic reemergence.[65] This seclusion was supervised by mothers, sisters, and loving friends. Nursing and weaning involved the advice and assistance of female friends and relatives. So did miscarriage.[66] Death, like birth, was structured around elaborate unisexed rituals. When Nelly Parke Custis Lewis rushed to nurse her daughter who was critically ill while away at school, Nelly received support, not from her husband, who remained on their plantation, but from her old school friend, Elizabeth Bordley. Elizabeth aided Nelly in caring for her dying daughter, cared for Nelly's other children, played a major role in the elaborate funeral arrangements (which the father did not attend), and frequently visited the girl's grave at the mother's request. For years Elizabeth continued to be the confidante of Nelly's anguished recollections of her lost daughter. These memories, Nelly's letters make clear, were for Elizabeth alone, "Mr. L knows nothing of this," was a frequent comment.[67] Virtually every collection of letters and diaries in my sample contained evidence of women turning to each other for comfort when facing the frequent and unavoidable deaths of the eighteenth and nineteenth centuries.[68] While mourning for her father's death, Sophie DuPont received elaborate letters and visits of condolence—all from women. No man wrote or visited Sophie to offer sympathy at her father's death.[69] Among rural Pennsylvania Quakers, death and mourning rituals assumed an even more extreme same-sex form, with men or women largely barred from the deathbeds of the other sex. Women relatives and friends slept with the dying woman, nursed her, and prepared her body for burial.[70]

Eighteenth- and nineteenth-century women thus lived in emotional proximity to each other. Friendships and intimacies followed the biological ebb and flow of women's lives. Marriage and pregnancy, childbirth and weaning, sickness and death involved physical and psychic trauma which comfort and sympathy made easier to bear. Intense bonds of love and intimacy bound together those women who, offering each other aid and sympathy, shared such stressful moments.

These bonds were often physical as well as emotional. An undeniably romantic and even sensual note frequently marked female relationships. This theme, significant throughout the stages of a woman's life, surfaced first during adolescence. As one teenager from a struggling pioneer family in the Ohio Valley wrote in her diary in 1808: "I laid with my dear R[ebecca] and a glorious good talk we had until about 4 [A.M.]—O how hard I do *love* her. . . ."[71] Only a few years later Bostonian Eunice Callender carved her initials and Sarah Ripley's into a favorite tree, along with a pledge of eternal love, and then waited breathlessly for Sarah to discover and respond to her declaration of affection. The response appears to have been affirmative.[72] A half-century later urbane and sophisticated Katherine Wharton commented upon meeting an old school chum: "She was a great pet of mine at school & I thought as I watched her light figure how often I had held her in my arms—how dear she had once been to me." Katie maintained a long intimate friendship with another girl. When a young man began to court this friend seriously, Katie commented in her diary that she had never realized "how deeply I loved Eng and how fully." She wrote over and over again in that entry: "Indeed I love her!" and only with great reluctance left the city that summer since it meant also leaving Eng with Eng's new suitor.[73]

Peggy Emlen, a Quaker adolescent in Philadelphia in the 1760s, expressed similar feelings about her first cousin, Sally Logan. The girls sent love poems to each other (not unlike the ones Elizabeth Bordley wrote to Nelly Custis a generation later), took long solitary walks together, and even haunted the empty house of the other when one was out of town. Indeed Sally's absences from Philadelphia caused Peggy acute unhappiness. So strong were Peggy's feelings that her brothers began to tease her about her affection for Sally and threatened to steal Sally's letters, much to both girls' alarm. In one letter that Peggy wrote the absent Sally she elaborately described the depth and nature of her feelings: "I have not words to express my impatience to see My Dear Cousin, what would I not give just now for an hours sweet conversation with her, it seems as if I had a thousand things to say to thee, yet when I see thee, everything will be forgot thro' joy. . . . I have a very great friendship for several Girls yet it dont give me so much uneasiness at being absent from them as from thee. . . . [Let us] go and spend a day down at our place together and there unmolested enjoy each others company."[74]

Sarah Alden Ripley, a young, highly educated woman, formed a similar intense relationship, in this instance with a woman somewhat older than herself. The immediate bond of friendship rested on their atypically intense scholarly interests, but it soon involved strong emotions, at least on Sarah's part. "Friendship," she wrote Mary Emerson, "is fast twining about her willing captive the silken hands of dependence, a dependence so sweet who would renounce it for the apathy of self-sufficiency?" Subsequent letters became far more emotional, almost conspiratorial. Mary visited Sarah secretly in her room, or the two women crept away from family and friends to meet in a nearby woods. Sarah became jealous of Mary's other young woman friends. Mary's trips away from Boston also thrust Sarah into periods of anguished depression. Interestingly, the letters detailing their love were not destroyed but were preserved and even reprinted in a eulogistic biography of Sarah Alden Ripley.[75]

Tender letters between adolescent women, confessions of loneliness and emotional dependency, were not peculiar to Sarah Alden, Peggy Emlen, or Katie Wharton. They are found throughout the letters of the thirty-five families studied. They have, of course, their parallel today in the musings of many female adolescents. Yet these eighteenth- and nineteenth-century friendships lasted with undiminished, indeed often increased, intensity throughout the women's lives. Sarah Alden Ripley's first child was named after Mary Emerson. Nelly Custis Lewis's love for and dependence on Elizabeth Bordley Gibson only increased after her marriage. Eunice Callender remained enamored of her cousin Sarah Ripley for years and rejected as impossible the suggestion by another woman that their love might some day fade away.[76] Sophie DuPont and her childhood friend, Clementina Smith, exchanged letters filled with love and dependency for forty years while another dear friend, Mary Black Couper, wrote of dreaming that she, Sophie, and her husband were all united in one marriage. Mary's letters to Sophie are filled with avowals of love and indications of ambivalence toward her own husband. Eliza Schlatter, another of Sophie's intimate friends, wrote to her at a time of crisis: "I wish I could be with you present in the body as well as the mind & heart—I would turn your *good husband out of bed*—and snuggle into you and we would have a long talk like old times in Pine St.—I want to tell you so many things that are not *writable*. . . ."[77]

Such mutual dependency and deep affection is a central existential reality coloring the world of supportive networks and rituals. In the case of Katie, Sophie, or Eunice—as with Molly, Jeannie, and Sarah—their need for closeness and support merged with more intense demands for a love which was at the same time both emotional and sensual. Perhaps the most explicit statement concerning women's lifelong friendships appeared in the letter abolitionist and reformer Mary Grew wrote about the same time, referring to her own love for her dear friend and lifelong companion, Margaret Burleigh. Grew wrote, in response to a letter of condolence from another woman on Burleigh's death: "Your words respecting my beloved friend touch me deeply. Evidently . . . you comprehend and appreciate, as few persons do . . . the nature of the relation which existed, which exists, between her and myself. Her only surviving niece . . . also does. To me it seems to have been a closer union than that of most marriages. We know there have been other such between two men and also between two women. And why should there not be. Love is spiritual, only passion is sexual."[78]

How then can we ultimately interpret these long-lived intimate female relationships and integrate them into our understanding of Victorian sexuality? Their ambivalent and romantic rhetoric presents us with an ultimate puzzle: the relationship along the spectrum of human emotions between love, sensuality, and sexuality.

One is tempted, as I have remarked, to compare Molly, Peggy, or Sophie's relationships with the friendships adolescent girls in the twentieth century routinely form—close friendships of great emotional intensity. Helene Deutsch and Clara Thompson have both described these friendships as emotionally necessary to a girl's psychosexual development. But, they warn, such friendships might shade into adolescent and postadolescent homosexuality.[79]

It is possible to speculate that in the twentieth century a number of cultural taboos evolved to cut short the homosocial ties of girlhood and to impel the emerging women of thirteen or fourteen toward heterosexual relationships. In contrast, nineteenth-century American society did not taboo close female relationships but rather recognized them as a socially viable form of human contact—and, as such, acceptable throughout a woman's life. Indeed it was not these homosocial ties that were inhibited but rather heterosexual leanings. While closeness, freedom of emotional expression, and uninhibited physical contact characterized women's relationships with each other, the opposite was frequently true of male–female relationships. One could thus argue that within such a world of female support, intimacy, and ritual it was only to be expected that adult women would turn trustingly and lovingly to each other. It was a behavior they had observed and learned since childhood. A different type of emotional landscape existed in the nineteenth century, one in which Molly and Helena's love became a natural development.

Of perhaps equal significance are the implications we can garner from this framework for the understanding of heterosexual marriages in the nineteenth century. If men and women grew up as they did in relatively homogeneous and segregated sexual groups, then marriage represented a major problem in adjustment. From this perspective we could interpret much of the emotional stiffness and distance that we associate with Victorian marriage as a structural consequence of contemporary sex-role differentiation and gender-role socialization. With marriage, both women and men had to adjust to life with a person who was, in essence, a member of an alien group.

I have thus far substituted a cultural or psychosocial for a psychosexual interpretation of women's emotional bonding. But there are psychosexual implications in this model which I think it only fair to make more explicit. Despite Sigmund Freud's insistence on the bisexuality of us all or the recent American Psychiatric Association decision on homosexuality, many psychiatrists today tend explicitly or implicitly to view homosexuality as a totally alien or pathological behavior—as totally unlike heterosexuality. I suspect that in essence they may have adopted an explanatory model similar to the one used in discussing schizophrenia. As a psychiatrist can speak of schizophrenia and of a borderline schizophrenic personality as both ultimately and fundamentally different from a normal or neurotic personality, so they also think of both homosexuality and latent homosexuality as states totally different from heterosexuality. With this rapidly dichotomous model of assumption, "latent homosexuality" becomes the indication of a disease in progress—seeds of a pathology which belie the reality of an individual's heterosexuality.

Yet at the same time we are well aware that cultural values can effect choices in the gender of a person's sexual partner. We, for instance, do not necessarily consider homosexual-object choice among men in prison, on shipboard or in boarding schools a necessary indication of pathology. I would urge that we expand this relativistic model and hypothesize that a number of cultures might well tolerate or even encourage diversity in sexual and nonsexual relations. Based on my research into this nineteenth-century world of female intimacy, I would further suggest that rather than seeing a gulf between the normal and the abnormal we view sexual and emotional impulses as part of a continuum or spectrum of affect gradations strongly effected by cultural norms and arrangements, a continuum influenced in part by observed and thus learned behavior. At one end of the continuum lies committed heterosexuality, at the other uncompromising homosexuality; between, a wide latitude of emotions and sexual feelings. Certain cultures and environments permit individuals a great deal of freedom in moving across this spectrum. I would like to suggest that the nineteenth century was such a cultural environment. That is, the supposedly repressive and destructive Victorian sexual ethos, may have been more flexible and responsive to the needs of particular individuals than those of mid-twentieth century.

Notes

1. The most notable exception to this rule is now eleven years old: William R. Taylor and Christopher Lasch, "Two 'Kindred Spirits': Sorority and Family in New England, 1839–1846," *New England Quarterly* 36 (1963): 25–41. Taylor has made a valuable contribution to the history of women and the history of the family with his concept of "sororial" relations. I do not, however, accept the Taylor-Lasch thesis that female friendships developed in the mid-nineteenth century because of geographic mobility and the breakup of the colonial family. I have found these friendships as frequently in the eighteenth century as in the nineteenth and would hypothesize that the geographic mobility of the mid-nineteenth century eroded them as it did so many other traditional social institutions. Helen Vendler (*Review of Notable American Women, 1607–1950,* ed. Edward James and Janet James, *New York Times*) [November 5, 1972]: sec. 7) points out the significance of these friendships.

2. I do not wish to deny the importance of women's relations with particular men. Obviously, women were close to brothers, husbands, fathers, and sons. However, there is evidence that despite such closeness relationships between men and women differed in both emotional texture and frequency from those between women. Women's relations with each other, although they played a central role in the American family and American society, have been so seldom examined either by general social historians or by historians of the family that I wish in this article simply to examine their nature and analyze their implications for our understanding of social relations and social structure. I have discussed some aspects of male–female relationships in two articles: "Puberty to Menopause: The Cycle of Femininity in Nineteenth-Century America," *Feminist Studies* 1 (1973): 58–72, and, with Charles Rosenberg, "The Female Animal: Medical and Biological Views of Women in 19th Century America," *Journal of American History* 59 (1973): 331–56.

3. See Freud's classic paper on homosexuality, "Three Essays on the Theory of Sexuality," in *The Standard Edition of the Complete Psychological Works of Sigmund Freud,* trans. James Strachey (London: Hogarth Press, 1953), 7:135–72. The essays originally appeared in 1905. Prof. Roy Shafer, Department of Psychiatry, Yale University, has pointed out that Freud's view of sexual behavior was strongly influenced by nineteenth-century evolutionary thought. Within Freud's schema, genital heterosexuality marked the height of human development (Schafer, "Problems in Freud's Psychology of Women," *Journal of the American Psychoanalytic Association* 22 [1974]: 459–85).

4. For a novel and most important exposition of one theory of behavioral norms and options and its application to the study of human sexuality, see Charles Rosenberg, "Sexuality, Class and Role," *American Quarterly* 25 (1973): 131–53.

5. See, e.g., the letters of Peggy Emlen to Sally Logan, 1768–72, Wells Morris Collection, Box 1, Historical Society of Pennsylvania; and the Eleanor Parke Custis Lewis Letters, Historical Society of Pennsylvania, Philadelphia.

6. Sarah Butler Wister was the daughter of Fanny Kemble and Pierce Butler. In 1859 she married a Philadelphia physician, Owen Wister. The novelist Owen Wister is her son. Jeannie Field Musgrove was the half-orphaned daughter of constitutional lawyer and New York Republican politician David Dudley Field. Their correspondence (1855–98) is in the Sarah Butler Wister Papers, Wister Family Papers, Historical Society of Pennsylvania.

7. Sarah Butler, Butler Place, S.C., to Jeannie Field, New York, September 14, 1855.

8. See, e.g., Sarah Butler Wister, Germantown, Pa., to Jeannie Field, New York, September 25, 1862, October 21, 1863; or Jeannie Field, New York, to Sarah Butler Wister, Germantown, July 3, 1861, January 23 and July 12, 1863.

9. Sarah Butler Wister, Germantown, to Jeannie Field, New York, June 5, 1861, February 29, 1864; Jeannie Field to Sarah Butler Wister, November 22, 1861, January 4 and June 14, 1863.

10. Sarah Butler Wister, London, to Jeannie Field Musgrove, New York, June 18 and August 3, 1870.

11. See, e.g., two of Sarah's letters to Jeannie: December 21, 1873, July 16, 1878.

12. This is the 1868–1920 correspondence between Mary Hallock Foote and Helena, a New York friend (the Mary Hallock Foote Papers are in the Manuscript Division, Stanford University). Wallace E. Stegner has written a fictionalized biography of Mary Hallock Foote (*Angle of Repose* [Garden City, N.Y.: Doubleday & Co., 1971]). See, as well, her autobiography: Mary Hallock Foote, *A Victorian Gentlewoman in the Far West: The Reminiscences of Mary Hallock Foote*, ed. Rodman W. Paul (San Marino, Calif.: Huntington Library, 1972). In many ways these letters are typical of those women wrote to other women. Women frequently began letters to each other with salutations such as "Dearest," "My Most Beloved," "You Darling Girl," and signed them "tenderly" or "to my dear dear sweet friend, good-bye." Without the least self-consciousness, one woman in her frequent letters to a female friend referred to her husband as "my other love." She was by no means unique. See, e.g., Annie to Charlene Van Vleck Anderson, Appleton, Wis., June 10, 1871, Anderson Family Papers, Manuscript Division, Stanford University; Maggie to Emily Howland, Philadelphia, July 12, 1851, Howland Family Papers, Phoebe King Collection, Friends Historical Library, Swarthmore College; Mary Jane Burleigh to Emily Howland, Sherwood, N.Y., March 27, 1872, Howland Family Papers, Sophia Smith Collection, Smith College; Mary Black Couper to Sophia Madeleine DuPont, Wilmington, Del.: n.d. [1834] (two letters), Samuel Francis DuPont Papers, Eleutherian Mills Foundation, Wilmington, Del.; Phoebe Middleton, Concordiville, Pa., to Martha Jefferis, Chester County, Pa., February 22, 1848; and see in general the correspondence (1838–49) between Rebecca Biddle of Philadelphia and Martha Jefferis, Chester County, Pa., Jefferis Family Correspondence, Chester County Historical Society, West Chester, Pa.; Phoebe Bradford Diary, June 7 and July 13, 1832, Historical Society of Pennsylvania; Sarah Alden Ripley, to Abba Allyn, Boston, n.d. [1818–20], and Sarah Alden Ripley to Sophia Bradford, November 30, 1854, in the Sarah Alden Ripley Correspondence, Schlesinger Library, Radcliffe College; Fanny Canby Ferris to Anne Biddle, Philadelphia, October 11 and November 19, 1811, December 26, 1813, Fanny Canby to Mary Canby, May 27, 1801, Mary R. Garrigues to Mary Canby, five letters n.d. [1802–8], Anne Biddle to Mary Canby, two letters n.d., May 16, July 13, and November 24, 1806, June 14, 1807, June 5, 1808, Anne Sterling Biddle Family Papers, Friends Historical Society, Swarthmore College; Harriet Manigault Wilcox Diary, August 7, 1814, Historical Society of Pennsylvania. See as well the correspondence between Harriet Manigault Wilcox's mother, Mrs. Gabriel Manigault, Philadelphia, and Mrs. Henry Middleton, Charleston, S.C., between 1810 and 1830, Cadwalader Collection, J. Francis Fisher Section, Historical Society of Pennsylvania. The basis and nature of such friendships can be seen in the comments of Sarah Alden Ripley to her sister-in-law and long-time friend, Sophia Bradford: "Hearing that you are not well reminds me of what it would be to lose your loving society. We have kept step together through a long piece of road in the weary journey of life. We have loved the same beings and wept together over their graves" (Mrs. O. J. Wister and Miss Agnes Irwin, eds., *Worthy Women of Our First Century* [Philadelphia: J. B. Lippincott & Co., 1877], p. 195).

13. Mary Hallock [Foote] to Helena, n.d. [1869–70], n.d. [1871–72], Folder 1, Mary Hallock Foote Letters, Manuscript Division, Stanford University.

14. Mary Hallock [Foote] to Helena, September 15 and 23, 1873, n.d. [October 1873], October 12, 1873.

15. Mary Hallock [Foote] to Helena, n.d. [January 1874], n.d. [Spring 1874].

16. Mary Hallock [Foote] to Helena, September 23, 1873; Mary Hallock [Foote] to Richard, December 13, 1873. Molly's and Helena's relationship continued for the rest of their lives. Molly's letters are filled with tender and intimate references, as when she wrote, twenty years later and from 2,000 miles away: "It isn't because you are good that I love you—but for the essence of you which is like perfume" (n.d. [1890s?]).

17. I am in the midst of a larger study of adult gender-roles and gender-role socialization in America, 1785–1895. For a discussion of social attitudes toward appropriate male and female roles, see Barbara Welter, "The Cult of True Womanhood: 1820–1860," *American Quarterly* 18 (Summer 1966): 151–74; Anne Firor Scott, *The Southern Lady: From Pedestal to Politics, 1830–1930* (Chicago: University of Chicago Press, 1970), chaps. 1–2; Smith-Rosenberg and Rosenberg.

18. See, e.g., the letters of Peggy Emlen to Sally Logan, 1768–72, Wells Morris Collection, Box 1, Historical Society of Pennsylvania; and the Eleanor Parke Custis Lewis Letters, Historical Society of Pennsylvania.

19. See esp. Elizabeth Bott, *Family and Social Network* (London: Tavistock Publications, 1957); Michael Young and Peter Willmott, *Family and Kinship in East London*, rev. ed. (Baltimore: Penguin Books, 1964).

20. This pattern seemed to cross class barriers. A letter that an Irish domestic wrote in the 1830s contains seventeen separate references to women and but only seven to men, most of whom were relatives and two of whom were infant brothers living with her mother and mentioned in relation to her mother (Ann McGrann, Philadelphia, to Sophie M. DuPont, Philadelphia, July 3, 1834, Sophie Madeleine DuPont Letters, Eleutherian Mills Foundation).

21. Harriett Manigault Diary, June 28, 1814, and passim; Jeannie Field, New York, to Sarah Butler Wister, Germantown, April 19, 1863; Phoebe Bradford Diary, January 30, February 19, March 4, August 11, and October 14, 1832, Historical Society of Pennsylvania; Sophie M. DuPont, Brandywine, to Henry DuPont, Germantown, July 9, 1827, Eleutherian Mills Foundation.

22. Martha Jefferis to Anne Jefferis Sheppard, July 9, 1843; Anne Jefferis Sheppard to Martha Jefferis, June 28, 1846; Anne Sterling Biddle Papers, passim, Biddle Family Papers, Friends Historical Society, Swarthmore College; Eleanor Parke Custis Lewis, Virginia, to Elizabeth Bordley Gibson, Philadelphia, November 24 and December 4, 1820, November 6, 1821.

23. Phoebe Bradford Diary, January 13, November 16–19, 1832, April 26 and May 7, 1833; Abigail Brackett Lyman to Mrs. Catling, Litchfield, Conn., May 3, 1801, collection in private hands; Martha Jefferis to Anne Jefferis Sheppard, August 28, 1845.

24. Lisa Mitchell Diary, 1860s, passim, Manuscript Division, Tulane University; Eleanor Parke Custis Lewis to Elizabeth Bordley [Gibson] February 5, 1822; Jeannie McCall, Cedar Park, to Peter McCall, Philadelphia, June 30, 1849, McCall Section, Cadwalader Collection, Historical Society of Pennsylvania.

25. Peggy Emlen to Sally Logan, May 3, 1769.

26. For a prime example of this type of letter, see Eleanor Parke Custis Lewis to Elizabeth Bordley Gibson, passim, or Fanny Canby to Mary Canby, Philadelphia, May 27, 1801; or Sophie M. DuPont, Brandywine, to Henry DuPont, Germantown, February 4, 1832.

27. Place of residence is not the only variable significant in characterizing family structure. Strong emotional ties and frequent visiting and correspondence can unite families that do not live under one roof. Demographic studies based on household structure alone fail to reflect such emotional and even economic ties between families.

28. Eleanor Parke Custis Lewis to Elizabeth Bordley Gibson, April 20 and September 25, 1848.

29. Maria Inskeep to Fanny Hampton Correspondence, 1823–60, Inskeep Collection, Tulane University Library.

30. Eunice Callender, Boston, to Sarah Ripley [Stearns], September 24 and October 29, 1803, February 16, 1805, April 29 and October 9, 1806, May 26, 1810.

31. Sophie DuPont filled her letters to her younger brother Henry (with whom she had been assigned to correspond while he was at boarding school) with accounts of family visiting (see, e.g., December 13, 1827, January 10 and March 9, 1828, February 4 and March 10, 1832; also Sophie M. DuPont to Victorine DuPont Bauday, September 26 and December 4, 1827, February 22, 1828; Sophie M. DuPont, Brandywine, to Clementina B. Smith, Philadelphia, January 15, 1830; Eleuthera DuPont, Brandywine, to Victorine DuPont Bauday, Philadelphia, April 17, 1821, October 20, 1826; Evelina Dupont [Biderman] to Victorine DuPont Bauday, October 18, 1816). Other examples, from the Historical Society of Pennsylvania, are Harriet Manigault [Wilcox] Diary, August 17, September 8, October 19 and 22, December 22, 1814; Jane Zook, Westtown School, Chester County, Pa., to Mary Zook, November 13, December 7 and 11, 1870, February 26, 1871; Eleanor Parke Custis [Lewis] to Elizabeth Bordley [Gibson], March 30, 1796, February 7 and March 20, 1798; Jeannie McCall to Peter McCall, Philadelphia, November 12, 1847; Mary B. Ashew Diary, July 11 and 13, August 17, Summer and October 1858, and, from a private collection, Edith Jefferis to Anne Jefferis Sheppard, November 1841, April 5, 1842; Abigail Brackett Lyman, Northampton, Mass., to Mrs. Catling, Litchfield, Conn., May 13, 1801; Abigail Brackett Lyman, Northampton, to Mary Lord, August 11, 1800. Mary Hallock Foote vacationed with her sister, her sister's children, her aunt, and a female cousin in the summer of 1874; cousins frequently visited the Hallock farm in Milton, N.Y. In later years Molly and her sister Bessie set up a joint household in Boise, Idaho (Mary Hallock Foote to Helena, July [1874?] and passim). Jeannie Field, after initially disliking her sister-in-law, Laura, became very close to her, calling her "my little sister" and at times spending virtually every day with her (Jeannie Field [Musgrove] New York, to Sarah Butler Wister, Germantown, March 1, 8, and 15, and May 9, 1863).

32. Martha Jefferis to Anne Jefferis Sheppard, January 12, 1845; Phoebe Middleton to Martha Jefferis, February 22, 1848. A number of other women remained close to sisters and sisters-in-law across a long lifetime (Phoebe Bradford Diary, June 7, 1832, and Sarah Alden Ripley to Sophia Bradford, cited in Wister and Irwin, p. 195).

33. Rebecca Biddle to Martha Jefferis, 1838–49, passim; Martha Jefferis to Anne Jefferis Sheppard, July 6, 1846; Anne Jefferis Sheppard to Rachael Jefferis, January 16, 1865; Sarah Foulke Farquhar [Emlen] Diary, September 22, 1813, Friends Historical Library, Swarthmore College; Mary Garrigues to Mary Canby [Biddle], 1802–8, passim; Anne Biddle to Mary Canby [Biddle], May 16, July 13, and November 24, 1806, June 14, 1807, June 5, 1808.

34. Sarah Alden Ripley to Abba Allyn, n.d., Schlesinger Library.

35. Phoebe Bradford Diary, July 13, 1832.

36. Mary Hallock [Foote] to Helena, December 23 [1868 or 1869]; Phoebe Bradford Diary, December 8, 1832; Martha Jefferis and Anne Jefferis Sheppard letters, passim.

37. Martha Jefferis to Anne Jefferis Sheppard, August 3, 1849; Sarah Ripley [Stearns] Diary, November 12, 1808, January 8, 1811. An interesting note of hostility or rivalry is present in Sarah Ripley's diary entry. Sarah evidently deeply resented the husband's rapid remarriage.

38. Martha Jefferis to Edith Jefferis, March 15, 1841; Mary Hallock Foote to Helena, n.d. [1874–75?]; see also Jeannie Field, New York, to Sarah Butler Wister, Germantown, May 5, 1863, Emily Howland Diary, December 1879, Howland Family Papers.

39. Anne Jefferis Sheppard to Martha Jefferis, September 29, 1841.

40. Frances Parke Lewis to Elizabeth Bordley Gibson, April 29, 1821.

41. Mary Jane Burleigh, Mount Pleasant, S.C., to Emily Howland, Sherwood, N.Y., March 27, 1872, Howland Family Papers; Emily Howland Diary, September 16, 1879, January 21 and 23, 1880; Mary Black Couper, New Castle, Del., to Sophie M. DuPont, Brandywine, April 7, 1834.

42. Harriet Manigault Diary, August 15, 21, and 23, 1814, Historical Society of Pennsylvania; Polly [Simmons] to Sophie Madeleine DuPont, February 1822; Sophie Madeleine DuPont to Victorine Bauday, December 4, 1827; Sophie Madeleine DuPont to Clementina Beach Smith, July 24, 1828, August 19, 1829; Clementina Beach Smith to Sophie Madeleine DuPont, April 29, 1831; Mary Black Couper to Sophie Madeleine DuPont, December 24, 1828, July 21, 1834. This pattern appears to have crossed class lines. When a former Sunday school student of Sophie DuPont's (and the daughter of a worker in her father's factory) wrote to Sophie she discussed her mother's health and activities quite naturally (Ann McGrann to Sophie Madeleine DuPont, August 25, 1832; see also Elizabeth Bordley to Martha, n.d. [1797], Eleanor Parke Custis [Lewis] to Elizabeth Bordley [Gibson], May 13, 1796, July 1, 1798; Peggy Emlen to Sally Logan, January 8, 1786. All but the Emlen/Logan letters are in the Eleanor Parke Custis Lewis Correspondence, Historical Society of Pennsylvania).

43. Mrs. S. S. Dalton, "Autobiography," (Circle Valley, Utah, 1876), pp. 21–22. Bancroft Library, University of California, Berkeley; Sarah Foulke Emlen Diary, April 1809; Louisa G. Van Vleck, Appleton, Wis., to Charlena Van Vleck Anderson, Göttingen, n.d. [1875]; Harriet Manigault Diary, August 16, 1814, July 14, 1815; Sarah Alden Ripley to Sophy Fisher [early 1860s], quoted in Wister and Irwin (n. 12 above), p. 212. The Jefferis family papers are filled with empathetic letters between Martha and her daughters, Anne and Edith. See, e.g., Martha Jefferis to Edith Jefferis, December 26, 1836, March 11, 1837, March 15, 1841; Anne Jefferis Sheppard to Martha Jefferis, March 17, 1841, January 17, 1847; Martha Jefferis to Anne Jefferis Sheppard, April 17, 1848, April 30, 1849. A representative letter is this of March 9, 1837 from Edith to Martha: "My heart can fully respond to the language of my own precious Mother, that absence has not diminished our affection for each other, but has, if possible, strengthened the bonds that have united us together & I have had to remark how we had been permitted to mingle in sweet fellowship and have been strengthened to bear one another's burdens. . . ."

44. Abigail Brackett Lyman, Boston, to Mrs. Abigail Brackett (daughter to mother), n.d. [1797], June 3, 1800; Sarah Alden Ripley wrote weekly to her daughter, Sophy Ripley Fisher, after the latter's marriage (Sarah Alden Ripley Correspondence, passim); Phoebe Bradford Diary, February 25, 1833, passim, 1832–33; Louisa G. Van Vleck to Charlena Van Vleck Anderson, December 15, 1873, July 4, August 15 and 29, September 19, and November 9, 1875. Eleanor Parke Custis Lewis's long correspondence with Elizabeth Bordley Gibson contains evidence of her anxiety at leaving her foster mother's home at various times during her adolescence and at her marriage, and her own longing for her daughters, both of whom had married and moved to Louisiana (Eleanor Parke Custis [Lewis] to Elizabeth Bordley [Gibson], October 13, 1795, November 4, 1799, passim, 1820s and 1830s). Anne Jefferis Sheppard experienced a great deal of anxiety on moving two days' journey from her mother at the time of her marriage. This loneliness and sense of isolation persisted through her marriage until, finally a widow, she returned to live with her mother (Anne Jefferis Sheppard to Martha Jefferis, April 1841, October 16, 1842, April 2, May 22, and October 12, 1844, September 3, 1845, January 17, 1847, May 16, June 3, and October 31, 1849; Anne Jefferis Sheppard to Susanna Lightfoot, March 23, 1845, and to Joshua Jefferis, May 14, 1854). Daughters evidently frequently slept with their mothers—into adulthood (Harriet Manigault [Wilcox] Diary, February 19, 1815; Eleanor Parke Custis Lewis to Elizabeth Bordley Gibson, October 10, 1832). Daughters also frequently asked mothers to live with them and professed delight when they did so. See, e.g., Sarah Alden Ripley's comments to George Simmons, October 6, 1844, in Wister and Irwin, p. 185: "It is no longer 'Mother and Charles came out one day and returned the next,' for mother is one of us; she has entered the penetratice, been initiated into the mystery of the household gods, . . . Her divertissement is to mend the stockings . . . whiten sheets and napkins, . . . and take a stroll at evening with me to talk of our children, to compare our experiences, what we have learned and what we have suffered, and, last of all, to complete with pears and melons the cheerful circle about the solar lamp. . . ." We did find a few exceptions to this mother-daughter felicity (M. B. Ashew Diary, November 19, 1857, April 10 and May 17, 1858). Sarah Foulke Emlen was at first very hostile to her stepmother (Sarah Foulke Emlen Diary, August 9, 1807), but they later developed a warm supportive relationship.

45. Sarah Alden Ripley to Sophy Thayer, n.d. [1861].

46. Mary Hallock Foote to Helena [winter 1873] (no. 52); Jossie, Stevens Point, Wis., to Charlena Van Vleck [Anderson], Appleton, Wis., October 24, 1870; Pollie Chandler, Green Bay, Wis., to Charlena Van Vleck [Anderson], Appleton, n.d. [1870]; Eleuthera DuPont to Sophie DuPont, September 5, 1829; Sophie DuPont to Eleuthera DuPont, December 1827; Sophie DuPont to Victorine Bauday, December 4, 1827; Mary Gilpin to Sophie DuPont, September 26, 1827; Sarah Ripley Stearns Diary, April 2, 1809; Jeannie McCall to Peter McCall, October 27 [late 1840s]. Eleanor Parke Custis Lewis's correspondence with Elizabeth Bordley Gibson describes such an apprenticeship system over two generations—that of her childhood and that of her daughters. Indeed Eleanor Lewis's own apprenticeship was

quite formal. She was deliberately separated from her foster mother in order to spend a winter of domesticity with her married sisters and her remarried mother. It was clearly felt that her foster mother's (Martha Washington) home at the nation's capital was not an appropriate place to develop domestic talents (October 13, 1795, March 30, May 13, and [summer] 1796, March 18 and April 27, 1797, October 1827).

47. Education was not limited to the daughters of the well-to-do. Sarah Foulke Emlen, the daughter of an Ohio Valley frontier farmer, for instance, attended day school for several years during the early 1800s. Sarah Ripley Stearns, the daughter of a shopkeeper in Greenfield, Mass., attended a boarding school for but three months, yet the experience seemed very important to her. Mrs. S. S. Dalton, a Mormon woman from Utah, attended a series of poor country schools and greatly valued her opportunity, though she also expressed a great deal of guilt for the sacrifices her mother made to make her education possible (Sarah Foulke Emlen Journal, Sarah Ripley Stearns Diary, Mrs. S. S. Dalton, "Autobiography").

48. Maria Revere to her mother [Mrs. Paul Revere], June 13, 1801, Paul Revere Papers, Massachusetts Historical Society. In a letter to Elizabeth Bordley Gibson, March 28, 1847, Eleanor Parke Custis Lewis from Virginia discussed the anxiety her daughter felt when her granddaughters left home to go to boarding school. Eleuthera DuPont was very homesick when away at school in Philadelphia in the early 1820s (Eleuthera DuPont, Philadelphia, to Victorine Bauday, Wilmington, Del., April 7, 1821; Eleuthera DuPont to Sophie Madeleine DuPont, Wilmington, Del., February and April 3, 1821).

49. Elizabeth Bordley Gibson, a Philadelphia matron, played such a role for the daughters and nieces of her lifelong friend, Eleanor Parke Custis Lewis, a Virginia planter's wife (Eleanor Parke Custis Lewis to Elizabeth Bordley Gibson, January 29, 1833, March 19, 1826, and passim through the collection). The wife of Thomas Gurney Smith played a similar role for Sophie and Eleuthera DuPont (see, e.g., Eleuthera DuPont to Sophie Madeleine DuPont, May 22, 1825; Rest Cope to Philema P. Swayne [niece] West Town School, Chester County, Pa., April 8, 1826, Friends Historical Library, Swarthmore College). For a view of such a social pattern over three generations, see the letters and diaries of three generations of Manigault women in Philadelphia: Mrs. Gabrielle Manigault, her daughter, Harriet Manigault Wilcox, and granddaughter, Charlotte Wilcox McCall. Unfortunately the papers of the three women are not in one family collection (Mrs. Henry Middleton, Charleston, S.C., to Mrs. Gabrielle Manigault, n.d. [mid 1800s]; Harriet Manigault Diary, vol. 1, December 1, 1813, June 28, 1814; Charlotte Wilcox McCall Diary, vol. 1, 1842, passim. All in Historical Society of Philadelphia).

50. Frances Parke Lewis, Woodlawn, Va., to Elizabeth Bordley Gibson, Philadelphia, April 11, 1821, Lewis Correspondence; Eleuthera DuPont, Philadelphia, to Victorine DuPont Bauday, Brandywine, December 8, 1821, January 31, 1822; Eleuthera DuPont, Brandywine, to Margaretta Lammont [DuPont], Philadelphia, May 1823.

51. Sarah Ripley Stearns Diary, March 9 and 25, 1810; Peggy Emlen to Sally Logan, March and July 4, 1769; Harriet Manigault [Wilcox] Diary, vol. 1, December 1, 1813, June 28 and September 18, 1814, August 10, 1815; Charlotte Wilcox McCall Diary, 1842, passim; Fanny Canby to Mary Canby, May 27, 1801, March 17, 1804; Deborah Cope, West Town School, to Rest Cope, Philadelphia, July 9, 1828, Chester County Historical Society, West Chester, Pa.; Anne Zook, West Town School, to Mary Zook, Philadelphia, January 30, 1866, Chester County Historical Society, West Chester, Pa.; Mary Gilpin to Sophie Madeleine DuPont, February 25, 1829; Eleanor Parke Custis [Lewis] to Elizabeth Bordley [Gibson], April 27, July 2, and September 8, 1797, June 30, 1799, December 29, 1820; Frances Parke Lewis to Elizabeth Bordley Gibson, December 20, 1820.

52. Anne Jefferis Sheppard to Martha Jefferis, March 17, 1841.

53. Peggy Emlen to Sally Logan, March 1769, Mount Vernon, Va.; Eleanor Parke Custis [Lewis] to Elizabeth Bordley [Gibson], Philadelphia, April 27, 1797, June 30, 1799; Jeannie Field, New York, to Sarah Butler Wister, Germantown, July 3, 1861, January 16, 1863, Harriet Manigault Diary, August 3 and 11–13, 1814; Eunice Callender, Boston, to Sarah Ripley [Stearns], Greenfield, May 4, 1809. I found one exception to this inhibition of female hostility. This was the diary of Charlotte Wilcox McCall, Philadelphia (see, e.g., her March 23, 1842 entry).

54. Sophie M. DuPont and Eleuthera DuPont, Brandywine, to Victorine DuPont Bauday, Philadelphia, January 25, 1832.

55. Sarah Ripley [Stearns] Diary and Harriet Manigault Diary, passim.

56. Sophie Madeleine DuPont to Eleuthera DuPont, December 1827; Clementina Beach Smith to Sophie Madeleine DuPont, December 26, 1828; Sarah Faulke Emlen Diary, July 21, 1808, March 30, 1809; Annie Hethroe, Ellington, Wis., to Charlena Van Vleck [Anderson], Appleton, Wis., April 23, 1865; Frances Parke Lewis, Woodlawn, Va., to Elizabeth Bordley [Gibson], Philadelphia, December 20, 1820; Fanny Ferris to Debby Ferris, West Town School, Chester County, Pa., May 29, 1826. An excellent example of the warmth of women's comments about each other and the reserved nature of their references to men are seen in two entries in Sarah Ripley Stearns' diary. On January 8, 1811 she commented about a young woman friend: "The amiable Mrs. White of Princeton . . . one of the loveliest most interesting creatures I ever knew, young fair and blooming . . . beloved by everyone . . . formed to please & to charm. . . ." She referred to the man she ultimately married always as "my friend" or "a friend" (February 2 or April 23, 1810).

57. Jeannie Field, New York, to Sarah Butler Wister, Germantown, April 6, 1862.

58. Elizabeth Bordley Gibson, introductory statement to the Eleanor Parke Custis Lewis Letters [1850s], Historical Society of Pennsylvania.

59. Sarah Foulke [Emlen] Diary, March 30, 1809.

60. Harriet Manigault Diary, May 26, 1815.

61. Sarah Ripley [Stearns] Diary, May 17 and October 2, 1812; Eleanor Parke Custis Lewis to Elizabeth Bordley Gibson, April 23, 1826; Rebecca Ralston, Philadelphia, to Victorine DuPont [Bauday], Brandywine, September 27, 1813.

62. Anne Jefferis to Martha Jefferis, November 22 and 27, 1840, January 13 and March 17, 1841; Edith Jefferis, Greenwich, N.J., to Anne Jefferis, Philadelphia, January 31, February 6 and February 1841.

63. Edith Jefferis to Anne Jefferis, January 31, 1841.

64. Eleanor Parke Custis Lewis to Elizabeth Bordley, November 4, 1799. Eleanor and her daughter Parke experienced similar sorrow and anxiety when Parke married and moved to Cincinnati (Eleanor Parke Custis Lewis to Elizabeth Bordley Gibson, April 23, 1826). Helena DeKay visited Mary Hallock the month before her marriage; Mary Hallock was an attendant at the wedding; Helena again visited Molly about three weeks after her marriage; and then Molly went with Helena and spent a week with Helena and Richard in their new apartment (Mary Hallock [Foote] to Helena DeKay Gilder [Spring 1874] (no. 61), May 10, 1874 [May 1874], June 14, 1874 [Summer 1874]). See also Anne Biddle, Philadelphia, to Clement Biddle (brother), Wilmington, March 12 and May 27, 1827; Eunice Callender, Boston, to Sarah Ripley [Stearns], Greenfield, Mass., August 3, 1807, January 26, 1808; Victorine DuPont Bauday, Philadelphia, to Evelina DuPont [Biderman], Brandywine, November 25 and 26, December 1, 1813; Peggy Emlen to Sally Logan, n.d. [1769–70?]; Jeannie Field, New York, to Sarah Butler Wister, Germantown, July 3, 1861).

65. Mary Hallock to Helena DeKay Gilder [1876] (no. 81); n.d. (no. 83), March 3, 1884; Mary Ashew Diary, vol. 2, September–January, 1860; Louisa Van Vleck to Charlena Van Vleck Anderson, n.d. [1875]; Sophie DuPont to Henry DuPont, July 24, 1827; Benjamin Ferris to William Canby, February 13, 1805; Benjamin Ferris to Mary Canby Biddle, December 20, 1825; Anne Jefferis Sheppard to Martha Jefferis, September 15, 1884; Martha Jefferis to Anne Jefferis Sheppard, July 4, 1843, May 5, 1844, May 3, 1847, July 17, 1849; Jeannie McCall to Peter McCall, November 26, 1847, n.d. [late 1840s]. A graphic description of the ritual surrounding a first birth is found in Abigail Lyman's letter to her husband Erastus Lyman, October 18, 1810.

66. Fanny Ferris to Anne Biddle, November 19, 1811; Eleanor Parke Custis Lewis to Elizabeth Bordley Gibson, November 4, 1799, April 27, 1827; Martha Jefferis to Anne Jefferis Sheppard, January 31, 1843, April 4, 1844; Martha Jefferis to Phoebe Sharpless Middleton, June 4, 1846; Anne Jefferis Sheppard to Martha Jefferis, August 20, 1843, February 12, 1844; Maria Inskeep, New Orleans, to Mrs. Fanny G. Hampton, Bridgeton, N.J., September 22, 1848; Benjamin Ferris to Mary Canby, February 14, 1805; Fanny Ferris to Mary Canby [Biddle], December 2, 1816.

67. Eleanor Parke Custis Lewis to Elizabeth Bordley Gibson, October–November 1820, passim.

68. Emily Howland to Hannah, September 30, 1866; Emily Howland Diary, February 8, 11, and 27, 1880; Phoebe Brandford Diary, April 12 and 13, and August 4, 1833; Eunice Callender, Boston, to Sarah Ripley [Stearns], Greenwich, Mass., September 11, 1802, August 26, 1810; Mrs. H. Middleton, Charleston, to Mrs. Gabrielle Manigault, Philadelphia, n.d. [mid 1800s]; Mrs. H. C. Paul to Mrs. Jeannie McCall, Philadelphia, n.d. [1840s]; Sarah Butler Wister, Germantown, to Jeannie Field [Musgrove], New York, April 22, 1864; Jeannie Field [Musgrove] to Sarah Butler Wister, August 25, 1861, July 6, 1862; S. B. Raudolph to Elizabeth Bordley [Gibson], n.d. [1790s]. For an example of similar letters between men, see Henry Wright to Peter McCall, December 10, 1852; Charles McCall to Peter McCall, January 4, 1860, March 22, 1864; R. Mercer to Peter McCall, November 29, 1872.

69. Mary Black [Couper] to Sophie Madeleine DuPont, February 1827, [November 1, 1834], November 12, 1834, two letters [late November 1834]; Eliza Schlatter to Sophie Madeleine DuPont, November 2, 1834.

70. For a few of the references to death rituals in the Jefferis papers see: Martha Jefferis to Anne Jefferis Sheppard, September 28, 1843, August 21 and September 25, 1844, January 11, 1846, summer 1848, passim; Anne Jefferis Sheppard to Martha Jefferis, August 20, 1843; Anne Jefferis Sheppard to Rachel Jefferis, March 17, 1863, February 9, 1868. For other Quaker families, see Rachel Biddle to Anne Biddle, July 23, 1854; Sarah Foulke Farquhar [Emlen] Diary, April 30, 1811, February 14, 1812; Fanny Ferris to Mary Canby, August 31, 1810. This is not to argue that men and women did not mourn together. Yet in many families women aided and comforted women and men, men. The same-sex death ritual was one emotional option available to nineteenth-century Americans.

71. Sarah Foulke [Emlen] Diary, December 29, 1808.

72. Eunice Callender, Boston, to Sarah Ripley [Stearns], Greenfield, Mass., May 24, 1803.

73. Katherine Johnstone Brinley [Wharton] Journal, April 26, May 30, and May 29, 1856, Historical Society of Pennsylvania.

74. A series of roughly fourteen letters written by Peggy Emlen to Sally Logan (1768–71) has been preserved in the

Wells Morris Collection, Box 1, Historical Society of Pennsylvania (see esp. May 3 and July 4, 1769, January 8, 1768).

75. The Sarah Alden Ripley Collection, the Arthur M. Schlesinger, Sr., Library, Radcliffe College, contains a number of Sarah Alden Ripley's letters to Mary Emerson. Most of these are undated, but they extend over a number of years and contain letters written both before and after Sarah's marriage. The eulogistic biographical sketch appeared in Wister and Irwin (n. 12 above). It should be noted that Sarah Butler Wister was one of the editors who sensitively selected Sarah's letters.

76. See Sarah Alden Ripley to Mary Emerson, November 19, 1823. Sarah Alden Ripley routinely, and one must assume ritualistically, read Mary Emerson's letters to her infant daughter, Mary. Eleanor Parke Custis Lewis reported doing the same with Elizabeth Bordley Gibson's letters, passim. Eunice Callender, Boston, to Sarah Ripley [Stearns], October 19, 1808.

77. Mary Black Couper to Sophie M. DuPont, March 5, 1832. The Clementina Smith–Sophie DuPont correspondence of 1,678 letters is in the Sophie DuPont Correspondence. The quotation is from Eliza Schlatter, Mount Holly, N.J., to Sophie DuPont, Brandywine, August 24, 1834. I am indebted to Anthony Wallace for informing me about this collection.

78. Mary Grew, Providence, R.I., to Isabel Howland, Sherwood, N.Y., April 27, 1892, Howland Correspondence, Sophia Smith Collection, Smith College.

79. Helena Deutsch, *Psychology of Women* (New York: Grune & Stratton, 1944), vol. 1, chaps. 1–3; Clara Thompson, *On Women,* ed. Maurice Green (New York: New American Library, 1971).

Cancer in Two Voices

Living in an Unstable Body

Sandra Butler
Barbara Rosenblum

Sandra Butler (1938–   ) was born in Massachusetts and received both a B.A. (1976) and an M.A. (1978) from Goddard College, San Francisco, California. She is the author of the groundbreaking work Conspiracy of Silence: the Incest Trauma *(1985), based in part on her work as director of the Sexual Trauma Center in San Francisco. Barbara Rosenblum (1944–1988), sociologist, is the author of* Photographers at Work *(1978). Together, Butler and Rosenblum faced the diagnosis of Rosenblum's cancer. This selection, from* Cancer in Two Voices *(1988), is part of their account of the battle that was lost and the knowledge gained from that experience.*

Barbara

My doctor put it to me very clearly: I had to have chemotherapy, surgery, and radiation, in that order. I had to have chemotherapy for three months before surgery because the tumor in my breast was too large to remove surgically. It had grown too quickly and was now virtually inoperable. Chemotherapy would shrink the tumor, permitting surgery without skin graft. There was another reason for chemotherapy first: the cancer had spread to my lymph nodes, including a supraclavicular node near my collarbone. That was an indicator that metastatic processes were already occurring throughout my body. It was a serious, aggressive cancer and I would require the most aggressive treatment available.

Before the first treatment, my doctor prepared me for the various side effects I might experience: my hair would fall out; I'd have mouth sores; I'd vomit; and I'd lose my period. So after the first treatment, I vomited about thirty times in forty-eight hours, had tired muscles and aching joints, and was exhausted from spasmodic vomiting. And that was just the first week.

The second week, I had low blood counts, extreme fatigue, and breathlessness from the lack of sufficient hemoglobin—and consequently oxygen—in my blood. Almost exactly on the twenty-first day following the first set of three injections, my hair began to fall out. Not just on my head. I lost my pubic hair as well. But I still had my period.

After the second treatment, I had all the side effects again. And I still had my period. I thought for sure I'd beat this: I wouldn't go into menopause.

Following the third treatment, I had all the same side effects but, this time, I had a shorter period. Still I didn't attend to it much because, by this time, my nose and anus were bleeding from

"Living in an Unstable Body" and "Living in My Changing Body—And Hers" by Sandra Butler and Barbara Rosenblum. From *Cancer in Two Voices,* Sandra Butler and Barbara Rosenblum, pp. 129–143. Minneapolis: Spinsters Ink, 1991. Available from Spinsters Ink, PO Box 300170, Minneapolis, MN 55403. Reprinted by permission.

chemotherapy and I had grown alarmed. It seemed like I was bleeding from new places and losing the familiar bleeding from familiar places.

Three weeks later, after the fourth treatment, my period stopped. I began to get hot flashes, sometimes as frequently as one an hour. My ears glowed bright red, my face darkened, and sweat collected on the surface of my skin. I felt like a vibrating tuning fork for the next two minutes. Then my internal air conditioning took over, but didn't know when to stop. I got cold; I'd quickly cover myself to avoid the chill of perspiration. I could never find the right amount of clothing because my internal thermostat was completely out of balance. I no longer had any sense of what "room temperature"—that euphemism for a shareable external reality—was. I had no reliable information from my body about the temperature of the outside world. My only information, which I knew was distorted and unreliable, came from deep inside my body.

Then all the hair on my head fell out. Frantically I searched for a good wig before this occurred, but nothing fit my small head. I found a hairdresser who worked for the opera company and he used his connections to get a wig for me. The wig fit but felt foreign and made my scalp hot and itchy. I decided, like many other women who become bald from chemotherapy, not to disguise my loss.

Hats now hang off any available hook in my apartment. I have cotton hats, wool hats, berets, hats with brims, ski caps. Friends have knitted caps for me. And, even now, every time I go into the street, I'm still aware that people look at me. A vital aspect of my social identity has been taken away. In the last six months, I've lost my hair twice. And before that, three times. Practice does not make it easier.

Losing my hair has been much harder than losing my breast. No one can see underneath my clothes. But everyone can see my hair. I never thought my hair was beautiful: it was a simple, brown mop that I combed and washed. It grew out of my scalp. It was a part of me. It was mine.

But as I saw it cover my pillow, as I saw gobs of it come out on the comb, and masses of it clog the shower drain, I sank powerlessly into resignation.

I knew my hair would grow back when I went off the powerful chemotherapy to another combination of chemicals. It did, but thinly. And then I went off chemotherapy completely and all my hair came back, thick and spiky. But during that time when I didn't take chemotherapy, the cancer spread to my liver and then my lungs. I had to have chemotherapy, the strong stuff, again. Now it is clear that I will never have a full head of hair again. I now lose my hair once a month. I will always look like a Buddhist monk until the day I die.

My pudenda is as smooth as a fig. Even a peach with its infantile fuzziness is too hairy to describe it. Bald, completely smooth except for one Fu Manchu-like hair, straight and long, that resisted decimation. It is a dark, sturdy branch that extends from my skin. It is my mysterious hair, this proud survivor.

Losing my pubic hair, I felt naked and embarrassed, inadvertently returned to pre-pubescence. I was too exposed and didn't want to be touched.

My vagina was changing too. The vaginal tissue was thinning and becoming more sensitive to pressure and friction. It began to hurt when Sandy and I had sex. Then I noticed that my ordinary levels of dampness seemed to be changing: I was becoming less moist. Worst of all I stopped lubricating when I became sexually excited. That single, physiological fact made me realize that the agreements and understandings I had with my body were no longer in effect. If I no longer lubricated when I got sexually aroused, then how could I know I was feeling sexy?

Until I began chemotherapy, my relationship with my body was simple, direct, and uncomplicated. I had a friendly, warm, and pleasurable relationship with my body. Sex was always fun and untroubled. The cycles of my ability to become aroused were exquisitely dependent on my hormones. Ten days before my period, like clockwork, I would begin to feel sexual. This would continue for the next ten days and when my period came the urge would fizzle out. In other words, I had a physiologically based definition of my own sexual excitement: if my body produced some of the sensations that, through experience, had become my standard set of signals for sexual excitement, then I knew what to do with my behavior. But when chemotherapy induced an early and rapidly onsetting menopause and my hormone levels dropped dramatically, I was no longer on a monthly hormone cycle. I could no longer tell when I felt sexy or premenstrual. I got very confused about what I was feeling and when I was feeling it.

These questions of semantic meaning were urgently pre-empted by the necessity of finding practical solutions. Without body clues to signal me as to when and how I was feeling sexy, I consulted my head. Sandy and I re-created situations that had a proven record of creating the right mood in me. We purposefully incorporated the old, reliable environmental cues that had worked so well in the past: excellent food, candlelight, intimate conversation, music. I felt as close as could be, but nothing was happening in my body. We tried romantic meals at cozy restaurants. Nothing. Massage with scented oils. Nothing. Morning hiking in the country followed by steaming coffee and good pancakes. Nothing. Everything in my head told me this should be the right moment to make love but there were no signals coming from my body. Sandy touched me in all the loving, familiar ways. It was soothing and pleasant but not sexy. Nothing. The conclusion: for me sex does not work in the head.

We stopped making love. Instead we found new ways of being intimate. Sandy, who is a very light sleeper and consequently sleeps far away from me so as not to be disturbed by my twists and turns, began to hold me through the night. Our hands found new ways to console each other. I was reminded of how animals touch, lick, and chew each other. They pick at and groom each other, making the other feel secure and loved with their paws. I would touch Sandy's throat in a spot I knew contained all her tears: she would sob. And right in the midst of chemotherapy infusions, when the chemicals were flowing into my veins from huge syringes, Sandy helped me relax by touching my back and neck lightly.

I confess I was still nervous about not making love. Without telling Sandy I still tried to make myself feel sexy. I believed that if I tried hard enough, I could discover a more subtle sexual language in my body. I thought maybe I could pick up these signals when alone. So when Sandy was busy or out of the house, I tried to get in the mood to masturbate. Nothing. But our new intimacy helped ease the passage. I accepted this nonsexual period as part of my life. Ultimately the rock bottom question remains: when facing one's own death, what happens to one's sexuality? I suppose for some women sexual feelings become intensified. They become hungry for life, hungry for life through sex. Erotic energy keeps them alive. I suspect Sandy would have liked it better if I experienced the life force as erotic energy, as libido. But I don't. My life energy comes in another form, in the passion to learn everything, to feel everything, to live every moment with presence and intensity. To study new things. To master new areas of knowledge. To write—alone and with Sandy. Together we have developed a new form that can accommodate our individual and unique voices into a dialogue. We write about things that are important to us. We make love at the typewriter, not in the bedroom.

As I write now, I see that I was learning a new language of the body but it was the language of symptoms, not of sexuality. I became sensitive to when my body was retaining water. I could glance at my various parts, my legs, arms, stomach, and chest and notice a puffiness that had not been there the day before. I learned that when I became puffy, my metabolism was off and that meant my liver wasn't functioning properly. I calculated the ebbs and flows of my energy because my daily activities, as simple as taking a walk, depended on an exact calibration of that energy. I observed how it wavered, how much time I had between the waves, how it disappeared all at once, without forewarning. I discovered how close I could come to throwing up without actually having to do it. I studied the gradations of nausea and their subdivisions, and how to assess when nausea would pass or when I had to take an anti-nausea pill. I learned how to move quickly to the curb while walking the dog, emptying the contents of my stomach there, not on the sidewalk, and how to look reasonably dignified afterward. I learned how to run fast while compressing my anal sphincter muscles so that I wouldn't shit in my pants from the diarrhea that chemo induced. Sometimes I didn't make it.

In the last two and a half years, I peed in my pants three times. Chemotherapy irritates the bladder. That's why doctors tell you to drink half a gallon of liquid whenever you get chemotherapy. The chemicals are so strong that they can even cause cancer of the bladder. On the few occasions I couldn't control my urine, I noticed that I didn't get the usual signal that told me it was time to think about going to the bathroom. It didn't begin as a small pressure or urge, as it normally does, and then build up. No, rather it came on with a burst of urgency, as if I'd been holding it for hours. I had to learn this new language too.

The form of my body changed too. I lost a breast. When I had the mastectomy, I was too worried about my life to worry about my breast. I hoped that the doctors would "get" all the cancer in my breast and that postoperative radiation would control any errant cells that had not been excised by surgery. Losing a breast did alter my body image, as well as my body, but I never felt a diminishment of my femininity. My breasts were never the center of my womanness.

From the responses of other women in my support group and also from my cancer counselor, I knew that losing a breast was very hard for some women. In my cancer support group, most women were concerned about reconstructive surgery. They swapped names of good plastic surgeons. They talked about aesthetic criteria for evaluating a good job, such as the surgeon's ability to make breasts match in color, tone, weight, density, shape, and identicality of nipple placement with appropriate tones of darkness. To me, they expressed a fetishistic quality in their talk; they were desperate and afraid.

One woman in the support group told the story of someone whose husband left her from the time of the mastectomy until she got her reconstructed breast. She explained matter-of-factly that he couldn't bear the sight of his wife. Then there's the letter I got from a distant acquaintance who told me that she, too, had had breast cancer. She wrote that it wasn't so dangerous now that they could control it with early detection. She also wrote that, since her surgery a few years before, she, herself, never got undressed in front of her husband. When they made love, she always wore her bra with the prosthesis tucked inside.

I couldn't even imagine how these women might feel about their partners. I would feel enraged. I cannot count the number of stories I've heard about couples, both lesbian and straight, breaking up after a mastectomy. Illness places enormous strains on couples and many separate afterwards. Each person may feel guilt and abandonment simultaneously.

I'm very lucky. Sandy has been exceptionally steadfast and easy about the changes in my body. She did not compel me to pay attention to her needs, her anxieties, her worries. She never made me feel inadequate or freakish. Her face never revealed shock or terror. She was easy with my scar, touching it delicately. During vomiting bouts she simply got the bucket, never cringing or complaining. She was always softly, gently there, through everything.

Signals about hunger also got confused when I began chemotherapy. Up until that time, food was one of the great pleasures of my life. Over the years I'd become very sophisticated about food and very knowledgeable about its preparation. Eating was a supremely aesthetic experience for me. I always tried to eat and cook well for myself. Unlike many people who don't cook for themselves when they are alone, I didn't need the company of another person to stimulate me to cook: my own pleasure was sufficient. I would cook sweetbreads in a cream sauce or chicken with lemon and tarragon. Tastes would explode on my tongue, clear and definite tastes.

So when chemotherapy caused painful sores in my mouth and the only thing I could consume was a blenderful of fruit and yogurt, I became despondent. It hurt even to put solid food in my mouth. My appetite and desire for particular flavors and sensations was annihilated. I could no longer tell when I was hungry or when I wanted a specific texture or flavor. All I wanted to do was to get the food down and keep it down and to make sure it didn't hurt as I ate. I treated myself like a hospital patient, making an eating schedule and sticking to it, making sure I had enough protein, liquid, and caloric content.

Now there is never a time in my treatment cycle when my mouth isn't sore or sensitive. I can't have spices—I can't eat hot Chinese food or savor my favorite cuisine, Indian food. My diet resembles that of an ulcer patient: bland and creamy. My relationship to food has been permanently altered and I grieve this loss every day.

In the last two years, my clothes have increased by three sizes. My legs filled with fluid and were puffy and large. My arms and shoulders, usually slender, looked bulky and strong. I remember when Sandy and I saw a beautiful pair of green loafers in a shop window in Amsterdam. They were the first expensive, European shoes I ever owned, but I can no longer wear them. My feet became swollen with fat and fluids. I consulted Shizuko Yamamoto, a well-known macrobiotic practitioner in New York. She slapped my thighs and said in a thick accent, "Water jugs, your legs are like water jugs."

I watched my body stretch to accommodate all the fluid that was collecting in my tissues. I could not believe how rapidly my body shape was changing. I needed new clothes immediately, but going shopping was a horrendous experience. Sandy was kind and patient. She had reached her full height of six feet by the age of thirteen and shopping for clothes that didn't fit was a familiar experience. Turning what was humiliating into an adventure was an old defense for her and now served us both well. I'd be crying from frustration in the fitting room and Sandy would quietly leave and cheerfully return with a few items in the next size.

One day I stopped going to department stores. It was too hard. I decided to go to a shop for larger women. While walking to it, I passed a maternity shop and thought that these clothes might fit me. They did.

The surface of my skin changed too. My veins became more prominent because the fluid in my tissues pressed them against my skin. Even the tiniest capillaries started bursting and my skin became marbled with designs. On my inner thighs, where the pressure was greatest, the capillaries looked like calligraphy. My body oils disappeared and my skin became parched and crusty. Flakes of skin fell from my face. My fingernails first turned black from chemotherapy, then they became ridged with white bands. My fingernails became like alum, soft and whitish, and they ripped rather than broke.

Two and a half years since the first diagnosis and I am still getting chemotherapy six days a month. For two days I'm in the hospital, where I get Adriamycin, and for four days I'm attached to an ambulatory pump filled with Velban, another type of chemotherapy. It hangs from my waist on a velcro belt, buttressed by a safety pin. It looks like a Walkman. Tubes extend from its square form into a one-inch needle that is inserted into my chest. It is attached to a Port-A-Cath, a plastic container that is surgically placed in my chest, the purpose of which is to receive chemotherapy. My veins are too fragile and unstable. They've stabbed me too many times and missed. They have had too many veins burst open with gushing blood. The chemo has burned my veins too many times, making them fibrotic and painfully sensitive.

When I wear the portable pump, I am bombarded by images: of being attached to a bomb, having an artificial limb, having additional plumbing, like there's a giant opening in me, like it's a bionic extension. It's like having shrapnel inside you, like an artificial hip or a metal plate instead of your skull.

My hand rests on the pump: I sense its vibrations and hear it churning along. With the aid of Valium and sleeping pills, I sleep with it tied to my waist. It runs on batteries. It is saving my life. Other people wear pumps too: diabetics get insulin, older people get liquid nutrition, people with AIDS get antibiotics, and people with intractable pain get a continuous infusion of painkilling drugs like morphine. I have cancer and I get chemotherapy. I hate the pump.

Yesterday I called a woman who is on the pump all the time, twenty-four hours a day, 365 days a year, getting chemotherapy for liver cancer. She was helpful and gave me words of encouragement. Maybe I can learn from her.

What is it like to live in a body that keeps on changing? It's frightening, terrifying, and confusing. It generates a feeling of helplessness. It produces a slavish attention to the body. It creates an unnatural hypervigilance toward any and all sensations that occur within the landscape of the body. One becomes a prisoner to any perceptible change in the body, any cough, any difference in sensation. One loses one's sense of stability and predictability, as well as one's sense of control over the body. It forces you to give up the idea that you can will the body to behave in ways you would like. Predictability ends. One grieves over its loss, and that further complicates the process of adjustment to an unstable body. Time becomes shortened and is marked by the space between symptoms.

In our culture it is very common to rely on the body as the ultimate arbiter of truth. We consult our bodies like an oracle. While every emotion may not be consciously available to be experienced, the body knows the truth. We cannot conceal the truth from the body.

We turn to the body to decipher its coded language, to apprehend its grammar and syntax. By noticing the body's responses to situations, we have an idea about how we "really feel about things." For example, if you get knots in your stomach every time a certain person walks into the room, you have an important body clue to investigate. Or if your eyes tear up during a yawn, you might suspect that you may be experiencing some deep and underlying sadness that has not yet come to the surface or, as Wordsworth put it, a thought too deep for tears.

We trust that the body will tell us the truth about emotions that are hidden from consciousness. We trust that the body knows things before the mind does. Our job is to mind the body, to mine the body, to interpret its language.

Interpretations of bodily signals are premised on the uninterrupted stability and continuity of the body. We experience the continuity of the body as taken for granted. Only when there are interruptions does the body become problematic. We usually associate the same continuous sensations with the same stimulations. When the body, like my body, is no longer consistent over time, when it gives different signals every month, when something that meant one thing in April may have a different meaning in May, then it's hard to rely on the stability—and therefore the truth—of the body. And because of that, it's hard to interpret and hard to predict.

I was thrown into a crisis of meaning. I could no longer assess and evaluate what sensations meant. I could no longer measure the intensity of sensations. I was no longer fluent in the language of my body, its signs and symbols, and I felt lost.

Living in the world has become an existential problem for me. How to interpret my very existence is problematic. Am I living because I am alive? Am I dying because I'd be dead in three months without chemotherapy? Am I living and dying? Are all of us living and dying, except that I'm doing it faster?

And all of this confusion is predicated on time because the human mind can experience the simultaneity of the past and the present and can project into the future. The human mind has memory. Time past can color the present and the future. If there were only present time, I could joyfully embrace my body and delight in whatever it brings, whatever form it takes, whatever is given to me. If there were only the past, I would remember swimming naked six months after my surgery in the Pacific waters off the coast of Australia's Great Barrier Reef, when my body, without breast, without much hair, looked whole, healthy, and perfect.

If there were only time past. I remember the time Sandy and I went away with friends of ours who were fighting all weekend. We were at a loss. What could we do to make them stop? Distancing myself from their anger, I put on some old Motown music and started dancing. I had just come out of the hot tub and there I was, naked as a jaybird, having a wonderful time, laughing, singing, and dancing unselfconsciously to rock and roll. There I was, with one breast flopping, and one big body dancing. Our friends, stunned at what they called "the life force," stopped fighting and started dancing.

But there is not just the past and not just the present. There is the future. And I can imagine worse scenarios with just as much vividness as I can remember the past. I can envision more chemotherapy, more tubes, more degeneration of body function, more loss of energy and loss of control, more desperation. There may be more physical pain, more ambiguous sensations arising from a body I can no longer interpret, more confusion.

When you have cancer, the body no longer contains the old truths about the world. Instead you must learn a new language, a new vocabulary, and over time, as symptoms converge and conflate, you learn the deeper structure of its grammar. The patient's task is to learn the new language, hoping that the body will remain stable enough. You can no longer rely on the previous systems of interpreting the body you have used before. When you have cancer, the ground is pulled out from under you. Existence is problematic and anxious. You must look for new, stable ground.

When you have cancer, you have a new body each day, a body that may or may not have a relationship to the body you had the day before. When you have cancer, you are bombarded by sensations from within that are not anchored in meaning. They float in a world without words, without meanings. You don't know from moment to moment whether to call a particular sensation a "symptom" or a "side effect" or a "sign." It produces extreme anxiety to be unable to distinguish those sensations that are caused by the disease and those that are caused by the treatment. Words and their referents are uncoupled, uncongealed, no longer connected. You live in a mental world where all the information you have is locked into the present moment. The past, what the doctors may call "your medical history," is useless and irrelevant for your construction of meanings. Sensations come and go; they disappear for a while and they return; they change. They may add up to something; they may not. They may have meaning; they may not. That pain in my stomach may mean something new or it may not. I must wait until something else happens, until I have an accretion of evidence, until a pattern emerges, if I'm lucky enough to have a pattern. Interpretation of a sensation always depends on having at least two bodily events close enough in time to make meaning of seemingly random events. And most of the time, I live in a world of random body events. I'm hostage to the capriciousness of my body, a body that sabotages my sense of a continuous and taken-for-granted reality.

Sometimes I can hardly use human language to tell how I feel. When I am frightened or feel alone and can't sleep, I need to take sleeping pills because I lie there thinking about dying. I explain to Sandy, "If I were a dog, I'd be shaking and trembling." Animals don't use words; their bodies speak for them. While I'm not mute, I am often frustrated by the way the limits of language circumscribe my ability to communicate events in my body. But I am not an animal. I am a human being, an articulate one at that, who is challenged to find words to apply to sensations I've never had before, challenged to find meaning and stability despite a changing body. I'm caught in a relentless metamorphosis. You cannot imagine how stable and firm and fixed your body looks to me. You cannot imagine that I can actually feel my molecules moving around, wondering what miraculous shape they will prefer next time.

Cancer in Two Voices

Living in My Changing Body – And Hers

Sandra Butler
Barbara Rosenblum

Sandra Butler (1938–) was born in Massachusetts and received both a B.A. (1976) and an M.A. (1978) from Goddard College, San Francisco, California. She is the author of the groundbreaking work Conspiracy of Silence: The Incest Trauma *(1985), based in part on her work as director of the Sexual Trauma Center in San Francisco. Barbara Rosenblum (1944–1988), sociologist, is the author of* Photographers at Work *(1978). Together, Butler and Rosenblum faced the diagnosis of Rosenblum's cancer. This selection, from* Cancer in Two Voices *(1988), is part of their account of the battle that was lost and the knowledge gained from that experience.*

"Living in an Unstable Body" and "Living in My Changing Body—And Hers" by Sandra Butler and Barbara Rosenblum. From *Cancer in Two Voices,* Sandra Butler and Barbara Rosenblum, pp. 129–143. Minneapolis: Spinsters Ink, 1991. Available from Spinsters Ink, PO Box 300170, Minneapolis, MN 55403. Reprinted by permission.

Sandy

I BEGIN WRITING THIS SITTING AT THE KITCHEN table drinking tea and listening to the eager clacking of Barbara's typing. She has just begun to write a piece about her changing relationship to her body and has announced quite firmly that she wants to write it alone. I chafe, wishing we could work together, wondering what she will write about our sex life, our changing intimacies. Wanting to be included.

Last week I spoke at the Women's Building about sexuality in the relationship of a couple dealing with life-threatening illness. My talk was very well received and many of the women seemed relieved to hear me describe the physical or emotional isolation they were experiencing. I was both moved by and grateful for the response and it deepened my conviction that the writing Barbara and I are doing is vital in the lives of others who are living through many of the same realities.

I spoke about our sex life: how it used to be, how it is now, how we have accommodated to the physical changes in Barbara's body, the emotional changes in her psyche, and the relational changes in our daily lives. I didn't talk like that though.

I talked in a daily language. One of need and dependency. Mostly mine. Of an inwardness and sometimes excruciating thoughtfulness. Mostly hers. I talked about the way I was socialized to be an appropriate heterosexual and had lived for nearly thirty-five years in response to the sexual needs of others, and how hard I had struggled against that early conditioning when I came out as a lesbian. I spoke of how easily I find myself slipping back into those old roles again. How I find myself feeling Barbara's needs are the real needs and that mine are not. That her feelings are the ones that matter, and mine don't. That the frequency, the form, the intensity of the sexual dimension of our lives will—no—should be determined by her. Not by me and rarely by us. Just like it was before when I was in my twenties and thirties. Actually I know it isn't like before, but I do admit to an uneasy similarity sometimes.

Now I sit wishing she would call to me from her office down the hall and ask me what I would add to her piece. What is it like for me, as her partner? How does it feel to live with a woman who now has advanced cancer spreading through her body?

If she did ask, I would begin by writing about her breast. The one they excised soon after her diagnosis. The surgeon and the oncologist, both women, remarked after the surgery was over that we seemed to be "handling" the experience so well. I think what they meant was that we were not acting like some heterosexual couples. Barbara expressed no shame about "disfigurement," no embarrassment about being less of a woman, or worry that desire would never return. Unlike many husbands I did not awkwardly avert my glance from her wound but, instead, kissed her scar, her chest and her body after the surgery with the same love, passion, tenderness that I had before. She was still Barbara. This was still the body of the woman I had loved all those years. It was only that the body had assumed a different shape. Quieter now. More mood swings. But she was still Barbara inside herself.

Then I would write about the loss of her pubic hair and how unusual it was for me to see her vulva exposed in that way. I had been shaved twice in preparation for the birth of my two daughters nearly thirty years ago but had never seen another adult woman without hair. I found myself intrigued at the odd juxtaposition of a girlish pudenda and a woman's body. I wanted to touch and stroke it but she was uncomfortable and wouldn't allow me to. The hair on her head was gone, too, which caused her more public shyness and uncertainty. But the loss of pubic hair made her feel like a child, utterly vulnerable and exposed. It was not possible for her to open further—to open beyond the vulnerability of her body being so uncovered, so unprotected.

Then I would write about her edema. How her body became swollen with fluids that were not being processed properly by her liver. Barbara gained twenty-five pounds in barely a month. She described her body as being unfamiliar and alien: bloated, hairless, and always with some level of discomfort, weakness, achiness, or nausea—the endless variety of symptoms chemotherapy produces in the body.

At first I was unthinkingly delighted as her hips spread and grew wider. I reassured her that her hips (indeed hips in general) were my favorite part of a woman's body. Bigger hips meant, to me at least, better hips. I found her body very exciting and was filled with renewed desire. She, however, felt trapped and alienated in this stranger's body and was unable or unwilling to respond.

She has just come down the hall carrying the pages she has written. As I read them my eyes fill with tears of recognition. I read how she experiences us making love at the typewriter. How each morning we would walk laboriously to my office, resting every few blocks, and sit beside each other, one of us at the keyboard, the other sitting closely alongside. We typed, interrupted, criticized, added, paced, drank coffee, laughed, then grew thoughtful, intense, or joyous with relief when just the right word or image emerged. It was a making of love. An honoring of our bond. Lovemaking. The work we did had the focus, the passion, the sense of completion our lovemaking once had. I often felt similarly spent when a work session ended. But so loved. So known. So deeply connected to this woman.

In rereading these thoughts about my response to Barbara's changing body, I notice that I am present only in response, in relationship to Barbara. As her body changes, as her needs, strength, and focus shift—I respond. I notice now, for the first time, that, slowly, imperceptibly, gradually, Barbara's body has become the body in our lives. I have ceased to have a body and, instead, have Barbara's. Her stamina, her vitality, her appetites delineate our day. When we awoke, if she felt strong enough for a long walk, we would walk. If she felt sluggish or weak, the morning would be spent in a more sedentary way—reading, writing, visiting with friends. When her appetite was good and there were none of the monthly mouth sores making anything but creamy shakes impossible, we would go to eat spicy, ethnic food. When she was unable to, or had lost the appetite for complex flavors, we ate very little and simply, at home.

I, too, have put on a lot of weight but never noticed. I never felt full, or overly full, or stuffed, or bloated, or sated. I cannot remember thinking about if I was hungry, what I wanted to eat, or when I had had enough. We ate. We filled our body with what we liked when we were hungry.

I exercised in relation to Barbara's body. I ate in relation to Barbara's appetite. I had somehow neglected to make a parallel assessment of my own energy, my own desires, my own need for fresh air and exercise. Just as I had been "responsive to her sexual needs," I had become an extension of her physical capacities. Mornings when I had awakened and done yogic stretches had stopped, and I didn't remember why. The feeling of being strong and vital in my body has evaporated as well. I can't remember the last time I felt powerful, the last time my skin tingled with the rush of blood that comes from vigorous exercise.

In much the same way her sexuality has become "our" sexuality—now her body has become "our" body. If she couldn't have a strong, powerful, healthy body—then I simply wouldn't have one either. At least insofar as I could encourage that sameness. It felt impossible to leave Barbara, feeling weak or depleted, reading quietly on the sofa, while I went out to exercise or swim. It felt impossible to enjoy and delight in my body—an act of disloyalty. I can no longer take my body for granted and assume that it will be reliable, strong, and healthy since Barbara can no longer do that, feel that, have that possibility. Even the thought fills me with guilt.

The guilt of survival. The guilt of comparison. The guilt of randomness—being selected out as the one of us who will outlast the other. The one of us who will live beyond the "us" that has been the foundation of my life. The guilt of the relief that it is not me. But what is the same for both of us is that the illusion of endless time no longer exists. There is not going to be enough time for her. And there may not be for me. I no longer imagine my life as an old woman but hope I live long enough to become an old woman. No certainty remains.

I remember how shaken and guilty I felt when she was misdiagnosed. The guilt of having been impatient with what I felt was her hypochondriacal pattern of going to the doctor over "every little thing," a pattern all the women in my family have followed. It was only when her breast started to swell and the lump was clearly palpable that I began to take it as seriously as I should have. Going with her to the Kaiser clinic, I saw the passivity of the patients, the waiting, the fear of taking too much time, of asking too many questions, of being a "nuisance." I felt guilty that I hadn't encouraged her to have her own doctor. A private doctor. That I had ignored her complaints until they were too advanced to contain.

I suppose it is always necessary to rewrite history—to replay a series of "what if," "if only," "how could I have not seen" questions that are the inevitable outgrowth of illness and accidents. I'm no different in this effort to impose retrospective meaning and responsibility. The doctors were responsible. Not me. But I hadn't paid enough attention. I hadn't listened clearly enough to her words. Somehow it was my fault that this was happening to her body. And because it was my fault, I began to deny my own body and my pleasure in it as well.

I have guilty feelings about my thick, heavy, rapidly growing hair. During our ceremony of commitment, now nearly seven months ago, Barbara expressed dismay over her patchy, balding, very short, thin hair.

"It's not as unattractive as you imagine," I assured her.

"Oh?" she responded tartly. "If it's so attractive, why haven't you cut your hair to look like mine?" Hours later I remembered her words, and even though I knew they were said in irritation and frustration, I decided to have my hair cut as a gesture of love and support. When I look back over the photograph album of our ceremony, we both have near crewcuts, decorated with festive earrings and glowing faces.

But now she is bald again and has been for many months, and my hair is growing out—a luxuriant and lovely shade of salt and pepper. I am aware of closing the bathroom door when I brush it and being very careful to take all the hair out of the drain in the shower when I shampoo.

But there is also the gratitude that balances my loss. Gratitude that I can call home and hear her voice rise with eagerness at the sound of my voice. That her sculpted, hairless skull contains her piercing eyes without brows, without lashes. Her unadorned face smiles at the phone when she hears my voice. She is still there inside her changing body—the body so different from the body I first touched and held. One breast, still high and firm. I have two breasts, somewhat fallen and considerably less firm. My body, too, has changed, grown older, and softened. We have become clearer to each other and to ourselves though, our bodies less opaque. We can see through, into each other. We are living in changed and changing bodies—living with full hearts and open minds and great love.

The Four-Year Itch

Helen E. Fisher

Helen E. Fisher (1945–   ) was born in New York City, graduated from New York University, and received her Ph.D. in anthropology from the University of Colorado in 1975. Intellectually, she says, she has grown out of two errors: the belief that the human infant is a blank slate onto which culture writes its dictates, and the belief that human beings are entirely different from the animal world. She states that current research demonstrates that "many of our sexual emotions and behavior patterns are not learned but the product of predispositions inherited by natural selection through evolution. Most predominant of these is the human tendency to bond." In the following selection, Fisher examines the bond of marriage in different cultures and times.

SAMUEL JOHNSON DEFINED REMARRIAGE AS THE triumph of hope over experience. Anthropologists call this human habit "serial monogamy." Americans joke about the "seven-year itch." Call it what you will, the human penchant for divorce and remarriage is worldwide.

Among the !Kung Bushmen of southern Africa's Kalahari Desert, for example, men and women often marry more than once. Although the !Kung are rapidly adopting Western values and twentieth-century technology, divorce is not a new development. The traditional !Kung, who were studied by anthropologists, lived in semipermanent groups. During the rainy season, ten to thirty individuals—including couples, their children, and other kin—interacted daily. Friends and relatives traveled between communities, connecting a fluid network of several hundred people. Every two or three days some of the women of a band went collecting. They returned from their expeditions with roots, melons, nuts, berries, honey, and occasionally, small mammals, insects and birds' eggs. !Kung men went hunting about three days a week. Often they came home with meat: sometimes just a hare; sometimes an antelope large enough to be divided among all community members.

Sixty to 80 percent of the daily staples were provided by women; women shared the rights to waterholes in the desert, too. During their reproductive years, women held high status, and older women had an important say in community affairs. When a woman found herself in a desperate marriage, she often assembled her few belongings and departed for another camp nearby.

Sometimes !Kung couples argued for months before splitting up. Neighbors also got involved. But eventually, many unhappy marriages ended; either the man or the woman walked out. Perhaps they could do so because both partners were relatively self-sufficient. Of the 331 marriages reported by !Kung women to sociologist Nancy Howell, 134 ended in divorce. Some men and women had more than four consecutive spouses.

Divorce is also common in other societies

With permission from *Natural History*, October 1987.

where men and women are relatively economically independent. Among the Yoruba of West Africa, where women traditionally control the complex marketing system, as much as 46 percent of all marriages end in divorce. In highland Nepal, the Tamang give little girls a chicken or other livestock, corn, or a small amount of money and encourage them to increase this wealth. By their late teens, Tamang women often own substantial movable property and the right to distribute it. When she first marries, a young woman rarely transfers all of her livestock or other wealth to her husband's farmland. If the marriage goes poorly, she just walks home. The divorce rate among the Tamang is also high.

The Hadza live in the rocky grasslands of Tanzania. During the dry season, men hunt impala, buffalo, and other large game, but meat is a luxury. Both men and women collect vegetable foods, which are never in short supply. Among the Hadza, marriage is a casual affair; divorce occurs when a couple cease to live together for more than a few days. Anthropologist Ernestine Friedl, reporting on research done in the 1960s, says that divorce rates are "roughly five times as high as in the United States."

Divorce is less common where women and men are economically dependent on one another—most notably in societies that use the plow for agriculture. In such societies, spouses need each other to make ends meet. Examples are India and China and, in the past, preindustrial Europe and America. For example, in 1700 a woman living on a small farm in Massachusetts depended on her husband to move the rocks, fell the trees, and plow the land. He depended on her to sow, weed, pick, prepare, and store the vegetables. Together they worked the farm. More important, whoever elected to leave the marriage left empty-handed; neither spouse could dig up half the land and relocate. Farming women and men were tied to the land, to one another, and to a network of stationary kin. Under these ecological circumstances, divorce was not a practical alternative, and cultural mores made marital separation very difficult.

The Industrial Revolution changed this relationship between the sexes. When factories began to appear beyond the barns of agricultural America, men and women began to leave home for the workplace, bringing back money—movable, divisible property. During much of the 1800s, middle-class women still ran the home. But in the early decades of the twentieth century, American women began to join the labor force in greater numbers. With time, the steady influx of women into the job market began to give them economic autonomy; not coincidentally, the American divorce rate began a slow but steady rise. For an unhappy man will leave a wife who brings home an income long before he will desert a woman he depends on to weed his garden. And a woman with a salary may be less tolerant of marital despair than one dependent on her spouse to provide the evening meal. Since 1960, the number of women in the job market has doubled. The American annual divorce rate has doubled too. Many demographers identify women's employment as a prime factor in this rising frequency of divorce.

The relationship between rising divorce rates and female–male economic autonomy has been seen before in Western culture. Shortly after the Romans conquered Carthage in the third century B.C., an urban upper class emerged. Wealthy Roman patricians were apparently no longer willing to let massive dowries pass into the hands of potentially errant sons-in-law, as was customary under the traditional religious marriage forms. Instead, they married off their daughters in civil unions, and the women themselves were able to control their fortunes. As a class of economically self-sufficient women emerged in ancient Rome, the divorce rate soared.

Since 1947, census takers in places as culturally dissimilar as South Africa, Morocco, Japan, the Soviet Union, Greece, El Salvador, and the United States have periodically asked about divorce. Among their survey questions are: How many years were you married at the time of your divorce? How old were you when you divorced? How many children did you have when you divorced? These data, compiled every decade by the Statistical Office of the United Nations, present a surprisingly consistent global picture.

Most striking, in a sample of fifty-eight populations where data are complete, there are three divorce peaks—among couples married for four years, among people between the ages of 25 and 29, and among couples with no children or one dependent child. Although the data are not sufficient to show the relationship between these three peaks, the relatively high frequency of divorce after about four years of marriage probably accounts in large part for the divorce peak among couples with one or no children. The risk of divorce for men and women in their late twenties is always high, however, regardless of where the divorce peak falls with respect to numbers of years married.

The three-peak pattern appears unrelated to high or low divorce rates. Finland is a typical example. In the 1950s, the divorce rate was relatively low; it has risen steadily since. But the "profile" of divorce has remained almost the same. In 1950, divorces peaked among couples married four years and among women aged 25 to 29 and men aged 35 to 39. Seventy-one percent of divorces involved couples with one dependent child. In 1966, divorce peaked after the third year of marriage, then shifted back to the four-year peak in 1974 and 1981; for these years, the peak for men and women was in the 25 to 29 age group. The overall pattern remained remarkably similar in all four decades, despite a doubling of divorces. With some variation, this pattern is seen around the world. Across the United Nations sample, an average of 48 percent of the divorces occur within seven years of marriage; they cluster around the four-year peak. So divorce commonly occurs early in marriage, among couples at the height of their reproductive and parenting years.

A comparable statistical breakdown of divorce practices is not available for most so-called primitive cultures. But anthropologist Napoleon Chagnon recently began studying the "decay rate" of the nuclear family in thirteen Yanomamö villages along the upper Orinoco River in Venezuela. He reported that among these hunters and gardeners, nearly all children younger than five lived with their natural mother; the majority had their biological father living with them too. But the cohabitation of biological parents declined sharply among children older than five.

This divorce pattern among the Yanomamö is consistent with the United Nations data on fifty-eight industrial and agricultural peoples. And it is difficult to attribute this pattern to the forces of society. These peoples vary widely in religion, social structure, economy, political views, and per capita income. Why are their divorce profiles similar?

There is a possibility that the common pattern is a result of brain physiology. Psychiatrists divide the love between a man and woman into two fundamental stages: the "attraction phase" and the "attachment phase." During the attraction phase, infatuation engulfs lovers with giddiness, euphoria, optimism, and energy. Michael Liebowitz, a psychiatrist at the New York State Psychiatric Institute, thinks these feelings may be caused by increased activity in the brain of phenylethylamine or other natural brain stimulants. John Money, a sexologist from Johns Hopkins University, suggests that among lovers who see each other regularly, this stage of intense emotion can last only about two or three years—long enough, however, to foster pregnancy.

Liebowitz theorizes that the brain's tolerance for these natural aphrodisiacs grows, eventually dulling the sensation of intense infatuation. Now stage two, the attachment stage, sets in. This is the stage of peaceful, secure, comfortable love that so many couples report. Liebowitz suspects that the attachment stage is associated with a different set of brain chemicals, the endorphins—the opiates of the mind: "Biologically, it appears that we have evolved two distinct chemical systems for romance; one basically serves to bring people together and the other to keep them together." He attributes these systems to our evolutionary heritage:

> *For primitive man two aspects of relating to the opposite sex were important for survival as a species. The first was to have males and females become attracted to each other for long enough to have sex and reproduce. The second was for the males to become strongly attached to the females so that they stayed around while the females were raising their young and helped to gather food, find shelter, and teach the kids certain skills.*

But Liebowitz cautions that even with this brain circuitry, "if you want a situation where you and your long-term partner can still get very excited about each other—you have to work on it. In some ways you are bucking a biological tide."

Nature seems quite determined that we fall in love; she has dedicated less evolutionary energy to maintaining that state. Anthropologists have, in fact, argued about the essence of the human pair bond for decades. Some think it does not exist. They will tell you that less than one-fifth of human cultures practice monogamy, while more than four-fifths permit men to have several wives simultaneously. But in the vast majority of these polygynous cultures, only about 10 percent of men actually have more than a single wife at one time; moreover, women in polygynous households marry only one man at a time. So monogamy—a mating and marriage system in which an individual forms a social, economic, and sexual union with a single member of the opposite sex at one time—is pretty standard for the human species.

This is not to say that spouses are necessarily faithful to each other; monogamy does not imply fidelity. In the late 1940s and early 1950s, Alfred Kinsey and his colleagues estimated that, based on their sample, about one-third of all American married men and about one-fourth of American married women were sexually unfaithful to their spouses. Since then these statistics have gone up. And American patterns of adultery are not unusual; extramarital affairs are reported in many cultures, even where participants are punished with death. But records taken by the United Nations show that an average of 93 percent of women and 92 percent of men in industrial and agricultural societies marry. The ethnographic literature confirms that marriage is nearly universal in traditional societies.

And in cultures where divorce is common, so too is remarriage. The U.S. National Center for Health Statistics has projected that, if current trends continue, 47.4 percent of all first marriages that were contracted in 1974 will end in divorce. But Andrew Cherlin, a sociologist at Johns Hopkins University, reports that about five out of six men and about three out of four women who divorce remarry, half the time within three years. Statistics on marriage and divorce recorded in other countries, as well as anthropological data on traditional societies, indicate that remarriage among couples of reproductive age occurs regularly.

Monogamy is rare in nonhuman mammals. Less than 3 percent of mammalian species form a pair bond and, as "husband and wife," raise their young. Monogamy is much more common among birds, however. About 90 percent of avian species pair up to raise a brood (in some cases, as among humans, the pair bond does not entail fidelity).

Monogamous species practice this reproductive strategy for several reasons. Gibbons, primate relatives of ours, probably originally evolved monogamy for an ecological reason. In the jungles of Indonesia the resources are so scattered that two females cannot raise their young in the same home range; therefore they must spread out. A male and female pair up shortly after puberty and establish a permanent territory containing fresh water and a few dispersed but continually renewing fruit trees. Here they mate for life, raising their young and defending their small home range. In a fundamental respect, a man and woman living on a small farm in Massachusetts in 1700 displayed the same mating strategy—marrying for life and raising their children on a small plot of land with a continually renewing food supply.

Monogamy is also common in species where more than one parent, the female, may be needed to rear the young successfully. Females of some species bear many infants at once or bear young that are altricial (relatively undeveloped). The female red fox, for example, may deliver too many pups to raise by herself. The male and female form a pair bond in winter and raise a litter together during the spring and summer months. But as autumn leaves pile up around the den, and the young begin to wander, the parents split up to forage independently. The bond only functions to raise the young.

The formation of bonds in association with a breeding season is also common among birds. Most birds bear altricial young and form pair bonds to raise them. Half of this group, like the robin, form a pair bond that lasts only through the breeding season. Some pairs stay together and raise more than one brood in the same season. But after the last fledglings leave the nest, the parents split up. And they do not always mate with the same partner the following year.

Human beings have some things in common with robins and foxes. Human females bear altricial babies and need help in caring for them. Moreover, they do not necessarily mate for life. In societies where men and women are not economically dependent on one another, some bond serially—typically dissolving their marriages after about four years.

Four years may be the length of our ancestral, biological "breeding season." Scientists have observed that among the traditional !Kung Bushmen, women tended to nurse their infants for three or four years. And because !Kung mothers breast-fed regularly throughout the day and night, as well as offered their breasts as pacifiers, ovulation and subsequent pregnancy were postponed; births were about four years apart. Births are spaced about four years apart among groups of Australian aborigines, too. These data have led scientists to suggest that four-year intervals were the natural pattern of birth spacing among our forebears. Human brain physiology for infatuation and attachment also seems to fit this interval. So here is my theory: Perhaps, like serial monogamy in robins, foxes, and other species that mate only for a breeding season, the human pair bond originally evolved to last long enough to raise a single child through infancy. The seven-year itch, recast as a four-year human reproductive cycle, may be a biological phenomenon.

Pair bonding must have evolved when ancestral hominid females first began to deliver helpless young and needed the support of a mate to raise them. Nobody knows when selection for altricial babies occurred. Primates generally bear immature young, but human infants are born much less developed in some respects than are the infants of even our closest relatives, the apes. And human childhood is by far the longest of any primate species. This characteristic may be linked to two critical developments in human history: the evolution of upright walking, about four million years ago, and the expansion of the human brain, about two million years ago.

When our ancestors first began to walk erect, the front-to-back diameter of the pelvic inlet, the bony sides of the birth canal, began to get smaller. Anthropologists Robert Tague and C. Owen Lovejoy conclude that Lucy, the well-known hominid that walked through the woodlands of what is today Ethiopia almost three and a half million years ago, experienced slow, difficult birth. Then, by two million years ago, this obstetric difficulty was complicated by the expanding human brain. Along with others who have studied this question, I believe that at some stage ancestral females must have begun to experience an obstetric crisis—bearing babies that were too large to squeeze through the smaller birth canal. Over time, many must have died in childbirth; but a few, by genetic chance, bore their young earlier—delivering more immature babies that easily slipped through the birth canal. These females and their babies survived more often, passing the critical trait to bear highly immature infants across the eons to women around the world today.

Exactly when this occurred has still to be settled. Recent comparisons of growth patterns in the teeth of modern humans with those of fossil hominids suggest that it was one and a half million years ago or even more recently. But other data on dental growth support the conclusion that females bore babies in the human pattern by two million years ago. In either case, along with this fundamental change in female reproductive physiology must have come modern human mating patterns. Why? Because small groups of these early females, encumbered with infants, were walking through the dangerous grasslands of Africa, from nut grove to berry thicket to fishing pond. They must have begun to need a mate to help feed and protect the helpless babies, and pair bonding between male and female was the solution. The brain physiology of infatuation and attachment—all of the mechanisms that initiate and maintain a bond today—must have evolved with monogamy.

But I see no reason why these early human pair bonds always needed to be permanent. Once a child had been weaned, it could join play groups or become the responsibility of several community members. Why should a couple necessarily remain together unless a second infant was conceived? While there may have been strong evolutionary selection for couples to remain together at least long enough to raise a single baby through infancy, there may have been no stringent selection for permanent monogamy during the reproductive years.

Americans idealize lifelong marriage; they equate divorce with failure. But among our ancestors, there may even have been biological advantages to changing mates during the reproductive years. For instance, a prehistoric male who "divorced" his partner after seeing one offspring through infancy would have had the opportunity to pick a younger "spouse" more capable of bearing and raising babies. A female might leave one mate to "marry" a better provider for her and her forthcoming children. More significant, a male or female who changed mates during his or her reproductive years would have produced genetically more varied young, probably enhancing the likelihood that his or her lineage would survive in fluctuating environments.

There may have been cultural advantages to divorce and remarriage, too. Edward Tylor, one of the founding fathers of anthropology, observed in 1889 that "among tribes of low culture there is but one means known of keeping up alliances, and that means is inter-marriage." More recently, Ernestine Friedl of Duke University noted that in horticultural societies, where men and women garden without the plow, divorce is extremely high, particularly for first marriages arranged by the kin of the married couple. She reports that, nevertheless, there are few permanent negative consequences of divorce for the couple involved or their kin. If this is the case, why not marry more than once and create associations with two or more neighbors?

Similarly, for early human groups, serial monogamy, as opposed to lifelong bonding, would have extended ties. Contemporary observers have commented on the growing role of the "new" extended family, which includes stepparents and other step-relatives. Given the hypothesis that serial pair bonding evolved on the grasslands of Africa two million years ago, these multiconnected households are not new at all.

I am not suggesting that ancestral couples consciously engaged in serial monogamy to further their genetic lines. They probably fell in and out of love for many of the same psychological reasons we do today. But those who did change mates bore genetically more varied children that grew up in environments of extended cultural resources. These young survived disproportionately, passing to modern humankind our nagging restlessness during long relationships, our penchant for divorce, and our perennial optimism about our next relationship.

I also do not wish to suggest that lifelong monogamy was an inferior reproductive strategy. Permanent relationships between compatible partners, in the right ecological circumstances, must have had genetic and cultural payoffs too. Today, about half of American marriages last for life, and about half the spouses are faithful to their partners. Human beings are certainly capable of enduring relationships, particularly as they age. In fact, other things being equal, the statistics bode well for the American family. America is getting older. Our huge baby boom generation is in its late thirties and early forties, past the age of highest divorce risk. As this large group moves beyond its reproductive years, we may experience a few decades of relative family stability.

Love Is Not a Pie

Amy Bloom

Amy Bloom (1943–) is a New York–born writer who works as a psychotherapist and now lives in Durham, Connecticut. The story "Love Is Not a Pie" is contained in her book-length collection of short stories, Come to Me *(1993), nominated for a National Book Award. Of this collection, critic Sherri Hallgren says, "What sets her stories apart is her complete lack of meanness, cynicism or sentimentality. . . . The urgency to speak about how things really are, how people really do behave, the kinds of things they really feel, informs all her stories, suggesting there just is no time for pretending that things are prettier or simpler than they really are."*

IN THE MIDDLE OF THE EULOGY AT MY MOTHER'S boring and heartbreaking funeral, I started to think about calling off the wedding. August 21 did not seem like a good date, John Wescott did not seem like a good person to marry and I couldn't see myself in the long white silk gown Mrs. Wescott had offered me. We had gotten engaged at Christmas, while my mother was starting to die. She died in May, earlier than we had expected. When the minister said, "She was a rare spirit, full of the kind of bravery and joy that inspires others . . . ," I stared at the pale blue ceiling and thought, "My mother would not have wanted me to spend my life with this man." He had asked me if I wanted him to come from Boston to the funeral, and I said no. So he didn't, respecting my autonomy and so forth. I think he should have known that I was just being considerate.

After the funeral, we took the little box of ashes back to the house and entertained everybody who came by to pay their respects. Lots of my father's colleagues, other law professors, a few of his former students, my Uncle Steve and his new wife, my cousins (whom my sister and I always referred to as Thing One and Thing Two), friends from the old neighborhood, before my mother's sculpture started selling, my mother's art world friends, her sisters, some of my friends from high school, some people I used to baby-sit for, my best friend from college, some friends of my sister's, a lot of people I didn't recognize. I've been living away from home for a long time, first at college, now at law school.

My sister, my father and I worked the room. And everyone that came in, my father embraced. It didn't matter whether they started to pat him on the back or shake his hand, he pulled them to him and hugged them so hard, I saw some people's feet lift right off the floor. My sister and I took the more passive route, letting people do whatever they wanted to us—patting, stroking, embracing, cupping our faces in their hands.

My father was in the middle of squeezing Mrs. Ellis, our cleaning lady, when he saw Mr. DeCuervo come in, still carrying his suitcase. He about dropped Mrs. Ellis and went charging over to Mr. DeCuervo, wrapped his arms around him, and the two of them moaned and rocked together, in a passionate, musicless waltz. My sister and I sat down on the couch, our arms pressed against each other, watching our father cry all over his friend, our mother's lover.

When I was eleven and my sister was eight, her last naked summer, Mr. DeCuervo and his daughter, Gisela, who was just about to turn eight, spent part of the summer with us at the cabin in Maine. The cabin was from the Spencer side, my father's side of the family, and he and my Uncle Steve were co-owners. We went there every July (colder water, better weather) and they came in August. My father felt about his brother the way we felt about our cousins, so we would only overlap for lunch on the last day of our stay.

That July, the DeCuervos came, but without Mrs. DeCuervo, who had to go visit a sick someone in Argentina, where they were from. That was okay with us; Mrs. DeCuervo was a professional mother, a type that made my sister and me very uncomfortable. She told us to wash the berries before we ate them, to rest after lunch, to put on more suntan lotion, to make our beds. She was a nice lady; she was just always in our way. My mother had a few very basic summer rules: don't eat food with mold or insects on it; don't swim alone; don't even think about waking your mother before 8 A.M., unless you are fatally injured or ill. That was about it and Mrs. DeCuervo was always amending and adding to the list, one apologetic eye on my mother. Our mother, as usual, was pleasant and friendly and did things the way she always did. She made it pretty clear that if we were cowed by the likes of Mrs. DeCuervo, we were on our own. They got divorced when Gisela was a sophomore at Mount Holyoke.

We liked pretty, docile Gisela, and bullied her a little bit, and liked her even more because she didn't squeal on us, on me in particular. We liked her father, too. We saw the two of them, sometimes the three of them, at occasional picnics and lesser holidays. He always complimented us, never made stupid jokes at our expense and brought us unusual, perfect little presents. Silver barrettes for me, the summer I was letting my hair grow out from my pixie cut; a leather bookmark for Lizzie, who learned to read when she was three. My mother would stand behind us as we unwrapped the gifts, smiling and shaking her head at his extravagance.

When they drove up, we were all sitting on the porch; Mr. DeCuervo got out first, his curly brown hair making him look like a giant dandelion, with his yellow T-shirt and brown jeans. Gisela looked just like him, her long, curly brown hair caught up in a bun, wisps flying around her tanned little face. As they walked toward us, she took his hand and I felt a rush of warmth toward her, for showing how much she loved her daddy, like I loved mine, and for showing that she was a little afraid of us, of me, probably. People weren't often frightened of Lizzie, she never left her books long enough to bother anyone.

My parents got down from the porch, my big father in his faded blue trunks, drooping below his belly, his freckled back pink and moist in the sun, as it was every summer. The sun caught the red hair on his head and shoulders and chest and he shone. The Spencers were half Viking, he said. My mother was wearing her summer outfit, a black two-piece bathing suit. I don't remember her ever wearing a different suit. At night, she'd add one of my father's shirts and wrap it around her like a kimono. Some years, she looked great in her suit, waist nipped in, skin smooth and tan; other years, her skin looked burnt and crumpled and the suit was too big in some places and too small in others. Those years, she smoked too much and went out on the porch to cough. But that summer, the suit fit beautifully, and when she jumped off the porch into my father's arms, he whirled her around and let her black hair whip his face, while he smiled and smiled.

They both hugged Mr. DeCuervo and Gisela; my mother took her little flowered suitcase and my father took his duffel bag and they led them into the cabin.

The cabin was our palace; Lizzie and I would say, very grandly, "We're going to the cabin for the summer, come visit us there, if it's okay with your parents." And we loved it and loved to act as though it was nothing special, when we knew, really, that it was magnificent. The pines and birches came right down to the lake, with just a thin lacing of mossy rocks before you got to the smooth, cold water, and little gray fish swam around the splintery dock and through our legs, or out of reach of our oars when we took out the old blue rowboat.

The cabin itself was three bedrooms and a little

kitchen and a living room that took up half the house. The two small bedrooms had big beds with pastel chenille spreads; yellow with red roses in my parents' room, white with blue pansies in the other. The kids' room was much bigger, like a dormitory, with three sets of bunk beds, each with its own mismatched sheets and pillowcases. The pillows were always a little damp and smelled like salt and pine and mine smelled of Ma Griffe perfume as well, because I used to sleep with my mother's scarf tucked under my pillow. The shower was outside, with a thin green plastic curtain around it, but there was a regular bathroom inside, next to my parents' room.

Mr. DeCuervo and Gisela fit into our routine as though they'd been coming to the cabin for years, instead of just last summer. We had the kind of summer cabin routine that stays with you forever as a model of leisure, of life being enjoyed. We'd get up early, listening to the birds screaming and trilling, and make ourselves some breakfast: cold cereal or toast if the parents were up, cake or cold spaghetti or marshmallows, if they were still asleep. Then the parents would get up, my mother first, usually. She'd make a cup of coffee and brush and braid our hair and set us loose. If we were going exploring, she'd put three sandwiches and three pieces of fruit in a bag, with an army blanket. Otherwise, she'd just wave to us as we headed down to the lake.

We'd come back at lunchtime and eat whatever was around and then go out to the lake, or the forest, or down the road to see if the townie kids were around and in a mood to play with us. I don't know what the grown-ups did all day; sometimes they'd come out to swim for a while, and sometimes we'd find my mother in the shed she used for a studio. But when we came back at around five or six, they all seemed happy and relaxed, drinking gin-and-tonics on the porch, watching us run toward the house. It was the most beautiful time.

At night, after dinner, the fathers would wash up and my mother would sit on the porch, smoking a cigarette, listening to Aretha Franklin or Billie Holiday or Sam Cooke, and after a little while, she'd stub out her cigarette and the four of us would dance. We'd twist and lindy and jitterbug and stomp, all of us copying my mother. And pretty soon, the daddies would drift in, with their dishtowels and their beers, and they'd lean in the doorway and watch. My mother would turn first to my father, always to him, first.

"What about it, Danny? Care to dance?" And she'd put her hand on his shoulder and he'd smile, tossing his dishtowel to Mr. DeCuervo, resting his beer on the floor. And my father would lumber along, gamely, shuffling his feet and smiling. Sometimes, he'd wave his arms around and pretend to be a fish or a bear, while my mother swung her body, easily and dreamily, sliding through the music. They'd always lindy together, to Fats Domino. That was my father's favorite and then he'd sit down, puffing a little.

My mother would stand there, snapping her fingers, shifting back and forth.

"Gaucho, you dance with her, before I have a coronary," said my father.

Mr. DeCuervo's real name was Bolivar, which I didn't know until Lizzie told me after the funeral. We always called him Mr. DeCuervo because we felt embarrassed to call him by a nickname.

So, Mr. DeCuervo would shrug gracefully, and toss the two dishtowels back to my father. And then he'd bop toward my mother, his face still turned toward my father.

"We'll go running tomorrow, Dan, get you back into shape, so you can dance all night."

"What do you mean, 'back'? I've been exactly this same svelte shape for twenty years. Why fix it if it ain't broke?"

And they all laughed and Mr. DeCuervo and my mother rolled their eyes at each other and my mother walked over and kissed my father, where the sweat was beading up at his temples. Then she took Mr. DeCuervo's hand and they walked to the center of the living room.

When she and my father danced, my sister and I giggled and interfered and treated it like a family badminton game in which they were the core players but we were welcome participants. When she danced with Mr. DeCuervo, we'd sit on the porch swing or lean on the windowsill and watch, not even looking at each other.

They only danced the fast dances, and they danced as though they'd been waiting all their lives for each song. My mother's movements got deeper and smoother and Mr. DeCuervo suddenly came alive, as though a spotlight had hit him. My father danced the way he was—warm, noisy, teasing, a little overpowering; but Mr. DeCuervo, who was usually quiet and thoughtful and serious, became a different man when he danced with my mother. His dancing was light and happy and soulful, edging up on my mother, turning her, matching her every step. They would smile at all of us, in turn, and then face each other, too transported to smile.

"Dance with Daddy some more," my sister said, speaking for all three of us. They had left us too far behind.

My mother blew Lizzie a kiss. "Okay, sweetheart."

She turned to both men, smiling, and said, "That message was certainly loud and clear. Let's take a little break, Gauch', and get these monkeys to bed. It's getting late, girls."

And the three of them shepherded the three of us through the bedtime rituals, moving us in and out of the kitchen for water, the bathroom for teeth, potty and calamine lotion, and finally to our big bedroom. We slept in our underwear and T-shirts, which impressed Gisela.

"No pajamas?" she had said, the first night.

"Not necessary," I said smugly.

We would lie there after they kissed us, listening to our parents talk and crack peanuts and snap cards; they played gin and poker while they listened to Dinah Washington and Odetta.

One night, I woke up at around midnight and crossed the living room to get some water in the kitchen and see if there was any strawberry shortcake left. I saw my mother and Mr. DeCuervo hugging, and I remember being surprised, and puzzled, too. I had seen movies; if you hugged someone like you'd never let them go, surely you were supposed to be kissing, too. It wasn't a Mommy-Daddy hug, partly because their hugs were defined by the fact that my father was eight inches taller and a hundred pounds heavier than my mother. These two looked all wrong to me; embraces were a big pink-and-orange man enveloping a smaller, leaner black-and-white woman who looked up at him. My mother and Mr. DeCuervo looked like sister and brother, standing cheek-to-cheek, with their broad shoulders and long, tanned, bare legs. My mother's hands were under Mr. DeCuervo's white T-shirt. She must have felt my eyes on her because she opened hers slowly.

"Oh, honey, you startled us. Mr. DeCuervo and I were just saying goodnight. Do you want me to tuck you in after you go potty?" Not quite a bribe, certainly a reminder that I was more important to her than he was. They had moved apart so quickly and smoothly I couldn't even remember how they had looked together. I nodded to my mother; what I had seen was already being transformed into a standard goodnight embrace, the kind my mother gave to all of her close friends.

When I came back from the bathroom, Mr. DeCuervo had disappeared and my mother was waiting, looking out at the moon. She walked me to the bedroom and kissed me, first on my forehead, then on my lips.

"Sleep well, pumpkin pie. See you in the morning."

"Will you make blueberry pancakes tomorrow?" It seemed like a good time to ask.

"We'll see. Go to sleep."

"Please, Mommy."

"Okay, we'll have a blueberry morning. Go to sleep, now. Goodnight, nurse." And she watched me for a moment, from the doorway, and then she was gone.

My father got up at five to go fishing with some men at the other side of the lake. Every Saturday in July, he'd go off, with a big red bandanna tied over his bald spot, his Mets T-shirt, and his tackle box, and he'd fish until around three. Mr. DeCuervo said that he'd clean them, cook them and eat them, but he wouldn't spend a day with a bunch of guys in baseball caps and white socks to catch them.

I woke up smelling coffee and butter. Gisela and Liz were already out of bed and I was aggrieved; I was the one who had asked for the pancakes and they were probably all eaten by now.

Mr. DeCuervo and Liz were sitting at the table, finishing their pancakes. My mother and Gisela were sitting on the blue couch in the living room, while my mother brushed Gisela's hair. She was brushing it more gently than she brushed mine, not slapping her on the shoulder to make her sit still. Gisela didn't wiggle and she didn't scream when my mother hit a knot.

I was getting ready to be mad when my mother winked at me over Gisela's head and said, "There's a plate of pancakes for you on top of the stove, bunny. Gauch', would you please lift them for Ellen? The plate's probably hot."

Mr. DeCuervo handed me my pancakes, which were huge brown wheels studded with smashed, purply berries; he put my fork and knife on top of a folded paper towel and patted my cheek. His hand smelled like coffee and cinnamon. He knew what I liked and pushed the butter and the honey and the syrup toward me.

"Juice?" he said.

I nodded, trying to watch him when he wasn't looking; he didn't look like the man I thought I saw in the moonlight, giving my mother a funny hug.

"Great pancakes, Lila," he said.

"Great, Mom." I didn't want to be outclassed by the DeCuervos' habitual good manners. Even Gisela remembered her please and thank you for every little thing.

My mother smiled and put the barrettes in Gisela's hair. It was starting to get warm, so I swallowed my pancakes and kicked Liz to get her attention.

"Let's go," I said.

"Wash your face, then go," my mother said.

I stuck my face under the kitchen tap and my mother and Mr. DeCuervo laughed. Triumphantly, I led the two little girls out of the house, snatching our towels off the line as we ran down to the water, suddenly filled with longing for the lake.

"Last one in the water's a fart," I screamed, cannonballing off the end of the dock. I hit the cold blue water, shattering its surface. Liz and Gisela jumped in beside me and we played water games until my father drove up in the pickup with a bucket of fish. He waved to us and told us we'd be eating fish for the next two days, and we groaned and held our noses as he went into the cabin, laughing.

There was a string of sunny days like that one: swimming, fishing with Daddy off the dock, eating peanut-butter-and-jelly sandwiches in the rowboat, drinking Orange Crush on the porch swing.

And then it rained for a week. We woke up the first rainy morning, listening to it tap and dance on the roof. My mother stuck her head into our bedroom.

"It's monsoon weather, honeys. How about cocoa and cinnamon toast?"

We pulled on our overalls and sweaters and went into the kitchen, where my mother had already laid out our mugs and plates. She was engaged in her rainy-day ritual: making sangria. First she poured the orange juice out of the big white plastic pitcher into three empty peanut-butter jars, then she started chopping up all the oranges, lemons and limes we had in the house. She let me pour the brandy over the fruit, Gisela threw in the sugar and Lizzie came up for air long enough to pour the big bottle of red wine over everything. I cannot imagine drinking anything else on rainy days.

That day, my mother went out onto the porch for her morning cigarette and when my father came down, he joined her on the porch, while we played Go Fish; I could see them snuggling on the wicker settee. After a while, Mr. DeCuervo came down, looked out on the porch and picked up an old magazine and started reading.

We decided to play Monopoly in our room, since the grown-ups didn't want to entertain us. After two hours, in which I rotted in jail and Lizzie forgot to charge rent, little Gisela beat us and the three of us went back to the kitchen for snacks. Rainy days were basically a series of snacks, more and less elaborate, punctuated by board games, card games and whining. We drank soda and juice all day, ate cheese, bananas, cookies, bologna, graham crackers, Jiffy popcorn, hard-boiled eggs. The grown-ups ate cheese and crackers and drank sangria.

The daddies were reading in the two big armchairs; my mother had gone off to her room to sketch. We were getting bored, so I started writing my name in the honey that had spilled on the kitchen table, while Gisela and Liz pulled the stuffing out of the hole in the bottom of the blue couch.

My mother came downstairs for a cigarette and started swearing. "Jesus Christ, Ellen, get your hands out of the goddamned honey. Liz, Gisela, that's absolutely unacceptable, you know that. Leave the poor couch alone. If you're so damned stir-crazy, go outside and dance in the rain."

The two men looked up, slowly focusing, from a great distance.

"Lila, really," said my father.

"Lila, it's pouring. We'll keep an eye on them, now," said Mr. DeCuervo.

"Right. Like you were." My mother was grinning.

"Can we, Mommy, can we go in the rain? Can we take off our clothes and go in the rain?"

"Sure, go naked, there's no point in getting your clothes wet and no point in suits. There's not likely to be a big crowd in the yard."

We ran to the porch and, before my mother could get rational, stripped and ran whooping into the rain, leaping off the porch onto the muddy lawn, screaming and feeling superior to every child in Maine who had to stay indoors.

We played goddesses-in-the-rain, which consisted of caressing our bodies and screaming the names of everyone we knew, and we played ring-around-the-rosie and tag and red light, green light and catch, all of which were deliciously slippery and surreal in the sheets of gray rain. Our parents watched us from the porch.

When we finally came in, thrilled with ourselves and the extent to which we were completely, profoundly wet, in every pore, they bundled us up and told us to dry our hair and get ready for dinner.

My mother brushed our hair and then she made sauce for spaghetti, while my father made a salad and Mr. DeCuervo made a strawberry tart, piling the berries into a huge, red, shiny pyramid in the center of the pastry. We were in heaven. The grown-ups were laughing a lot, sipping their rosy drinks, tossing the vegetables back and forth.

After dinner, my mother took us into the living room to dance and then the power went off.

"Shit," said my father in the kitchen.

"Double shit," said Mr. DeCuervo, and we heard them stumbling around in the dark, laughing and cursing until they came in with two flashlights.

"The cavalry is here, ladies," said Daddy, bowing to us all and twirling his flashlight.

"American and Argentinian divisions, senora y senoritas." I had never heard Mr. DeCuervo speak Spanish before, not even that little bit.

"Well, then, I know I'm safe—from the bad guys, anyway. On the other hand . . ." My mother laughed, and the daddies put their arms around each other, and they laughed, too.

"On the other hand, what? What, Mommy?" I tugged at her the way I did when I was afraid of losing her in a big department store.

"Nothing, honey. Mommy was just being silly. Let's get ready for bed, munchkins. Then you all can whisper in bed for a while. We're shut down for the night, I'm sure."

The daddies accompanied us to the bathroom and whispered that we could skip everything except peeing, since there was no electricity. The two of them kissed us goodnight, my father's moustache tickling, Mr. DeCuervo's sliding over my cheek. My mother came into the room a moment later, and her face was as smooth and warm as a velvet cushion. We didn't whisper for long; the rain dance and the eating and the storm had worn us out.

It was still dark when I woke up, but the rain had stopped and the power had returned, so that there was a light burning in our hallway. It made me feel very grown-up and responsible, getting out of bed and going around the house turning out the lights that no one else knew were on; I was conserving electricity.

I went into the bathroom and was squeezed by stomach cramps, probably from all the burnt popcorn kernels I had eaten. I sat on the toilet for a long time, watching a brown spider crawl along the wall; I'd knock him down and then watch him climb back up again toward the towels. My cramps were better, but not gone, so I decided to wake my mother. My father would have been more sympathetic, but he was the heavier sleeper, and by the time he understood what I was telling him my mother would have her bathrobe on and be massaging my stomach, kindly, but without the excited concern that I felt was my due as a victim of illness.

I walked down to my parents' room, turning the hall light back on. I pushed open the creaky door and saw my mother spooned up against my father's back, as she always was, and Mr. DeCuervo spooned up against her, his arm over the covers, his other hand resting on the top of her head.

I stood up and looked and then backed out of the bedroom. They hadn't moved, the three of them breathing deeply, in unison. What was that, I thought, what did I see? I wanted to go back and take another look, to see it again, to make it disappear, to watch them carefully, until I understood.

My cramps were gone. I went back to my own bed, staring at Liz and Gisela, who looked, in their sleep, like little girl versions of the two men I had just seen. Just sleeping, I thought, the grown-ups were just sleeping. Maybe Mr. DeCuervo's bed collapsed, like ours did two summers ago, or maybe it got wet in the storm. I thought I would never be able to fall asleep, but the next thing I remember is waking up to more rain and the sounds of Liz and Gisela begging my mother to take us to the movies in town. We went to see *The Sound of Music,* which had been playing at the Bijou for about ten years.

I don't remember much else about the summer; all of the images run together. We went on swimming and fishing and taking the rowboat out for little adventures, and when the DeCuervos left, I hugged Gisela, but wasn't going to hug him, until he whispered in my ear, "Next year, we'll bring up a motorboat and I'll teach you to water-ski," and then I hugged him very hard and my mother put her hand on my head, lightly, giving benediction.

The next summer, I went off to camp in July and wasn't there when the DeCuervos came. Lizzie said they had a good time without me. Then they couldn't come for a couple of summers in a row, and by the time they came again, Gisela and Lizzie were at camp with me in New Hampshire; the four grown-ups spent about a week together, but then I heard my father say that another vacation with Elvira DeCuervo would kill him or he'd kill her. My mother said she wasn't so bad.

We saw them a little less after that. They came, Gisela and Mr. DeCuervo, to my high school graduation, to my mother's opening in Boston, to my father's fiftieth birthday party and then to Lizzie's graduation. When my mother went down to New York, she'd have dinner with the three of them, she said, but sometimes her plans would change and they'd have to substitute lunch for dinner.

Gisela couldn't come to the funeral; she was in Argentina for the year, working with the architectural firm that Mr. DeCuervo's father had started.

After all the mourners left, Mr. DeCuervo gave us a sympathy note from Gisela, with a beautiful pen-and-ink of our mother inside it. The two men went into the living room and took out a bottle of Scotch and two glasses. It was like we weren't there; they put on Billie Holiday singing "Embraceable You," and they got down to serious drinking and grieving. Lizzie and I went into the kitchen and decided to eat everything sweet that people had brought over: brownies, strudel, pfeffernuss, sweet potato pie, Mrs. Ellis' chocolate cake, with chocolate mousse in the middle. We laid out two plates and two mugs of milk and got to it.

Lizzie said, "You know, when I was home in April, he called every day." She jerked her head toward the living room.

I couldn't tell if she approved or disapproved, and I didn't know what I thought about it either.

"She called him 'Bolivar.'"

"What? She always called him 'Gaucho' and so we didn't call him anything."

"I know, but she called him 'Bolivar.' I heard her talk to him every fucking day, El; she called him 'Bolivar.'" Tears were running down Lizzie's face, and I wished my mother was there to pat her soft, fuzzy hair and keep her from choking on her tears. I held her hand across the table. I was still holding my fork in my other hand and I could feel my mother looking at me, smiling and narrowing her eyes a little, the way she did when I was balking. I dropped the fork onto my plate and went over and hugged Lizzie, who leaned into me as though her spine had collapsed.

"I asked her, after the third call, about his calling," she said, into my shoulder.

"What'd she say?" I straightened Lizzie up, so I could hear what she was saying.

"She said, 'Of course, he calls at noon, he knows that's when I'm feeling strongest.' And I told her that's not what I meant, that I hadn't known they were so close."

"You said that?"

"Yeah. And she said, 'Honey, nobody loves me more than Bolivar.' And I didn't know what to say, so I just sat there feeling like 'Do I really want to hear this?' and then she fell asleep."

"So what do you think?"

"I don't know. I was getting ready to ask her again . . ."

"You're amazing, Lizzie," I interrupted. She really is, she's so quiet but she goes out and has conversations that I can't even imagine having.

"But I didn't have to ask because she brought it up herself, the next day after he called. She got off the phone, looking just so exhausted, she was sweating, but she was smiling. She was looking out at the crabapple trees in the yard, and she said, 'There were apples trees in bloom when I met Bolivar, and the trees were right where the sculpture needed to be in the courtyard, so he offered to get rid of the trees, and I said that seemed arrogant, and he said that they'd replant them. So I said okay and he said, 'What's so bad about arrogance?' And the first time he and Daddy met, the two of them drank Scotch and watched soccer while I made dinner. And then they washed up, just like at the cabin. And when the two of them are in the room together and you two girls are with us, I know that I am living in a state of grace.'"

"She said that? She said 'in a state of grace'? Mommy said that?"

"Yes, Ellen. Christ, what do you think, I'm making up interesting deathbed statements?" Liz hated to be interrupted, especially by me.

"Sorry. Go on."

"Anyway, we were talking and I sort of asked what were we actually talking about. I mean, close friends or very close friends, and she just laughed. You know how she'd look at us like she knew exactly where we were going when we said we were going to a friend's house for the afternoon but we were really going to drink Boone's Farm and skinny-dip at the quarry? Well, she looked just like that and she took my hand. Her hand was so light, El. And she said that the three of them loved each other, each differently, and that they were both amazing men, each special, each deserving love and appreciation. She said that she thought Daddy was the most wonderful husband a woman could have and that she was very glad that we had him as a father. And I asked her how she could do it, love them both, and how they could stand it. And she said, 'Love is not a pie, honey. I love you and Ellen differently, because you are different people, wonderful people, but not at all the same. And so who I am with each of you is different, unique to us. I don't choose between you. And it's the same way with Daddy and Bolivar. People think that it can't be that way, but it can. You just have to find the right people.' And then she shut her eyes for the afternoon. Your eyes are bugging out, El."

"Well, Jesus, I guess so. I mean, I knew . . ."

"You knew and you didn't tell me?"

"You were eight or something, Lizzie, what was I supposed to say? I didn't even know what I knew then."

"So what did you know?" Lizzie was very serious. It was a real breach of our rules not to share inside dirt about our parents, especially our mother; we were always trying to figure her out.

I didn't know how to tell her about the three of them; that was even less normal than her having an affair with Mr. DeCuervo with Daddy's permission. I couldn't even think of the words to describe what I had seen, so I just said, "I saw Mommy and Mr. DeCuervo kissing one night after we were in bed."

"Really? Where was Daddy?"

"I don't know. But wherever he was, obviously he knew what was going on. I mean, that's what Mommy was telling you, right? That Daddy knew and that it was okay with him."

"Yeah. Jesus."

I went back and sat down and we were halfway through the strudel when the two men came in. They were drunk, but not incoherent. They just weren't their normal selves, but I guess we weren't either, with our eyes puffy and red and all this destroyed food around us.

"Beautiful girls," Mr. DeCuervo said to my father. They were hanging in the doorway, one on each side.

"They are, they really are. And smart, couldn't find smarter girls." My father was going on and on about how smart we were. Lizzie and I just looked at each other, embarrassed but not displeased.

"Ellen has Lila's mouth," Mr. DeCuervo said. "You have your mother's mouth, with the right side going up a little more than the left. Exquisite."

My father's nodding his head, like this is the greatest truth ever told. And Daddy turns to Liz and says, "And you have your mother's eyes. Since the day you were born and I looked right into them, I thought, 'My God, she's got Lila's eyes, but blue, not green.'"

And Mr. DeCuervo is nodding away, of course. I wondered if they were going to do a complete autopsy, but they stopped.

My father came over to us at the table and put one hand on each of us. "You girls made your mother incredibly happy. There was nothing she ever created that gave her more pride and joy than you two. And she thought that you were both so special . . ." He started crying and Mr. DeCuervo put an arm around his waist and picked up for him.

"She did, she had two pictures of you in her studio, nothing else. And you know, she expected us all to grieve, but you know how much she wanted you to enjoy, too. To enjoy everything, every meal, every drink, every sunrise, every kiss . . ." He started crying too.

"We're gonna lie down for a while, girls. Maybe later we'll have dinner or something." My father kissed us both, wet and rough, and the two of them went down the hall.

Lizzie and I just looked at each other.

"Wanna get drunk?" I said.

"No, I don't think so. I guess I'll go lie down for a while unless you want my company." She looked like she was about to sleep standing up, so I shook my head. I was planning on calling John anyway.

Lizzie came over and hugged me, hard, and I hugged her back and brushed the chocolate crumbs out of her hair.

Sitting alone in the kitchen, I thought about John, about telling him about my mother and her affair and how the two men were sacked out in my parents' bed, probably snoring. And I could hear John's silence and I knew that he would think my father must not have really loved my mother, if he'd let her go with another man; or that my mother must have been a real bitch, forcing my father to tolerate an affair "right in his own home," John would think, maybe even say. I thought I ought to call him, before I got myself completely enraged over a phone call that hadn't taken place. Lizzie would say I was projecting anyway.

I called John and he was very sweet, asking how I was feeling, how the memorial service had gone, how my father was. And I told him all that and then I knew I couldn't tell him the rest and that I couldn't marry a man I couldn't tell this story to.

"I'm so sorry, Ellen," he said. "You must be very upset. What a difficult day for you."

I realize that that was a perfectly normal response; it just was all wrong for me. I didn't come from a normal family, I wasn't ready to get normal.

I felt terrible, hurting John, but I couldn't marry him just because I didn't want to hurt him, so I said, "And that's not the worst of it, John. I can't marry you, I really can't. I know this is pretty hard to listen to, over the phone . . ." I couldn't think of what else to say.

"Ellen, let's talk about this when you get back to Boston. I know what kind of a strain you must be under. I had the feeling that you were unhappy about some of Mother's ideas. We can work something out when you get back."

"I know that you think this is because of my mother's death and it is, but not the way you think, John, I just can't marry you. I'm not going to wear your mother's dress and I'm not going to marry you and I'm very sorry." He was quiet for a long time and then he said, "I don't understand, Ellen. We've already ordered the invitations." And I knew that I was right. If he had said, "Fuck this, I'm coming to see you tonight," or even "I don't know what you're talking about, but I want to marry you anyway," I would have probably changed my mind before I got off the phone. But as it was I said goodbye sort of quietly and hung up.

It was like two funerals in one day. I sat at the table, poking the cake into little shapes and then knocking them over. My mother would have sent me out for a walk. I started to clear the stuff away when my father and Mr. DeCuervo appeared, looking more together.

"How about some gin, El?" my father said.

"If you're up for it," said Mr. DeCuervo.

"Okay," I said. "I just broke up with John Wescott."

"Oh?" I couldn't tell which one spoke.

"I told him that I didn't think we'd make each other happy." Which was what I had meant to say.

My father hugged me and said, "I'm sorry if it's hard for you." Then he turned to Mr. DeCuervo and said, "Did she know how to call them or what? Your mother knew you weren't going to marry that guy."

"She was almost always right, Dan."

"Almost always, not quite," said my father, and the two of them laughed at some private joke and shook hands like a pair of old boxers.

"So it's your deal," my father said, leaning back in his chair.

"Penny a point," said Mr. DeCuervo.

First Love

R. A. Sasaki

R. A. Sasaki (1952–) was born in San Francisco, where her story "First Love" takes place. Her degrees are from the University of California at Berkeley (B.A., 1974) and San Francisco State University (M.A., 1988). As a third-generation Japanese American (sansei), *she grew up in a community that suffered "cultural amnesia" inflicted by the internment—the result of Executive Order 9066, which forced 120,000 Japanese Americans into ten "relocation camps"—and the atomic bomb. Through her stories, Sasaki wishes to restore "a history that was almost lost when the voices of the first generation* (issei) *and the second generation* (nissei) *were silenced by the burden of shame imposed on them because of their ancestry."*

It was William Chin who started the rumor. He had been crossing California Street on a Saturday afternoon in December when he was almost struck down by two people on a Suzuki motorcycle. As if it weren't enough to feel the brush of death on the sleeve of his blue parka, a split second before the demon passed, he had looked up and caught sight of two faces he never would have expected to see on the same motorcycle—one of which he wouldn't have expected to see on a motorcycle at all. No one would have imagined these two faces exchanging words, or thought of them in the same thought even; yet there they were, together not only in physical space, but in their expressions of fiendish abandon as they whizzed by him. He was so shaken, first by his nearness to death, then by seeing an F.O.B. hood like Hideyuki "George" Sakamoto in the company of a nice girl like Joanne Terasaki, that it was a full five minutes before he realized, still standing in amazement on the corner of California and Fourth, that Joanne had been driving.

When William Chin's story got around, there was a general sense of outrage among the senior class of Andrew Jackson High—the boys, because an upstart newcomer like George Sakamoto had done what they were too shy to do (that is, he had gotten Joanne to like him), and the girls, because George Sakamoto was definitely cool and Joanne Terasaki, as Marsha Aquino objected with utter contempt, "doesn't even like to dance." Joanne's friends remained loyal and insisted that Jo would come to her senses by graduation. George's motorcycle cronies were less generous. "Dude's fuckin' crazy," was their cryptic consensus. Opinions differed as to which of the two lovers had completely lost their minds; however, it was unanimously held that the pairing was unsuitable.

And indeed, the two were from different worlds.

Hideyuki Sakamoto ("George" was his American name) was Japanese, a conviction that eight years, or half his life, in the States had failed to shake. He had transferred into Jackson High's senior class that year from wherever it was that

---

F.O.B.s (immigrants fresh off the boat) transferred from; and though perhaps in his case the "fresh" no longer applied, the fact that he had come off the boat at one time or another was unmistakable. It lingered—rather, persisted—in his speech, which was ungrammatical and heavily accented, and punctuated by a mixture of exclamations commonly used on Kyushu Island and in the Fillmore District.

An F.O.B. at Jackson High could follow one of two routes: he could be quietly good at science or mathematics, or he could be a juvenile delinquent. Both options condemned him to invisibility. George hated math. His sympathies tended much more toward the latter option; however, he was not satisfied to be relegated to that category either. One thing was certain, and that was that George wanted no part of invisibility. As soon as his part-time job at Nakamura Hardware in Japantown afforded him the opportunity, he went out and acquired a second-hand Suzuki chopper (most hoods dream of owning a Harley, but George was Japanese and proud of it). He acquired threads which, when worn on his tall, wiry frame, had the effect—whether from admiration, derision, or sheer astonishment—of turning all heads, male and female alike. He had, in a short span of time, established a reputation as a "swinger." So when William Chin's story got around about George Sakamoto letting Joanne Terasaki drive his bike, the unanimous reaction among the girls who thought of themselves as swingers was voiced by Marsha Aquino: "God dog, what a waste."

Joanne Terasaki, or "Jo," as she preferred to be called, was, in popular opinion, a "brain." Although her parents were living in Japantown when she was born, soon afterwards her grandparents had died and the family moved out to "the Avenues." Jo was a product of the middle-class, ethnically mixed Richmond District. She had an air of breeding that came from three generations of city living, one college-educated parent, and a simple belief in the illusion so carefully nurtured by her parents' generation, who had been through the war, that she was absolutely Mainstream. No one, however, would have thought of her in conjunction with the word "swing," unless it was the playground variety. Indeed, there was a childlike quality about her, a kind of functional stupidity that was surprising in a girl so intelligent in other respects. She moved slowly, as if her mind were always elsewhere, a habit that boys found mysterious and alluring at first, then exasperating. Teachers found it exasperating as well, even slightly insulting, as she earned As in their classes almost as an afterthought. Her attention was like a dim but powerful beacon, slowly sweeping out to sea for—what? Occasionally it would light briefly on the world at hand, and Jo would be quick, sharp, formidable. Then it would turn out to faraway places again. Perhaps she was unable to reconcile the world around her, the world of Jackson High, with the fictional worlds where her love of reading took her. In her mind, she was Scarlett O'Hara, Lizzy Bennet, Ari Ben Canaan. Who would not be disoriented to find oneself at one moment fleeing the Yankees through a burning Atlanta, and the next moment struggling across the finish line in girls' P.E.? Tart repartee with Mr. Darcy was far more satisfying than the tongue-tied and painful exchanges with boys that occurred in real life. Rebuffed boys thought Jo a snob, a heartless bitch. The world of Andrew Jackson High was beneath her, that was it—a passing annoyance to be endured until she went out into the wider world and entered her true element. It must be on this wider world, this future glory, that her vision was so inexorably fixed.

Or perhaps it was fixed on a point just across San Francisco Bay, on the imposing campanile of the Berkeley campus of the University of California. She had always known she would go there, ever since, as a child, she had often gone to her mother's dresser and surreptitiously opened the top drawer to take out the fuzzy little golden bear bearing the inscription in blue letters, "CAL." It was one of the few "heirlooms" that her mother had salvaged from the wartime relocation. She had taken it with her to internment camp in the Utah desert, an ineffectual but treasured symbol of a shattered life. The government could take away her rights, her father's business, her home, but they could never take away the fact that she was U.C. Berkeley, Class of '39. Jo would have that, too. People often said of Jo that she was a girl who was going places; and they didn't mean on the back (or front) of George Sakamoto's bike.

Only love or drama could bring together two people cast in such disparate roles. When auditions began for the play that was traditionally put on by the senior class before graduation, Jo, tired of being typecast as a brain, tried out for the part most alien to her image—that of the brazen hussy who flings herself at the hero in vain. For a brief moment she stood before her fellow classmates and sang her way out of the cramped cage that their imaginations had fashioned for her. The moment was indeed brief. Marsha Aquino got the part.

"You have to admit, Jo," said William Chin apologetically, "Marsha's a natural." And Jo agreed, somewhat maliciously, that Marsha was.

George, for his part, went for the lead. It was unheard of for a hood (and an F.O.B, at that) to aspire to the stage, much less the leading part. So thoroughly did George's aspect contradict conventional expectations of what a male lead should be, that the effect was quite comic. His good-natured lack of inhibition so charmed his audience that they almost overlooked the fact that his lines had been unintelligible. At the last moment, a voice of reason prevailed, and George was relegated to a nonspeaking part as one of six princes in a dream ballet, choreographed by Jo's friend Ava.

And so the two worlds converged.

"Grace," Ava was saying. "And—flair." She was putting the dream princes and princesses through their paces. "This is a ballet."

The dancers shuffled about self-consciously. After hours of work the princes and princesses, trained exclusively in soul, were managing to approximate a cross between a square dance and a track-and-field event.

"You've got to put more energy into it, or something," Jo, who was a princess, observed critically as a sheepish William Chin and Ed Bakowsky leaped halfheartedly across the floor.

"Like this, man!" George yelled suddenly, covering the stage in three athletic leaps. He landed crookedly on one knee, arms flung wide, whooping in exhilaration. There was an embarrassed silence.

"Yeah," Jo said. "Like that."

"Who is that?" she asked Ava after the rehearsal.

"I don't know," Ava said, "but what a body."

"That's George Sakamoto," said Marsha Aquino, who knew about everyone. "He's bad."

Jo, unfamiliar with the current slang, took her literally.

"Well, he seems all right to me. If it wasn't for him, our dream ballet would look more like 'The Funeral March.' Is he new?"

"He transferred from St. Francis," Marsha said. "That's where all the F.O.B.s go."

Jo had always had a vague awareness of Japanese people as being unattractively shy and rather hideously proper. Nothing could have been further from this image than George. Jo and her friends, most of whom were of Asian descent, were stunned by him, as a group of domesticated elephants born and bred in a zoo might have been upon meeting their wild African counterpart for the first time. George was a revelation to Jo, who, on the subject of ethnic identity, had always numbered among the ranks of the sublimely oblivious.

George, meanwhile, was already laying his strategy. He was not called "*Sukebe* Sakamoto" by his friends for nothing.

"This chick is the door-hanger type," he told his friend Doug. "You gotta move real slow."

"Yeah," Doug said. "Too slow for you."

"You watch, sucker."

He called her one weekend and invited her and Ava to go bowling with him and Doug. Jo was struck dumb on the telephone.

"Ha-ro, is Jo there?"

"This is Jo."

"Hey, man. This is George."

"Who?"

"George, man. Sakamoto."

"Oh." Then she added shyly, "Hi."

The idea of bowling was revolting, but Jo could bowl for love.

She told her mother that she had a date. Her mother mentally filed through her list of acquaintances for a Sakamoto.

"Is that the Sakamoto that owns the cleaner on Fillmore?"

"I don't think so," Jo said.

"Well, if Ava's going, I guess it's all right."

When George came to pick her up, Jo introduced him to her father, who was sitting in the living room watching television.

"Ha-ro," George said, cutting a neat bow to her startled father.

"Was that guy Japanese?" her father asked later when she returned.

"Yeah," Jo said, chuckling.

There was an unspoken law of evolution which dictated that in the gradual march toward Americanization, one did not deliberately regress by associating with F.O.B.s. Jo's mother, who was second generation, had endured much criticism from her peers for "throwing away a college education" and marrying Jo's father, who had graduated from high school in Japan. Even Jo's father, while certainly not an advocate of this law, assumed that most people felt this way. George, therefore, was a shock.

On their second date, Jo and George went to see Peter O'Toole in a musical. From then on, they decided to dispense with the formalities, a decision owing only in part to the fact that the musical had been wretched. The main reason was that they were in love.

They would drive out to the beach, or to the San Bruno hills, and sit for hours, talking. In the protective shell of George's mother's car they found a world where they were not limited by labels. They could be complex, vulnerable. He told her about his boyhood in Kyushu, about the sounds that a Japanese house makes in the night. He had been afraid of ghosts. His mother had always told him ghost stories. She would make her eyes go round and utter strange sounds: "*Ka-ra . . . ko-ro . . . ka-ra . . . ko-ro . . .*"—the sound made by the wooden sandals of an approaching ghost. Japanese ghosts were different from American ghosts, he said. They didn't have feet.

"If they don't have feet," Jo asked curiously, "how could they wear sandals?"

George was dumbfounded. The contradiction had never occurred to him.

They went for motorcycle rides along the roads that wound through the Presidio, at the edge of cliffs overlooking the Golden Gate. Then, chilled by the brisk winter fog, they would stop at his house in Japantown for a cup of green tea.

He lived in an old Victorian flat on the border between Japantown and the Fillmore, with his mother and grandmother and cat. His mother worked, so it was his grandmother who came from the kitchen to greet them. (But this was later. At first, George made sure that no one would be home when they went. He wanted to keep Jo a secret until he was sure of her.)

The Victorian kitchen, the green tea, all reminded Jo of her grandparents' place, which had stood just a few blocks away from George's house before it was torn down. Jo had a vague memory of her grandmother cooking fish in the kitchen. She couldn't remember her grandfather at all. The war had broken his spirit, taken his business, forced him to do day work in white people's homes, and he had died when Jo was two. After that, Jo's family moved out of Japantown, and she had not thought about the past until George's house reminded her. It was so unexpected, that the swinger, the hood, the F.O.B. George Sakamoto should awaken such memories.

But they eventually had to leave the protective spaces that sheltered their love. Then the still George of the parked car and Victorian kitchen, the "real" George, Jo wanted to believe, evolved, became the flamboyant George, in constant motion, driven to maintain an illusion that would elude the cages of other people's limited imaginations.

He took her to dances Jo had never known existed. Jo had been only to school dances, where everyone stood around too embarrassed to dance. The dances that George took her to were dark, crowded. Almost everyone was Asian. Jo knew no one. Where did all these people come from? They were the invisible ones at school, the F.O.B.s. They *dressed* (unlike Jo and her crowd, who tended toward corduroy jeans). And they danced.

George was in his element here. In his skintight striped slacks flared at the calf, black crepe shirt open to the navel, billowing sleeves and satiny white silk scarf, he shimmered like a mirage in the strobe lights that cut the darkness. Then, chameleonlike, he would appear in jeans and a white T-shirt, stocking the shelves of Nakamura Hardware. At school, George shunned the striped shirts and windbreaker jackets that his peers donned like a uniform. He wore turtleneck sweaters under corduroy blazers, starched shirts in deep colors with cuff links. When he rode his bike, he was again transformed, a wild knight in black leather.

"The dudes I ride with," George confided to Jo in the car, "see me working in the store, and they say, 'Hey, what is this, man? You square a-sup'm?' Then the guys in the store, they can't believe I hang out with those suckers on bikes. 'Hey George,' they say, 'you one crazy son-of-a-bitch.' In school, man, these straight suckers can't believe it when I do good on a test. I mean, I ain't no hot shit at English, but I ain't no dumb sucker neither. 'Hey George,' they say, 'you tryin' to get into college a-sup'm?' 'Hey, why not, man?' I say. They can't take it if you just a little bit different, you know? All them dudes is like that—'cept you."

Jo was touched, and tried to be the woman of George's dreams. It was a formidable endeavor. Nancy Sinatra was the woman of George's dreams. For Christmas Jo got a pair of knee-high black boots. She wore her corduroy jeans tighter in the crotch.

"Hey, George," Doug said. "How's it goin' with Slow Jo?"

"None of your fuckin' business, man," George snapped.

"Oh-oh. Looks bad."

On New Year's Eve Jo discovered French kissing and thought it was "weird." She got used to it, though.

"You tell that guy," her father thundered, "that if he's gonna bring that motorcycle, he doesn't have to come around here anymore!"

"Jesus Christ!" Jo wailed, stomping out of the room. "I can't wait to get out of here!"

Then they graduated, and Jo moved to Berkeley in the spring.

The scene changed from the narrow corridors of Andrew Jackson High to the wide steps and manicured lawns of the university. George was attending a junior college in the city. He came over on weekends.

"Like good ice cream" he said. "I want to put you in the freezer so you don't melt."

"What are you talking about?"

They were sitting outside Jo's dormitory in George's car. Jo's roommate was a blonde from Colusa who had screamed the first time George walked into the room with Jo. ("Hey, what's with that chick?" George had later complained.)

"I want to save you," George said.

"From what?" Jo asked.

He tried another analogy. "It's like this guy got this fancy shirt, see? He wants to wear it when he goes out, man. He don't want to wear it every day, get it dirty. He wears an old T-shirt when he works under the car—get grease on it, no problem. It don't matter. You're like the good shirt, man."

"So who's the old T-shirt?" Jo asked, suddenly catching on.

"Hey, nobody, man. Nobody special. You're special. I want to save you."

"I don't see it that way," Jo said. "When you love someone, you want to be with them and you don't mind the grease."

"Hey, outasight, man."

So he brought her to his room.

George's room was next to the kitchen. It was actually the dining room converted into a young man's bedroom. It had the tall, narrow Victorian doors and windows, and a sliding door to the living room, which was blocked by bookshelves and a stereo. The glass-doored china cabinet, which should have housed Imari bowls, held tapes of soul music, motorcycle chains, Japanese comic books, and Brut. In Jo's grandparents' house there had been a black shrine honoring dead ancestors in the corner of the dining room. The same corner in George's room was decorated by a life-sized poster of a voluptuous young woman wearing skintight leather pants and an equally skintight (but bulging) leather jacket, unzipped to the waist.

George's mother and grandmother were delighted by Jo. In their eyes she was a "nice Japanese girl," something they never thought they would see, at least in conjunction with George. George had had a string of girlfriends before Jo, which had dashed their hopes. Jo was beyond their wildest expectations. It didn't seem to matter that this "nice Japanese girl" didn't understand any Japanese; George's grandmother spoke to her anyway, and gave her the benefit of the doubt when she smiled blankly and looked to George for a translation. They were so enthusiastic that George was embarrassed, and tried to sneak Jo in and out to spare her their effusions.

They would go to his room and turn up the stereo and make love to the lush, throbbing beat of soul. At first Jo was mortified, conscious of what her parents would say, knowing that "good girls" were supposed to "wait." But in the darkness of George's room, all of that seemed very far away.

So her first experiences of love were in a darkened room filled with the ghosts of missing Japanese heirlooms; in the spaces between the soul numbers with which they tried to dispel those ghostlike shadows, sounds filtered in from the neighboring kitchen: samurai music from the Japanese program on television, the ancient voice of his grandmother calling to the cat, the eternal shuffle of slippers across the kitchen floor. When his mother was home and began to worry about what they were doing in his room, he installed a lock, and when she began pounding on the door, insisting that it was getting late and that George really should take Jo home, George would call out gruffly, "Or-righ! Or-righ!"

But there was that other world, Jo's weekday world, a world of classical buildings, bookstores, coffee shops, and tear gas (for the United States had bombed Cambodia).

Jo flitted like a ghost between the two worlds so tenuously linked by a thin span of steel suspended over San Francisco Bay. She wanted to be still, and at home, but where? On quiet weekday mornings, reading in an empty courtyard with the stillness, the early morning sun, the language of Dickens, she felt her world full of promise and dreams. Then the sun rose high, people came out, and Jo and her world disappeared in a cloak of invisibility, like a ghost.

"Her English is so good," Ava's roommate remarked to Ava. "Where did she learn it?"

"From my parents," Jo said. "In school, from friends. Pretty much the same way most San Franciscans learn it, I guess."

Ava's roommate was from the East Coast, and had never had a conversation with an 'Oriental' before.

"She just doesn't know any better," Ava apologized later.

"Well where has that chick been all her life?" Jo fumed.

Then she would long for George, and he would come on the weekend to take her away. Locked together on George's bike, hurtling back and forth between two worlds, they found a place where they could be still and at peace.

George tried to be the man of her dreams. They went on hikes now instead of soul dances. He would appear in jeans and a work shirt, and he usually had an armload of books. He was learning to type, and took great pains over his essays for Remedial English.

But they began to feel the strain. It began to bother George that Jo made twenty-five cents an hour more at her part-time job in the student dining room than he did at the hardware store. He had been working longer. He needed the money. Jo, on the other hand, never seemed to buy anything. Just books. Although her parents could afford to send her to college, her high-school record had won her a scholarship for the first year. She lived in a dream world. She had it so easy.

He asked to borrow fifty dollars, he had to fix his car, and she lent it to him immediately. But he resented it, resented his need, resented her for having the money, for parting with it so easily. Everything, so easily. And he tortured her.

"Hey, is something wrong, man?" George asked suddenly, accusing, over the phone.

"Wrong?" Jo was surprised. "What do you mean?"

"You sound funny."

"What do you mean, funny?"

"You sound real cold, man," George said. His voice was flat, dull.

"There's nothing wrong!" Jo protested, putting extra emphasis in her voice to convince him, then hating herself for doing so. "I'm fine."

"You sound real far away," George went on, listlessly.

"Hey, is something bothering *you?*"

"No," George said. "You just sound funny to me. Real cold, like you don't care." He wanted her to be sympathetic, remorseful.

And at first she was—repentant, almost hysterical. Then she became impatient. Finally, she lapsed into indifference.

"I have the day off tomorrow," George said over the phone. "Can I come?"

Jo hesitated.

"I have to go to classes," she warned.

"That's okay," he said. "I'll come with you."

There was another long pause. "Well . . . we'll see," she said.

As soon as she saw him the next day, her fears were confirmed. He had gone all out. He wore a silky purple shirt open halfway to his navel, and skintight slacks that left nothing to the imagination. There was something pathetic and vulnerable about the line of his leg so thoroughly revealed by them. As they approached the campus, George pulled out a pair of dark shades and put them on.

He was like a character walking into the wrong play. He glowed defiantly among the faded jeans and work shirts of the Berkeley campus.

Jo's first class was Renaissance Literature.

"If you want to do something else," she said, "I can meet you after class."

"That's okay, man," George said happily. "I want to see what they teaching you."

"It's gonna be real boring," she said.

"That's okay," he said. "I have my psych book."

"If you're going to study," Jo said carefully, "maybe you should go to the library."

"Hey," George said, "you tryin' to get rid of me?"

"No," Jo lied.

"Then let's go."

They entered the room. It was a seminar of about ten people, sitting in a circle. They joined the circle, but after a few minutes of discussion about *Lycidas*, George opened his psychology textbook and began to read.

Jo was mortified. The woman sitting on the other side of George was looking curiously, out of the corner of her eye, at the diagram of the human brain in George's book.

"Would you care to read the next stanza aloud?"

the lecturer asked suddenly. "You—the gentleman with the dark glasses."

There was a horrible moment as all eyes turned to George, bent over his psychology textbook. He squirmed and sank down into his seat, as if trying to become invisible.

"I think he's just visiting," the woman next to George volunteered. "I'll read."

Afterwards, Jo was brutal. Why had he come to the class if he was going to be so rude? Why hadn't he sat off in the corner, if he was going to study? Or better yet, gone to the library as she had suggested? Didn't he know how inappropriate his behavior was? Didn't he care if they thought that Japanese people were boors? Didn't he know? Didn't he care?

No, he didn't know. He was oblivious. It was the source of his confidence, and that was what she had loved him for.

And so the curtain fell on their little drama, after a predictable denouement—agreeing that they would date others, then a tearful good-bye one dark night in his car, parked outside her apartment. Jo had always thought it somewhat disturbing when characters who had been left dead on the set in the last act, commanding considerable emotion by their demise, should suddenly spring to life not a minute later, smiling and bowing, and looking as unaffected by tragedy as it is possible to look. She therefore hoped she would not run into George, who would most certainly be smiling and bowing and oblivious to tragedy. She needn't have worried. Their paths had never been likely to cross.

Jo was making plans to study in New York when she heard through the grapevine that George was planning a trip to Europe. He went that summer, and when he returned, he brought her parents a gift. Jo's parents, who had had enough complaints about George when Jo was seeing him, were touched, and when Christmas came around Jo's mother, in true Japanese fashion, prepared a gift for George to return his kindness. Jo, of course, was expected to deliver it.

She had had no contact with him since they had broken up. His family was still living in Japantown, but the old Victorian was soon going to be torn down for urban renewal, and they were planning to move out to the Avenues, the Richmond District where Jo's parents lived.

As Jo's dad drove her to George's house, Jo hoped he wouldn't be home, hoped she could just leave the gift with his mother. She was thankful that she was with her father, who had a habit of gunning the engine as he sat waiting in the car for deliveries to be made, and was therefore the ideal person with whom to make a quick getaway.

George's grandmother opened the door. When she saw who it was, her face changed and she cried out with pleasure. Jo was completely unprepared for the look of happiness and hope on her face.

"Jo-chan!" George's grandmother cried; then, half-turning, she called out Jo's name twice more, as if summoning the household to her arrival.

Jo was stunned.

"This is for George," she said, thrusting the gift at George's grandmother, almost throwing it at her in her haste. "Merry Christmas."

She turned and fled down those stairs for the last time, away from the doomed Victorian and the old Japanese woman who stood in the doorway still, calling her name.

The Virgin's Passion

Lucía Guerra

Translated by Richard Cunningham
and Lucía Guerra

Lucía Guerra (1943–) came to the United States on a Fulbright Scholarship from her birthplace of Santiago, Chile. She was awarded a Ph.D. following her studies in Spanish and Portuguese at the University of Kansas, and is now a professor of Spanish at the University of California, Irvine. She and her Irish American husband, Richard Cunningham, are the award-winning translators of the work of María Luisa Bombal. The following story, originally published in Spanish and later translated into English by the author and her husband, was awarded first prize by the Mexican magazine Plural *when it first appeared in 1988. Guerra and Cunningham are the parents of two sons—Shannon and Pablo.*

I AM WRITING THIS ONLY TO FULFILL A PROMISE that I made long, long ago. Last night, after finishing the hem on Marita's skirt, I said to myself that if I have answered my duties to the family, surely I have the right to be dutiful to myself. Of course in that far-off time I didn't know that promises are little more than illusive pacts which give voice to hope. ("Oh Lord, I promise to pray four hours every day if Gustavo stops drinking!" I remember Aunt Adela whispering in every corner of the old house, without knowing, the poor thing, that her husband would die of cirrhosis—taking his untimely leave of her amid tears and horrifying screams.) My promise was also anchored in a hope. But being so young, how could I have known that some of us are born and yet do not truly exist until just before we die? In a movie I saw about ten years ago, or maybe it was fifteen, yes fifteen, because my nephew Jorge Javier had just graduated from high school, there appeared on the screen the image of an aborted child, which seemed to me the true reflection of myself: a body visible but without life.

A poor spinster you remain, without illusion, without faith; your heart grown sick with anguish; and today your mutilated life is but the setting of the sun. So goes the Tango that was so much in fashion in my youth, yet which still moves me—although it also makes me very angry. Mutilated life, yes (shouldn't I know!), but the real torment is that one never loses the illusion, nor the faith, or the hope that one day . . .

This is why I made the promise, which may sound ridiculous, especially at my age, but it was the most important thing in my life, and so it continues to be. The truth is that I do not recall when I stopped associating the word "virgin" with that statue cast in plaster and wrapped with Chantilly lace, wearing the crown of a queen on her head, that perfect profile tilted so tenderly toward the baby she never quite breast feeds, that tearful silhouette holding in her arms the wasted body of

From *Short Stories by Latin American Women: The Magic and the Real,* edited by Celia de Correas De Zapata. Reprinted by permission of the publisher, Arte Público Press.

her son. Without knowing how or when "virgin" started to mean "not yet to be," and as I started accumulating details on the loss of virginity, I began to wish with all my heart for the pain and the blood. (Stains on nuptial sheets; hoarse cries of pain; a sharp storm penetrating so deep as to damage the uterus; newlywed young girls, victims of an oversized mate, bleeding and pale in an emergency clinic—these were some of the colorful patches that covered the quilt of my adolescence, handed down in whispers by the older girls in the family.) The sword the young prince ceremoniously receives from his father's hands seemed therefore a dull image when set beside this other initiation of vagina and vocal chords, this act of becoming with your whole body. And I was seized by the intense desire to become a woman through this rite of blood and kisses, to open myself like a flower under the penetrating ray of a man who would be forever after the solar star of all my constellations. That is why it seemed to me silly and even profane that my cousins and my sisters one night agreed (they even signed an oath!) to share all the details of their wedding night. To me, my passage into real life would be a written and sacred text, an intimate testimonial which, as years went by, I would re-read the way one re-reads sacred scripture, and thereby reenacting the ritual, resubmerging myself in that dark and bloody night of my true birth.

I and my sixteen years in front of the window naively making a promise that dragged inside me like a large snake with no head or tail. I, bent over this sheet of paper, giving form to this wet and scaly weight inhabiting my body. I, the young girl of marriageable age who thought it would be so easy to take pen in hand and write a tale faithful to reality. I, to the relatives of now three generations, the kind old maid, expert in making flan and sewing silk. I, the deflowered old woman trying to start a tale that lengthens the wished-for wedding night into a burning chain of hours, days and years . . . Unlike the stories whispered by my cousins and my sisters, pregnant with details, and well-defined actions and sensations, I only have images, built up like barnacles inside me, not in my soul or my innocent heart, as they might think, but in this fiery box covered with hair as gray as ashes.

Tonight I see myself again in the back yard of the country house in that long-ago time of my childhood. Under the burning sun of a summer afternoon, I walk on a path of dry weeds, staring at the fruit of the trees which hide themselves among leaves covered with dust. We children of the house had already made off with the plums and apricots and figs that we could reach, but higher up, shiny as sin, hung a few that tempted my childish gluttony. Taking the long pole that supported the clothesline and climbing up onto two big stones, I started to hit at a plum growing between two branches. But the pole got stuck in the leaves, which fell on my freshly-cut hair, and in anger I began lashing out in all directions, and so fell to the ground. It was then that I heard a laugh from beneath the fig tree.

"No use swinging crazy like that. To grab fruit you gotta use tricks, same as with women!" said Antuco the gardener. "Come here, I'll pick you some ripe figs."

Happy and anxious, I parted the rough fig leaves which hung to the ground, and, putting my hands on my hips like the housekeeper did when she gave orders to the servants, I told Antuco to be quick about it. He took off his shirt, jumped onto a branch like a cat, and began crawling upward, filling his pockets with dark fruit.

"Didn't I tell you? You get what you want with tricks and strength. Look how fat and juicy they are! Melt in your mouth, they're so sweet. Only I don't know how the hell you're gonna carry them all. Listen, it'd be better to just eat them here, so's the other kids don't take them away from you." He jumped to the ground, landing nimbly on all fours. "Here, sit on my jacket, I always use it to take a nap about this time."

I sat down and he lay beside me, laughing. His face was full of mischief, and I, with my mouth stuffed with pink seeds and sweet juice, smiled gratefully back at him. Suddenly he put his hands between his legs and his smile faded.

"Shoot, kid, this old animal is getting hard again."

"What animal!" I asked, half curious and thinking it a game.

"A real nice little animal that rears up each time it sees a pretty girl," he said, closing his eyes.

And opening his pants, little by little he started showing me a piece of pink flesh that looked at first like a newborn mouse but then, as he stroked it, I saw it jump up furiously between his thighs.

"Lay down here beside me," he said, and I, still clutching two figs, obediently moved closer.

Rubbing my neck and back with his calloused hands, he led me into a lethargy of sun, fruit, and tenderness that recurred often throughout the rest of the summer.

I didn't know then that all the other suns in my life would prove to be so cruel, setting far too fast—callers who shone briefly and then went into an abrupt eclipse, leaving dark craters in my yearning soul. Now that time has taught me to know men, I think that I frightened them away with my eagerness, this passion for the other, angular body with its hard muscles which God ordained could only find rest and peace on the rounded spongy flesh of a woman. At this very moment I can see myself again, poring over movie magazines, cutting with frenzy the pictures of the famous actors of that era. Clark Gable smiling at me through cigar smoke! Tyrone Power in a bullfighter's costume, inviting me to enter the ring! Riding off into the sunset, Alan Ladd waves a reluctant goodbye! (Can still see myself, surrounded by all these irresistible men, trying to forget my sisters' trousseaus, their fussed-over pregnancies, and their children's birthday parties and First Communions.)

To this day I don't remember when I came to be considered the spinster of the family. In all honesty, I think that I was quite silly to allow them to dress me in garments which even now, at my age, seem foreign. The simple truth is that, through a kind of moral laziness, I allowed myself to become the kind and patient aunt who beat the eggs and embroidered the baby clothes, who with equal amounts of peroxide and love treated all the children's scratches. Poor little Inez, who irons clothes and sleeps alone, says another song; and that's what I was for them—the best housecleaner, a glorified maid who dreamed in her corner of a prince who never came. They didn't know, could not possibly have known that under those chaste garments, my body muzzled as it were, beat a primitive and tribal chant, a rhythm of horses running wild that made me moan in my sleep, tossing and tearing at my bonds like one lost at sea, pulled along by a tide as heavy as fruit ripening under the sun.

But Antuco came to save me. I cannot forget the day he arrived at our house. My father had just died, and my mother had gathered all of us together to distribute what she called the sentimental part of his legacy. On the dining room table she began to place his pocket watch, several pairs of fine French cuffs, tie pins he had collected on all his journeys, old postcards where radiant couples stood framed by violets, fountain pens, wooden chests which we had never seen opened. With an almost ritual seriousness, she started to parcel out our inheritance. Taking up a leather-bound photo album, she handed it to me, saying, "This is for you. We all know how much you like pictures." That night, half asleep, I began leafing through the sepia images of young men with walking sticks and derby hats, of gentlemen who stared back at me with solemn expressions made even more serious by the size of their thick mustaches, ladies in white hats and high lacy collars. Suddenly I came upon a photo that altered this landscape of solemnity, one taken at a picnic: a row of well-dressed men stood at the rear; in front of them, seated, a group of ladies holding parasols; before them crouched boys in short trousers and little girls with ribbons in their braids; and in the foreground, as though he were the center of all attention, lay Antuco, holding up, with an amused and mischievous air, a demijohn of wine. We looked at each other for a long time, my eyes on his even as I opened the drawer of the night table and groped for a pair of scissors. "Many things have happened during all these years, Antuco; but nothing has happened to me," I told him as I rescued him from that bourgeois and ornamental group of unrelaxed correctness. He lowered his eyes in sadness, then looked at me again with the same expression he wore when I entered that lair of his within the overhanging branches of the fig tree.

With Antuco's arrival, it no longer irked me to wear the dark blue and gray dresses my family liked to see me in (although of course they never said so openly), and I ceased to grumble every time one of my sisters phoned me to ask that I stop by the San Camilo Bakery to pick up pastry, or to buy at the Cordonería Alemana the bronze buttons which absolutely had to be ready for my nephew's school uniform the following morning. All these mundane chores became as seaweed carried away in the undertow of evening when, as I dozed, Antuco would caress my back, and once again I tasted the ripe fruit of summer as he lulled me to sleep . . . Writing this, I cannot pinpoint the exact night when those seeds soaked in sweetness started to descend like mysterious ants, moving from my palate to awaken my womb. Antuco's fingertips seemed to multiply, roaming every inch of my skin while, face down and trembling with pleasure, I bounced on the hard sheet, listening to the wet sound of his thighs and picturing the pink flesh of his excited organ. In those moments my whole body became a huge wave about to break on the sand, and I felt, if such a thing is possible, like a sealed volcano rumbling under the moon. And thus suspended on this wave, caught and held in an impending storm that never burst, I would find myself watching the first rays of dawn creep across my bed.

To my family's alarm, dark lines appeared under my eyes, and my countenance took on that gray aspect of someone seriously ill. Diligently, my oldest niece took me to various specialists, who examined me in laboratories full of strange objects—slabs of lead, transparent tubes, hidden screens, metallic devices they inserted down my throat. (And all for nought—How could anyone have imagined my nocturnal torment?) At dusk my hands started trembling, and my chin began to feel the tickling that announced the Calvary of my body. In vain I would implore Antuco to help me; only he could release this scream that was stuck in my lips like a bloody wound. "I can't," he whispered one night. "I'd best be off . . ." And waving goodbye in the mirror, he vanished into air. I sat up in bed with a start, and with my hands on my hips I ordered him to return immediately. My heart heaving, I waited in vain until the sun illuminated the window curtains, and then I felt that reptilian weight of my promise coiling itself tight around my body.

They all thought I couldn't hear them criticizing me under their breath. Naturally my hearing isn't what it used to be, especially in my left ear—although this particular defect, as they well knew, was due not to old age but to the ball my nephew Gustavo accidentally hit me with when he was fourteen years old. They don't seem to need me anymore, but I feel certain that should an emergency arise, they will all run in search of their good old auntie.

It was Mercedes, the kindest of my sisters, who convinced me to take a vacation. ("Inesita, my dear, it's been a long time since you've had a real rest. Señora María's daughter tells me that in Puerto Montt there is a wonderful boarding house with a very quiet atmosphere.") I was so weary of their ill-concealed gossip about me, so tired of entering rooms where the conversation suddenly ceased, that four days later I found myself bidding goodbye to my niece Angélica and her children on the boarding platform of the Estación Central.

The trip was very uncomfortable, but I didn't mind, because I had already made up my mind to give Albertito a big surprise. I was going to look for some shells to add to the precious collection he had started on his fifteenth birthday. He always said that on the shores of Chiloé one could find spectacular molluscs from long-extinct species, and that truly fine fossilized clams lay on the sand like fallen fruit, ripe for the picking. I would wait until we were alone to hand him this new treasure and, picking me up in his strong arms, he would say, "Thank you, mamicha, thank you!" Albertito was the only one who did not call me aunt. And rightly so, for he is the only one who is like a true son to me. I was already forty years old when he was born, but I took him to live with me barely six months later, and he did not return to his parents until he entered grammar school. He was the only one who met Antuco, one day during his fourth year of school when he stopped by for tea after football practice. That afternoon I was sewing a button in his blue jacket, and I asked him to hand me the thimble that I always keep in the drawer of my night table. When he saw Antuco, he asked me who he was, and I told him that Antuco was my secret fiancé. (There were so many secrets that I shared with Albertito!)

Immediately after settling into the boarding house I went to ask about the excursion boats that regularly visited the nearby islands. The following morning, after a leisurely and delightful journey down the coast, we docked at Chiloé. Once ashore, I stopped to ask an old fisherman about the shells. "The only one who keeps such things," he said, "is Ignacio, because he's a kind of witch, you know? He lives up there," he added, pointing over his shoulder. Under the midday sun I started walking toward a hut almost hidden among the trees on a nearby hill. Parting the waist-high weeds as I went, I arrived at the hut with my shoes covered with burrs. The door was made of upright logs, and I knocked on it with a rock I presume was the owner's doorstop.

"There's no bread in this house for beggars or curious people," shouted a voice from within. Shouting back, I told him that I had come to attend to very important business. I heard movement, and I had the impression of someone hurriedly washing his face, and then the door swung open.

"Come right on in, mam," said Antuco, much younger, and wearing a mustache.

The dark room was like a cave strewn with shells of all sizes and shapes and colors. The bone-white stalks of picoroco shells hung down from the ceiling like blunt stalactites. Large shells as deep as basins were attached to the walls like some growth, reflecting and refracting color, they shimmered in pink and gray as though alive. On a heavy wooden table slept enormous conch snails; clams that kept watch, opening and closing their slimy mouths; mussels sheltering small crustaceans in their thick black hair. "You shouldn't have disobeyed me, Antuco," I said. And, making the sign of the cross, he knelt and started to kiss my feet. "I am still the virgin girl who lay beside you under the fig tree," I added, taking off my black, cotton dress.

He nodded and said, "Holy Mary, mother of God." And then he began climbing my body with burning kisses that melted the scales of the long-hated snake. Solemnly he led me to a bed reeking of algae and sea water, and my thighs finally sheltered him in that pulsating ritual of blood and hot, spurting wax.

I returned to the continent at twilight, staring at the black clouds menacing the horizon, my hands folded on my placidly aching lap. At long last I was the owner of all dawns, and as I write the last words of the testimony of my true birth, I hear outside the steps of Antuco—returning, to stay with me forever.

To Have & To Hold

Christine Schutt

Christine Schutt (1948–   ) was born in Heartland, Wisconsin, and received her bachelor's and master's degrees from the University of Wisconsin. Moving to New York City, she entered the Columbia University School of Arts, earned a Master of Fine Arts degree, and became a New Yorker, teaching English and writing short stories. About "To Have & To Hold" (1992) she says, "The story came to me very quickly, and I took pleasure in the speed with which it came together. I was able to say something about the threat of the other woman and the wife's curiosity about her. People enjoy this story. They laugh when they read it."

I HAVE ACCIDENTS IN THE FIFTH AVENUE KITCHEN—cuts, falls, scaldings. What could I be thinking of when I scissor through a plugged cord? My sleeve catches fire on the burner, and all I do is watch its crinkling into nothing. Fast as paper, it burns, filling the kitchen with a stink of burnt hair, my hair, and that is what finally makes me run for the salt, the smell of me catching fire.

Worse things happen in the kitchen—my husband tells me he is in love with someone else, and what do I do? I go out and buy he- and she-gerbils to make us feel more like a family.

I hate the gerbils. Nothing about them is cute; they twitch and gnaw. The animals live in a plastic, night-glow cage set next to the stove, because this kitchen is small, even if it is on Fifth Avenue, and here they scrabble and play and shred their tray paper—dirty animals that eat their own tails.

The girl was the first at it. One morning I found her dragging her rump through the shavings, scooting around the cage, past the boy. His tail was whole; hers was stubbed, pink, wet-looking. I saw her dizzying chase of it. I thought, maybe this is a mating ritual, maybe this is natural. What do I know? Except a few days later, some of the boy's tail was missing; now both of these cannibals are nearly tailless.

This eating has nothing to do with making baby gerbils. I don't think they even like one another. When the gerbils escape from their cage, and they escape every night, squiggling through a gnawed-away part, I never find them huddling. I might find the boy under the sink, the girl near the warm and coiled back of the refrigerator. I catch them up with a dishcloth; I can't stand to touch these silly savages—who could?—especially since they started eating themselves.

I want to know why my husband picked this woman to love, this woman who has been in my kitchen, who once helped me dry the silverware. This woman my husband loves is always, always on my mind here in the kitchen, where she once hugged me good-bye in her fur and pearls. I split open the coals of feeling to feel the buckle on her belt heat up in my hand. I touch her skirt and the stitched spine of her high heels. I am in a kind of hurry. I snatch at her nylons, her bag. Her bag is the color of toffee; I could eat it, I could gnaw off the clip to where the lining riffles with the scent of her, perfume and pennies and lipstick. Would she want to trade her clothes for my kitchen? Does she want babies?

The Fifth Avenue kitchen is so bright and clean. My husband says the counters are still gritty with cleanser. He says the food's embarrassed to be seen.

I admit it, I am driven. Last thing I do each night is wash my floor. One of the reasons the gerbils are such a problem is that they are so ridiculously dirty.

I should get out of the kitchen.

I should set the gerbils free.

I should let the scrub pads rust and the inky vouchers stain the counters. I should mess up.

My husband says the fridge door reads like an advertisement. He says the door is not a bulletin board. He says, Why don't you get a datebook, act like other people?

I thought that's what I was doing—acting like other people. So much space glinting off the white dune of Fifth Avenue, I thought, other people must want this, but not, it seems, the woman my husband wants. She, he says, wants to pitch her umbrella elsewhere.

Where?

I am standing here with the gerbils, who are loose again and scrabbling over my bare feet.

There is broken glass on the floor.

I can't help what happens.

The kitchen is sprung like an army knife, and I am in a hurry.

I have thrown open the window and am moving fast to catch these gerbils with only my hands. First the girl, who is trembling and trying to nip me, I swing her by the leg and out the window, she is gone. Then I make for the boy, hiding in a corner.

I think he thinks he is safe; he doesn't move. Lost, pointless, filthy boy.

I toss him underhand—just like rice.

Vase

Ou-yang Tzu

Translated by Limin Chu

Ou-yang Tzu (1939–) was born of Chinese parents in Hiroshima, Japan. She studied English at National Taiwan University before coming to the United States to enter the Creative Writing Workshop at the University of Iowa where she earned an M.F.A. Her stories are collected in Girl with the Long Hair *(1967) and* Leaves of Autumn *(1971). As a writer of fiction, she specializes in psychological studies which are marked by precise language and a rejection of sentimentalism.*

"Vase" was first published in Hong Kong but reprinted in 1990 as part of the collection *Bamboo Shoots After the Rain: Contemporary Stories by Women Writers of Taiwan.*

SHIH CHIH-CHUAN, PUTTING DOWN THE CHOPsticks, took up the bowl of soup from the table. With both hands holding fast the bowl, his fingers continued to tremble slightly. Sitting opposite him, Feng Lin was finishing her last bit of rice. Shih, bowing his head, lifted his soup and began to sip it.

He was resentful of his own mood of uneasiness. After all, he was not in the least at fault. But he knew that he would never be able to face himself again for the rest of his life if he did not do as he had planned this evening.

"We're going to see the movie at the Far East this evening," he said finally.

But, after blurting that out, he immediately felt a little regretful since the tone of his statement wasn't exactly what he intended, wasn't quite the thing. He had had no intention of making the statement sound like an order.

Feng said nothing in reply for the moment. Shih, watching her from the corner of his eye, saw her put down her chopsticks and stare straight at the table. An inexplicable bit of a smile began to play around the corners of her mouth.

"We haven't been to the movies together for quite some time," Shih added. He put down his soup bowl and looked up. He had a rather pale face and a slightly upturned nose, but his jaw and cheekbones were well shaped. You wouldn't call him handsome, but it could be said that he was rather good-looking.

He found Feng staring at him with a challenging look. That vague light of hostility in her eyes aroused in Shih an extraordinarily thrilling sensation. "I hold an advantage over her after all," he thought. "She believes she is superior to me; everyone believes she is superior to me, but actually I have been the victor. I hold the trump card."

He waited patiently for Feng's answer. To cover up his curiosity, he began to sip his soup again. He secretly heaved a sigh of relief, because it was now his wife's turn to say something; if she would say nothing, that wouldn't be his fault.

"This time I have really succeeded in making her face the impossible," he thought. He really was anxious to see how she was going to answer him. Would she dare to admit it? Would she dare to say, "No, I can't go with you. I have a date with somebody else"? Or, would she be able to think of some other excuse? Shih felt himself in control of the situation; now it was obvious he could do with her as he pleased. He couldn't think of anywhere she could escape to.

For the last two years, what had most piqued Shih was his mad love for Feng. He loved her so much that he began to hate her. Her existence was forever tormenting him, making him feel ill at ease. She was twenty-eight, only two years his junior, but she appeared to be just past twenty. With abundant black hair set against her milky white complexion, she was extremely attractive; the thinness of her lips made them even more appealing. She herself was especially proud of the beauty mark on her right cheek. Feng Lin was a real beauty and, like all beautiful women, she liked to dominate others, always demanding that others adjust themselves to her and never willing to try and adjust herself to accommodate others. In front of his wife, Shih never felt like a man or her husband. For this, he hated her, and hated himself. He could not forgive Feng Lin for lacerating his manly dignity.

Often Shih felt the desire to rebel surging in his heart, but when he discovered that it was just "desire" with no "power," he became as desperate as he was angry, like a beast at bay.

But what made him most desperate was his consciousness that there was no way for him to resist her spell. Burning jealousy kept torturing him. He was jealous of Feng Lin's every movement, every gesture. Even her smile was intolerable because he thought she had no right to feel happy behind his back. But if she cried (notwithstanding the fact that this was rare), he would find it even more intolerable; he was jealous of and hated any tears that were not shed for his sake.

However, in order to maintain his dignity, he kept suppressing this kind of almost abnormal jealousy. Not to betray himself, he even went so far as to deliberately appear indifferent and refrained from making inquiries about Feng Lin's private matters. Shih Chih-chuan was very proud—at least he showed himself to be terribly proud because of his feelings of inferiority. He would often keep himself distant from her so that she might not suspect his desire, his need of her. But secretly he was always watching her and whenever possible took in every little gesture of hers. Gradually he found himself hating her out of jealousy more than loving her; he could stand not possessing her himself, but found it difficult to tolerate any contact between her and the world. The world, to him, was so spacious—there was so much going on in the world that he couldn't know!

Feng Lin, however, appeared to be totally unaware of her husband's secret sensations. She was forever busy about her own activities, writing letters, seeing friends, etc. There were so many things to occupy, to amuse her. This couple were used to the idea of respecting each other as husband and wife should, but each felt a strange shadow between them—the existence of a certain kind of hypocrisy. It was as if the two of them were engaged in a fierce fight over something unnameable on an invisible battleground.

"She thinks she has an edge on me," thought Shih Chih-chuan, "but she doesn't understand me, she doesn't comprehend what's on my mind. I'm far cleverer than she. She doesn't know that in this psychological warfare I'm in control of her—she's unaware that she's being deceived! I never interfere with her, but does this mean I've given up? No, of course not! I know everything about her! I know everything that she thinks I don't and more!"

"What's on at the Far East?" Feng Lin asked, eyes still on the table.

"*Fated Love*," answered Shih, his hands still holding the soup bowl, watching Feng Lin from above its brim.

Feng frowned slightly.

Now just look at that frown, observed Shih. A sharp thrill flashed like electricity through his consciousness. His greatest wish today was to hurt her in order to ease the pain of his own tormented love these past days. Love! Terrifying love!

Again he couldn't help remembering that terrible night not so long before. That night, in a friend's house, he drank a lot of wine; feeling flushed and perspiring, he was quite full of tipsy sensations. When he got home, Feng Lin glanced at him and shrugged her shoulders slightingly and, in an insulting tone, told him he had had too much to drink. Thereupon he suddenly lost his usual composure. With one hand seizing her dress, another fastened on her arm, he pulled her into their bedroom and brutally pushed her onto the bed. "Don't think I dare not!" he cried hoarsely, "Don't think I dare not!" When he saw the contempt on her face, his anger instantly shot up to the boiling point. Brutally he began peeling off her clothes, one piece after another, and threw them on the ground as if his life depended on it. "Who are you anyway to slight me! What have you got anyway to slight me so!" He ground his teeth, but his voice began to quiver, sobs intermingled with words.

That was indeed a horrible night! He had almost committed an unforgivable crime. Awakened in the middle of the night, he discovered Feng Lin sleeping in his arms, a half-moon shining through the screen window upon her naked body. He remembered his drunken loss of manners. Shame and disgust, regret and chagrin shot through his heart. But Feng Lin was sleeping so peacefully, her breathing even, her chest rising and falling normally. At that moment nothing like contempt was on her face. She belonged to him at that moment, was completely and totally his. He was a man, a complete man. Shih Chih-chuan sat up, single-mindedly watching this beautiful woman bathed in moonlight. Slowly he began to caress her flesh. First he put a hand on her calf, then gradually moving upwards he caressed her smooth legs and thighs, her plump buttocks, then he turned his attention to her soft triangle and bulging breasts. Finally his hand stopped on her neck.

Her neck was small and delicate, so small and delicate that it could all be over in a matter of minutes if he exerted some pressure. He believed he could do it. Everything would then be so simple. She would never be awake but forever rest in peace and remain his woman. He could do as he pleased with her body, like other husbands with their wives, without feeling ashamed, nor suffering from looks of contempt. No longer necessary to guard against being controlled by her, no more fear of losing his dignity before her. When her body began to decay, he might lose her, but never again would he have to worry about losing her or feel insecure from morning till night. All pains would disappear. He could be released from bondage and obtain his freedom . . .

But Feng Lin was sleeping so serenely. On her marblelike face, the nose lifted high, with eyelash shadows below her eyelids. Shih Chih-chuan's fingers trembled, his whole frame was on fire; his eyes were dry and perspiration oozed out of the corners of his forehead. Just as he was about to concentrate all his might to . . . suddenly Feng Lin stopped breathing. Although her eyes remained shut, her eyelashes appeared under the somber moonlight to be stirring slightly. Shih felt himself suddenly paralyzed, and whatever energy he was gathering up was all lost in an instant. Falling back, he desperately bit into the pillow case, shedding tears of despair.

Not unexpectedly, a mysterious, inexplicable expression appeared on Feng Lin's face. She placed the bowls and plates one on top of the other in a pile, stood up, left the dining room, and went into the bedroom. The maid came in and took the dishes away. She returned with a piece of cloth and began to wipe the dining table. Finishing the job and turning to leave, her plump figure bumped against a small table near the wall. Shih Chih-chuan's heart suddenly contracted and he nearly cried out loud.

The flower vase shook but did not fall.

Shih sighed with relief, stepped across and carefully lifted the vase and pressed it against his cheek.

A thrilling stream of icy coolness coursed through his whole body.

This porcelain vase, brought over by a friend from Kyoto two months before, was a thing of delicate grace and beauty, smooth and refined, with surface designs of rare flowers, radiating extraordinarily gleaming colors. Shih fell in love with it the moment he saw it. Whenever his fingers slowly caressed its smooth coolness, he never failed to experience an indescribable thrill, sharp and akin to pain. But he couldn't stand to let others finger it or touch it. At first he was going to lock up the vase, but Feng Lin laughed at him. No, she did not laugh at him, but he felt that her eyes were laughing at him. This angered him so that he changed his mind, took out the vase and placed it on the small table in a corner of the dining room. But he wouldn't let any flowers be put in the vase. Every morning he would personally wipe the dust off it carefully with a piece of wool. He would begin to feel uneasy the moment any guest stepped in and wished the intruder would not look in the direction of that corner table. He would feel bad if his treasure were discovered. "How handsome! Where on earth did you get it?" It would then be handled and admired. At such moments his pain was like having his own heart cut out and fingered and admired by others.

Shih Chih-chuan stepped into the bathroom, hurriedly washed his face, and turned into the bedroom. Sitting in front of her dresser, Feng Lin suddenly looked up and her eyes clashed with his in the glass. Both seemed shocked at the same time, but it lasted only for a fraction of a second. Immediately Feng looked down, picked up a brush and began combing her hair. Shih squinted at her. "She has guilty feelings," he thought, "and I'd like to see what kind of pretext she can think up."

"The show doesn't start until nine," he said, "it's only seven now. Rather too early to dress up."

Feng Lin set her mind on combing her hair, saying nothing and not looking up.

"But you might as well begin dressing now, because tonight I want you to look particularly beautiful," Shih Chih-chuan said, feeling he had an absolutely superior edge on her. Without guilty feelings, he thought, she would not have appeared so submissive. All of a sudden he felt his "masculinity" recovered since Feng Lin was in an abyss of despair, unable to fight him.

"Make yourself beautiful," he said again, "for we haven't been out together for quite a long time." He was determined to hurt her and conclude this long drawn out war tonight. He knew the victory would be his.

Feng Lin put down the brush and ever so slightly shrugged her shoulders.

"I didn't say I was going out with you," she replied.

"What, you're not going? You're not going to the movie?" cried Shih. He was well prepared to fight this battle.

"I haven't decided," said Feng, smearing cold cream on her face with her delicate thin fingers.

"Not decided? What's the matter? You're putting on your makeup, getting ready to leave." Shih kept his eyes on her.

With both hands spreading the cold cream evenly over her forehead and cheeks, she slowly and softly massaged them. She had on a chemise, revealing two bare arms, very sexy looking. Staring at her, Shih really would have liked to bite her.

"What I mean is," Feng began, without looking at him as usual. "What I mean is, I haven't decided which date to keep."

"What? Oh, good heavens, you have another date tonight?" Shih, staring with widening eyes, pretended surprise and disappointment.

Feng quickly lifted her eyes and boldly looked at him in the glass without blinking.

"You know it," she said, every word loud and clear and cold.

Shih shuddered.

"You know it, why pretend," she repeated, eyes flashing with obvious hostility.

Shih's complexion paled. His estimate went wrong. For the moment he couldn't think of anything new.

"I—I know it? You, what—what do you mean?" he blurted.

A little vague smile flashed across her face, but she said nothing.

Suddenly a huge wave of indignation overwhelmed him. Completely beside himself, Shih rushed toward Feng, seized her shoulders and roughly turned her around. The action caught her by surprise and she couldn't help crying out. The two stared at each other. Shih kept both his hands fastened on her sexy arms. Feng tried to struggle a while but soon gave up. She didn't cry out again, remained extraordinarily composed, but turned very pale.

"Speak up! What do you mean?" shouted Shih, shuddering with rage.

Cold flame darted out of Feng's two fiery sockets.

"You really want to know?" she asked darkly.

"Tell me!" Shih roared, pressing his fingers more tightly around her arms.

Around the corners of her mouth gradually appeared a smile of contempt.

"All right, then, listen well," she began, coldly and brutally. "You thought I didn't know? You're jealous of me, insanely jealous. Yesterday when my cousin called me, you were eavesdropping behind the door and heard that I was invited out to a play. You really think I don't know? Ever since my cousin returned from the States half a year ago, you've been watching me every step of the way as if I were going to elope with him any moment. It's really extremely comical. If you're jealous, why didn't you come right out and say so? Why didn't you act like a man and simply stop me from seeing him? Why didn't you do it? Why?" she ceased, turning crimson in her paleness.

Shih's face turned ashy. His breathing became difficult. Releasing Feng, he weakly let fall his hands.

"You—you—" he wanted to say something, but only stammered.

"And that's not all," Feng continued indicting him. "I kept the letters from friends in my desk drawer and you examined every one of them in my absence. I wouldn't be surprised at all if you were able to recite their contents from memory. Whenever you do something, whatever it is, you're afraid that I will laugh, that others will laugh, so you always do things secretly, behind one's back, like a night cat.

When I went out, you shadowed me, didn't you? Didn't you? You thought I didn't know?

"Maybe you thought you were putting one over on me, but let me tell you something—I know you didn't know I knew. I merely pretended and you thought I didn't understand you. Why should you be so jealous? I'm your wife, you have certain rights concerning me. When did I ever refuse you? It's all your own fault. You deliberately stood apart and pretended to be aloof. If you were really aloof and inaccessible, why then didn't you set me free? I know you. You wanted to have me under your control, to put me in your pocket, and yet you didn't dare. You don't have guts enough, so you began to hate me and schemed to take revenge. All right, why didn't you screw up your courage to avenge yourself? You played with eavesdropping. You learned I had a date with my cousin, and then asked me to see *Fated Love* in the same evening deliberately—did you really think that would hurt me and make it impossible for me? How wrong, how utterly wrong you are!"

The longer she talked the more triumphant and eloquent she became. She ceased now, breathing hard a while, her face all flushed with excitement.

Shih struggled with himself.

"Nonsense! A whole pack of nonsense!" he finally blurted out these few words, both hands holding fast the back of a chair, his face completely contorted.

"Nonsense?" Feng began to smile triumphantly, her attitude entirely at ease, her tone totally contemptuous. "You say I was talking nonsense? Ha! Never was there more truth! You really felt yourself unmanly; you hated me because I saw through you. Don't deny it, you cannot deceive me."

"Cheat! You—a cheat!" Shih hoarsely hissed, cold sweat oozing all over his forehead.

Insolently shrugging her shoulders and turning to the mirror, Feng ignored him. She picked up an eyebrow pencil and carefully started to paint her eyebrows.

All this took Shih completely by surprise. On the psychological battlefield he thought the victory was his; it was entirely unexpected that he should have suffered such ignominious defeat and humiliation. Feng was sitting there, aloof and serene, painting her eyebrows with one bare arm lifted high. He always thought that he was clever, intellectually far superior to Feng. He didn't realize she knew everything. He had failed! He had always failed!

Shih could hear his own heavy breathing. In the reflection of the dresser's glass, he saw Feng secretly glancing at him.

Feng soon finished painting her lips. She stood up, walked over to the bureau and took out a purple *ch'i-p'ao** with flower designs, a dress ordered two years before especially for their wedding, and a special favorite of Shih's. Feng loosened her chemise, let it fall to the ground, and stood there, almost completely naked. Shih hurriedly shifted his gaze. Gracefully, and taking her time, Feng put on her slip and the *ch'i-p'ao.* She twisted herself into the *ch'i-p'ao* and made it fit closely to every part of her voluptuous body.

"Shall we go?" She broke silence eventually, her voice surprisingly soft. "Let's go a little earlier so we'll be sure to get tickets."

At this, Shih suddenly turned around to face her. His complexion became greenish, lips purplish, eyes darting with hellish flame.

"Go! Go!" He shouted madly. "Go and find your cousin! Go away! Who wants you! Who wants you, anyway!" He waved his arms like an idiot. Then, his strength utterly exhausted, he stopped screaming and sank paralyzed into a chair.

He was feeling dizzy.

Although in a daze, he felt Feng drawing near and finally standing before him.

"Chih-chuan," she called him, softly, her hand touching his forehead.

As if shocked by electricity he jumped up from the chair.

"Get out!" He shouted with all his might. "You slut! Slut! Get out of here!"

Feng's face, at one moment so softened, now turned ghastly pale, but she stood facing him without flinching and a fierce light of hostility began to flash out from her sockets once more.

"You really want me to leave?" she asked in an icy tone.

"Scram! Bitch . . . ! Get the hell out of here!"

He suddenly gave her a push and she stumbled out of the bedroom and almost fell.

"Scram! Bitch . . . ! Get the hell out of here!"

"Since you want me to leave," she said, "since you're forcing me to leave, forcing me to elope—oh, to elope!" And she broke into laughter without restraint all of a sudden.

"Scram . . . ! Scram!" he shouted, stepping toward her menacingly.

* A close-fitting dress with a high neck and a slit skirt.

"All right, don't worry, I'm going this instant, but remember, it's you who wanted me to leave," she was saying as she was walking forward. But she stopped short, turned and asked him:

"Guess, did I ever love you?"

"Scram . . . !" he roared, eyes flashing with fire.

She tossed her head lightly, raised her hand to touch her hair and then smiled a vague smile—an icy smile.

"Oh, yes, I did love you once," she said. "Too bad it was only for one short moment—that instant when you were prepared to strangle me."

"Get out . . . !"

Feng was leaving, passing through the drawing room, opening the door. Shih, eyes bloodshot, was still angrily looking at her, standing at the bedroom threshold.

"That night, why didn't you strangle me?" She turned around again, taunting him. "You want me to say it? It was because—because you were afraid! You were afraid! Afraid!"

Shih plunged forward, but Feng had already stepped out and banged the door shut. He leaned against it, breathing hoarsely. It was as if the sky were about to fall.

Shutting his eyes, he kept breathing hoarsely for almost five minutes. When he opened his eyes, the first object in his line of vision was the vase on the corner table. Unexpectedly his heart contracted all of a sudden.

The light reflected from its polished surface and its flowery designs seducingly drew him toward it, making him feel itchy all over. He walked over and picked up the vase. A thrilling coolness stole through his heart, stimulating, sharply stimulating. With both hands on the neck of the vase, he strangled it mightily, wishing above all else to crush it into powder. But it was so sturdy. So delicate in appearance, but so surprisingly indestructible.

Tomorrow, there would be guests again. Certain enough they would again begin to admire it as they pleased, touching it, caressing it, making it smudgy. "Look, how pretty! How refined!" they would say, thinking such compliments would please him.

And then, at some time or other the stupid, fat body of the maid would again bump into the corner table, causing the vase to shake. Sooner or later it would be broken by he didn't know who. He had to be careful and guard against such an accident all the time. But that would make him so nervous. He had been suffering from nervous depression. This precious flower vase was indeed a little too much for him. It was beautiful, too beautiful, so beautiful as to pain him, so painful as to make the whole situation unbearable. Everybody has eyes that can see the vase. Nobody is likely to shut his eyes so as not to look at it. Who knows, one of these days it may simply disappear—stolen by a thief or burnt to ashes when the house catches fire. He had to take care of it and worry about it, but his nerves—they were in such bad shape.

Ah, since eventually the day would come so that . . . Why not now? Why not now?

Shih lifted his arms high. He set his face rigid, whirled the vase madly around in the air, and then violently threw it on the floor.

Unexpectedly this frail and graceful vase flew across the floor and fell before the sofa onto the center of a thick and soft nylon carpet. It somersaulted lightly until it sat on its base, proud and still, without the slightest scratch.

For quite a while, Shih stared straight at this marvelous, shining vase, with unbelief and curiosity on his face. It was as if he could not trust his own eyes. But the vase was haughtily sitting there still, as if smiling at him. Finally he bent his knees, knelt and began to crawl forward, single-mindedly intending to recapture it. But before he could reach the vase, his whole frame suddenly became paralyzed, exhausted, unable to move. With his hands on the ground, he started to cry like a helpless child.

My Man Bovanne

Toni Cade Bambara

Toni Cade Bambara (1939–) was born in New York City. With a master's degree in literature (City College of New York, 1964) and interests in linguistics, film, theater, and mime, she is also a writer and civil rights activist. As a screen writer, she has scripted "Zora" (1971) and "Tar Baby" (1984), based on Toni Morrison's novel. Novelist Anne Tyler says that, as a writer of fiction, "what pulls us along is the language of [her] characters, which is startlingly beautiful without once striking a false note." Bambara is to street talk what Ella Fitzgerald is to jazz. Critic C. D. B. Bryan writes that Bambara's real subject is love: "love for one's family, one's friends, one's race, one's neighborhood, . . . the sort of love that comes with maturity and inner peace."

BLIND PEOPLE GOT A HUMMIN JONES IF YOU NOTICE. Which is understandable completely once you been around one and notice what no eyes will force you into to see people, and you get past the first time, which seems to come out of nowhere, and it's like you in church again with fat-chest ladies and old gents gruntin a hum low in the throat to whatever the preacher be saying. Shakey Bee bottom lip all swole up with Sweet Peach and me explainin how come the sweet-potato bread was a dollar-quarter this time stead of dollar regular and he say uh hunh he understand, then he break into this *thizzin* kind of hum which is quiet, but fiercesome just the same, if you ain't ready for it. Which I wasn't. But I got used to it and the onliest time I had to say somethin bout it was when he was playin checkers on the stoop one time and he commenst to hummin quite churchy seem to me. So I says, "Look here Shakey Bee, I can't beat you and Jesus too." He stop.

So that's how come I asked My Man Bovanne to dance. He ain't my man mind you, just a nice ole gent from the block that we all know cause he fixes things and the kids like him. Or used to fore Black Power got hold their minds and mess em around till they can't be civil to ole folks. So we at this benefit for my niece's cousin who's runnin for somethin with this Black party somethin or other behind her. And I press up close to dance with Bovanne who blind and I'm hummin and he hummin, chest to chest like talkin. Not jammin my breasts into the man. Wasn't bout tits. Was bout vibrations. And he dug it and asked me what color dress I had on and how my hair was fixed and how I was doin without a man, not nosy but nicelike, and who was at this affair and was the canapés dainty-stingy or healthy enough to get hold of proper. Comfy and cheery is what I'm tryin to get across. Touch talkin like the heel of the hand on the tambourine or on a drum.

But right away Joe Lee come up on us and frown for dancin so close to the man. My own son who knows what kind of warm I am about; and don't grown men all call me long distance and in the middle of the night for a little Mama comfort?

But he frown. Which ain't right since Bovanne can't see and defend himself. Just a nice old man who fixes toasters and busted irons and bicycles and things and changes the lock on my door when my men friends get messy. Nice man. Which is not why they invited him. Grass roots you see. Me and Sister Taylor and the woman who does heads at Mamies and the man from the barber shop, we all there on account of we grass roots. And I ain't never been souther than Brooklyn Battery and no more country than the window box on my fire escape. And just yesterday my kids tellin me to take them countrified rags off my head and be cool. And now can't get Black enough to suit em. So everybody passin sayin My Man Bovanne. Big deal, keep steppin and don't even stop a minute to get the man a drink or one of them cute sandwiches or tell him what's goin on. And him standin there with a smile ready case someone do speak he want to be ready. So that's how come I pull him on the dance floor and we dance squeezin past the tables and chairs and all them coats and people standin round up in each other face talkin bout this and that but got no use for this blind man who mostly fixed skates and skooters for all these folks when they was just kids. So I'm pressed up close and we touch talkin with the hum. And here come my daughter cuttin her eye at me like she do when she tell me about my "apolitical" self like I got hoof and mouf disease and there ain't no hope at all. And I don't pay her no mind and just look up in Bovanne shadow face and tell him his stomach like a drum and he laugh. Laugh real loud. And here come my youngest, Task, with a tap on my elbow like he the third grade monitor and I'm cuttin up on the line to assembly.

"I was just talkin on the drums," I explained when they hauled me into the kitchen. I figured drums was my best defense. They can get ready for drums what with all this heritage business. And Bovanne stomach just like that drum Task give me when he come back from Africa. You just touch it and it hum thizzm, thizzm. So I stuck to the drum story. "Just drummin that's all."

"Mama, what are you talkin about?"

"She had too much to drink," say Elo to Task cause she don't hardly say nuthin to me direct no more since that ugly argument about my wigs.

"Look here Mama," say Task, the gentle one. "We just tryin to pull your coat. You were makin a spectacle of yourself out there dancing like that."

"Dancin like what?"

Task run a hand over his left ear like his father for the world and his father before that.

"Like a bitch in heat," say Elo.

"Well uhh, I was going to say like one of them sex-starved ladies gettin on in years and not too discriminating. Know what I mean?"

I don't answer cause I'll cry. Terrible thing when your own children talk to you like that. Pullin me out the party and hustlin me into some stranger's kitchen in the back of a bar just like the damn police. And ain't like I'm old old. I can still wear me some sleeveless dresses without the meat hangin off my arm. And I keep up with some thangs through my kids. Who ain't kids no more. To hear them tell it. So I don't say nuthin.

"Dancin with that tom," say Elo to Joe Lee, who leanin on the folks' freezer. "His feet can smell a cracker a mile away and go into their shuffle number post haste. And them eyes. He could be a little considerate and put on some shades. Who wants to look into them blown-out fuses that—"

"Is this what they call the generation gap?" I say.

"Generation gap," spits Elo, like I suggested castor oil and fricassee possum in the milk-shakes or somethin. "That's a white concept for a white phenomenon. There's no generation gap among Black people. We are a col—"

"Yeh, well never mind," says Joe Lee. "The point is Mama . . . well, it's pride. You embarrass yourself and us too dancin like that."

"I wasn't shame." Then nobody say nuthin. Them standin there in they pretty clothes with drinks in they hands and gangin up on me, and me in the third-degree chair and nary a olive to my name. Felt just like the police got hold to me.

"First of all," Task say, holdin up his hand and tickin off the offenses, "the dress. Now that dress is too short, Mama, and too low-cut for a woman your age. And Tamu's going to make a speech tonight to kick off the campaign and will be introducin you and expecting you to organize the council of elders—"

"Me? Didn nobody ask me nuthin. You mean Nisi? She change her name?"

"Well, Norton was supposed to tell you about it. Nisi wants to introduce you and then encourage the older folks to form a Council of the Elders to act as an advisory—"

"And you going to be standing there with your

boobs out and that wig on your head and that hem up to your ass. And people'll say, 'Ain't that the horny bitch that was grindin with the blind dude?' "

"Elo, be cool a minute," say Task, gettin to the next finger. "And then there's the drinkin. Mama, you know you can't drink cause next thing you know you be laughin loud and carryin on," and he grab another finger for the loudness. "And then there's the dancin. You been tattooed on the man for four records straight and slow draggin even on the fast numbers. How you think that look for a woman your age?"

"What's my age?"

"What?"

"I'm axin you all a simple question. You keep talkin bout what's proper for a woman my age. How old am I anyhow?" And Joe Lee slams his eyes shut and squinches up his face to figure. And Task run a hand over his ear and stare into his glass like the ice cubes goin calculate for him. And Elo just starin at the top of my head like she goin rip the wig off any minute now.

"Is your hair braided up under that thing? If so, why don't you take it off? You always did do a neat cornroll."

"Uh huh," cause I'm thinkin how she couldn't undo her hair fast enough talking bout cornroll so countrified. None of which was the subject. "How old, I say?"

"Sixtee-one or—"

"You a damn lie Joe Lee Peoples."

"And that's another thing," say Task on the fingers.

"You know what you all can kiss," I say, gettin up and brushin the wrinkles out my lap.

"Oh, Mama," Elo say, puttin a hand on my shoulder like she hasn't done since she left home and the hand landin light and not sure it supposed to be there. Which hurt me to my heart. Cause this was the child in our happiness fore Mr. Peoples die. And I carried that child strapped to my chest till she was nearly two. We was close is what I'm tryin to tell you. Cause it was more me in the child than the others. And even after Task it was the girlchild I covered in the night and wept over for no reason at all less it was she was a chub-chub like me and not very pretty, but a warm child. And how did things get to this, that she can't put a sure hand on me and say Mama we love you and care about you and you entitled to enjoy yourself cause you a good woman?

"And then there's Reverend Trent," say Task, glancin from left to right like they hatchin a plot and just now lettin me in on it. "You were suppose to be talking with him tonight, Mama, about giving us his basement for campaign headquarters and—"

"Didn nobody tell me nuthin. If grass roots mean you kept in the dark I can't use it. I really can't. And Reven Trent a fool anyway the way he tore into the widow man up there on Edgecomb cause he wouldn't take in three of them foster children and the woman not even comfy in the ground yet and the man's mind messed up and—"

"Look here," say Task. "What we need is a family conference so we can get all this stuff cleared up and laid out on the table. In the meantime I think we better get back into the other room and tend to business. And in the meantime, Mama, see if you can't get to Reverend Trent and—"

"You want me to belly rub with the Reven, that it?"

"Oh damn," Elo say and go through the swingin door.

"We'll talk about all this at dinner. How's tomorrow night, Joe Lee?" While Joe Lee being self-important I'm wonderin who's doin the cookin and how come no body ax me if I'm free and do I get a corsage and things like that. Then Joe nod that it's O.K. and he go through the swingin door and just a little hubbub come through from the other room. Then Task smile his smile, lookin just like his daddy, and he leave. And it just me in this stranger's kitchen, which was a mess I wouldn't never let my kitchen look like. Poison you just to look at the pots. Then the door swing the other way and it's My Man Bovanne standin there sayin Miss Hazel but lookin at the deep fry and then at the steam table, and most surprised when I come up on him from the other direction and take him on out of there. Pass the folks pushin up towards the stage where Nisi and some other people settin and ready to talk, and folks gettin to the last of the sandwiches and the booze fore they settle down in one spot and listen serious. And I'm thinkin bout tellin Bovanne what a lovely long dress Nisi got on and the earrings and her hair piled up in a cone and the people bout to hear how we all gettin screwed and gotta form our own party and everybody there listenin and lookin. But instead I just haul the man on out of there, and Joe Lee and his wife look at me like I'm terrible, but they ain't said boo to the man yet.

Cause he blind and old and don't nobody there need him since they grown up and don't need they skates fixed no more.

"Where we goin, Miss Hazel?" Him knowin all the time.

"First we gonna buy you some dark sunglasses. Then you comin with me to the supermarket so I can pick up tomorrow's dinner, which is goin to be a grand thing proper and you invited. Then we goin to my house."

"That be fine. I surely would like to rest my feet." Bein cute, but you got to let men play out they little show, blind or not. So he chat on bout how tired he is and how he appreciate me takin him in hand this way. And I'm thinkin I'll have him change the lock on my door first thing. Then I'll give the man a nice warm bath with jasmine leaves in the water and a little Epsom salt on the sponge to do his back. And then a good rubdown with rose water and olive oil. Then a cup of lemon tea with a taste in it. And a little talcum, some of that fancy stuff Nisi mother sent over last Christmas. And then a massage, a good face massage round the forehead which is the worryin part. Cause you gots to take care of the older folks. And let them know they still needed to run the mimeo machine and keep the spark plugs clean and fix the mailboxes for folks who might help us get the breakfast program goin, and the school for the little kids and the campaign and all. Cause old folks in the nation. That what Nisi was sayin and I mean to do my part.

"I imagine you are a very pretty woman, Miss Hazel."

"I surely am," I say just like the hussy my daughter always say I was.

The Promise

Toi Derricotte

Toi Derricotte (1941–   ) was born in Detroit, Michigan. She earned a bachelor's degree at Wayne State University in 1965 and a master's degree from the creative writing department of New York University in 1984. Since 1988 she has worked as associate professor of creative writing and minority literature at Old Dominion University, Norfolk, Virginia. Her three volumes of poetry are informed by her experiences as a Catholic and a black woman: "In Catholic school, we learned that by confessing our sins, admitting faults and weaknesses, we were forgiven, made 'whole' and acceptable, put back into the state of grace. In my writing, truthtelling as a way to self-integrity operates as a strong impulse."

I will never again
expect too much of you. I have
found out the secret of marriage:
I must keep seeing your beauty
like a stranger's, like the face
of a young girl passing on a train
whose moment of knowing illumines
it—a golden letter in a book.
I will look at you in such
exaggerated moments, lengthening
one second and shrinking eternity
until they fit together like man and wife.
My pain is expectation:
I watch you for hours sleeping, wanting
you to roll over
and look me in the eye;
my days are seconds of waiting
like the seconds between the makings
of boiling earth and sweating rivers.
What am I waiting for if not
your face—like a fish rising

---

to the surface, a known
but forgotten expression that
suddenly appears—or like myself,
in a strip of mirror, when, having
passed, I come back to that image
hoping to find the woman
missing. Why do you think I sleep
in the other room, planets away,
in a darkness where I could die solitary,
an old nun wrapped in clean white sheets?
Because of lies I sucked
in my mother's milk, because
of pictures in my first grade reader—
families in solid towns as if
the world were rooted and grew down
holding the rocks, eternally;
because of rings in jewelers' windows
engraved with sentiments—*I love you*
forever—as if we could survive
any beauty for longer than just after . . .
So I hobble down a hall
of disappointments past where
your darkness and my darkness have
had intercourse with each other.
Why have I wasted my life
in anger, thinking I could have more
than what is glimpsed in recognition?
I will let go, as we must
let go of an angel called
back to heaven; I will not hold
her glittering robe, but let it
drift above me until I see
the last shred of evidence.

VI

Parents and Children

The way we institutionalize motherhood in our society—assigning sole responsibility for child care to the mother, cutting her off from the easy help of others in an isolated household, requiring round-the-clock tender, loving care, and making such care her exclusive activity—is not only new and unique, but not even a good way for either women or—if we accept as a criterion the amount of maternal warmth shown—for children. It may, in fact, be the worst. It is as though we had selected the worst features of all the ways motherhood is structured around the world and combined them to produce our current design.

–Jessie Bernard, "The Mother Role"

In the late 1920s my mother ran away from home to marry my father. Marriage, if not running away, was expected of seventeen-year-old girls. By the time she was twenty she had two children and was pregnant with a third. Five children later, I was born. And this is how I came to know my mother: she seemed a large, soft, loving-eyed woman who was rarely impatient in our home. Her quick, violent temper was on view only a few times a year, when she battled with the white landlord who had the misfortune to suggest to her that her children did not need to go to school.

–Alice Walker, "In Search of Our Mothers' Gardens"

I want the whole family!
Their courage and faith
to make something good
and try to keep it that way.
Even though the light falls behind the hills.
Even though the water grows dark.

–Susan Browne, "By the River"

The Chair

Susan Browne

Susan Browne (1952–) was born in Long Beach, California, and has lived most of her life in the San Francisco Bay Area. She received a bachelor's degree from the California State University at Chico and a master's degree in creative writing from the University of Colorado at Boulder. She lives in Berkeley and teaches writing and literature at Diablo Valley College, where she has edited the literary magazine Agape. *The Wildwood Poetry Competition selected her work for a Poetry Prize in 1992. While she works primarily alone, she also meets with a poet-friend every month. She has also worked with "great poets of this century: Sharon Olds, Galway Kinnell, Jack Gilbert, Brenda Hillman, Robert Hass, Dorianne Laux, Kate Braverman."*

The night I came home too early,
the living room chair was on fire,
and my mother, a beautiful woman,
drunk on the floor.
She whispered, "He hit me,"
then slurred an obscenity,
a guttural growl.
I edged my way past her
as if she could burn me,
out the sliding glass door
and into the yard.
There were so many stars,
and a terrible fire on every one.
They looked calm and gold,
arranged in an orderly constellation;
you wouldn't know how dead they are,
you wouldn't know looking at our house
from the street, shining lawn,
flowers beaming, warm lights on,
that everything wasn't perfect, under control,
except for the small fire now blazing in the window.

I found the hose and dragged the uncoiling thing
across the patio, into the house, past my mother
who remarked, "I think my arm is broken."
The fire hadn't spread, and the chair just looked
like it had grown an orange tuft of hair.
The room was tidy, everything in its place,
and a place for everything. Above the flames,
on the bookshelf, pictures of the family,
everybody smiling, teeth white and straight,
arms around each other, nicely shaped arms
and none in a sling. I had to go back outside
to turn on the water. I didn't want to get water on anything
that wasn't burning. My mother still lay on the floor,
on her side, her black hair gleaming, and I could see
her long eyelashes brushing her cheeks. I saw
her tying my shoe as I sat on my bed, dolls and puppets
and pink curtains, rays of sun, my foot on her knee,
her head curved toward me. Her hair was navy blue
it was so black and smelled like lavender. I told everyone
in kindergarten I had the most beautiful mother.
It was true.
I turned on the faucet
and looked up at the stars,
listening to the water
rush through the hose, probably ruining
the carpet. There was a shooting star,
but I knew wishing was a waste of time.
I went back into the house to put out the fire,
get my mother off the floor,
and maybe see what had happened to my father.

Death By Brute Force

Susan Browne

In my mom's hospital room,
waiting for her to die, my dad
is drinking bourbon or something dark.
Earlier, I could have gone
for a beer myself. The surgery
took so long, twelve hours to cut
one quarter of my mom's brain out.
The surgeon hadn't been able to tell
what kind of life she would have
after, but what the hell, why not go
for it, he was in the business
of saving lives in any form, and hey,
the odds were sixty/forty. I needed
a drink. I like to drink when I gamble,
and it had been a tough day, working
and commuter traffic, driving up
to Sacramento on Highway 80 over the spot
where my mom's head cracked open
as the car turned over and ejected her
partly from the window. My throat is parched.
My dad takes another swig,
then stuffs the square bottle
into his back pocket. I am amazed
how perfectly it fits, as if the makers
of bourbon designed it for that purpose.
My two sisters and I stand on the side of the bed
where the brain monitor is. The nurses explained,
because I asked, that if the line goes flat
my mom is brain dead. I have many questions, though:
If you are brain dead, are you dead? For instance,
my dad is heart dead but he is alive.
If other parts of your body aren't dead,
(the nurses explained that my mom's heart
is strong because my older sister asked),

---

but your brain is dead, are you dead?
What if my mom's brain clicked back on
in the coffin, for example. I am confused.
My dad doesn't ask any questions.
He stands by the door and takes a big, sucking
drink from the bottle. Is he a person?
When do you stop being called a person
and instead a Walking Coma? He has lost
so many parts of himself how come he is still
believed to be human? This is getting complicated,
and I want to ask my dad for a drink.
I want to say, kind of buddy-like, *Fuck you,*
I don't like you, I don't like your face, guy,
let's step outside so I can punch it in, like
my mom's face, which is black and blue and bloated
and one of her smashed eyes is huge, swollen,
and the other is open just a slit looking at nothing.
Her head is bandaged, her hands are bandaged,
there are bags underneath her bed filling
with red, orange and yellow liquid. My dad
is done with his bottle. He says, "Excuse me.
I have to go to the bathroom." But I know
he is going to the bar on E Street.
I want to toss him some chump change, "Get me
a Coors or a Miller, something American, domestic
and cheap, that tastes like piss." In fact, I want
to go with him. Maybe there's a game on. We can bet
on the winner. He hobbles out of the room, his pants
slumped down like he's shit in them, flooding over
his heels. One of his shoes is untied. A pink bald spot
on the back of his head. He tacks out of the room,
shipwrecked sailor. If I were drunk I might pity him,
but I am completely sober, more awake than ever before,
watching my mom die. And I hate him, I hate him,
I feel no pity, no empathy, no compassion. I am sick
of pretending I do. My dad killed my mom, and I am sick
of lying about it. The insurance claim will say she died
a Wrongful Death. The police report will say Death
By Brute Force. They are both correct. My dad
killed my mom. He killed her dead.

The Mother Role

Jessie Bernard

Jessie Bernard (1903–) now resides in Washington, D.C., after a long and distinguished career as professor of sociology at Pennsylvania State University. Educated at the University of Minnesota and Washington University, Dr. Bernard belongs to a generation of women scholars who pioneered in academic life but were challenged in the sixties by the new feminists. In The Future of Marriage *(1972), she writes that her own discipline, sociology, was furiously attacked by radical women of the 60s, forcing her to recognize that "a value judgment is implicit in the choice of any research topic." She notes that before their consciousness was raised, sociologists "documented ad nauseam the dependencies of wives rather than how to overcome them."*

A New and Unique Institution

Motherhood as we know it today is a surprisingly new institution. It is also a unique one, the product of an affluent society. In most of human history and in most parts of the world even today, adult, able-bodied women have been, and still are, too valuable in their productive capacity to be spared for the exclusive care of children. They have been necessary for tilling the fields or fishing or gathering. In a study of six cultures around the world, including our own, for example, a team of anthropologists and psychologists found only our culture following our model.[1]

Among the Nyansongo of Kenya, for example, "during much of the day . . . the mother is working the nearby fields and around the house, and the infant is carried and cared for by a child nurse . . . six to ten years old . . . usually an older sibling . . . who plays an important part in the infant's life."[2] Sometimes co-wives help; sometimes fathers do also. For "Nyansongo mothers are over-burdened with an agricultural and domestic work load which limits the attention they can pay to their weaned children. In consequence, they delegate a good deal of caretaking and training to older children in the homestead, and they reduce their maternal role to what they consider its bare essentials. . . . Another important consequence of the mother's heavy work load is that she trains the children to share it with her as soon as they are able."[3] Similarly, among the *Rajputs* of India, "during the months when the baby is too old to lie quietly on a cot and too young to walk itself, it is, if possible, turned over to an older girl to carry when the mother is busy working. As a rule, this caretaker will be an older sister, but a cousin may take the child if the sisters-in-law are on good terms."[4] Old men may also help in baby-tending. And once the child begins to walk, if he is a boy, the men—fathers, uncles, or grandfathers—may take over. And so, too, among the villagers of Taira, Okinawa. "From the time he is a month old until shortly before the arrival of the next baby, he [the infant] is constantly carried during the day-time on the back of . . . an adult or an older child. . . . His carriers include parents, paternal grandparents, unmarried aunts and uncles, older siblings in an extended household, and parents and older siblings in a nuclear household."[5] And the Mixtecans of Mexico where "the transference of the primary caretaking responsibilities from the mother to the sibling group . . . takes place . . . about a year after weaning."[6] And among the residents of Tarong, an Ilocos barrio in the Philippines: "in no household did a mother have sole responsibility for her children—it would be unthinkable. . . . If the house is relatively isolated and the family nuclear, the father may well hold the baby whenever he is not in the fields, bathe it, change its clothes, feed it tidbits. If the house has many women or older girls, he will rarely do more than play with the child while it is still young."[7] After weaning, caretakers may be aunts, grandmothers, siblings, or even fathers. "More often than not . . . the child . . . eventually obtains care from the socially approved source—the neighbor-kin group, both adults and peers."[8] For pre-schoolers there are many caretakers, all the children belonging to all in the housing group. "We all help to raise our children."[9] Among the Alors, "since women are primarily responsible for garden work and the subsistence economy, mothers return to regular field work ten days to two weeks after the birth of the child. It is not customary for the mother to work with the child on her back or even near her, as it is in some societies. Instead the infant is left at home in care of some kin, for example the father, an older sibling of either sex, or a grandmother whose field labor is less effective or necessary than that of a younger woman."[10] By way of contrast, we find that in our society today "parents . . . generally discourage older siblings . . . from assuming responsibility for infants on the grounds that the older child will be irresponsible and that it would also be imposing unduly on him or her. It is thought to be too trying for an older child to face the baby's antisocial behavior and maintain reasonable control over it."[11]

And Not a Good One

The way we institutionalize motherhood in our society—assigning sole responsibility for child care to the mother, cutting her off from the easy help of others in an isolated household, requiring round-the-clock tender, loving care, and making such care her exclusive activity—is not only new and unique, but not even a good way for either women or—if we accept as a criterion the amount of maternal warmth shown—for children. It may, in fact, be the worst. It is as though we had selected the worst features of all the ways motherhood is structured around the world and combined them to produce our current design.

This charge is based on the findings of the research teams previously quoted. They found that women in cultures where they were given the heaviest load of child care were more changeable in expressing warmth than those in other cultures and more likely to have hostilities not related to the behavior of the children.[12] In fact, the greater the burden of child care assigned to these mothers, the less likely they were to be able to supply the warm care infants require. "Mothers," they reported, "who spend a high proportion of their time caring for children are somewhat more unstable in their emotional reactions to their children than are mothers who do not have such exclusive responsibility."[13] The so-called harassment aspect of child care was also greater among them. Maternal warmth was more likely to occur when there was a grandmother present to spell the mother off. "Mothers who must cope more than others, either with their own children or their children's cousins, are muted in their warmth, while mothers who have the help of a grandmother are free in their expression of affection."[14] Maternal instability likewise decreased when additional caretakers eased the mother's burden and when there were relatively few children requiring her care.

Life-style was also found to be related to maternal warmth. "Mothers who are really isolated from their relatives and substitute caretakers may control expressiveness . . . to avoid further wear and tear on their own frayed nerves and fights among siblings for their own praise and affection."[15] Another study of forty-five cultures for which data were available found a relationship between a high incidence of mother–child households (as, for example, in polygyny) and the inflicting of pain on the child by the nurturant agent. And, conversely, although less markedly, a negative relationship between maternal warmth and incidence of mother–child households.[16]

The two requirements we build into the role of mother—full-time care of children and sole responsibility for them—seem, in brief, to be incompatible with one another, even mutually exclusive. In view of these findings it is sobering to note that in our society we seem to maximize this contradiction in the role so that mothers here "have a significantly heavier burden (or joy) of baby care than the mothers in any other society."[17] Today young mothers who "spend a high proportion of their time caring for children" are corroborating the researchers' report. Yes, they are beginning to tell us, it's true: they find joy in their children, but they do not like motherhood.[18]

Home and Mother

The isolated home as we know it, like motherhood with which it is intrinsically related, is also a fairly new institution in human history. The privacy of the home originated as a form of protective isolation, though what it was guarding against changed with time. In the fifteenth century, for example, it was protection against the evils of communal festivities.[19] Later it was protection against too great demands being made upon it:

> *In the eighteenth century, the family began to hold society at a distance, to push it back beyond a steadily extending zone of private life. The organization of the house altered in conformity with this new desire to keep the world at bay. . . . People began defending themselves against a society whose constant intercourse had hitherto been the source of education, reputation and wealth. . . . The history of modern manners can be reduced in part to this long effort to break away from others, to escape from a society whose pressure had become unbearable.*[20]

In the nineteenth century the cloistering of the home was a protection against the evils of industrialization and urbanization.

In the new economic order that accompanied the industrial revolution, hard, driving, competitive men were creating a male-oriented civilization in which a dog-eat-dog philosophy prevailed; the survival of the fittest as it was then interpreted, called for an extremely rugged individualism. Let the best man win. It was a world of achievement at almost any human price.

But even for those who could operate successfully in such an atmosphere, as well as for those who could not, there had to be some place where relief was possible. That place was provided by the sheltering home. And it was woman's role to supply the healing balm to the victors as well as to the victims of the cruel outside world. "The Feminine as the giver of shelter and protection" encompassed "the life of the family and group in the symbol of the house."[21]

The Queen's Walled Garden

The home was a sacred place. Even for non-believers and agnostics it was a "secular temple," a place for social altruism. In order for the mother to perform her sheltering and protective function she herself had to be protected from the outside world, isolated from it, immured in a walled garden.

> *. . . the conception of the home as a source of virtue and emotions which were nowhere else to be found, least of all in business and society . . . made it a place radically different from the surrounding world. It was much more than a house where one stopped at night for temporary rest and recreation—or procreation—in the midst of a busy career. It was a place apart, a walled garden, in which certain virtues too easily crushed by modern life could be preserved and certain desires of the heart too much thwarted be fulfilled.*[22]

This isolated home, protected from the outside world for whatever reason, was the mother's responsibility to maintain as a sanctuary. She ruled over it contributing order, arrangement, decision, as well as faithful and wise counseling. In an essay that has been called "the most important single document . . . for the characteristic idealization of love, woman, and the home in Victorian thought,"[23] John Ruskin laid out the province of mothers:

> *This is the true nature of home—it is the place of Peace; the shelter, not only from all injury, but from all terror, doubt, and division. In so far as it is not this, it is not home; so far as the anxieties of the outer life penetrate into it, and the inconsistently-minded, unknown, unloved, or hostile society of the outer world is allowed by either husband or wife to cross the threshold, it ceases to be home; it is then only a part of that outer world which you have roofed over, and lighted fire in. But so far as it is a sacred place, a vestal temple, a temple of the hearth watched over by Household Gods . . . so far as it is this, and roof and fire are types only of a nobler shade and light,—shade as of the rock in a weary land, and light as of the Pharos in the stormy sea;—so far it vindicates the name, and fulfills the praise, of Home.*[24]

A man might have to sally forth to meet the perils of the outside world, to struggle on that grim, harsh stage, become hardened, but "he guards the woman from all this; within his house, as ruled by her, unless she herself has sought it, need enter no danger, no temptation, no cause of error or offense."[25] George Eliot put it succinctly: "A loving woman's world lies within the four walls of her own home; and it is only through her husband that she is in any electric communication with the world beyond."[26] Protected, sheltered, isolated, safe within the walls of their gardens, women as mothers became the repositories of all the humane virtues. It was the mother who made of home a school of virtue.

Mother As Symbol

The idealization of the maternal role in society's taboos indicates that in the interest of the survival of the species the mother–child relationship has to be buttressed by social regulation, and also that this is often not sufficient, and that deficiencies have therefore to be covered up by idealization.[27]

Increasingly idealized—by definition loving, gentle, tender, self-sacrificing, devoted, limited in interests to creating a haven for her family—the mother became in time almost a parody. Mothers have been honored from time immemorial, assessed above rubies in value, as the Proverbial woman was, or as the Roman matron was, or the chatelaine of a medieval castle might be. But the mother adored for her self-abnegation, her "altruistic surrender,"[28] even for her self-immolation, was a nineteenth-century Victorian creation. This image reached its heyday at the turn of the century and lingered on until yesterday.

Even today, in fact, one catches glimpses of the Victorian mother in debates about the place of women.[29] The image still lurks behind the battle cry "A woman's place is in the home." It has retained a tenacious hold on our minds long after the environment that created and supported it has disappeared. And its extension into the future is suggested by its persistence in children's schoolbooks, where mother is still the ever-loving homebody.[30]

It has taken a long time to overcome this concept of the home as a walled garden presided over by a cherishing mother, an isolated, cut-off, protected temple where people could huddle together against a cruel outside world. It may be that only certain members of the post-war generation carry no vestige of it. So far as they are concerned, they want no part of it. For them—and even, increasingly, for their mothers as well—the isolated, walled garden became a prison long ago, keeping them in rather than the world out.

Furthermore, the outside world changed, changing the part played both by the home and by the workshop. The home was no longer a sanctuary for men in a hostile world. They were deriving as much—or as little—satisfaction from their work as from their marriages.[31]

Mothers As Women

Victorian motherhood was a male—and a middle-class—conception. The more female historians study it from the point of view of the women themselves the less authentic it looks. It was never a genuine portrait even of the Victorian mother, let alone the mother of any other age. Women are just not like that. Now or ever.

Mothers in the home were already becoming a "social problem" a hundred years ago. They were already champing at the bit. They were already complaining of being boxed in. Even then they were fretting and wearied by motherhood's "daily round of trivial tasks, occupying the time and absorbing the energies."[32] Then as now they felt shut in "from the larger life of the world, which courses freshly past the home within which they are imprisoned." Many who "once dreamed of great things" sighed "sadly in the thought of the nursery bondage and . . . looked out wistfully on the noble labors awaiting mind and heart in the outer world."[33] Then, as now, those who fretted "under its [motherhood's] burdens of care, threw off from them in every way possible their divinely imposed charge" in order to "escape from the home to society, to find for themselves pleasure, or to make for themselves work other than that providentially ordered."[34] As early as 1879, Ibsen's Nora, in reply to her husband's dictum that "before all else" she was "a wife and mother," said: "that I no longer believe. I believe that before all else I am a human being, just as much as you are—or at least that I should try to become one."

By the turn of the century it was already becoming apparent that there was something wrong about the nineteenth-century model for the role of mother. Women were finding it increasingly difficult to perform it. Invoking the idealized model did no good. "Putting on a Madonna-like pedestal the often impatient, irritable mother who feels chained to her duties, may suffice for the aims of idealism and wishful thinking, but makes life easier neither for mothers nor for children. True, it saves society the feeling that it should change itself."[35] But aggrieved women were not to let "society" spare itself the comfort of standing pat. If they were poor, they were protesting against having too many children;[36] if they were affluent, they were protesting against the confinement of the doll's house. They wanted out.

But never until this very historical moment have women rebelled as many are now doing against the very way we institutionalize motherhood. They are daring to say that although they love children, they hate motherhood. That they object to being assigned sole responsibility for child care. That they object to having child care conceived as their only major activity. That they object to the isolation in which they must perform the role of mother, cut off from help, from one another, from the outside world. For the first time they are protesting the false aura of romanticism with which motherhood is endowed, keeping from young women its terrible "hidden underside," which "is hardly talked about." One young mother feels "obsessed with the need to tell people what really happens when you have children," to expose "the terrible weight of responsibility, the way it affects a woman's personality." A group of women, basing their conclusions on their own experiences as participant observers—or, rather, as observant participators—note almost point for point how the way we institutionalize motherhood is bad for women. They call on women to organize "to fight those aspects of our society that make childbearing and child rearing stressful rather than fulfilling experiences." One young woman speaks of "the baby trap."[37] Another writes a book to tell us that "mother's day is over," to inform us that "until now millions of women have secretly shared, and silently endured, a profound guilt: they love their children, but they do not love being mothers." She hopes her book "will end their solitude and reduce their guilt and make them more dignified human beings."[38]

Nor is motherhood as we institutionalize it good for children. The anger and irritability it fosters in women reverberates on the children. "When it is realized how difficult woman's present situation makes her full self-realization, how many desires, rebellious feelings, just claims she nurses in secret, one is frightened at the thought that defenseless infants are abandoned to her care."[39] It is no less serious because "most women have the morality and decency to repress their spontaneous impulses; nevertheless these impulses suddenly flash out at times in angry scenes, slaps, punishments, and the like." The mother may feel remorse; but the child feels the pain.

The "smother-love" fostered in women with no other channel for self-actualization came in time to be resented by the sons and daughters. These children of the women struggling to fill their lives with the mother role were as much victimized as the women themselves. They began to see their mothers as not all that saintly after all. Sometimes, in fact, they saw them as devouring vultures. Instead of honoring mother they had to fight to rid themselves of their enforced dependencies on her. Mothers were attacked as a generation of vipers[40] who had ruined their sons by their momism[41] and had produced sons full of sexual compulsions.[42] The virtues of the nineteenth-century mother were turned inside out: the angels became monsters. The Great Mother archetype became the Terrible Mother archetype.[43] Once worshipfully hoisted on a pedestal, mothers were now pelted with abuse.

> *... mothers are held responsible for juvenile delinquency, problem children, neurotic children, vandalism, communism, and the many other woes of society. Now, on bearing a child, one automatically loses any semblance of common sense one may have had earlier when one was in business, in a profession or in some other career. ... [Mothers] are maligned, insulted, and treated like an evil spirit.*[44]

Whether the denigration of the mother resulted, as some alleged, from neglect by working mothers or, as others alleged, from "smother-love" by home-bound mothers, whether too little or too much mothering was the basis of the denigration, it was, in fact, quite real. Whatever was wrong in our society, it had to be the mother's fault.

Role, home, and symbol as components of Victorian motherhood were, then, all relatively new when they arose, but they were already in process of becoming anachronisms when the twentieth century inherited them. What we see today is the tail end of a comet, the tail of a model of motherhood that began to disintegrate as it struck the twentieth century. The comet itself was a model of motherhood that appeared in Victorian times in response to a set of circumstances unique in human history, circumstances that resulted finally in the severance of the two most fundamental aspects of human life, family and work. Two worlds separated out, one an outside work world, one an almost cloistered family world.

It was not the protests of mothers that finally battered down the walls of the queen's garden. It was the outside forces that were taking much of the work of women out of the home and attenuating much that remained within it. The shock waves of industrialization and urbanization that began to break at the end of the eighteenth century were to be felt throughout all of nineteenth-century society. Nothing was to be left untouched, even motherhood. The nature of work, the nature of the home, the nature of all human relations, were all to be transformed. We have to go back more than ten thousand years, to the beginnings of agriculture, to find anything comparable to the events we now call *the* industrial revolution, actually only one of many, before and since.

The walls that had surrounded the home proved unable to withstand the maelstrom of industrialism and urbanism. They crumbled first among the poor. Then among the unmarried daughters of the not-so-poor. Then among the valiant well-to-do, among women who began to see the walls as keeping them in rather than as keeping the world out. Then among wives, even mothers. The walls, however symbolic, remain today as only reminders of the past. They have come to be seen by more and more women as gilded cages, if not as prisons.

The current revolt of many women against the role of mother as institutionalized in our society will no more force us to rethink the structure of motherhood today than did the protests of mothers a century ago. But a host of other forces, including—in addition to continuing technological changes—the antinatalism engendered by the environment movement, are already at work to bring about such a restructuring. We can't go home again. Not, at least, to the Victorian home.

Notes

1. Beatrice B. Whiting, ed., *Six Cultures, Studies of Child Rearing* (Wiley, 1963).

2. Robert A. LeVine and Barbara B. LeVine, "Nyansongo: A Gusii Community in Kenya," in Beatrice B. Whiting, ed., *Six Cultures*, p. 139.

3. *Ibid.*, p. 161.

4. Leigh Minturn and John T. Hitchcock, "The Rajputs of Khalapur, India," *Ibid.*, p. 314.

5. Thomas W. Maretzki and Hatsumi Maretzki, "Taira: An Okinawan Village," *Ibid.*, p. 462.

6. Kimball Romney and Romaine Romney, "The Mixtecans of Juxtlahuaca, Mexico," *Ibid.*, p. 650.

7. William F. Mydegger and Corinne Mydegger, "Tarong: An Ilocos Barrio in the Philippines," *Ibid.*, p. 821.

8. *Ibid.*, p. 833.

9. *Ibid.*, p. 834.

10. Cora DuBois, *The People of Alors* (University of Minnesota Press, 1944), p. 36. "'Lazy' women use the care of the child as an excuse to slight their field work" (p. 34).

11. John L. Fischer and Ann Fischer, "The New Englanders of Orchard Town, U.S.A.," in Beatrice B. Whiting, ed., *Six Cultures*, p. 946. Alorese mothers face the same problem of irresponsibility in older siblings as "baby sitters." It might be noted in passing that despite the much-publicized community child-care facilities in China today a newspaper report in 1972 pointed out that "an older child always seems to be taking care of a younger one" (Wes Gallagher, "Unexpected U.S. Visitors Stir a Tiny Chinese Hamlet," *The Washington Post*, August 17, 1972).

12. Leigh Minturn and William L. Lambert, *Mothers of Six Cultures: Antecedents of Child Rearing* (Wiley, 1964), p. 56.

13. *Ibid.*, p. 66.

14. *Ibid.*, pp. 282–83.

15. *Ibid.*, p. 283.

16. James W. Prescott and Cathy McKay, "Child Abuse and Child Care: Some Cross-Cultural and Anthropological Perspectives," paper prepared for research workshop of the National Institute of Child Health and Human Development, June, 1973, Table 2.

17. Minturn and Lambert, *Mothers of Six Cultures*, p. 97.

18. Shirley Radl, *Mother's Day Is Over* (Charterhouse, 1973), *passim*.

19. Arthur W. Calhoun, *A Social History of the American Family: Volume 1. Colonial Period* (Cleveland: Arthur H. Clark, 1917), pp. 38–40.

20. Philippe Ariès, *Centuries of Childhood* (Knopf, 1962), pp. 398, 406–7.

21. Erich Neumann, *The Great Mother, An Analysis of the Archetype*, trans. Ralph Manheim (Princeton-Bollinger, 1963), p. 137.

22. Walter E. Houghton, *The Victorian Frame of Mind* (Yale University Press, 1957), p. 343.

23. *Ibid.*, p. 343.

24. John Ruskin, "Of Queens' Gardens," Section 68, in *Works,* Vol. 8, p. 122.

25. *Ibid.*, p. 122.

26. George Eliot, "Amos Barton," in *Scenes from Clerical Life,* Vol. 1, p. 85.

27. Alexander Mitscherleck, *Society Without Father, A Contribution to Social Psychology* (Harcourt Brace & World, 1968), p. 56.

28. The concept of altruistic surrender was originally developed by Anna Freud to refer to a form of identification with another person in which one all-but-gave-up one's own identity. Arlie Hochschild has developed the concept as a component of the mother role among women sixty-five years of age and older as related to grown sons and daughters (*The Unexpected Community,* Prentice-Hall, 1973, pp. 100ff.). It may be noted in passing that even Mary, who in the folk mind had been something of a roustabout, became, in effect, a Victorian mother in the nineteenth century, the very model of "the heart of the home." Although she had always been full of maternal warmth and kindness, though amoral, generous with mercy, assistance, and healing even for sinners, she had also been patroness of prostitutes and, in the Mexican folk mind, suspected of promiscuity. Folk tales had her giving milk from her own breast to horribly diseased patients, delivering the baby of a reverend abbess, substituting for a nun who went off to live it up as a prostitute (Wolfgang Lederer, *The Fear of Women,* Harcourt Brace Jovanovich, 1968, pp. 175–77). Not until the middle of the nineteenth century did she become completely domesticated.

29. As late as 1967, 34 percent of the respondents in a Gallup poll believed women's place was in the home. Even among college freshmen, usually an avant garde, 51.9 percent of the men queried in 1971 and 30.6 percent of the women, professed that belief.

30. New Jersey NOW Task Force, *Dick and Jane As Victims* (1972). Published by authors.

31. See Chapter 18, *The Future of Motherhood.*

32. R. Heber Newton, *Womanhood* (Putnam's, 1881), p. 123.

33. *Ibid.*, p. 123.

34. *Ibid.*, p. 123.

35. Alexander Mitscherleck, *Society Without Father,* p. 57.

36. Margaret Sanger, *Motherhood in Bondage* (Brentano's, 1928).

37. Shirley Radl, *Mother's Day Is Over,* p. 10.

38. Simone de Beauvoir, *The Second Sex* (Bantam, 1952), pp. 484–85.

39. *Ibid.*, p. 485.

40. Philip Wylie, *A Generation of Vipers* (Farrar, 1942).

41. William Streckert, *Their Mothers' Sons* (Lippincott, 1956).

42. Philip Roth, *Portnoy's Complaint* (Random House, 1969).

43. Erich Neumann, *The Great Mother,* pp. 148–49. The archetype of the Terrible Mother is the negative side of the Great Mother, witches, vampires, ghouls, specters.

44. Helen E. Peixotto, "Mothers Had Mothers Too," in Edgar J. Schmiedeler, ed., *The Mother the Heart of the Home* (St. Meinard, Ind.: Grail Publications, 1955), pp. 135–36.

In Search of Our Mothers' Gardens

Alice Walker

Alice Walker (1944–) was born in Eatonton, Georgia, and attended Spelman College in Atlanta before transferring to Sarah Lawrence College in Bronxville, New York. In 1983 she published The Color Purple, *which Gloria Steinem describes as "the kind of literary event which transforms a small and intense reputation into a popular one." Within Walker's work two voices are united: that of the emerging African American and of the creative artist who happens to be female. Influenced by the work of Virginia Woolf, Walker has searched for models among the neglected African American writers of the past, among them Phillis Wheatley and Zora Neale Hurston. In the following essay, she asks what the oppressed women of the past did with their energy and gifts.*

I described her own nature and temperament. Told how they needed a larger life for their expression. . . . I pointed out that in lieu of proper channels, her emotions had overflowed into paths that dissipated them. I talked, beautifully I thought, about an art that would be born, an art that would open the way for women the likes of her. I asked her to hope, and build up an inner life against the coming of that day. . . . I sang, with a strange quiver in my voice, a promise song.

–Jean Toomer, "Avey," *Cane*

The poet speaking to a prostitute who falls asleep while he's talking—

When the poet Jean Toomer walked through the South in the early twenties, he discovered a curious thing: black women whose spirituality was so intense, so deep, so *unconscious,* that they were themselves unaware of the richness they held. They stumbled blindly through their lives: creatures so abused and mutilated in body, so dimmed and confused by pain, that they considered themselves unworthy even of hope. In the selfless abstractions their bodies became to the men who used them, they became more than "sexual objects," more even than mere women: they became "Saints." Instead of being perceived as whole persons, their bodies became shrines: what was thought to be their minds became temples suitable for worship. These crazy Saints stared out at the world, wildly, like lunatics—or quietly, like suicides; and the "God" that was in their gaze was as mute as a great stone.

Who were these Saints? These crazy, loony, pitiful women?

Some of them, without a doubt, were our mothers and grandmothers.

In the still heat of the post-Reconstruction South, this is how they seemed to Jean Toomer: exquisite butterflies trapped in an evil honey, toiling away their lives in an era, a century, that did not acknowledge them, except as "the *mule* of the world." They dreamed dreams that no one knew—not even themselves, in any coherent fashion—and saw visions no one could understand. They wandered or sat about the countryside crooning lullabies to ghosts, and drawing the mother of Christ in charcoal on courthouse walls.

They forced their minds to desert their bodies and their striving spirits sought to rise, like frail whirlwinds from the hard red clay. And when those frail whirlwinds fell, in scattered particles, upon the ground, no one mourned. Instead, men lit candles to celebrate the emptiness that remained, as people do who enter a beautiful but vacant space to resurrect a God.

Our mothers and grandmothers, some of them: moving to music not yet written. And they waited.

They waited for a day when the unknown thing that was in them would be made known; but guessed, somehow in their darkness, that on the day of their revelation they would be long dead. Therefore to Toomer they walked, and even ran, in slow motion. For they were going nowhere immediate, and the future was not yet within their grasp. And men took our mothers and grandmothers, "but got no pleasure from it." So complex was their passion and their calm.

To Toomer, they lay vacant and fallow as autumn fields, with harvest time never in sight: and he saw them enter loveless marriages, without joy; and become prostitutes, without resistance; and become mothers of children, without fulfillment.

For these grandmothers and mothers of ours were not Saints, but Artists; driven to a numb and bleeding madness by the springs of creativity in them for which there was no release. They were Creators, who lived lives of spiritual waste, because they were so rich in spirituality—which is the basis of Art—that the strain of enduring their unused and unwanted talent drove them insane. Throwing away this spirituality was their pathetic attempt to lighten the soul to a weight their work-worn, sexually abused bodies could bear.

What did it mean for a black woman to be an artist in our grandmothers' time? In our great-grandmothers' day? It is a question with an answer cruel enough to stop the blood.

Did you have a genius of a great-great-grandmother who died under some ignorant and depraved white overseer's lash? Or was she required to bake biscuits for a lazy backwater tramp, when she cried out in her soul to paint watercolors of sunsets, or the rain falling on the green and peaceful pasturelands? Or was her body broken and forced to bear children (who were more often than not sold away from her)—eight, ten, fifteen, twenty children—when her one joy was the thought of modeling heroic figures of rebellion, in stone or clay?

How was the creativity of the black woman kept alive, year after year and century after century, when for most of the years black people have been in America, it was a punishable crime for a black person to read or write? And the freedom to paint, to sculpt, to expand the mind with action did not exist. Consider, if you can bear to imagine it, what might have been the result if singing, too, had been forbidden by law. Listen to the voices of Bessie Smith, Billie Holiday, Nina Simone, Roberta Flack, and Aretha Franklin, among others, and imagine those voices muzzled for life. Then you may begin to comprehend the lives of our "crazy," "Sainted" mothers and grandmothers. The agony of the lives of women who might have been Poets, Novelists, Essayists, and Short-Story Writers (over a period of centuries), who died with their real gifts stifled within them.

And, if this were the end of the story, we would have cause to cry out in my paraphrase of Okot p'Bitek's great poem:

> O, my clanswomen
> Let us all cry together!
> Come,
> Let us mourn the death of our mother,
> The death of a Queen
> The ash that was produced
> By a great fire!
> O, this homestead is utterly dead
> Close the gates
> With *lacari* thorns,
> For our mother
> The creator of the Stool is lost!
> And all the young women
> Have perished in the wilderness!

But this is not the end of the story, for all the young women—our mothers and grandmothers, *ourselves*—have not perished in the wilderness. And if we ask ourselves why, and search for and find the answer, we will know beyond all efforts to erase it from our minds, just exactly who, and of what, we black American women are.

One example, perhaps the most pathetic, most misunderstood one, can provide a backdrop for our mothers' work: Phillis Wheatley, a slave in the 1700s.

Virginia Woolf, in her book *A Room of One's Own,* wrote that in order for a woman to write fiction she must have two things, certainly: a room of her own (with key and lock) and enough money to support herself.

What then are we to make of Phillis Wheatley, a slave, who owned not even herself? This sickly, frail black girl who required a servant of her own at times—her health was so precarious—and who, had she been white, would have been easily considered the intellectual superior of all the women and most of the men in the society of her day.

Virginia Woolf wrote further, speaking of course not of our Phillis, that "any woman born with a great gift in the sixteenth century [insert "eighteenth century," insert "black woman," insert "born or made a slave"] would certainly have gone crazed, shot herself, or ended her days in some lonely cottage outside the village, half witch, half wizard [insert "Saint"], feared and mocked at. For it needs little skill and psychology to be sure that a highly gifted girl who had tried to use her gift for poetry would have been so thwarted and hindered by contrary instincts [add "chains, guns, the lash, the ownership of one's body by someone else, submission to an alien religion"], that she must have lost her health and sanity to a certainty."

The key words, as they relate to Phillis, are "contrary instincts." For when we read the poetry of Phillis Wheatley—as when we read the novels of Nella Larsen or the oddly false-sounding autobiography of that freest of all black women writers, Zora Hurston—evidence of "contrary instincts" is everywhere. Her loyalties were completely divided, as was, without question, her mind.

But how could this be otherwise? Captured at seven, a slave of wealthy, doting whites who instilled in her the "savagery" of the Africa they "rescued" her from . . . one wonders if she was even able to remember her homeland as she had known it, or as it really was.

Yet, because she did try to use her gift for poetry in a world that made her a slave, she was "so thwarted and hindered by . . . contrary instincts, that she . . . lost her health. . . ." In the last years of her brief life, burdened not only with the need to express her gift but also with a penniless, friendless "freedom" and several small children for whom she was forced to do strenuous work to feed, she lost her health, certainly. Suffering from malnutrition and neglect and who knows what mental agonies, Phillis Wheatley died.

So torn by "contrary instincts" was black, kidnapped, enslaved Phillis that her description of "the Goddess"—as she poetically called the Liberty she did not have—is ironically, cruelly humorous. And, in fact, has held Phillis up to ridicule for more than a century. It is usually read prior to hanging Phillis's memory as that of a fool. She wrote:

> The Goddess comes, she moves divinely fair,
> Olive and laurel binds her *golden* hair.
> Wherever shines this native of the skies,
> Unnumber'd charms and recent graces rise. [My italics]

It is obvious that Phillis, the slave, combed the "Goddess's" hair every morning; prior, perhaps, to bringing in the milk, or fixing her mistress's lunch. She took her imagery from the one thing she saw elevated above all others.

With the benefit of hindsight we ask, "How could she?"

But at last, Phillis, we understand. No more snickering when your stiff, struggling, ambivalent lines are forced on us. We know now that you were not an idiot or a traitor; only a sickly little black girl, snatched from your home and country and made a slave; a woman who still struggled to sing the song that was your gift, although in a land of barbarians who praised you for your bewildered tongue. It is not so much what you sang, as that you kept alive, in so many of our ancestors, *the notion of song.*

Black women are called, in the folklore that so aptly identifies one's status in society, "the *mule* of the world," because we have been handed the burdens that everyone else—*everyone* else—refused to carry. We have also been called "Matriarchs," "Superwomen," and "Mean and Evil Bitches." Not to mention "Castraters" and "Sapphire's Mama." When we have pleaded for understanding, our character has been distorted; when we have asked for simple caring, we have been handed empty inspirational appellations, then stuck in the farthest corner. When we have asked for love, we have been given children. In short, even our plainer gifts, our labors of fidelity and love, have been knocked down our throats. To be an artist and a black woman, even today, lowers our status in many respects, rather than raises it: and yet, artists we will be.

Therefore we must fearlessly pull out of ourselves and look at and identify with our lives the living creativity some of our great-grandmothers were not allowed to know. I stress *some* of them because it is well known that the majority of our great-grandmothers knew, even without "knowing" it, the reality of their spirituality, even if they didn't recognize it beyond what happened in the singing at church—and they never had any intention of giving it up.

How they did it—those millions of black women who were not Phillis Wheatley, or Lucy Terry or Frances Harper or Zora Hurston or Nella Larsen or Bessie Smith; or Elizabeth Catlett, or Katherine Dunham, either—brings me to the title of this essay, "In Search of Our Mothers' Gardens," which is a personal account that is yet shared, in its theme and its meaning, by all of us. I found, while thinking about the far-reaching world of the creative black woman, that often the truest answer to a question that really matters can be found very close.

In the late 1920s my mother ran away from home to marry my father. Marriage, if not running away, was expected of seventeen-year-old girls. By the time she was twenty, she had two children and was pregnant with a third. Five children later, I was born. And this is how I came to know my mother: she seemed a large, soft, loving-eyed woman who was rarely impatient in our home. Her quick, violent temper was on view only a few times a year, when she battled with the white landlord who had the misfortune to suggest to her that her children did not need to go to school.

She made all the clothes we wore, even my brothers' overalls. She made all the towels and sheets we used. She spent the summers canning vegetables and fruits. She spent the winter evenings making quilts enough to cover all our beds.

During the "working" day, she labored beside—not behind—my father in the fields. Her day began before sunup, and did not end until late at night. There was never a moment for her to sit down, undisturbed, to unravel her own private thoughts; never a time free from interruption—by work or the noisy inquiries of her many children. And yet, it is to my mother—and all our mothers who were not famous—that I went in search of the secret of what has fed that muzzled and often mutilated, but vibrant, creative spirit that the black woman has inherited, and that pops out in wild and unlikely places to this day.

But when, you will ask, did my overworked mother have time to know or care about feeding the creative spirit?

The answer is so simple that many of us have spent years discovering it. We have constantly looked high, when we should have looked high—and low.

For example: in the Smithsonian Institution in Washington, D.C., there hangs a quilt unlike any other in the world. In fanciful, inspired, and yet simple and identifiable figures, it portrays the story of the Crucifixion. It is considered rare, beyond price. Though it follows no known pattern of quilt-making, and though it is made of bits and pieces of worthless rags, it is obviously the work of a person of powerful imagination and deep spiritual feeling. Below this quilt I saw a note that says it was made by "an anonymous Black woman in Alabama, a hundred years ago."

If we could locate this "anonymous" black woman from Alabama, she would turn out to be one of our grandmothers—an artist who left her mark in the only materials she could afford, and in the only medium her position in society allowed her to use.

As Virginia Woolf wrote further, in *A Room of One's Own:*

> *Yet genius of a sort must have existed among women as it must have existed among the working class. [Change this to "slaves" and "the wives and daughters of sharecroppers."] Now and again an Emily Brontë or a Robert Burns [change this to "a Zora Hurston or a Richard Wright"] blazes out and proves its presence. But certainly it never got itself on to paper. When, however, one reads of a witch being ducked, of a woman possessed by devils [or "Sainthood"], of a wise woman selling herbs [our root workers], or even a very remarkable man who had a mother, then I think we are on the track of a lost novelist, a suppressed poet, of some mute and inglorious Jane Austen. . . . Indeed, I would venture to guess that Anon, who wrote so many poems without signing them, was often a woman. . . .*

And so our mothers and grandmothers have, more often than not anonymously, handed on the creative spark, the seed of the flower they themselves never hoped to see: or like a sealed letter they could not plainly read.

And so it is, certainly, with my own mother. Unlike "Ma" Rainey's songs, which retained their creator's name even while blasting forth from Bessie Smith's mouth, no song or poem will bear my mother's name. Yet so many of the stories that I write, that we all write, are my mother's stories. Only recently did I fully realize this: that through years of listening to my mother's stories of her life, I have absorbed not only the stories themselves, but something of the manner in which she spoke, something of the urgency that involves the knowledge that her stories—like her life—must be recorded. It is probably for this reason that so much of what I have written is about characters whose counterparts in real life are so much older than I am.

But the telling of these stories, which came from my mother's lips as naturally as breathing, was not the only way my mother showed herself as an artist. For stories, too, were subject to being distracted, to dying without conclusion. Dinners must be started, and cotton must be gathered before the big rains. The artist that was and is my mother showed itself to me only after many years. This is what I finally noticed:

Like Mem, a character in *The Third Life of Grange Copeland,* my mother adorned with flowers whatever shabby house we were forced to live in. And not just your typical straggly country stand of zinnias, either. She planted ambitious gardens—and still does—with over fifty different varieties of plants that bloom profusely from early March until late November. Before she left home for the fields, she watered her flowers, chopped up the grass, and laid out new beds. When she returned from the fields she might divide clumps of bulbs, dig a cold pit, uproot and replant roses, or prune branches from her taller bushes or trees—until night came and it was too dark to see.

Whatever she planted grew as if by magic, and her fame as a grower of flowers spread over three counties. Because of her creativity with her flowers, even my memories of poverty are seen through a screen of blooms—sunflowers, petunias, roses, dahlias, forsythia, spirea, delphiniums, verbena . . . and on and on.

And I remember people coming to my mother's yard to be given cuttings from her flowers; I hear again the praise showered on her because whatever rock soil she landed on, she turned into a garden. A garden so brilliant with colors, so original in its design, so magnificent with life and creativity, that to this day people drive by our house in Georgia—perfect strangers and imperfect strangers—and ask to stand or walk among my mother's art.

I notice that it is only when my mother is working in her flowers that she is radiant, almost to the point of being invisible—except as Creator: hand and eye. She is involved in work her soul must have. Ordering the universe in the image of her personal conception of Beauty.

Her face, as she prepares the Art that is her gift, is a legacy of respect she leaves to me, for all that illuminates and cherishes life. She has handed down respect for the possibilities—and the will to grasp them.

For her, so hindered and intruded upon in so many ways, being an artist has still been a daily part of her life. This ability to hold on, even in very simple ways, is work black women have done for a very long time.

This poem is not enough, but it is something, for the woman who literally covered the holes in our walls with sunflowers:

They were women then
My mama's generation
Husky of voice—Stout of
Step
With fists as well as
Hands
How they battered down
Doors
And ironed
Starched white
Shirts
How they led
Armies
Headragged Generals
Across mined
Fields
Booby-trapped
Kitchens
To discover books
Desks

A place for us
How they knew what we
Must know
Without knowing a page
Of it
Themselves.

Guided by my heritage of a love of beauty and a respect for strength—in search of my mother's garden, I found my own.

And perhaps in Africa over two hundred years ago, there was just such a mother; perhaps she painted vivid and daring decorations in oranges and yellows and greens on the walls of her hut; perhaps she sang—in a voice like Roberta Flack's—*sweetly* over the compounds of her village; perhaps she wove the most stunning mats or told the most ingenious stories of all the village storytellers. Perhaps she was herself a poet—though only her daughter's name is signed to the poems that we know.

Perhaps Phillis Wheatley's mother was also an artist.

Perhaps in more than Phillis Wheatley's biological life is her mother's signature made clear.

Loving My Boys

Laura Chester

Laura Chester (1949–) was born in Cambridge, Massachusetts. In 1969 she married Geoffrey Young and bore the two sons, Clovis and Ayler, the subjects of this article. Her college career, which was distinguished by prizes in poetry, resulted in a B.A. from the University of New Mexico in 1972. The next year she and Sharon Barba edited Rising Tides, *an anthology of twentieth-century women poets. At the age of thirty-three, Chester was diagnosed with lupus, a disease of the immune system which primarily affects women between the ages of fifteen and forty.* Lupus Novice: Toward Self-Healing *(1987) is the story of her struggle with this disease.*

Reprinted from *Deep Down,* edited by Laura Chester, 1988.

I HAVE TO BE CAREFUL IN LOVING MY BOYS, TO DO so with distance, as from my desk, where I sit now, hearing him bellow, gleeful, as he drives the tractor and his full young voice bounces against the forest, the edge of which he cuts. My big boy, as tall as I am, with his twelve-and-a-half size shoe—I watch him in our Levi jacket, as he takes his lariat and ropes a chair on the patio, returning a call from "Wendy." He's got a date tonight, my baby, only thirteen. My friend Francine says he's going to be a killer, with that look in his eye, and he's got the meat already. I like to push on him to feel the playful resistance, the teen-force in him, ram-like. He walks into my bedroom first thing in the morning, looking for his brother to shoot. They kill each other, over and over, using red and blue ink that dries without a mark. They drag each other across the lawn, hoist one another from the downstairs up, by an ankle on a rope. My younger son is still innocent enough to come crawl into bed, and I gather his warmth, his blondness, into my arms, even hug him in with a leg, and often we fall back to sleep that way, arms around each other's necks. Soon, he too won't be able to come to me, tenderness met with a shrug. "Oh Mom!" They will be loved by many girls. I was simply the first. They both have heart as well as head. They both will undoubtedly devour sex. But leaving the nest is never graceful. My applause holds back, as they tumble and wave. I know I will have to let go, the hardest act—pretending to turn away, as if I had someone better to love. And it is already beginning. This summer my eldest flew off to the Tetons. When he returned, he had veins in his arms, the way a man has muscles and veins. My younger son *leaps.* I imagine a baby. They will go into manhood with their good bodies, confident, ready, whole. Take life on and plunge it. Make it thrive and yield.

Invisible Fathers

Mary Crow Dog with Richard Erdoes

Mary Crow Dog (1953–) is the author, with Richard Erdoes, of Lakota Woman *(1990). She grew up among Sioux on the Rosebud reservation near Pierre, South Dakota. She describes herself as* iveska, *or half-blood. In this selection, she describes her life with her mother and grandparents before she had to leave for boarding school. In 1968 she and her husband, Leonard Crow Dog, joined the American Indian Movement (AIM) and participated in the Trail of Broken Treaties, a caravan that followed the Cherokee Trail of Tears. Leonard, the movement's chief medicine man, revived the sacred but outlawed Ghost Dance. They have three children.*

The father says so—E'yayo!
The father says so—E'yayo!
You shall see your grandfather!
You shall see your kindred—E'yayo!
The father says so.
A'te he'ye lo.

Child let me grasp your hand,
Child let me grasp your hand.
You shall live,
You shall live!
Says the father.
A'te he'ye lo.

—*Ghost Dance song*

Our people have always been known for their strong family ties, for people within one family group caring for each other, for the "helpless ones," the old folks and especially the children, the coming generation. Even now, among traditionals, as long as one person eats, all other relatives eat too. Nobody saves up money because there is always some poor relative saying, "Kanji, I need five bucks for food and gas," and he will not be refused as long as there is one single dollar left. Feeding every comer is still a sacred duty, and Sioux women seem always to be cooking from early morning until late at night. Fourth and fifth cousins still claim relationship and the privileges that go with it. Free enterprise has no future on the res.

At the center of the old Sioux society was the tiyospaye, the extended family group, the basic hunting band, which included grandparents, uncles, aunts, in-laws, and cousins. The tiyospaye was like a warm womb cradling all within it. Kids were never alone, always fussed over by not one but several mothers, watched and taught by several fathers. The real father, as a matter of fact, selected a second father, some well-thought-of relative with special skills as a hunter or medicine man, to help him bring up a boy, and such a person was called "Father" too. And the same was true for the girls. Grandparents in our tribe always held a special place in caring for the little ones, because they had more time to devote to them, when the father was out hunting, taking the mother with him to help with the skinning and butchering.

The whites destroyed the tiyospaye, not accidentally, but as a matter of policy. The close-knit clan, set in its old ways, was a stumbling block in the path of the missionary and government agent, its traditions and customs a barrier to what the white man called "progress" and "civilization." And so the government tore the tiyospaye apart and forced the Sioux into the kind of relationship now called the "nuclear family"—forced upon each couple their individually owned allotment of land, trying to teach them "the benefits of wholesome selfishness without which higher civilization is impossible." At least that is how one secretary of the interior put it. So the great brainwashing began, those who did not like to have their brains washed being pushed farther and farther into the back country into isolation and starvation. The civilizers did a good job on us, especially among the half-bloods, using the stick-and-carrot method, until now there is neither the tiyospaye nor a white-style nuclear family left, just Indian kids without parents. The only thing reminding one of the old Sioux family group is that the grandparents are playing a bigger role than ever. With often no mother or father around, it is the old folks who are bringing up the kids, which is not always a bad thing.

My father, Bill Moore, was part Indian, but mostly white, French with a little Spanish mixed in—Spanish not chicano. He was in the navy and later became a trucker. He lives in Omaha—I think. All that's left of him is his picture on the mantelpiece showing him in navy uniform, a lean-faced, sharp-eyed man. He stayed around just long enough until mom got pregnant with me. Then he split, telling my mother he was tired of all that baby shit. He just left. He was not interested in us, nor in the kids he had with another wife whom he did not want either and placed on welfare. I don't know what became of them. So there is just that one picture left to remind me that I, too, had a father like everybody else. My mother never talked of him; my grandfather—his own father—never talked of him. So all I know is that he wanted no part of me and liked to drink. That's the only things I was ever told about him.

I saw him twice in the flesh. He came back when I was eleven in order to ask his father for some money. The second time I saw him was when he came for his brother's funeral. He looked right through me as if I had not been there. His eyes were dead. He did not even ask who I was. As a matter of fact he did not talk at all, just grinned when some jokes were told and looked uncomfortable in his tight, new cowboy boots. After the funeral he just shook hands all around, without uttering a word, in a hurry to be off again. My mother divorced him in 1954 when I was one year old.

When I was nine or ten my mother married again. This stepfather was even worse than my real father, who at least was not around. My stepfather was. He was a wino and started us kids drinking when I was barely ten years old. After my mother married this man I did not want to be around. I did not like the way he stared at me. It made me uncomfortable. So I just kept away from my mother's place. I rather was on my own, took care of myself, hating myself for having allowed him to teach me to drink. On the rare occasions when I went home I always got into arguments with my mother, telling her, "Why did you marry that man? He's no dad. He doesn't love us. He does nothing for us."

So I and my mother did not get along then. I was a natural-born rebel. They were married and I could do nothing about it. So I drank and ripped off as I got older, living like a hobo, punishing my mother that way. I had to mature. My mother had to mature also. We get along now, really like and respect each other. I realize that I was very intolerant. My mother could not help herself. The little settlements we lived in—He-Dog, Upper Cut Meat, Parmelee, St. Francis, Belvidere—were places without hope where bodies and souls were being destroyed bit by bit. Schools left many of us almost illiterate. We were not taught any skills. The land was leased to white ranchers. Jobs were almost nonexistent on the reservation, and outside the res whites did not hire Indians if they could help it. There was nothing for the men to do in those days but hit the bottle. The men were psychologically crippled and thus my mother did not have much choice when it came to picking a husband. The men had nothing to live for, so they got drunk and drove off at ninety miles an hour in a car without lights, without brakes, and without destination, to die a warrior's death.

There were six of us kids. A seventh had died as a baby. First, my oldest sister, Kathie, then my brother

Robert, then Barbara, who is closest to me in life-style and has had experiences almost exactly like mine. Then came Sandra, and then myself, the youngest. After me came a little boy. We adopted him. This came about when my mother visited his parents for some reason or other. She found nobody at home except this baby boy, dirty, bawling with hunger, and soaking wet, in a box under the dresser. All alone. Everybody gone. Barhopping, most likely. It got my mother mad and somehow she worked it out so we could adopt the baby. He was very spoiled. Everything he wanted he got. So at least one kid in the family got pampered.

After father left, mother became our sole financial support. In order to earn a living she went to be trained as a nurse. When she had finished her training the only job she could find was in Pierre, some hundred miles away. There was nobody there to take care of us while she worked, so she had to leave us behind with our grandparents. We missed her at times. We would see her only rarely. She did not have many chances to come home because she had no transportation. She could not afford a car and it was impossible to get around without one. So she was not there when we needed her because she had to care for white patients. It was only after I was almost grown-up that I really became acquainted with her.

Like most reservation kids we wound up with our grandparents. We were lucky. Many Indian children are placed in foster homes. This happens even in some cases where parents or grandparents are willing and able to take care of them, but where the social workers say their homes are substandard, or where there are outhouses instead of flush toilets, or where the family is simply "too poor." A flush toilet to a white social worker is more important than a good grandmother. So the kids are given to wasičun strangers to be "acculturated in a sanitary environment." We are losing the coming generation that way and do not like it.

We were lucky, having good, warm-hearted grandparents until we, too, were taken away to a boarding school. My grandma was born Louise Flood and she was a Sioux. Her first husband's name was Brave Bird. I have tried to find out about this ancestor of mine. I looked in all the Lakota history books. There were Brave Bears, and Brave Bulls, and Brave Wolves, but no Brave Birds listed. I should have asked when grandma was still alive. They lived on their allotted land way out on the prairie. When grandma was young the whole tribe lived on commodities. Every head of household had a ration card, keeping this precious object in a small, beautifully beaded pouch around his neck, the kind which now costs collectors as much as three hundred dollars. Once a month everybody had to go for their supplies—coffee, sugar loaves, sacks of flour, bacon—mostly starch but filling enough while it lasted, and if we were not cheated out of part of it. Sometimes there was a beef issue of living cattle, the stringiest, skinniest beasts imaginable. This meat-on-the-hoof was driven into a huge corral and then our men were allowed to play buffalo hunters for a couple of hours and ride after them and shoot down those poor refugees from the glue factory and butcher them. This was always a big occasion, good entertainment one could talk about. One day, Grandfather Brave Bird hitched up his wagon and team to drive six hours to town to get his government issue. He went all by himself. On the way home he ran into a thunderstorm. Lightning spooked the horses. They raced off at a dead run, upsetting the wagon. The box seat got ripped off with Brave Bird still in it, entangled in the reins. The horses dragged him through the brush, over rocks, and finally for a couple of miles along a barbed-wire fence. He was dead when they found him.

At that time my grandmother had two girls and two boys. These uncles of mine got TB as they grew up, were taken to an institution, and died from this disease. Tuberculosis is still a problem with us, striking men more often than women. At least they died when they were grown-up, not as children as often happens. At least my grandmother thinks that is where and how they died. She never got any records. All she got was a box to bury.

There was a man called Noble Moore. He had a family and his wife died, and grandma had a family and her husband had died. So the widow and the widower got together and married. By this time my mom was already grown-up. Now Moore had a son of the same age called Bill. One thing led to another and mom married Bill, our absentee head of family, the ex-navy trucker in Omaha. Grandma had the father and my mother wound up with the son. In this kind of lottery grandma won the big prize, because the old man was as good and sober and caring as his son was the opposite.

Grandpa and Grandma Moore were good to us, raising us ever since we were small babies. Grandfather Noble Moore was the only father I knew. He took responsibility for us in his son's place. He gave us as good a home as he could. He worked as a janitor in the school and had little money to take care of a large family, his own and that of his son. Nine people in all plus always some poor relatives with no jobs. I don't know how he managed, but somehow he did.

The old couple raised us way out on the prairie near He-Dog in a sort of homemade shack. We had no electricity, no heating system, no plumbing. We got our water from the river. Some of the things which even poor white or black ghetto people take for granted we did not even know existed. We knew little about the outside world, having no radio and no TV. Maybe that was a blessing.

Our biggest feast was Thanksgiving because then we had hamburgers. They had a wonderful taste to them which I still remember. Grandpa raised us on rabbits, deer meat, ground squirrels, even porcupines. They never seemed to have money to buy much food. Grandpa Moore and two of his brothers were hunting all the time. It was the only way to put some fresh, red meat on the table, and we Sioux are real tigers when it comes to meat. We can't do without it. A few times grandpa came back from fishing with a huge mud turtle and threw it in the pot. That was a feast for him. He said one could taste seven different kinds of meat flavors in a turtle stew—chicken, pork, beef, rabbit, deer, wild duck, antelope, all these. We also got the usual commodities after OEO came in.

Our cabin was small. It had only one room which served as our kitchen, living room, dining room, parlor, or whatever. At night we slept there, too. That was our home—one room. Grandma was the kind of woman who, when visitors dropped in, immediately started to feed them. She always told me: "Even if there's not much left, they gonna eat. These people came a long ways to visit us, so they gonna eat first. I don't care if they come at sunrise or at sundown, they gonna eat first. And whatever is left after they leave, even if it's only a small dried-up piece of fry bread, that's what we eat." This my grandmother taught me. She was Catholic and tried to raise us as whites, because she thought that was the only way for us to get ahead and lead a satisfying life, but when it came to basics she was all Sioux, in spite of the pictures of Holy Mary and the Sacred Heart on the wall. Whether she was aware of how very Indian she had remained, I cannot say. She also spoke the Sioux language, the real old-style Lakota, not the modern slang we have today. And she knew her herbs, showing us how to recognize the different kinds of Indian plants, telling us what each of them was good for. She took us to gather berries and a certain mint for tea. During the winter we took chokecherries, the skin and the branches. We boiled the inside layers and used the tea for various sorts of sicknesses. In the fall she took us to harvest chokecherries and wild grapes. These were the only sweets we had. I never discovered candy until much later when I was in school. We did not have the money for it and only very seldom went to town.

We had no shoes and went barefoot most of the time. I never had a new dress. Once a year we would persuade somebody to drive us to the Catholic mission for a basement rummage sale. Sometimes we found something there to put on our feet before it got cold, and maybe a secondhand blouse or skirt. That was all we could afford. We did not celebrate Christmas, at least not the kind of feast white people are used to. Grandma would save a little money and when the time came she bought some crystal sugar—it looked like small rocks of glass put on a string—some peanuts, apples, and oranges. And she got some kind of cotton material, sewing it together, making little pouches for us, and in each put one apple, one orange, a handful of peanuts, and some of that crystal sugar which took forever to melt in one's mouth. I loved it. That was Christmas and it never changed.

I was too small to know about racism then. When I was in third grade some relative took me to Pine Ridge and I went into a store. It was not very big, a small country grocery. One of my teachers was inside. I went right to the vegetable and fruit bins where I saw oranges just like the one I always got on Christmas. I sure wanted one of them. I picked the biggest one. An uncle had given me a nickel to go on a wild spree with and I wanted to use it paying for the orange. The store owner told me, "A nickel ain't enough to pay for one of them large Sunkist navel oranges, the only ones I got. Put it back." I still remember that. I had to put that damned orange back. Next to me, the wasičun teacher saw me do it and she made a face saying out loud, so that everyone in the store could hear it: "Why can't those dirty Indians keep their hands off this food? I was going to buy some oranges, but they put their dirty hands on them and now I must try to find some oranges elsewhere. How disgusting!" It made a big impression on me, even though I could not understand the full meaning of this incident.

Grandma told me: "Whatever you do, don't go into white people's homes. 'Cause when they come into our homes they make fun of us, because we are poor." When we were growing up at He-Dog there were a few Indian shacks and the garage for buses and the filling station and that was totally it. Then the government started to move us to Parmelee where they put up new OEO houses, small, matchstick structures without cellars which the people called "poverty houses." A school was also built and a few white teachers moved there. I made friends with a little white girl. She said, "Come to my house." I answered, "No, I ain't supposed to go to nobody's house." She said, "My ma ain't home. She's visiting neighbors. Just come!" So I sneaked over there without grandma knowing it. The white girl had many toys, dolls, a dollhouse. All the things I used to admire in the *Sears, Roebuck Catalogue* which I always studied in the outhouse. She had everything. She said, "Sit down and play with my toys." I did. I thought she was my friend. Suddenly I heard the door banging, banging, banging. It was the little girl's mother and she was yelling, "You open this door! You got some nerve coming into my home. You locked me out." She was screaming and I was shaking. I did not know what to do. I told her, "I did not lock you out. I did not even know that door was locked." She yelled, "Where is my whip?" She went into the hallway and got hold of a big, thick leather belt. She said, "Get over here!"

I ran as fast as I could back to my grandmother's house. I told her, "That white woman is going to whip me."

"What did you do?"

"Nothing. I just went into her house and she wants to whip me. Her little girl got me into trouble. I didn't do nothing. Hide me, grandma!" I was so scared.

By about that time the lady was coming. Grandma told me, "You stay in here!" Then she got her big butcher knife. She went out standing in the doorway and told that woman, "You goddam white trash, you coming any closer and I'll chop your ears off." I never saw anybody run as fast as did that white lady.

In South Dakota white kids learn to be racists almost before they learn to walk. When I was about seven or eight years old, I fought with the school principal's daughter. We were in the playground. She was hanging on the monkey bar saying. "Come on, monkey, this thing is for you." She also told me that I smelled and looked like an Indian. I grabbed her by the hair and yanked her down from the monkey bar. I would have done more, but I saw the principal coming.

As I said, grandma spoke Sioux fluently. So does my mother. But we were not allowed to speak it and we were not taught. Many times I asked my grandmother, "Why don't you teach me the language?" Her answer always was: "'Cause we want you to get an education, to live a good life. Not have a hard time. Not depend on nobody. Times coming up are going to be real hard. You need a white man's education to live in this world. Speaking Indian would only hold you back, turn you the wrong way."

She thought she was helping me by not teaching me Indian ways. Her being a staunch Catholic also had something to do with it. The missionaries had always been repeating over and over again: *"You must kill the Indian in order to save the man!"* That was part of trying to escape the hard life. The missions, going to church, dressing and behaving like a wasičun—that for her was the key which would magically unlock the door leading to the good life, the white life with a white-painted cottage, and a carpet on the floor, a shiny car in the garage, and an industrious, necktie-wearing husband who was not a wino. Examples abounded all around her that it was the wrong key to the wrong door, that it would not change the shape of my cheekbones, or the slant of my eyes, the color of my hair, or the feelings inside me. She had only to open her eyes to see, but could not or would not. Her little dream was nourished and protected by the isolation in which she lived.

Grandma had been to mission school and that had influenced her to abandon much of our traditional ways. She gave me love and a good home, but if I wanted to be an Indian I had to go elsewhere to learn how to become one. To grandma's older sister, Mary, for instance, the one who is married to Charlie Little Dog. I call them grandfather and grandmother, too, after the Sioux manner. He is a hundred and four years old now and grandma Little Dog about ninety-eight. They are very traditional people, faithful to the ancient rituals. They still carry their water from the river. They still chop wood. They still live like the Sioux of a hundred years ago. When Charlie Little

Dog talks, he still uses the old words. You have to be at least sixty or seventy years old to understand what he is talking about—the language has changed that much. So I went to them if I wanted to hear the old tales of warriors and spirits, the oral history of our people.

I also went to grand-uncle Dick Fool Bull, the flute maker, who took me to my first peyote meeting, and to people like the Bear Necklaces, the Brave Birds, Iron Shells, Hollow Horn Bears, and Crow Dogs. One woman, Elsie Flood, a niece of grandma's, had a big influence upon me. She was a turtle woman, a strong, self-reliant person, because a turtle stands for strength, resolution, and long life. A turtle heart beats and beats for days, long after the turtle itself is dead. It keeps on beating all by itself. In traditional families a beaded charm in the shape of a turtle is fastened to a newborn child's cradle. The baby's navel cord is put inside this turtle charm, which is believed to protect the infant from harm and bad spirits. The charm is also supposed to make the child live to a great old age. A turtle is a strength of mind, a communication with the thunder.

I loved to visit Aunt Elsie Flood to listen to her stories. With her high cheekbones she looked like grandma. She had a voice like water bubbling, talking with a deep, throaty sound. And she talked fast, mixing Indian and English together. I had to pay strict attention if I wanted to understand what she told me. She always paid her bills, earning a living by her arts and crafts, her beautiful work with beads and porcupine quills—what she called "Indian novelties." She was also a medicine woman. She was an old-time woman carrying her pack on her back. She would not let a man or younger woman carry her burden. She carried it herself. She neither asked nor accepted help from anybody, being proud of her turtle strength. She used turtles as her protection. Wherever she went, she always had some little live turtles with her and all kinds of things made out of tortoiseshell, little charms and boxes. She had a little place in Martin, halfway between Rosebud and Pine Ridge, and there she lived alone. She was very independent but always glad to have me visit her. Once she came to our home, trudging along as usual with the heavy pack on her back and two shopping bags full of herbs and strange things. She also brought a present for me—two tiny, very lively turtles. She had painted Indian designs on their shells and their bottoms. She communicated with them by name. One she called "Come" and the other "Go." They always waddled over to her when she called them to get their food. She had a special kind of feed for them, leaving me whole bags of it. These small twin turtles stayed tiny. They never grew. One day the white principal's son came over and smashed them. Simply stomped them to death. When she heard it my aunt said that this was an evil sign for her.

The turtle woman was afraid of nothing. She was always hitchhiking, constantly on the road thumbing her way from one place to the other. She was a mystery to some. The Indians held her in great respect, saying that she was "wakan," that she was some sort of holy person to whom turtles had given their powers. In the summer of 1976 she was found beaten to death in her home. She was discovered under the bed, face down and naked, with weeds in her hair. She had never hurt anyone or done an unkindness to anybody, only helped people who needed it. No Indian would have touched a single hair on her head. She died that way. I still grieve for her. Her death has never been investigated. The life of a Indian is not held in great value in the State of South Dakota. There is no woman like her anymore.

So many of my relations and friends who were ever dear to me, or meant something to me, or meant something to the people, have either been killed or found dead on some out-of-the-way road. The good Indians die first. They do not grow old. This turtle aunt of mine was one of the traditionally strongest women of her generaton. To bring back what knowledge she had is going to take time. It will take another generation or two to bring it back.

In spite of our grandparents trying so hard to be good Christians, some Indian beliefs rubbed off on them. I remember when I was little, if someone was sick, Grandfather Moore would fill one of the tubs used for watering the cattle and put live ducks in it, saying: "If those birds stay in and swim awhile, swim around, that sick person is gonna be all right. But if the ducks just jump out and leave, the sick one won't get better." He never explained it, just expected everybody to take it on faith. Much later, when my sister Barbara lost her baby, some relatives and friends held a peyote meeting for her. Barb asked our mother and grandmother to come and they actually did. They must have been a little uneasy among all these heathenish goings-on, but they lasted all night and behaved well, as if they had been doing it all their lives. I am sure they worried that the priest would hear about it. I also remember having been told that once, when a person living in a tent behind our shack fell ill, grandfather got a medicine man to doctor him and suck the evil poisons out of his system.

I lived the simple life at He-Dog until I had to go to boarding school. We kids did not suffer from being poor, because we were not aware of it. The few Indians nearby lived in the same kind of want, in the same kind of dilapidated shacks or one-room log cabins with dirt floors. We had nothing to compare our life to. We existed in a vacuum of our own. We were not angry because we did not know that somewhere there was a better, more comfortable life. To be angry, poverty has to rub shoulders with wealth, as for instance ghetto people in squalid tenements living next door to the rich in their luxury apartments as I have seen during my visits to New York. TV has destroyed the innocence, broken through the wall that separates the rich whites from the poor nonwhites. The "boob tube" brainwashes people, but if they are poor and nonwhite, it also makes them angry seeing all those things advertised that they can never hope to have—the fancy homes and cars, the dishwashers and microwaves, the whole costly junk of affluent America. I wonder whether the advertisers who spend a hundred thousand dollars on a commercial are aware of broadcasting a revolutionary message.

As we had no electricity we also had no "idiot box" and therefore felt no envy. Except for that one incident in the white lady's home, I had not yet encountered racism in its varied forms, and that one event I had not fully comprehended. It left me afraid of white people, though, that and some stories I had heard. As I hardly met any white people, they did not bother me. I liked the food I got; I did not know any other, and hunger is a good cook. I liked our shack. Its being overcrowded only meant womblike security to me. Again, except for that white lady's house, I only knew the kind that looked like ours, except for the filling station, but that was not a home. I had food, love, a place to sleep, and a warm, potbellied, wood-fed stove to sit near in the winter. I needed nothing more. Finally, I had something white kids don't usually have—horses to ride. No matter how poor we Sioux are, there are always a few ponies around. When I was a small girl you could buy a nice-looking pinto for ten dollars. So I was riding from as early an age as I can remember. I liked the feel of a horse under me, a feeling of mastery, of freedom, of wildness, of being Indian. It is a feeling shared by everybody on the reservation. Even the most white-manized Sioux is still half horse. I never particularly wished for anything during my earlier childhood except to own an Appaloosa, because I had seen a picture of one in a magazine and fell in love with it. Maybe one day, if I live, I'll get my wish.

Grandfather Moore died in 1972. He passed away peacefully in his sleep. I was glad he had such an easy death. He was a good, loving man, a hard-working janitor. I miss him. I miss grandma. They protected us as long as they were able, but they could not protect us from being taken away to boarding school.

Trying to Read the Tea Leaves

Penelope Kramer

Penelope Kramer (1947–) was born in Shaker Heights, Ohio. Her degrees are from Duke University in North Carolina and the University of Michigan (M.A. in American studies, 1974). After moving to the San Francisco Bay Area in 1974, she studied journalism at the graduate level at the University of California at Berkeley and has worked as a reporter and television newswriter since. Her coverage of environmental issues and the homeless, as well as her human interest and feature stories, has appeared in the San Francisco Examiner, *the* San Francisco Chronicle, *and the* Oakland Tribune. *A longer version of the present article (1992) was published in the* Boston Globe.

In my favorite picture of my dad, he's leaning against a dark oak bar, smiling confidently at the camera from under the brim of his fedora, a cigarette hanging from the corner of his mouth, looking every inch the ace reporter that he was. He was the perfect '30's hero, a cross between William Powell's *Thin Man* and Cary Grant's wisecracking reporter in *His Girl Friday,* the kind of guy who not only does everything well, but does it with ease, while tossing off a joke and tossing back a cocktail.

When my father was 17 he was a reporter with his own column in his home town paper. By the time he graduated from college, he'd landed a job at a major metropolitan daily where he soon became an award-winning editor and foreign affairs columnist. In his spare time he gave after-dinner speeches, ran his own nationally-recognized polling service, invented a new product and turned it into a business to finance his four children's college education. At 44, he quit the paper to manage his expanding company, which he ran for thirty years. And then he began forgetting things.

At 75, my father was like a finely-tuned jet sailing along at cruising speed just after the first engine warning light has come on. By the time he was 80, he'd gone into a screaming dive. And now at 85, all that's left is scattered wreckage.

But the wreckage of my father still crawls, tries to feed himself, needs his diapers changed, throws his dentures across the room in frustration, and realizes, at some elemental level, what he's lost.

The former dapper sophisticate now finds long pants too constricting, and spends his days with his knobby legs hanging out of an oversized lemon yellow diaper. More often than not, he can't remember how to walk, so he sits on the floor, scooting around in frantic circles like a grotesque go-cart. Last time I was home, he suddenly stopped scooting, grabbed my arms and looked pleadingly into my eyes. "I want to be in the stronger time," he begged. "I want to be in the stronger time."

Oh Dad, I know. Oh Dad.

When I look at my father, I am flooded with pain. Then I think of my own future and the pain turns to fear.

The fear began seven years ago, when we were just beginning to admit to ourselves that Dad might have Alzheimer's disease. I was in a department store about to try something on when I realized I couldn't remember the word for dressing room. I stood, rooted to the spot, dumbfounded, while pictures of dressing rooms bobbed through my mind with no words attached. The only word that came to mind was "box." It took a full two minutes of serious concentration before I could come up with "the place where you change your clothes."

Since then I've taken note whenever I forget a word or a name, or absent-mindedly open the refrigerator door to toss my laundry in or cruise oblivious past my freeway exit. For most people, bloopers like these are good for a laugh. For me, each slip makes me wonder—is this how it started for him?

The folks at the Alzheimer's Association say I'm not alone; many people panic about midlife memory loss, especially if they've heard the rumor that half the children of this country's four million Alzheimer's victims are destined to get the disease.

They assure callers in soothing tones that confusion and forgetfulness are normal in middle age, especially if one is "maybe experiencing anxiety or depression about a parent's Alzheimer's."

I'm grateful for the reassurance and hope they're right, but it's hard to shake the feeling that they don't really know. Late onset Alzheimer's disease wasn't identified until 16 years ago. Research is just beginning, preliminary results are inconclusive and contradictory, and it would seem impossible to tell whether a disease is inherited when it wasn't even recognized in earlier generations.

At this point, researchers say the only Alzheimer's known to be inherited by 50% of victims' children is a rare form which strikes in middle age. They say late onset Alzheimer's is an entirely different disease, caused by the combination of one or more abnormal genes and an "environmental trauma." Rumors about aluminum aside, no one knows what trauma or which genes.

Nor does anyone know how many children of victims inherit the disease. All researchers can say is that children are somewhere between two and four times as likely to get it as the general population. At this point they estimate that something like 3–5% of them have Alzheimer's by age 65, 20% by age 75, and 50% by age 85.

Victim's children cope with the lack of solid information by swapping rumors and folklore and reading their parents' symptoms like tea leaves for clues to their own future. When they get together, they often talk about seeing warning signs of a parent's disease years or even decades before it was recognized—in fact when the parents were . . . about the age the children are now. The subtext, of course, is either I'm safe because I don't have these symptoms, or I'm in trouble because I do.

Experts laugh this off as "retrospective diagnosis," claiming patients don't change more than five years before their disease surfaces. But how can they know what was happening in another person's mind?

My father's friends say that in social situations, he was brilliant and entertaining until he was 75. But twenty years earlier, after we'd moved away from the city to be closer to his business, Dad began spending his evenings sitting alone watching television hour after hour in a stupefied trance. Maybe he was missing old friends—but maybe he was avoiding conversation because the clever banter he'd enjoyed all his life was beginning to elude him.

In his 60s, Dad would hang uncertainly outside the door of his grandchildren's playroom, "as if," one said later, "he wanted to talk, but couldn't think of anything to say." And when he was 65, I found him on his way out to dinner at his country club, carefully stowing a hand-printed list of the members' names in his breast pocket. "I don't much care for most of these folks, so I can never remember their names," he explained with a rueful smile, "but there's no need to hurt their feelings."

What if Dad's disease started earlier than we knew, forcing him to work harder and harder to compensate for accumulating losses? What if he was able to mask these losses until late in life so that what happened only looked like a sudden decline?

My fear is not that I have full-blown Alzheimer's now, or that I'll get it tomorrow or next year. I can even live with the idea that at 85 I'll be wearing my own diaper. My real fear is this: What if Alzheimer's isn't a sudden slide down a precipice into living death? What if it doesn't grab hold of the controls of your mind when you reach 65, randomly flipping channels until it settles on permanent white sound?

What if it's more like a gradual erosion of words while a fine mist seeps slowly into your brain, turning imperceptibly into a dense fog?

What if it's already started?

Everyone has different ways of coping with the fear of Alzheimer's. The terminally well-adjusted claim that since they can't do anything about it, they never think about it—except for every time they forget something. Of course, they do keep an informal tally of their average number of slips per day, so they'll know when to shop for a nursing home. Other than that, it never crosses their minds.

None of my three brothers' Alzheimer's scenarios includes actually living with the disease. One insists "they" will find a cure before we get it. Another says the minute his symptoms get bad, he'll commit suicide—neatly bypassing the question of how a mind too disabled to organize a trip to the bathroom will pull that off. The third claims to have that problem covered; he's made his daughter promise that as soon as he's incapacitated, she'll kill him. (Oh yeah, there's a plan that's bound to go like clockwork when the time comes.)

My brothers know I deal with Alzheimer's the way I deal with life—by worrying. They advise me, in that comforting way men have, to cut it out.

But I continue to swing between hope and fear. Whenever I forget something, I tell myself it could be anything: anxiety, hormones, fatigue. Then I think, "or it could be," and my mind flips to its own white sound born of pure terror.

The Alzheimer people say this kind of panic subsides as people accept their parents' disease. In the meantime, in their own way, my brothers are right. I have to cut it out. A mind made blank by terror is not all that much more desirable than one wiped clean by Alzheimer's.

Sometimes I think dwelling on the panic is my inverted way of saying I hate this. Make it go away. I can't bear watching my father torn down like an old building. I don't want to have my mind erased as surely and relentlessly as his—to be alive, but empty, a helpless, incorrigible burden.

I was born in the age of medical miracles and raised to think that life could only get better and longer for me and mine. My father's disease has brought me smack up against the reality that life isn't endless; there isn't always a cure; we can't count on always being ourselves. And I don't like it.

In his final days, even without his mind, my father has taught me one last thing which I should have already known—that every day of consciousness is a gift.

And in the end I am just like him. I want to stay in the stronger time.

Altered Loves

Mothers and Daughters during Adolescence

Terri Apter

Terri Apter (1949–) was born in Chicago and educated in the United Kingdom, receiving her M.A. from the University of Edinburgh in 1969 and her Ph.D. from Cambridge University in 1987. She is married and the mother of two daughters. In addition, she teaches English and American literature at Cambridge University and is the author of eight books, the most recent of which is Altered Loves: Mothers and Daughters during Adolescence *(1990). This work, which collects the interviews of sixty-five pairs of mothers and daughters, develops a positive hypothesis about the distance that daughters put between themselves and their mothers during adolescence.*

My Mother, My Father

The worst she can do is tell my father.

Usually we think of adolescents on the one hand and parents on the other. Then we speak of an adolescent's relationship with parents, and the problems she has with them. But these adolescent girls clearly had two very different relationships with their different parents, one with their mother and one with their father.[1] These differences covered every aspect of the relationship—her feelings, her sense of trust, and her sense of self. For what was remarkable was how she saw herself to be different in the company of each parent, and how she proved herself to be different by exercising a different level of maturity in the way she viewed each parent.

The range of differences began at a very simple level. Most girls enjoyed doing different things with their mothers and with their fathers. With their mothers they preferred unstructured activities, vaguely described as 'doing things in the kitchen' or shopping—which most girls thought of as an extra special treat, 'like just the two of us taking a holiday', or 'being able to get her attention, without her always thinking about dinner or my little sister or when my Dad's coming home'. They also liked 'just sitting and talking'. When adolescent girls described what they liked doing with their fathers, however, they did not emphasise activities which offered opportunities for conversation, but on activities which involved a specific task. Usually they liked the father helping them with something, or they liked him to teach them a certain skill. Girls spoke fondly of fathers helping them, or teaching them how to connect a plug safely to the wires, or how to mend a chair with doweling and glue, or how to fasten a door on its hinges. Most girls enjoyed their father teaching them a sport. Most girls had been taught to ride a bicycle by their father, and they all smiled as they said this. They also enjoyed a wide range of recreational activities with him, such as camping, or hiking.

Adolescent girls clearly value time with both their mothers and fathers, but they seek—or expect—very different things from each parent. Not only was there little emphasis in talking to the father, in confiding feelings and sharing ideas (except if the ideas were shared in a structured argument, as they would be if they would discuss politics or social issues) but whereas girls often said their mother was the person they would most likely confide in, many of them said that their father was the least likely person they would confide in.[2] 'Are you kidding?' was the amazed reply when I suggested that if the mother were not available, they might turn to the father. 'I'd die before I told my father about my boyfriend—I mean about how I really feel.' 'Oh, sure', 14-year-old Mary muttered sarcastically, 'Can't you see us sitting down to have a heart-to-heart with Dad? About sex!' she screeched. She had that irritable petulance common in mid-adolescence. She gave the impression of feeling that she was overweight, and her hairstyle showed she was not yet used to her plumper and larger face, and she slouched like a tired 9-year-old, except for the disconsolate look she cast upon her developed body.'Can you imagine it?' she demanded of her older sister, who laughed easily, unperturbed by the younger girl's irritation. 'He'd be as uncomfortable as we would. He'd say "Yeah, yeah", squirm in his seat and change the subject.' The father as confidant did not merely pale beside the mother, the father was someone they would positively avoid, the person they would turn to last. The father was not so much feared or distrusted in this role. He simply was thought to look ridiculously inept.

These very marked differences in what a girl likes to do with a mother and with a father are merely the more obvious of an entire range of differences. A daughter not only plays with her parents in different ways, she argues with them in different ways. She has different expectations about the course and resolution of the argument. She uses different tactics for resolving a quarrel, and harbours a different sense of who is to blame. It is far easier, apparently, to bear a grudge against the father than the mother. 'He knows I'm mad at him, so he won't expect much more than sulking for the next few days', Jenny explained. Believing that her father expected her to hold a grudge, she thought it was all right, or even necessary to do so. At 16, Jenny had that spark of many young black girls—keen, sly, wry and hopeful. She lived with both parents in an Oakland house which, like many houses built just after the big earthquake in 1906, were spacious, elegant, and so under-insulated that, 'My Dad only has to sneeze upstairs, for us to jump in the kitchen.' The notion of space but no insulation was clear in her description of her fights with her response to her mother. 'Mum and I had a terrible fight. We were both torn up about it. But it's hard to stay angry. Well, no, it's easy to get real angry. But even when I'm panting in my room, I feel like she's near me. I know she's panting—crying inside, really angry—on the other side of the door, and it starts ticking over in my mind, "How are we going to get over this? Who's going to make the first move?" Not that either one of us will admit we're in the wrong', Jenny added with a smile.

Most girls had a very different sense of how to 'make up' with or 'make amends to' the mother and father. To make up with the mother, they might say 'sorry' or try to 'talk things out.' 'I know I hurt her', a classmate of Jenny's admitted, 'when I get mad at her. Even when I'm spitting out all those rude words, I'm thinking about what's at the end of this. And I know there are some arguments she'll listen to—she's a real sucker for me saying it's all her fault. You know, I'll say, "The reason I did this was that you let my brother do it", or I'll say, "but you do it to me, and I'm not supposed to mind", and that will sort of distract her, so she'll stop and think, and when she does that I know we can begin to ease off each other, because she's not so sure anymore and I don't feel so beaten.' 'I can always just say "I'm sorry"', a third classmate, Alecia, boasted. 'Even if she gets real nasty with me and mimics me—"You're sorry, nah, nah",—I know the fight's over.'

Few girls assumed that they had this reciprocal power—to hurt and to heal—with their father. Instead of meeting the problems arising from a quarrel with her father head on, daughters were inclined to wait until things 'cooled down' or 'calmed down' and then just 'pretend nothing happened'. 'If I said "sorry" to my dad', Jenny explained, 'I'd be giving away too much'. 'I sometimes apologise to my Dad', Alecia said. 'But every time I do it, I'm sorry, and I say to myself "I'm never going to do this again. Never-ever." He sniffs—'. She gave a wonderful imitation of a complacent snort. 'You know, takes it like that, like I'm saying he's right and I'm wrong. I only mean to say "I'm sorry we're fighting." But he doesn't take it like that.' 'Yeah, that's what my Dad does', Lydia concurred. 'He's sweeter than that. I mean, he can go all soggy when I say I'm sorry, and then he says "That's all right honey", but it's that same thing. It's thinking that "I'm sorry" means "I was in the wrong and you were in the right." So I don't apologise any more—not unless I'm feeling real sneaky, and want something from him. I just go away, and let the pot cool.'

Girls did not always want to mitigate the effects of a quarrel, or their anger. Sometimes they wanted to punish a parent. They wanted to see a parent hurt. They wanted to show a parent how much they had been hurt. And just as they would make up in different ways with a mother and with a father, they would use different methods to punish a mother or a father. 'Getting back at mother' was very different from 'getting back at father'. In some sense the mother had the worse of it, with more 'back talk' or 'disrespect' or 'shouting' as her punishment, whereas the father was ignored, and would 'just get real brief answers'. The adolescent daughter would attack the mother directly. She would 'punish', or try to hurt the father by giving him the silent treatment. She was hot in her anger towards the mother, and icy towards the father.

Adolescents, for all their self-involvement, are emerging from the self-centredness of childhood. Their perception of other people has more depth. They are better equipped at appreciating others' reasons for action, or the basis of others' emotions. But this maturity functions in a piecemeal fashion. They show more understanding of their friends, but not of their teachers. What is even more striking is that adolescent daughters view their mothers with more depth than they view their fathers. Daughters see a mother and a father in different ways, and have a different relationship with each of them. That is not surprising. They are two very different people. But not only do they respond to the mother and the father in different ways, they view them with different levels of perceptual maturity.

Parents and children always have difficulty seeing one another clearly. Objectivity does not thrive within the family. But girls saw their mothers with far greater clarity than they saw their fathers. The generosity and empathy they easily expended on their mother was hoarded like a miser in relation to their father. An adolescent girl tends to be remarkably good at seeing things from her mother's perspective. She can explain why her mother behaves as she does. 'She's worried sick about cars and car accidents.' 'She's always more edgy when my Dad's away.' 'She doesn't want to have the trouble with me that she did with my sister.' 'She thinks I'm a little lazy, and always need an extra push.' She can explain why her mother reacts as she does. 'She's flustered because we're having guests this evening. That's always a bit too much for her.' 'She can't stand it when I have to work out at the gym all weekend. When I come home in the evening all she can do is snap, just because she missed me.' These girls could take a mother's perspective, in the sense of understanding it, even when they did not share it. It seemed that they were reciprocating what they felt to be her greater ability to see things from their point of view. For however much a daughter complained that her mother 'did not see' or 'would not see' what she was, she also judged her mother not only to try to understand her, but to be generous in this understanding—in contrast to the father's tendency to 'lay down the law'.

Girls see their fathers as exercising authority over them. Even when they consider their fathers kind and supportive, they describe their relationship with him in terms of control. Yet daughters describe their interactions with mothers in terms of intimate exchanges. It is not that the mother has no authority, it is that her authority is transformed by intimacy, or utilised in intimacy to support these exchanges. The mother listens, comforts, offers advice. The way she exercises authority is by 'insisting on knowing what is going on'. What threatens her power is ignorance of her daughter's feelings, whereas the father wants to control what she does without this close reference to the daughter's feelings. It isn't that fathers do not care what their adolescent daughters feel. It is that they do not go about finding out how they feel. They do not tend to engage in the kind of exchanges whereby they would have the opportunity to sense the ebb and flow of feeling. They do not have the information—about school, friends, hopes, anxieties—which would allow them to link moods with deeper emotions. Lacking a rich contextual picture, the father's understanding is less intimate and less elastic. He is concerned for the daughter's well-being, but the daughter interprets this concern in terms of control, whereas the concern coming from the mother is experienced first as emotional involvement, and only subsequently, if something goes wrong, as control or intrusion.

Accompanying the different ways of each parent,

and the different depth of the views, was a difference in how they tried to be nice or 'good' to each parent—should they happen to want to be so. To a mother, a girl was likely to help her ('make her life easier') by 'telling her I love her', whereas to a father she would reciprocate, or show gratitude, by 'keeping out of trouble' or 'doing well in school', especially if he was paying for school. These girls were aware of a financial debt to their fathers, but they saw the way to make their mothers happy, or to be good to them, was to reaffirm their closeness.

This reaffirmation came easy for them. Here I was, speaking to girls in mid-adolescence, which is a time that is generally thought to be characteristic of the greatest conflict between parent and child, and most girls said the person they felt closest to, the person they felt most loved by, the person who offered them the greatest support, was their mother. She was likely to be closer to her mother than to her friends, and closer to her mother than to any other member of the family; if there was an exception to this the closest family member would be a sibling, most often a sister. 'Sometimes I feel closest to my sister. We can talk about anything, and we don't mind feeling ridiculous. It's more serious, though, with my mother, and I know she'll listen—well, not every time. She can be busy—she's often "too busy right now"—but when I talk to her, I feel she's "there" for me, and even when the things I say make her cross—like I'll tell her what I said to my boyfriend, and she'll say, "You shouldn't have said that! What is he going to think of you now" or I'll tell her what I did with some friends, and her eyes will pop out of her head. You know, she's still surprised that I can take the lead with my friends, and sort of form groups, and get them to do things. But if she gets cross when she hear things, I just wait it out—usually—and then she'll calm down, and give me advice, and—I don't know, sometimes it's real funny, and I wouldn't follow it—no way!—but it somehow helps, anyway.' In contrast, the father seemed to have 'no time' or 'no patience' or 'no interest' in the girl's feelings—at least this is how the adolescent girl tended to describe her father, who never admitted to the charge of 'not caring' or 'not wanting to know'. But, according to the daughter, her father 'just doesn't try to understand me. He comes in and says what he thinks, or what I should do, and that's that. I don't get a chance to give him my side. So I just stay out of his way.' In addition to the father not hearing what she had to say, or refusing to see her point of view, she complained that he actually did not see her. 'He doesn't see how much I've grown. He still treats me like a little girl. I feel myself clamming up when he's around.'

Because the father would not listen, because the father would not see them, the adolescent girl who had a fair degree of control over her actions, and a keen sense of strategy within the family, would avoid the father, either by 'keeping out-of his way' or 'clamming up', that is, not necessarily avoiding him, but keeping a lid on self-expression and self-exposure. Such tactics were not simply defences against being ignored or misunderstood or misperceived. This was a form of deliberate punishment. If her father did not listen to her, then she would not speak to him. If her father was not ready to see her, then she would in some way hide from him, disguise herself in his presence. The daughter would punish her father by not giving him any part of her. Because he lacked the flexibility to listen and to see, she would cut herself off from him. Separation was brought about by anger. It was induced as punishment for not allowing her to grow close.

Adolescent girls are not close to their fathers. They often increase the distance between them in order to punish the father. They tend to be less close to their fathers during adolescence than they have been during childhood. It is terribly difficult to understand precisely what is going on as the girl draws away from her father. It is tempting to see this failure of intimacy between father and daughter during adolescence as some repercussion of an earlier state, when the father simply let the mother do most of the caring and even much of the loving for him. The distance between father and adolescent daughter made me wonder whether they had ever been very close.

In the early stages of the women's movement, the institution of parenthood and the traditional divided roles of mother and father came under criticism and scrutiny. The emphasis at that time was on parenting of infants and very young children. Since gender identity emerged in very early childhood, it seemed reasonable to look to early child rearing practices to explain different gender characteristics. The infant's initial bond with the mother was thought to be responsible for gender identity as we know it. The girl's early identification with the mother would set her on the course towards a female who would find meaning through attachment to others. The boy's early identification with the mother would always haunt him, so that, to preserve his masculine identity he would seek control over strong emotions, close bonds, and tender merging. If this theory was right, then gender identity could be changed. If the father were to care for an infant in the same way a mother did, or if the father had an equal share in caring for the child, then the gender stereotypes would be destroyed. The infant girl, cared for by both the male and female parent, would not see herself so closely bound to the mother and so separate from the father. The infant boy, being cared for by both female and male parents, will (it was predicted) not associate those early feelings of boundless love, attachment and dependence as a purely female phenomenon. His masculine identity would not be threatened by deep feeling, for he will direct such emotion, and receive such emotions from his father as well as his mother.

Many parents, believing that the traditional institution of motherhood is beneficial neither to the parents nor to the children, shifted the old balance of parental responsibilities. The shift is not so easily put into effect, however. Parenting can be established as a time-share job, but mothers are less good at 'switching off' their parent identity and turning to something else.[3] Many women envy the father's ability to set clear boundaries between home and work, between being an on-duty and an off-duty parent. But few women envy the father his emotional distance or psychological disengagement from the child.[4] Women work very hard to maintain a closeness to their child. Fathers value intimacy with a child, but often do not know how to work to maintain it.

In the past fifteen years, women have increasingly extended their roles outside the home, but their roles within the home have not drastically changed. Most of them do continue to be the primary parent, the primary caretaker. However determined both mother and father may be to share the parenting load, the woman is more likely to do more because she is quicker to see what there is to be done and quicker to respond to the child's demands. She has the opportunity to teach her husband the skills she is naturally better at and for which she has been more intensively trained, but often the task of teaching him is too costly. She feels that in reminding him she is 'nagging'. She feels that in correcting him she arouses impatience and irritation. It is easier, and safer for the marriage, to take full domestic responsibility than to engage in the reminders, the teaching, the insistence that may be necessary to change a father's domestic and parenting patterns.

However, some couples do stick with this determination to share, fair and square, early parenting tasks. Many of the adolescents I spoke to, both in England and America (though the majority were in America) had, as infants, a larger than typical share of father care. The differences to the adolescents, however, were far more marked among boys than among girls. It was boys who had been close to their father during infancy, and boys who remained close to their fathers in adolescence who were 'better' at friendship—that is, they valued friendship highly and sought self-exploration through friendship. The boys whose fathers participated fully in their care (that is, who did about fifty per cent of the parenting jobs) saw friendship as more than a means of getting buddies or 'mates' to do things with, more than a companion or accomplice. Boys whose father had spent more time caring for them had more sophisticated aims in forming friendships with girls. They did not seek girl friends simply for the purpose of having someone to go out with or make out with, but saw relationships as having developmental potential.[5] They wanted to 'get to know the girl', but also to get to know themselves through the girl. Dating itself was seen as an opportunity for psychological intimacy. For whatever the reason—whether boys with fathers who devoted more time caring for them simply had fathers who were more expressive and warmer than boys whose fathers maintained a traditional paternal role, or whether the father's time and care itself made the difference—these male adolescents were different from the stereotype of the male adolescent. They valued intimacy more, and they saw relationships as an important facet of their identity. In this respect having two parents caring for them, having the father assume many maternal tasks was highly effective in shifting the stereotype. But dual parenting does not seem to have the same effect on girls. However close the father's participation in caring for the girl, her aims and self-image during adolescence remain indistinguishable from those of girls whose parents have stuck to the traditional division of labour.[6] The primacy of the mother/daughter bond is such that it is not altered by the close, caring presence of a father during infancy, and in fact, the father is often crowded out during the girl's adolescence.

The strange, disturbing and sad picture of father and daughter seems to be that during the daughter's adolescence, the distance between them increases. Most fathers become extremely attached to an infant daughter. This closeness is usually sustained in early childhood, but thereafter gradually diminishes. Girls who are very close to their fathers in early childhood, are less close at 9, and less close again, at 13. They confide in them less, spend less time with them, enjoy their company less, receive less encouragement and support from them. Frustrated, hurt and angered by this distance, an adolescent girl will 'punish' her father for his lack of empathy, for his unwillingness to understand her, by aggravating the separation between them.[7] Thus she aggravates the separation for which she is punishing him.

The Battle for Recognition

If she gives up on a father's understanding or empathy, a daughter will avoid discussion with him. She lowers the level of conflict by avoiding contact. Seldom, however, does a daughter avoid a mother, even to diminish conflict. She tries to avoid conflict with her father because it is unproductive. She may find conflict with her mother painful, but she does not avoid it. She seeks out contact to analyse, explain and even expand conflict. Being closer to her mother, she has far more problems with her.

The adolescent girl repeatedly complains about how the mother sees her. She engages in vigorous argument to correct and redress and defend her mother's image of her. She fights not so much for freedom as for her mother's belief in her judgement and trust in her independence. These are not the responses of people trying to separate from one another. These are the responses of people who remain preoccupied with the relationship, and who are hoping for something to happen within the relationship. For girls in mid-adolescence are looking for and trying to inspire new responses for their parents. Earlier, in the first stages of adolescence, girls suffered a keen sense of separation, but this was separation from themselves—from their familiar world of childhood. Their loneliness was confusion about the physical and hormonal changes taking place within them. They were thrust into a world where change differed from the innocent, exciting growth of childhood, when development was greeted with unambiguous delight. Instead, at puberty, they met with mixed responses, and saw that their development, though containing some good, some excitement, some promise, also changed the network of responses and expectations. The girl who develops early, before her peers, suffers a special loneliness and a special self-consciousness. With the high visibility of her physical maturity, she sees herself as awkward, . . .

■ ■ ■

The Life-Long Dialogue

The adolescent daughter needs her mother. She needs to fight with her, to come to self-awareness by forcing her mother to see the new person within her. The mother often finds this exhausting work. She may also find it disheartening, for she may not like the person her daughter is becoming. She knows that she is playing a large part in this development. Her daughter's demands upon her make this very clear. Yet she does not always believe she has control upon her influence. She tries to influence her daughter in one direction, but her wishes push her daughter in another direction. It is maddening, having this powerful influence yet being unable to direct it, to feel that what she does has enormous impact on her daughter without being able to predict the impact. Her daughter's responses seem, given the twists of psychological logic, bizarre and irrational. Though her daughter continues to use her as a mirror or a bouncing board, the mother herself has lost her daughter as a simple and direct reflector of the mother's love.

If people close to us change, and change rapidly, we may be thrilled, but we may also be threatened. We may not like what they are. In some ways mothers are more 'objective' about a teenage daughter than about a much younger daughter. As she changes, they see her more clearly. They see her from a greater distance. If they do not like what they see, they feel that bitter anger which only a disappointed parent feels. But not liking them, they continue to love them, and try to change them.

As a very young adult, a woman often has, towards her mother, a cooling off or brushing off phase. Disappointed by her 'failure' to separate during adolescence, she tries to draw boundaries between them. She is a woman, too, now, and an equal of her mother. Her self-boundaries should be well-defined, should they not? If she is fortunate, if she has some success, some direction, and formed some good attachments outside her family, then these 'boundaries' will take good shape within new contexts, and her demands upon her mother will diminish. Yet many young women, as they receive the first thrills of adult confirmation in their work, stack up these successes like a pile of grudges, reserved ammunition against the mother, who did not believe in her enough, or failed to recognise that skill, that capacity. 'My mother thought I couldn't be a lawyer. She thought I wanted to go to law school just to stay in school a few years longer. She didn't think I was career-minded. And now she sees my salary cheque—well, that impresses her. I never could convince her, but this pay-in slip sure does.' 'My mother was always sure I wouldn't make it through college. She thought I had the brains, but somehow not the stamina. I want her to come to my graduation—she'd better come—because I want her to sit there and see that I've done it. Without a slip. Without a tremor. I've done it, and she was wrong to be afraid.' 'When I walk on to the stage', said a young opera singer, 'the most nervous person in the hall is my mother. She told me she had dreams, just before I first performed at the Wigmore Hall, that I forgot the music, that I just broke off, and there was nothing she could do to help me. I always feel particularly sassy [smug, impudent] when she's watching me. I want to prove I have all the confidence I need.' 'Here I am, living on my own—and living pretty well—miles away from her', explained an apparently highly independent woman of 23, 'but each time—a hundred times a day!—I'll find myself talking to her, as though she's here, arguing with me. It could be any little thing. She might be asking me why I'm buying this or that at the supermarket, and I'll find myself trying to come up with an explanation that will suit her. Or it might be a conversation with a much larger framework. I'll be telling her how satisfying I find this job, what good work I can hope to do as a lawyer, and how right she was to back me. Anything in my life that wouldn't appeal to her tends to crop up. Sometimes I'm annoyed and sometimes I feel as though I'm getting somewhere, that she's really able to understand and accept all of me. It's not a huge issue—it doesn't take up my whole consciousness. I'll just catch myself doing it. It can be peripheral—but then of course I can also brood long and hard over it.'

The desire to make the mother proud is twisted into anger, anger that it is still necessary to fight for recognition. The mother's protectiveness is so ingrained that it takes some time to get used to her daughter's ability to plough through life without her. The daughter offers her independence like a gift, and then finds that it is received with suspicion. Or, when she has proved that her life as an adult is pretty much in order, a less dependent sister may seem to absorb the greater part of passion and attachment that parents retain for their adult children. The good work done between them during adolescence creates high expectation, and hence offers many grounds for disappointment and complaint.

Mothers and daughters continue to quarrel because neither gives up on the other. Underlying the continuing quarrels is the hope that needs will be met. Each quarrel is an attempt to get, this time, the right response, the correct effect. A mother continues to haunt her daughter, for better or for worse, throughout her life. This intimacy is due not only, and perhaps not primarily, to the emotional bonding of infancy, but to the type of personal growth she battles through during adolescence, a growth which is like a persuasion. It is impossible ever to forget the role she has played in this development, and it is impossible ever to forgive those bad patches which reside within us all. Well into adulthood, long past adolescence, daughters ponder over the meaning their mothers had for them. A woman may fear becoming a mother herself as she acknowledges the terrible burden of her personality, as something which is bound to affect her daughter as much as her mother's affected her. This intimate exchange of identity is a secret dread of many women, which can be heightened as they themselves become mothers of daughters. The daughter's need for her mother's confirmation cannot be conceived as a weakness, but as a fact of female psychology. Letters between mothers and daughters document this continued need for the daughter to explain herself, to justify herself through explanation, through making her mother see, understand, accept, verify, confirm.[8] This form of written communication is particularly revealing. Sometimes it urges forward the more positive feelings, which may be buried under daily, minor irritations.[9] Sometimes the negative feelings surface, which are normally buried under the fear of causing pain, or of retaliation. In letters the daughter takes on a more adult and circumspect persona. The daughter feels she has the chance to have her full say, without interruption. She can qualify her remarks at her own pace. The hectic ping-pong effect of the adolescent smashing with a spin each remark her mother hands to her, turns into a more refined dialogue, wherein the mother is able to explain herself and her love anew, to someone who has known it all along, but who can now understand it. This dialogue continues in some form as long as the mother and daughter can look at one another, and acknowledge what they see.

The greatest change in adulthood is not the final breaking of the bond between mother and daughter, but the daughter's acceptance of the fact that it is not the mother who forces the bond upon her. Whereas the daughter may continue to pick fights, or to seek confirmation, or to expect praise, the mother herself loosens her hold, and wonders at the tenacity of her daughter's complaints, her continued fantasy that the mother is 'governing' her life. 'In a voice remarkably free of emotion—a voice, detached, curious, only wanting information—she says to me, "Why don't you go already? Why don't you walk away from my life? I'm not stopping you"', demands an elderly mother of her middle-aged daughter, finding her demands and complaints exhausting and confusing. Standing 'half in, half out' of the mother's room, the adult daughter acknowledges, 'I know you're not Ma'.[10] The daughter grows into womanhood, still puzzled by that tricky equation between her identity and her mother's, still prepared to fight one more battle to make their different positions clear, and for her mother to offer the banner of acceptance and admiration. In moments of enlightenment, she sees that the argument is no longer between her mother and herself, but between her self and the history which formed that self.

Notes

1. Steinberg, 1981.
2. Youniss and Smollar, 1985.
3. Ehrensaft, 1987.
4. Apter, 1985.
5. Cooper and Grotevant, 1987, pp. 247–64.
6. Earlier writings indicate that women who become professionally successful have a closer bond to their fathers than their mothers. See, for example, Hennig and Jardim, 1977; 1978. I did not find this true for a later generation of professionally successful women (cf. Apter 1985). Nor do current studies show this for adolescent girls (cf. Cooper and Grotevant, 1987).
7. Youniss and Smollar, 1985.
8. Payne, 1983.
9. Plath, 3 March 1956.
10. Gornick, 1987.

The Child That Never Was

María Virginia Estenssoro

Translated by John Benson

María Virginia Estenssoro (1902–1970) was born in Bolivia. Her short stories have been collected under the title El Occiso *(The Slain) (1937). Her work is translated here from the Spanish. Sirius (the "Dog Star" in the constellation Canus Major), mentioned in this story, is the brightest star in the heavens. Because it appeared at about the time the Nile began its annual floods, the Egyptians associated Sirius with fertility and called it "the creator of all green growing things." Sirius is also noted for having a companion star, a "white dwarf," that influences its orbit, while remaining almost invisible.*

THEY WERE LAUGHING ON THEIR WAY BACK FROM A spin in the car.

Out in the open country, the sky was jet black in the depths of the night.

Suddenly, Ernesto pointed at something: "Sirius!" And he recounted the affair in bitter-sad-cynical-mordant phrases.

"It was in New York. Her name was Caroline. I loved her. She arrived one afternoon at the park where I was waiting for her and she told me, 'It's all taken care of.' I was looking at Sirius, just like I am now, and replied, 'Yeah?' I was a little out of it. She was happy: 'Yes, I'm free now. What a relief! Aren't you happy?' 'Yeah, yeah . . .' 'Well, what's wrong with you now? I'm going.' And I watched her stride away, pulling on her gloves, swallowed by the subway entrance. Sirius kept on shining like a sparkling diamond. I thought about God and the old curse: 'Be fruitful and multiply!' Nowadays nobody pays much attention to it, what with prophylactics and abortion. What do you think He thinks of his handiwork? What must God think about this anthropoid, this overgrown monkey that dares to be intelligent enough to invent things that abrogate his eternal laws, unchangeable laws, eternal and irresistable as God Himself?"

"Did you ever see her again?" asked Magdalena.

"No. I loved her a lot, almost as much as you. And that night I thought about how easy it is to lose someone in a city as vast as New York. So I looked up at Sirius—shining like a tear in the sky—and drummed on the window with my fingers, thinking about my son, the son that never was, that never became a . . . a lawyer." Ernesto cut off suddenly with a short, sarcastic laugh.

Magdalena meditated on Sirius and on the moon that lit up the sky and seemed to bathe them in pearls. She slowly turned around, looked

From *Short Stories by Latin American Women: The Magic and the Real*, edited by Celia de Correas De Zapata. Reprinted by permission of the publisher, Arte Público Press.

straight into his eyes and said, "But I will love your child."

Then he kissed her hand, all tenderness as in their best moments together, murmuring softly like a child about to break out in tears, "My God!"

Magdalena moaned monotonously on the operating table, "No more, please, no more."

The doctor stanched the blood with bits of sterilized cotton. She could smell the iodine, alcohol, disinfectant. The pain pierced her and she implored again, "Enough, for the love of God, enough!"

Suddenly the instrument drove home and, as she screamed, a muffled, babbled appeal came from within, "Mommy . . ."

The doctor was drying his hands as he remarked, "That's all, ma'am. Rather squeamish, aren't we?"

"Please don't make fun of me."

And then she heard, "Mommy . . ."

And then she left. Though she was still in pain, she lengthened her stride and tried to put some spring into her step as she walked along: Click, click, click, click, click, click. Mom, my Mom, my . . .

A ragged, barefoot newsboy looked up at her imploringly. Magdalena bought a paper from him as she searched his face: "Mommy."

Her child was waiting for her at home, her boy, the one from her marriage. He came running out like always, little arms out, tripped and fell: "Mommy!"

Dejected, depressed, she lay down. Her little boy dozed happily at her side, his little brown-haired head nestled in the pillow. She looked at him, a lovely flower rooted in her heart. Now in that same heart she now felt another little one, something that could have bloomed forth in innocence, just like the first one which she had allowed the surgeon to cruelly uproot.

"Mommy."

But the dark head cut off in its beginning, torn from her, destroyed, sabred in her very womb, the little dark head had left its imprint, a small, indelible trace, uneraseable, adorable. And in the mother's soul the little shade stretched forth his arms and cried: "Mommy! Mommy!"

"My poor baby!" Magdalena moaned, pressing the fair hand of the other son who slept on her breast, smiling and content. "My poor baby! You're half-frozen like a little bird. Come here and warm up, go to sleep. Poor dear, so cold, so unloved, little star, my little treasure. Poor baby, sleep, sleep."

And the little shadow kept on: "Mommy, Mommy . . ."

She thought she was going crazy. The heart of the child sleeping next to her went "Mommy!"

The clock seemed to go "Mommy!"

She got up. Walking back and forth, she remembered the afternoon Ernesto mused about what God must think of his piteous creatures, and what Caroline said: "It's all taken care of."

She lay down again and dreamt.

The sky was jet black in the depths of the night. The tremulous light of a candle came and went up and down in the darkness. Wherever it passed, beads of light came to life like in electric signs: red letters, green letters and white ones.

"Mommy, Mommy, Mommy . . ."

And then, a cold chill and everything went black again. Was it limbo? There was a stirring of shadows and wings. Were they newborns? Then, deep sighing and little sobs: "Mommy, Mommy, Mommy . . ."

Suddenly a large figure hurried by, a skeleton in surgeon's costume and rubber gloves. Death / The Surgeon grasped a package that squirmed and cried: "Mommy."

She awoke in a cold sweat. She got up again. Striding around the estate, feverish, she peered inward in anguish.

"Does it take courage to raise a fatherless child?" she asked herself.

"Does it?"

Yes, it does. But I have one already—my husband's; he never had any use for him, and all I have is love, love and instinct, tenderness and impulses. And happiness. And gratitude. I'm not courageous, not heroic. I'm happy. And what do I give him? Everything and nothing. He—weak, small, defenseless as he is—gives me his laughter, his happiness, the light in his eyes, the life I first gave him. He gives me back enchantment, fantasy, poetry. He transmutes even money—the filthy, worn bills I get I handle avidly, impatiently as though they were fine cloth or satin. It turns into his little shoes, toys, candies, his grabby little hands and his inquiring eyes excited at the prospect of a present. He is my supreme happiness, constantly renewed, hope, life itself. I'm not courageous, just happy.

Courage is something else. Terrifying, abominable. Magnificent yet infernal. Courage to forgo happiness, kill contentment, destroy the enchantment, rip the veil of fantasy, turn the knife to one's very bowels and against one's own life.

"But I will love your child."

"Mommy, Mommy, Mommy."

Mommy, I do love you so much! Mothers are supposed to sacrifice themselves for their children, but I will sacrifice myself for you. Mommy, dear Momma, I'll never bother you again. You'll never have to listen to me cry, although sometimes you'll wish you could. I'll never tear pages out of your books, never knock over and break a vase. You'll never have to worry about my getting sick, or fret over not being able to buy me a toy. I'll never be bad, or awkward or make you uncomfortable. I'm the nice boy, the good boy. I won't bother you with my noisy games and you'll never lose time dressing, washing or feeding me. Want me to go, Mommy? I'm the obedient one. No cradle, no Mother Goose, I'll disappear in the cold, in the night, out there somewhere . . . Want me to go? All right, I'll go. But I do love you so much, dear Momma, Mommy, Mommy, Mommy . . .

The Management of Grief

Bharati Mukherjee

Bharati Mukherjee (1940–   ) born in Calcutta, India, has lived in England and Canada, and came to the United States in 1961 to study at the Iowa Writer's Workshop. She received a Ph.D. from the University of Iowa in 1969 and is currently a professor of English at the University of California at Berkeley. Her novels include The Tiger's Daughter *(1972),* Wife *(1975), and, most recently,* The Holder of the World *(1993). Based on historical documents, the novel tells the story of Hannah Easton, a blond Caucasian woman who went to live in India in the seventeenth century and who experienced the transformation that immigration can bring about.*

A WOMAN I DON'T KNOW IS BOILING TEA THE Indian way in my kitchen. There are a lot of women I don't know in my kitchen, whispering, and moving tactfully. They open doors, rummage through the pantry, and try not to ask me where things are kept. They remind me of when my sons were small, on Mother's Day or when Vikram and I were tired, and they would make big, sloppy omelets. I would lie in bed pretending I didn't hear them.

Dr. Sharma, the treasurer of the Indo-Canada Society, pulls me into the hallway. He wants to know if I am worried about money. His wife, who has just come up from the basement with a tray of empty cups and glasses, scolds him. "Don't bother Mrs. Bhave with mundane details." She looks so monstrously pregnant her baby must be days overdue. I tell her she shouldn't be carrying heavy things. "Shaila," she says, smiling, "this is the fifth." Then she grabs a teenager by his shirttails. He slips his Walkman off his head. He has to be one of her four children, they have the same doomed and dented foreheads. "What's the official word now?" she demands. The boy slips the headphones back on. "They're acting evasive, Ma. They're saying it could be an accident or a terrorist bomb."

All morning, the boys have been muttering, Sikh Bomb, Sikh Bomb. The men, not using the word, bow their heads in agreement. Mrs. Sharma touches her forehead at such a word. At least they've stopped talking about space debris and Russian lasers.

Two radios are going in the dining room. They are tuned to different stations. Someone must have brought the radios down from my boys' bedrooms. I haven't gone into their rooms since Kusum came running across the front lawn in her bathrobe. She looked so funny, I was laughing when I opened the door.

The big TV in the den is being whizzed through American networks and cable channels.

"Damn!" some man swears bitterly. "How

can these preachers carry on like nothing's happened?" I want to tell him we're not that important. You look at the audience, and at the preacher in his blue robe with his beautiful white hair, the potted palm trees under a blue sky, and you know they care about nothing.

The phone rings and rings. Dr. Sharma's taken charge. "We're with her," he keeps saying. "Yes, yes, the doctor has given calming pills. Yes, yes, pills are having necessary effect." I wonder if pills alone explain this calm. Not peace, just a deadening quiet. I was always controlled, but never repressed. Sound can reach me, but my body is tensed, ready to scream. I hear their voices all around me. I hear my boys and Vikram cry, "Mommy, Shaila!" and their screams insulate me, like headphones.

The woman boiling water tells her story again and again. "I got the news first. My cousin called from Halifax before six A.M., can you imagine? He'd gotten up for prayers and his son was studying for medical exams and he heard on a rock channel that something had happened to a plane. They said first it had disappeared from the radar, like a giant eraser just reached out. His father called me, so I said to him, what do you mean, 'something bad'? You mean a hijacking? And he said, *behn,* there is no confirmation of anything yet, but check with your neighbors because a lot of them must be on that plane. So I called poor Kusum straightaway. I knew Kusum's husband and daughter were booked to go yesterday."

Kusum lives across the street from me. She and Satish had moved in less than a month ago. They said they needed a bigger place. All these people, the Sharmas and friends from the Indo-Canada Society had been there for the housewarming. Satish and Kusum made homemade tandoori on their big gas grill and even the white neighbors piled their plates high with that luridly red, charred, juicy chicken. Their younger daughter had danced, and even our boys had broken away from the Stanley Cup telecast to put in a reluctant appearance. Everyone took pictures for their albums and for the community newspapers—another of our families had made it big in Toronto—and now I wonder how many of those happy faces are gone. "Why does God give us so much if all along He intends to take it away?" Kusum asks me.

I nod. We sit on carpeted stairs, holding hands like children. "I never once told him that I loved him," I say. I was too much the well brought up woman. I was so well brought up I never felt comfortable calling my husband by his first name.

"It's all right," Kusum says. "He knew. My husband knew. They felt it. Modern young girls have to say it because what they feel is fake."

Kusum's daughter, Pam, runs in with an overnight case. Pam's in her McDonald's uniform. "Mummy! You have to get dressed!" Panic makes her cranky. "A reporter's on his way here."

"Why?"

"You want to talk to him in your bathrobe?" She starts to brush her mother's long hair. She's the daughter who's always in trouble. She dates Canadian boys and hangs out in the mall, shopping for tight sweaters. The younger one, the goody-goody one according to Pam, the one with a voice so sweet that when she sang *bhajans* for Ethiopian relief even a frugal man like my husband wrote out a hundred dollar check, *she* was on that plane. *She* was going to spend July and August with grandparents because Pam wouldn't go. Pam said she'd rather waitress at McDonald's. "If it's a choice between Bombay and Wonderland, I'm picking Wonderland," she'd said.

"Leave me alone," Kusum yells. "You know what I want to do? If I didn't have to look after you now, I'd hang myself."

Pam's young face goes blotchy with pain. "Thanks," she says, "don't let me stop you."

"Hush," pregnant Mrs. Sharma scolds Pam. "Leave your mother alone. Mr. Sharma will tackle the reporters and fill out the forms. He'll say what has to be said."

Pam stands her ground. "You think I don't know what Mummy's thinking? *Why ever?* that's what. That's sick! Mummy wishes my little sister were alive and I were dead."

Kusum's hand in mine is trembly hot. We continue to sit on the stairs.

She calls before she arrives, wondering if there's anything I need. Her name is Judith Templeton and she's an appointee of the provincial government. "Multiculturalism?" I ask, and she says, "partially," but that her mandate is bigger. "I've been told you knew many of the people on the flight," she says. "Perhaps if you'd agree to help us reach the others . . . ?"

She gives me time at least to put on tea water and

pick up the mess in the front room. I have a few *samosas* from Kusum's housewarming that I could fry up, but then I think, why prolong this visit?

Judith Templeton is much younger than she sounded. She wears a blue suit with a white blouse and a polka dot tie. Her blond hair is cut short, her only jewelry is pearl drop earrings. Her briefcase is new and expensive looking, a gleaming cordovan leather. She sits with it across her lap. When she looks out the front windows onto the street, her contact lenses seem to float in front of her light blue eyes.

"What sort of help do you want from me?" I ask. She has refused the tea, out of politeness, but I insist, along with some slightly stale biscuits.

"I have no experience," she admits. "That is, I have an MSW and I've worked in liaison with accident victims, but I mean I have no experience with a tragedy of this scale—"

"Who could?" I ask.

"—and with the complications of culture, language, and customs. Someone mentioned that Mrs. Bhave is a pillar—because you've taken it more calmly."

At this, perhaps, I frown, for she reaches forward, almost to take my hand. "I hope you understand my meaning, Mrs. Bhave. There are hundreds of people in Metro directly affected, like you, and some of them speak no English. There are some widows who've never handled money or gone on a bus, and there are old parents who still haven't eaten or gone outside their bedrooms. Some houses and apartments have been looted. Some wives are still hysterical. Some husbands are in shock and profound depression. We want to help, but our hands are tied in so many ways. We have to distribute money to some people, and there are legal documents—these things can be done. We have interpreters, but we don't always have the human touch, or maybe the right human touch. We don't want to make mistakes, Mrs. Bhave, and that's why we'd like to ask you to help us."

"More mistakes, you mean," I say.

"Police matters are not in my hands," she answers.

"Nothing I can do will make any difference," I say. "We must all grieve in our own way."

"But you are coping very well. All the people said, Mrs. Bhave is the strongest person of all. Perhaps if the others could see you, talk with you, it would help them."

"By the standards of the people you call hysterical, I am behaving very oddly and very badly, Miss Templeton." I want to say to her, *I wish I could scream, starve, walk into Lake Ontario, jump from a bridge.* "They would not see me as a model. I do not see myself as a model."

I am a freak. No one who has ever known me would think of me reacting this way. This terrible calm will not go away.

She asks me if she may call again, after I get back from a long trip that we all must make. "Of course," I say. "Feel free to call, anytime."

Four days later, I find Kusum squatting on a rock overlooking a bay in Ireland. It isn't a big rock, but it juts sharply out over water. This is as close as we'll ever get to them. June breezes balloon out her sari and unpin her knee-length hair. She has the bewildered look of a sea creature whom the tides have stranded.

It's been one hundred hours since Kusum came stumbling and screaming across my lawn. Waiting around the hospital, we've heard many stories. The police, the diplomats, they tell us things thinking that we're strong, that knowledge is helpful to the grieving, and maybe it is. Some, I know, prefer ignorance, or their own versions. The plane broke into two, they say. Unconsciousness was instantaneous. No one suffered. My boys must have just finished their breakfasts. They loved eating on planes, they loved the smallness of plates, knives, and forks. Last year they saved the airline salt and pepper shakers. Half an hour more and they would have made it to Heathrow.

Kusum says that we can't escape our fate. She says that all those people—our husbands, my boys, her girl with the nightingale voice, all those Hindus, Christians, Sikhs, Muslims, Parsis, and atheists on that plane—were fated to die together off this beautiful bay. She learned this from a swami in Toronto.

I have my Valium.

Six of us "relatives"—two widows and four widowers—choose to spend the day today by the waters instead of sitting in a hospital room and scanning photographs of the dead. That's what they call us now: relatives. I've looked through twenty-seven photos in two days. They're very kind to us, the Irish are very understanding. Sometimes understanding means freeing a tourist bus for this trip to the bay, so we can pretend to spy our loved ones through the glassiness of waves or in sunspeckled cloud shapes.

I could die here, too, and be content.

"What is that, out there?" She's standing and flapping her hands and for a moment I see a head shape bobbing in the waves. She's standing in the water, I, on the boulder. The tide is low, and a round, black, head-sized rock has just risen from the waves. She returns, her sari end dripping and ruined and her face is a twisted remnant of hope, the way mine was a hundred hours ago, still laughing but inwardly knowing that nothing but the ultimate tragedy could bring two women together at six o'clock on a Sunday morning. I watch her face sag into blankness.

"That water felt warm, Shaila," she says at length.

"You can't," I say. "We have to wait for our turn to come."

I haven't eaten in four days, haven't brushed my teeth.

"I know," she says. "I tell myself I have no right to grieve. They are in a better place than we are. My swami says I should be thrilled for them. My swami says depression is a sign of our selfishness."

Maybe I'm selfish. Selfishly I break away from Kusum and run, sandals slapping against stones, to the water's edge. What if my boys aren't lying pinned under the debris? What if they aren't stuck a mile below that innocent blue chop? What if, given the strong currents. . . .

Now I've ruined my sari, one of my best. Kusum has joined me, knee-deep in water that feels to me like a swimming pool. I could settle in the water, and my husband would take my hand and the boys would slap water in my face just to see me scream.

"Do you remember what good swimmers my boys were, Kusum?"

"I saw the medals," she says.

One of the widowers, Dr. Ranganathan from Montreal, walks out to us, carrying his shoes in one hand. He's an electrical engineer. Someone at the hotel mentioned his work is famous around the world, something about the place where physics and electricity come together. He has lost a huge family, something indescribable. "With some luck," Dr. Ranganathan suggests to me, "a good swimmer could make it safely to some island. It is quite possible that there may be many, many microscopic islets scattered around."

"You're not just saying that?" I tell Dr. Ranganathan about Vinod, my elder son. Last year he took diving as well.

"It's a parent's duty to hope," he says. "It is foolish to rule out possibilities that have not been tested. I myself have not surrendered hope."

Kusum is sobbing once again. "Dear lady," he says, laying his free hand on her arm, and she calms down.

"Vinod is how old?" he asks me. He's very careful, as we all are. *Is,* not was.

"Fourteen. Yesterday he was fourteen. His father and uncle were going to take him down to the Taj and give him a big birthday party. I couldn't go with them because I couldn't get two weeks off from my stupid job in June." I process bills for a travel agent. June is a big travel month.

Dr. Ranganathan whips the pockets of his suit jacket inside out. Squashed roses, in darkening shades of pink, float on the water. He tore the roses off creepers in somebody's garden. He didn't ask anyone if he could pluck the roses, but now there's been an article about it in the local papers. When you see an Indian person, it says, please give him or her flowers.

"A strong youth of fourteen," he says, "can very likely pull to safety a younger one."

My sons, though four years apart, were very close. Vinod wouldn't let Mithun drown. *Electrical engineering,* I think, foolishly perhaps: this man knows important secrets of the universe, things closed to me. Relief spins me lightheaded. No wonder my boys' photographs haven't turned up in the gallery of photos of the recovered dead. "Such pretty roses," I say.

"My wife loved pink roses. Every Friday I had to bring a bunch home. I used to say, why? After twenty odd years of marriage you're still needing proof positive of my love?" He has identified his wife and three of his children. Then others from Montreal, the lucky ones, intact families with no survivors. He chuckles as he wades back to shore. Then he swings around to ask me a question. "Mrs. Bhave, you are wanting to throw in some roses for your loved ones? I have two big ones left."

But I have other things to float: Vinod's pocket calculator; a half-painted model B-52 for my Mithun. They'd want them on their island. And for my husband? For him I let fall into the calm, glassy waters a poem I wrote in the hospital yesterday. Finally he'll know my feelings for him.

"Don't tumble, the rocks are slippery," Dr. Ranganathan cautions. He holds out a hand for me to grab.

Then it's time to get back on the bus, time to rush back to our waiting posts on hospital benches.

Kusum is one of the lucky ones. The lucky ones flew here, identified in multiplicate their loved ones, then will fly to India with the bodies for proper ceremonies. Satish is one of the few males who surfaced. The photos of faces we saw on the walls in an office at Heathrow and here in the hospital are mostly of women. Women have more body fat, a nun said to me matter-of-factly. They float better.

Today I was stopped by a young sailor on the street. He had loaded bodies, he'd gone into the water when—he checks my face for signs of strength—when the sharks were first spotted. I don't blush, and he breaks down. "It's all right," I say. "Thank you." I had heard about the sharks from Dr. Ranganathan. In his orderly mind, science brings understanding, it holds no terror. It is the shark's duty. For every deer there is a hunter, for every fish a fisherman.

The Irish are not shy; they rush to me and give me hugs and some are crying. I cannot imagine reactions like that on the streets of Toronto. Just strangers, and I am touched. Some carry flowers with them and give them to any Indian they see.

After lunch, a policeman I have gotten to know quite well catches hold of me. He says he thinks he has a match for Vinod. I explain what a good swimmer Vinod is.

"You want me with you when you look at photos?" Dr. Ranganathan walks ahead of me into the picture gallery. In these matters, he is a scientist, and I am grateful. It is a new perspective. "They have performed miracles," he says. "We are indebted to them."

The first day or two the policemen showed us relatives only one picture at a time; now they're in a hurry, they're eager to lay out the possibles, and even the probables.

The face on the photo is of a boy much like Vinod; the same intelligent eyes, the same thick brows dipping into a V. But this boy's features, even his cheeks, are puffier, wider, mushier.

"No." My gaze is pulled by other pictures. There are five other boys who look like Vinod.

The nun assigned to console me rubs the first picture with a fingertip. "When they've been in the water for a while, love, they look a little heavier." The bones under the skin are broken, they said on the first day—try to adjust your memories. It's important.

"It's not him. I'm his mother. I'd know."

"I know this one!" Dr. Ranganathan cries out suddenly from the back of the gallery. "And this one!" I think he senses that I don't want to find my boys. "They are the Kutty brothers. They were also from Montreal." I don't mean to be crying. On the contrary, I am ecstatic. My suitcase in the hotel is packed heavy with dry clothes for my boys.

The policeman starts to cry. "I am so sorry, I am so sorry, ma'am. I really thought we had a match."

With the nun ahead of us and the policeman behind, we, the unlucky ones without our children's bodies, file out of the makeshift gallery.

From Ireland most of us go on to India. Kusum and I take the same direct flight to Bombay, so I can help her clear customs quickly. But we have to argue with a man in uniform. He has large boils on his face. The boils swell and glow with sweat as we argue with him. He wants Kusum to wait in line and he refuses to take authority because his boss is on a tea break. But Kusum won't let her coffins out of sight, and I shan't desert her though I know that my parents, elderly and diabetic, must be waiting in a stuffy car in a scorching lot.

"You bastard!" I scream at the man with the popping boils. Other passengers press closer. "You think we're smuggling contraband in those coffins!"

Once upon a time we were well brought up women; we were dutiful wives who kept our heads veiled, our voices shy and sweet.

In India, I become, once again, an only child of rich, ailing parents. Old friends of the family come to pay their respects. Some are Sikh, and inwardly, involuntarily, I cringe. My parents are progressive people; they do not blame communities for a few individuals.

In Canada it is a different story now.

"Stay longer," my mother pleads. "Canada is a cold place. Why would you want to be all by yourself?" I stay.

Three months pass. Then another.

"Vikram wouldn't have wanted you to give up things!" they protest. They call my husband by the name he was born with. In Toronto he'd changed to Vik so the men he worked with at his office would find his name as easy as Rod or Chris. "You know, the dead aren't cut off from us!"

My grandmother, the spoiled daughter of a rich

zamindar, shaved her head with rusty razor blades when she was widowed at sixteen. My grandfather died of childhood diabetes when he was nineteen, and she saw herself as the harbinger of bad luck. My mother grew up without parents, raised indifferently by an uncle, while her true mother slept in a hut behind the main estate house and took her food with the servants. She grew up a rationalist. My parents abhor mindless mortification.

The zamindar's daughter kept stubborn faith in Vedic rituals; my parents rebelled. I am trapped between two modes of knowledge. At thirty-six, I am too old to start over and too young to give up. Like my husband's spirit, I flutter between worlds.

Courting aphasia, we travel. We travel with our phalanx of servants and poor relatives. To hill stations and to beach resorts. We play contract bridge in dusty gymkhana clubs. We ride stubby ponies up crumbly mountain trails. At tea dances, we let ourselves be twirled twice round the ballroom. We hit the holy spots we hadn't made time for before. In Varanasi, Kalighat, Rishikesh, Hardwar, astrologers and palmists seek me out and for a fee offer me cosmic consolations.

Already the widowers among us are being shown new bride candidates. They cannot resist the call of custom, the authority of their parents and older brothers. They must marry; it is the duty of a man to look after a wife. The new wives will be young widows with children, destitute but of good family. They will make loving wives, but the men will shun them. I've had calls from the men over crackling Indian telephone lines. "Save me," they say, these substantial, educated, successful men of forty. "My parents are arranging a marriage for me." In a month they will have buried one family and returned to Canada with a new bride and partial family.

I am comparatively lucky. No one here thinks of arranging a husband for an unlucky widow.

Then, on the third day of the sixth month into this odyssey, in an abandoned temple in a tiny Himalayan village, as I make my offering of flowers and sweetmeats to the god of a tribe of animists, my husband descends to me. He is squatting next to a scrawny *sadhu* in moth-eaten robes. Vikram wears the vanilla suit he wore the last time I hugged him. The *sadhu* tosses petals on a butter-fed flame, reciting Sanskrit mantras and sweeps his face of flies. My husband takes my hands in his.

You're beautiful, he starts. Then, *What are you doing here?*

Shall I stay? I ask. He only smiles, but already the image is fading. *You must finish alone what we started together.* No seaweed wreathes his mouth. He speaks too fast just as he used to when we were an envied family in our pink split-level. He is gone.

In the windowless altar room, smoky with joss sticks and clarified butter lamps, a sweaty hand gropes for my blouse. I do not shriek. The *sadhu* arranges his robe. The lamps hiss and sputter out.

When we come out of the temple, my mother says, "Did you feel something weird in there?"

My mother has no patience with ghosts, prophetic dreams, holy men, and cults.

"No," I lie. "Nothing."

But she knows that she's lost me. She knows that in days I shall be leaving.

Kusum's put her house up for sale. She wants to live in an ashram in Hardwar. Moving to Hardwar was her swami's idea. Her swami runs two ashrams, the one in Hardwar and another here in Toronto.

"Don't run away," I tell her.

"I'm not running away," she says. "I'm pursuing inner peace. You think you or that Ranganathan fellow are better off?"

Pam's left for California. She wants to do some modelling, she says. She says when she comes into her share of the insurance money she'll open a yoga-cum-aerobics studio in Hollywood. She sends me postcards so naughty I daren't leave them on the coffee table. Her mother has withdrawn from her and the world.

The rest of us don't lose touch, that's the point. Talk is all we have, says Dr. Ranganathan, who has also resisted his relatives and returned to Montreal and to his job, alone. He says, whom better to talk with than other relatives? We've been melted down and recast as a new tribe.

He calls me twice a week from Montreal. Every Wednesday night and every Saturday afternoon. He is changing jobs, going to Ottawa. But Ottawa is over a hundred miles away, and he is forced to drive two hundred and twenty miles a day. He can't bring himself to sell his house. The house is a temple, he says; the king-sized bed in the master bedroom is a shrine. He sleeps on a folding cot. A devotee.

There are still some hysterical relatives. Judith Templeton's list of those needing help and those who've "accepted" is in nearly perfect balance. Acceptance means you speak of your family in the past tense and you make active plans for moving ahead with your life. There are courses at Seneca and Ryerson we could be taking. Her gleaming leather briefcase is full of college catalogues and lists of cultural societies that need our help. She has done impressive work, I tell her.

"In the textbooks on grief management," she replies—I am her confidante, I realize, one of the few whose grief has not sprung bizarre obsessions—"there are stages to pass through: rejection, depression, acceptance, reconstruction." She has compiled a chart and finds that six months after the tragedy, none of us still reject reality, but only a handful are reconstructing. "Depressed Acceptance" is the plateau we've reached. Remarriage is a major step in reconstruction (though she's a little surprised, even shocked, over *how* quickly some of the men have taken on new families). Selling one's house and changing jobs and cities is healthy.

How do I tell Judith Templeton that my family surrounds me, and that like creatures in epics, they've changed shapes? She sees me as calm and accepting but worries that I have no job, no career. My closest friends are worse off than I. I cannot tell her my days, even my nights, are thrilling.

She asks me to help with families she can't reach at all. An elderly couple in Agincourt whose sons were killed just weeks after they had brought their parents over from a village in Punjab. From their names, I know they are Sikh. Judith Templeton and a translator have visited them twice with offers of money for air fare to Ireland, with bank forms, power-of-attorney forms, but they have refused to sign, or to leave their tiny apartment. Their sons' money is frozen in the bank. Their sons' investment apartments have been trashed by tenants, the furnishings sold off. The parents fear that anything they sign or any money they receive will end the company's or the country's obligations to them. They fear they are selling their sons for two airline tickets to a place they've never seen.

The high-rise apartment is a tower of Indians and West Indians, with a sprinkling of Orientals. The nearest bus stop kiosk is lined with women in saris. Boys practice cricket in the parking lot. Inside the building, even I wince a bit from the ferocity of onion fumes, the distinctive and immediate Indianness of frying *ghee*, but Judith Templeton maintains a steady flow of information. These poor old people are in imminent danger of losing their place and all their services.

I say to her, "They are Sikh. They will not open up to a Hindu woman." And what I want to add is, as much as I try not to, I stiffen now at the sight of beards and turbans. I remember a time when we all trusted each other in this new country, it was only the new country we worried about.

The two rooms are dark and stuffy. The lights are off, and an oil lamp sputters on the coffee table. The bent old lady has let us in, and her husband is wrapping a white turban over his oiled, hip-length hair. She immediately goes to the kitchen, and I hear the most familiar sound of an Indian home, tap water hitting and filling a teapot.

They have not paid their utility bills, out of fear and the inability to write a check. The telephone is gone; electricity and gas and water are soon to follow. They have told Judith their sons will provide. They are good boys, and they have always earned and looked after their parents.

We converse a bit in Hindi. They do not ask about the crash and I wonder if I should bring it up. If they think I am here merely as a translator, then they may feel insulted. There are thousands of Punjabi-speakers, Sikhs, in Toronto to do a better job. And so I say to the old lady, "I too have lost my sons, and my husband, in the crash."

Her eyes immediately fill with tears. The man mutters a few words which sound like a blessing. "God provides and God takes away," he says.

I want to say, but only men destroy and give back nothing. "My boys and my husband are not coming back," I say. "We have to understand that."

Now the old woman responds. "But who is to say? Man alone does not decide these things." To this her husband adds his agreement.

Judith asks about the bank papers, the release forms. With a stroke of the pen, they will have a provincial trustee to pay their bills, invest their money, send them a monthly pension.

"Do you know this woman?" I ask them.

The man raises his hand from the table, turns it over and seems to regard each finger separately before he answers. "This young lady is always coming here, we make tea for her and she leaves papers for us to sign." His eyes scan a pile of papers in the corner of the room. "Soon we will be out of tea, then will she go away?"

The old lady adds, "I have asked my neighbors and no one else gets *angrezi* visitors. What have we done?"

"It's her job," I try to explain. "The government is worried. Soon you will have no place to stay, no lights, no gas, no water."

"Government will get its money. Tell her not to worry, we are honorable people."

I try to explain the government wishes to give money, not take. He raises his hand. "Let them take," he says. "We are accustomed to that. That is no problem."

"We are strong people," says the wife. "Tell her that."

"Who needs all this machinery?" demands the husband. "It is unhealthy, the bright lights, the cold air on a hot day, the cold food, the four gas rings. God will provide, not government."

"When our boys return," the mother says. Her husband sucks his teeth. "Enough talk," he says.

Judith breaks in. "Have you convinced them?" The snaps on her cordovan briefcase go off like firecrackers in that quiet apartment. She lays the sheaf of legal papers on the coffee table. "If they can't write their names, an X will do—I've told them that."

Now the old lady has shuffled to the kitchen and soon emerges with a pot of tea and two cups. "I think my bladder will go first on a job like this," Judith says to me, smiling. "If only there was some way of reaching them. Please thank her for the tea. Tell her she's very kind."

I nod in Judith's direction and tell them in Hindi, "She thanks you for the tea. She thinks you are being very hospitable but she doesn't have the slightest idea what it means."

I want to say, humor her. I want to say, my boys and my husband are with me too, more than ever. I look in the old man's eyes and I can read his stubborn, peasant's message: *I have protected this woman as best I can. She is the only person I have left. Give to me or take from me what you will, but I will not sign for it. I will not pretend that I accept.*

In the car, Judith says, "You see what I'm up against? I'm sure they're lovely people, but their stubbornness and ignorance are driving me crazy. They think signing a paper is signing their sons' death warrants, don't they?"

I am looking out the window. I want to say, *In our culture, it is a parent's duty to hope.*

"Now Shaila, this next woman is a real mess. She cries day and night, and she refuses all medical help. We may have to—"

"—Let me out at the subway," I say.

"I beg your pardon?" I can feel those blue eyes staring at me.

It would not be like her to disobey. She merely disapproves, and slows at a corner to let me out. Her voice is plaintive. "Is there anything I said? Anything I did?"

I could answer her suddenly in a dozen ways, but I choose not to. "Shaila? Let's talk about it," I hear, then slam the door.

A wife and mother begins her new life in a new country, and that life is cut short. Yet her husband tells her: Complete what we have started. We, who stayed out of politics and came halfway around the world to avoid religious and political feuding have been the first in the New World to die from it. I no longer know what we started, nor how to complete it. I write letters to the editors of local papers and to members of Parliament. Now at least they admit it was a bomb. One MP answers back, with sympathy, but with a challenge. You want to make a difference? Work on a campaign. Work on mine. Politicize the Indian voter.

My husband's old lawyer helps me set up a trust. Vikram was a saver and a careful investor. He had saved the boys' boarding school and college fees. I sell the pink house at four times what we paid for it and take a small apartment downtown. I am looking for a charity to support.

We are deep in the Toronto winter, gray skies, icy pavements. I stay indoors, watching television. I have tried to assess my situation, how best to live my life, to complete what we began so many years ago. Kusum has written me from Hardwar that her life is now serene. She has seen Satish and has heard her daughter sing again. Kusum was on a pilgrimage, passing through a village when she heard a young girl's voice, singing one of her daughter's favorite *bhajans.* She followed the music through the squalor of a Himalayan village, to a hut where a young girl, an exact replica of her daughter, was fanning coals under the kitchen fire. When she appeared, the girl cried out, "Ma!" and ran away. What did I think of that?

I think I can only envy her.

Pam didn't make it to California, but writes me from Vancouver. She works in a department store, giving make-up hints to Indian and Oriental girls. Dr. Ranganathan has given up his commute, given up his house and job, and accepted an academic position in Texas where no one knows his story and he has vowed not to tell it. He calls me now once a week.

I wait, I listen, and I pray, but Vikram has not returned to me. The voices and the shapes and the nights filled with visions ended abruptly several weeks ago.

I take it as a sign.

One rare, beautiful, sunny day last week, returning from a small errand on Yonge Street, I was walking through the park from the subway to my apartment. I live equidistant from the Ontario Houses of Parliament and the University of Toronto. The day was not cold, but something in the bare trees caught my attention. I looked up from the gravel, into the branches and the clear blue sky beyond. I thought I heard the rustling of larger forms, and I waited a moment for voices. Nothing.

"What?" I asked.

Then as I stood in the path looking north to Queen's Park and west to the university, I heard the voices of my family one last time. *Your time has come,* they said. *Go, be brave.*

I do not know where this voyage I have begun will end. I do not know which direction I will take. I dropped the package on a park bench and started walking.

By the River

Susan Browne

Susan Browne (1952–   ) was born in Long Beach and currently teaches English at Diablo Valley College in Pleasant Hill, California. Of her writing process, she says, "I get feedback on my writing from other writers who are my friends and who take writing seriously. I only truly listen to the comments on my work from people who are also writers, who work hard at their craft." Of the discipline needed to be productive, she says, "My writing time is precious. I need solitude to write, and I demand it for myself. Writing is a profession, an art, a great joy, and a liberation to my spirit."

I'm in love with this baby
wearing a yellow straw hat,
blue ribbon wound round the crown,
the brim trimmed with flowers,
her wide, quiet eyes
wise and astonished.
She stands on the stones
near the edge of the river,
reaching to touch
the bright, fast water.
Her father's large hands
hold her legs
so she won't fall.
He strokes her skin's new translucence,
from the perfect arcs of her bottom
to the tiny bones in her feet.
I've been staring a long time,
and I don't know if I'm in love
with the baby or the father,
and here comes the mother
bringing food, thick sandwiches,
strawberries, wine.
A cold bottle of milk shines in the sun.

I'm starving!
I want the whole family!
Their courage and faith
to make something good
and try to keep it that way.
Even though the light falls behind the hills.
Even though the water grows dark.

VII

Spirituality

Archaeological, anthropological, and historical evidence indicates that woman was the focus of human life and spirituality for millennia. This spirituality was the basis of a holistic worldview encompassing human relationships, material survival, and coexistence with all forms of life. Women's natural abilities to create life and food, plus their menstrual coordination with the cycles of the moon, were probably regarded as evidence of their intimate relationship with the mysteries of the universe. Thus women were revered as shamans, healers, priestesses, and oracles.

–Hallie Austen Iglehart, *WomanSpirit*

If I had asked myself at age twenty, thirty, or forty what matters most in life, I would have said being independent and having many choices. But there are lots of things I didn't get to choose: the decent and loving family I was born into; the social, religious or economic circumstance of that family; or to be 5′10″ tall, have brown hair, a thin frame, a hearty constitution, or a questioning nature.

When I stopped resisting, when I stopped trying to change, when I trusted that there was nothing missing inside, that I didn't have to choose between one part of me over another, I rediscovered me.

–Sue Bender, *Plain and Simple*

Nothing so inevitably blackened my heart as an obligatory Sunday at the Shadyside Presbyterian Church: the sight of orphan-girl Liz's "Jesus" tricked out in gilt; the minister's Britishy accent; the putative hypocrisy of my parents, who forced me to go, though they did not; the putative hypocrisy of the expensive men and women who did go. I knew enough of the Bible to damn these people to hell, citing chapter and verse. My house shall be called the house of prayer; but ye have made it a den of thieves. Every week I had been getting madder; now I was going to plain quit. One of these days, when I figured out how.

–Annie Dillard, *An American Childhood*

Because I Could Not Stop for Death

Emily Dickinson

Emily Dickinson (1830–1886) was born in Amherst, Massachusetts. As a student at Mount Holyoke Seminary, she realized that she could not honestly profess a faith in Christ. While her sister Lavinia stayed on to study, she returned to her parents' home, where she remained the rest of her life. Dickinson wrote constantly, often enclosing poems in gifts or letters. Following Dickinson's death, Lavinia discovered she had inherited sixty packets tied in twine—a life's work of 900 poems. Of the following poem, critic Allen Tate has written, "The terror of death is objectified through this figure of the genteel driver, who is made ironically to serve the end of Immortality."

Because I could not stop for Death—
He kindly stopped for me—
The Carriage held but just Ourselves—
And Immortality.

We slowly drove—He knew no haste
And I had put away
My labor and my leisure too,
For His Civility—

We passed the School, where Children strove
At Recess—in the Ring—
We passed the Fields of Gazing Grain—
We passed the Setting Sun—

Or rather—He passed Us—
The Dews drew quivering and chill—
For only Gossamer, my Gown—
My Tippet—only Tulle—

We paused before a House that seemed
A Swelling of the Ground—
The Roof was scarcely visible—
The Cornice—in the Ground—

Since then—'tis Centuries—and yet
Feels shorter than the Day
I first surmised the Horses' Heads
Were toward Eternity—

1890

A Book of Showings

[*God the Mother*]

Julian of Norwich

Julian of Norwich(1342–1416/1423), also called Juliana, was an English mystic who wished for three gifts from God: recollection of Christ's passion; an illness at thirty; and three wounds—true contrition, loving compassion, and affective longing for God. At the age of thirty, she became ill and lay near death. As she gazed at the crucifix, she experienced a series of sixteen visions or "showings" and was miraculously cured. These revelations became the subject of her writing for the next twenty years. Her characterization of the Trinity as Father, Mother, and Lord speak to many in search of a contemporary spirituality.

The Fifty-Ninth Chapter

. . .

As truly as God is our Father, so truly is God our Mother, and he revealed that in everything, and especially in these sweet words where he says. I am he;[1] that is to say: I am he, the power and goodness of fatherhood; I am he, the wisdom and the lovingness of motherhood; I am he, the light and the grace which is all blessed love; I am he, the Trinity;[2] I am he, the unity; I am he, the great supreme goodness of every kind of thing; I am he who makes you to love; I am he who makes you to long; I am he, the endless fulfilling of all true desires. For where the soul is highest, noblest, most honourable, still it is lowest, meekest and mildest.

And from this foundation in substance we have all the powers of our sensuality by the gift of nature, and by the help and the furthering of mercy and grace, without which we cannot profit. Our great Father, almighty God, who is being, knows us and loved us before time began. Out of this knowledge, in his most wonderful deep love, by the prescient eternal counsel of all the blessed Trinity he wanted the second person to become our Mother, our brother and our saviour. From this it follows that as truly as God is our Father, so truly is God our Mother. Our Father wills, our Mother works, our good Lord the Holy Spirit confirms. And therefore it is our part to love our God in whom we have our being, reverently thanking and praising him for our creation, mightily praying to our Mother for mercy and pity, and to our Lord the Holy Spirit for help and grace. For in these three is all our life: nature, mercy and grace, of which we have mildness, patience and pity, and hatred of sin and wickedness; for the virtues must of themselves hate sin and wickedness.

And so Jesus is our true Mother in nature by our first creation, and he is our true Mother in grace by his taking our created nature. All the lovely works and all the sweet loving offices of beloved motherhood are appropriated to the second person, for in him we have this godly will, whole and safe forever, both in nature and in grace, from his own goodness proper to him.

I understand three ways of contemplating motherhood in God. The first is the foundation of our nature's creation; the second is his taking of our nature, where the motherhood of grace begins; the third is the motherhood at work. And in that, by the same grace, everything is penetrated, in length and in breadth, in height and in depth without end; and it is all one love.

The Sixtieth Chapter

But now I should say a little more about this penetration, as I understood our Lord to mean: How we are brought back by the motherhood of mercy and grace into our natural place, in which we were created by the motherhood of love, a mother's love which never leaves us.

Our Mother in nature, our Mother in grace, because he wanted altogether to become our Mother in all things, made the foundation of his work most humbly and most mildly in the maiden's womb. And he revealed that in the first revelation, when he brought that meek maiden before the eye of my understanding in the simple stature which she had when she conceived; that is to say that our great God, the supreme wisdom of all things, arrayed and prepared himself in this humble place, all ready in our poor flesh, himself to do the service and the office of motherhood in everything. The mother's service is nearest, readiest and surest: nearest because it is most natural, readiest because it is most loving, and surest because it is truest. No one ever might or could perform this office fully, except only him. We know that all our mothers bear us for pain and for death. O, what is that? But our true Mother Jesus, he alone bears us for joy and for endless life, blessed may he be. So he carries us within him in love and travail, until the full time when he wanted to suffer the sharpest thorns and cruel pains that ever were or will be, and at the last he died. And when he had finished, and had borne us so for bliss, still all this could not satisfy his wonderful love. And he revealed this in these great surpassing words of love. If I could suffer more, I would suffer more.[3] He could not die any more, but he did not want to cease working; therefore he must needs nourish us, for the precious love of motherhood has made him our debtor.

The mother can give her child to suck of her milk, but our precious Mother Jesus can feed us with himself, and does, most courteously and most tenderly, with the blessed sacrament,[4] which is the precious food of true life; and with all the sweet sacraments he sustains us most mercifully and graciously, and so he meant in these blessed words, where he said: I am he whom Holy Church preaches and teaches to you.[5] That is to say: All the health and the life of the sacraments, all the power and the grace of my word, all the goodness which is ordained in Holy Church for you, I am he.

The mother can lay her child tenderly to her breast, but our tender Mother Jesus can lead us easily into his blessed breast through his sweet open side, and show us there a part of the godhead and of the joys of heaven, with inner certainty of endless bliss. And that he revealed in the tenth revelation,[6] giving us the same understanding in these sweet words which he says: See, how I love you, looking into his blessed side, rejoicing.

This fair lovely word "mother" is so sweet and so kind in itself that it cannot truly be said of anyone or to anyone except of him and to him who is the true Mother of life and of all things. To the property of motherhood belong nature, love, wisdom and knowledge, and this is God. For though it may be so that our bodily bringing to birth is only little, humble and simple in comparison with our spiritual bringing to birth, still it is he who does it in the creatures by whom it is done. The kind, loving mother who knows and sees the need of her child guards it very tenderly, as the nature and condition of motherhood will have. And always as the child grows in age and in stature, she acts differently, but she does not change her love. And when it is even older, she allows it to be chastised to destroy its faults, so as to make the child receive virtues and grace. This work, with everything which is lovely and good, our Lord performs in those by whom it is done.[7] So he is our Mother in nature by the operation of grace in the lower part, for love of the higher part. And he wants us to know it, for he wants to have all our love attached to him; and in this I saw that every debt which we owe by God's command to fatherhood and motherhood is fulfilled in truly loving God, which blessed love Christ works in us. And this was revealed in everything, and especially in the great bounteous words when he says: I am he whom you love.[8]

The Sixty-First Chapter

And in our spiritual bringing to birth he uses more tenderness, without any comparison, in protecting us. By so much as our soul is more precious in his sight, he kindles our understanding, he prepares our ways, he eases our conscience, he comforts our soul, he illumines our heart and gives us partial knowledge and love of his blessed divinity, with gracious memory of his sweet humanity and his blessed Passion,[9] with courteous wonder over his great surpassing goodness, and makes us to love everything which he loves for love of him, and to be well satisfied with him and with all his works. And when we fall, quickly he raises us up with his loving embrace and his gracious touch. And when we are strengthened by his sweet working, then we willingly choose him by his grace, that we shall be his servants and his lovers, constantly and forever.

And yet after this he allows some of us to fall more heavily and more grievously than ever we did before, as it seems to us. And then we who are not all wise think that everything which we have undertaken was all nothing. But it is not so, for we need to fall, and we need to see it; for if we did not fall, we should not know how feeble and how wretched we are in ourselves, nor, too, should we know so completely the wonderful love of our Creator.

For we shall truly see in heaven without end that we have sinned grievously in this life; and notwithstanding this, we shall truly see that we were never hurt in his love, nor were we ever of less value in his sight. And by the experience of this falling we shall have a great and marvellous knowledge of love in God without end; for enduring and marvellous is that love which cannot and will not be broken because of offences.

And this was one profitable understanding; another is the humility and meekness which we shall obtain by the sight of our fall, for by that we shall be raised high in heaven, to which raising we might never have come without that meekness. And therefore we need to see it; and if we do not see it, though we fell, that would not profit us. And commonly we first fall and then see it; and both are from the mercy of God.

The mother may sometimes suffer[10] the child to fall and to be distressed in various ways, for its own benefit, but she can never suffer any kind of peril to come to her child, because of her love. And though our earthly mother may suffer her child to perish, our heavenly Mother Jesus may never suffer us who are his children to perish, for he is almighty, all wisdom and all love, and so is none but he, blessed may he be.

But often when our falling and our wretchedness are shown to us, we are so much afraid and so greatly ashamed of ourselves that we scarcely know where we can put ourselves. But then our courteous Mother does not wish us to flee away, for nothing would be less pleasing to him; but he then wants us to behave like a child. For when it is distressed and frightened, it runs quickly to its mother; and if it can do no more, it calls to the mother for help with all its might. So he wants us to act as a meek child, saying: My kind Mother, my gracious Mother, my beloved Mother, have mercy on me. I have made myself filthy and unlike you, and I may not and cannot make it right except with your help and grace.

And if we do not then feel ourselves eased, let us at once be sure that he is behaving as a wise Mother. For if he sees that it is profitable to us to mourn and to weep, with compassion and pity he suffers that until the right time has come, out of his love. And then he wants us to show a child's characteristics, which always naturally trusts in its mother's love in well-being and in woe. And he wants us to commit ourselves fervently to the faith of Holy Church, and find there our beloved Mother in consolation and true understanding, with all the company of the blessed. For one single person may often be broken, as it seems to him, but the entire body of Holy Church was never broken, nor ever will be without end. And therefore it is a certain thing, and good and gracious to will, meekly and fervently, to be fastened and united to our mother Holy Church, who is Christ Jesus. For the flood of mercy which is his dear blood and precious water is plentiful to make us fair and clean. The blessed wounds of our saviour are open and rejoice to heal us. The sweet gracious hands of our Mother are ready and diligent about us; for he in all this work exercises the true office of a kind nurse, who has nothing else to do but attend to the safety of her child.

It is his office to save us, it is his glory to do it, and it is his will that we know it; for he wants us to love him sweetly and trust in him meekly and greatly. And he revealed this in these gracious words: I protect you very safely.[11]

1393?

Notes

1. In a series of visions in the previous chapters, Christ showed himself to Julian and spoke words which she then interprets in the later chapters.

2. The first person of the Trinity is God, the second person is Jesus Christ, and the third is the Holy Spirit; all three, however, may bear the name God.

3. In the ninth revelation, Christ spoke these words to Julian.

4. The bread and wine consumed during the Catholic mass, which represent the body and blood of Christ.

5. In the twelfth revelation.

6. In the tenth revelation Christ showed Julian a wound in his side, through which she saw "his blessed heart riven in two."

7. I.e., in disciplining her child the mother acts as an agent of God's will.

8. In the twelfth revelation.

9. The crucifixion, in which Christ sacrificed his own life as payment for humanity's sins.

10. Allow.

11. In Chapter Thirty-Seven after the thirteenth revelation.

Life, Death, and Life after Death

Elisabeth Kübler-Ross

Elisabeth Kübler-Ross (1926–) was born in Zurich, Switzerland, and received an M.D. from the University of Zurich in 1957. In 1958 she married and began an internship at Community Hospital, Glen Cove, New York. In 1965 she conceived of a teaching seminar at the Billings Hospital of the University of Chicago, described as "a series of conversations with the terminally ill which would make it possible for them to talk about their feelings and thoughts in this crisis situation." These conversations led to On Death and Dying *(1969) and* Questions and Answers on Death and Dying *(1972).* On Children and Death *(1983) discusses "premature" death and the problems of survivors. In the following selection, Kübler-Ross discusses an extraordinary personal experience.*

One of my first lessons was during a research project where I had an out-of-body experience, induced by iatrogenic means, in a laboratory in Virginia, observed by several skeptical scientists. It was during one of these out-of-body experiences that I was slowed down by the laboratory chief who felt that I went too fast. Much to my dismay, he interfered with my own needs and my own personality. During a second attempt at having an out-of-body experience, I was determined to circumvent this problem by giving myself a self-induction to go faster than the speed of light and further than any human being has ever gone during an out-of-body experience. The moment the induction was given I literally left my body at an incredible speed.

The only memory I had when I returned into my physical body were the words *Shanti Nilaya.* I had no idea about the meaning and significance of this, and had no concept of where I had been. The only awareness I had was that I was healed of an almost complete bowel obstruction, and also of a very painful slipped disc which made it impossible for me to even pick up a book from the floor. When I came out of this experiment my bowel obstruction was healed, and I was literally able to lift a hundred-pound sugar bag from the floor without any discomfort or pain. I was told that I radiated, that I looked twenty years younger. Everyone present tried to press me for information, but I had no idea where I had been until the night following the experiment. A night spent in a lonely guest-house, alone in the forest of the Blue Ridge Mountains. Gradually, and not without trepidation, the awareness came to me that I had gone too far and that I now had to accept the consequences of my own choices. I tried to fight sleep during that night, having a vague, inner-knowledge that "it" would happen, but not knowing what "it" would mean. And the moment I let go I had probably the most painful, most agonizing experience any human being has ever lived through. I literally experienced the thousand deaths of my thousand patients. It was a total physical, spiritual, emotional, and intellectual agony causing the inability to breathe, a doubling up of my body, an agonizing physical pain and a total knowledge and awareness that I was out of reach of any human being. And I had to somehow make it through that night.

In those agonizing hours I had only three reprieves. It was very similar to labor pains, and after each labor pain another one followed immediately without an instant to breathe in between. In those three brief moments when I was able to catch a breath, there were some significant symbolic occurrences which I understood only much later.

During the first reprieve, I begged for a shoulder to lean on. I literally expected a man's left shoulder to appear so I could put my head on it and bear the agony somewhat better. In the same instance that I asked for the shoulder to lean on, a deep, caring, compassionate and severe voice simply stated: "You shall not be given."

Endless time later, when I had another moment to catch a breath, I begged for a hand to hold. Again, I expected a hand to show up at the right side of my bed, so I could grab onto it and endure the agony somewhat easier. And the same voice spoke again: "You shall not be given."

The third and last time I was able to catch a breath, I contemplated asking for a fingertip. But, very much in character for me, I said: "No, if I can't get the hand I don't want the fingertip either." The meaning of the fingertip was simply the awareness of the presence of a human being, with the full knowledge that I could not hold onto that fingertip. It became, for the first time in my life, an issue of faith. And the faith had something to do with a deep, inner knowledge that I had the strength and the courage to endure this agony by myself. But it also included the faith and the knowledge that we are never given more than we can bear. I suddenly became aware that all I needed to do was to stop my fight, to stop my rebellion, to stop being a warrior and move from rebellion to a simple, peaceful, positive submission—to an ability to simply say "yes" to it.

Once I did that, the agony stopped and my breathing was easier. My physical pain disappeared at the moment I uttered the word "yes," not in words but in thoughts. And instead of the thousand deaths, I lived through a rebirth beyond human description.

It started with a very fast vibration, or pulsation, of my abdominal area which spread through my entire body and then to anything that my eyes could see—the ceiling, the walls, the floor, the furniture, the bed, the window, the horizons outside of my window, the trees, and eventually the whole planet earth. It was as if the whole planet was in a very high speed vibration, every molecule vibrated. At the same time, something that looked like a lotus flower bud appeared and opened into an incredible, beautiful, colorful flower. Behind the lotus flower appeared the light that my patients so often talk about. And as I approached this light through the open lotus flower, with a whirl in a deep, fast vibration, I gradually and slowly merged into this incredible unconditional love, into this light. I became one with it.

At the moment of merging into this source of light, all vibrations stopped. A deep silence came over me, and I fell into a deep trance-like sleep from which I awoke knowing that I had to wear a robe, put my sandals on, and walk down the hill. This would occur at the moment the sun was rising from below the horizon.

Approximately an hour and a half later I woke up, put on my robe and sandals and walked down the hill. I experienced probably the greatest ecstasy of existence that human beings can ever experience on this physical plane. I was in total love and awe of all life around me. I was in love with every leaf, every cloud, every piece of grass, every living creature. I felt the pulsation of the pebbles on the path, and I literally walked above the pebbles, conveying to them: "I cannot step on you, I cannot hurt you." As I reached the bottom of the hill I became aware that I had not touched the ground on this path. Yet, there was no questioning the validity of this experience, it was simply an awareness of a cosmic consciousness of life in every living thing, and of a love that can never ever be described in words.

It took me several days to come back to my physical existence with the trivialities of washing dishes, doing the laundry and cooking a meal for my family. And it took several months before I was able to verbalize my experience and share it with a beautiful, non-judgmental, understanding group, a group who had invited me to speak at a conference on transpersonal psychology in Berkeley, California. After I shared my experience, I was given a label for it. It was called cosmic consciousness. As usual, I had to go to the library to find a book with the same title to learn intellectually, and to comprehend, the meaning of such a state. I was also told at that moment that as I merged into this spiritual energy, the source of all light, the words that were given to me, Shanti Nilaya, mean the final home of peace, the home all of us will return to when we have gone through all the agonies, the pains, the sorrows, the griefs. It is where we will be able to let go of the pain and become what we were created to be, a being of harmony between the physical, the emotional, the intellectual and the spiritual quadrants, a being that understands that love, true love, has no claims and no "ifs." If we could understand this state of love, then all of us would be whole and healthy, and all of us would be able to fulfill our destiny in a single lifetime.

This experience has touched and changed my life in ways that are very difficult to put into words. But I think it was because of this experience that I understood that if I ever shared my understanding of life after death, I would literally have to go through a thousand deaths. The society in which I live would try to shred me to pieces, but the experience and the knowledge, the joy, the love and the sensation of what followed the agony, the rewards would always be far greater than the pain.

The Spirit Within

Anita Feder-Chernila

Anita Feder-Chernila (1937–   ) was born in Buffalo, New York. When she was thirteen years old, her family moved to Colorado, where she continued to live while studying for her B.A. in psychology from the University of Denver. She has also studied with Fritz Perls and Dr. Robert Assagioli of Florence, Italy, and was enrolled for a time in the Ph.D. program at the University of California, Berkeley. Currently, she lives and works in Berkeley as a therapist and Buddhist practitioner. She and her husband have two daughters. The following selection is a transcription of a conversation between Feder-Chernila and another therapist.

I REMEMBER AS A CHILD—MAYBE SIX, SEVEN YEARS old, roller skating around the block, having a dialogue with God. It was like talking with an inner friend. That really continues for me now. It is this great, enormous friendship I have inside my mind. That translates as being my guidance, and my intuition. This is how I have always related to God—as an internal friendship. Prayer and formal religion were totally meaningless to me; fortunately for me, my parents did not intrude with any strong religious training. My internal friendship has never been connected with any kind of dogma. God did not identify Himself to me; He spoke to me through the deepening of my intuition. I learned to pay very close attention to my own inner guidance. God is a state of inner openness, a state of total receptivity inside myself. For people with an aversion to talking about God, it is necessary to find a way to translate Higher Power. They need a way to transform the idea of God into an internal receptivity and openness to healing power.

Our whole society is not geared to openness or receptivity, but rather, it is focused on being independent, to operating alone and on our own. Calling on God says "I can't do this by myself." This fear of dependence creates tremendous isolation from any kind of emotional support, interdependence with other people or guidance from all the levels of consciousness that send guidance. But it must start on a simple level—inside, in the heart. It is really a matter of real commitment to awareness, a moment-to-moment awareness to learn to recognize fear and be aware of it in the mind, and then find ways to deal with it.

I find people becoming very creative in dealing with fear. It is often a real revelation once they are aware of it! In my work, people can really hear their fear and give it a voice. They can hear their parents. They can hear someone else's voice internalized in themselves which makes it easier to identify. Once it is identified, they turn toward it, face it, acknowledge it and release it. They constantly release it and return to the present, for fear is always the future. So, if they always come back to the present and affirm the present again and again, it gets to be a habit of mind.

Another way to deal with fear and increase awareness is to meditate every day. This causes clearer minds and heightened awareness of the thoughts that go through the mind. Meditation is a tremendous tool for getting in the present, to *be* present. I like meditation and I like it stripped of any religious dogma. I prefer meditation as just a way to be internal and aware and mindful of thoughts. People sometimes get into meditation as the religious ritual that is saving them, rather than simply for the awareness of themselves. Meditation helps you be here, to be mindful. To be mindful, you must be in the present. To be present, you have to get rid of all the extraneous distractions that go on all the time in the mind. You breathe, you notice your breath, you notice your fear, and you let it go.

Increasing awareness and releasing fear allows you to learn to trust yourself in your own heart and that is what God is. God is inside each of us and this prayer sums that up for me—it is Maitreya's Prayer for the New Age.

I am the creator of the Universe.
I am the Father and Mother of the Universe.
Everything came from me.
Everything shall return to me.
Mind, spirit and body are my temples,
for the self to realize in them
My Supreme Being and Becoming.

Walking on Water

Reflections on Faith and Art

Madeleine L'Engle

*Madeleine L'Engle (1918–   ) was born in New York City and graduated from Smith College in 1941. In her long career, she has written fiction for children and adults, as well as poems, nonfiction based on her journals, and a verse drama—*The Journey with Jonah *(1967). Of her writing, Mara McFadden says, "L'Engle's works are linked by a challenge to conventional religious pieties and an assertion of the dignity and creativity of each individual." The following selection is taken from one of several nonfiction works based on her journals:* Walking on Water: Reflections on Faith and Art *(1980).*

WE ARE HURT; WE ARE LONELY; AND WE TURN TO music or words, and as compensation beyond all price we are given glimpses of the world on the other side of time and space. We all have glimpses of glory as children, and as we grow up we forget them, or are taught to think we made them up; they couldn't possibly have been real, because to most of us who are grown up, reality is like radium, and can be borne only in very small quantities.

But we are meant to be real, and to see and recognize the real. We are all more than we know, and that wondrous reality, that wholeness, holiness, is there for all of us, not the qualified only.

I am glad that in the communion of my church we are baptized as infants, because this emphasizes that the gift of death to this world and birth into the Kingdom of God is, in fact, gift—it is nothing we have earned, or even, as infants, chosen. It is God's freely bestowed love.

Juan Carlos Ortiz, a priest in South America, uses this baptismal formula, "I kill you in the name of the Father and of the Son and of the Holy Spirit, and I make you born into the Kingdom of God to serve and please him."

It is baptism itself that I am talking about, not "immersion" or "splashing." My husband, being properly submerged in the First Baptist Church when he was ten, experienced the same undeserved glory that I did, who was baptized before the age of reason. It is the gift that matters. It is death, and life.

It is as radical as that, and it is gift. Through no virtue of our own we are made dead to the old and alive in the new.

And for each one of us there is a special gift, the way in which we may best serve and please the Lord whose love is so overflowing. And gifts should never be thought of quantitatively. One of the holiest women I have ever known did little with her life in terms of worldly success; her gift was that of bringing laughter with her wherever

---

she went, no matter how dark or grievous the occasion. Wherever she was, holy laughter was present to heal and redeem.

In the Koran it is written, "He deserves Paradise who makes his companions laugh."

Plain and Simple

Sue Bender

Sue Bender (1933–), born in New York City, studied at Simmons College and has earned two master's degrees, in education from Harvard University and in psychiatric social work from the University of California at Berkeley. She is married to "a very patient man"; they are the parents of two sons. Having worked all her life as an artist, in ceramics and collage, Bender was drawn to the quilts of the Amish, but surprised at the depth of her attraction to them. She persisted in following an inner voice that directed her to leave her family and go to live with the Amish, then to write the book Plain and Simple *(1989).*

When I told people I wanted to live with an Amish family everybody laughed. "Impossible," they said. "No Amish family will take you in."

I didn't know when I first looked at an Amish quilt and felt my heart pounding that my soul was starving, that an inner voice was trying to make sense of my life.

I didn't know that I was beginning a journey of the spirit, what Carlos Castaneda calls following "a path that has heart."

I thought I was going to learn more about their quilts, but the quilts were only guides, leading me to what I really needed to learn, to answer a question I hadn't formed yet:

"Is there another way to lead a good life?"

I went searching in a foreign land and found my way home.

Perhaps each of us has a starved place, and each of us knows deep down what we need to fill that place. To find the courage to trust and honor the search, to follow the voice that tells us what we need to do, even when it doesn't seem to make sense, is a worthy pursuit. This story is about that search.

Maybe you have a dream, incubating, not fully formed. Maybe you are on a similar quest. I hope you will listen to my story and at the same time hear yours. That way it will be our journey.

Lessons

"How is your life different?" friends asked. "How have you changed?" I hated the question.

"Give us answers," I heard, but the demand was really coming from me. I wanted to say, "Look at me. Look what I've done."

I wished I could say, "Simplicity, and doing your own cooking, and washing the dishes are wonderful pursuits and will make you happy."

But I wasn't happy.

"You haven't done anything because you have nothing to show for it!" a judging voice inside me said.

Maybe I should have been content to have experienced a way of life that had a quality that seemed elusive to me. Maybe I should have understood that the splendor of another's life doesn't need to be incorporated into one's own—nor is it possible.

But the need to produce something is so ingrained in me that I spent a very long time searching for answers. I still believed there was "something out there" and if only I could find it I could give myself a gold star for coming up with a happy ending.

■ ■ ■

I had picked a practical people who value the "homey virtues." Is this how love affairs begin? Opposites attract? The Amish didn't talk about their values, they lived them. I couldn't live as the Amish, but I knew their spirit was there, inside, and that was as real as anything that was going on outside.

Now when I'm frantic, I feel particularly awful. "Rushing for what?" I stop and ask. It takes time for the "chatter" to quiet down—and in the silence of "not doing," I begin to know what I feel.

My lists are still full, often bursting with possibilities, but I can see what's filling up my life with busyness and what's important—even if I don't always act on that information.

Housework hasn't changed, but my attitude toward the work has changed. Early each morning I squeeze fresh orange juice for my husband, clean off the surface where the juice has spilled, look around the kitchen and take great pleasure seeing it sparkle. Then I go out for a long, early morning walk with a beloved friend. I don't have to try to make these simple activities more interesting.

Before the visit to the Amish, I was proud to make art—precious objects to be seen in a gallery or placed ever so carefully just in the right place in the living room, where they could be admired and protected.

Now, for the first time, I began to make practical ceramics that our family could use every day: dishes, bowls, and plates—sturdy objects, no two alike—irregular, ever so slightly off-balance, hand-painted, crooked black-and-white squares. Their role was to be useful, but I also liked how they looked and loved holding them in my hands. Deciding which cup matched the spirit of which guest gave me considerable pleasure.

When I had tried to achieve without first knowing who I was or what really mattered, the achievement was empty. Those first old quilts I saw—proscribed, ordered, and intense—told me something about the women who made them and their view of the world. I was beginning to understand that our attitude toward the world resonates in the objects around us. They reveal our intention.

■ ■ ■

"Do you know what your trouble is?" a friend asked one day. "You're more an Amish housewife than you realize."

"How can you say that about me? I'm not an Amish housewife! That's a *homebody, and I'm not a homebody."*

But it was true. Just as home is the center for Emma Yoder and Sarah and Becky, my home reflects who I am and what I value. My house is a self-portrait. It has an aesthetic leanness, a paring down that I have come to appreciate. That spare, quiet quality makes me feel calm.

And it's still a struggle. I have giant lapses—when the house is a mess and I'm frantically spinning, and I resent the time it would take to wash even one dish. At those times, when there isn't a single calm moment in the day, I think of the tranquility of the Amish and realize I've made a choice.

Unlike the unhurried and even life of the Amish, I *did* want to go overboard, be consumed by a project, and at times lose all sense of proportion. Maybe I needed to give myself totally to something, to feel the ache that goes along with the joy, to realize how much I have to give up when I'm being single-minded. What

I carry in my heart is an awareness of the values intrinsic to their way of life, something to aim for.

Finding a balance I can live with—that's what I was after. The proportions need constant attention and readjusting. How much red, blue, and yellow do I need, both in my art and in my life?

■ ■ ■

I had been afraid to tell friends what touched me most deeply, because it might sound simplistic, corny, banal. On one of those days when I was feeling particularly miserable, a friend told me about her six-year-old grandson who was helping his father puzzle out how to mend a broken lamp while his grandfather looked on.

"Do you know how talented your father is at fixing things?" the proud grandfather asked.

"Yes," the boy said with a serious expression on his face, "but do you know what he's really best at?"

"What?" the surprised grandfather asked.

"He's best at loving."

Is loving banal?

I went back to the dictionary and looked up *banal.* The first definitions were "trite" and "insipid." I knew that. But then I read on and found "commonness." Maybe the things we share in common are the most important things.

Is loving simple?

Listening to your heart is not simple. Finding out who you are is not simple. It takes a lot of hard work and courage to get to know who you are and what you want.

■ ■ ■

I never knew what to say if someone asked me at a party, "What do you do?" Artist, writer, therapist, wife, mother—I would be judged by the label I chose. The Amish make no distinction. No one is labeled cook, quilter, or housewife. In fact, standing out would be a sign of false pride. I remembered Miriam saying,

"Making a batch of vegetable soup, it's not right for the carrot to say I taste better than the peas, or the pea to say I taste better than the cabbage. It takes all the vegetables to make a good soup!"

Maybe one of these days I'll be able to give myself a gold star for being ordinary, and maybe one of these days I'll give myself a gold star for being extraordinary—for persisting. And maybe one day I won't need to have a star at all.

■ ■ ■

Following a "path that has heart" offers many lessons.

I saw the old, folk-art image "heart in the hand." That's a fine guide, I thought. As an artist I started by using my hands, making things out of clay. Clay needed patience and respect. I could not will it to harden if it was a damp day. The clay took its time, and I had to learn to watch and listen—to yield to its timing. My task was to reconnect with my nature, a nature that had been bent out of shape.

If I had asked myself at age twenty, thirty, or forty what matters most in life, I would have said being independent and having many choices. But there are lots of things I didn't get to choose: the decent and loving family I was born into; the social, religious or economic circumstance of that family; or to be 5′10″ tall, have brown hair, a thin frame, a hearty constitution, or a questioning nature.

When I stopped resisting, when I stopped trying to change, when I trusted that there was nothing missing inside, that I didn't have to choose between one part of me over another, I rediscovered me.

Reclaiming my past, knowing where I came from, getting to know and love my brother and cousins, wanting tradition, rituals, needing to have Thanksgiving dinner at my home every year for thirty years, and being an active participant in a culture that forever romanticizes change is what I am.

"The first principle of a warrior is not being afraid of who you are," a wise Tibetan leader once said. I was beginning to feel what he meant.

And I have another choice—to accept what I didn't get to choose. I could have wished for a calmer nature and on and on, a very long list, but what I finally get to choose is that tiny space between all the givens.

In that tiny space is freedom.

The Emerging Ninepatch

When I set out to live with the Amish, my life had seemed like a crazy quilt—fragmented, with no overall order. I had wanted to get rid of my frenzied life because it was driving me crazy. I kept hoping another image would appear, but there was nothing I could willfully do to change it. For years I used the ninepatch as the basis for the Amish squares, but I never felt a personal connection to the pattern. Then one day, while talking to a friend about the squares, the image of the ninepatch suddenly became intensely personal in a way I couldn't yet put into words.

I knew I'd been given another important message.

An American Childhood

Annie Dillard

Annie Dillard (1945–) was born in Pittsburgh, Pennsylvania, and grew up in the Homewood branch of the Carnegie Library there. She graduated from Hollins College, Virginia, in 1967. Her first book, Pilgrim at Tinker Creek *(1974), won the Pulitzer Prize. Following her divorce and remarriage, she wrote* Holy the Firm *(1977), a book of religious musing centered on a child burn victim named after Julian of Norwich (q.v.).* Teaching a Stone to Talk: Expeditions and Encounters *(1982) continues Dillard's "personal narratives of the fringes and hollows in which life is lived and death is rife."*

THAT MORNING IN CHURCH AFTER OUR FIRST SUBscription dance, we reconvened on the balcony of the Shadyside Presbyterian Church. I sat in the first balcony row, and resisted the impulse to stretch my Charleston-stiff legs on the balcony's carved walnut rail. The blond boy I'd met at the dance was on my mind, and I intended to spend the church hour recalling his every word and gesture, but I couldn't concentrate. Beside me sat my friend Linda. Last night at the dance she had been a laughing, dimpled girl with an advanced sense of the absurd. Now in church she was grave, and didn't acknowledge my remarks.

Near us in the balcony's first row, and behind us, were the boys—the same boys with whom we had traveled on a bus to and from the Sewickley Country Club dance. Below us spread the main pews, filling with adults. Almost everyone in the church was long familiar to me. But this particular Sunday in church bore home to me with force a new notion: that I did not really know any of these people at all. I thought I did—but, being now a teenager, I thought I knew almost everything. Only the strongest evidence could penetrate this illusion, which distorted everything I saw. I knew I approved almost nothing. That is, I liked, I adored, I longed for, everyone on earth, especially India and Africa, and particularly everyone on the streets of Pittsburgh—all those friendly, democratic, openhearted, sensible people—and at Forbes Field, and in all the office buildings, parks, streetcars, churches, and stores, excepting only the people I knew, none of whom was up to snuff.

The church building, where the old Scotch-Irish families assembled weekly, was a Romanesque chunk of rough, carved stone and panes of dark slate. Covered in creeper, long since encrusted into its quietly splendid site, it looked like a Scottish rock in the rain.

Everywhere outside and inside the church and parish hall, sharp carved things rose from the many dim tons of stone. There were grainy crossed keys, pelicans, anchors, a phoenix, ivy

---

vines, sheaves of wheat, queer and leering mammal heads like gargoyles, thistles for Scotland, lizards, scrolls, lions, and shells. It looked as if someone had once in Pittsburgh enjoyed a flight or two of fancy. If your bare hand or arm brushed against one of the stone walls carelessly, the stone would draw blood.

My wool coat sat empty behind me; its satin lining felt cool on the backs of my arms. I hated being here. It looked as if the boys did, too. Their mouths were all open, and their eyelids half down. We were all trapped. At home before church, I had been too rushed to fight about it.

I imagined the holy war each boy had fought with his family this morning, and lost, resulting in his sullen and suited presence in church. I thought of Dan there, ruddy-cheeked, and of wild, sweet Jamie beside him, each flinging his silk tie at his hypocrite father after breakfast, and making a desperate stand in some dark dining room lighted upward by snowlight from the lawns outside—struggling foredoomed to raise the stone and walnut weight of this dead society's dead institutions, battling for liberty, freedom of conscience, and so forth.

The boys, at any rate, slumped. Possibly they were hung over.

While the nave filled we examined, or glared at, the one thing before our eyes: the apse's enormous gold mosaic of Christ. It loomed over the chancel; every pew in the nave and on the balcony looked up at it. It was hard to imagine what long-ago board of trustees had voted for this Romish-looking mosaic, so glittering, with which we had been familiarizing ourselves in a lonely way since infancy, when our eyes could first focus on distance.

Christ stood barefoot, alone and helpless-looking, his palms outcurved at his sides. He was wearing his robes. He wasn't standing on anything, but instead floated loose and upright inside a curved, tiled dome. The balcony's perspective foreshortened the dome's curve, so Christ appeared to drift flattened and clumsy, shriveled but glorious. Barefoot as he was, and with the suggestion of sandstone scarps behind him, he looked rural. Below me along the carpeted marble aisles crept the church's families; the women wore mink and sable stoles. Hushed, they sat and tilted their hatted heads and looked at the rural man. His skies of shattered gold widened over the sanctuary and almost met the square lantern tower, gold-decorated, over the nave.

The mosaic caught the few church lights—lights like tapers in a castle—and spread them dimly, a dusting of gold like pollen, throughout the vast and solemn space. There was nothing you could see well in this rich, Rembrandt darkness—nothing save the minister's shining face and Christ's gold vault—and yet there was no corner, no scratchy lily work, you couldn't see at all.

It was a velvet cord, maroon, with brass fittings, that reserved our ninth-grade balcony section for us. We sat on velvet cushions. Below us, filling the yellow pews with dark furs, were the rest of the families of the church, who seemed to have been planted here in dignity—by a God who could see how hard they worked and how few pleasures they took for themselves—just after the Flood went down. There were Linda's parents and grandparents and one of her great-grandparents. Always, the same old Pittsburgh families ran this church. The men, for whose forefathers streets all over town were named, served as deacons, trustees, and elders. The women served in many ways, and ran the Christmas bazaar.

I knew these men; they were friends and neighbors. I knew what they lived for, I thought. The men wanted to do the right thing, at work and in the community. They wore narrow, tight neckties. Close-mouthed, they met, in volunteer boardrooms and in club locker rooms, the same few comfortable others they had known since kindergarten. Their wives and children, in those days, lived around them on their visits home. Some men found their families bewildering, probably; a man might wonder, wakened by reports of the outstanding misdeeds of this son or that son, how everyone had so failed to understand what he expected. Some of these men held their shoulders and knuckles tight; their laughter was high and embarrassed; they seemed to be looking around for the entrance to some other life. Only some of the doctors, it seemed to me, were conspicuously interested and glad. During conversations, they looked at people calmly, even at their friends' little daughters; their laughter was deep, long, and joyful; they asked questions; and they knew lots of words.

I knew the women better. The women were wise and strong. Even among themselves, they prized gaiety and irony, gaiety and irony come what may. They coped. They sighed, they permitted themselves a remark or two, they lived essentially alone. They reared their children with their own two hands, and did all their own cooking and driving. They had no taste for waste or idleness. They volunteered their considerable energies, wisdom, and ideas at the church or the hospital or the service organization or charity.

Life among these families partook of all the genuine seriousness of life in time. A child's birth was his sole entrée, just as it is to life itself. His birthright was a regiment of families and a phalanx of institutions which would accompany him, solidly but at a distance, through this vale of tears.

Families whose members have been acquainted with each other for as long as anyone remembers grow not close, but respectful. They accumulate dignity by being seen at church every Sunday for the duration of life, despite their troubles and sorrows. They accumulate dignity at club luncheons, dinners, and dances, by gracefully and persistently, with tidy hair and fitted clothes, occupying their slots.

In this world, some grown women went carefully wild from time to time. They appeared at parties in outlandish clothes, hair sticking out, faces painted in freckles. They shrieked, sang, danced, and parodied anything—that is, anything at all outside the tribe—so that nothing, almost, was sacred. These clowns were the best-loved women, and rightly so, for their own sufferings had taught them what dignity was worth, and every few years they reminded the others, and made them laugh till they cried.

My parents didn't go to church. I practically admired them for it. Father would drive by at noon and scoop up Amy and me, saying, "Hop in quick!" so no one would see his weekend khaki pants and loafers.

Now, in unison with the adults in the dimness below, we read responsively, answering the minister. Our voices blended low, so their joined sound rose muffled and roaring, rhythmic, like distant seas, and soaked into the rough stone vaults and plush fittings, and vanished, and rose again:

> The heavens declare the glory of God:
> AND THE FIRMAMENT SHOWETH HIS HANDYWORK.
> Day unto day uttereth speech,
> AND NIGHT UNTO NIGHT SHOWETH KNOWLEDGE.
> There is no speech nor language, where their voice is not heard.

The minister was a florid, dramatic man who commanded a batch of British vowels, for which I blamed him absolutely, not knowing he came from a Canadian farm. His famous radio ministry attracted letters and even contributions from Alaskan lumberjacks and fishermen. The poor saps. What if one of them, a lumberjack, showed up in Pittsburgh wearing a lumberjack shirt and actually tried to enter the church building? Maybe the ushers were really bouncers.

I had got religion at summer camp, and had prayed nightly there and in my bed at home, to God, asking for a grateful heart, and receiving one insofar as I requested it. Inasmuch as I despised everything and everyone about me, of course, it was taken away, and I was left with the blackened heart I had chosen instead. As the years wore on, the intervals between Julys at camp stretched, and filled with country-club evenings, filled with the slang of us girls, our gossip, and our intricately shifting friendships, filled with the sight of the boys whose names themselves were a litany, and with the absorbing study of their nonchalance and gruff ease. All of which I professed, from time to time, when things went poorly, to disdain.

Nothing so inevitably blackened my heart as an obligatory Sunday at the Shadyside Presbyterian Church: the sight of orphan-girl Liz's "Jesus" tricked out in gilt; the minister's Britishy accent; the putative hypocrisy of my parents, who forced me to go, though they did not; the putative hypocrisy of the expensive men and women who did go. I knew enough of the Bible to damn these people to hell, citing chapter and verse. My house shall be called the house of prayer; but ye have made it a den of thieves. Every week I had been getting madder; now I was going to plain quit. One of these days, when I figured out how.

After the responsive reading there was a pause, an expectant hush. It was the first Sunday of the month, I remembered, shocked. Today was Communion. I would have to sit through Communion, with its two species, embarrassment and tedium—and I would be late getting out and Father would have to drive around the block a hundred times. I had successfully avoided Communion for years.

From their pews below rose the ushers and elders—everybody's father and grandfather, from Mellon Bank & Trust et cetera—in tailcoats. They worked the crowd smoothly, as always. When they collected money, I noted, they were especially serene. Collecting money was, after all, what they did during the week; they were used to it. Down each pew an usher thrust a long-handled velvet butterfly net, into the invisible interior of which we each inserted a bare hand to release a crushed, warm dollar bill we'd stored in a white glove's palm.

Now with dignity the ushers and elders hoisted the round sterling silver trays which bore Communion. A loaded juice tray must have weighed ten pounds. From a cunning array of holes in its top layer hung wee, tapered, lead-crystal glasses. Each held one-half ounce of Welch's grape juice.

The seated people would pass the grape-juice trays down the pews. After the grape juice came bread: flat silver salvers bore heaps of soft bread cubes, as if for stuffing a turkey. The elders and ushers spread swiftly and silently over the marble aisles in discreet pairs, some for bread cubes, some for grape juice, communicating by eyebrow only. An unseen organist, behind stone screens, played a muted series of single notes, a restless, breathy strain in a minor key, to kill time.

Soon the ushers reached the balcony where we sat. There our prayers had reached their intensest pitch, so fervent were we in our hopes not to drop the grape-juice tray.

I passed up the Welch's grape juice, I passed up the cubed bread, and sat back against my coat. Was all this not absurd? I glanced at Linda beside me. Apparently it was not. Her hands lay folded in her lap. Both her father and her uncle were elders.

It was not surprising, really, that I alone in this church knew what the barefoot Christ, if there had been such a person, would think about things—grape juice, tailcoats, British vowels, sable stoles. It was not surprising because it was becoming quite usual. After all, I was the intelligentsia around these parts, single-handedly. The intelligentsium. I knew why these people were in church: to display to each other their clothes. These were sophisticated men and women, such as we children were becoming. In church they made business connections; they saw and were seen. The boys, who, like me, were starting to come out for freedom and truth, must be having fits, now that the charade of Communion was in full swing.

I stole a glance at the boys, then looked at them outright, for I had been wrong. The boys, if mine eyes did not deceive me, were praying. Why? The intelligentsia, of course, described itself these days as "agnostic"—a most useful word. Around me, in seeming earnest, the boys prayed their unthinkable private prayers. To whom? It was wrong to watch, but I watched.

On the balcony's first row, to my right, big Dan had pressed his ruddy cheeks into his palms. Beside him, Jamie bent over his knees. Over one eye he had jammed a fist; his other eye was crinkled shut. Another boy, blond Robert, lay stretched over his arms, which clasped the balcony rail. His shoulders were tight; the back of his jacket rose and fell heavily with his breathing. It had been a long time since I'd been to Communion. When had this praying developed?

Dan lowered his hands and leaned back slowly. He opened his eyes, unfocused to the high, empty air before him. Wild Jamie moved his arm; he picked up a fistful of hair from his forehead and held it. His eyes fretted tightly shut; his jaws worked. Robert's head still lay low on his outstretched sleeves; it moved once from side to side and back again. So they struggled on. I finally looked away.

Below the balcony, in the crowded nave, men and women were also concentrating, it seemed. Were they perhaps pretending to pray? All heads were bent; no one moved. I began to doubt my own omniscience. If I bowed my head, too, and shut my eyes, would this be apostasy? No, I'd keep watching the people, in case I'd missed some clue that they were actually doing something else—bidding bridge hands.

For I knew these people, didn't I? I knew their world, which was, in some sense, my world, too, since I could not, outside of books, name another. I knew what they loved: their families, their houses, their country clubs, hard work, the people they knew best, and summer parties with old friends full of laughter. I knew what they hated: labor unions, laziness, spending, wildness, loudness. They didn't buy God. They didn't buy anything if they could help it. And they didn't work on spec.

Nevertheless, a young father below me propped his bowed head on two fists stacked on a raised knee. The ushers and their trays had vanished. The people had taken Communion. No one moved. The organist hushed. All the men's heads were bent—black, white, red, yellow, and brown. The men sat absolutely still. Almost all the women's heads were bent down, too, and some few tilted back. Some hats wagged faintly from side to side. All the people seemed scarcely to breathe.

I was alert enough now to feel, despite myself,

some faint, thin stream of spirit braiding forward from the pews. Its flawed and fragile rivulets pooled far beyond me at the altar. I felt, or saw, its frail strands rise to the wide tower ceiling, and mass in the gold mosaic's dome.

The gold tesserae scattered some spirit like light back over the cavernous room, and held some of it, like light, in its deep curve. Christ drifted among floating sandstone ledges and deep, absorbent skies. There was no speech nor language. The people had been praying, praying to God, just as they seemed to be praying. That was the fact. I didn't know what to make of it.

I left Pittsburgh before I had a grain of sense. Who IS my neighbor? I never learned what the strangers around me had known and felt in their lives—those lithe, sarcastic boys in the balcony, those expensive men and women in the pews below—but it was more than I knew, after all.

The Door to the Soul

Carolyn McVickar Edwards

Carolyn McVickar Edwards (1954–) was born in Carmel, California, and grew up in Lakewood. She moved to Berkeley at eighteen to attend the University of California. In creating her book The Storyteller's Goddess *(1991), she included three types of stories: existing stories that she has retold, stories that she has substantially revised, and stories that she invented herself. In the selection "Shekina, Keeper of Wisdom," she says the student could be either a man or a woman because in this case "gender is merely the mask of the archetype." Edwards says, "I want these stories to become threads in a new myth that we are weaving."*

Shekina (shuh-KEE-nuh)—Keeper of Wisdom (Hebrew People)

People who are uncovering psychological and spiritual truth experience the power of knowing something in the body—not just in the head or even in the heart. Jewish mystical writings, called the Kabbalah, used the word *daath* for the insight that is true because it is accompanied by great feeling. *Daath* is the knowledge that comes from the union of conscious and unconscious minds, a kind of knowing that is a deeply erotic experience. *Daath* is the word used by Kabbalistic writers to refer to the union of God with His Bride, the Sabbath, or the Shekina. The Zohar, the principal book of the Kabbalah, says, "[On the Sabbath] all is found in one body, complete, for the Matronit clings to the King and is become one body, and this is why blessings are found on that day."

Shekina, meaning Sabbath, is the name for the Feast of the Full Moon, which once celebrated the menstruation of the Great Goddess. Originally honored once a month, Her holiness came to be observed once every quarter moon (once a week). The Friday evening that began Her honor was the night in which the husband of the home made love with his wife, recapitulating the union of the God and Goddess. The following day, Saturday, was devoted to the postcoital reverie of washed perceptions and the leisurely depth of feeling that should not be disturbed by mundane doings or materialism.

Patriarchal influence, however, lessened interest in the power of love between the male and female deities within and outside of humans. Consequently, the Sabbath became more an observance obsessed with the minutiae of the law, and the Shekina, once Goddess of Babylon and then of the Jews, went underground.

Her light still glows, however, in the holiness of passionate love, and the braids of Her hair are suggested in the shape of challah bread. Study of the Torah, said to be Her outer garments, can be symbolized in erotic imagery: like a Bride within Her curtained chamber, the Shekina must be courted with the heart, soul, and entire being of those who would know Her wisdom and joy.

Silver candlesticks, white candles, and challah bread all help me to call the Shekina. I wrote this story from the point of view of the young ascetic in me who is still waking to the peace of her own body. Sections of *The Wise Wound* by Penelope Shuttle and Peter Redgrove were invaluable for my understanding of the Shekina.

Once a young man asked himself these questions: Who am I? And how am I connected to all others? He wondered and wandered and asked the questions again and again. He yearned for the answers.

One day he approached a teacher and asked, "Who am I? And how am I connected to all others?" The teacher said, "Study will answer those riddles."

"What must I study?" asked the young man.

"Study the thousand and one books," said the teacher. "It is through your study that you will gain wisdom."

So the young man piled the thousand and one books, some dry bread, and some candles on a cart. Then he took himself in cap and shawl, with paper in his shoes for warmth, to a small house at the edge of a town.

Inside the house, at the desk he sat, day after day, reading the thousand and one books. "Who am I?" he wrote on a paper. "How am I connected to all others?" he wrote on a second. Outside the trees turned fiery and lost their leaves. Inside, the young man filled page after page with learning from his books. He stopped only to swallow a little of the dry bread and sometimes to renew his candle or to drop his aching shoulders before him on the desk to sleep. The young man's wrists grew thin and his eyes burned. The thousand and one books stacked themselves around him in wobbly towers, and the pages of his writings heaped themselves before him like a fence.

One night a freezing rain beat in a torrent against the walls of the house. The young man pulled his shawl tight about him, but he felt the damp like a knife in his back. His feet were numb. The marks on the page before him began to swim. Suddenly the young man let out a moan and flung the book toward the window. "I don't know!" he yelled. "I DON'T KNOW!"

At that very second the rain outside halted and a howl of wind blew up. It clattered the panes and then, in a rush of power, ripped open the catch of the window. The room was filled with the shock of cold air. The candle blew out, and the papers on the desk spattered apart and lifted like the feathers of some giant white bird.

The young man staggered to the window and wrenched it shut. Then turning slowly and looking across the room, he drew back to see that a small light had formed on the other side of the swinging doors that led to the next room. "How can that be?" said the young man. "There is no one in this house but me."

The young man felt afraid. But the light glowed so softly. After a moment, the young man followed the glow to the other side of the doors. The pale light went on before him. This time he had to part a curtain to enter the next room. Still the glow went forward, and the young man found himself walking through room after room. He had not known the house had so many rooms. Was it possible he'd forgotten them? Had they been here before?

Finally the light drew him to a tightly closed door. He pushed it open, and the light settled on a bed in the small room. The young man breathed out as he saw the light falter, then flare up, and then turn before his eyes into a beautiful Woman.

The Woman's skin was dark and Her hair curled about Her face. Her garment was like the shadows of leaves. She looked quietly at the young man. The bed on which She sat was covered with quilts the color of shells. The walls seemed soft as clouds.

"Who are you?" asked the young man.

"I am your Soul," said the Woman. "I am the Shekina. Eat and be full."

The Woman turned and lifted to the bed a great tray laden with a feast. The young man felt ravenous. Fruit of every sort filled the tray. He fell to it and ate his fill.

The Shekina handed him a cup of steaming broth. The young man felt the warmth seep into his bones. "Bathe now," said the Shekina.

Around him the young man could feel hot, lapping, washing water. Afterward a towel folded around him held in the sweet heat.

"Now. Come. Sleep," said the Shekina. She helped the young man into the bed.

For six days the young man clung to the Shekina, wrapped now in the deepest sleep, then awake and gazing into Her eyes, and then holding Her completely as he could. And then again drifting into the lovely snow of sleep.

On the seventh day, the Shekina rose up and kissed the young man on his lips. Then Her skin seemed to melt and he could no longer see Her features. She faded again to a glow of light. The young man lay unable to move, his breath caught in his throat.

The young man didn't know how long he slept after that. But the next time he opened his eyes, the sun was shining. He gathered up the pits of the fruits he'd eaten and went outside. There in the soil he planted a garden. At the center of the garden he placed a stone. On the stone he wrote these words: "I am one with all. All is one."

Years passed by. The seeds of the fruits grew into a mighty orchard. The young man was no longer young. Now he was an old man who carried his grandchildren.

Always on the seventh day, the old man lit the candles and whispered the story of the calling of the Soul. "Come, Shekina," he would say to the breeze that flickered the candle flames bright. "Come, Shekina, come. Fill this garden with Your rest."

Womanspirit: A Guide to Women's Wisdom

Hallie Austen Iglehart

Hallie Austen Iglehart (1947–), born in New York City, grew up in a family of five children in Baltimore County, Maryland. In 1969 she graduated from Brown University in classics and literature. Traveling to England and India catalyzed a recognition that traditional religion in the West subtly flattens and distorts a woman's sense of the Spirit. In 1974 she began teaching Womanspirit classes in San Francisco. The following selection from Womanspirit: A Guide to Women's Wisdom *(1983) was written before she decided to use "Austen" as her family name, to honor her matrilineal line. Since then, she has written a book on multicultural art and mythology,* The Heart of the Goddess.

The Mother of Songs, the mother of our whole seed, bore us in the beginning. She is the mother of all races and the mother of all tribes. She is the mother of the thunder, the mother of the rivers, the mother of the trees and all kind of things. She is the mother of songs and dances. She is the mother of the stones. She is the mother of the dance paraphernalia and of all temples and the only mother we have. She is mother of animals, the only one, and the mother of the Milky Way. She is the mother of the rain, the only one we have. She alone is the mother of things, she alone.[1]

From the Kagaba, a South American Indian culture

In cultures throughout the world, woman has long been recognized as the creation maker. She has been revered for her ability to give birth, to create food with her own body, to provide a large part (in many cases, most) of her people's food through gathering, and for her contributions to the spiritual and everyday life of the community.

The dominance of man as creation maker is a relatively recent phenomenon; yet today we have all been raised in a culture created almost exclusively by men, a culture that recognizes a male god as the creator of all physical life. And now some of man's creations, in particular his technology, offer him the role of the destruction maker, as we face the possibility of nuclear annihilation of the planet. We also face the possible destruction of our souls; for competitiveness and separation of mind from body, and human from nature, have caused an alienation of the psyche greater than any previously known.

We have become too imbalanced. It is time for women to rediscover and fulfill our roles as creation makers if this planet is to survive and women and men are to be able to live creative, harmonious, and truly productive lives. We must bring back the power of women's wisdom. This strength is not a power over anything else, but a force emanating from deep within each of us, radiating out into the world and connecting and interacting with others, creating a new definition of strength.

I believe that the synthesis of feminism and spirituality, called Womanspirit, is a major key to rediscovering this knowledge and power. Spirituality and politics are not separate, nor have they ever been. By examining our spiritual life we can see how it affects our material and everyday lives. Many of our images of who we are and of our power, or powerlessness, come from early spiritual and religious teaching. Even if we do not have a formal religious education, the values of established religions permeate all forms of education and media. Here are a few of these attitudes that we all grew up with: the creator is male; the body is separate from and inferior to the spirit; matters of the spirit need not affect those of politics; women are to follow men; power ultimately lies in someone else's hands.

I use the name Womanspirit to describe the path of the new creation makers for several reasons. I believe that the knowledge and wisdom evolving from women, individually and in groups, are essential to the healing and continued growth of our world. I have found that most meditations and spiritual practices taught by male-dominated religions and spiritual traditions are generally inappropriate for myself and other women. Certain approaches and techniques recur in women's spiritual groups, conferences, and rituals, and these seem particularly useful to women. All of the tools I describe in this book were created by myself or are my adaptations of teachings by other women or cultures in which women have leading roles as creation makers.

I am a woman giving birth to myself.
We are women giving birth to ourselves.

Contemporary chant

The development of our power comes from daily practices that strengthen our bodies, psyches, and souls. This book is written for women who want to learn techniques that they can use to become stronger and wiser in everyday life. By rediscovering our history as women myth-makers, artists, and healers, and by developing tools for creating new forms of consciousness through meditation, dreamwork, and ritual, we can recreate ourselves according to our own image. To develop a whole person, it is important to work on all parts of the self, and this can be done by approaching one's being through personal and collective history and mythology as well as inner meditation and dreamwork, natural healing as well as ritual. At some happy point, all the forms blend together and one learns to intuit and use whatever one needs. I use the female pronoun throughout the book, although these techniques may also be used by men who want to develop their more intuitive, gentle, deeper selves and better understand their own Womanspirits. In sum, the work is for all who want to learn from women's wisdom and rediscover the true nature of Womanspirit. Only by tapping our deep spiritual power and integrating it with action can we effect any lasting changes in our social, political, and economic condition.

▪ ▪ ▪

I realized that as a twentieth-century western woman, I could no longer look for answers outside myself and my culture. I wanted to find out whether other women shared my spiritual discoveries and perplexities. I hoped it was possible to uncover a women's spiritual consciousness as powerful as that which I had experienced with the Tibetans, but which was closer to my own inner being, and less oppressive.

Women's Spiritual Heritage

My traveling days over, I returned to the United States once again, found a job, and began to do volunteer work at the San Francisco Women's Health Center and the Women's Switchboard. I joined a consciousness-raising group and a women's studies program. The things I began to learn were more powerful than I expected.

Many of the experiences I had working in women's health care showed me that my "spiritual" self and my "political" self are not separate from one another. I had always hated the word "spiritual" because it implied that my meditations, my dreams, my creativity, and many other parts of my life were independent from the rest of myself. I realized that the division between my spiritual, political, and personal lives perpetuated my powerlessness. If I dismissed an intuition or meditation that related to my work, I denied my own wisdom and power. I felt this was a source that women were especially close to, whether biologically or sociologically. I was beginning to feel the connections between many of my parts. If the word "spirituality" meant anything to me, it meant integrating and acting from my whole self—my mind, my body, and my emotions—the union of personal and political, spiritual and material, inner and outer.

Although at the time, spirituality and holistic health were generally considered irrelevant and impractical in most feminist groups, I began to find others who were making discoveries and connections similar to my own. I wrote in my journal:

> *It is so simple. All I have to do is look inside myself, and to other women, and trust us and what I have intuited and known all along. We grow up thinking we didn't know anything—that our teachers and bosses and boyfriends and husbands knew better. But now I realize that we really do know—and that the world badly needs our ideas and our ways of being to regain its balance. I feel as though I have "come home."*

I began reading about prepatriarchal history. At first, rather than accepting that women had indeed contributed many of the basic building blocks of civilization, I often doubted what I read or heard in classes, thinking that I simply "wanted to believe" in women's past power and authority. The roots of the fiction of male supremacy were deep in my soul. It took me a long time to dig them out and realize that women and women's work have in fact been overlooked and "written out" of history.

I read Elizabeth Gould Davis's *The First Sex* and Helen Diner's *Mothers and Amazons* and found that, contrary to what most conventional history books had taught us, women had a primary role in ancient culture.[2] They were honored as leaders, priestesses, healers, artists, inventors, and builders, as well as mothers, homemakers, and food providers. I learned that the biases that omitted women from history books had also labeled many cultures "primitive" when they were nothing of the sort. In fact, some early matrifocal cultures were egalitarian, communal, peaceful, and, for their time, highly developed culturally and technologically.[3]

Much evidence indicates that these societies were far more peaceful, creative, and communal than ours, with few of the radical social and economic imbalances that predominate today's world. Cultures that find their main source of food by gathering, as did the majority of prepatriarchal cultures, are generally communal, with everyone helping run the community's affairs. Archaeology shows us that there were no separate structures for rulers, for everyone lived and ruled together. The lack of fortifications and weapons in archaeological remains of such cultures as Catal Huyuk (Turkey, c. 3000 B.C.) and Crete (3000–1500 B.C.) indicates that both of these societies existed in peace for at least a thousand years. Significantly, there were altars and shrines everywhere, with no separate temples, indicating that spirituality was an integral part of everyday life. In *When God Was a Woman,* Merlin Stone makes the point that sexism, classism, racism, violence, and religious hierarchies came in with the patriarchy. For example, the concept of light being superior to dark (rather than being simply another part of the spectrum) was brought into India by the Aryans, the northern patriarchal invaders, to help assert their dominance over the peaceful, darker-skinned, goddess-worshipping Dravidian inhabitants.

Archaeological, anthropological, and historical evidence indicates that woman was the focus of human life and spirituality for millennia. This spirituality was the basis of a holistic worldview encompassing human relationships, material survival, and coexistence with all forms of life. Women's natural abilities to create life and food, plus their menstrual coordination with the cycles of the moon, were probably regarded as evidence of their intimate relationship with the mysteries of the universe. Thus women were revered as shamans, healers, priestesses, and oracles.[4]

Learning about women's cultures has given me a new perspective on myself and my society, as well as inspiration for making changes in both. My deep belief that the world need not be and has not always been as sexist, racist, classist, and violent as it is now has been confirmed. In fact, research into other cultures made me realize that our society is even more unbalanced than I had thought. An emphasis on female energy is needed to restore the balance in the lives and psyches of both women and men. Ignorance about women and women's cultures perpetuates women's powerlessness and men's imbalance. Knowing about strong women of the past has provided me with models and has helped me believe in myself and in the potential of all women for growth and survival. Meditating on these women and their lives gives me a deeper understanding of my own potential.

These discoveries, and a desire to find other women with whom I could explore spirituality, led me to teach my first Womanspirit class. We focused on women's history, healing, and meditation. As we sparked one another with our information and excitement, I felt my spiritual and political worlds come together; we had tapped the power of a spirituality that affirms and strengthens women. As the past decade has unfurled itself, Womanspirit has helped me discover unimagined strength within myself and learn how to channel that power to help create peace in the world. I hope that Womanspirit will help you as much as it has helped me.

Notes

1. As reprinted and edited by Judy Chicago for The Birth Project Exhibition, Unit 3, 1983.

2. Elizabeth Gould Davis, *The First Sex* (Baltimore: Penguin Books, 1971); Helen Diner, *Mothers and Amazons* (Garden City, New York: Anchor Press/Doubleday, 1973).

3. See also: Merlin Stone, *When God Was a Woman* (New York: The Dial Press, 1976).

4. Anne Kent Rush, *Moon Moon* (New York and Berkeley: Moon Books/Random House, 1976).

My Life for the Poor

Silence and Kindness

Mother Teresa of Calcutta

Mother Teresa (1910–) was born in Skopje, Albania, and named, originally, Agnes Gonxha Bejaxhia. In 1929 she joined the congregation of Loretto nuns in Calcutta as Sister Teresa. In 1946 she received a clear call from God to leave the convent and serve the poor while living among them. In 1950, with an initial membership of twelve, she set up the new congregation of the Missionaries of Charity in the slums of Calcutta. Her book Gift from God *appeared in 1975. In 1979 she received the Nobel Peace Prize, and in 1985 the Presidential Medal of Freedom in the USA.*

From *My Life for the Poor, 1985.* Reprinted by permission of Harper Collins.

MAN NEEDS SILENCE.

To be alone or together looking for God in silence.

There it is that we accumulate the inward power which we distribute in action, put in the smallest duty and spend in the severest hardships that befall on us.

Silence came before creation, and the heavens were spread without a word.

Christ was born in the dead of night; and though there has been no power like his, "He did not strive nor cry, neither was his voice heard in the streets."

Once I was asked by someone what I consider most important in the training of the sisters. I answered:

Silence. Interior and exterior silence. Silence is essential in a religious house. The silence of humility, of charity, the silence of the eyes, of the ears, of the tongue. There is no life of prayer without silence.

Silence, and then kindness, charity; silence leads to charity, charity to humility. Charity among themselves, accepting one another when they are different; charity for union in a community. Charity leads to humility. We must be humble. It strikes me how God is humble. He humbled himself. He who possessed the fullness of the Godhead took the form of a servant. Even today God shows his humility by making use of instruments as deficient as we are, weak, imperfect, inadequate instruments.

Then, there must be joy in the heart, the joy of serving God, the joy of doing his work. That is not incompatible with humility.

Indeed, in her Magnificat, Mary exclaimed that she rejoiced because "He who is mighty has done great things to me!"

Yes, I tell the sisters not to fear to do good before the eyes of men. Our Lord said, "Let your light shine before men, that seeing your good deeds they may praise your Father in heaven!"

So, let men see your good deeds: it is Christ who does them through you.

When people praise us for what we are doing, I do not mind it at all. Rather, I rejoice because it all leads to the glory of God.

Index of Authors and Titles